THE POLITICS OF THE COMMON LAW

Perspectives, Rights, Processes, Institutions

The Politics of the Common Law offers a critical introduction to the legal system of England and Wales. Unlike other conventional accounts, this revised and updated second edition presents a coherent argument, organised around the central claim that contemporary post colonial common law must be understood as an articulation of human rights and open justice.

The book examines the impact of human rights on the structures and ideologies of the common law and engages with the politics of the rule of law. These themes are read into normative accounts of civil and criminal procedure that stress the importance of due process. The final sections of the book address the reality of civil and criminal procedure in the light of recent civil unrest in the UK and the growing privatisation of public services. The book questions whether it is possible to find a balance between the requirements of economics and the demands of justice.

Professor Adam Gearey, Birkbeck College, University of London; visiting professor in the Faculty of Law at Makerere University, Uganda (2001–2); the University of Pretoria, South Africa (2004) and the University of Peace, Costa Rica (2008–9); visiting fellow in the Center for Law and Society, University of California, Berkeley (2008–9).

Professor Wayne Morrison LLD, PhD, LLM, LLB, (Barrister and Solicitor of the High Court of New Zealand) is Professor of Law, Queen Mary, University of London and former Director of the University of London's International Programmes for Law.

Robert Jago MPhil. (cantab.) is a Senior Lecturer and Deputy Head of the School of Law at the University of Surrey. He is also a regular visitor to HKU SPACE where he teaches Public Law.

THE POLITICS OF THE COMMON LAW

Perspectives, Rights, Processes, Institutions

Second Edition

Adam Gearey, Wayne Morrison and Robert Jago

Routledge
Taylor & Francis Group

LONDON AND NEW YORK

Second edition published 2013
by Routledge
2 Park Square, Milton Park, Abingdon, Oxon OX14 4RN

Simultaneously published in the USA and Canada
by Routledge
711 Third Avenue, New York, NY 10017

*Routledge is an imprint of the Taylor & Francis Group,
an informa business*

First edition published by Routledge-Cavendish 2008

British Library Cataloguing in Publication Data
A catalogue record for this book is available from the British Library

Library of Congress Cataloging in Publication Data
Gearey, Adam.
 The politics of the common law / Adam Gearey, Wayne Morrison and
 Robert Jago. – Second Edition.
  pages cm
 Includes bibliographical references and index.
 ISBN 978-0-415-66236-9 (pbk : alk. paper) – ISBN 978-0-203-07199-1 (ebk)
 1. Common law–Great Britain. 2. Justice, Administration of–Great Britain.
 3. Law–Political aspects–Great Britain. I. Morrison, Wayne. II. Jago, Robert.
 III. Title.
 KD671.G43 2013
 340.5'70942–dc23   2012051037

ISBN: 978–0–415–66236–9 (pbk)
ISBN: 978–0–203–07199–1 (ebk)

Typeset in Sabon
by RefineCatch Limited, Bungay, Suffolk

MIX
Paper from
responsible sources
FSC   FSC® C013056
www.fsc.org

Printed and bound in Great Britain by
TJ International Ltd, Padstow, Cornwall

Praise for *The Politics of the Common Law*:

'Finally, a book that brings the political, the personal, the economic and the aesthetic into the heart of the institution and into the method of law. A perfect paradox, *The Politics of the Common Law* is a strikingly radical introduction to a grindingly conservative discipline. This book seeks to forge a plural identity for a tradition adrift between memories of empire and continental confusions of human rights. This book is a necessity for any student eager to engage with contemporary transformations of the common law.'

– Professor Peter Goodrich, Cardozo School of Law, USA

'All too often in recent years democratic politics and the law have seemed to be at odds. Yet *The Politics of the Common Law* brings them dramatically back together. Gearey, Morrison and Jago do all of us an enormous favour by revealing so powerfully the democratic potential of a reimagined common law. The book should be required reading for everyone who wishes to reconcile human rights, individual liberties and the collective politics of participation.'

– Professor Marc Stears, Professor of Political Theory,
University of Oxford and Visiting Fellow,
Institute for Public Policy Research, UK

'This is an invaluable book. At one level it is an introduction to the study of the common law in the post-Human Rights Act environment. But unlike many books of this type it also sets out an ambitious thesis which weaves together an account of the common law in a post-colonial context with an argument about the centrality of participation and public reason to the legitimacy of the law. As such it is not only an excellent student textbook, but also makes a contribution to academic debates about the theory and politics of the common law.'

– Professor Lindsay Farmer, University of Glasgow, UK

'The authors of this book present the common law around three key themes – a concern with legal culture; the politics of the judiciary and the legitimacy of the common law; and the integrity of civil and criminal procedure. They strongly support the view that the authentic common law tradition embraced difference and plurality in the past and argue for this understanding to be followed through in present times. An important focus in their approach is the recognition of and remembrance of law's complicity in the process of Empire. They underscore the necessity of law's authority to rest on transparency, integrity, participation and open justice. Common law procedures are addressed through human rights, thereby disclosing a critical perspective on common law. The book raises a question that should be central to the study of common law no matter where, namely "To what extent can the common law help build plural communities that are committed to democracy and the rule of law?" This book brings forth fresh and alternative angles on the study of the common law … [it] illustrates a deep reflection and contemplation of some of the most important and difficult questions confronting legal scholars and students of law and opens possibilities for further reflection by way of textured engagement.'

– Karin van Marle, Professor and Head of the
Department of Jurisprudence,
Faculty of Law, University of Pretoria, South Africa

'*The Politics of the Common Law* (2nd ed) throws down a challenge that no law student should be spared. The authors eschew formalist depictions of law and legal process that typify introductory texts. They interweave the normative present and historical past to lay bare, with disturbing clarity, the tensions which shape the law and its institutions. Their unique text takes the reader *inside* the law, as something organic and living, not lifeless and detached as standard texts so often portray.'

– Philip A Joseph LLD, Professor of Law,
University of Canterbury, New Zealand

CONTENTS

AUTHORS' ACKNOWLEDGEMENTS

My love and great thanks to Mary Gearey – still il miglior fabro; also thanks to my comrades at Birkbeck. Honourable mention to Arthur and Niamh Gearey – fans of Tom Paine and innate philosophers of justice. Thanks to Emma Nugent for patience and calm advice. Gilly Shapiro selflessly laid down her weekend to ensure that this book was published. Finally, in the real world: Deadeye Douglas, the Chailey Kid, El Machiato and The Rustler. This, my friends, was not written on the back of my hand.

The Gay Hussar, Soho, remains the only place to dine, drink and discuss serious matters.

A.G.

During this process Lynsey and Karen provided worthwhile distractions with Boris; Julia kept the beer, wine and all things alcoholic flowing; Paul, as a keen chronicler, kept Facebook relevant; Indira telephoned with reminders of why we do this job and Jane proved herself worldly wise. Charlie provided loving support and constant encouragement. Love to my parents, as always. I continue to be lucky with my family and friends. Emma Nugent deserves a medal for coordinating us authors and once again fellas it has been a pleasure working with you both.

Hear, hear for The Gay Hussar!

R.J.

Love and thanks to Michele for all her support and to Tzu Hsi for keeping me on the go. Respect to a multitude of London International students who study in the most diverse situations imaginable, to those at Queen Mary for the quality of their attention and thanks Terry for the conversations and the emails detailing our remarkable, if challenged, world. My memory of Johti Ram and the places we drank at KL side remains, RIP mate.

W.J.M.

PUBLISHER'S ACKNOWLEDGEMENTS

———•◆•———

Routledge and the authors wish to thank the institutions and individuals that have kindly provided photographic material for use in this book. Full caption and source information is listed below.

Chapter 3

3.2, 3.3, 3.4, 3.6, 3.8 – Mary Evans Picture Library

3.5 – Frontispiece to *Leviathan or the Matter, Forme and Power of a Common Wealth Ecclesiasticall and Civil*, 1651, by Thomas Hobbes (1588–1679) of Malmesbury (engraving) (b&w photo), English School, (17th century)/Private Collection/The Bridgeman Art Library

3.7 – *The Polling*, engraved by George Presbury, from *The Works of William Hogarth*, published 1833 (litho) by Hogarth, William (1697–1764) (after), Private Collection/Ken Welsh/The Bridgeman Art Library

Extract from *Law, like Love* by W.H. Auden. Copyright © 1940 by W.H. Auden, renewed. Reprinted by permission of Curtis Brown, Ltd. "Law Like Love", copyright 1940 and renewed 1968 by W.H. Auden, from COLLECTED POEMS OF W.H. AUDEN by W.H. Auden. Used by permission of Random House, Inc. Any third party use of this material, outside of this publication, is prohibited. Interested parties must apply directly to Random House, Inc. for permission.

Chapter 4

4.1 – © Victoria and Albert Museum, London

4.2 – Mary Evans Picture Library

4.3, 4.4 – Joseph Mallord William Turner, English, 1775–1851, *Slave Ship (Slavers Throwing Overboard the Dead and Dying, Typhoon Coming On)*, 1840, Oil on canvas, 90.8 × 122.6 cm (35 3/4 × 48 1/4 in.), Museum of Fine Arts, Boston, Henry Lillie Pierce Fund 99.22. Photograph © 2012 Museum of Fine Arts, Boston. All rights reserved.

Chapter 5

5.1 – Ian Waldron, *Hey Bros*, 1998. Acrylic on canvas. 122 × 176 cm. © Ian Waldron

5.2 – Unknown artist, *Illustrated London News*, 1870

5.3 – Mary Evans Picture Library

5.4 – Yala Yala Gibbs Tjungurrayi Kaarkurutinytja, Lake McDonald 1997 © estate of the artist 2012 licensed by Aboriginal Artists Agency Ltd

5.5 – Eugenics poster entitled 'The Nuremberg Law for the Protection of Blood and German Honor'. United States Holocaust Memorial Museum, courtesy of Hans Pauli. © United States Holocaust Memorial Museum. 'The views or opinions expressed in this book, and the context in which the images are used, do not necessarily reflect the views or policy of, nor imply approval or endorsement by, the United States Holocaust Memorial Museum.'

Chapter 6

6.1 – Mary Evans Picture Library

Chapter 11

11.1 – Mary Evans Picture Library

Chapter 15

15.1 – Photo by Oli Scarff/Getty Images, Copyright 2012 Getty Images

15.2 – © Victoria and Albert Museum, London

Chapter 16

16.1 – Photo by Oli Scarff/Getty Images, Copyright 2009 Getty Images

Chapter 17

17.1 – © Peter Finnemore

Every effort has been made to trace and contact copyright holders prior to publication. If notified, the publisher will undertake to rectify any errors or omissions at the earliest opportunity.

1

INTRODUCTION PART I

OUTLINE OF THE STRUCTURE OF THE BOOK

> Justice is not a cloistered virtue: she must be allowed to suffer the scrutiny and respectful, even though outspoken, comments of ordinary men.[1]

For us the contemporary common law is defined by the Human Rights Act 1998, the presence of European Convention[2] rights in English law and the reality of European Union law.[3] Equally important is the political situation of the United Kingdom in a world characterised by the globalised flows of capital, commodities, information, images and people.

The common law needs to be understood against the backdrop of the cultural heritage of post colonialism. The original 'home' of common law was England. The history of the common law is inseparable from the patterns of trade and colonial 'adventure' that defined the British Empire. In the colonial period common law combined with 'local' jurisdiction that ranged from customary law to Islamic law, to provide the foundations for the legal systems of countries as diverse as the United States, Malaysia, Bangladesh, and Cyprus. However, to think properly about the common law today we need to appreciate its part in a complex postcolonial reality. Wherever we look, the common law is inseparable from broader historical, political, cultural and economic contexts. In particular, the sense that democracy is in 'decline' in the United Kingdom[4] opens pressing questions about legal and political institutions.

---

1   Milton's *Areopagitica*, cited by Lord Atkin, in *Ambard v. A-G for Trinidad and Tobago* [1936] AC 322, 335.
2   The European Convention for the Protection of Human Rights [ECHR] was signed in Rome in 1950 and entered into force in 1953. The Convention guarantees certain rights including the right to life, freedom from torture, freedom from arbitrary arrest, the right to a fair trial, the right to privacy, freedom of religion, freedom of expression, and freedom of assembly and association. Institutionally, the Convention provided for an international court, the European Court of Human Rights [ECtHR] and a Commission to consider complaints and decide whether or not to remit them to the court.
3   The European Union was founded in 1992 by the Treaty on European Union. It was formally known as the European Community. Defining the Union is a difficult task; and indeed, the political implications of various definitions of the Union are currently being fought out in European politics. A basic working definition is, however, possible. The European Union is essentially a common market. Linked to the common market, and open to varying degrees of acceptance by the member states of the Union is an ongoing experiment in social democracy. This means that the common market is subject to regulation, and, that there is a commitment to various social, economic and welfare rights. From a legal perspective the most important aspect of the Union is that fact that it is a supranational institution. Lawyers have tended to link law to the nation state. There is thus something of a challenge in conceiving of a legal order that is international but creates rights that can be used in national courts.
4   Democracy Audit 17.

This introduction provides a brief overview of our argument, followed by a more substantive development of our key themes and introduces major ideas we will take up throughout the book.

Our presentation of the common law is organised around three key themes. The first theme – our concern with legal culture – can be disaggregated into sub themes: a reading of the cultures of the postcolonial common law, an understanding of the aims of legal education, and our commitment to notions of public reason and scrutiny concerning judicial practice. Such ideas and practices of normative visibility also inform our engagement with Article 6 of the European Convention: a key organising instrument that declares a human right to a fair trial.

The development of the first theme runs through Chapters 1 to 9. Chapters 3 to 5 are primarily concerned with the postcolonial common law, Chapters 6 to 9 are focused on public reason and judicial practices, and Chapters 12 to 14 deal with Article 6 and the norms, rules and principles of fair trials.

The second theme, developed in Chapters 10 and 11 is focused on the politics of the judiciary and the legitimacy of the common law. We will discuss the transformation of the judicial role since the Human Rights Act 1998 and the so called dialogue between the courts and Parliament over human rights.

Our third theme – articulated in Chapters 15 and 16 – confronts the material realities of civil and criminal procedure. We will be particularly concerned with how we can, in imagination if not reality, retain a sense of the integrity of procedures beyond the messy compromises of their operation.

We now want to elaborate the first two themes in a little more detail. It is apt that we start – in Chapter 3 – in an (ex) colonial location: the law school at the University of Canterbury in New Zealand. Chapter 3 begins by fore fronting the theme of legal education. Our narrative attempts to disturb this 'scene' of the transmission of legal knowledge to the 'subjects' of the law. We argue that law cannot be narrowly seen as the rules articulated by a sovereign power that 'states' the law for its subjects. We also criticise the idea that law can somehow be 'owned' by a culture. Against the view that law must defend a homogeneity of identity and community (articulated by the German theorist Carl Schmitt above all), we argue that the authentic common law tradition embraced difference and plurality and attempted, not always fully successfully, to accommodate that difference in wholeness. As Sir Matthew Hale put it in the seventeenth century: 'tho' the Britains were, as is supposed, the most ancient inhabitants, yet there were mingled with them, the Romans, the Picts, the Saxons, the Danes, and . . . the Normans'.[5] We need to remember law's complicity in the process of Empire. However, we also need to hold onto concepts and understandings embedded in the history and myths of the common law tradition that resonate with contemporary ideas about equality and democracy.

Chapter 6 develops these thoughts. Our argument about public reason and judicial practice stresses that in a democracy law's authority rests on openness, and on principles of reasoned adjudication of disputes by independent courts staffed by unbiased judges. Law is not the domain of a sovereign and its subjects. Rather, as Lord

---

5   Sir Matthew Hale, *The History of the Common Law of England*, p. 39.

Bingham and others have argued, due process and the rule of law defend the independence and integrity of the law: central values in a democratic culture.

Present constitutional arrangements in the United Kingdom show a degree of strain; whilst fundamental constitutional structures remain largely unchanged, the conventional concept of the deference of an unelected judiciary to a sovereign Parliament is being slowly redefined by the impact of the Human Rights Act of 1998. There are a host of questions. In what ways are judges engaged in a 'dialogue' with Parliament; a dialogue that also requires us to examine the relationship between the domestic courts and the European Court of Human Rights (ECtHR) in Strasbourg and the state of British politics. Moreover, how are judges appointed? How representative are they of the democracy they serve?

Our approach to Article 6 is focused on principles of integrity, participation and open justice. Framing this concern as one of human rights needs to be carefully understood; certainly the common law principles that regulated criminal and civil trials were not framed in the language of human rights. The 'language' of human rights is a fairly recent invention. Whilst remaining cognizant of the immanent principles of the common law, we will argue that looking at common law procedures through human rights allows us a critical perspective to the common law. Utilising Article 6 also means that we can examine the extent to which the common law measures up to international standards of due process. This is a salutary reminder that the common law cannot be studied in a vacuum.

Our third theme picks up and develops concerns at the level of the criminal and civil justice systems. Whilst Chapters 12 to 14 stress the values that should underlie the criminal process, Chapter 16 shows how, in reality, it is somewhat chaotic. High minded ideals of integrity and participation come up against a reality of dysfunctional agencies and the prison industrial complex. Criminal 'justice' appears almost as a bad joke when we realise that the system is a complex and expensive means of 'constituting', marginalising and condemning a 'criminal population'.

Our study of civil justice in Chapter 15 works its way through similar themes. However, we will attempt to show that a somewhat more principled idea of justice can be used to think about the way in which the civil system operates. But a reality of discrimination and compromise means a just system for the resolution of civil disputes is still some way from being achieved.

We want to turn from this overview of the themes and structure of the book to a more detailed discussion of our core ideas.

THE POSTCOLONIAL COMMON LAW

The opening chapters of this book are concerned with presences and absences in what we can term the postcolonial common law.[6] From the perspective of British history,

----

6   The postcolonial is a difficult term to define. We mean it in its least problematic sense: the period after 1945 when European Empires are either dismantled or fall apart. See Costas Douzinas and Adam Gearey, *Critical Jurisprudence* (Oxford: Hart Press, 2005).

the common law was central to the production of a 'nation' and an 'English speaking people'. The common law was fundamental to the centralisation of power, and it was mobilised in subtle and not so subtle networks that brought together forms of direct and indirect rule over colonised territories.

Whilst the story of nation building and Empire has been the dominant account of the common law, contemporary understandings of this subject are concerned with a different problematic. To what extent can the common law help build plural communities that are committed to democracy and the rule of law?

This question requires another historical perspective on the common law. This is why Chapter 4 examines two 'slave' cases from the seventeen and eighteen hundreds. In these cases we can see a struggle taking place over the proper role of the law; we are also concerned with the proper language in which to talk about the law. Is the proper task of the common law the protection of property rights, even if this extends to the right of a master to own his slaves? Or must the common law realise the exemplification of the spirit of liberty, equality and dignity – and affirm that a human being is not a chattel? There are a number of compromises between these positions – and it could no doubt be seen as traditional English duplicity to affirm that there can be no slavery in mainland Britain, whilst enjoying the economic products of systems of slave holding safely located on the colonial periphery.

The slave cases show how different narratives about the law circulate, how different political claims about the values of law oppose one another. Law's 'open texture' has allowed (at least to some extent) legal challenges to be mounted on even the most seemingly settled of cultural institutions; even if the courts prefer not to develop the law in a progressive manner. This connects with our engagements with the colonial and the state of emergency in Chapter 5. We will argue that we can learn a great deal from the act of declaring a state of emergency: indeed, the state of emergency provides an insight into what passes as the normal 'state' of the law. Can law ever protect itself? That is a question of law and politics. It is inseparably connected with what we call the realisation of plural communities, and a concern that takes us back to the rule of law.

These themes are explicated in a little more detail in Chapter 2. However, to conclude this section of the introduction, we want to refer to one of the most intriguing contemporary articulations of the rule of law. This is important as it provides a focus for our development of notions of plurality and equality:

> The rule of law is thus [the establishment] of a space accessible to everyone in which it is possible to affirm and defend a commitment to human dignity *as such*, [we have to be aware that all communities] have to come to terms with the actuality of human diversity – and that the only way of doing this is to acknowledge the category of 'human dignity as such' – a non-negotiable assumption that each agent . . . could be expected to have a voice in the shaping of some common project for the well-being and order of a human group.[7]

---

7   Dr Rowan Williams, Archbishop of Canterbury, at http://www.guardian.co.uk/uk/2008/feb/07/religion. world3.

This is an account of the rule of law by the former Archbishop of Canterbury, Dr Rowan Williams. It is worth thinking about this statement, even though (at least for a lawyer) it is expressed in a rather unfamiliar language. Dr Williams is suggesting that within a polity composed of 'plural communities' (i.e. different beliefs, values and mores) the rule of law creates a 'space' (we will return to this word in a moment) where a common value ('dignity as such') is both 'affirm[ed] and defend[ed]'. There is, then, a fundamental value that underlies political community (or, crudely put, a load of people living together in a nation state): dignity. Dignity is a difficult concept to define. We will do so in Chapter 2, and again in Chapter 17, but the basic contour of our understanding can be sketched as follows. Dignity corresponds with the idea of the moral worth of the human being. The moral worth of the human being means that all human beings are equal in dignity. This corresponds with equality before the law, and, as we will suggest, other (controversial) values that are both human rights and claims to substantive equality.

The idea that the rule of law is a 'space' is a metaphor that we would interpret in the light of our understanding of dignity. The rule of law is a space because it is more than simply legal rules. To claim that the rule of law is a space is to refer (implicitly) to legal institutions. The legal institutions that we are primarily concerned with in this book are courts. Thus, as we will argue, courts require moral authority to deal justly with individuals. However, the notion of space (in an institutional sense) also refers to what takes place in legal institutions: legal speech. Later, in Chapter 2, we will link this notion of legal speech to the principles of integrity, participation and open justice that define fair trial rights. But, there is still more to be said about the 'space' of the rule of law.

Note that Dr Williams suggests that dignity relates to 'a non-negotiable assumption that each agent . . . could be expected to have a voice in the shaping of some common project for the well-being and order of a human group'. If an 'agent' is a person (an individual with moral personhood), then to acknowledge the 'voice' of the person is to allow people the opportunities or structures that enable them to take some control over the decisions that affect their 'well being'. We will argue that this concern can be linked with the idea of the fair trial, and (in Chapter 17) – with an understanding of democracy.

One final point: we are aware of 'relativist' arguments. The relativist would seek to criticise our position in the following terms: 'it's all very well to assert the rule of law, dignity and human rights as fundamental "master" values, but aren't these ideas ultimately too linked to colonialism and western hegemony to be critical? In the name of a "critical" account of the common law, you have in fact merely reproduced a neo-colonial account that ignores, silences or marginalises the ideas and values of those non western others who have become subjects of human rights in the same way that they were subjects of colonial law'.

How would we reply? Our defence (in outline only) would be to acknowledge the force of these arguments. Given time, we would hope to produce a defence of dignity and solidarity that – at both a pragmatic and more principled levels – articulates the rule of law as a 'space' where – in a 'properly' democratic sense – the terms of our common life could be worked out. We will touch upon these themes again in Chapter 17. However, the terms of our arguments in this book are deliberately 'thin'.

Thus, in the following section our analysis of public reason is not an argument that public reason of law has to necessarily defend any substantive values (i.e. equality of opportunity). We stress that public reason is best understood as authority's commitment to provide reasons for its decisions. This, in the terms of Dr Williams' definition of the rule of law, is perhaps the most minimal element in defining the 'space' of the rule of law.

PUBLIC REASON: JUDICIAL PRACTICES, LEGITIMACY AND DEMOCRACY

The doctrines of precedent and techniques of statutory interpretation have to be understood as judicial practices.[8] To describe precedent and statutory interpretation as practices draws attention to the way in which judges interpret the law and act on the basis of those interpretations. Practices take shape within a culture that determines how they are composed.[9] Judicial practices link to structures of adjudication. Adjudication, as we will argue, is a particular form of public reason. These terms will be described in much more detail in Chapter 6. At this stage we just want to outline the basic terms of our argument.

The American jurist Lon L. Fuller has most famously argued that adjudication requires certain structural features: 'it confers on the affected party a peculiar form of participation in the decision, that of presenting proofs and reasoned arguments for a decision in his favor'.[10] For Fuller: 'participation through reasoned argument loses its meaning if the arbiter of the dispute is inaccessible to reason because he is insane, has been bribed, or is hopelessly prejudiced'.[11] In other words, adjudication has its inherent structures, which require a neutral judge and the participation of the parties to the dispute. This is another way of thinking about what defines the limits of adjudication: what makes adjudication principled is the fact that it concerns reasoned argument.

Whilst Fuller is not referring to Article 6, his argument is entirely compatible with our understanding of fair trial rights. This extends beyond the prohibition of bias and equality of arms (a principle which itself stresses that the law is about reason) to the very idea that a judgement needs to be publically justified. But this is to jump ahead with our argument. For the moment we want to stress that the proper role of the judge relates to adjudication and public reason.

The judicial practice of precedent is an exercise in public reason to the extent that judges must give reasoned judgments that show how they have reached their conclusions, and how these conclusions are justified. These are democratic practices to the

---

8   The philosophical orientating points for a proper understanding of the practice of precedent would have to draw on Wittgenstein – perhaps even as mediated by Michel de Certeau in *The Practice of Everyday Life* (Berkeley: University of California Press, 2006).

9   Any sensible development of these themes would have to take into account Peter Goodrich's work – especially *Reading the Law* (London: Basil Blackwell, 1986) and *Languages of Law* (London: Weidenfeld and Nicolson, 1990). These are essential texts for understanding the dynamics of the common law traditions.

10   Fuller (1978: 364).

11   Ibid.

extent that these reasoned judgments are not exercises of naked power; rather, power justified through reason. They can, within the institutional terms of the law, be challenged and criticised. But, perhaps most importantly, they provide accountable and transparent grounds for the exercise of judicial power.

Chapters 8, 9, 10 and 11 will elaborate these arguments. Our approach will allow us to discuss judicial law making and to understand its contemporary dynamic, and the centrality of the Human Rights Act (HRA) 1998 to these concerns. This raises fundamental questions about British democracy.[12]

A central principle of the British constitution is the doctrine of the sovereignty of Parliament. That Parliament should be able to make or unmake any law that it so chooses is justified by the claim that it is elected by 'the people'. It is thus entirely proper (so the argument goes) that in a democracy, the legislature should be sovereign and the executive's domination of the legislature is justified by the fact that the majority of people have voted for it and its legislative programme. The sovereignty of Parliament thus rests on a majoritarian thesis about its 'popular' legitimacy.

However, one of the central themes of constitution in recent years has been the extent to which a political party with a large majority can exploit the sovereignty of Parliament to push through its policies unhindered by checks or balances on its power. The political accountability of the executive to Parliament appears too remote to make much of a difference to the activities in which government engages.

Commentators on relationships between the courts and Parliament have increasingly made use of the idea of a democratic dialogue.[13] However, as Young has commented, it can be difficult to determine precisely how this dialogue is meant to operate. Indeed, some have rejected the idea more or less out of hand. To credit the criticisms, it is difficult to find hard evidence of Parliament somehow working alongside the judiciary to create a human rights culture, if, as Young notes, 'MPs regard the decisions of the judiciary as final determinations of the content of human rights, causing some to regret the presence of the HRA and its consequent restriction on democratic decision-making'.[14] However, the idea of dialogue should not be abandoned too quickly, and we will make use of it to examine ways of thinking about judicial law making, and the problematic distinction between law and politics.

We will also use the idea of dialogue to examine the relationship between the European Court of Human Rights in Strasbourg and the domestic courts. We will see this relationship as a work in progress. It is based on the 'mirror principle' that

---

12 See Lord Steyn, 'Democracy, The rule of Law and the Role of Judges' E.H.R.L.R. 2006, 3, 243–253.
Lord Steyn posits two 'strands' to the 'democratic ideal'. The first relates to the notion that Parliament is an elected body, accountable to the people. The second is that 'the basic values of liberty and justice for all and respect for human rights and fundamental freedoms must be guaranteed'. Where there is conflict between these values, an 'impartial and independent judiciary' must find the balance 'in accordance with principles of institutional integrity'.

13 For a useful elaboration of this themes, see T.R.S. Allan, 'Constitutional Dialogue and the Justification of Judicial Review' (2003) 23 O.J.L.S. 563. T.R.S. Allan writes: '[w]e may imagine a dialogue between the judge and the representative legislator . . . [t]he opposition between parliamentary sovereignty and the rule of law has been conceived too starkly. On close examination these principles are more interdependent than independent, enabling legislative will and common law reason to be combined in accordance with the demands of justice and the common good'.

14 Young (2010: 773).

articulates the fundamental relationship between an international court, responsible for the coherent development of human rights principles, and the elaboration of human rights principles in common law by the domestic courts. Whilst domestic courts have to follow Strasbourg's lead, the development of human rights law has to be seen as a creative partnership within the terms that we will outline. Indeed, we will see human rights as an important intervention into British politics, and one that might make for a more principled public life.

IMAGINING CIVIL AND CRIMINAL JUSTICE

To imagine a system of justice is to imagine a process which is fair both procedurally and substantively. Laws mean nothing if their application goes unconsidered. Our chapters on imagining civil and criminal justice ask some critical questions about how these areas of procedure operate.

In our consideration of civil justice, we use the work of John Rawls to demonstrate why civil justice is important. This also allows us to move away from traditional accounts of civil procedure which tend to merely summarise the detailed bodies of rules. We prefer to encourage our readers to think about how the civil justice system 'actually' works. To this end we will critically describe the problematic way in which civil justice has attempted to deal with three concerns: the allocation of medical resources; claims made to land by a minority group and the operation of legal aid.

There is a second difference between our work on procedure and traditional text book accounts. The latter tend to present the law and its processes in a 'whiggish' fashion where the history of an institution is a story of its gradual improvement. Thus, the injustice of civil law in the 1800s is demonstrated by reference to Charles Dickens' novel *Bleak House*. Contemporary civil justice can then be triumphantly presented as the realisation of a rational form of civil procedure and the achievement of a better future. In our consideration of Lord Woolf's reforms, we want to show how many problems remain.

Whilst the criminal justice process is also characterised by intractable problems, it is also worth pointing out that the issues raised in this area are quite different from the problems we describe in civil justice. For a start, state punishment impacts more seriously upon an individual's liberty than the remedies available in a civil trial. Furthermore, the competing aims and values at play in the criminal justice system tend to undermine the consistent functioning of the system. We want to raise some questions about the legitimacy and integrity of criminal justice processes.

We begin with a study of police powers to stop and search. Whilst this practice can be justified as necessary to effective policing, the operation of stop and search powers impacts upon minorities in a disproportionate way. We then turn our attention to the way in which the criminal justice system increasingly relies on scientific evidence. This form of evidence is meant to allow the court to find out the truth in any given case. In the words of Jerome Frank, science serves as something of 'a procedural opiate'. We will show that scientific evidence is far more problematic than most would want to believe.

The final section of the chapter looks at prison overcrowding. Once again we come across profound tensions within the system. Although the battle between the judiciary and the executive over sentencing powers is not new, in the last decade it has assumed a particularly 'sharp' form. This is driven, in part, by the executive's commitment to an expansionist prison policy which appears to have popular support. To pick up on themes developed earlier on in the book, we feel that this is another area in which the judges, rather than Parliament, have stood up for the principles of individual liberty.

The excessive use of the prison comes at a time when the population of incarcerated people is at its highest in this country. Prisons are packed to such a degree that overcrowding has a severe detrimental impact upon the conditions prisoners must endure when serving their sentences. The public, fuelled by the press, may imagine a room with a view, a satellite dish and a few cuddly toys. This is far from the reality of Britain's prisons.

We are often told that problems and abuses within civil and criminal justice are inevitable. This is a lazy excuse to forget those who suffer at the hands of the system. It is a failure of imagination!

So as not to overburden our explication of the themes of *The Politics of the Common Law*, we will turn to elaborate our concerns with fair trials, the rule of law and due process in Chapter 2.

2

INTRODUCTION PART II

◆•◆

PROCEDURAL FAIRNESS, THE RULE OF LAW
AND DUE PROCESS

> . . . that he produce his body ['et nunc praecipietur viceomiti quod habeat corpus'] on another day by a writ of this kind: The King to the viscount greeting. We enjoin you before our justiciaries etc. On such a day the body of A., to answer to B. Concerning such a plea.[1]

In turning to issues of due process and Article 6 we are focusing on the structure of the law at the specific levels of civil and criminal procedure. How do we approach these themes? Article 6 relates to central ideas of the rule of law and due process. How do we understand these terms? The conventional starting point is Dicey's definition.[2] The rule of law is understood in terms of the 'supremacy of regular law as opposed to arbitrary power and equality before the law'.[3] We could suggest that common law provides the parties to both criminal and civil proceedings with a number of protections and safeguards which, taken together, form the framework of a common law right to fair trial. There are two minimum fair trial principles: 'nobody should be a judge in his/her own case' and 'allow both sides to be heard'. These are the principles of natural justice and have evolved as the principles of administrative law.

Now consider Lord Bingham's definition of the rule of law.[4] It begins in terms reminiscent of Dicey. The 'core of the existing principle' is that 'all persons and authorities within the state, whether public or private, should be bound by and entitled to the benefit of laws publicly and prospectively promulgated and publicly administered in the courts'. This clearly expands the sense of Dicey's definition. It stresses that we are concerned with law that is both publicly stated and administered. The law both binds its subjects, and entitles them to the benefit of its protection. At the centre of this concept of publicly visible law is the requirement that 'adjudicative procedures provided by the state should be fair' and that one guarantee of fairness is 'open hearings'. This is linked to 'the dictum that justice must manifestly and undoubtedly be seen to be done'. Lord Bingham's use of this maxim of normative visibility is

---

1   Bracton, in *De Lgibus et Consuetudinibus Angliae* (1883 ed.: 474–477), discussing the writ or petition of habeas corpus, a foundational petition that gives a procedural norm of visibility to common law processes. The body (the person) must not be held in secret but must be open to the scrutiny of the justices who may see for themselves if the body bears the marks of torture and so forth.
2   *Thomas v. Baptiste* [1999] 3 WLR 249.
3   Richard Clayton and Hugh Tomlinson, *Fair Trial Rights* (Oxford: Oxford University Press, 2001), 7.
4   Lord Bingham, *The Rule of Law*, at http://www.cpl.law.cam.ac.uk/Media/THE%20RULE%20OF%20LAW%202006.pdf

particularly interesting. If we refer back to Dicey it would seem that one of the principles of natural justice (admittedly always part of the definition of the rule of law) has moved to the centre of the concept.

These themes are not only present in judicial writings on the rule of law; they are also a pervasive and important theme in contemporary legal philosophy. If we take Hart's *The Concept of Law* (1961) as one of the most important statements of the philosophy of English law in the period after 1945, then we can note two important concerns. Due process and fair procedures do not occur as specific themes in *The Concept of Law*. Although Hart was writing in a period much later than Dicey we could account for the absence of these concepts from the book by arguing that Hart, like Dicey, assumed common law procedures were fair. We cannot reconstruct the debates in legal philosophy on procedure in this short book; but we can observe that – again paralleling our point above – fair procedures have emerged as a defining theme in the most influential accounts of the nature of law. Joseph Raz, for instance, affirms that the rule of law should include the requirement that 'the principles of natural justice must be observed', that procedures are 'open . . . fair' and free of 'bias'; and that 'the courts are easily accessible'.[5]

What, then, is the link between fair procedures, the rule of law and due process? In order to briefly illustrate our argument we will start with a case that exemplifies our main claims:

> [D]ue process, unlike some legal rules, is not a technical conception with a fixed content unrelated to time, place and circumstances . . . [D]ue process cannot be imprisoned within the treacherous limits of any formula. Representing a profound attitude of fairness between man and man, and more particularly between the individual and government, 'due process' is compounded of history, reason, the past course of decisions, and stout confidence in the strength of the democratic faith we profess. Due process is not a mechanical instrument. It is not a yardstick. It is a process. It is a delicate process of adjustment inescapably involving the exercise of judgment.[6]

This passage is exemplary: we have to be careful not to reduce due process to some timeless formula. It is a way of thinking about the relationship between legal procedures and the values of the rule of law. It would follow that, to understand contemporary ideas of due process, we need to approach the matter historically; aware that the concept has changed over time – and has only recently been articulated as a right. Note, however, that despite the changes in ideas of due process it would appear to have some kind of content relating to 'attitude[s] of fairness between man and man'. More than that: due process is 'compounded' or made of 'reason', 'the past course of decisions' and 'stout confidence in the strength of the democratic faith we profess'. This is a democratic understanding of due process, congruent with the notions of public reason that we outlined above; it does, of course, go beyond this idea. We will pick up

---

5   Raz, 'The Rule of Law and its Virtue', in *The Authority of Law: Essays on Law and Morality* (Oxford: Clarendon Press, 1979), at 216–17. See also Jeremy Waldron, *The Rule of Law and the Importance of Procedure*, NYU School of Law, Public Law Research Paper No. 10–73 (2010).

6   *Joint Anti-Fascist Refugee Comm. v. McGrath*, 341 U.S. 123, 162–63 (1951)

on these themes in the final section of the introduction when we relate fair trial rights to the values of participation and integrity. For the moment, we want to show how due process becomes linked to the right to a fair trial.

A (very) brief history of due process

Prior to the Human Rights Act, English law provided no explicit general statement of rights in relation to the conduct of the legal process. However, due process does appear as part of a general legal inheritance. Scholars of the common law have traced the first use of the term 'due process' to a statute of 1354:

> No man of whatever state or condition he be, shall be put out of his lands or tenements nor taken, nor disinherited, nor put to death, without he be brought to answer by due process of law.

These terms can themselves be traced back to chapter 39 of Magna Carta (1215):

> No free man shall be taken or imprisoned or deprived of his freehold or his liberties or free customs, or outlawed or exiled, or in any manner destroyed, nor shall we come upon him or send against him, except by a legal judgment of his peers or by the law of the land.[7]

However, there is a risk in tracing due process back to Magna Carta. Some scholars argue that the understandings of law in this document were limited to a very precise context; and certainly cannot be linked with ideas of equality and democracy. The fundamental concern of the drafters of Magna Carta lay in asserting the privileges and power of the nobles against the King. Magna Carta did not speak for 'the common man' or indeed, the common woman. This does not stop the document being read in this way; but it does suggest that we need to see Magna Carta as a document that has been understood in different ways at different times.[8]

The argument that due process can be found in the Magna Carta owes a great deal to Sir Edward Coke's work. Coke was writing in a time of constitutional tension between King and Parliament, in the days before the English Civil War. As Lord Chief Justice, his rulings went against James I's claims to power and privilege. Coke's attempt to define the law of England must therefore be seen, at least in part, in this historical context. In 1627 and 1628 the king had been challenged over his 'arbitrary imprisonment' of his subjects, and there had been legal arguments over the precise meaning of the statutes of Edward and the terms 'process of law'. Coke's *Second Institute* reflects these disputes. Coke can be read as making a claim for the limited nature of the King's power:

> But by the Law of the Land. For the true sense and exposition of these words, see the Statute of 37. Edw. 3. cap. 8. where the words, by the law of the Land, are rendred, without due process of Law, for there it is said, though it be

---

7   This is the form of words in Chapter 29 of the *Third Reissue of Henry III* in 1225; which added the important words: 'To no one will we sell, to no one will we deny or delay right or justice'.

8   McIlwain (1914: 27–51).

contained in the great Charter, that no man be taken, imprisoned, or put out of his free-hold without proces of the Law; that is, by indictment of present-ment of good and lawfull men, where such deeds be done in due manner, or by writ originall of the Common law.

Coke's argument is that the 'true sense' of the words of the Statutes of Edward render the law of the land as 'due process of law' – an authority buttressed by Magna Carta itself. Due process is then linked to the 'original common law'; the upshot of the argument being that the common law itself requires procedures of lawful arrest and the sanctity of property.

There are a number of problems with this argument that relate not only to Coke's citation of the Edwardian statute, but to his creative re-interpretation of the narrow notion of process.[9] Nevertheless, one can appreciate the success of Coke's rhetoric. Coke has suggested that the common law itself enshrines those very values which the King is threatening. It would follow that the Crown is acting illegitimately; the King is against the law of due process.[10]

So, perhaps this bold equation of the common law and due process has to be understood in the context of the constitutional struggles of the time. Certainly later commentaries did not follow Coke – and tended to use process in the narrow sense.[11] This more limited understanding of process fed into Blackstone's Commentaries (1765–1769). Blackstone is an important writer because his work on law engages with the transformation of old structures, without necessarily being able to grasp the shape of the new forms.[12] Blackstone writes of process as the means by which a person is brought before a court. This reflects earlier understandings of procedure. However, it is interesting that Blackstone adds in parenthesis: 'according to the rules of equity in all'. This suggests a broader claim – that links process to equity.

Commentators have not made much of this point – so we should not over-emphasise it. It does, however, suggest something more than a narrow sense of process – and whilst it might be straining the interpretation to suggest that equity means something like fair process, it does indicate that there is the desire to at least intimate an understanding of process that invokes a claim to wider values. Whether or not Blackstone had some idea of the fairness of law is an open question. Crucial to our argument are a set of political and legal developments that certainly opened far reaching and dramatic questions about the nature of law and society.

....

9   Process related to writs, but there is also evidence that it referred to 'summons, attachment, warrants for appearance, and subpoena' (Jurow 273). Jurow argues that this narrow meaning of process can also be found in Pollock and Maitland's *A History of English Law Before the Time of Edward the First* (2 vols.; 1898), V. 2, p. 578.

10   Corwin 'The Doctrine of Due Process Before the Civil War', 24 *Harv. L. Rev.* 366–85, 460–79 (1911); Robert P. Reeder, 'The Due Process Clause and the Substance of Individual Rights', 58 *Univ. of Penn. L. Rev.* 191, 204 (1910); Charles M. Hough, 'Due Process of Law Today', 32 *Harv. L. Rev.* 218 (1919).

11   Jurow, 278.

12   Kennedy (1979).

With the constitutional upheavals of the late 1700s, a new understanding of law came into being. Reflecting on 'revolutionary' law, Max Weber wrote: '[i]t is clear that these postulates of formal equality and economic mobility paved the way for the destruction of all patrimonial and feudal law . . .'[13] The background of these ideas is found in enlightenment philosophy and its drive to subject all forms of authority to reason. Although a proper examination of these ideas would have to engage with diverse figures from different traditions, we will (for sake of space alone) make reference to Tom Paine's *The Rights of Man* (1791). The concept of the rights of man was not original to Paine. It is part of traditions that predated the enlightenment and can be traced back to the very origins of western political and philosophical thought.[14] Paine was, however, a great populariser of the idea of rights. His work influenced the American Revolution and *The Rights of Man* defended the French Revolution from its detractors. The American Declaration of Independence of 1789 reflected enlightenment thinking in its assertion that 'all men are created equal'. The Declaration of Independence denounced the colonial order. It contained, amongst its grievances at breaches of 'American rights and liberties' the suspension of trial by jury and the tyrannical and arbitrary rule of King George. Ideas of rights and equality fed into the Bill of Rights of the Constitution of the United States (ratified in 1791). The Bill of Rights contains in its fifth, sixth, seventh and eight amendments a powerful statement of due process and equality before the law.

What of France? *The Declaration of the Rights of Man and of Citizens* (1789) articulated the values of the French Revolution. A number of provisions are relevant to our study of due process:

> 7. No person shall be accused, arrested, or imprisoned except in the cases and according to the forms prescribed by law. Any one soliciting, transmitting, executing, or causing to be executed, any arbitrary order, shall be punished. But any citizen summoned or arrested in virtue of the law shall submit without delay, as resistance constitutes an offense.

> 8. The law shall provide for such punishments only as are strictly and obviously necessary, and no one shall suffer punishment except it be legally inflicted in virtue of a law passed and promulgated before the commission of the offense.

> 9. As all persons are held innocent until they shall have been declared guilty, if arrest shall be deemed indispensable, all harshness not essential to the securing of the prisoner's person shall be severely repressed by law.

For the framers of *The Declaration*, 'law is an expression of the will of the community'. Law, it might be said, creates the community; or, in the language we have used above, defines that network of reciprocal rights and duties that define how people will relate to each other. If 'the people' or 'the will of the community' creates the law, then Articles 7, 8

13   Weber (1978: 641).
14   See Douzinas (2000), Wall (2011).

and 9 determine the legal processes that will institutionalise this democratic relationship. Thus, the very idea of due process stands against the exercise of arbitrary power: the law can only work legitimately through processes that are defined by rules. The power of the community to punish must likewise be subject to processes; processes which, as Article 9 stresses, must be limited to the end that they serve.

It would seem, then, that the constitutional revolutions of the late seventeen hundreds produced bold, new ideas of due process linked to the rights of man and the right to hold property. Matters were slightly more complicated. Mary Wollstonecraft's *Vindication of the Rights of Women* (1792) revealed how the logic of the rights of man required the extension of rights to women. Furthermore, as Guardiola-Rivera has pointed out, the constitutional revolutions in America and France appear somewhat partial when viewed from different parts of the world. One way into this issue is to read Marx's comments on *The Declaration*. Marx argued that the so called rights of man were an invention by a newly dominant social class who had assumed political, economic and social power after the break down of the old feudal and early modern world. Marx famously commented on the French and American revolutions that: '[p]olitical emancipation is the reduction of man . . . to an egoistic, independent individual . . . to a juridical person'.[15] The juridical person or citizen brought into being by the French and American revolutions was not a properly democratic citizen: rather, the values of the revolutions reflect the 'sanctity of property'. Marx is suggesting that the new order – which proclaimed emancipation and equality, was not true to its word. The new political order made supreme the right to hold property. Indeed, when the great proclamations of the rights of man were announced, many people were considered to be 'things'. As have often been pointed out, the American Bill of Rights was promulgated by slave holders. Although Marx does not spell it out, it would follow that legal procedures would likewise effectively privilege the values of property over all others.

Marx's criticisms can be extended to colonial law. As far as the European empires were concerned, the rights of man – or at least liberties at law – were to be reserved for white men – the full possessors of reason and civilisation: the rest were treated somewhat differently. Certainly the British had high ideas about the project of Empire. As Lord Lugard wrote: '[i]t was the task of civilisation to put an end to slavery, to establish Courts of Law, to inculcate in the natives a sense of individual responsibility, of liberty, and of justice, and to teach their rulers how to apply these principles . . .' (Lugard 1965, 5). In reality, imperial law was about control.

For Marx the Empire was a vast network to extract commodities and labour from colonised peoples. Slavery was abolished because it was inefficient: not a good way of making money. As the colonial period developed, the British developed a system called indirect rule. Indirect rule manifested itself in dual legal systems, in regimes that 'differentiated' between the indigenous and the settler, the native and the European at both a doctrinal and institutional level. Legal power included 'the native' within a framework that granted rights, but simultaneously marginalised 'native' subjects in customary legal

---

15 Marx, *On the Jewish Question*.

systems. Mamdani calls this a 'dual' system.[16] The British defined a system of indirect rule that allowed a small group of administrators to control the vast conquered or acquired territories. Thus, although there was some commitment to due process and the rule of law, these values were perhaps secondary to economic objectives.

The 13 American colonies had joined together and achieved independence by 1779: 80 years later one of the most notorious cases in legal history, *Dredd Scott* v. *Sandford* (1857), also concerned due process. Indeed, Lord Chief Justice Taney stressed that under the Fifth Amendment to the Constitution: 'the rights of property are united with the rights of person, and placed on the same ground by . . . which provides that no person shall be deprived of life, liberty, and property, without due process of law'. So, we could say that this is a case about property and people. People *with* property are protected by due process of law. This seems entirely in keeping with the declaration of the sanctity of property in the Declaration of the Rights of the Citizen. However, we need to question the distinction between people and things. Today, we would see these two concepts as opposed; people are not things. This was not the case in America in 1857. Chief Justice Taney put the point succinctly:

> The question is simply this: Can a negro, whose ancestors were imported into this country, and sold as slaves, become a member of the political community formed and brought into existence by the Constitution of the United States, and as such become entitled to all the rights, and privileges, and immunities, guaranteed by that instrument to the citizen? One of which rights is the privilege of suing in a court of the United States in the cases specified in the Constitution.

If Dredd Scott was a slave, then he would be incapable of suing for his freedom in a court of law. As the Supreme Court argued, the circuit court that had originally considered Scott's case lacked jurisdiction. As a thing, or a chattel, a slave could not be considered a citizen of the United States. This was elaborated in the following way:

> The question before us is, whether the class of person [slaves] . . . compose a portion of this people . . .? We think they are not, and that they are not included, and were not intended to be included, under the word 'citizens' in the Constitution, and can therefore claim none of the rights and privileges which that instrument provides for and secures to citizens of the United States.

It is worth reading this passage against those of Tom Paine we cited above. A citizen is a 'constituent member' of the sovereign body which founds law making power. As such, a citizen is entitled to be respected and protected by the body so empowered. This is, after all, the revolutionary basis of both democracy and due process: the political community and its laws are not somehow the gift of the Crown. The crucial issue, therefore, is who is included, and who is excluded from this sovereign body. To be excluded is not to count

---

16   Mamdani (1996).

as a citizen; in the case of slaves, it is to be a 'thing' – an object, rather than the subject of the law.

It is still shocking to read Dredd Scott. The reasoned legal language conceals such a horrific denial of humanity. As Daniel Bell has written[17] the history of racism is bound up with the history of the United States (but note that Chief Justice Taney's opinion shows the complicity of English common law in the legal regime that protected the rights of slave holders). Whether or not the Civil War was fought to free the slaves, the aftermath of the conflict saw a concerted attempt to reconstruct American law and society. The Fourteenth Amendment of the Constitution over-ruled *Dredd Scott* v. *Sandford*, and stated an elaboration of due process that brought all within the 'equal protection of the laws':

> All persons born or naturalized in the United States, and subject to the juris-
> diction thereof, are citizens of the United States and of the state wherein they
> reside. No state shall make or enforce any law which shall abridge the privi-
> leges or immunities of citizens of the United States; nor shall any state deprive
> any person of life, liberty, or property, without due process of law; nor deny
> to any person within its jurisdiction the equal protection of the laws.

If we turn our attention from America and back to England, we can see another set of distinctive principles about due process developing in the early 1800s. Jeremy Bentham's work proved influential. Bentham wanted to 'make it new' – to sweep away the inefficient and the ancient, to modernise and rationalise. His work is animated by the spirit of utility. These themes feed into his thinking on due process. Bentham invested his energies in devising a Procedure Code that would prevent the country from being 'saddled' with insti-tutions that were costly and ineffective.[18] He saw the trial as a procedure that is meant to achieve an accurate outcome through the application of clear legal principle to the facts.[19] Whilst this interpretation of procedure was certainly influential, contemporary writers have criticised the fundamental reduction of procedure to the single notion of accuracy. Bentham's hostility to safeguards in the criminal trial also detracts from the contemporary relevance of his work. Thus, those scholars drawing on Bentham's work have argued that his funda-mental insight should be updated, to allow us to see that 'legal standards' are 'supplemented by other normative standards and values'.[20]

Perhaps Bentham ultimately failed to appreciate the forces that animated modernity. In other words, we have to look elsewhere for the 'normative standards and values' that will allow us to address law in its contemporary context. The normative standards that we will use are those of human rights. Why? In terms of the brief history that we are presenting here, we see human rights (at least in some ways) as an inheritance of a radical, democratic

....
17   Bell (1992).
18   Bentham (1838).
19   Opposed to the law of evidence of his day, Bentham argued that this last objective would be provided by a system of 'natural proof' that offered a common sense approach to forensic proof, rather than the arcane rituals that he saw taking place in the court room.
20   Galligan (1996).

inheritance that can be traced back to Tom Paine and the rights of man. It is also worth remembering that in the period when Bentham was writing women did not have the vote, and were not accorded the same civic status as men. The principle of utility is too narrow a basis to think about law and rights. At the same time (and to return to Marx's criticism) the rights of man are, in modern language, distinctly dodgy. To update this insight: we cannot accept human rights in an uncritical way, even though we see them as the underpinnings of our normative argument. We will return to this point in the conclusion to the chapter. For the moment, we need to take stock of our argument. So far, 'revolutionary law' has swept away the feudal hierarchies of privilege and deference. The development of modern law, largely driven by the economics of capitalism and the need for a rational and calculable form of market economy, has continued this re-definition of the social world. To what extent might it be possible, in the new social, economic and political conditions of 'modernity' to continue a tradition of critical thinking about human rights?

Modernity is characterised by the industrial revolution, the growth of market economy and scepticism towards 'metaphysical' values. Rational law becomes the only source of legitimate authority in the state. The concept of formal legal rationality as the definition of authority means that medieval and early modern beliefs about either the divinity of the king, or the 'natural' justice of the rights of man, now have to be subordinated to a new way of thinking and acting. Authority must be held to account through rational principles that apply to all people.

What does this mean for due process? Elaborating this argument would give us a clearer sense of legal procedures: they are specifically legal, existing with a distinct staff of experts, and characterised by their own autonomous institutions. Legal rules – whether relating to procedure or substance, have to have sources that can be delineated; and 'tested'. In other words, if substantive law is defined by its own body of doctrine that determines its rules and principles, the same must be true of procedural law. If this was not the case, we could not speak of a rational order with empirical validity. Law 'develops bodies of rules, which are applied through formal procedures guaranteeing that the rules will be followed in all cases'.

The second important theme for an account of modernity is the growth of modern notions of democracy. As far as the perspective of British politics is concerned, modern democracy is based on the progressive extension of the franchise, so that, with the realisation of votes for women in the early nineteen hundreds, the right to vote was enjoyed by most adults. This is a complex theme, but, we could argue that it is linked to other major concerns such as the growth of political and economic organisation of the working class and the creation of the welfare state. Democracy becomes linked to more than formal equality. It requires government action to manage the economy and ensure at least some measure of social protection against poverty, unemployment and destitution.

Whilst we recognise certain problems with the welfare state, we would also argue that something like the welfare state is a precondition for a functioning market that provides for the needs of human beings. This, of course, takes us away from our consideration of the law, but, we hope to show later in this book how these concerns are inseparable from a proper consideration of law and justice, and remain a real concern for any proper doctrine of human rights. However, we must return to our sketch of the contemporary situation of the law.

When Weber referred to the 'iron cage' of rational capitalism, he was describing the 'legal rational' state and the network of bureaucracy and management that grew up more or less simultaneously as a result of the forces that we have been describing. The pressing question, especially with the welfare state, is how are these networks to be regulated and controlled? We have to appreciate the contradiction that Weber was addressing. The rational management of economy and the state was meant to create a better society. However, the 'administrative density'[21] of the mechanisms that regulate the social and economic worlds are such that they appear to largely operate in their own interests. How can they be made more responsive to the demands of citizens? The point is that these processes of administration and economic regulation frequently either bypass the law, or do not make use of courts. How can we ensure that they are fair? Once again, our argument returns (at least in part) to human rights, but, we need to deal with one last theme before we can develop our answer.

We cannot go into the complex historical factors that link modernity to world war. What is important to our sketch of the history of due process, however, is an acknowledgement that the reconstruction after the global devastation wrought by World War II (1939–45) brought with it an epochal moment at least as significant as the declarations of the rights of man three hundred years earlier: *The Universal Declaration of Human Rights*. To understand the context, we have to remember that the end of WWII was contemporary with processes that brought to an end the European colonial empires, a further refinement of economics around world markets and the integration of nation states into networks of international governance defined by the UN, as well as bodies like the World Bank and the World Trade Organization (WTO). In the aftermath of war, states assumed unprecedented duties of social, economic and political management. To what extent can the administrative and bureaucratic processes inseparable from the tasks of the modern state be accountable, transparent and answerable to the citizens they are meant to serve? These remain pressing questions. We need to focus our analysis on the issues of courts and due process.

DUE PROCESS AS A HUMAN RIGHT

A highly important development is the notion of due process as a human right. This is a very distinct claim. Human rights require us to think about law in a very specific way; the history we recounted in the section above should help make more sense of these themes. The claims to due process, to 'equal protection of the laws' that we examined were implicated in exclusivity; a distinction between men and women, or freemen and slaves, or the colonisers and the colonised. Human rights require law to reflect values of non discrimination, equality and human dignity.

---

21   Habermas (1989).

The Universal Declaration has a number of relevant sections that allow us to link these foundational values to due process. Article 7 is perhaps the core:

> All are equal before the law and are entitled without any discrimination to equal protection of the law. All are entitled to equal protection against any discrimination in violation of this Declaration and against any incitement to such discrimination.

Note how specific this article is about discrimination. Discrimination is in breach of the fundamental principles of human rights – and hence this statement of due process is explicit about the relationship between these two terms. Article 10 provides the essential elaboration of the idea of due process:

> Everyone is entitled in full equality to a fair and public hearing by an independent and impartial tribunal, in the determination of his rights and obligations and of any criminal charge against him.

Note the key terms: the requirement for an impartial and independent tribunal and the fact that due process has to cover both civil rights and criminal charges. The Declaration then goes on to provide specific provisions for criminal law in Article 11:

> (1) Everyone charged with a penal offence has the right to be presumed innocent until proved guilty according to law in a public trial at which he has had all the guarantees necessary for his defence.

> (2) No one shall be held guilty of any penal offence on account of any act or omission which did not constitute a penal offence, under national or international law, at the time when it was committed. Nor shall a heavier penalty be imposed than the one that was applicable at the time the penal offence was committed.

We will presently link these concerns with a much broader understanding of due process. However, to complete our overview of *The Universal Declaration*, we need to refer to Article 5:

> No one shall be subjected to torture or to cruel, inhuman or degrading treatment or punishment.

This can be read alongside Article 9:

> No one shall be subjected to arbitrary arrest, detention or exile.

And finally, Article 8:

> Everyone has the right to an effective remedy by the competent national tribunals for acts violating the fundamental rights granted him by the constitution or by law.

These Articles can perhaps be generally summed up by reference to Article 6: 'Everyone has the right to recognition everywhere as a person before the law'. What does this mean? To be a person with civic status, to be a citizen, requires recognition by the law. We saw above that a slave lacks the recognition of the law. S/he is an it. A non person, a 'thing'. Dignity is a vital concept to explain the fundamental idea at stake in our discussion, as it articulates the moral 'personhood' that defines the human being. Although the idea of moral personhood raises many interesting and demanding philosophical issues, we think the basic idea is fairly easy to understand.

To describe a human being as having dignity is to claim that human beings have distinctive qualities. We could relate this to any number of features that human beings share, such as the capacity to reason, to use language, or even to suffer. If we use the idea of moral personhood, and relate this to dignity, then we are claiming that these features define the equal worth or value of all human beings. The moral personhood of the human being thus relates to the inherent value of human beings; a value linked to the fact that we are reasoning, language using 'creatures' that can be made to suffer. There is another feature of dignity that is of vital importance. Human beings are sociable creatures: they live in society with each other. Dignity describes our 'being together'. This is a somewhat contentious argument. We will return to it in the conclusion as it concerns a philosophical/political point that, whilst it underpins our argument at a depth level, does not (at least in this book) 'operate' in our analysis of the law and the cases. However, it would follow from our arguments about dignity and moral personhood that human beings must be respected by the political, economic and legal institutions that define our common life together.

So, the point that we want to carry forward is that human rights give moral personhood symbolic and material form. The argument that law should respect human rights principles is another way of expressing this central claim: the law needs to treat all citizens as human beings. Surely this is rather anodyne. To what extent does it allow us the critical purchase on law that we advertised above as a central feature of our argument? Our answer would run as follows. The contemporary problem is not simply that of slavery reducing people to things. There are subtler ways of preventing the recognition of people as citizens. This takes us back to our discussion of colonial law (the 'apartheid' regimes of South Africa, and the doctrine of 'equal but different' in American law operated in similar ways). Colonial law did not deprive 'natives' of rights; rather the 'rights' of natives confirmed their inferior status to their masters. The language of *The Universal Declaration* takes seriously the fact that the twentieth century is marked by acts of apartheid and colonialism. We will pick up on these themes, in a somewhat different 'key', in Chapter 5. We also want to stress that our critical approach to due process is an attempt to deal with the administrative and bureaucratic form of the modern state. In contemporary times, the desire to achieve 'value for money' and 'efficiency' means that other values tend to be either forgotten or downplayed, especially in these times of austerity. We need to re-assert different ideas of value and worth. The key point is this: we need to develop a set of general principles that allow us to think about due process as defined in such a way as to ensure that law trial processes are transparent, accountable and allow access to justice for all citizens.

To be precise, we need a normative theory based on principles that allow us to analyse trials as processes that protect the equality and dignity of citizens. Normative, in this context, means that we see a set of principles as underlying due process. At a depth level (the level of philosophical argument) our principles are those of equality, dignity and moral personhood. However, we also need principles that 'translated' these principles into ones of more immediate relevance for law. As our focus is on a particular order of human rights – the European Convention – we will base our normative account of the trial on Article 6. We now turn to the task of developing the outline of a normative theory.

PARTICIPATION, INTEGRITY AND OPEN JUSTICE

We need to be clear about the precise terms of Article 6 before we can develop this argument. Article 6 of the European Convention on Human Rights states:

(1) In the determination of his civil rights and obligations or of any criminal charge against him, everyone is entitled to a fair and public hearing within a reasonable time by an independent and impartial tribunal established by law. Judgement shall be pronounced publicly but the press and public may be excluded from all or part of the trial in the interest of morals, public order or national security in a democratic society, where the interests of juveniles or the protection of the private life of the parties so require, or the extent strictly necessary in the opinion of the court in special circumstances where publicity would prejudice the interests of justice.

1   Everyone charged with a criminal offence shall be presumed innocent until proved guilty according to law.
2   Everyone charged with a criminal offence has the following minimum rights:
    (a) to be informed promptly, in a language which he understands and in detail, of the nature and cause of the accusation against him;
    (b) to have adequate time and the facilities for the preparation of his defence;
    (c) to defend himself in person or through legal assistance of his own choosing or, if he has not sufficient means to pay for legal assistance, to be given it free when the interests of justice so require;
    (d) to examine or have examined witnesses against him and to obtain the attendance and examination of witnesses on his behalf under the same conditions as witnesses against him;
    (e) to have the free assistance of an interpreter if he cannot understand or speak the language used in court.

We can see that Article 6 expressly confers fair hearing rights in broad and unqualified terms.[22] In our consideration of the Article, we will see that the Court has also recognised the 'implied rights' of access to the courts and a series of other fair trial rights. So, to think of due process in human rights terms, we need to have regard to values which contemporary scholars have shown to provide an underpinning normative foundation to both civil and criminal trials. The idea of the normative underpinning of a trial is based on the recent work of scholars who have tried to find the principles

22   Supra, n. 21.

that allow us to think critically about law in a democracy.[23] Although their work is primarily focused on the criminal trial, we can generalise it to think about the underlying structures of both civil and criminal trials. The starting point is the idea that the trial is a holding to account. A criminal trial obviously holds to account in a different way to a civil trial. The former is concerned with criminal conduct, the latter with liability for a breach of civil law. The normative account of the trial stresses the 'communicative' processes that should underlie the way in which a trial seeks to come to an accurate decision. But (to refer back to our comments on Bentham above) whilst accurate decision making is central to the operation of a court, a fair trial requires much more than accuracy. To argue that a trial is a communicative process elaborates this very point.

Communicative processes are clearly ones that involve communication; but to understand this idea, we need to remember that it relates to the idea of a citizen in a democracy. Democratic institutions must treat citizens with respect. The power to fine or imprison, for instance, cannot be based on an arbitrary whim, but must be justified by reference to clear and public principles of law. The idea of the normative, communicative order of the trial, then, is a sophisticated way of thinking about the rule of law at the level of the citizen who finds him or herself before a court. In order to make our discussion manageable within the terms of this book we will stress three essential groupings of principles: those that concern participation, those that concern the integrity of legal procedures and those that relate to open justice. We want to analyse these principles in a little more detail.

How can we think about the integrity of legal proceedings, and how can we relate this concept to Article 6? As far as a criminal court is concerned, the integrity of its proceedings preserves the 'moral authority' of the court which justifies its punishment of citizens who are criminally liable for their acts.[24] We could add that in a civil trial, the court requires a similar moral authority to determine the liability of the defendant for a breach of civil law. Integrity also reflects the requirement that the evidence is true and accurate and that the rights of the defendant or the parties to the action are protected. For a criminal trial this principle is of central importance. Defendants have rights to protect them from the coercive power of the state. Whilst the coercive power of the state is perhaps less present in civil process, the rights of the plaintiff and the defendant need to be balanced to ensure that the court is able to come to an accurate decision. We will see that this issue means that we need to think about access to the courts; a particularly pressing concern in a time when legal aid has contracted significantly and litigation between powerful commercial actors is big business.

In the terms of Article 6, our key point of reference will be the idea that a fair trial requires 'an independent and impartial tribunal established by law'. We will see that this principle applies to the court, the judge and that peculiar common law institution, the jury. We will develop these arguments in Chapter 12. The contemporary jurisprudence of Article 6 also requires us to engage with many of the specialist courts and tribunals that, standing outside the structure of regular courts, deal with matters such

---

23   Duff, Farmer, Marshall and Tadros (2007).
24   Ibid., at 236.

as mental health, the custody of children, welfare benefits and military discipline. These specialist tribunals are central to the regulation of many areas of social life and so – just like the regular courts, must operate in a principled way.

We can briefly deal with a more general theme at this point in our discussion. Our argument about fair trials is clearly focused on courts. For many scholars on civil and criminal justice, our approach could be criticised as it takes our attention away from the variety of other tribunals and mechanisms that characterise, in different ways, the modern approach to dispute resolution which either bypass or downplay the formality of courts. For instance, there is strong evidence that most determinations of criminal liability are based on guilty pleas or plea bargaining that avoids the need for a full trial. In the civil justice system there is increasing use of forms of alternative dispute resolution or mediation that also avoid the need for expensive and time consuming trials.

We have already mentioned that – at least as far as our discussion of integrity is concerned – we will engage with the ways in which 'alternative' tribunals resolve disputes (our focus is on military justice). Our response to criticisms of ignoring alternatives to courts would be similar. Even plea bargaining and the submission of a guilty plea take place 'in the shadow of the courts'.[25] to the extent that the decisions made by the actors involved require them to think about what would happen if the matter did go to trial. Our approach to civil justice in Chapter 15 also shows what is at stake in privileging alternative ways of resolving disputes. The increasing use of alternatives to courts might suggest something about the political choices that require civil and criminal processes to be structured around less costly forms of dispute resolution.

Participation[26] as a principle of a fair trial can be linked to a diverse set of themes: a person should be able to influence processes in which their interests are at stake.[27] But it is not just this ethics of citizenship that underpins participation. The importance of participation also lies behind procedural principles that enable a person to give evidence and respond to questions aimed at elucidating the issues and the possibilities of their resolution. By making information available in this way, it enables the adjudicator to make a full and 'balanced' decision. Participation of the accused in the criminal trial requires that the defendant has a chance to reply to the charge and to take part in the search for 'truth' that requires the accused to question their own behaviour. As a form of 'moral criticism', the trial attempts to confront the accused with the consequences of his or her act, and this would lack legitimacy if the findings of the court were simply thrust upon them.[28]

....

25   Ibid.
26   Participation is difficult to define, as it covers a range of different concerns. Participation in forensic processes relates to the rights of the parties to 'present their cases and respond to the cases against them' (Ibid., 130). Parties can also call witnesses and choose whether to give evidence themselves. This full adversarial model is perhaps the most realised form of participation, which can also include far more minimal forms of involvement, such as 'the barest opportunity to present a statement of facts and perhaps an expression of opinion'. At an administrative level, participation tends to be 'consultative' in nature – which again takes different forms from the full public inquiry to the mere chance to 'submit a written statement'. Participation in politics is generally expressed through voting either in local or general elections – but – it can also mean party activism.
27   Supra, n. 11.
28   Ibid., 138.

Our discussion of the principle of participation and Article 6 will engage with three doctrines that have developed in fair trial jurisprudence: the rights of the defence, equality of arms and access to justice. It is perhaps somewhat peculiar to consider the rights of the defence from the perspective of participation. One of the features of the criminal trial that we will discuss is the right of the defendant *not* to participate. For instance, as the prosecution bear the burden of proof, a defendant does not have to participate in his or her trial at all. There are also principles of evidence that limit the terms of participation by, for example, excluding prejudicial or self incriminatory evidence. There is still a qualified 'right to silence'. Furthermore, the 'professionalisation' of the criminal trial means that many defendants are represented by lawyers and play very little real part in their own defence. It would seem strange, and even possibly contradictory to privilege the importance of participation of the defendant in a criminal trial.

The point is that the participation principle is qualified by other important features of the trial. Whilst the criminal trial can be modelled as a 'holding to account', the coercive power of the state that mobilises resources to prosecute crime must be checked by principles that either limit the kind of evidence that can be used against the accused in the interests of accurate and fair decision making. The representation of the defendant's interests by a professional lawyer can be justified in a similar way. There is another argument that justifies the defendant's refusal to 'participate' in his/her defence, but we will discuss this below in the context of the principle of open justice.

The doctrine of equality of arms can also be thought about in terms of criminal evidence. The key point is that the trial should preserve a more or less equal balance between the defence and the prosecution, and we will examine a number of key authorities where Article 6 jurisprudence has impacted on the common law. The last section of the chapter considers access to the courts. We have already mentioned this concern in discussing the integrity principle, but, we will deal with it in more detail in our study of participation in both civil and criminal trials. A citizen should be able to access the courts to protect his or her rights; and cost or inefficiency should not impact unduly so as to restrict the use of the courts. Civil and criminal courts do not just deal with private individuals. There are commercial, industrial and business interests that both make use of the civil courts and find themselves subject to criminal penalties. The power of these bodies to mobilise resources can, in some instances, be equal or greater than that of national governments, and certainly goes far beyond those of individuals or groups of individuals. Due process does, to some extent, take this disparity of resources into account, as indeed it must do if it is linked to the concept that the courts must be open to all. It would arguably be a breach of due process if an individual was deprived of public resources that would enable him or her to sue a powerful company; or indeed to protect him or herself from aggressive assertions of economic power. We will see in Chapter 13 that one of the longest running pieces of civil litigation in English legal history concerns this very issue. Due process must take into account these issues of access.

The principle of open justice is related to both the participation principle, and the requirement for the integrity of procedures. The influence of the doctrine of natural justice is a clear influence on this concept of procedure: justice must be seen to be done.[29] We will relate this to the broader role of the criminal and civil courts in a democracy; and, indeed, back to the requirements of public reason. We will thus stress the importance of the 'duty to give reasons' under Article 6.[30] We will also argue that the right to open justice can be linked to the prohibition on torture evidence. To further stress the main points: torture evidence would 'make the whole trial not only immoral and illegal, but also entirely unreliable in its outcome'. Thus any use of torture evidence would amount to 'a flagrant denial of justice if such evidence were admitted in a criminal trial'.

The justification of open justice ultimately takes us to a peculiar principle of democracy. A public trial allows scrutiny of the courts which improves the quality of decision making. But, open justice is not simply founded on this 'instrumental' objective. We need to see the principle: 'in terms of the rights of citizens either to affirm verdicts or to distance themselves from them, rights that are grounded in the critical independence that liberal democracies ought to afford their citizens'.[31] Our defence of open justice takes us back to our arguments about public reason. Critical public reason, or the principle of open justice, may tell us a great deal about the role of the courts, but it also forces us to think about the values of the rule of law in a democratic polity.

There is a final point that we want to make. The principles of integrity, participation and open justice are not hard edged. We mean that there are significant over-laps between the three principles, and that we have only defined then in the way that we have for analytical convenience. One could, for instance, argue that the right of access to the courts is as much part of the principle of integrity as it is participation. The point is that, whatever the identity of the individual principles, they amount to an identification of those underlying jurisprudential themes that structure a fair trial.

JUSTICE, RIGHTS AND DEMOCRATIC CULTURE

To briefly recap: the right to a fair trial – to processes characterised by integrity, participation and openness is a core human right of citizens in a democracy.

Recall the brief history of due process that we sketched out above. From the perspective of the law, the equality of citizens is entirely formal. This means that procedural justice tends to accord rights on the basis of the principle that all are equal before the law. Anatole France's famous statement 'the law equally forbids the rich and the poor from sleeping in the street and stealing bread'[32] is a pithy way of explaining this concern. The law has no concern with the material inequalities that exist between people. This is a difficult theme, and one that we only touch upon in the last section of Chapter 13. We argue that the right of access to the court shows an acknowledgement within human rights law that formal equality requires at least some recognition of

29   Jacob (2007).
30   Ibid., 1403. Although Article 6 does not contain the duty to give reasons, 'the right to a fair hearing generally carries with it an obligation to give reasons'.
31   Supra, n. 28, at 270.
32   A rather free translation of: 'La majestueuse égalité des lois, qui interdit au riche comme au pauvre de coucher sous les ponts, de mendier dans les rues et de voler du pain'. From *Le Lys Rouge* (1894).

material inequality. Whilst this does not amount to a 'right to legal aid', a democratic system of formal justice does require the state to provide resources for those without the necessary means to defend themselves in court and to assert their rights. We pick up on this point in Chapter 15 where we make use of Rawls' (1971) theory of justice to think critically about the operation of the civil justice system.

In conclusion, we want to stress a final point. Our discussion of contemporary common law assumes a problematic political reality: '[l]ong-term survey evidence suggests that the public . . . regard democratic institutions such as Parliament as increasingly irrelevant; and have growing concerns about levels of corruption in politics and government'. There is a general perception that standards of conduct in public life have declined[33] and that the rise of both political and material equality 'is widening rapidly and even provisions intended to guarantee basic human rights are increasingly being brought into question'. Even the '"minimal" guarantee of key civil and political rights' under the Human Rights Act has been called into question.

There is another major area of concern: 'corporate power is growing, partly as a result of wider patterns of globalisation and deregulation'. The growth of corporate power 'threatens to undermine some of the most basic principles of democratic decision-making'. In particular, 'ways in which policy-making appears to have shifted from the democratic arena to a far less transparent set of arrangements in which politics and business interests have become increasingly interwoven'. One compelling piece of evidence is the 'closeness of relationships between senior politicians and large media corporations, most notably News International'.

These troubling themes do not just appear in social surveys and audits on the health of British democracy. They are increasingly present in legal scholarship. Nicol for one, has argued that the 'political elites [feel] threatened by democracy' and want 'their business-friendly policy preferences to be less effectively contested'. Nicol's concerns are part of a wider picture. Business friendly policies seek to 'promote privatisation and ward off socialistic encroachments by states'. The distortion of democracy places 'economic liberties beyond the reach of majoritarian control'.[34] Debates on human rights and politics are symptoms of these wider issues. In keeping with the argument we present on interpretative prejudice in Chapter 6, it is only reasonable to outline our own at the beginning of the book: it is necessary to re-assert the democratic credentials of the law.

THE HUMAN RIGHTS ACT 1998: A LEGAL AND POLITICAL OVERVIEW

This short chapter overviews the key provisions of the HRA. It is not intended as a detailed description of the Act – rather, it should be read as an introduction to some of the fundamental themes that will be discussed in this book. Thus, our main concern is to outline the interpretative provisions under s.2 and s.3. We will also be concerned

33   http://democracy-uk-2012.democraticaudit.com/assets/documents/how_democratic_is_uk.pdf
34   Nicol (2010: 18–19).

with declarations of incompatibility (s.4) and their effects on legislation (s.10). A final section will take a brief look at the politics of the Human Rights Act, and the possibility of a British Bill of Rights.

Section 2(1) of the Act specifies that in the interpretation of Convention rights,[35] a court or tribunal must take into account a number of sources of European human rights law[36] if 'in the opinion of the court or tribunal, it is relevant to the proceedings in which that question has arisen'. The court thus has a discretion to determine whether or not the authorities are relevant to the proceedings in question; even if they pre-date the Act.[37] The Act then goes on to state at 3(1), that as far as the interpretation of legislation is concerned, primary legislation and subordinate or delegated legislation must be read and given effect so that they are compatible with Convention rights, 'so far as it is possible to do so'. Once again, the court has a wide discretion to determine whether or not legislation is Convention compliant. Section 3(2) concerns the extent of this section's operation. It applies, first of all, to primary legislation and subordinate legislation whenever enacted. Bear in mind that incompatibility does not affect the validity or continuing operation of any provision, or the validity or continued operation of incompatible subordinate legislation, if the primary legislation from which it is derived prevents the removal of that incompatibility.[38]

What, then, should happen in the event of a court determining that legislation is incompatible with a Convention right? This takes us to section 4. Section 4(2) states that when a court[39] finds that a provision is incompatible with a Convention right, it may make a declaration of that incompatibility.[40] What effect does a declaration of incompatibility have? We need to look at section 10: 10(1) states that if a provision of legislation has been declared incompatible, and if certain conditions are satisfied with reference to the fact that there will not be an appeal against this incompatibility, then a minister may, under section 10(2) make such an order that the incompatibility

----

35   That is, those under the European Convention on Human Rights – ECHR.
36   These are:

    (a)   judgment, decision, declaration or advisory opinion of the European Court of Human Rights;
    (b)   opinion of the Commission given in a report adopted under Article 31 of the Convention.
    (c)   certain decisions of the Commission in connection with Articles 26 and 27 of the Convention; or
    (d)   decisions of the Committee of Ministers taken under Article 46 of the Convention.

37   Section 2(1) states that the relevant source can be taken into account 'whenever made or given'.
38   Lewis contrasts s.2 of the HRA with 3(1) of the EC Act 1972, which states that UK courts are bound by the decisions of the ECJ, 729. Later, he cites Masterman's rationale for the structure of the HRA, which in turn (at least for the first three points, are taken from statements of Lord Irvine during Parliamentary debate). Domestic courts are not bound to follow the ECtHR because: (a) the Convention is the 'ultimate' source of law; but has 'no strict rule of precedent' (731); (b) the Convention states that the UK is bound only by rulings in cases in which it was a party; (c) [from the White Paper], the common law courts must be free to develop Convention law; (d) as the judgments of the ECHR are 'declaratory' in nature, it is difficult to follow them as precedent decisions. Lewis cites Clayton's (below) argument that there is a difference between the way in which the ECtHR and common law courts produce their decisions. This makes it all the more necessary to qualify strict adherence to the mirror principle and to develop indigenous interpretations of the Convention.
39   A court is defined as (4(5)): the House of Lords; the Judicial Committee of the Privy Council; the Courts-Martial Appeal Court; in Scotland, the High Court of Justiciary sitting otherwise than as a trial court or the Court of Session; in England and Wales or Northern Ireland, the High Court or the Court of Appeal.
40   Note that, by 4(6), a declaration of incompatibility under this section affects neither the validity, continuing operation, nor the enforcement of the provision in respect of which it is given; and, secondly, the declaration is not binding on the parties to the proceedings in which it is made.

will be removed. The Act states that the minister 'may' make an order if there are 'compelling reasons' for so doing. It is not a duty to make an order, because this would effectively mean that a court could compel a change in the law. The Human Rights Act thus leaves the sovereignty of Parliament in place.[41]

A Ministry of Justice Report published in 2011,[42] made available the following figures on Declarations of Incompatibility:

> Since the Human Rights Act 1998 came into force on 2 October 2000, 27 declarations of incompatibility have been made. Of these. . . . 12 will have been remedied by primary legislation, 2 will have been remedied by a remedial order under section 10 of the Human Rights Act [and] 4 related to provisions that had already been remedied by primary legislation at the time of the declaration; 1 is under consideration as to how to remedy the incompatibility.

How can we assess the significance of these figures? The Department of Constitutional Affairs (published in 2006) report puts them in the context of the HRA's impact on policy and the policy-making process.[43] The fundamental problem is the difficulty of isolating the effect of the Act in the complex series of inputs that feed into policy.[44] The report asserts that overall, on the evidence available, there has been a 'significant' and 'beneficial' influence of the Act on central government.[45] The Act has led to the formalisation of policy making processes, and has arguably made for changes of behaviour within public authorities, as they become more sensitive to human rights issues. Moreover, litigation under the Act has led to changes in policy and the methods of its implementation. Furthermore, the Act has ensured that the needs of the diverse groups that make up the population of the UK are represented in policy making, promoting 'greater personalisation' and thus 'better public services'. This does indeed suggest that sections 3, 4, and 10 have created mechanisms that have enabled a dialogue to develop between the courts and central and local government. Any substantive assessment of these policy networks would take us beyond the scope of this short review but we could argue that the HRA has had a structural impact in these areas, and that human rights have become more central to the governmental processes and policies.

As we look at the impact of s.2 and s.3 in the context of the relationship between Strasbourg and the domestic courts in Chapters 7 and 8, developments in the area of statutory interpretation in Chapter 9, and broader questions around judicial

---

41   How often are Declarations of Incompatibility issued? Since 2000, there have been eight declarations relating to various areas of law: mental health, immigration, taxation, offences against the person, sentencing, and embryology. (Statistics based on information supplied to the Human Rights Unit by the Human Rights Act Research Unit, Doughty Street Chambers, London, based on cases reported in *Lawtel Human Rights Interactive* and Butterworths *Human Rights Direct* from case transcripts available from 2 October 2000 to 13 December 2001.)

42   http://www.justice.gov.uk/downloads/publications/moj/2011/responding-to-human-rights-judgments.pdf

43   DCA, Review of the Implementation of the Human Rights Act, July 2006, 20. In only one instance was a remedial order issued.

44   Any assessment also depends on the assessor's point of view: for instance, someone assessing whether or not targets for delivery of social services are met is unlikely to be particularly concerned with the role played by the HRA; any consideration of the regulatory framework of the delivery of public services would have to contend with the centrality of the HRA.

45   Supra, n. 22, at 22.

interpretation of the HRA in Chapters 10 and 11, we don't want to anticipate our conclusions at this point.

THE POLITICS OF HUMAN RIGHTS

The General Election of 2010 brought to an end over a decade of Labour government, but with no party commanding an overall majority, a Coalition of the Liberal Democrats and the Conservatives took office. Although we cannot assess the record of the Labour government in this short update, we do want to draw attention to some broad themes which are relevant to our argument. The change of government has, arguably, opened up a new approach to the HRA. In opposition, the Conservative Party had been crtical of the HRA. In May 2007 David Cameron stated that 'the civil liberties of the suspect' were being put 'first' by the courts.[46] Cameron has argued that the HRA has brought about a culture of 'rights without responsibilities'.[47]

This relates to the argument (put forward by New Labour Ministers, as well as the present government) that human rights are inconvenient and limit executive action (in particular, David Cameron alleges, in the areas of criminal justice and anti-terrorism policing). Another Tory Minister, Dominic Grieve, has argued that the new bill of rights 'would make it clear that British courts could allow UK common law to take precedence over decisions by the European court of human rights in Strasbourg'.[48] Grieve has stated that it would be necessary to 'reword' a British Bill of Rights to stress 'our own national jurisprudence and traditions' whilst still 'acknowledging the relevance of Strasbourg court decisions'.[49]

The Coalition's room for political manoeuvre is profoundly limited given the Conservative's reliance on their Liberal-Democrat partners, who are committed to the HRA. Lord McNally, the justice minister and a senior Liberal Democrat, has said he would resign from the government rather than see the UK withdraw from the European convention, to which Britain has been a signatory for more than 60 years. Writing in *The Guardian* in 2010, he stated that: 'the Convention is not "someone else's law". It was never imposed on Britain. The UK proposed the creation of the convention at the end of the second world war'. However Lord McNally did give some suggestion that a British bill might be possible. He stated that he wanted to look 'afresh at the way rights are protected in the UK, to see if things can be done better and in a way that properly reflects our legal traditions'. This seems quite general, and not that helpful as a way of trying to work out what Dominic Grieve means. Nor does it give unequivocal support to a British Bill of Rights.[50]

----

46   http://www.guardian.co.uk/politics/2006/jun/26/conservatives.constitution
47   Ibid.
48   Patrick Wintour, *The Guardian*, 16/1/11 at http://www.guardian.co.uk/law/2011/feb/16/bill-of-rights-review-imminent-david-cameron
49   Ibid.
50   Tom McNally, *The Guardian*, 21/11/10 at http://www.guardian.co.uk/commentisfree/libertycentral/2010/nov/21/convention-human-rights-britain-coalition. We have chosen not to analyse the arguments for a British Bill of Rights, as the final report has not yet been published.

3

'AS A SYSTEM . . . THE COMMON LAW IS A THING MERELY IMAGINARY'[1]

English legal development appears as a historical continuum. There is no obvious rupture, no wholesale wiping out of the legal wisdom of centuries and no division of the law into a pre- and a post-revolutionary era. In English law the present is never completely shut off from the past and its historical roots are easily perceived.[2]

Out of hard and bitter experience, Englishmen had come to learn that the remorseless, incalculable power of the past over the present was not to be dispelled by the strivings of a single generation. From 1660 onwards, England was never again entirely to forget that the secret of a nation's strength is to have the power of the historic past behind it, not against it.[3]

INTRODUCTION: ORIENTATION AND THE USE OF HISTORY

What is the role of history in the common law world?

Where did Australian law begin? According to traditional legal historiography the origins of Australian law are found in England, around the time of the Norman Conquest in 1066. The English law that developed in the succeeding centuries was ultimately imported to Australia by the British colonists, laying the foundations for an Australian law which grew to have a separate existence from its English parent. This account assumes that the history of law in Australia, like all other Australian histories, began only with the 'discovery' of Australia by Captain Cook in 1770.[4]

As with this account of Australian law so my [WJM] legal education. I attended law school at the University of Canterbury (New Zealand) in the mid to late 1970s. The first year of the four-year law degree contained only one law subject – *Legal*

---

1   This title is an edited version of a quote from Jeremy Bentham (1928: 125); the full quote reads 'as a system of rules'.
2   Van Caenegem (1986: 8).
3   S. Chrimes, discussing the events of the civil war, overthrow of Charles I and virtual replacement by the army under Oliver Cromwell and the attempt to create a new system of government (along with a written constitution), the failure of that enterprise and the recall to the throne of the heir of Charles Stuart, in the small work on English Constitutional History I [WJM] used as a supplementary text, S. Chrimes, 1st ed. (1948). We used the 3rd ed. (1965: 158).
4   Mathew, Hunter and Charlesworth (1995: 3).

System. This was a 'filter subject', which one had to pass along with the non-law subjects at a good grade to allow one to enter law school proper. It was not even called *New Zealand Legal System*. Perhaps that was as well, for it was a trawl through a set of historical events and institutions, images in words, of England. Beginning with an idea of rough and ready customs before the Norman Conquest of England in 1066, we sat in the same packed lecture hall (and the lectures were repeated twice as demand for places so great) week in and week out to construct a set of notes concerning such items as Shire Courts and the Curia Regis, the Magna Carta, the role of juries (which protected us subjects of England's great providential history from the terrors of continental torture), Chief Justice Coke's confrontation with the Crown in which he reminded the king that the king was not above the law but partly constituted by the law, the development of the 'spirit of judicial independence', the glories of equity (and Lord Mansfield's attempts to fuse equity and the common law), the development of the 'modern' courts (and there was a certain repugnance attached to the word 'modern'). Students and lecturer were in New Zealand, yet we were not working with New Zealand material and it seemed as if the lecturer did not particularly like being in New Zealand (the bearing that he presented was very much of a colonial administrator having worked as a public prosecutor in Kenya prosecuting, solid rumour had it, members of the Mau Mau uprising/insurgency against British rule), but he was sure that the common law – along with parliamentary democracy and cricket – were gifts that New Zealanders ought to appreciate. Later in the year we did legal method using a mixture of English and New Zealand cases, but legal method was prefaced by legal history; it was through legal history that we were told the identity of that strange phenomenon that we were to study – the common law legal system.

I was bemused by that lecturer and his style. He began sometimes with, 'Now last time I saw you I ended with [dramatic pause] . . . a comma, after the comma comes the word . . .', and on it would drone at a pace just sufficient for us to sit there writing down his words as a comprehensive set of 'lecture notes', but the impact of those classes lingers on and the implicit pedagogical answer to the issue of modern law's identity – history – needs evaluation. It is important to distinguish my distaste for the experience from the act of questioning what 'legal history' is a history of. And why was that presentation of *Legal System* a collection of 'images' from the past? And what now, located in London, can I make of it all?

Pedagogy, content and ideology

I now label this early experience 'instructionist teaching' that did not involve students in doing any real activities. We faced activities later in the second part of the course which focused on legal method and they were very much concerned with reading case reports, identifying key common law features (many defined in Latin such as *ratio decendidi* and *obiter dicta*), and getting to know how to find and use the 'sources' of law such as the techniques of finding case reports, digests and legislation in the library and then using these sources to construct arguments. I went faithfully to my Legal System lectures; I did not to *Introduction to Sociology*. The *Legal System* module was assessed by examinations (25 per cent mid-sessional and 75 per cent final year); two of my other subjects were largely coursework-based with the examinations only taking up 30 per cent of the assessment. In *Introduction to Politics* I completed projects on Japan (on the Liberal Democratic Party and the Japanese Constitution [written unlike New Zealand and the UK]), while in *Sociology* I was faced virtually from day one with the necessity of reading scholarly journals (with their rather peculiar language) to construct a series of assessed essays (on 'father figures' such as Weber and 'concepts' such as power and social development). I hardly attended the lectures in *Sociology* and my memory presents me with a rather different and revealing counter position to *Legal System*. As I remember it, I was put off by the presentation of a young lecturer (dressed in jeans and shirt) from the north of England who claimed that Marxism was the most relevant theoretical stance to explain then contemporary New Zealand (including its legal distribution of 'rights' and 'property') and if we would not see that then we were in the grip of 'ideological mystification'. Through his performance I sat, hardly taking notes, thinking, 'Who is this "outsider", this "whinging POM?" ' (as we termed anyone from England who complained about our country). Coming from a small town and partly raised on a farm, I gave more attention to the statements in *Introduction to Economics* on the role of pork bellies in the construction of the Chicago Futures Market (the 'MERC') and decided to invest what spare cash I had in the Stock Exchange (later taken out and the practice not continued at ongoing considerable loss to my potential economic benefit).

The small figure lecturing in full academic gown in *Legal System* carried more 'authority'; after all as a public prosecutor in Kenya he had defended the state (and possibly 'civilisation') from the Mau Mau 'emergency'. If he thought that legal history was our route into law, then who were we to question?

This, in both crude and sophisticated forms, has been until recently a standard view. Consider the following two quotations:

> Speculation about law and politics is an attractive pursuit. More especially is it attractive to the young. A small knowledge of the rules of law, a sympathy with hardships which have been observed, and a little ingenuity, are sufficient to make a very pretty theory . . . It is a harder task to become a master of Anglo-American law, by using the history of that law to discovery the principles which underlie its rules, and to elucidate the manner in which these principles have been developed and adapted to meet the infinite complexities of life in different ages. But those who have chosen to endure this harder task have chosen the better part . . . for, as Hale said, 'It is most certain that time and long experience is much more ingenious, subtle and judicious, than all the wisest and acutest wits in the world coexisting can be.'[5]

> The English legal system, which includes for this purpose that of the United States of America and most of the British Commonwealth of Nations, is peculiar among modern systems in this unbroken link with the past. It is the heritage of a profession which made its own law and whose debt to foreign systems is small.[6]

----

5   Holdsworth (1928: 104–105).
6   Potter (1943: 2).

Both date from the first half of the twentieth century. The first writer is William Holdsworth, a greatly respected legal historian; the second is a more mundane but respected law professor. While very much a history in which we have 'an eye on the end of the story' (perhaps a version of the progress wins in history meta-narrative), Holdsworth's legal history was self-consciously educative; 'effective legal history' rather than 'mere antiquarianism' enabled us to learn lessons about what was successful, about those things that underpinned the contemporary. By contrast I have little recollection of any normative thread to the 'history' I was recounted, perhaps there was but I took the message to be more celebratory, rejoice (New Zealanders) in what you are a product of. While Holdsworth was a comparativist, asserting that both the legal systems of England and of Rome had solved the 'difficult problem of combining stability with elasticity',[7] a Potter style history (as displayed in the second quotation above) disavowed that there was any worth in presenting a multiplicity of perspectives. The narrative we were implicitly presented with may be then of one story, one past and one future. Perhaps again I am simplifying my recollection of the pedagogy I experienced, or perhaps the lecturer had already dumbed-down the message or, more prosaically, had simply inherited the course and someone else's notes; alternatively this may have been just the first stage of the intellectual apprenticeship of joining the legal profession and we needed a course on its tradition as a precursor before we got down to the more practical task of learning the 'rules' and policy disputes of contemporary practice. After all, until relatively recently one did not learn the common law by going to university; one learnt it by observing others in practice, by apprenticeship, and there is justification for that. If we assume that law has its own realm, and it has developed in accordance with a set of processes and practices that have given it its own specificity then it follows that we learn what law is by entering into that realm and learning to accept and play the game by the 'rules' of its internal dynamics, customs, methods of arguing and persuading and ways of action, and that this is the true method of understanding, not seeking knowledge from some 'external' vision such as that of a sociologist. Take the words of the legal historian and writer on 'legal transplants', Alan Watson, who presents the growth and evolution of the law as largely determined by an autonomous legal tradition that exists and operates independently of the demands of societal factors.

> There is a lawyer's way to approach a problem. This mode of thinking inoculates them from too much concern with the demands of society.[8]

> Law . . . is above all and primarily the culture of the lawyers and especially of the law-makers, that is, of those lawyers who, whether as legislators, jurists, or judges, have control of the accepted mechanisms of legal change. Legal development is determined by their culture; and social, economic, and political factors impinge on legal development only through their consciousness . . . Law is largely autonomous and not shaped by societal needs; though legal institutions will not exist without corresponding social institutions, law evolves from the legal tradition.[9]

---

7   Ibid., 9.
8   Watson (1985: 42).
9   Ibid., 119.

For Watson the success of what he termed legal transplants provided a conclusive demonstration for his arguments:

> To a large extent law possesses a life and vitality of its own; that is, no extremely close, natural or inevitable relationship exists between law, legal structures, institutions and rules on the one hand and the needs and desires and political economy of the ruling elite or of the members of the particular society on the other hand. If there was such a close relationship, legal rules, institutions and structures would transplant only with great difficulty, and their power of survival would be severely limited.[10]

So then for us in New Zealand, and elsewhere in the lands affected by British imperialism (the common law world), the common law had been 'transplanted' and our law, New Zealand law, gained its identity not by politics or struggle in particular socio-economic domains but through the internal dynamics and culture of the common law 'tradition'. The small amount of New Zealand history that we did note consisted in the acts whereby we, seemingly without much more than instances of a little 'local trouble', adopted English common law as our law.[11]

But I knew from undertaking my *Introduction to Politics* course that the Japanese constitution (and legal system) adopted after the Meiji Restoration in 1889 was very much a political act in response to acts of an external power (the difficulty of maintaining Japan's isolation after the display of power by Commodore Perry of the US Navy). But that was a university course where we learnt about 'them'; it was a course in understanding another system and culture, undertaken on borrowed time (before I did proper legal studies); we did no such 'external' accounts to our own.

The difference may in part be explained as a matter of assigning identities to the different players: the sociologist is given the status of an observer, a spectator who seeks to attain a distancing from practices, the regularities, the human actors, to cast aside any familiarity he has from that what he is observing so that he can gain the grasp of an independent 'science' and return with greater insight and deeper familiarity. The lawyer, in counter-position, gains the status of an actor, who takes his or her meanings from the viewpoint of the internal participant, one who is engaged, who participates in practices that are value laden.

So what then of the images I had been presented with? What was my role as audience? Why do I have no recollection of any narrative binding them together? Should some intellectual order have been imposed so strongly upon them that I can still recollect a message as to what the 'system' added up to? But whose system was it? There was a certain existential imbalance. Why were we students given a history, but not of 'our' system? Did New Zealand have a legal system or a simple 'import'? What was, if

---

10   Watson (1978: 314–315).
11   So, in a small book we used as a back up in constitutional law: Chrimes (1965) 3rd ed. (my copy had been bought and sold in the law students' second-hand book sales eight times before my purchase, an indication of its centrality) we read: 'The English Constitution is remarkable for many reasons. Alone among existing Constitutions it is the product of a history never entirely broken over a period of some fourteen centuries. Notwithstanding its long history, it is in the highest degree adaptable to the needs of changing circumstances and conditions . . . It is remarkable also in having been exported whole-scale, often more or less *en bloc*, to distant lands. . .' (pp. 2–3).

any, the link between the history of the first term and the analytical training – the techniques of legal method in the second?

Now, years later, as a legal academic I accept there are at least two different ways of approaching the study of a 'legal system'; one is analytical, defining the constituent elements and tracing their functional or logical interconnections; another is historical. Contemporary legal system texts and courses largely ignore history; accounts of purposes, functions and social policy have replaced it.[12] I do not seek to analyse the reasons for this, merely to note it. I take this to be what Bentham – a great believer in the enlightenment drive for rationality, system and order – meant in his late eighteenth century criticism that the common law as presented by people such as Blackstone (who portrayed it as historical creation) was not really a system of law at all. Perhaps what I experienced was the repetition of an act of recounting that once was vital but had become a tired old trope. If so then that recounting of the history of the common law was an exercise that once had given it legitimacy and identity, but was now simply a genuflection to ritual where the real action was becoming learning sets of rules and proceedings with discussions of policy, or functions, or effectiveness, disentangled from history.[13] What can I re-imagine? Perhaps not a system of law, but elements of a tradition . . . .

ORIGINS

The Norman Conquest is a catastrophe which determined the whole future of English Law.[14]

Britain had not been conquered . . . she felt no need to exorcise the past.[15]

Time has a particular relationship with common law. On one level the acceptance of custom – historically the first major source of common law – was that it ran from time out of mind, from time immemorial, later accepted as from 1189 (the first year of the reign of Richard I). Another is of the common law as a unique combination of continuity and change. Sir Mathew Hale presented an analogy with the ship of the Argonauts: thus although continually changing, the common law kept its essential nature.[16] The two quotes immediately above reflect a dilemma at the heart of

---

12   See Partington (2003), beginning with 'Knowledge, themes and structure', then 'Law and Society: the purposes and functions of law'. Cownie and Bradney (1996) in *English Legal System* in Context begin by asking 'What is "the English Legal System"?'

13   Allison (2007) in a text entitled *The Historical Constitution: Continuity, Change and European Effects* presents the two sides of Dicey.

14   Pollock and Maitland (1898: 79).

15   Jean Monnet (one of the intellectual figures behind the EU), in his memoirs (Monnet, 1978) reflecting upon the different attitude Britain took to the European community than France and Germany.

16   'But tho' those particular Variations and Accessions have happened in the Laws, yet they being only partial and successive, we may with just Reason say, They are the same English Laws now, that they were 600 Years since in the general. As the Argonauts Ship was the same when it returned home, as it was when it went out, tho' in that long Voyage it had successive Amendments, and scarce came back with any of its former Materials; and as Titius is the same Man he was 40 Years since, tho' Physicians tells us, That in a Tract of seven Years, the Body has scarce any of the same Material Substance it had before.' From Hale (1971: 39) *The History of the Common Law*, written in the seventeenth century.

understanding the interconnections of common law tradition, British identity and constitutionalism. The history of gradualism and piecemeal change inherent in Monnet's succinct statement contrasts to most countries; the United Kingdom has few overriding constitutional movements or events of great change such as revolutions. One context for the argument for and practical creation of the European Community, now the European Union, was the catastrophic wars continental Europe experienced over the centuries and in particular in World War I and World War II. Whereas China, for example, had in the twentieth century three radically contrasting systems of government and three entirely rewritten constitutions; the twentieth century saw great changes in the UK but its land was never invaded and its constitutional developments, such as its reform Acts or devolution of power on Scotland and Wales, and the significance of the joining the evolving EEC/EU were gradual rather than revolutionary, evolutionary rather than imposed by events and people from outside.

Under the narratives of gradualist legal evolution the common law of England is traced back in its development as the oldest state law in Europe in the sense that England existed as a state (though not in the sense of a nation-state that was to become the popular motif of state formation in modern society) as old as the Anglo-Saxons with a relatively centralised currency, law (albeit customary based) and an administration of justice that gave a role for central officials. It developed as the oldest body of law that was common to a whole kingdom and administered by a central court with a nation-wide competence in first instance. In the rest of Europe at that time, the law was either European or local, not particular to a state. Some European countries adopted the cosmopolitan *jus commune* (Roman or canon law, shared by learned lawyers over Europe) to provide a national legal system that their divergent customs could not produce. In England, a common law was produced out of the mixture of Norman land law and the courts dealing with English customs and via an administrative class linked to the crown. Ironically that class was not English at all but kings and justices of continental extraction: the disputed point of origin was the invasion of the Anglo-Saxon kingdom by the Normans under William Duke of Normandy. I will begin by contrasting two images concerning the Norman Conquest: one of violence and the other of administration and centralisation.

First a central image to British historical consciousness is the famous Battle of Hastings, often called the cataclysm of 1066, when the Norman Duke William defeated the English King Harold and claimed the throne of England.

The victory of William Duke of Normandy poses a problem for any ideology of continuity and unbroken evolution for it led to the succession of a new dynasty, the dispossession of a native aristocracy and the creation of a split society. The *Franci* became the dominant minority, introducing values, rules and a language different from those of the native masses (the *Anglici*). This is dramatic change: how then is the image of the laws of England being the expression of national identity preserved?

The traditional explanation, which preserves the identity of the common law from being seen as actually foreign, is a paradox: William was a political victor (he who 'gained' the Throne) who left the law alone. But this is partly, at least, mythological. Of course, it was an important tool of ruling that one could present it as preserving an existing system, but there were many changes and introductions. The Anglo-Saxon system of administration had many features that we can see as more efficient than

Figure 3.1 Death of King Harold at the Battle of Hastings.
Source: Cassell's *Illustrated History of England* (1900) p. 81, which states 'the great battle of Hastings, which lasted from sunrise to sunset, and which, for the valour displayed by both armies and their leaders, was worthy to decide a contest for a crown'. The term 'Conqueror' here bears the original meaning of 'the Gainer'. William claimed not the right of a usurper but those of a lawful heir to the English throne.

those in use on the continent – such as the use of a centralised system of money exchange with taxation – and so preservation of the main features of the system was efficient as well as good rhetoric. Yet the fact remains that the resulting system was a blend. Take the situation of Henry II (1154–1189), who is often referred to as the father of the common law. Here the system was not just English: Henry was titled King of the English, Duke of the Normans and Aquitanians and Count of Angevins. Under his administration locally chosen sheriffs were changed into royally appointed agents charged with effectively enforcing the law and collecting taxes in the counties. Henry made use of juries (then used as instruments for the presentation of facts of the locality) and reintroduced the sending of justices (judges) on regular tours of the country to hear cases for the crown. His legal reforms led him to be called the father of the common law; he died in France in 1189 at war with his son Richard (later Richard I, the Lionheart).

My second image reflects the opportunity that the pre-existing system gave to this new energised and competent élite.

I use this image as symbolising the formation of central government. Baker relates that the earliest form of justice was not seen as coming from a ruler or the state

Figure 3.2 The Domesday Book.
Source: MEPL.
Twenty years after the Battle of Hastings, William I faced pressures from the Danes and the King of Norway in particular which necessitated a significant expenditure. William ordered a great survey be made and that a book be compiled containing information on who owned what throughout the country. This book would strengthen the tax revenue as it would provide the record against which nobody could dispute or argue against a tax demand. (One story [mythical] of the title is that it brought doom and gloom to the people of England – hence 'Domesday Book'.) Each record includes, for each settlement in England, its monetary value and any customary dues owed to the Crown at the time of the survey, values recorded before Domesday, and values from before 1066. The Domesday survey is far more than just a physical record though. It is a detailed statement of lands held by the king and by his tenants and of the resources that went with those lands. It records which manors rightfully belonged to which estates, thus ending years of confusion resulting from the gradual and sometimes violent dispossession of the Anglo-Saxons by their Norman conquerors. It was moreover a 'feudal' statement, giving the identities of the tenants-in-chief (landholders) who held their lands directly from the Crown, and of their tenants and under tenants. The fact that the scheme was executed and brought to complete fruition in two years is a tribute of the political power and formidable will of William the Conqueror. It was compiled by (1) collecting existing information about manors, people and assets, including documents dating from the Anglo-Saxon period and post-1066 which listed lands and taxes in existence, and each tenant-in-chief, whether bishop, abbot or baron, and each sheriff and other local official, was required to send in a list of manors and men; (2) verifying or correcting this information – commissioners were assigned sections of England called circuits and travelled around the country; in every town, village and hamlet, the commissioners asked the same questions to everyone with interest in land from the barons to the villagers; (3) recording all of this in three stages: as it was in the time of King Edward, as it was when King William gave it and as it is now.

employed learned judges but communal justice or the custom of the people.[17] As feudalism developed, the style of authority that came with being a lord gave rise to a set of courts relating from a developing personalisation of authority. The most important long-term effect of this, once England became a single kingdom in the tenth

....
17   Baker (2002).

century, was the constitutional ascendancy of the king. William and the new élite worked with and developed further the existing institutions. The growth of the common law was owed in great part to the ability of a central court to fashion and administer a set of remedies and in the process of deciding disputes articulate principles and rules. Without a developing strong central government it would not have been possible to unify the norms and customs of the country into a centralised form administered by a common set of courts and each area of the country would have been able to develop its own traditions and customs in conflicting and competing ways. The growth of the common law was in one sense a victory of centralised authority over a host of competing local forms.

Land law was central and here the rise of royal actions, in particular the royal order of *reseisin*. Here, as elsewhere, the crucial process was procedural. Fees had to be paid for this justice but 'the main attractions for the private litigant were no doubt the effective process and enforcement which royal writs procured, and the availability from the late twelfth century of a central written record which would end the dispute for all time'.[18] The common law developed because of the strength of the king's (institutional) power behind the writ (royal commands addressed to officials to 'do' something), and the development of a professional body of persons and settled behaviour in the processing of claims and the enforcement of judgment. Predictability of process was a key factor. Judgments were not ad hoc but followed from similar forms through real actions and the processes whereby cases were structured, presented and resolved in court.[19] Delegation of authority to decide led to the rise of a legal profession with judges at the peak. Another factor leading to the pre-eminence of English judges was the fact that the law was not placed in the first place in any one learned 'Holy Writ'; that is, codification, hence it did not fall into the hands of a guild of scholarly jurists who had sole access to its bookish sources. Although there were statutes, the central lawgiver remained largely inactive. By contrast there was the strength and continuity of the central courts competent in first instance for a wide variety of cases over the whole kingdom. They acted with royal power behind them and were staffed

18   Ibid., 14–15.
19   Judicial reasoning is not a mechanical process; it is better seen as an **art form** developed over time and through many political and social battles. For centuries, until the Judicature Acts of the 1870s, the common law of England consisted of a system of actions or legal remedies, each commanding its own procedure. It was crucial to get the procedure correct, to specify the right pleading (the oral presentation of the issues and facts); early books on English law tended to be compilations of correct procedures or collections of moves that had worked in the past. Breaking out of those procedure-based actions, legal doctrine developed but it was essential to use established concepts, principles and arguments that had been approved in earlier cases. In this way we say that English law prefers **precedent** as a basis for legal judgments, and moves empirically from case to case, from one reality (actual case) to another. Continental law (from the civil or Roman law tradition) tends to move theoretically by deductive reasoning, basing judgments on abstract principles. It is more conceptual, more scholastic and works with definitions and distinctions. The common law is for the most part not a codified law. Rules and principles are made clear by the examination of decided cases. We do this by drawing generalisations from the cases, but there is argument as to the exact status of decided cases: are they 'the law' or are they (as per Blackstone) 'evidence of the law'? In the declaratory theory, the common law is always something more than what is contained in the judgments. The legal reasoning and rules expounded in the cases can be good or bad, and we say that the law works itself out through the cases. This implies that the law is always something other than the cases, and being faithful to the law means being faithful to something beyond what we can see written down; it means being faithful to a tradition and to historically entrenched ideals.

by professionals. These royal judges shaped the common law in cooperation with barristers and serjeants (the small group of leading barristers of the time; in modern time that order has been replaced by King's/Queen's Counsel) and were at the same time its guardians.

The continental development of civil law is considerably different. Several countries in the European continent in the late middle ages came to adopt the law as contained in the *Corpus Juris*; the Code Civil became the lawyer's bible. These texts were treated by many as *Ratio scripta*, 'reason put into writing', so legal science was based on great authoritative texts and consisted in large part of glosses and commentaries. This was different from the Roman production of these texts and seems strange, almost religious, to the practically focused English frame of mind.

Thus the continent accepted a great law book of a society that had been gone for centuries as its ultimate authority, and entirely reshaped its own law through scholastic gloss, disputations and commentaries based on the Roman model.

The English way came to be to create relatively settled modes of presenting arguments, developing existing rules, modernising the courts and their procedures and gradually building up case law. Perhaps it would occasionally appeal to the lawgiver, but otherwise it let the professionals get on with the task of pleading and adjudicating. The conquest of Normandy by the French monarchy and the gradual introduction of Roman-inspired French law into the duchy turned Anglo-Norman law into purely English law. What became the common law tradition started as Anglo-Norman law, shared by a kingdom (England) and a duchy (the French duchy of Normandy) that were not separated but united by the Channel; what came to be the hallmark of England's difference from Europe was initially not insular at all.

I now look at another image which deals with a famous, if rather misunderstood legal document, the Magna Carta, which has for a long, long time held a place in popular consciousness, at least, as the nearest thing to a written foundational document. John's reign has been termed 'a career in tyranny'[20] and the document was not understood at the time as it became to be. A grasp of the rhetorical appeal of the Magna Carta may be gauged from Cassell's glowing tones in the 'century edition' of 1902:

> To the Englishman of modern times, the event of that day bears a deep and solemn interest, far surpassing that of battles or of conquests. He is surrounded now by many of the blessings that freedom gives to all who live beneath her sway. Under her warm smile civilisation grows and flourishes, knowledge sheds around her calm, undying light; wrong is redressed by free opinion; and man, with brow erect, throws off the tyranny of man. In the green meadow of the Thames was sown the seed which bears such fruits as these. Centuries more of toil and struggle may be needed to bring it to maturity. The progress of the human race is slow, and beset with difficulties: amidst the present material prosperity, with all the advantages of civil and religious liberty, we are still far from the goal which lies before us . . . Now at least, the way is open to us, and cannot be mistaken; the light of Heaven shines full upon it, the obstacles grow fewer

----

20   Cassell (1902: vol. I, 266).

Figure 3.3 *King John Granting Magna Charta (on the Thames island of Runnymede, near Windsor)* by
Ernest Normand (1859–1923), a notable painter in Victorian England for works on historical and orientalist scenes.
This is a painting in canvas the same as the *King John Granting the Magna Carta* fresco at the Royal Exchange in
London (painted 1900, restored 2001).
Source: Cassell's Frontispiece to Vol. I.

Figure 3.3 Continued

This image of course obscures (it does not present) the fact that on 15 June 1215, the action by King John, pressured by the barons and threatened by insurrection, was one of extreme reluctance. John assumed that the pope would give him permission to retract his agreement immediately once he could get himself into a better political position on the grounds that he signed under duress.

The charter, however, also established a council of barons who were to ensure that the sovereign observed the charter, with the right to wage war on him if he did not. The Magna Carta was the first formal document insisting that the sovereign was as much under the rule of law as his people, and that the rights of individuals (at least those of a certain status) were to be upheld even against the wishes of the sovereign. As a source of fundamental constitutional principles, the Magna Carta came to be seen as an important definition of aspects of English law, and in later centuries was popularly perceived as the basis of the liberties of the English people. It has of course long been superseded but in the absence of a written constitution it retained almost mythological status.

The Magna Carta lives on as a central trope to be deployed in narratives of democratic progress and struggle. For example in 2007 the British Cabinet Minister Jack Straw, as leader of the House of Commons, claimed that the 'fight now against unbridled terror' should be part of a story, 'alongside the Magna Carta, the fight for votes and emancipation of Catholics, women, ethnic minorities and World War II' which makes it 'clearer about what it means to be British' and its roots in democracy to challenge those opposed to Britain's core values. Some rights and responsibilities were a non-negotiable part of being a British citizen and it would help reduce segregation in an increasingly mixed society. While conceding that the British had often looked or acted like oppressors 'to the Irish and to many of the peoples of the British Empire', the freedom preached by Britain helped ensure that the empire had collapsed 'with less bloodshed than many other decolonisation struggles'. A stronger 'British story' would challenge those with a 'single, all-consuming identity' at odds with democratic values, such as minority fringe Muslim groups. Thus society should stress how democracy could serve 'as the means to allow different groups with often competing interests to live together in relative harmony'. But while there was room for 'multiple and different identities', they could not take precedence over the British 'core democratic values of freedom, fairness, tolerance and plurality'. 'To be a British citizen, fully playing your part in British society, you must subscribe to that. It is the bargain and it is non-negotiable.' (Cyril Foster Lecture at Oxford University, reported by the *Guardian*, 25 January 2007.)

In February 2008, when now Lord Chancellor (the reformed post) and Secretary of State for Justice, Jack Straw gave a lecture at George Washington University in the US, he began 'where so much of our legal, governmental and social systems begins – with the Magna Carta'. The Magna Carta, the Declaration of Independence, and the Bill of Rights and the Constitution constituted the 'political scriptures'. In Straw's narrative:

'In the late eighteenth century, the Founding Fathers searched for an historical precedent for asserting their rightful liberties from King George III and the English Parliament. They found it in a parley which took place more than 500 years before that, between a collection of barons, and the then impoverished and despotic King John, at Runnymede in 1215. On that unremarkable field they did a remarkable thing. They demanded of the king that their traditional rights be recognised, written down, confirmed with the royal seal and sent to every county to be read aloud to all freemen.

Let us, however, prick the illusion, that the Magna Carta was precipitated by the equivalent of thirteenth century civil rights campaigners. The Magna Carta was a feudal document – designed to protect the interests, rights and properties of powerful landowners with the temerity to stand up to the monarch. Given its provenance, it is a paradox that a document which was founded on the basis of class and self-interest has over centuries become one of the basic documents for our two constitutions, and one of the icons of the universal protection of liberty.

This is a measure of how constitutions evolve, grow and develop with changing circumstances; in this sense they can be very much like scripture. This is the process by which a document just shy of its eight-hundredth birthday still has a resonance and relevance today. In more than 100 decisions, the United States Supreme Court has traced dependence on the Magna Carta for understanding of due process of law, trial by one's peers, the importance of a fair trial, and protection against excessive fines and cruel and unusual punishment. These are principles which similarly have long formed the bedrock of our system of common law in the United Kingdom – as admired as it is emulated in democracies around the world.

I dwell on this historical point to demonstrate that in spite of the very different systems of governance in the UK and the US, there is an enduring bond between our two democracies, a shared legal culture, a common thread that can be followed back to the Magna Carta. At the heart of each, of both, is a powerful and everlasting idea of liberty and of rights.'

(Mr Jack Straw, Modernising the Magna Carta – Ministry of Justice, website, delivered 13 February 2008 at George Washington University, Washington, DC.)

and weaker by the day, the efforts to oppose them grow stringer, and the final triumph is secure. The value and importance of Magna Charta is not to be estimated by its immediate application to ourselves. Those positive laws and institutions of later times, all have their root in this charter.[21]

John ruled an England officially Catholic. He may have been an able administrator interested in law and government but he neither trusted others nor was trusted by them. His despotic tendencies, refusal to honour agreements, heavy taxation, disputes with the Church (John was excommunicated by the Pope in 1209) and unsuccessful attempts to recover his French possessions made him unpopular. Many of his barons rebelled and in June 1215 they forced the king to sign a peace treaty accepting their reforms. The barons took their stand on feudal law and followed its formalities. For, if the king was their divinely ordained ruler he was also their feudal lord and as such had obligations towards them. King and barons entered into a contract and the contractual nature of medieval feudalism coloured the constitutional outlook at this time.

As a peace treaty, the Magna Carta was a failure and the rebels invited Louis of France to become their king. When John died in 1216, England was in the grip of civil war. The treaty was later seen as a key constitutional document and the name Magna Carta has great rhetorical power; it limited royal powers, defined feudal obligations between the king and the barons, and guaranteed a number of rights. The most influential clauses concerned the freedom of the Church; the redress of grievances of owners and tenants of land; the need to consult the Great Council of the Realm so as to prevent unjust taxation; mercantile and trading relationships; regulation of the machinery of justice so that justice should be denied to no one; and the requirement to control the behaviour of royal officials. The most important clauses established the basis of the writ of habeas corpus ('you have the body, bring it to me'); that is, that no one shall be imprisoned except by due process of law, and that 'to no one will we sell, to no one will we refuse or delay right or justice'.

METHODS OF PROOF AND THE RISE OF THE JURY

While to the participant, who we assume believed deeply in God, the practices held respect, to modern senses early modes of procedure and proof 'in contentious matters was calculated to avoid reasoned decision-making'.[22] If the parties, either in a dispute we would now call criminal matters or civil, could not be persuaded to settle, then resort would be had to proof by oath, backed up by a physical test. The complainer would have to demonstrate that his case was believable and worthy of taking action by bringing a group of supporters who would back up his story, the defender may be allowed to respond by 'proof by oath', that is to swear on the holy book to the truth of the case and he was expected to bring neighbours as 'oath helpers' to back up his word. But if this form of proof was not allowed, either because of the gravity of the

---

21   Ibid., 268–70.
22   Baker (2002: 4).

Figure 3.4 Trial by ordeal by water (unattributed woodcut, probably of a supposed witch, sixteenth century).
Credit: MEPL

accusation or the unreliability of the party's word, the oath might have to be proved by test of an ordeal. There were two main ordeals, by fire or by water (and occasionally the oath was to be proved by making the oath taker swallow a large piece of hardened dry bread!). In the ordeal of fire a piece of iron was put into a fire and then into the party's hand, the hand was bound and inspected a few days later: if the burn had festered, God was taken to have decided against the party. The ordeal of water required the party to be tied and lowered into a pond; if she/he sank the water was deemed to have received her/him with God's blessing, and she/he was quickly fished out.

Ordeals were a unilateral appeal to the judgment of God. These relied upon the help of the Church for a priest was required to perform the rites necessary to call upon divine aid. The priest must heat the iron or *adjure* the pool of water to receive the innocent who, if they sank, were declared to have come clean from the ordeal (the ordeal of cold water). A priest bound up the hand that carried the hot iron and unbound it to see whether the burn had healed thereby showing a stainless conscience (ordeal of hot iron). The priest adjured the morsel of bread (*cosned*) to choke the swearer of a false oath. In 1215 the Lateran Council resolved to withdraw the sanction of the (Roman Catholic) Church from the ordeal. In consequence the ordeal soon became virtually obsolete (with the exception of 'witches').

Its disappearance enabled the jury trial to take its place. It is important to understand how this enabled law and facts to be separated and how the difference enabled
'law' to develop over time. The ordeal was inscrutable.

> There was a prolonged intellectual debate about the legitimacy of the ordeal. It was not
> clear how man could expect God to answer human questions: might He not, for
> instance, choose to absolve men who had broken the law but repented? And what if He
> decided not to intervene at all, but to leave the matter to be settled by His ordinary laws
> of nature? Could one be sure in a given case whether He has intervened? There is some
> evidence that those who administered ordeals, perhaps because of such doubts, began
> to feel a responsibility to facilitate the result they considered right: for instance, by
> letting the iron cool in cases where suspicion was weak, or by interpreting a burned
> hand liberally. In the last days of the ordeal, the acquittal rate was surprisingly high.
> Above all, it was not clear that humans had any right to invoke God's miraculous inter-
> vention in mundane affairs: indeed, the Church taught that is was wrong to tempt the
> Almighty. In 1215, the Lateran Council, after discussing these problems, took the deci-
> sive step of forbidding clergy to participate any more in ordeals.[23]

Under the old system 'judgment preceded proof: once it was adjudged that one of
the parties should swear or perform a test there was no further decision to make,
except whether he has passed it'.[24] However separating law and facts enabled judgments to be produced by the application of legal rules to accepted facts (it was the role
of the jury to rule on competing versions of facts) and judges to develop the rules and
issue directions to the jury on how, given what version of the facts they accepted, a
valid verdict was to be reached.

SOVEREIGNTY AND THE RISE OF POSITIVISM

My next image I will call an 'anti-common law' image. It was presented by the English
political theorist Thomas Hobbes in 1651 as the frontispiece of *Leviathan*, regarded as
a foundational text for English political liberalism. Writing against the backdrop of a
bloody civil war in England and widespread war and unrest in Europe, Hobbes sought
to present an image of authority and reason to avoid the dangerous and bloody quar-
rels over the respective claims of political and religious leaders by defining the law of
practical human association (the Commonwealth) as the command of the sovereign.
'[I]t is not wisdom but authority that makes a Law.'[25] If we did not agree on a stable
institutional authority for (human) law we would be lost in different claims about law
and reason, and everyone would have grounds for questioning laws validity. Positive
law was an instrument of power; where there is no sovereign, such as in the case of
so-called international law, there is no real law.

---

23   Ibid., 5.
24   Ibid., 5.
25   Hobbes, *Dialogue*, 55.

This simplifies Hobbes, but in *Leviathan* and his related *Dialogue* law fits the paradigm of the legislator; that is, the political power centre as the king of the law, and all further legal officials operating as deputies of that sovereign power.[26] Hobbes may be called an 'anti-common law' writer as he seems to present a theory of 'positive law' (or law posited by a human power centre) before its time. His essential themes were picked up in the late eighteenth and nineteenth centuries by the English legal philosophers Jeremy Bentham and John Austin to found a perspective entitled legal positivism, which for much of the 'modern' era has been the dominant approach to understanding law in Anglo-American jurisprudence.

Positivist sovereignty is hierarchy ('sovereign and subject' in John Austin's terms), law – whatever rational or theoretical justification for it – is an emanation of sovereignty. By contrast the idea of the rule of law presents another articulation of the relationship of sovereignty and law in which law is not the emanation of sovereignty but sovereignty operates subject to law. *Leviathan* presents hierarchy as the solution of the impasse of a harsh meta-narrative of the human condition, one which gives the natural condition of mankind as a state of 'warre' of all on all, where reason has little chance against the violent passions of man, and the life of man is solitary, poor, nasty, brutish and short. Humanity is rescued from this condition by fear and our use of reason to overcome the essential weakness of our natural condition. Fear of death drives man to act rationally and combine together, forming a strong, even totalitarian government, through accepting that power – might – lies at the heart of all social organisation and that whoever possesses power has both the ability and the right to dominate. The commands of the government – the sovereign – are the law and ultimately it is power that makes law effective. We are simplifying but Hobbes places the achievement of security – the pacification of violence – before all else and demands performability (the power to enforce or to make a predictable, repeatable occurrence) as his criteria for success.[27] In a Hobbesian world the sovereign must be effective; it was not feudal obligation but rational calculation that founded the social bond.

Leviathan, whether or not the author understood it as such, is a prototypical modernist text. Although the author tries to work with the allusions and language of the past (except that he wrote it in English and not Latin as was expected) he gives a new beginning to stories of our social life. He is termed the father of 'political liberalism' since he says we must start our notions of human interaction with the basic premises that we are first all relatively equal and that we are also to be treated as autonomous individuals, and he is a modernist when he gives us the task of creating, of moulding the conditions of social life anew and doing that through the use of scientific knowledge, not the historical narratives or epics of the traditions. The political power centre is to use law as our instrument of command, of enforcing political will, of getting social projects done.

---

26   Blackstone grasped this clearly; sovereign or supreme power articulated itself, made law, through legislation: 'For legislature . . . is the greatest act of superiority that can be exercised by one being over another.' (*Commentaries*, I, 46*).

27   In today's conditions – post-11 September 2001, and observing the instability of Iraq and many other countries around the globe – Hobbes' message rings true to many.

Figure 3.5 In the frontispiece of *Leviathan* (1651), we are presented with an image of sovereignty – it concerns both protected (civilised) space and embodiment. The body of the sovereign towers over the protected space; the sovereign is the highest, it is the summit towering over what it dominates and protects. Note that the body of the sovereign is composed of the bodies of the subjects and the reality of the body limits, of the vulnerability of all humans to pain and death, provides a key element in Hobbes' narrative of the human condition that he used to legitimate sovereign power. The frontispiece concerns the creation of civilised space, a realm of civil society where a civilised humanity can flourish beneath the watching gaze of the sovereign. We know that Hobbes placed the control of social violence, the widespread nature of which in the early seventeenth century could hardly even be described as the waging of 'war', as key.

Figure 3.5 Continued

On the page, an interlocking set of images gives a visual presentation of the benefits of security and stability; in effect an existential world picture. For us of course this is a classical text: we cannot recreate the experience of encountering it during the time of its writing. We acknowledge that it was written at the time of the passing in Europe of the superordinate authority of the Christian church; it was a time when religious authority, instead of being a binding force, had itself become a major source of conflict. What should replace the claims to loyalty of religious brotherhood or localised relations? The Thirty Years War – the most bitter European campaign then seen – had laid waste to much of central Europe and drastically reduced the German-speaking population. Few people thought globally as we mean it; but, using our current language, the major blocs of that time appear as a divided European Christendom, with the strongest world powers being the Chinese Empire, localised in its concerns, and the Islamic Ottoman Empire, somewhat at odds with Islamic Persia. For centuries Islam, not Christian Europe, had been the place of learning; but a grand European project was to change that world. Spain destroyed the last Muslim (Moorish) enclave in Western Europe – the Emirate of Granada – in 1492, in the aftermath of which Columbus was allowed to sail in search of a new route to India. From that time, the ships and military power of Europeans entered into the wider realms of the globe, overwhelming cultures and peoples that could not withstand the onslaught, and creating new social and territorial relations in a European image.

Driving this world shift in power was an existential perspective on life itself. Hobbes postulated the basis of the social bond – in place of dynasties, religious tradition or feudal ties – as rational self-interest exercised by calculating individuals. As bearers of subjective rationality, individuals were depicted as forming the social order and giving their allegiance to a government, a sovereign, because it was in their rational self-interest to do so and the metaphor for the social bond was contractual, not traditional. The sovereign was now to have a particular territory, which many have rather loosely termed the 'nation state', wherein he was the representative of a people and was ultimately composed of the people who occupied that territory. To ensure security and maintain peace, Hobbes knew the sovereign must be well armed. The armaments he gave him were dual: the public sword and the weapons of the military, but there are also the weapons of metaphysical awe, the emblems of the Church, of solace as well as respect. The sovereign would use the weapons of power and awe; his word would make law. But what of justice? The common law views of the time stressed that judges did not make law as a representative of the power centre – deputies of the sovereign – but either declared what the custom of the locality had been (and in this, as later writers such as Blackstone stated as if a legitimating factor, would be law by the acceptance of the people).

THE CENTRALITY OF JUDGES

To accompany the next image consider an extract from the English twentieth century poet W.H. Auden's poem *Law like love*.[28]

Law, says the judge as he looks down his nose,
Speaking clearly and most severely,
Law is as I've told you before,
Law is as you know I suppose,
Law is but let me explain it once more,
Law is The Law

I interpret this extract as representing a peculiarly English way of expressing an attitude and understanding of law that has become common sense. Is there any philosophical point being expressed there, and why should Auden have a 'judge' as the speaker?

In my own reading the quotation expresses the anti-theoretical leaning of much of English writing about law; law was simply the law, get on with it: work within the

....
28   Auden (1976).

Figure 3.6 Earl Mansfield, wearing the Robes of a Peer, engraved by H.T. Ryall after a painting by Sir Joshua Reynolds (MEPL). Mansfield is known as the father of English commercial law for his influence while Lord Chief Justice, but like the educationalist, William Blackstone, he became a judge through politics (and was better at law than politics). He was born 1705 in Scotland, the fourth son of the fifth Viscount Stormont. He was a King's Scholar at Westminster School (a leading private school), and Christ Church College, Oxford, and was called to the Bar at Lincoln's Inn in 1730. He became an MP and made his name in 1737 with his speech to the House of Commons in support of a merchants' petition to stop Spanish assaults on their ships. In 1742 he became Solicitor General. In 1754 he was appointed Attorney General and was leader of the House of Commons under the Duke of Newcastle. In 1756 he was appointed Chief Justice of the King's Bench, being raised to the peerage, a post he held until 1788. The role of the judge as the central actor in the legal system is displayed by the fact that he rationalised many of the rules of procedure, reduced expense and delay, and tried to fuse the principles of law and equity. Though not fully successful in renovating the medieval law of property, he developed a theory of contract that laid the foundation for modern commercial law. His role in the development of commercial law owed a lot to listening to commercial practitioners and coming up with a decision that fitted with their notions of practice (what we may call commercial custom). He attempted to apply continental analogies in order to bring English law closer to international practice. Mansfield was unpopular for his opinions on seditious libel and for his judgments in the case of the radical politician John Wilkes, and his house was burned (1780) in the anti-Catholic Gordon riots. In preparing *Commentaries on the Laws of England*, Blackstone was clearly influenced by Mansfield and incorporated many of his opinions into his exposition of the law.

tradition (and the tradition, of course, gave you ways of thinking that you took for granted). Law did not need defining, it did not need some overriding theoretical framework, it was better understood through practice, through the experience of it rather than some logical scheme and the prince of law was the judge. The judge, not the politician, not the academic commentator and certainly not the administrator, was the key figure, the controller of meaning, the arbitrator of application. Thus the imagery of English law abounds with portraits of judges, some famous (or infamous) at the time and now forgotten by history, others immortalised as famous figures of the common law. The image I present is of Lord Mansfield, perhaps the most famous of the classic common law judges. In the common law tradition the judges are central. Since the so-called constitutional settlement which gave the English throne to William and Mary in the late seventeenth century, judges have security of tenure; in other words the government cannot dismiss them at will. The Act of Settlement provided that judges' commissions should be during good behaviour and they should be removable only upon the address of both Houses of Parliament (a very unlikely event). Much of the actual law of England and Wales has been developed out of judges' decisions – this is often said to be the narrow meaning of the phrase 'common law'; that is, case law, as opposed to statute law which has been made by the legislature. In Chapters 3 and 4 we expand on the basic arguments that exist on how much law-making judges do when deciding cases and interpreting earlier decisions to draw out the principles earlier used therein, and apply them in fresh conditions; whatever position one holds on the extent of judicial law-making, all agree that in common law jurisdictions judges control the process of declaring what the law is in practical application of resolving disputes. You should note that even in the case of statutes – where it seems that that control is given to the legislature – the judges retain ultimate control, for they declare what the statute 'means'. They declare, in reality, how the statute is to be applied. Many scholars, however, hold that in declaring what the law is, the judges extend law; put starkly, they make law. How can this difference be reconciled? In practice the complexity of the issues – both factual and legal – presented in a particular case and the wealth of competing analogies available with the circumstances of previous cases ('precedents' or 'authorities') frequently allow a judge to make his own constructive choice without appearing to breach the doctrine of binding precedent (the key doctrine of the modern common law system, which is literally to stand by what has previously been decided).

INTERNAL AND EXTERNAL PERSPECTIVES IN LEGAL EDUCATION, INSIDERS AND OUTSIDERS

University education in common law is relatively recent and it was only in the 1960s and 1970s that the legal profession in England began to be a profession of law graduates. Law has been a subject of exposition and study in universities from the thirteenth century formation of 'university life' in Bologna, Italy, but it was study of Roman Law, the classical codes and glosses on them derived from the system of governance of the Roman Empire. As late as 1881 Dicey gave his inaugural lecture with the title 'Is English Law a fit topic for study at University?' The common law was learnt by apprenticeship and seemed unsuitable for university study; it was law without clear foundations, bastard law (law without a 'father' or sovereign, everywhere a mass of cases, or so it seemed). My assertion, simply put, is that these two sets of images – that of the sovereign power presented by Hobbes as above and directing society on the one side, with that of the judge epitomised by Earl Mansfield (or Blackstone himself) on the other – represent radically different ways of understanding law and its relation to social order. On the one side we have law as the expression of power, law as *imperium*, law as an instrument of the power élite moulding and changing society; on the other, law as community and tied in with the mysterious science of the common law, known primarily by the judges, where law reflects the organic social order that is built up from below and the judges when they decide actual disputes are conduits for this process and bring out its inherent rationality. This distinction has an inbuilt inside–outside distinction. On the one side the commentator stands outside the legal tradition and adopts an external perspective, ideally trying to understand the entirety of law and its role in society; on the other side one works within the tradition, within its narratives and its sets of meaning, adopting an internal attitude, one of striving to be faithful to your (interpretative) understanding of the enterprise you are part of.

While Hobbes was in many respects an outsider – performing a supportive role to members of the establishment (*Leviathan* was written to be presented to the members of the exiled English Court who at that time were living just outside Paris while conflict raged in England) – Blackstone, the author of the first comprehensive scholarly work presenting the common law as a whole (written at Oxford and published first in 1765–1769), was an insider, a person who desired to become a central member of the establishment élite. For Blackstone considered that the pinnacle for his life's achievements would be to become a judge, and he first studied law at Lincoln's Inn, was a junior barrister, became a scholar and lecturer at All Souls College, Oxford, a member of its governing body, then a Member of the National Parliament (when the Tory Party effectively bought the local MPship for him for two periods), before succeeding in becoming a judge. But it is as the author of the famed *Commentaries on the Laws of England* that Blackstone's place in the intellectual history of England and the common law is assured (we may note that the text also made him a wealthy man!).

I will not go into great detail on the *Commentaries on the Laws of England*, save to say that it stands as the great educational testament to the classic common law. The *Commentaries* is not a dry cataloguing of legal rules and maxims. It had been written by Blackstone principally in order to establish English law as a fit subject for university education, but it was also an extended essay which celebrated the genius and liberty of the English people. He also claimed it demonstrated how English common law exemplified 'the general spirit of laws and principles of universal jurisprudence' (*Commentaries*, Preface). The common law was held out as a product of English exceptionalism – that is to say that it could only have been created out of the heritage of England and its institutions. And yet (and here Blackstone seemed to imply it was as a result of God's divine providence) the result was of universal applicability and enshrined positions and concepts of value elsewhere. Blackstone presented the common law as both a particular product of a specific historical development and also an entity that could be taken elsewhere, perhaps partly explaining why he has been termed its saviour, preserving it from codification, founding its modern academic study, and popularising its study through teaching the lawyer not only to speak the language of a scholar and a gentleman, but also to present the common law as forming a system. The *Commentaries* were the legal publishing sensation of the eighteenth century and new editions appeared well into the nineteenth; in addition they spawned a diverse series of works which were at first based on the *Commentaries* but went on to have lives of their own. The text continued in smaller student editions in England well into the twentieth century. In America many copies of the editions printed in England circulated. Additionally a first American edition, Bell's, appeared almost immediately in 1771–1772. Tucker's 1803 five volume edition proved a benchmark in that Blackstone's *Commentaries* were taken as the authoritative statement of the common law by reference to which American writers could display the well-founded continuity of American law or choose to differentiate new, specifically American, paths. Future American editors felt able to preserve the original text of the ninth edition and add on their own commentaries in well-used editions until the late nineteenth century.

The imagery of Blackstone's *Commentaries* – of the common law as a traditional and customary system that contains in its present forms the features of the past and that would hand on that historical identity to the future – appears at odds with the rationalising impulse of modernity. Yet it is precisely this aspect that gave it its enduring appeal.

It is hard for outsiders to appreciate the interlocking nature of the common law heritage and the constitution of the United Kingdom. Both are in a sense unwritten – the constitution and indeed the common law cannot be found in one authoritative text (hence we say it is unwritten) – and yet there are so many written texts or judgments to consult. We look to the past, yet the past is always open to interpretation. So it was with the success of Blackstone's *Commentaries*; they are full of history, yet the aim was to expound and explain English law as history had organically produced it. He asserted the existence of the common law from time immemorial and followed the earlier judge and writer Sir Mathew Hale (who objected strongly to Hobbes' image of law) in denying that William the Conqueror had altered or could 'alter the laws of this kingdom, or impose laws upon the people *per modum conquestus or jure belli*'. A narrative of national identity of epic proportions runs throughout the text, one in which the common law, and the judges, preserve the liberty of the Englishman and develop a country whose air is even too pure to allow slavery.

I have called Blackstone an insider, by which I mean someone who lives, breathes and desires those things that the tradition bequeaths. Consider the places where Blackstone produced the *Commentaries*, his life as a member of one of the Inns of Courts in London and his academic base in All Souls College, Oxford. First consider Oxford University, with its traditions, solid feeling and robust buildings. The four volumes of the *Commentaries* were partly an essay heralding the past congratulating England upon its social constitution and offering images imbued with complacency. The past was to be a reservoir feeding confidence into future actions. A sense of general improvement had been established by the greater political stability and domestic peace after the turmoil of the sixteenth-century Wars of Religion and the Thirty Years War (1618–1648). The scientific revolution of the seventeenth century and the advent of capitalist industrialisation gave hope for progress through science and commerce. The test of legal identity for the common law offered in the Commentaries lay not in analytical consistency to any body of political or legal principles, but historical evolution. The legal scholar was to be asked to treat the common law as an intricate legacy, one to be carefully studied with no part easily vanquished.

CELEBRATING THE MYTHOLOGIES OF POPULAR HISTORY

There is more than one story of legal history. Consider the separation of powers and the rule of law. When Dicey came to formulate the analytical structure of the British constitution in the late nineteenth century it seemed that he could celebrate the first of its historical creation but now present the features of the constitution as if they could be henceforth divorced from history. Yet features of the constitution understood historically show the contingency and malleability of social institutions.

Another image comes from what we may term the 'subversive media'. In the early months of 1754, the painter and satirical engraver William Hogarth was working on what eventually became a set of four paintings and prints dealing with electoral corruption. This subject dominated London's newspapers and journals because of the general election of that year and in particular because of the notoriously corrupt election campaign in Oxfordshire. The first of these, *An Election Entertainment* was put on display just days before the election itself. In this quartet of pictures, Hogarth shows the various stages of an election campaign in the fictional country town of Guzzledown. The first scene depicts an electoral feast organised by the Whig Party to garner support. *Canvassing for Votes*, the second scene, is set outside the Royal Oak inn, and focuses on a farmer who is being offered bribes by representatives of both the Tories and the Whigs. The sense of a nation being failed by their political leaders is made even more explicit in the third scene, *The Polling*, where a broken-down coach, representing Britain itself, has ground to a halt. Meanwhile every available male is being dragged to a polling booth to vote. In the final scene the Tory victory parade is violently interrupted and upset by a riotous cluster of people and animals.

Dicey could by the late nineteenth century assert as an analytical principle of modern constitutional law that the Crown in Parliament is sovereign. Yet the composition and relationship between the analytical or constituent parts of government is no logical concept, Parliament evolved and for much of history was in a series of complex power struggles with the Crown, viewed then as separate. Crown (here directly referring to 'royal') patronage made the constitutional balance later called the separation of powers work by royal 'influence'.

Chrimes[29] summarises the revolution of 1688–1689 as bequeathing the eighteenth century as its form of government a partnership of king, lords, common and common law: 'The link between the executive and the Parliament which was most effective in keeping the wheels of government turning in the eighteenth century and the early

29   Chrimes (1965: 170–1).

Figure 3.7 The Polling (third engraving in *Four Prints Of an Election* by William Hogarth [1697–1764]) illuminates how a Member of Parliament is elected. Ballots were not secret but held under the watching eyes of clerks who may or may not be in the influence of one or either of the competing groups. First in line at the polling station is a soldier who has lost three of his limbs. A clerk tries to subdue his laughter as the veteran places his hook on the Bible. Lawyers from opposing parties flank him and argue the validity of his 'handless' oath. Next an imbecile locked in his chair is taking the oath. He is being prompted by an individual standing behind him whose leg is also manacled to the chair. Third in line is a dying man who is dragged up the stairs by his nurses. One is lacking his nose, a symptom of advanced venereal disease. A blind man – guided by his stick and a boy – walks up the stairs; behind him is a cripple. The two candidates appear in highchairs with a sleeping beadle between them. Other men around them share a ballad or drink merrily together. In the background, 'Britannia's' coach (the State) has broken down and is about to overturn. Involved in their game of cards, the coachmen ignore the dangerous situation. The ship of state is not in safe hands. The . . . *of an Election* set was published by William Hogarth from February 1755 to February 1758. It represents Hogarth's last great set of engravings and is loosely based upon the riotous Oxfordshire election of 1754, where the Whig candidate, the Duke of Marlborough, challenged the incumbent Tories. Hogarth's satirical works strove to provide images to mock and critique existing political and aristocratic methods to bribe, coerce and generally exploit the populace and manage the constitutional process. Hogarth partly engraved the pieces assisted by other engravers working in London to complete the series. (The Polling was designed by William Hogarth, engraved by Le Cave and published by William Heath in 1822.) William Hogarth is the unquestioned father of England's rich tradition of satire and remains one of the most original and lively minds in the entire history of British art. *The Election* series that he produced over 1754–1755 signalled a new kind of artistic venture on Hogarth's part, in which he offered a beautifully painted but severe indictment of modern electoral corruption. This turn to political subject matter became more pronounced with the publication of his print *The Times* in 1762, which saw Hogarth becoming actively involved in a bitter and personalised war of political images and texts. Largely thanks to this intervention into the field of political satire, Hogarth had become both the most celebrated and most vilified artist in Britain by the time of his death in 1764.

nineteenth century was what we would call bribery and corruption, but which was usually regarded as merely the obvious exercise of influence.' The settlement had led to recognition of the independence of the judiciary which enabled the courts to arbitrate within the law between the executive and the people subject to the overriding supremacy of Acts of Parliament, the royal prerogative of refusing assent to bills passed by both Houses of Parliament was not used after 1701, the Commons gained the rights to discuss any matter freely, to criticise executive power, and be supreme in matters of financial supply. But if a system of checks and balances was created, how was deadlock prevented? Normally the Crown, if it could not rely upon the loyal support of majorities in the House, 'could and did attach to its interest the needful balance of votes in either House by exercising its "influence" '. Without clear party organisation, Members of Parliament supported the Crown either because they saw it in the national interest to do so or as a result of personal advantage. 'The Crown's powers of patronage were ample; the favours, the honours, the pensions, the sinecures it could bestow were great – greater than those within the gift of any of the powerful and wealthy leaders of whichever group happened at any time to be resisting the "influence" of the Crown.' Factors which led to the contemporary balance include the rise of political parties, the changing electorate and the overriding principle of democracy.

RULE OF LAW AS INSTITUTIONAL FREEDOM FOR THE LEGAL PROCESS

To understand this, consider another image, that of the Queen's Bench, an important central court.

The rule of law means in social reality a *set of social conventions and practices* that enscribe concepts such as professional duty, respect for conventions, the power of restraining influences. Consider the image of the Court of Queen's Bench of 1870. The image presents a social space dominated by legal professionals, texts and counsel making oral presentation (argument) in front of judges. The Common Law Procedure Act of 1854 gave the possibility of trying facts by judges alone in civil cases and this led in time to the virtual disappearance of the jury from civil trials. This changed the nature of the judgment delivered with the resultant statement a combination of the trial judges' notes on evidence, the previous 'direction on law' (which would have been given to the jury), verdict and the courts decision (and often comment on the counsel's argument). Barker comments: 'Now that law and fact are no longer decided separately, it is never certain to what extent judgments turn on the facts and to what extent the judge's comment on particular facts are intended to create legal distinctions. In theory every case now establishes some new point, however minute.'[30]

The image opposite also represents adversarial proceedings. Litigation at common law was a system in which the parties themselves set the agenda and the pace of proceedings. At its apex was the image of the trial at which all the business was

---

30   Baker (2002: 93).

THE COURT OF QUEEN'S BENCH

Figure 3.8 The Court of Queen's Bench in session (1870) unattributed artist in *The Graphic.* After the reorganisation of the courts in the Judicature Act 1873 the court system returned to its foundational structure of a single Curia Regis and the distinction between courts of equity and common law was abolished.

conducted orally, even documents and legal authorities being read out in public court (in the above image clerks appear to be consulting reports, checking that counsel's statements are accurate). 'Co-operation was not expected, and the parties did their utmost to hinder or ambush their opponents. Costs were unpredictable and often disproportionate to the matter in dispute.'[31] From the time of the Victorian criticism (see Chapter 12 for Charles Dickens's critique of the Court of Chancery in *Bleak House*) reforms seemed unable to fundamentally change these elements. All socio-legal studies in the twentieth century, however, and the legal realism movement, stressed that the pre-trial stage had gained in importance, that the majority of 'cases' never culminated in final court trials, that retention of documents which would show the real 'facts' was substantially unfair, that 'ambush' infringed in spirit if not in the letter of the law the principles of due process, that 'expert witnesses' had increased in use, that many cases pitted parties against each other that were radically unbalanced in terms of resources and knowledge (for example, major corporations and insurance companies against sole litigants) and that the growing complexity of commercial transactions meant the old reliance on orality was counter-productive. How could the system gain

31   Ibid.

access to the array of complex documents buried deep in filing systems or in computer memories, easily shredded or wiped, multinational corporations could simply transfer information out of the jurisdiction. Early action was needed, such as discovery, pre-trial injunctions, freezing orders and orders to preserve evidence. Both sides could commission experts to provide technical evidence. But if these measures were designed to address one set of problems, they could be weapons to harass opponents and add unnecessarily to delay and cost.

In the 1980s and 1990s the solution increasingly was seen in changing the role of the judge: instead of the traditional role of umpire, the role of 'case manager' was envisaged. After a comprehensive review Sir Harry Woolf (later Lord Woolf) proposed radical changes aimed at simplifying litigation, encouraging alternative dispute resolution and reducing cost. His recommendations were mostly adopted and formed the basis of the Civil Procedure Rules adopted in 1999. Cases were to be differentiated on grounds of complexity and amount. Not only was English finally to replace some of the terms inherited from the French–Latin mixture of the formation of the common law but an overriding objective – to deal with cases 'justly' – was established with the court required to further this objective by 'actively managing cases'. The new proce-dures are designed to reduce the role of orality with a great deal of the work finding, reading and analysing the documentation taking place long before the trial, if one results at all. If this was a new landscape, its proponents also stressed it was a work in progress.

> The message for all those involved in the civil justice system, judges, practitioners and court staff alike, is that the changes being introduced in April (1999) are as much changes of culture as they are changes in the Rules themselves. We have to be ready to be proactive, not reactive. And we must see this as the beginning, not the end, of the process of change.[32]

CONCLUSION

This chapter began with reflection and questions to which I now think I have an answer. Today I am one person who speaks (along with many others) a particular language of law. Semantically it can be called a language frame that certain fellow lawyers – those who study and practise in the common law world (within the common law legal family) – recognise, understand and communicate within. This language, this set of tropes, rhetorical appeals, processes and shared invocations has an internal aspect in which we users think of it as some natural form of being, of its users as sharing if not a uniform concept of law then a set of concepts within a relatively friendly 'family' with a basic identity. From an external view, and that is a view adopted by both those who are not speaking the language of the common law (and it may also be said those who refute the whole idea of 'law' as some form of uniform entity) this

---

32   Lord Irvine of Lairg, 'Foreword' to the Civil Procedure Rules. (S.I. 1998 No. 3132 L. 17).

language use may give a greater confidence in identity and coherence than is warranted. But it is an evolving language and it has given us today basic legal concepts and rules, like the concept of rights, duties and remedies, due process, the concept of a sanction and a competence. This language is deeply penetrated by historical legal experiences, some of which have been imaged in this chapter and some we can put under broader headings, such as the struggle for democratic procedures of legitimate legislation. Many people who refer to law, who raise a legal claim assume, consciously or otherwise, these basic experiences. This idea of the common law and its politics is more than a theoretical hypothesis; it is living history.

RECORDING LAW'S EXPERIENCE: FEATURES OF THE 'CASE'

Last Friday morning early, two poor negroes came to inform me that one of their friends was [word illegible] by his Master on shipboard at Gravesend to be sent as a slave to Barbados. All the judges being out of town on the circuit I could not obtain either warrant or writ of habeas corpus after the most unwearied endeavours till late on Saturday night and in the meantime I had notice that the ship was sailed from Gravesend. However I sent [the writ] off by an attorney and the young man's friend in a post-chaise that same night to Deal in hopes that the ship might not yet have quitted the Channel and they happily arrived in the Downs just in time to save the poor despairing man: a delay even of a single minute more would have been fatal! However they brought the young man safe to me yesterday at noon and after proper consultation I sent him this morning with officers to catch his master but he had prudently decamped and fled to Scotland. The young man confessed that he had intended to jump into the sea as soon as it was dark in order to avoid slavery by death![1]

Figure 4.1 Granville Sharp (1735–1813), the abolitionist, rescuing a slave [Jonathan Strong] from the hands of his master, by James Hayllar (1829–1920). Oil painting, England, 1864.

....
1   Letter from Granville Sharp to the Archbishop of Canterbury about helping a slave, 1 August 1786 [Gloucestershire Archives, Ref D3549 13/1/C3].

CONSTRUCTING LAW'S EXPERIENCE

The American jurist and Supreme Court Judge Oliver Wendell Holmes Jr. (1841–1935) famously said that the life of the law was not logic but experience.[2] But how does the common law record and present its experience? For generations of lawyers and law students the answer is simple: through the institutional processing, deciding and recording of cases. Cases are not dry 'law', decided under the sway of some mechanical jurisprudence; they are more. They are collections of stories, narratives where human characters make appeals to the law (often in practice stopped by their lawyers who turn what they want to say into language that is regarded as legally relevant), ask for rights, assert that others owe them duties and seek remedies for supposed breaches of those duties. Within the context of the case, interpretation of legal sources takes place and arguments are engaged in. Some cases may be termed easy; there the facts are regarded in such a way that the interpretation of the legal sources seems to indicate that legal argument is one sided, that the strength of the arguments as to what the law is and how it applies to the factual situation are so unbalanced that only one outcome seems justified in good faith. But others, and – by dint of the institutional framework of the court structure of legal systems – most appeal cases, are harder; there the sources are open to an array of interpretations, both as to their importance and as to their 'meaning in application'. Whether hard or easy, whether reflected upon or not, within the confines of the case, propositions of law are advanced, contested, and in the adversarial setting of the common law institutions, success will flow to the party that has demonstrated their superiority in the argumentative practice.

A great deal of legal writing tends to obscure the reality that this is a very human process. Common law jurists, such as Ronald Dworkin,[3] may define the common law as the depository of a society's legal and political commitment to principle but others champion the joy of encountering the vagaries of human existence and story telling:

> The Common Law possesses a great deal of historical and contemporary colour: it is lively, realistic and, incidentally, eminently teachable. The student of common law rubs shoulders with Indian princes, fishwives, conjurors, shopkeepers and sea-captains of the East India Company. Translated into statutory language, only the pale shadows of this colourful assembly would remain, they would become plaintiffs, traffic accident witnesses, promisors of rewards, hire-purchasers and applicants for public office.

---

2   Justice Oliver Wendell Holmes, Jr., began his book The *Common Law* in 1881: 'The life of the law has not been logic: it has been experience. The felt necessities of the time, the prevalent moral and political theories, intuitions of public policy, avowed or unconscious, even the prejudices which judges share with their fellow-men, have had a good deal more to do than the syllogism in determining the rules by which men should be governed. The law embodies the story of a nation's development through many centuries, and it cannot be dealt with as if it contained only the axioms and corollaries of a book of mathematics. In order to know what it is, we must know what it has been, and what it tends to become. We must alternately consult history and existing theories of legislation. But the most difficult labor will be to understand the combination of the two into new products at every stage. The substance of the law at any given time pretty nearly corresponds, so far as it goes, with what is then understood to be convenient; but its form and machinery, and the degree to which it is able to work out desired results, depend very much upon its past.'
3   Dworkin (1986).

> The common law is a storehouse for worm tubs, ornamental broughams, snails in
> ginger beer bottles and fancy waistcoats, all of which would long since have turned to
> rust and rubbish had the cases which brought them into prominence been governed by
> some statute.[4]

Law's collective experience is recounted through narrative and the power of the
state to apply coercion in giving effect to legal judgment is in turn judged, in part at
least, by the aptness of that application in light of the events recounted in narrative.
The appeal to justice, the application of logic, the reference to past 'cases' (legal
precedents), the structuring of arguments so that they are legally relevant, so that they
fit the matter at hand, so that they carry substantive weight, is located amidst and
between many factors. We may mention for example, the court hierarchy, the adversarial profession, the variability of audiences, and one may start with the imbalance of
resources, both material and intellectual of the parties (the State against an individual
defendant, a well-resourced insurance company against an individual on state pension).
A great deal of this richness is lost in any legal education that deals with textbooks,
where, in the name of a positivist science of law, cases are reduced to one-line catch-
phrases, where we are told that such and such a case stands for a particular rule or
interpretation of principle. The desire to present the full 'syllabus' leads to teaching the
width of contract law, or insurance law, or of the law of Torts, a teaching that runs
against the desire to show depth, to uncover how, where and when, a principle came
out of the 'swamp' of law's existence in social life.[5] By contrast, problem-based modes
of learning start from a factual scenario and cast the student(s) in the semi-professional
role of legal advisors, asked to research and reconstruct the social situation into arguments, propositions in legal discourse that strive to command attention as valid assertions to conclude the argument. The successful conclusion is one that best fits with the
collective memory of law's enterprise, but this memory may be of tactics, of procedure,
of the actual and not the ideal which may manifest itself in the conclusion that the
outcome fits with what the law is, but is not 'just'. Law's stories are always partial,
incomplete and never fully innocent. Law's storytelling is purposeful, undertaken
within constraints of time, finance and the vagrancies of the adversarial profession.
There is no one story, although only one story may be told (and how that story, and
only that story surfaced, was allowed is again another story). The choices may reveal
an ongoing and constant contest between shifting narratives about the role of and
claims of law, government, political and social interests and identities. The resultant
decision, the decided case, is also not a simple plain fact; its holding is interpreted
and in the hands of future lawyers may be confined, extended, distinguished or even
overturned. A particular legal case may be formally located in terms of historical
categories, such as forms of 'trust' recognised in law, but these themselves are presented
in argumentative propositions structured in narrative (lawyers may say that such
and such judge got it wrong, and they got it wrong because they listened to that argument,
gave weight to this or that specific consideration, but if they had read the story of
the development of the principles in this area better, then they would have ...).

---

4   Luke (1982).
5   Maughan and Webb (2005).

Understood thus the appeal of law's experience is neither logical (analytical power) nor empirical (grasp of facts or secure reference) but historical.

> The life of the law is not a vision of the future but a vision of the past; its passions are unleashed, to use Benjamin's words, 'by the image of enslaved ancestors rather than that of liberated grandchildren'.[6]

Let us illustrate. This chapter began with a quotation from the 1 August 1786 entry in the diary of the eighteenth century social activist Glanville Sharp and another image, a painting of Sharp rescuing Jonathan Strong – formerly a slave but abandoned and later recaptured by his 'master' – from being sent back as a slave to Jamaica in 1767 by successfully pleading Strong's case before the Lord Mayor of London. Between that date and that of the diary quotation where the writ of *habeas corpus* was granted as a matter of normal legal course lies Sharp's historic legal victory in the Somerset case of 1772.[7] There, in a judgment barely 200 words long, Lord Mansfield responded to five days of arguments by England's finest barristers (spread over several months as he tried to arrange for the case to be settled out of court), including the legal and emotive appeals to him to recognise that the air of England was too pure for a slave to breathe and that the category of slavery must not be recognised by English courts. His judgment, often misunderstood as freeing all slaves in England, awarded the writ to free the black slave Somerset who had been bound in chains awaiting shipment to Jamaica. The impact on Somerset was a freedom, albeit socially restricted for Somerset would not have been on the same status as an Englishman, and we do not know the subsequent events in the personal narrative that was Somerset's life story.[8] The decision, more broadly, became a classic referent, a trope in the narrative of English law's protection of rights and adherence to due process, confirming that whoever was resident in England was able to use the law to protect their rights (other than those that had been expressly taken away by positive law).[9]

---

6   Luban (1994: 211).

7   The importance of this writ in the history (and mythology) of the common law may be gauged from the words of Chrimes (1965: 61): 'The writ of Habeas Corpus is the great and effective remedy to protect the individual from unlawful imprisonment and detention. Any imprisoned or detained person, or any person acting on his behalf, may apply for the writ to any judge of the High Court, who is bound, under heavy penalties, to issue the writ on prima facie cause being shown. The procedure is simple and expeditious. On cause being shown, the judge, as a matter of course, issues a peremptory order to the detainer to appear and show cause why a writ of Habeas Corpus should not be issued against him. If on appearance and argument, the judge is satisfied that the application is sound, the writ is forthwith issued, requiring the production of the prisoner in court on an appointed day, whereupon he is released if no sufficient cause for detention is proved. If sufficient cause is proved, then a speedy trial is ensured, thus making it impossible for the executive to detain a person for an indefinite period. The writ is issuable to anyone, whether a Secretary of State, a Minister, military authority, or any person whatsoever. It is a highly effective remedy for unlawful detention, but it does not of itself provide damages or penalties for unlawful detention or assault, to obtain which separate proceedings are required and available.'

8   Jonathan Strong never fully recovered from his beating and died in April 1773. Nothing is known of James Somerset after 1772. Extract from Granville Sharp's diary, 19 April 1773 [D3549 13/4/2 book G]: 'Poor Jonathan Strong, the first negro whose freedom I had procured in 1767, died this morning.'

9   Somerset had been taken from Africa as a slave to the Americas in 1749 where he was sold in Virginia to Charles Steuart, a Scottish merchant and slave trader in Norfolk who served after 1765 as a high-ranking British customs official. In 1769, Steuart took Somerset with him to England. After two years in England, Somerset escaped from Steuart, but was recaptured. Steuart decided to sell Somerset back into slavery in Jamaica, and, in late November 1771, Somerset was bound in chains on a ship on the Thames, the *Ann and Mary*, awaiting shipment.

In this image Granville Sharp is portrayed by the Victorian popular artist Hayllar as the protector of the black and the invoker of law's spirit. It fits with the symbolic invocation of the names of Somerset's case and Granville Sharp as a narrative demonstration of law's experience that whatever your social status you are the subject of the law, and are not subject to the arbitrary capriceness of man without legal protection and that the common law has due process values inscribed in it. It is an imaginary representation to the public of what Holdsworth later asked law schools to achieve, namely:

> To put and keep before the minds of their students that sense of the sanctity of the law, and of its great civilizing mission, which is and always has been present to the minds of the great administrators of the law.[10]

We may be more sceptical. Read from a 'subaltern' position the image is also the message that the civilisation that carries the spirit of the law, law's civilising mission, is white and male. The space of action in the painting is largely that inside the door of the courtroom where a substantial group (of white males), including lawyers and on the bench the Lord Mayor as judge, watch Sharp prevent a sea captain from taking Strong away from the court. This portrays the courtroom as the gateway to rights, to performance, the place where a claim is registered, heard and action ordered. This is in many ways a particular Western conception of law as an ensemble of rights and legal process as the establishment and authoritative pronouncement of those rights and court orders as their enforcement.

Hayllar's painting was a popular celebration:[11] yet the image is an illusion of law's justice and the ease of claiming rights. Images partly create illusions and illusions often create images. The artist had, of course, no first-hand knowledge of the events he portrayed; this was an image of historical recall, one of the victory of the spirit of English law in the protection of the rights of the oppressed.

There is in this story a narrative of distress and the appeal to the courts as the guardians of rights, and also of the reading of English history as such that it must grant rights.[12] But it is by no means a linear or autonomous story of law's progress. One question concerned standing, basic identity: who was the bearer of rights? Was the answer Free Englishmen, and only those of the correct Church (i.e. members of the Anglican Church), or any human that was in England?

At the time of the case Strong had been baptised and had English godparents. This ritual, this joining the Christian brotherhood, was undertaken to grant him a substance, a presence and a voice. In eighteenth century Britain and the colonies, it was popularly believed that baptism made African slaves free; common references to slaves as

---

10   Holdsworth (1928b: 183).
11   James Hayllar had come from a family of artists and came to London in 1848, studied with F.S. Cary and at the R.A. Schools. Having spent a fashionable two years in Italy he made money painting humorous genre pictures involving children and later adopted a style of painting historical paintings with a popular appeal.
12   The following story is in essence well known: my particular sources are Guildhall Library Manuscripts Section – Strong, Somerset and Sharp – liberating black slaves in England (Guildhall Library Manuscripts Section, online resources), Gloucestershire Council library resources.

'heathens' served to buttress the slave trade, and passages from the Bible were used to suggest that becoming a Christian conferred freedom. As a result, many plantation owners refused to allow their slaves baptism and several American colonies passed laws which explicitly outlawed freedom by baptism. However there was no British legal opinion until 1729, when the Attorney General and the Solicitor General ruled that 'baptism doth not bestow freedom' (the Yorke–Talbot ruling).

Nonetheless a popular belief persisted that coming to Britain and being baptised released you from slavery though not service – so that you could not be bought and sold, nor beaten. Many slaves brought to Britain by their masters did seek baptism, finding a sympathetic clergyman and English godparents.

Granville Sharp met the young runaway slave Jonathan Strong by chance in 1765. Strong had been brought as a slave from Barbados to London before being savagely beaten with a pistol by his master David Lisle and abandoned by Lisle in the street.

However, Strong found his way to the surgeon William Sharp's house, where Sharp treated the poor of the City of London for free. Sharp's brother Granville was taken by Strong's condition and enquired about his serious injuries.[13] He then arranged for Strong to be admitted to St Bartholomew's Hospital where Strong received treatment for four months. On his discharge, the Sharp brothers found him employment as errand boy with a surgeon, with whom he lived for two years. Lisle saw Strong by accident one day and having followed him home, entered into an agreement to sell the slave he had left for dead and obtained £30 for him, to be paid when Strong was aboard a West Indian ship ready to sail. Lisle therefore paid two slave-hunters to kidnap Strong and deliver him to the Poultry Compter (a jail in the City of London) until a West India ship was ready to sail.

Strong's employer was only interested in financial compensation for his loss. Strong realised his only chance of avoiding going back to Jamaica as a slave, was to contact Sharp who appealed to the Magistrates and used his influence to call a hearing in front of the Lord Mayor. The action was heard at Mansion House on 18 September 1767 where the Lord Mayor discharged Strong because 'the lad had not stolen anything, and was not guilty of any offence, and was therefore at liberty to go away'. As the painting presents it, in the courtroom, in front of the Lord Mayor, the captain of the ship attempted to seize Strong but Sharp prevented him being taken away. Another conflict then ensues: 'David Lisle, Esq. (a man of the law) called upon me . . . to demand gentlemanlike satisfaction . . . I told him, that, "as he had studied the law for so many years, he should want no satisfaction that the law should give him".' Lisle responded to Sharp's refusal to fight a duel by joining with the Jamaican planter who had bought Strong to sue the Sharp brothers for trespass in depriving them of their property. Sharp's success in gaining Strong his liberty had betrayed their property rights, guaranteed by law. The Sharp brothers engaged lawyers to defend them, but

---

13   The occasion is recorded in Sharp's own words (1820: 33): 'Nothing can be more shocking to Human Nature than the case of a Man or Woman who is delivered into the absolute Power of Strangers to be treated according to the New Masters Will & pleasure; for they have nothing but misery to expect; and poor Jonathan Strong, who was well acquainted with West India Treatment seemed to be deeply impressed with that extreme horror which the poor victims of the inhuman Traffic generally experience.'

those lawyers quoted the Yorke–Talbot ruling of 1729 that a slave did not become free on coming to England, he did not become free by baptism and that any master might compel his slave to return to the West Indies.

Sharp was shocked: he 'could not believe that the Laws of England were really so injurious to natural Rights' and began studying the law to conduct his own defence. He was a clerk in the Ordnance Office at Tower Hill and had 'never opened a lawbook (except the Bible) in my life'.

For over two years Sharp committed himself to legal research seeking to trace the original sources of the laws of England and interpret the history of villeinage, the British form of feudal serfdom. His was a well-known and socially connected family, he spoke with many of the leading legal officials and remained convinced that English law did not sanction slavery. He learnt the language in which to construct and frame his counter argument, his assertion as to what the law really was. The lawyers he commissioned presented Sharp's arguments to the opposing set with 'the desired effect, for it intimidated the Plaintiffs' lawyers from proceeding in their action' and in 1769 Sharp published his answer to Yorke–Talbot, *A Representation of the Injustice and Dangerous Tendency of Tolerating Slavery; or of Admitting the Least Claim of Private Property in the Persons of Men, in England*. The central proposition was that any person who came to England and lived there became a subject of the king and therefore subject to *habeas corpus* which prevented forcible removal to another country. And he cast the legal proposition against which he argued into a social language of humanitarian appeal: 'a toleration of slavery is, in effect, a toleration of inhumanity'.

Sharp, who had now left his job and was financially supported by his brothers, became the conduit for social activism in the cause of fighting slavery, assisting other runaway slaves to find safety and bringing a number of cases before the courts, seeking in vain a definitive judgment on the legality of slavery in four separate cases. The climax came with James Somerset. Somerset was an African slave sold in Virginia to Charles Steuart, a colonial customs official, later based in Boston. He arrived, with Steuart, in London in 1769 and was baptised as James Somerset on 20 February 1771 at St Andrew Holborn. He left Steuart's service on 1 October 1771. Steuart hunted him, and he was seized and confined in irons aboard a ship bound for Jamaica on 26 November 1771. His godparents, Thomas Walklin, Elizabeth Cade and John Marlow, applied for a writ of *habeas corpus* to prevent his removal and sale in Jamaica and paid for Somerset's bail. Somerset visited Granville Sharp and persuaded Sharp to become involved.

Sharp organised counsel to argue for Somerset and published an appendix to *The Injustice of Tolerating Slavery* which drew on the cases he had brought previously and implicitly criticised Lord Mansfield for impeding law's development. Indeed, he arranged for James Somerset to deliver a copy directly to Mansfield. West Indian planters rallied round Steuart, determined too that this should be a test case, and framed their response to the *habeas corpus* very carefully. Their position was simple: 'negro slaves' were chattel goods, and as Somerset was a slave according to the laws of Virginia and Africa, his master had rightfully detained him to send him to Jamaica for sale.

The hearing began in February 1772; Hochschild terms it 'high theatre, prolonged over several months by recesses when Mansfield vainly kept pushing for an out-of-court.[14] A central focus was whether slavery was legal in England and whether if not was it then possible for an English court to uphold colonial laws which did not have an English parallel. Steuart's lawyers stressed the harmful economics of letting slaves go; they did not appeal to a proposition that it was God's will that Blacks be inferior, or that it was even in line with natural justice that slavery exist, but that it was simply so: slavery was in their eyes a legal fact and the court must recognise that. It was the legal and social order and the court should not act so as to disturb that order. Mansfield wished to avoid a decision and tried to persuade Elizabeth Cade, Somerset's godmother, to buy him and Charles Steuart, his former owner, to set him free. Both refused because they wanted the case settled and the law made clear. Feeling the significance of the case Mansfield is said to have finally exclaimed: '*Fiat justicia, ruat coelum*' (Let justice be done, though the heavens fall) and delivered a carefully worded judgment on 22 June 1772.

> We feel the force of the inconveniences and consequences that will follow the decision of this question. Yet all of us are so clearly of one opinion upon the only question before us, that we think we ought to give judgment, without adjourning the matter to be argued before all the Judges, as usual in the Habeas Corpus, and as we at first intimated an intention of doing in this case. The only question then is, Is the cause returned sufficient for the remanding him? If not, he must be discharged. The cause returned is, the slave absented himself, and departed from his master's service, and refused to return and serve him during his stay in England; whereupon, by his master's orders, he was put on board the ship by force, and there detained in secure custody, to be carried out of the kingdom and sold. So high an act of dominion must derive its authority, if any such it has, from the law of the kingdom where executed. A foreigner cannot be imprisoned here on the authority of any law existing in his own country: the power of a master over his servant is different in all countries, more or less limited or extensive; the exercise of it therefore must always be regulated by the laws of the place where exercised. The state of slavery is of such a nature, that it is incapable of now being introduced by Courts of Justice upon mere reasoning or inferences from any principles, natural or political; it must take its rise from positive law; the origin of it can in no country or age be traced back to any other source: immemorial usage preserves the memory of positive law long after all traces of the occasion; reason, authority, and time of its introduction are lost; and in a case so odious as the condition of slaves must be taken strictly, the power claimed by this return was never in use here; no master ever was allowed here to take a slave by force to be sold abroad because he had deserted from his service, or for any other reason whatever; we cannot say the cause set forth by this return is allowed or approved of by the laws of this kingdom, therefore the man must be discharged.

A legal judgment is addressed to at least three audiences: the legal profession, the parties and the public. The narrow focus should be appreciated along with the wider impact.

----

14   Hochschild (2005: 50).

Focused on the legality of forcible deportation the decision looked extremely narrow: Steuart was not entitled to seize and deport Somerset under the laws of England and the writ was available to stop him and bring 'the man', the slave, before the courts so that they, and they alone, could determine his legal status.

The wider holding concerned the status of the applicable law: the laws of Virginia supported slavery but there was no law in England which did and in 'a case so odious as the condition of slaves' the master was not given the power claimed under common law and only a positive law could grant such power. 'No master ever was allowed here to take a slave by force to be sold abroad because he deserted from his service . . . and therefore the man must be discharged.'

A set of common distinctions characterise the many projects of understanding law in general: one is between law as power and law as reason; another is between law as the upholder of justice and law as the upholder of social order. In the later contrast, law as the upholder of justice requires a decision to be made that may result in social unrest, one seeks justice, not what the demands of utilitarian calculation advises; with law as the upholder of social order, one preserves and defends the institutional state of affairs, which may be achieved only at the expense of justice.

We know of Mansfield's attempts to have the case settled out of court (he is said to have muttered that he wished all blacks thought they were free and all masters thought they were slaves). At first sight his decision to 'let justice be done' is narrowly focused, a compromise image of law as the upholder of due process, a formal definition of justice as following the correct procedures, of sidestepping the arguments of Somerset's lawyers concerning the big picture of the inhumanity and injustice of slavery. Another reading is to see it as an example of law's characteristic role of mediating between the ideal and the real. The 'pure' legality of the decision seems to reduce the appeal of justice to a procedural calculation of due process: 'Is the cause returned sufficient for remanding him? If not, he must be discharged.' That is, a simple question, namely did the response to the writ reveal a reason recognised in law for holding the person. But the distinction drawn between the narrow procedural outcome and the wider holding becomes legally radical when one realises that the comments on the state of slavery, namely that it was not covered by common law, means that Mansfield is stating that the legal status and effectiveness of slavery must only flow from positive legislative enactment or long-standing custom: 'The state of slavery is of such a nature, that it is incapable of now being introduced by Courts of Justice upon mere reasoning or inferences from any principles, natural or political'; or for that matter, the courts cannot declare what was legal to be now illegal by resort to reasoning or inferences from principles, natural or political.

But if slavery was a creation of 'positive law'; that is, law consciously made by man as an act of legislative will, or simply a longstanding custom of that region, then we have a separation that is at the same time both conservative and radical. It is conservative in that we face a claim of the purity of legal process and reasoning that in this operation law can have a socially neutral realm; radical in that if the status of slave was a creation of positive law, then why not gender, class or race more generally?

Somerset confirms Sharp's legal analysis: English law protects certain fundamental 'rights of man' even for African slaves in England, including the right of access to the courts to protect against unlawful imprisonment or abuse, and freedom from chattel slavery. *Somerset* thus becomes a trope in the narrative of English laws protection of freedom: core legal freedoms such as access to the courts and protection from arbitrary, unlimited physical abuse, were available to all subjects as 'rights of man', not dependent upon birth, race, religion, or free status, and could only be denied by statute or express, longstanding custom. The decision separates a claim to the naturalness of the common law from the arbitrariness of positive law.

For Van Cleve, Lord Mansfield's decision that positive law, not common law, must authorise slavery both in England and in its colonies, as opposed to deciding Somerset under English common law and limiting its holding to slavery in England only, was a 'transformative decision'.

Mansfield's positive law holding, Van Cleve reads, was legally novel, unnecessary to Mansfield's substantive holding in Somerset, seemingly supportive of the status quo, and yet deliberately subversive of both metropolitan and colonial slavery. Mansfield's holding had both domestic and imperial political motives, but reflected Mansfield's beliefs as well. As to English domestic politics, Mansfield's holding was an effort to eliminate slavery litigation in the English courts and to commit the slavery issue to Parliament. As to imperial politics, Mansfield's positive law holding avoided a difficult imperial governance problem, but did so by exacting a substantial price from colonial slaveholders. Positive law holding also knowingly devalued slave property by making slave status wholly dependent on the law of individual jurisdictions, which he (and slave owners) knew meant that slave flight would increase because fugitive slaves could become free or protected against excessive force and compelled return, not just in England but in the colonies.[15]

The holding on slavery's status was 'profoundly destructive of the moral and legal legitimacy of slavery, since it made slave property an artificial creature of statute and deprived slavery of the sanction of the common law'.

As for the effect on the public, many thought that Mansfield's decision freed the slaves of England. The *St James' Chronicle and General Evening Post* and the *Middlesex Journal* (both of 23 June 1772) and Felix Farley's *Bristol Journal* thought so, reporting 'that every slave brought into this country ought to be free, and no master had a right to sell them here'. Other papers more accurately reported that the Somerset case had decided only that black slaves in England could not be forcibly removed from England. The trial had been attended by a large number of black people who celebrated the verdict with delight. A ball for black people only was arranged at a pub in Westminster where Lord Mansfield's health was drunk. James Somerset wrote to a friend that the judgment meant all slaves were now free. But there were still many slaves in England long after 1772 – adverts for finding and returning runaway slaves continued to appear in English newspapers, especially in Bristol. West India planters ignored Mansfield's judgment, or got round it by apprenticing their slaves. They lobbied, unsuccessfully, for an Act of Parliament to reinstate the Yorke–Talbot ruling.

Public opinion was changing. Somerset's case was influential, widely reported in newspapers that portrayed it as a drama with human interest as well as great legal importance. Many English people found that they could not tolerate a man or woman being owned as a chattel, especially in London, where a free (albeit poor) black

....

15   Van Cleve (2006: 109–113).

community developed in the late eighteenth century. The slave trading ports of Bristol and Liverpool were more aware of the foundations of their prosperity.

LOST PRECEDENTS? FROM DUDLEY AND STEPHENS BACK TO THE *ZONG*

R. *v.* Dudley and Stephens

On 9 December 1884 Lord Coleridge, C.J., read out the verdict of a five-judge court which on 4 December in Westminster, London had heard arguments around a rather unusual situation both legally and factually. At the Devon and Cornwall Winter Assizes, 7 November 1884, the jury, at the suggestion of the trial judge, had found the facts of the case in a special verdict in which they asked for a set of judges to take the responsibility of actually determining whether a conviction of murder should be given.[16] The special

JUSTICE COLERIDGE, WEARING THE BLACK CAP.

Figure 4.2 Lord Coleridge, Chief Justice, puts on the black cap which signifies that he is about to pass the death sentence. Source: Engraving by an unnamed artist in the *Illustrated London News*, 1845.

16   The jury in Dudley and Stephens' murder trial issued a 'special verdict', which included several findings of fact as reproduced in our text. It failed to reach a 'general verdict' regarding the men's guilt or innocence: 'But whether upon the whole matter by the jurors found the killing of Richard Parker by Dudley and Stephens be felony and murder the jurors are ignorant, and pray the advice of the Court thereupon.' This was highly unusual at the time. The judge, Baron Huddleston, persuaded the jury at the trial of Dudley and Stephens to enter a special verdict in lieu of a general verdict as he apparently wanted to ensure that the judges of the Queen's Bench, rather than a lay jury, would have the chance to resolve whether the killing constituted murder. See Simpson (1984: 208–223).

verdict revealed the facts of a case of human cannibalism on the high seas and the plea of necessity as a defence to the charge of murder. It stated:

That on July 5, 1884, the prisoners, Thomas Dudley and Edward Stephens, with one Brooks, all able-bodied English seamen, and the deceased also an English boy, between seventeen and eighteen years of age, the crew of an English yacht, a registered English vessel, were cast away in a storm on the high seas 1600 miles from the Cape of Good Hope, and were compelled to put into an open boat belonging to the said yacht. That in this boat they had no supply of water and no supply of food, except two 1lb. tins of turnips, and for three days they had nothing else to subsist upon. That on the fourth day they caught a small turtle, upon which they subsisted for a few days, and this was the only food they had up to the twentieth day when the act now in question was committed. That on the twelfth day the remains of the turtle were entirely consumed, and for the next eight days they had nothing to eat. That they had no fresh water, except such rain as they from time to time caught in their oilskin capes. That the boat was drifting on the ocean, and was probably more than 1000 miles away from land. That on the eighteenth day, when they had been seven days without food and five without water, the prisoners spoke to Brooks as to what should be done if no succour came, and suggested that some one should be sacrificed to save the rest, but Brooks dissented, and the boy, to whom they were understood to refer, was not consulted. That on the 24th of July, the day before the act now in question, the prisoner Dudley proposed to Stephens and Brooks that lots should be cast who should be put to death to save the rest, but Brooks refused to consent, and it was not put to the boy, and in point of fact there was no drawing of lots. That on that day the prisoners spoke of their having families, and suggested it would be better to kill the boy that their lives should be saved, and Dudley proposed that if there was no vessel in sight by the morrow morning the boy should be killed. That next day, the 25th of July, no vessel appearing, Dudley told Brooks that he had better go and have a sleep, and made signs to Stephens and Brooks that the boy had better be killed. The prisoner Stephens agreed to the act, but Brooks dissented from it. That the boy was then lying at the bottom of the boat quite helpless, and extremely weakened by famine and by drinking sea water, and unable to make any resistance, nor did he ever assent to his being killed. The prisoner Dudley offered a prayer asking forgiveness for them all if either of them should be tempted to commit a rash act, and that their souls might be saved. That Dudley, with the assent of Stephens, went to the boy, and telling him that his time was come, put a knife into his throat and killed him then and there; that the three men fed upon the body and blood of the boy for four days; that on the fourth day after the act had been committed the boat was picked up by a passing vessel, and the prisoners were rescued, still alive, but in the lowest state of prostration. That they were carried to the port of Falmouth, and committed for trial at Exeter. That if the men had not fed upon the body of the boy they would probably not have survived to be so picked up and rescued, but would within the four days have died of famine. That the boy, being in a much weaker condition, was likely to have died before them. That at the time of the act in question there was no sail in sight, nor any reasonable prospect of relief. That under these circumstances there appeared to the prisoners every probability that unless they then fed or very soon fed upon the boy or one of themselves they would die of starvation.

That there was no appreciable chance of saving life except by killing some one for the others to eat. That assuming any necessity to kill anybody, there was no greater necessity for killing the boy than any of the other three men. But whether upon the whole matter by the jurors found the killing of Richard Parker by Dudley and Stephens be felony and murder the jurors are ignorant, and pray the advice of the Court thereupon, and if upon the whole matter the Court shall be of opinion that the killing of Richard Parker be felony and murder, then the jurors say that Dudley and Stephens were each guilty of felony and murder as alleged in the indictment.

We have an opportunity to decide denied to the jury, whom we suppose may have found a verdict of 'not guilty' on humane grounds. If a verdict of 'guilty' was to be found the penalty was death. Coleridge's judgment relates a story wherein he is conscious of the human appeal: 'The prisoners were subject to terrible temptation, to sufferings which might break down the bodily power of the strongest man, and try the conscience of the best. Other details yet more harrowing, facts still more loathsome and appalling, were presented to the jury.' Yet he finds the facts clear: 'The prisoners put to death a weak and unoffending boy upon the chance of preserving their own lives by feeding upon his flesh and blood after he was killed, and with the certainty of depriving him of any possible chance of survival.'

The first major argument put to the court was that it had no jurisdiction to try the matter. This was quickly disposed of, for it had been 'declared by Parliament to have been always the law' that:

All offences against property or person committed in or at any place either ashore or afloat, out of her Majesty's dominions by any master seaman or apprentice who at the time when the offence is committed is or within three months previously has been employed in any British ship, shall be deemed to be offences of the same nature respectively, and be inquired of, heard, tried, determined, and adjudged in the same manner and by the same courts and in the same places as if such offences had been committed within the jurisdiction of the Admiralty of England.

The only real question in the case was whether 'killing under the circumstances set forth in the verdict be or be not murder'. Coleridge then relates how the argument that it could be anything other seemed absurd:

The contention that it could be anything else was, to the minds of us all, both new and strange, and we stopped the Attorney General in his negative argument in order that we might hear what could be said in support of a proposition which appeared to us to be at once dangerous, immoral, and opposed to all legal principle and analogy.

He then sums up the arguments to the ploy that the only possible excuse in law could be that the killing was justified by what has been called 'necessity'.

But the temptation to the act which existed here was not what the law has ever called 'necessity'. Nor is this to be regretted. Though law and morality are not the same, and many things may be immoral which are not necessarily illegal, yet the absolute divorce of law from morality would be of fatal consequence; and such divorce would follow if the temptation to murder in this case were to be held by law an absolute defence of it. It is not so. To preserve one's life is generally speaking a duty, but it may be the plainest and the highest duty to sacrifice it. War is full of instances in which it is a man's duty not to live, but to die. The duty, in case of shipwreck, of a captain to his crew, of the crew to the passengers, of soldiers to women and children, as in the noble case of the Birkenhead; these duties impose on men the moral necessity, not of the preservation, but of the sacrifice of their lives for others, from which in no country, least of all, it is to be hoped, in England, will men ever shrink, as indeed, they have not shrunk.

The narrow point is positioned within a story of law's relationship to morality and to the past and Coleridge was certain: Englishmen had never shrunk from those duties, the law never knew of a defence of necessity. On a positivist reading that was true; the law, the collective experience of previous cases, did not know, but this is not innocent, it did not know because it had not been allowed to.

The voyage of the *Zong*: a precedent that never was

The basic facts are clear. The *Zong* was a slave ship owned by James Gregson and a number of others who were directors of a large Liverpool slaving company. In 1781 it travelled the triangle from Liverpool to West Africa and onwards with a cargo of slaves to the Caribbean, thence to return with a cargo of sugar for the English tea-houses. The *Zong* left West Africa on 6 September with a cargo of 470 slaves bound for Jamaica; when it approached its destination some 12 weeks later more than 60 Africans and 7 of the 17-man crew had died.[17] The captain, Luke Collingwood, was more used to being a ship's surgeon (a position it should be noted that meant he was responsible for picking out the slaves most likely to survive the journey) and had packed even more slaves on board than usual. Shyllon[18] states that 'chained two by two, right leg and left leg, each slave had less room than a man in a coffin'. The result was a high mortality level, for both black and white, but commentators consider it far less than the catastrophic losses suffered by some other slave ships. The British ship the *Hero*, for example, once lost 360 slaves (over half of its cargo), while the *Briton* lost over half of its 375 slaves on one voyage. The main cause of death in the middle passage was generally virulent dysentery that the sailors called the 'flux', though some slaves could be lost by being beaten to death or, in the case of women, killed when resisting sexual abuse. Slaves also tried to starve themselves to death as an act of resistance and had to be force-fed using mechanical devices that prised open their jaws.

On 29 November Collingwood called his officers together and proposed that the sick slaves should be jettisoned – thrown overboard – in order to secure the rapidly dwindling supplies of water and to allow the shipping company to claim their loss on

---

17   A voyage with favourable trade winds from Senegambia to Barbados might take as little as three weeks, but a ship travelling from Guinea or Angola might be becalmed by lack of wind or be driven back by storms and take as long as three months.
18   Shyllon (1974).

insurance. In Walvin's words: 'It was, even in the age of the slave trade, a grotesque suggestion.'[19]

Given the conditions, there were plenty of slaves who appeared sick. Collingwood explained to his officers that 'if the slaves died a natural death, it would be the loss of the owners of the ship; but if they were thrown alive into the sea, it would be the loss of the underwriters'. As a 'humane', though obviously specious, justification, he suggested that 'it would not be so cruel to throw the poor sick wretches into the sea, as to suffer them to linger out a few days, under the disorders with which they were afflicted'. Of course, no such proposal was made to put an end to the suffering of sick crewmen. Charles MacInnes explains that such actions were not uncommon:

> If the ship proved unseaworthy or if the food and water began to run short in conse-
> quence of an unduly prolonged voyage resulting from calms, adverse winds, or any
> other difficulties, a simple remedy lay at hand. A sufficient number of slaves would be
> thrown overboard.[20]

What was Collingwood's understanding of the law? He would have been familiar with the terms and conditions of the voyage which would have been covered by a 'standard' marine insurance policy. In that same year, a digest of insurance laws and practice was published in London on behalf of the Clarendon Press of Oxford. It stated:

> The insurer takes upon him the risk of the loss, capture, and death of slaves, or any
> other unavoidable accident to them: but natural death is always understood to be
> excepted:– by natural death is meant, not only when it happens by disease or sickness,
> but also when the captive destroys himself through despair, which often happens: but
> when slaves are killed or thrown into the sea in order to quell an insurrection on their
> part, then the insurers must answer.[21]

So the 'law' was clear! But was sickness alone a sufficient reason for drowning the slaves? Collingwood's excuse was that the ship was running short of water, due in part to his own navigational error that had mistaken Hispaniola for their destination, Jamaica. His argument was that to kill the sick slaves would mean that the healthy could be sustained on the dwindling supplies. Not to kill the slaves would be to jeop-ardise the safety and health of everyone on board. This was later to be the crucial factual issue at the court and seemed to others to be an unconvincing line of self-justification not least because water was not rationed until after the killing of the slaves had begun and, second, because no attempt was made to put ashore to replenish supplies. Moreover, according to the sailors' accounts, before all the sick slaves had been killed, 'there fell a plentiful rain' that was admitted to have 'continued a day or two'. They collected six casks of water, which was 'full allowance for 11 days, or for

19   Walvin (1992).
20   Charles MacInnes (1934).
21   Weskett (1781: 525).

23 days at half allowance'. When the *Zong* landed in Jamaica on 22 December, it had 420 gallons of water on board. It had left in its wake 132 drowned Africans.

The chief mate James Kelsal at first opposed the proposal to drown the slaves but Collingwood insisted, and the killings began. The crew selected those who 'were sick, and thought not likely to live'. On 29 November, the first batch of 54 was pushed overboard and a day later 42 more were drowned, while on the third day the slaves were fighting back with the result that 26 were thrown overboard with their arms still shackled. The remaining ten 'sprang disdainfully from the grasp of their tyrants, defied their power, and, leaping into the sea, felt a momentary triumph in the embrace of death'. One of the jettisoned slaves managed to catch on to a rope and climbed back safely on board. In Walvin's words: 'A total of 131 slaves were coolly murdered from the deck of a Liverpool vessel, for no good reason save the economic calculations of Captain Luke Collingwood and the physical compliance of his crewmen'.

Walvin has no trouble calling this 'murder', but we are concerned with the process whereby it avoided ever becoming recorded or labelled murder in the legal literature. On 19 March 1783 Sharp was visited by Olaudah Equiano (sometimes called Gustavus Vassa), an African and former slave who was emerging as the most prominent spokesman for the black community living in London: 'Gustavus Vassa, Negro, called on me with an account of 130 [sic] Negroes being thrown alive into the sea, from on Board an English Slave Ship'. The *Zong* affair was already before the courts some two weeks earlier, when the case of *Gregson* v. *Gilbert* had been heard in the Guildhall in London. Gregson, on behalf of himself and the other ship owners, were claiming for the loss of their slaves (£30 each) from their underwriters (Gilbert). The latter refused to pay, and the case was presented as a simple matter of maritime insurance.

The jury in that trial sided with the ship owners, ordering the insurance company to pay compensation for the dead slaves. In a letter to the *Morning Chronicle*, an eye-witness at the trial wrote: 'The narrative seemed to make every one present shudder; and I waited with some impatience, expecting that the jury, by their foreman, would have applied to the Court for information how to bring the perpetrators of such a horrid deed to justice.' Perhaps one way out was the suggestion that Captain Luke Collingwood – by now safely dead – 'was in a delirium, or a fit of lunacy when he gave the orders'. This was not to happen: the case was to retain its basic inhuman simplicity: a claim for insurance. Yet the correspondent went on to identify the *Zong* as involving questions beyond the particularities of an argument about insurance:

> That there should be bad men to do bad things in all large communities, must be expected: but a community makes the crime general, and provokes divine wrath, when it suffers any member to commit flagrant acts of villainy with impunity . . . it is hardly possible for a state to thrive, where the perpetration of such complicated guilt, as the present, is not only suffered to go unpunished, but is allowed to glory in the infamy, and carries off the reward for it.

Walvin's language is clear and is worth reading for his invocation of the close ties between the law and the economic system:

The crime had been committed on board a British ship, and was so startling in the crudity and extent of its violence that it clearly shook observers. But where would the pursuit of criminality end if, let us say, the crew were arraigned for their crimes? Although the murder of African slaves was unusual, it was common enough in pursuit of slaves, in securing the safety of a slave ship, in defeating ship-board resistance – to say nothing of the endemic violence which helped keep slavery in place throughout the American slave colonies. Slavery begat the slave trade, and the slave trade was, in origin, in conduct and in its very being, the crudest of violations, which encompassed, when necessary, the death of its victims. For the system to survive in its economic viability, some slaves had to pay the ultimate sacrifice. It took no great leap of the imagination to appreciate that the logic of pursuing the murderers of the slaves on the *Zong* would be the first tug which would unravel the entire garment of the slave system. And in some respects this is precisely what happened, for it was around the small band of men of sensibility, outraged by events on the *Zong*, that there developed the first powerful body of abolitionist feeling and action. The line of dissent from the *Zong* to the successful campaign for abolition was direct and unbroken, however protracted and uneven.

Granville Sharp tried to get together a body of like-minded men to pursue the prosecution of the *Zong* sailors. He was not to succeed. The *Zong* affair came to trial again on a matter of insurance for the underwriters refused to pay the compensation ordered, and the matter came before Lord Justice Mansfield sitting with two other judges in May 1783. The slave owners, claiming the insurance on the slaves, were represented by John Lee, the Solicitor-General. What was Lee's professional and ethical interest in the case? He certainly seemed aware of the potential implications of the case. At the trial he turned towards Granville Sharp in the public gallery and argued that there was a person in court who intended to bring on a criminal prosecution for murder against the parties concerned: 'But it would be madness: the Blacks were property'. Walvin describes the line he adopted as 'casually dismissive':

> What is all this vast declaration of human beings thrown overboard? The question after all is, was it voluntary, or an act of necessity? This is a case of chattels, of goods, it is really so: it is the case of throwing over goods – for to this purpose, and the purpose of the Insurance, they are goods and property: whether right or wrong, we have nothing to do with it. This property – the human creatures if you will – have been thrown overboard: whether or not for the preservation of the rest – that is the real question.

The slave system hinged on the concept of the slave as a thing: a chattel, a piece of property. Both law and economic practice had, from the early days of the Atlantic slave trade, accepted the chattel status of the slave, thus what objection could there be to the killing of chattel? Mansfield himself accepted the point: 'They had no doubt (though it shocks one very much) that the case of the slaves was the same as if horses had been thrown overboard'.

Mansfield conceded the importance of the case but contended that the owners had not definitively established that the ship's water supply was so low that there was an absolute 'necessity' to throw the slaves overboard to be drowned and so ordered a new trial (no one has found any evidence of a further trial being held or even identified the next legal step in the *Zong* affair). The owners of the *Zong* were not the last slave-ship owners to claim insurance for dead slaves. Granville Sharp continued his campaign and tried to persuade government officers to bring murder charges against those involved, telling Admiralty officials that he had 'been earnestly solicited and called upon by a poor Negro for my assistance, to avenge the blood of his murdered countrymen'. Marshalling all the supporting evidence he could find, Sharp hoped to present an unanswerable case for a prosecution.[22] But as Walvin concludes:

> Again, he confronted that official silence and inactivity born of the realisation that any such action would corrode the system. Once an English court began to discuss murder and cruelty in the conduct of the slaving system, there was no knowing where the questions – and the consequent material damage – would end.

How was the case contained?

The image with which this chapter began depicted the courtroom as an ethical space wherein the rights of man were defended. The modern rule of law finds its institutional space in the proceedings of a case, in the barrier of the courtroom and the inside–outside distinction. Inside the courtroom law provides the discourse for resolution. But legal discourse has its own distinction between what is relevant and what is irrelevant. Movement occurs between the formal and the specific, between abstract and the concrete.

As Baucom[23] relates, Sharp's appeal to use criminal discourse and test necessity is at odds with the meaning it held in Mansfield's courtroom. The use of necessity in the criminal law case of *R. v. Dudley and Stephens* and another could not be called upon since necessity was understood as a particular stipulation within the *Zong*'s insurance contract and to the general insurance principle underlying that stipulation. Inside the courtroom, whatever the appeal from the public gallery, whatever the concern of those who sat with Sharp observing to 'see' justice done, the question of necessity was circumscribed by the terms of an insurance contract. Necessity thus meant for Mansfield not an ethical or moral question, not an issue of man's treatment of man, not whether or not it had been necessary for Collingwood to sacrifice some lives to save others; necessity meant whether his actions met the standard of necessity (for the throwing overboard of 'goods') of his contract's jettison clause and whether, accordingly, the owners were or were not entitled to compensation for those lost 'goods' in accord with the rules laid down by the bedrock insurance principle of the 'general average'. In their appeal for a new trial following the Guildhall jury's initial ruling in favour of the owners (and initial determination that Collingwood's actions had indeed met his contract's standard of necessity), the underwriters were clear: 'The [owners]

---

22   Although there was no further legal action Parliament was petitioned. It refused to intervene, accepting that only 'cargo' was involved. The Quakers organised a general petition for the abolition of the slave trade but encountered the strong resistance of commercial interests. Four years later Granville Sharp joined with many others to form the Anti-Slave Trade Society. Today, this society continues to fight against modern forms of slavery and child trafficking that occur in many places around the world.
23   Baucom (2005: 139ff).

have since pretended that the Sd. 133 slaves which were thrown alive out of the Sd. Ship Zong into the sea and perished . . . were at the rate of 30 per head and according to the Stipulation and Agreement in the Afsd. Policies of Insurance of the value of 3990 & that the loss of the Sd. Slaves was a general Average Loss which ought to be born & paid for by the Underwriters.' The question before the court was whether or not the loss to the overall value of the *Zong*'s cargo was or was not a general average loss 'according to the Stipulation and Agreement' of its insurance policy. There were two main ways in which the underwriters' attorney could have pursued that question: either by suggesting that that policy did not include slaves among the list of 'goods' that could be treated as a general average loss or by suggesting that the policy did include slaves among that full list of 'commodities that had become the subject of insurance', but that, in this case, it had not been necessary for Collingwood to destroy these 'goods' and thus no compensation was owed. The first option would have entailed a fundamental engagement with the legality of slavery and the extant theory of property. The second, which is the option that the attorney chose to pursue, depended more simply on a matter of fact.

The 'standard' marine insurance policy of the period stipulated that:

> Whatever the master of a ship in distress, with the advice of his officers and sailors, deliberately resolves to do, for the preservation of the whole, in cutting away masts or cables, or in throwing goods overboard to lighten his vessel, which is what is meant by jettison or jetson, is, in all places, permitted to be brought into a general, or gross average: in which all concerned in ship, freight, and cargo, are to bear an equal or proportionate part of what was so sacrificed for the common good, and it must be made good by the insurers in such proportions as they have underwrote: however, to make this action legal, the three following points are essentially necessary; viz – 1st. That what was so condemned to destruction, was in consequence of a deliberate and voluntary consultation, held between the master and men: – 2dly. That the ship was in distress, and the sacrificing the things they did was a necessary procedure to save the rest: – and 3dly. That the saving of the ship and the cargo was actually owing to the means used with that sole view.

The *Zong* then is a referent both for the ship, the decision of its captain and crew towards their 'cargo' (not passengers), and it is also referent for the legal event and for absence. The *Zong*'s identity is as an exemplar of the contemporary, of the success of legal relevancy and the failure of the ethical appeal.

How can this be represented?

I pose another image, that by J.M.W. Turner and one which was the chief Academy picture of the Exhibition of 1840; when it was said later, 'Nothing could exceed the critical violence with which it was attacked.'[24]

---

24   The view is today different: Simon Schama: 'Though almost all of his critics believed that the painting represented an all time low in Turner's reckless disregard for the rules of art, it was in fact his greatest triumph in the sculptural carving of space.' See http://www.bbc.co.uk/arts/powerofart/turner.shtml.

Figure 4.3 Joseph Mallord William Turner, English, 1775–1851, *Slave Ship (Slavers Throwing Overboard the Dead and Dying, Typhoon Coming On)*, 1840, Oil on canvas, 90.8 × 122.6 cm (35 3/4 × 48 1/4 in.), Museum of Fine Arts, Boston, Henry Lillie Pierce Fund 99.22. Photograph © 2012 Museum of Fine Arts, Boston. All rights reserved (The original is of course in vibrant colour). The painting was accompanied by a poem that described a slave ship caught in a typhoon, and based on the *Zong*. The critic John Ruskin, wrote, 'If I were reduced to rest Turner's immortality upon any single work, I should choose this.' When Turner exhibited the work at the Royal Academy in 1840 he paired it with the following extract from his unfinished and unpublished poem Fallacies of Hope (1812): 'Aloft all hands, strike the top-masts and belay;/Yon angry setting sun and fierce-edged clouds/Declare the Typhon's coming/ Before it sweeps your decks, throw overboard/ The dead and dying – ne'er heed their chains/Hope, Hope, fallacious Hope!/ Where is thy market now?' (For the full text of Turner's verse see Finberg (1961). Ruskin: 'I think, the noblest sea that Turner has ever painted, and if so, the noblest, certainly, ever painted by man, is that of the Slave-ship. It is a sunset on the Adriatic [sic, he means Atlantic], after prolonged storm; but the storm is partially lulled, and the torn and streaming rain clouds are moving in scarlet lines to lose themselves in the hollow of the night. The whole surface of sea included in the picture is divided into two ridges of enormous swell, not high, nor local, but a low, broad heaving of the whole ocean, like the lifting of its bosom by deep-drawn breath after the torture of the storm. Between these two ridges, the fire of the sunset falls along the trough of the sea, dyeing it with an awful but glorious light, the intense and lurid splendour of which burns like gold, and bathes like blood. Along this fiery path and valley, the tossing waves by which the swell of the sea is restlessly divided, lift themselves in dark, indefinite, fantastic forms, each casting a faint and ghastly shadow behind it along the illumined foam. They do not rise everywhere, but three or four together in wild groups, fitfully and furiously, as the under strength of the swell compels or permits them; leaving between them treacherous spaces of level and whirling water, now lighted with green and lamp-like fire, now flashing back the gold of the declining sun, now fearfully dyed from above with the indistinguishable images of the burning clouds, which fall upon them in flakes of crimson and scarlet, and give to the reckless waves the added motion of their own fiery flying. Purple and blue, the lurid shadows of the hollow breakers are cast upon the mist of the night, which gathers cold and low, advancing like the shadow of death upon the guilty ship as it labours amidst the lightning of the sea, its thin masts written upon the sky in lines of blood, girded with condemnation in that fearful hue which signs the sky with horror, and mixes its foaming flood with the sunlight, – and, cast far along the desolate heave of the sepulchral waves, incarnadines the multitudinous sea.'

The Victorian art critic and one time owner of the picture Ruskin understood that Turner presented nature about to punish guilty human beings. In his eyes it was a masterpiece in its combination of inspiration and technique:

> Its daring conception – ideal in the highest sense of the word – is based on the purest truth, and wrought out with the concentrated knowledge of a life; its colour is absolutely perfect, not one false or morbid hue in any part or line, and so modulated that every square inch of canvass is a perfect composition; its drawing as accurate as fearless; the ship buoyant, bending, and full of motion; its tones as true as they are wonderful; and the whole picture dedicated to the most sublime of subjects and impressions.

The work counter-poses detail and distance: in the left distance the guilty vessel is about to meet its deserved end, while in the right and central foreground we see the cast off slaves being devoured by the sea and its creatures.

Turner presents us with fanciful ocean predators to play on the gothic fear of imagined consequences and while John McCoubrey states Turner painted this image specifically for an anti-slavery campaign, the image is ambiguous when we understand the full context. The year 1840 was to be a celebration of Britain's stance on slavery and the abolitionist movement were to hold an international convention of the great and good to express righteous indignation against slavery in the United States. Turner had been introduced to the cause many years before by his patron, Walter Fawkes, and wanted to make a contribution, but his work punctures any feeling of superiority. By going back to the *Zong*, Turner points to the failure of human justice; turned by the courts into the discourse of insurance and the claim of necessity, it is nature, the same nature that has terrible fates for the cast off slaves, that will punish those on the ship that threw them overboard. Turner's words in his poem 'Hope, Hope, fallacious Hope!/Where is thy market now?' is an attack not just on the slave trade but the way in which the humans of the *Zong* had not even gained a recognition as passengers but

Figure 4.4 Detail of the *Slave Ship* by Turner.

only as items of cargo that bore an insurance value. Turner's work opposes vantage points to communicate both sympathy and judgment leading the viewer to sympathise with the victims of those about to receive deserved retribution. Since this opposition of near and far in this way demonstrates for the viewer the essential justice of the ship's destruction, the very closeness of the dying slaves to the spectator creates a second effect, which is the recognition that the nature which will justly punish the ship is the same nature that is already unjustly devouring the ship's innocent victims. The law has denied justice: only nature will deliver it, but can we trust this nature? Turner may be with the classical Greek poet Hesiod: 'The immortals are ever present among men, and they see those who with crooked verdicts spurn divine retribution and grind down one another's lives . . . [They] keep a watchful eye over verdicts and cruel acts as they move over the whole earth, clothed in mist . . . so that people pay for the reckless deeds and evil plans of kings whose slanted words twist her straight path.'[25] We, however, may not share this confidence.

CONCLUSION: LAWS OPENNESS AND CLOSURE

Murphy reminds us that the common 'law is a matter of judgment in a particular place from which things can be seen in their proper arrangement'.[26] In this chapter we have been concerned with rights, due process, discourse, decision and vision: the ability to see and decide, whether 'justly' or not. Turner reminds us that the visibility of the courtroom is consequent to the structuring of the case. The court's ability to see, to have the facts and issues brought before a judge or panel of judges, is at the end of processes of inclusion and exclusion, both in terms of legal discourse (conceptualisation) and justicability (of allowing issues and facts to be in issue at the court). We will not in this text do more than note the widespread concerns over access to justice deserving of greater attention (the name of Bhopal and the denial of justice to the victims of that chemical disaster in the 1980s is but illustrative). Our concern is primarily the politics of the common law system in England and Wales and we shall look at some access to justices issues when we come to consider the values associated with legal aid, but viewed globally the rise of rights discourse also demonstrates how so few of the victims of abuses of rights can access any form of 'international justice'.[27] And while transatlantic slavery no longer exists, people trafficking is still extensive and monthly some choices are made in boats and containers over which illegal immigrant is to be taken on or sometimes pushed off into the sea – bodies of the not so lucky regularly wash up in the Mediterranean.

Law's domain is ambiguous: expansive and yet particular. Law appears to be able to answer any question that is turned into its particular forms of discourse, discourse that fits the constraints of the 'case'. Understood contextually, we need to be aware of

---

25   Hesiod (1983: vol. II, 73).
26   Murphy (1997: 116).
27   On the rise of rights discourse see Sellars (2002); among the growing list of works defining the twentieth century as one of mass crimes and little prosecution see Ball (1999); Rubenstein (2000); Morrison (2005).

the social, political and economic forces that structure the case and in scholarly terms there is much to be gained in knowledge from sociological, anthropological, historical, political and economic analysis to position the case, to position law's operation and its ability (or forgetfulness) to record laws experience. In this sense whatever the outcome of the (to law students often arbitrary) disputes as to whether multidisciplinary study should take 'law and society' or 'law in society' as its target law in the sense of the case is law in society. This might give rise to optimism: structure our understanding of the case so that we are aware of these constraints and law is free to be law and not politics, the case contains the interests, the law is impartial. However, the boundaries are not clear and are increasingly complex. We witness an expansion of the range of issues, parties and inherent conflict (if not outright contradiction) between them. The rise of the global economy presents environmental, economic and political interdependency as never before. Complex multinational organisations make identifying responsibility, cause and effect, extremely difficult. New technologies push out the boundaries of the possible, and create, for example, forms of bio-power that allow for the state to regulate 'life' – the rise of biotechnologies present ethical and political dilemmas that the courts struggle to cope with. The factors to be taken into account in the construction of a case expand, the outcomes of particular 'cases' may increasingly reflect compromises, criticised by observers as not settling the issues, but can such issues be settled?

For example, the seemingly relative simplicity of R v. *Dudley and Stephens* – and the patronising language of Coleridge's judgment – came back to play in the case of *Re: A (Children)* [2000]. Jodie and Mary were conjoined twins, joined at the pelvis, born to devout Roman Catholic parents. Mary was the weaker of the two twins and would not have survived if she had been born alone. She was being kept alive by virtue of Jodie's own circulatory system. Jodie was considered to be capable of surviving a separation procedure; Mary was not. The courts accepted that if no separation took place, both would die within a matter of months, due to the added strain on Jodie's circulatory system. The medical team looking after the twins wished to separate them, in the knowledge that Mary would die as a direct result of the operation. The twin's parents, however, would not sanction the operation. In their eyes, both twins were God's creatures, each having a right to life. They could not sanction the shortening of Mary's life in order to extend that of Jodie. If it was God's will that they die, then so be it. The medical team sought a ruling from the High Court that an operation to separate the twins, knowing that such a procedure would result in the death of Mary, would not be unlawful; that is, murder.

At the first instance trial, Johnson J tried to avoid calling this murder by ruling that such an operation would not be unlawful because in his view the proposed operation was not a positive act but represented a 'withdrawal of blood', a situation analogous to the withdrawal of feeding and hydration in *Airedale NHS Trust* v. *Bland* [1993]. The parents appealed on the grounds that Johnson J was wrong in finding that the proposed operation was in either Mary's or Jodie's best interests, and that the operation should not be held legal. Ward LJ, Brook LJ and Walker LJ of the Court of Appeal therefore considered submissions from all interested parties, and came to the same outcome – that the separation would not be unlawful. But they rightly saw the operation in terms of the doctors doing an intentional action and each judge used different routes to find the operation lawful. Each decided to concentrate on dealing with different spheres of principles of medical law, family law, criminal law and human rights principles and legislation. Each concluded that the operation would result in the death of Mary, an act that was intentional and was therefore murder. In order to be considered 'lawful', the operation would therefore have to be carried out under the auspices of an exception or defence to murder, or be 'excused' in some way. They considered the defence of 'necessity' to be applicable to this situation, Brook LJ giving the most detailed assessment of the relevant law (Brook LJ in *Re: A (Children)* part 4 sections 16–24). The defence was accepted with the compromise to restrict the applicability of this defence, for the purposes of public policy, to the very 'unique circumstances' of this case. But how did this fit in the narrative structure of law's predictability? Did the case give a result that ensured predictability? In other words could other doctors know whether the principles of 'necessity' will be applied in other aspects of medical practice, where decisions are made as to the relative worth of an individual's life, in comparison with that of another? It seemed not.

There were two sets of criticisms: one that the judgment did not enter into a deep enough discussion of the ethical and moral responsibilities. The other that the issues were not reconciled in law. The following was representative:

> Future criminal cases will find little material with which to generalise in Re A. Robert Walker LJ's judgment can largely be disregarded, and the analyses of Ward and Brooke LJJ tread different paths. Indeed, their Lordships' mutual declarations of agreement are undermined by the reasoning in their judgments. No ratio decidendae emerges with clarity from the decision. Nonetheless, authoritative dicta may be drawn upon to support arguments about the scope of self-defence (in Ward LJ's judgment) and especially necessity (in Brooke LJ's judgment). And one may be confident in future that a defence to murder will be available to D in situations where a blameless victim is, by her conduct, posing an unjustified threat to the lives of others, at least provided the victim's death is not directly sought and is only a virtually certain side-effect of the life-preserving actions taken by D.[28]

We will not go into further detail, we may or may not agree that 'the extension of what it is possible to do, from more efficient ways of killing people to the cloning of humans, have fast outstripped the ability of society to come to a consensus on what is permissible or right'. But one message is that more and more factors, parties and issues may be packed into a case; we have to accept that law's ability to see, in the confines of the case, seems destined to become simultaneously more opaque and more complex. If the common law's traditional practicality can provide answers, they will be increasingly temporary and open to analysis from many perspectives. But as this chapter has alluded to, the connection between law and truth may always have been the product of the confines of the 'case'.

---

28   Case Note, *Criminal Law*, Simester and Sullivan, Hart Publishing, updated 14 October 2002 (http://www.hartpublishingusa.com/updates/crimlaw/crimlaw_med.htm)

5

THE POSTCOLONIAL, THE VISIBLE AND THE INVISIBLE: THE NORMAL AND THE EXCEPTIONAL

... Good order is the foundation of all things. To be able to acquire, the people, without being servile, must be tractable and obedient. The magistrate must have his reverence, the laws their authority. The body of the people must not have the principles of natural subordination by art rooted out of their minds. They must respect that property of which they cannot partake. They must labour to obtain that which by labour can be obtained, and when they find, as they commonly do, their success disproportional to their endeavour, they must be taught their consolation in the final proportions of eternal justice.

... In this choice of inheritance [of the common law], we (the British) had given to our frame of polity the image of a relation in blood; binding up the constitution of our country without deepest domesticities; adopting our fundamental laws into the bosom of our family affections; keeping inseparable, and cherishing with the warmth of all their combined and mutually reflecting charities, our states, our hearths, our sepulchres and our altars.[1]

In the colonies the truth stood naked, but the citizens of the mother country preferred it with cloths on: the natives had to love them, something in the way mothers are loved.[2]

The colonial world is a world cut in two. The dividing line, the frontiers are shown by barracks and police stations. In the colonies it is the policeman and the soldier who are the official, instituted go-betweens, the spokesmen of the settler and his rule of oppression. ... In the colonial countries ... the policeman and the soldier, by their immediate presence and their frequent and direct action maintain contact with the native and advise him by means of rifle-butts and napalm not to budge [i.e. to stay in his place]. It is obvious here that the agents of government speak the language of pure force. The intermediary does not lighten the oppression, nor seek to hide the domination; he shows them up and puts them into practice with the clear conscience of an upholder of the peace; yet he is the bringer of violence into the home and into the mind of the native.[3]

---

1   Edmund Burke, 1970, pp. 120 and 372.
2   J.P. Sartre, Preface to Fanon, 1963, p. 7.
3   Fanon, 1963, p. 38.

INTRODUCTION: THE LONG VIEW, WHOSE PERSPECTIVE?

This text began in New Zealand in the 1970s with an act of reverence to the body and authority of the Law. It was to the figure wearing a black academic gown who had been a public prosecutor in Kenya and whom, it was rumoured, laid claim to have hung a considerable member of the Mau Mau, that the 'I' of an earlier chapter listened to in first year Legal System lectures on (English) legal history in preference to the figure of sociology 'I' in jeans and tee shirt who expressed critical views on property relationships and ideology. The 'I' voice of that first chapter is white (as are the other two co-authors), a *Pakeha*, as the Maori would call the white settlers – predominantly from Europe – who came (with superior technology, i.e. guns) to the lands they occupied.

The contemporary common law world – as with the civil law world – was built through the global spread of colonialism and capitalism.[4] Legal education can be in large part a celebration of law's effectivity, of its powers of juridification, to the spread of its networks that today underpin and constitute globalisation. Yet the interaction of race and law is not innocent; European expansion carried a story of delivering law as its gift, bringing order to chaos, light to darkness. But imperialism relied on violence and the violence of imperialism was 'legitimate'. For Fitzpatrick 'racism' solved the contradiction between enlightenment ideal of universal freedom and equality and the undeniable fact of European colonialism (and the inherent violence to the other inherent in that).[5] For Patricia Tuitt, the colonial state was 'monstrous' in its racial denial of what should be the 'most fundamental of securities, the persistent recognition of the human state to all, irrespective of race'. Race allows types of pairings or conjunctions with the now disputed human subject: the human subject's universality is demarcated and partitioned. Learning law is in part learning a language, a vision and an inheritance.[6] For many, and with considerable justification, the story of the development of modern law is a story of overcoming slavery, of developing ideas of subjective rights and then institutionalising those ideas in law and in international conventions.[7] For the French writer Kriegel the law provides the only route out of slavery: 'the chains of oppression can be broken and a community of men (sic) freed from bondage only by passing through a narrow gate', that of law.[8] And he is clear as to the origins of that 'law': . . . it was the British idea of the rule of law that . . . guaranteed free disposition of one's own body, a shift that constitutites the origin of both liberty and property.

---

4   Admitting there is no one form of colonialisation, and generalisations are always subject to qualification, the spread of Europe into the globe owned much to its technological, military and naval supremacy and its competitively minded nation states. It also owed greatly to its private entrepreneurs who had or organised capital to export, and its crowded populations that gave human resources for ships, military and people to settle other lands.

5   Fitzpatrick, 1992, cf. pp. 63–72.

6   'The knowledge of the law is like a deepe well out of which each man draweth according to the strength of his understanding. He that reacheth deepest, he seeth aimiable and admirable secrets of the law, wherein, I assure you, the sages of the law in former times . . . have had the deepest reach.' (Coke Upon Littleton, 71a)

7   Slavery is unfortunately still practised today in far too many places – see Bales, 1999 and the regular postings of Anti-Slavery International. It is of course officially condemned by virtually every government, even those of states that tolerate it.

8   Kriegel, 1995, p. 148.

Liberty is not exhausted by the right to make contracts; it begins with the protection of life secured by law. Consequently subjective rights are directly linked to the conception of power that rejects slavery and domination. They are inseparable from the new political arrangements and a new conception of rights as law.'[9] But for Kriegel and for the authors of this text, law is no simple fact, no positive thing, it is a complex that needs human action and ethical responsibility for it to live up to this narrative, else it may falsify, entrap. For others, such as Tuitt, modern law cannot be divorced from the violence and violent counter-violence of colonialism.[10] What is the responsibility in legal education of considerations of time, place and race?

If one narrative of the common laws development *within* its homeland of England (and Wales) (allowing for the constant and, one suspects, deeply ontological, engagement with continental Europe) is of the levelling of hierarchy, of the claiming (and acceptance) of legitimacy though democracy and 'the rule of law', what of the places 'other'? For many, particularly non-white Europeans (and I include as quasi-Europeans the white inhabitants of the Americas, Australia and sectors of Asia and Africa), the foundations of modern law are cast in the violence of colonisation – the other side of the European Enlightenment. We cannot here offer a major essay or series of reflections, only a small engagement with perspectives, walls and the fractured division of the human world. Law categorises, that is part of its utility; it seems to reflect division, it can demarcate, differentiate with precision. Oppositions seem also existentially inbuilt to conceiving of law; much thinking and speaking (and although not often articulated, of experiencing) about law is done in terms of internal and external, of inside and outside, perhaps better understood as by the insider and the outsider.

So with the university beginning of the first chapter: I (WJM) sat in a class of white faces, listening to a legal history and various courses on law delivered by white males (almost entirely) that had little role for the Maori (the brown skinned Polynesian inhabitants of the islands to be called New Zealand at the time of European arrival). Was the silence of these lectures towards the Maori and the Aboriginal, the absence of the 'other' to our real Australasian history, a form of institutional racism? I have ambivalence. I had no consciousness of any absence, but I am white and now conscious of the words of Patricia Williams that it is one of the privileges of whiteness to appear 'unraced'.[11] I was not so conscious of being and not-being then. In the concluding section of *Peau noire, masques blancs* (translated as Black Skins, White Masks), the Caribbean social theorist Frantz Fanon existentially denies any plain fact view of the world, stating words to the effect that the black man is not; nor is the white.[12] The English translation of his work subdues his existential sense (such as the title of Chapter 5 being presented as 'The Fact of Blackness', rather than a more subtle 'The Lived Experience of the Black Man'). Fanon is no positivist, the blackness of race is not a 'fact', not a reflection of natural state (and the same goes for whiteness); both are

9   Kriegel, 1995, p. 37.
10   Tuitt, 2004.
11   Patricia Williams, 1997.
12   Fanon, 1952.

a form of lived experience (*expérience vécue*). The ontology of social reality is lived experience. Existentially we have an abyss of meaning: the black man and the white man are not, and yet they are. The reality of their being is co-joined. Practical concern and much scholarly work on racism has emphasised the 'victim': key concepts – such as racism, discrimination, prejudice – seem to carry a certain direction that leads legal discourse and practical legal measures being orientated to helping, to avoiding harm to (an)other cast as the 'victim'. There is in this a certain one sidedness. The 'coloured', the 'black', fight as terms to reclaim a human dignity for those who they were once addressed to in disdain, in placement beneath; by contrast whiteness does not seem to exist. To the revisionist post-colonialists, by contrast, being white 'means that God put you on the planet to rule, to dominate, and occupy the center of the national and international universe – because you're white'.[13] For Toni Morrison whiteness is not static but defined in relationship to 'otherness'.[14] At times those who were 'white' were seen as dangerous and not-really-white. The identity of the white-non-white (and potential contagion) varies. In the US the 'Irish were niggers turned inside out'; and only by a combination of fortunate political and religious alliances were they recast as part of the mainstream.

Today in New Zealand the monolithic history has fractured,[15] and there are many ceremonies which declare the heritage of the space constituting New Zealand/ Aotearoa as one of diverse life experiences that have made and make the life that exists. But is this superficial or a real recognition of what has structured this space and life, impacting on how and what is currently lived? Certainly, first year Law students in New Zealand in the 2000s face a different heritage – the treaty of Waitangi (signed in 1840 by representatives of the British government and over 500 Maori chiefs) is now seen as the foundational legal document of the 'partnership' at the basis of New Zealand constitutional arrangement.[16] At the time I attended first year lectures the Maori had engaged in sustained land marches that claimed 150 years of broken promises and absent legal presence. If for the Maori the Treaty was a solemn legal compact in which they had surrendered certain things for recognition of *tino rangatiratanga* of the chiefs, tribes and people, and promises of equal protection, including protection of Maori property rights, then much of the 'real' history of New Zealand was of broken promises and denial of legal recognition. In Maori subject position the lesson of the rule of law appeared largely one-sided, of a violence being done to them (either through the taking of land or military action when they resisted). The words of

....

13   June Jordan, 1995, p. 21.

14   Toni Morrison, 1992.

15   Beginning in large part with the groundbreaking work of Andrew Sharp, *Justice and the Maori*, 1990, continued by others, notably Paul McHugh (*Aboriginal Societies and the Common Law*, 2004; and *Aboriginal Title*, 2011).

16   It is interesting to trace the slightly different interpretations of the partnership and success in raising claims in the successive editions of Joseph, *Constitutional and Administrative Law in New Zealand*, 1st ed. 1993, 2nd ed. 2001 and 3rd ed. 2007, 4th ed. 2013. There are debates over what exactly the Treaty 'meant' to both parties, and the difficulties in translation between the English and the Maori copies. As Seuffert points out, 2006, the process of settling Treaty claims undertaken from the mid 1980s and continuing is government sponsored and one can identify one aim as the re-creation of the story of national identity, now with the Maori being incorporated as economic entrepreneurs.

Judge F.R. Chapman, sentencing a Maori activist to prison in 1917 for resisting arrest are illustrative:

> You have learnt that the law has a long arm, and that it can reach you, however far back into the recesses of the forest you may travel, and that in every corner of the great Empire to which we belong, the King's law can reach anyone who offends against him. This is the lesson your people should learn from this trial.[17]

However, Maori activism had won from the Labour Government the Treaty of Waitangi Act 1975; it was to be largely a dead letter for some years until another Labour Government in 1985 extended the Waitangi Land tribunal to reopen old transactions, to look into historical breaches of the treaty and give financial compensation. The Tribunal became flooded with claims, and Pakaha-orientated history was turned into an unsettled history of claim, counter-claim and anxious race relations.[18]

Anderson reminds us that nations are imagined political communities.[19] The words of the conservative Eighteenth century British writer Edmund Burke with which this chapter began, against the ideas of the rights of 'mankind', gives notions of due deference, natural subordination and the fear of the judgment in the life to come (such notions of Heaven and Hell were familiar to me from the Catholic schools I had attended prior to University), but most strongly sees the common law heritage in the idea of a polity in 'the image of a relation in blood', 'adopting our fundamental laws into the bosom of our family affections'.[20] Burke speaks to the need to belong, to partake; to feel that law has a communal and almost transcendental presence. This offers another take at odds with the Hobbes-Bentham-Austin tradition of the clarity of Sovereign and subject, where law ('positive', or law strictly so-called, it must be admitted) was the commands of the politically superior to the politically inferior backed by sanctions. In the 1970s our legal education located us in the jurisprudence of H.L.A. Hart (the dominant figure since 1961), and ourselves as learning, and adopting, the 'insiders' view of law, for while the ordinary person may not think much about law we were to take our roles as 'the officials or experts of the system'. Our education was in part a socialisation into what Hart called 'the rule of recognition', the social practice by which members of the society recognised such and such rules, documents and so forth as the law. And this was knowable through descriptive tests: 'so long as the laws which are valid by the systems tests of validity are obeyed by the bulk of the population this is surely all the evidence we need in order to establish that a given legal order exists.'[21] And so we also learnt the weakness of Lon Fuller's claim of an 'inner morality to law'. For while Fuller wanted to identify law with substantially moral practices, with just procedures, as part of a morality of 'aspiration', Hart

17   Quoted, King, 2003, p. 222.
18   To note the title of one book, *An Unsettled History: Treaty Claims in New Zealand Today* (Alan Ward, 1999).
19   Anderson, 1991.
20   See concluding remarks on the cover image to the 1st edition of this text for a somewhat questioning take on this heritage.
21   Ibid., p. 111.

Figure 5.1 Yala Yala Gibbs Tjungurrayi, *Kaarkurutinytja, Lake McDonald* (1997). © estate of the artist 2012, licensed by Aboriginal Artists Agency Ltd.

What of this painting? Hart had in part constructed his theory of law in contrast to a 'primitive' state that was uncertain and static. For a considerable time the view, represented by Fraser, was one in which Aboriginal people lived in 'unbearable conditions' and created primitive art that served as 'memory aids for elders'; their 'art' was generally the 'more or less fossilized survival of art of the Old Stone Age' (Fraser, Primitive Art, 1962). By contrast the above painting represents Pintupi law (see discussion by Cunneen, 2010; Isaacs, 1999, pp. 41–43). Here the way of the Law relates to 'the footprints of the Ancestor', the law is a form of path-finding, a mapping, an ethical and practical relating of ways and resources in the journey of the ancestors that we learn from and reproduced on the painted 'map'. This represents their knowledge of the content of the land and the right way to live and act within it (Isaacs, 1999: 8). The particular image shows ceremonial activities of the Tingari, a journey undertaken by 'a group of Creation Ancestors, who travelled over vast areas of desert country performing rituals, singing the animals, plants and natural features into being and forming particular sites, which are now regarded as scared to their descendents, today's custodians of these places. The Tingari took different forms, some human, some animal. They also laid down social custom and law as it should be practised today to ensure harmony. Their journeys form the basis of sacred and secret men's law.' (Isaacs, p. 24) In this painting the circles and connecting linear tracks represent the activities of the Tingari men at Kaarkurutinytja. In this form of law the spirit of the country, the spirit of the past is to be learnt, revered, internalised.

stressed the purely descriptive practices of officials and experts, who had learnt the language of the law and followed its practices and learnt its techniques so that they may make claims, defend positions and empower themselves.

Hart's way was to learn to be equipped for practice in the normal operation of a modern municipal legal order (the perspectives of 'insiders'). But what if we were to attempt to look with the eyes of the colonial subject, what does the rule of law *look*

Figure 5.2 Hey Bros, Ian Waldron, 1998, acrylic on canvas.

At first sight this looks like a straight copy from a very famous English painting (*the Hay Wain* by John Constable painted in 1821) and then one notices a small aboriginal figure with the aboriginal flag and the caption Hey Bros . . . what is going on? Constable desired to be a landscape painter, though this was not popular and he had to produce portraits to ensure a good living, However, he made many sketches in pencil and oil paint in the open air as he observed the natural world and the effects of the weather and changing seasons on the countryside with the final paintings composed back in his studio, using the sketches as component parts. The resulting landscapes have a spontaneous appeal, despite the fact that they have been so carefully arranged. In *The Hay Wain* we see on the left-hand side, a mill-house, rented by a farmer called Willy Lott from Constable's father, who owned both the house and surrounding land. The house is often referred to as 'Will Lott's cottage' to reinforce the quaintness and rusticity of the scene, but it was in fact a much more sizeable property. To the extreme right, beside the fisherman's boat on the far side of the river, we can see the beginning of a red brick wall belonging to a water-mill, just out of sight in this view. Constable drew much of his initial inspiration for scenes such as this one from memories of the childhood he had spent in the area. The wisps of smoke curling from the chimney of the house, and the woman beside it, drawing water from the river, give the scene a harmonious, domesticated atmosphere. In the background, in the yellow and green fields, dappled with sunlight, we can see workers, one sharpening his scythe, others pitchforking hay onto an already laden wagon, and one man stacking the load from the top. The time of year must be between June and early August – haymaking season. The cloudy, wind-swept sky would seem to indicate the possibility of rain and certainly evokes English summertime weather. The hay wain itself ('wain' is an old word for 'wagon') is crossing the river at a ford to continue into the fields. The driver has stopped for a moment, perhaps to let the horses drink. Constable's innovative technique, with looser brushwork and the use of white paint to suggest reflections of light upon the water, was not very popular with contemporary English critics, who preferred a more traditional style of painting and more 'serious' subject matter. He did, however, achieve considerable success in France, winning a Gold Medal at the Paris Salon of 1824 with this painting. The painting by the Australian aboriginal artist is actually a play on the politics of colonialisation in Australia. The Common Law incorporated settled international (i.e. European) rules for the 'acquisition' of territory and added it own rules regarding the application of English law within the colonies established in the acquired areas. Blackstone explains in the *Commentaries* (I, p. 107–8*): 'Plantations or colonies in distant countries are either such where the lands are claimed by rights of occupancy only, by finding them desert and uncultivated, and peopling them from the mother country; or where, when already cultivated, they have been either gained by conquest, or ceded to us by treaties. And both these rights are founded upon the law of

Figure 5.2 Continued

nature, or at least upon that of nations. But there is a difference between these two species of colonies, with respect to the laws by which they are bound. For it has been held, that if an uninhabited country be discovered and planted by English subjects, all the English laws then in being, which are the birthright of every subject, are immediately then in force. But this must be understood with very many and very great restrictions. Such colonists carry with them only so much of the English law, as it is applicable to their own situation and the condition of an infant colony . . . But in conquered or ceded countries, that have already laws of their own, the King may indeed alter and change those laws; but, till he does actually change them, the ancient laws of the country remain, unless such as are against the law of God, as in the case of an infidel country.'

In a 'desert and uncultivated' land one could occupy and 'people from the mother country', i.e. settle, than the law in force would be all the English laws then in being as applicable to their situation. A 'settled colony' drew upon the notion of *terra nullius* (a Latin expression deriving from Roman Law signifying 'land belonging to no one', i.e. 'empty land'). In the 16th and 17th century expansion this blended into meaning in practice land that was unclaimed by a sovereign state recognized by European powers. The Swiss philosopher and international law theorist Emerich de Vattel, building on the philosophy of John Locke and others, proposed that terra nullius applied to uncultivated land. As the indigenous people were not (in this view) using the land, those who could cultivate the land had a right to claim it. English political and legal authorities accepted that the Australian colonies were 'settled', as opposed to conquered, colonies. On his later voyage after his 'discovery' of the lands in the south Cook could not nor was he instructed to specifically conclude any treaty with any of the Aboriginal peoples but he had been given vague instructions to take possession of land 'with the consent of the natives'. Cook recorded that he took possession through symbolic acts of planting a flag and firing a gun, ignoring some Aboriginal people, 'who follow'd us shouting'. Both Cook and Sir Joseph Banks concluded that there were few inhabitants, living only in the coastal area, and they could not be in possession of the land as they did not cultivate it.

The historian Henry Reynolds (1987, p. 31) argues that, regardless of the first impressions of Cook and Banks, it became clear to the British settlers who followed that the Australian colonies were not *terra nullius*. On the basis of a detailed examination of historical evidence he argues that the Imperial government was prepared to accept that, while English law applied in the Australian colonies, that law should and could recognise Aboriginal title to land. Reynolds contends that the colonists failed to observe Imperial instructions by continuing to ignore the Aborigines, and the common law followed suit. The Aboriginal artist is asking what would happen if an aboriginal came to England and claimed the territory on the grounds that the English had misused the land. Would it be a question of force?

like? What does one see? We will consider two images: one of the aboriginal perspectives of the settlement of Australia and the other of the Mau Mau 'emergency'.

REPLYING TO HEY BROS

It is now widely acknowledged that European incursion into the Americas, Australia and New Zealand led to the displacement and genocide of the indigenous populations of these areas, not by accident but in order to create the optimum conditions for white domination.

In the Caribbean, Newfoundland, and Tasmania all but a remnant of the resident aboriginal peoples had been murdered. In practice, the choice between killing and 'a temperate line of conduct' was often beyond the control of colonial administrators. As settlement expanded, aboriginal peoples were deprived of their lands and conflict was inevitable. However, once a sufficient number of aboriginal peoples had been killed (i.e., enough to ensure British dominance), a set of policies based on a 'temperate line of conduct' frequently became possible. These policies relied upon a dominant military or civil police force for their ultimate enforcement and were aimed at managing aboriginal peoples by controlling their land use, settlements, government, and daily life. They also called for the introducing of aboriginal peoples to missionaries.[22]

Against Armitage, the author of the extract above, it is *not* now widely acknowledged that genocide universally occurred throughout the lands mentioned; the earlier conquest and settlement of the Americas is now labelled genocide by some of those who claim descent from the original inhabitants, and the claim for genocide in Australia is hotly contested.[23] It is undeniable, however, that genocide has occurred when settler interests were threatened and where the means and authorisation (at least implicit) was available; the culmination of European colonialisation was the Nazi pursuit of life space in eastern Europe and the calculated denial of life to the 'sub-human Jews and lesser-human Poles.[24]

Access to and recognition in space – land in time – is central and here the prime place of law reveals itself: 'law as an ultimate and authoritarian assertion of position.'[25] The Imperial (European) law, brought from outside, enabled the colonist's claim to objectivity in relations. Consider the personal history and the most remembered judgment of Prendergast, first Chief Justice of New Zealand to be appointed from among the persons actually practising in New Zealand.

Born in London in 1826 the youngest son of a QC, James Prendergast graduated from Queens' College, Cambridge and enrolled in the Middle Temple in London in 1849. However he joined the gold rush in 1852 to Victoria, Australia. While not unsuccessful in the diggings he contracted dysentery and moved back to town where he became a magistrate's clerk and in 1856 met another Londoner, the young Julius Vogel, later to be a famous Prime Minister of New Zealand. Prendergast crossed over to New Zealand in 1862 and was admitted to the Bar in Otago that year. His arrival in Dunedin coincided with the great gold rush and dramatic expansion of legal business in Otago. Thirty-three lawyers were enrolled in Dunedin in 1862, and twenty more over the next three years (Prendergast's first client was Julius Vogel, then editor of the *Otago Daily Times* in Dunedin). Prendergast prospered in practice, in 1863 he was appointed acting solicitor for the Otago Province, in 1865 becoming Crown Solicitor. In 1865 Prendergast was appointed as a Member of Parliament to the Legislative Council, the then upper house of parliament; in 1865 he also became a non-political Attorney-General of New Zealand. As Attorney-General Prendergast's task was to consolidate the criminal law and in the process he drafted 94 Acts. He also helped to create order in the legal profession – in 1870 the New Zealand Law Society was formed with Prendergast as its first president. Prendergast was appointed Chief Justice of New Zealand on 1 April 1875 on the advice of Vogel. His most (in)famous decision came in *Wi Parata* v. *Bishop of Wellington* in 1871, where he sidestepped two New Zealand precedents and asserted that the British government had never recognised Maori law and custom because such an entity had never existed.

22   Armitage, 1995, p. 5.
23   For the lively claims of a part American Indian see Ward Churchill, 1977; for a damming indictment of the whole settlement of the Americas see Stannard, 1992, who gives his text the controversial title of *American Holocaust*. For the Australian situation see Reynolds early work, 1971, *An Indelible Stain? The Question of Genocide in Australia's History*.
24   See Zimmerer, 2004; Morrison 2006.
25   Fitzpatrick, 2001, p. 180.

The case involved land that was given by local Maori to the Anglican Church for the purpose of building a school. The school was never built and Parata asked the land given to the Church be returned to the Ngati Toa iwi. In his judgment, Prendergast took the view that 'native' or 'aboriginal' customary title, not pursuant to a Crown grant, could not be recognised or enforced by the courts; the Treaty of Waitangi was a 'simple nullity' as 'no body politic existed capable of making cession of sovereignty, nor could the thing itself exist'. The Maori tribe had no juridical status, but neither did individual Maori have the rights of Englishmen; British subjecthood and the rights that went with that apparently conferred by Article 3 of the Treaty, were denied (this was standard practice as it was legally recognised until – in practice – into the 1980s that for it to take effect the Treaty would have had to be incorporated into New Zealand law by specific statutory adoption). Instead relations between Crown and Maori were 'to be regarded as acts of State, and therefore are not examined by any Court'. Maori were labelled 'primitive barbarians', 'incapable of performing the duties, and therefore of assuming the rights, of a civilised community': consequently, 'in the case of primitive barbarians, the supreme executive Government . . . of necessity must be the sole arbiter of its own justice'. 'At common law, then, Maori lacked any original or subsisting juridical status. Their relations with the crown, including any "rights" they might hold, were judicially recognised as being at the absolute discretion of the crown.'[26] In Nan Seuffert's words: 'his decision literally remembers the nation by erasing or cutting off not only any recognition of Maori laws and practices in colonial law, but any existence at all of those laws and practices. He recreates the nation as one in which Maori laws and customs never existed.'[27]

The decision was extremely convenient for the Crown: native title matters involving the Crown now fell entirely within the jurisdiction of the Crown's prerogative powers, and so were outside the jurisdiction of the municipal Courts. This meant that native title claims were not enforceable against the Crown within these Courts, nor could these Courts refer such matters to the Native Land Court against the wishes of the Crown. Rather, the Crown was to be the 'sole arbiter of its own justice' on native title matters. The subsequent case law largely follows this case – even in the face of an open breach with the Privy Council in 1903 over this issue – and much of Prendergast's reasoning was not clearly rejected until 1938 when *Te Heuheu Tukino* v. *Aotea District Maori Land Board* was decided, where the Court ruled that the Treaty was seen as valid in terms of the transfer of sovereignty, but as it was not part of New Zealand statute law it was not binding on the Crown.

Prendergast's judgment contains various conflicting positions and almost certain contradictions. John Tate explains it in terms of a 'colonial consciousness' which shaped the way in which issues of land settlement were understood within settler societies largely.[28] While seeming to accept a view of the land before the British settlement as *terra nullis*, the decision, and consequent decisions, were more a logical game of being a servant to crown interests and perogative: Pendergast accepts that the common law could recognise native title but if it would have existed as a matter of fact – if

26   McHugh, 2001, p. 194.
27   Seuffert, 2006, p. 36.
28   Tate, 2003.

native title could be shown to have existed as a form of (customary) legal right – then the common law as understood in New Zealand courts and legislature would already have recognised it. In other words he assumes that the New Zealand government would have taken that into account in framing its statutes. The fact that they had not served to demonstrate that no such legal rights existed! But there were phrases in Crown statutes that implied customary ownership; in so far as they made reference to 'the rightful and necessary occupation and use' of land by the 'aboriginal inhabitants': such as in the Land Claims Ordinance of 1841. Prendergast blankly denied that they implied Crown recognition of native title. As he stated: 'These measures were avowedly framed upon the assumption that there existed amongst the natives no regular system of territorial rights nor any definite ideas of property in land'. He insisted that the absence of stated legal recognition of such 'territorial rights' or 'definite ideas of property in land' among Maori was due not to any oversight on the part of the Crown, rather, it was due to their non-existence in fact. He stated: 'Had any body of law or custom, capable of being understood and administered by the Courts of a civilised country, been known to exist, the British Government would surely have provided for its recognition, since nothing could exceed the anxiety displayed to infringe no just right of the aborigines'. Given this assumption of the Crown's desire to do everything in favour of the natives the fact that they had not recognised native title was proof of the absence of a 'body of law or custom' relating to property within Maori society which, Prendergast believed, rendered English law incapable of recognising any native title rights to which Maori tribes might be able to lay claim![29]

What was the threat to settler society? The Native Land Court posed a threat to Crown title in that if the Act recognised native title than matters would be referred to the Court and Maori understandings as to possession rights may determine the issue. If, however, Prendergast could claim that all native title matters involving the Crown were subject to the Crown's prerogative, this would exclude the jurisdiction of the municipal Courts, and so undermine their capacity to refer native title matters to the Native Land Court under the Native Rights Act 1865. Further, if he could claim that this Act itself was not intended to intrude on the Crown's prerogative, the jurisdiction of the Native Land Court would be limited as well.

Tate defines a 'colonial consciousness' as an outlook informed by the material interests of a settler society. Foremost among these interests is a necessary concern for the process of land settlement, since it is this process which, more than anything else, defines a 'settler' society. These material concerns were exacerbated in New Zealand society because of the open military conflict that had erupted between Maori tribes and the Crown over precisely this issue in the middle decades of the nineteenth century. For Tate the members of the New Zealand Bench were affected by these interests and concerns and these intruded on their legal outlook and judgment in native title cases. 'In particular, this "colonial consciousness" explains the Court of Appeal's tenacious commitment to the precedent of Wi Parata, its willingness to misread previous native title cases as consistent with this precedent, and its willingness to defend Wi Parata even to the point of an open breach with the Privy Council.' This colonial consciousness then manifested itself in some very traditional legal language, namely the defence

---

29   Discussion, pp. 77–78 Wi Parata . . .

NEW ZEALAND WAR-DANCE OF THE PAST.

Figure 5.3 New Zealand war dance of the past. Unknown artist, *Illustrated London News*, 1870.
Source, collection WJM.

King argues that one feature that saved the Maori from the genocidial practices elsewhere under colonial settlement was their ability to be imaged as proud, independent and fighters. Note that this image, presented in the popular *Illustrated London News* is titled New Zealand war dance *of the past*. Many assumed that the Maori, as with other native groups, would die out; that the future would not contain them; in this way it was assumed nature was genocidal. In Wi Parata the colonial law rejects Maori as any form of partner in the colonial nation's development. Nan Seuffert analyses another case, less known, *Rira Peti* v. *Ngaraihi To Paku*, 1888, where Prendergast effectively denies Maori custom in marriage effective legal recognition in colonial marriage law (Seuffert, 2006, p. 37 ff). This was at odds with social reality – most marriages between Maori up until c. 1936 were customary rather than conducted according to settler ritual and legal form. Earlier New Zealand legislation and court decisions COULD have been interpreted so as to recognise Maori customary practices and 'law'. This would, however, have meant that there were two narratives of original sources for New Zealand law. This, as the extract from Blackstone (see our pp 90–91) specifies was able to be recognised by the common law: the argument then must be that it was Colonial consciousness or settler interests that shaped the court's reasoning. The post-colonial court structure in New Zealand gave a different story in *Ngat Apa* v. *Attorney-General* relegating Wi Parata 'to an appendix of colonial injustices' (Ibid., p 133). But while this decision overturns much of the past, Seuffert argues that 'the founding violence of the nation . . . as a result of the repression of the Maori version of the Treaty remains unrepaired. Common law native title is a colonial legal invention, a view of indigenous law, customs and relationship with the land through the lenses of colonial courts. . . . It is not power sharing or self-determination (Ibid., p 135). We may note that the New Zealand war dance, the Haka, is now ritualised as the central feature of the New Zealand Rugby team, the All Blacks, a title itself a misspelling of a English reporter's text to London on watching the first New Zealand team to tour England (he actually sent 'all backs'.)

of the stability and security of the young nation. It also surfaced in the implicit defence of the New Zealand bench that they were – more than the Privy Council in London – being faithful to the law – the inherited 'common law'. Defined as the bearers of one universal law, the lack of a jurisprudence of legal pluralism, meant that to deny competing legal foundations meant that everything was to be decided in accordance with 'principle of law', 'settled principles of our law', and 'the common law of

England'. So the Bench reacted furiously to the Privy Council accusing the Lord Lords of not being as familiar with the operation of the common law in settings outside of the UK as they were and not following the precedent of Wi Parata.

The end of empire frees up the writing of history, post-colonial histories and institutional arrangements are heavily debated, though it is also a melancholy observation that the debate may be tangential to the power flows establishing the institutional re-recognition and re-defining of forms of association of the indigenous peoples as constituting 'indigenous law' and giving historical redress to the lack of recognition of that law. This is a politics of recognition, identity and imaging the nation. Recognising that the indigenous peoples had law, complicates the historical picture of settlement, and raises the issue of its relationship to the law of the new state in a 'post-colonial' era; post-colonial here meaning not just 'independence' but a reworking of historical narratives of foundation and identity. In New Zealand an alternative story of foundations – the recognition of the Waitangi treaty – could be constructed and is under critique and re-construction. But what of Australia?

In recent time the question of settlement came up in *Mabo* (1992), a claim to recognise native title. Before the arrival of the Europeans, the lands in question (three islands constituting the Murray Islands, Mer, Dauar and Waier) were already occupied by the Meriam people. In 1879, they were annexed to the colony of Queensland, although a few years later, the islands were reserved by proclamation for the 'native inhabitants'. Some years later still, in 1912, the islands were permanently reserved, being placed in trust in 1939. In this case Meriman people were arguing that they had good title to lands that they had never been 'Crown lands'. In 1992, after a decade of litigation, the High Court ruled that the land title of the Indigenous Peoples, the Aborigines and Torres Strait Islanders, was recognised at common law. This Indigenous Peoples' land title, or native title, stemmed from the continuation within common law of their rights over land which pre-date European colonisation of Australia. In the absence of an effective extinguishment by the crown, this title presents through inheritance the original occupants' right to possession of their traditional lands in accordance with their customs and lores. The judgment rejected the *Terra Nullius* concept, bringing Australia almost in line with other common law countries, i.e. USA, Canada and New Zealand.

Reynolds provides some evidence that aboriginal ownership of land has always been recognised by Britain, providing extracts from early dispatches to Australia from the British Colonial Office, proclamations in the House of Commons and private correspondence between officials.[30]

One of the central themes in *Mabo* was a question of the authority of the court. The court had to affirm its own authority to develop the law of Australia; to deal with the problem of native title from the perspective of a nation that considers itself to be a modern democracy. At the same time, the court is a product of its history. It cannot simply be a question of departing from the common law if jurisprudence is out of step with a contemporary political reality. The view then is that Australian law is both

---

30   Reynolds, 1987. The 1837 House of Commons select committees report on Australian Colonies, for example, stated 'that the native inhabitants of any land have an incontrovertible right to their own soil however, which seems not to have been understood'.

more than English common law, but enabled by the English common law tradition. Thus, it can develop 'independently' from the authorities of the English courts, and it is 'free' of the control of the 'Imperial' Centre. However, to retain its common law tradition Legal principles can be updated, but not to the extent that they completely break or throw over the basic 'skeleton of principles'.

We are dealing with a politics of memory. Clearly, the settlement in accordance with *terra nullis* rested on the notion that those living in the territory were without law. *Mabo* now rereads the position of indigenous peoples and gives them legal being, as far as the common law was concerned. However, in Mabo, the people who are to be one under the law are included into a common law history, are given an 'origin' synonymous with the arrival of the common law. Effectively, while the common law is recognised as a particular relationship to time – existing from time immemorial – the Australian aboriginal existence is recognised only as at the time of settlement. Under this assumption native 'law' is draw unproblematically into the fold of a common law that can adapt to history, and a foreign clime. After all, this grounds the claim that the common law is able to resolve the issue of native title by drawing into itself those social relations that it can order, determine and articulate in the best possible way. Behind this claim, is a far more difficult and subtle operation. *Mabo* effectively denies the reality of the indigenous claim, at the same time as acknowledging it. The *Mabo* judgment in no way challenges the legality of non-Aboriginal land tenure; settler interests are undisturbed. The Court went to considerable lengths to establish that the impact of its judgment will be minimal on non-Aboriginal Australians. Only land such as vacant crown land, national parks and possibly some leased land, where the lease is subject to Aboriginal rights of access to the land, can be subject to Aboriginal claims. Further, no native title is automatically recognised in law. The Aboriginal claimants have either to go to court, or possibly tribunals, and prove that they continually maintained their traditional association with the land they are claiming. Anyone can appeal against the claims and the Mabo judgment ensures that whenever there is conflict between titles granted by the crown and the native title, the native title loses. It is only in the case of titles newly established since 1975 that Aborigines can even claim compensation for extinguishment of title.

Thus, any claim to Aboriginal title or law has to be made through the medium of the common law of the colonist. It appears unlikely, especially in the wake of the *Mabo* decision and the law's retreat from a notion of native title that the ongoing violence of the original imposition of settlor's law can move towards reconciliation.

THE MAU MAU 'EMERGENCY'

What of our lecturer? As students we knew little of what the reference to the Mau Mau emergency was; all we understood was that it had been important and that our lecturer was to be respected for his role as an official operating the rule of law. Perhaps even if we had known that the Colonial Authorities in Kenya had declared a 'state of emergency', and that this provided a space of exception to the normal rule of law, we would not have understood what lessons can be learnt about the normal from the exceptional. In the last decade two books have appeared that have shattered any illusions about the heroic defence of the civilising mission in Kenya. I now read:

> State execution is a mighty weapon, and in the colonial context it has generally been used sparingly. Not so in the Mau Mau emergency. Kenya's hanging judges were kept busy. Between April 1953 and December 1956 the Special Emergency Assize Courts tried a total of 2609 Kikuyu on capital charges relating to Mau Mau offences in 1211 trials. Around 40% of those accused were acquitted, but 1574 were convicted and sentenced to hang over this period. Others still had been convicted in the Supreme Court before the Special Emergency Assize Courts were created in April 1953, and there would be a smattering of further Mau Mau trials throughout 1957 and even into 1958. In total, approximately 3000 Kikuyu stood trial between 1952 and 1958 on capital charges relating to the Mau Mau movement. In all, over the course of the emergency, 1090 Kikuyu would go to the gallows for Mau Mau crimes. In no other place, and at no other time in the history of British imperialism, was state execution used on such a scale as this. This was more than double the number of executions carried out against convicted terrorists in Algeria, and many more than in all the other British colonial emergencies of the post-war period – in Palestine, Malaya, Cyprus and Aden.[31]

Of the accounts in the western media of the Mau Mau – branded a terrorist group – a telling account concerns a small event in 1955, reported in *Time* magazine Monday, March 21, 1955, under the heading 'Mau Mau in the Cathedral'.

> In the blue-black darkness of an African night last week, a gang of Mau Mau warriors crept out of the squalid shantytown where the huge Negro majority of Nairobi's population lives, and moved, unseen, into the heart of the white city. It was Sunday evening, and the sexton had locked the doors of the Anglican cathedral after the evening service, but the Mau Mau broke in and gathered in a group in the chancel. They splashed water from the font for more than an hour in a weird pagan ceremony performed at an altar that faces Mt. Kenya (17,040 ft.). The mountain is the Mau Mau's sacred symbol, and British officers who investigated concluded that the terrorists had been ordaining a new Mau Mau general for the Nairobi area.

Consider again the foundational image Hobbes gave as the frontspiece of the *Leviathan*. There, in the protected space of the Sovereign's gaze and reach, lies civilised space, at the centre of which is the Cathedral. Hobbes had set up the natural necessity of the sovereign because of the natural condition of humanity as (relative) equality and (relative) autonomy. Since no one was naturally superior to the other, any could be killed by the other; since each was similar, yet not the same, all were in competition. Social order came from a social contract setting up a powerful figure/institution and law was its command. Many have misunderstood Hobbes. He has become a name called into action (intellectually) to defend authoritarian states and the radicalism of Hobbes was denied. His message has been (mis)presented as an issue of autonomy and identity, of

---

31   Anderson, 2005, pp. 6–7.

essential blocs of sameness in competition – i.e. as stating that the difference of humanity (grades of humans) was a basic feature of existence rather than recognising that above relative difference was an essential equality. The spatial protection offered by the sovereign was in principal open to everyone, and global in space; in practice it pertained only to civilised space.[32] David Sibley provides a helpful discussion of spatial purification. Purification reflects deep-seated paranoias concerned with defilement and pollution, the language of leaking and contamination refers both to individual bodies and national borders.[33] Perhaps both are inherent in the images which appeared in the western media after the attack upon a white settler's farm which killed the farming couple and their young son.

What was presented in the western media in 1952/3 as a sudden explosion of violence, reversion to cannibalism and rejection of the civilising mission had deep roots. Kenya displayed settlement colony tactics but in a land clearly not empty. Railway construction toward Uganda had opened up land and it appeared sensible to the colonialists to reserve the supposedly 'empty' and climatically suitable highlands for the Europeans. Consequently the African tribes were forced into reservations and excluded from the thinly settled highlands in order to create the pre-requisites for gentleman farming. Little analysis appeared on the conditions of the natives.

In 1999 a new imaginary of the Mau Mau was shown in Britain: *How Britain crushed the 'Mau Mau rebellion'* was a controversial episode in Channel Four TV's Secret History series (screened 15 September 1999). This presented an opposing story to the previous orthodoxy. The Mau Mau 'rebellion' (from 1952 to 1959) and the response to it by the colonial government and European settlers was presented through documentary footage, narration and interviews with participants from both sides, plus background material on the Channel Four web site. The programme began by reversing the terrorist label describing a 'gang of freedom fighters' called Mau Mau, who had vowed 'to free Kenya from colonialism at any cost'. It was the British response that was now to be seen as 'brutal and shocking'. Film footage of Kenya before the uprising, showed smug Europeans living a life of idle luxury based on African land and labour, a life that was increasingly resented after WWII. Having fought with the British the Kenyans now wanted some return, while the settlers were presented as living in an ideological mist of superiority. The Kikuyu tribe had 50 years earlier been evicted from their traditional areas to make way for the European farmers. By the end of the Second World War, 3,000 European settlers owned 43,000 square kilometres of the most fertile land, only 6 percent of which they cultivated while the African population of 5.25 million occupied – without ownership rights – less than 135,000 square kilometres of the poorest land. Pushed into 'native reserves' on which much of the land was unsuitable for agriculture, the rural African were not able to operate their traditional methods of extensive agriculture, but nor did they have access to the new technology that would make intensive agriculture viable. Presenting a picture where the population was having severe problems feeding itself a dramatic dislocation existed between the rural black African population and a white (and small black elite), the programme pointed to a rumour-led situation where a

32   Developed further in Morrison, 2006.
33   Sibley, 1995, p. 77.

Donne intrepide. Un gruppo di negri kikuyu, appartenenti alla setta dei Man Mau, ha aggredito due signore, Kitty Heselburger e Doroty Raines Simson, che erano sole in una fattoria nei pressi di Nyeri (Kenia). Le due donne non si sono perse d'animo, ma estratte le pistole hanno fatto fuoco sui selvaggi uccidendone due e facendo fuggire gli altri.
(Disegno di Walter Molino)

Figure 5.4 'Kitty Heselburger and Dorothy Raines-Simpson successfully defend themselves against the Mau Mau terrorists'.
Source: Walter Molinoin in 'La Domenica del Corriere', 18 January 1953 (Credit MEPL).

Kenya looks beautiful this week. The Nandi flame trees are ablaze with crimson against the clear blue sky, and in the sky glisten the snowy crests of Mount Kenya and Kilimanjaro. The giraffes gracefully nod their tall necks on the plains. Even the Aberdares, if you do not know what they shelter, could be called beautifully peaceful.

But it is really a land of murder and muddle. And there is little likelihood that either murder or muddle will halt soon. The sullen masses of evicted blacks in the overrun reserves; the white farmers and their wives besieged in their farmhouses with revolvers next to the dinner plates; the bearded commandos stumbling through forests after the elusive Mau Mau; the brittle Mayfair-in-suburbia life of spuriously gay Nairobi; the purple-faced ex-colonels in the very, very particular Rift Valley Club – none of them seeming to know what to do. Not even the Mau Mau themselves seem to know what they really want – except to kill and disembowel as many whites, chiefs, head men, and non-Mau Mau Kikuyu as possible.

Figure 5.4 Continued

Nobody can guess how long it may drag on, how far Mau Mauism may spread, how infectious its example might prove to be. What thoughts pass through the minds of Samburu, Turkana, Wakamba or Masai tribesmen as they watch the white man harried by the hitherto despised and pacific Kikuyu? What thoughts down in Central Africa, where the British plan a political federation opposed by the natives, or in Uganda or the Belgian Congo? In South Africa, the Negro-hating Boers use the Mau Mau's terror to win support for even more brutal suppression of the nonwhites. Kenya, the Land of the Shining Mountain, has become a smoldering ember in Africa. And the surrounding brush vast, white-run, black-populated, miles of it, is tinder-dry.'

'A Report from Kenya', *Time* Magazine, Monday, March 30 1953.

This report by *Time* was representative of the first wave of reporting in western media on the events in Kenya, labelled terrorists the Mau Mau were depicted as a primitive return to barbarism and rejection of western civilisation.

Corpses & Orgies.

Like African leaders everywhere, the men who organised the Mau Mau faced one basic difficulty in forging a nationalist spirit: for the ordinary African, a man's overriding loyalties are to his family and his tribe. By compelling Mau Mau members to violate not only Christian ethics but every tribal taboo as well, says Corfield, Mau Mau leaders deliberately reduced their victims to a state where a man who took the Mau Mau oath was cut off 'from all hope, outside Mau Mau, in this world or the next'. To achieve this, the Mau Mau leadership forced its recruits, voluntary or involuntary, to seal their oaths by digging up corpses and eating their putrefied flesh, copulating with sheep, dogs or adolescent girls, and by drinking the famed 'Kaberichia cocktail' – a mixture of semen and menstrual blood. And when he was assigned to kill an enemy of the movement, a sworn Mau Mau pledged himself to remove the eyeballs of his victim and drink the liquid from them. Once the blood lust had been aroused to this pitch, the oath taker was easily led to kill his own father or mother, wife, child or master at Mau Mau command. And any local Mau Mau leader devising a fouler ritual was under obligation to pass along his recipe immediately to his less inventive colleagues. Since there were seven basic oaths, which could be taken over and over again, Mau Mau ceremonies thus became perpetual orgies. The result was that, when a Mau Mau convert did repent and vomit out his story to authorities, he sometimes ended by humbly asking to be taken out and shot. His sense of absolute degradation and 'absolute sin', says the Corfield report, left him no choice.

The Expert.

Personally responsible for the 'general pattern' of this horror, charges the Corfield report, was Jomo ('Burning Spear') Kenyatta, sixtyish, longtime Kikuyu nationalist leader still under house arrest in a remote Kenya mountain village. A mission-educated nationalist fanatic who spent 17 years in England and Europe, where he made himself an expert in primitive anthropology and published a scholarly work on Kikuyu customs, Kenyatta diabolically parodied the traditional religion of his people in Mau Mau ritual – much as occultists did in the legendary Black Mass. In fact, reports Corfield, Kenyatta's work showed 'at least a passing acquaintance' with European witchcraft.

'The Oath Takers', *Time* magazine, Monday, June 13 1960). (Note: Kenyatta was released from prison and in 1963 became Kenya's first Prime Minister.)

secret society had been formed amongst the Kikuyu, Kenya's largest tribe, one-fifth of the population, called the Land Freedom Army (LFA). The society involved forcing Kikuyu to swear an oath to take back the land the white man had stolen. The term that was applied to this group, the 'Mau Mau', was never used by the Kikuyu and does not exist in their language and could have been coined by the British as part of an attempt to demonise the Kikuyu people. The core of the LFA was the Kikuyu Central Association (KCA), which was formed in 1924. Its original programme was a combination of radical demands such as the return of expropriated lands and the elimination of the passbook scheme, (similar to the internal passport system in South Africa), with a striving to return to the traditional pre-colonial past. In the late 1930s the KCA led a wave of mass peasant struggles against the forced sale of their livestock to the government. In the 1950s the KCA began conscripting support from the Kikuyu masses, believing it was possible to consolidate their support through the administration of 'the oath'. When a staunch British loyalist, Chief Waruhu, was killed on 7 October 1952, the government saw the LFA as the first serious threat to colonial rule in post-war Africa. Two weeks later, on 20 October, a state of emergency was declared. Thousands of British troops and equipment were flown in to 'clear the colony of the menace of Mau Mau'. Over 100 leading members of the Kenya African Union, a political party demanding greater African self-rule, were arrested. Along with others, Jomo Kenyatta was put on trial for subversion.

What of due process? Kenyatta had publicly denounced Mau Mau and advocated peaceful change, however, the British and the white settlers were convinced that he was the driving force behind the movement; there was no evidence. Nevertheless, Kenyatta was found guilty of incitement and imprisoned in a remote part of Kenya for seven years hard labour. In the first ten days of emergency rule, almost 4,000 Africans had been arrested, but the attacks from the LFA continued. A wave of hysteria swept through the European settlers. In January 1953, a European farmer and his family were killed and angry settlers stormed government house demanding stronger action. In fact, more white settlers died in road accidents on the streets of Nairobi during the emergency than at the hands of the LFA. On 25 March a loyalist village was destroyed and most of the inhabitants were killed, including Chief Luka and his family. This clearly seemed to be the slaughter of innocent Kikuyu but a short time before almost 100,000 Kikuyu farm workers and their families had been evicted from their homes in the Rift Valley – where they had been living as squatters on settler farms – and driven back to the reserve. Some of them had already been evicted 20 years earlier, to make way for European settlers. Chief Luka, who had been personally rewarded with good land, had negotiated this government 'land exchange scheme'. The farm workers vented their anger against the chief, whom they considered to be responsible for their plight. In a revenge attack the following day, 10 times more Kikuyu were killed by government forces and more houses were destroyed. The LFA faced the full force of British colonial power. The forests of Mount Kenya, where the LFA had their base camps, were designated a 'prohibited area' and heavily bombed. Peasants living on the fringes of the forest were evicted from the land, their animals confiscated and crops and huts burned to clear the way for the 'free fire zone'. Thousands were herded into overcrowded, heavily militarised 'protected villages' and a policy of 'terror' and 'containment' employed by the British. The programme reports various atrocities culminating in the death from beating of 11 men and serious injury of 60 at Hola camp. The reports of the beatings and deaths caused political uproar in Britain as it was now the British authorities that were exposed as brutal thugs. Within weeks the camps were close and the detainees released. The Mau Mau oaths became irrelevant. In 1960 the state of emergency was lifted. The LFA death toll during the emergency was 11,500, of whom around 1,000 were hanged. Eighty thousand Kikuyu were imprisoned in concentration camps and it is now claimed that one hundred and fifty thousand Africans, mostly Kikuyu, lost their lives, with many dying of disease and starvation in the 'protected villages'. On the other side, the KFA killed around 2,000 people, including 32 European civilians and 63 members of the security forces. In 1961 Jomo Kenyatta was freed from jail and in 1963, four years after the Hola massacre, Kenya was granted independence. The Mau Mau fighters were mostly excluded in independent Kenya from public life and preferment, the spoils of independence going to the wealthy and educated Africans who had a vested interest in marginalising them; a black-African elite simply replaced the white one.[34]

Writers in critical legal studies, feminist, and race theory field have stressed the complexity of the violence of colonial regimes. Patricia Tuitt sees the formation of the colonial state in terms of 'casual' and '(a)causal'. Drawing on Fanon and others, Tuitt locates a world of 'casual' relations and flows of events and an (a)causal world in which normal, expected, relations are inverted, in which there is a perversity of moral connections. A casual world experiences 'the constant sequence or conjunction of events, relations, state and moral precepts', which in (a)causal world these relations are suspended (an example of this chapter 'the state of emergency', which allowed the repression of the other as part of the state apparatus). The latter is inherently racist in the sense that it displaces 'the most fundamental of securities, the persistent recognition of human state to all, irrespective of race'.[35] This state form signifies sustained systemic violence by the dominant, going beyond the immediate realities of the racially dominated. It persists as well as a diffuse contemporary form in which 'the project of the history of racial harm, domination, and violence' stands subjected to other histories of past wrongs, in all their unending, even infinite, assertions of 'innocent causes' and to 'the unreliability of memory and testimony'.[36]

Tuitt argues, for example, that the 'counter-violence' of colonial subjects as needing to be understood by the 'full gaze of history', but this is no easy or certain task.[37] In our contemporary times, we are awash with narratives and counter narratives and the idea of modernity as a coherent, transparent whole, in which truth and reason would be the guides to policy and law is undone. A lot of so called post-modern (or post-structural or post-Marxist, or hyper-liberal) writings stress the difficulty of viewing, asking whose gaze is it that determines understanding, policy and connections between law and justice? We may take the Kenya case as an example of the intellectual, political and ethical problems associated with understanding resistance and insurgency. How may reading divergent stories found in postcolonial law and literature enable us to resituate the law of violence and violence of law discourse?

---

34   Kenya was not alone in achieving political independence. In 1960 Prime Minister Harold Macmillan, in his 'wind of change' speech, recognised the necessity for Britain to find a new form of rule in its colonial possessions in Africa. In Kenya political control was passed into Kenyatta's 'safe pair of hands' and the European settler farmers found that they were more prosperous after independence than they were before.

35   Tuitt, 2004, p. 32.

36   Tuitt, 2004, p. 33.

37   Tuitt, 2004, p. 96. For an idea of some of the contemporary discussion on the history of the 'emergency', see Anderson, 2005, pp. 2–3. This article highlights the division of the Kenyan nation over the efforts of the former members of Mau Mau, a nationalist and former insurgent organization in Kenya, to mount a prosecution of Great Britain for war crimes. Anderson, David; Bennett, Huw; and Branch, Daniel, 2006, pp. 20–22 is an article that asserts that the Freedom of Information Act is being used to protect the perpetrators of a war crime that took place in Kenya in June 1953. It tells the story of an atrocity committed by British military forces in colonial Kenya. The story of the shooting of twenty Kenyan civilians at Chuka in June 1953 has been hidden behind a veil of official secrecy. The British Ministry of Defence has still retained some of the papers on the case relating to the role of the two junior British officers in the massacre. 'Britain's Gulag: The Brutal End of Empire in Kenya'. *History Today*, Nov. 2005, Vol. 55 Issue 11, pp. 66–33.

FROM THE POSTCOLONIAL TO THE GLOBAL:
IS THE COLONIAL POST?

It takes under three hours to travel by Eurostar from London to Brussels, the home of the European Parliament and the administrative capital of the EU. The Channel Tunnel is a late modern testament to decreasing fears of European contamination and hopes for European integration. It can also appear as a conduit of crime:

> A man from the Congo, living in Brussels, travelled regularly to London on Eurostar to collect housing benefit, an Old Bailey jury heard today.
>
> Ngolompati Moka, 33, who is a Belgian national, used fake tenancy agreements to persuade the boroughs of Hounslow and Haringey to pay him a total of £4,653.36, said the prosecution. The court was told that Moka, who was born in the Congo, used a series of identities to claim the cash. After he was arrested in a Hounslow JobCentre last August, police found a number of documents that incriminated him. These included bogus tenancy agreements, a Belgian ID card and receipts from Eurostar trains. 'These show he was making trips from Brussels to claim benefit in this country,' said counsel.
>
> (*Evening Standard*, 28 January 1999)

For the media this was an everyday crime, one that was moreover evidence of the need to strengthen immigration control and border policing. Doing justice meant punishing an individual. It did not invite analysis as to the complex intertwining of the Congo and Brussels, nor of past exploitation justice and reparations. In this exercise of justice – concerning 'a man from the Congo, living in Brussels' – we are dealing with politics of the visible and the invisible.

Awareness of the colonial upsets the comfortable narrative where law represents the totality of shared habits, conventions and traditions; law and its institutions are seen as embodying the spirit of the nation or at least as representing a nation's historical and cultural achievements.[38] Colonialism shaped both geographical centres and margins (the cities in Europe are in many ways the product of the colonial).[39] Post war immigration provides a particular challenge to this construction of the present and

---

38   See Peter Fitzpatrick, 1987. One development of Marxism would understand racism as alien to capitalism's ideology of universal rights; another approach would see a symbiotic relationship where migrant workers provide cheap labour. Fitzpatrick's point is not that Marxism must be rejected, but that questioning race can also lead to a different understanding of Marxism. This appears coherent with the work of cultural theorists such as Paul Gilroy. More importantly, Fitzpatrick is concerned with a dynamic of liberalism that both links race to law, and then denies that racism is a central problem. Understanding the reach of this problem demands a work of historical and philosophical acumen that can trace the inter-relations between liberalism, enlightenment reason and a colonial project. Fitzpatrick is clear: 'liberal capitalism [both] opposes and is maintained by racism' (1987, p. 121), a particularly pithy summary of a central tension that runs in different ways through British and American law.

39   For reflections on Brussels and its connection with the imperial project of King Leopold II see Morrison, 2006, Chapters 5 and 6.

the past.[40] As Gilroy writes, the contemporary perception of the problem was not so much the volume of black settlement but rather its character and effects, specifically the threat to legal institutions.[41] Immigration was perceived as a threat to English constitutional values, and in its most paranoid form, saw the destiny of the west at stake.[42] This perception of immigration as threat, rather than an opportunity to create a different history, a different institutional response, represents the continual failure to overcome the role of the 'other'.

> December 4, 2012 – Online News Report Al Jazeera. Greece's growing chain of detention camps for undocumented migrants came under strong criticism from the United Nations with Francois Crepeau, Special Rapporteur for the Human Rights of Migrants, describing conditions in some of the camps as 'shocking' and the detention of children and families 'utterly unacceptable'. 'It's difficult to see families, it's difficult to see children, three or five years old, behind bars.' Migrants were often detained without proper heat, hygiene or legal representation: 'They are not informed properly about their rights, about what is going to happen to them, about recourses. They don't see lawyers, or the lawyers take the money and run.' Greek police spokesperson told Al Jazeera that the detention policy was partly undertaken for migrants' own good. 'In the camps a migrant has a certain level of comfort, regular meals, a lawyer and medical attention,' Crepeau said the worst camp he saw was in the town of Vena, '28 people are crowded into a room [of about 35 square metres] with beds which are concrete slabs, filthy toilets and nothing to do and no light . . . No television, nothing to read, no information – these are not places where I would care to spend more than an hour'. Greece adopted a detain-and-deport policy for undocumented migrants in March. Police stop migrants on the street to check their residence papers every day, and regular police sweep operations have rounded up migrants en masse. The Greek-Turkish border is the main entry point of irregular migration in the European Union. Estimations say that 85–90 per cent of irregular migrations go through that point. Prime Minister Antonis Samaras has called the influx 'an unarmed invasion'. . . . Despite the political pressure, Crepeau believes the Greek policy is ultimately untenable. 'The policy is not viable either legally or practically: Legally you can only detain if the person is dangerous to herself or others, or if the person is at risk of not coming back for proceedings. "These are the only two reasons for administrative detention. If you only have a policy of detaining everyone at all times it's against international law and it's against international human rights. It's not legally viable."' Greek Government passed legal amendments ratified this year to criminalise illegal entry onto Greek soil, and make it possible for the government to detain undocumented migrants for up to 18 months.

---

40   See Fitzpatrick, 1992. The nation is defined in terms of race; the colonised people are everything that the English are not. Whilst sustaining this division, the constitution of Englishness is largely left unexamined. In the wider colonial worldview, although there are differences between, say, the English and the French, they are still united by a 'something' that allows them to be posited as the colonisers and the natives as the colonised. Race, is therefore is some senses empty. It can be filled with the contents of Englishness and Frenchness yet still opposed to the otherness of the savage. Moreover, it raises a standard against which the 'new' nations can be judged, but which they must always fall short. The native can only be civilized to a certain extent, they can never quite be 'one of us'.
41   Gilroy, 1987.
42   For instance, following Enoch Powell's 'rivers of blood speech' in 1968, race was presented in the terms of the disastrous encounter of two different civilizations.

Crepeau did not lay the blame on Greece's door alone. He said the European Union had to collectively resolve the problem of undocumented migration, because EU member states have unrecognised labour market needs which attract migrants.

This is part of a broader cultural and political failure that reveals blindness to the wider problem. The industrialisation of the first world at the expense of the third has produced a developed core, and an underdeveloped and exploited periphery.[43] The political will to deal with the redistribution of resources that would help repair this situation does not exist; but the dislocations wrought by the process continue to cause social and economic effects.

FROM COLONIALISM TO GLOBALISM: THE FATE OF THE EXCEPTIONAL?

In our world, it is not only the violent exception that links people together across borders; the very nature of everyday problems and processes joins people in multiple ways. From the movement of ideas and cultural artefacts to the fundamental issues raised by genetic engineering, from the conditions of financial stability to environmental degradation, the fate and fortunes of each of us are thoroughly intertwined.[44]

In her study of postcolonial reason Gayatri Spivak refers to the creation of a class of indigenous functionary-intelligentsia who were not-quite-not-white and acted as buffers between the foreign rulers and the native ruled. This is part of the making of the so-called colonial subject, a narrative that supports the master narrative of the dominant European subject. What happened to these elites as decolonialisation happened? For many it is a continuation of forms of dominance,[45] but now as agents of a new globalising capital and privatisation. What of transnational literacy in the new world order?

---

43   In the sense developed by Etienne Balibar: the (shifting) distinction between the core and the periphery of the world economy corresponds also to the geographical and politico-cultural distribution of strategies of exploitation' 1991, p. 177.

44   David Held, 'Violence and Justice in a Global Age', in *After Sep. 11: Perspectives from the Social Sciences.* At http://www.ssrc.org/sept11/essays/held.htm, 2001.

45   In her study of *Britain's Gulag: the brutal end of Empire in Kenya*, 2005, Caroline Elkins relates a meeting between the previous governor, Sir Evelyn Baring and the new president in 1965. "Baring was uncharacteristically nervous as he visited his old office, especially because Kenyatta was standing just opposite him. Indeed, what do you possibly say to a man whose trial you rigged and who, because of your signature, spent years of his life banished to a desert wasteland? There was no avoiding the subject, so after some initial pleasantries the former jailer turned to his one-time captive, gestured, and said, "By the way, I was sitting at that actual desk when I signed your detention order 20 years ago." "I know," Kenyatta told him. "If I had been in your shoes at the time I would have done exactly the same." The nervousness evaporated, and the room erupted in relieved laughter. With everyone still chuckling, the new president chimed in, "And I have myself signed a number of detention orders sitting right there too." As the two later strolled through the gardens admiring the Naivasha thorns that Baring's wife had planted years before, Kenya's jails were already beginning to fill up with the detainees whom the new independent government deemed threats to the country's young democracy.' (pp. 354–355)

In 1988, the World Conservation Union Red Book of Endangered Species listed the hundreds of endemic fishes of Lake Victoria under a single heading: 'Endangered'. The most exuberant expression of vertebrate adaptive radiation in the world, the haplo-chromine species, is now in the midst of the first mass extinction of vertebrates that scientists have ever had the opportunity to observe, an event as exciting as it is depressing.[46]

It is not, it seems too difficult to visualise globalisation. And it's exciting, exciting to witness great extinctions, part of the process in which at a local level everything appears as if it has been determined from somewhere else.

Darwin's Nightmare is a 2004 Austrian-French-Belgian documentary film dealing with the environmental and social effects on the fishing industry around Lake Victoria which is shared by Tanzania, Kenya and Uganda of the introduction of exotic fish species.[47] The film opens with a Soviet made cargo plane landing on Mwanza airfield – the town with the largest fish processing plants in Tanzania. It will take back a cargo of processed fillets of Nile Perch, a predator species of fish which can grow up to two metres in length which was introduced into Lake Victoria, either as a sport resource or more calculatingly to turn the local biomass into commercially useful stock. While in the 1970s the perch made up less that 20 percent of the Lake's fish biomass it now accounts for over 80 percent and hundreds of endemic species are extinct. The film is a catalogue of witnessing; interviews with the relatively rich Russian and Ukrainian plane crew who bring in vodka and seek out women, well off local factory owners, nearly destitute guards (who are allowed to kill intruders into the 'Fishing Research Station'), prostitutes, fishermen and other villagers. The Nile perch has dramatically changed the ecosystem and economy of the region. As European aid is funnelled into Africa and NGOs make a business as middle organisations, the flights also bring in munitions and weapons from European arms dealers. Dima, the radio engineer of the plane crew, puts it crisply: the children of Angola receive guns for Christmas, the children of Europe receive grapes. Through images of the appalling living and working conditions of the indigenous people, we confront the continuing reality of Fannon's wretched of the earth in which basic sanitation is completely absent and many children turn to drugs and prostitution; the Nile perch is fished and filleted for export. The metropolitan consumer rules, each market demands particular forms of fillet, some markets use up 25 percent of the individual fish, others up to 45 percent; the festering carcasses of the gutted fish are then available for local consumption. Local news reports relayed in the film indicated Northern and Central Tanzania were facing famine, while the stocks of local fish are described as 'too expensive' to use locally. And while the reported cannibalism of the Mau Mau was doubtful, there is no doubting the arrival of a new form: having rendered so many local species extinct the perch have little to feed on and so now eat their own smaller kind.

....

46   Lake Victoria Case Study, Sect. 8 Legal Standing, found at www1.american.edu/ted/victoria.htm
47   Written and directed by Hubert Sauper *Darwin's Nightmare* premiered at the 2004 Venice Film Festival, and was nominated for the 2006 Academy Award for Documentary Feature.

THE LESSON? LAW'S BLAME OR LAW'S ESCAPE?

> The common law was corrupted in Australia by the nature of the relationship between settlers and aborigines in the same way it was corrupted in Britain's slave colonies . . . Forced and uncompensated dispossession was frowned on by the Imperial government but in one way or another colonists continued to take aboriginal land and convince themselves it was not theft.[48]

Law needs its authority. Thus we see a distinguishing: colonial violence is presented as being within the purview of the colonial government and distinct from the inherited legal system; the purity of (real) law is somehow protected. Today, in Australia, *Mabo* 'is transformed into a vindication of British common law, rather than an indictment of the system that denied aboriginal peoples fully human status for more than 200 years'.[49]

On October 5, 2012, the High Court on London ruled that three elderly Kenyans, representatives of the approximately 2,000 still alive of the tens of thousands incarcerated, had permission to claim damages for the grave abuses they suffered when imprisoned during the state of emergency. Rejecting the government's claim that too much time had elapsed for there to be a fair trial, it had earlier rejected the claim that the Mau Mau veterans should be suing the Kenyan government, not the British. The government accepted that all three were tortured by the colonial authorities and had suffered what their lawyers describe as 'unspeakable acts of brutality', including castration, beatings and severe sexual assaults. Mr Justice McCombe said a fair trial was possible and highlighted the fact that thousands of documents had been found in a secret Foreign Office archive containing files from dozens of former colonies; at an earlier hearing he had said there was 'ample evidence even in the few papers that I have seen suggesting that there may have been systematic torture of detainees during the Emergency'. The Government warned of possible floodgates of suits from other former colonies and pledged to appeal.

The case threatens to turn the exceptional – the state of emergency – into the normal, the act of suing and gaining damages. It thus can construe law's violence as History.

How can we both account for the exceptional situation and yet the normal legal? Perhaps the ultimate case of trying to save law from the violence of the colonial lies in the treatment of the Nazi legal order between 1933 and 1944. In a common image the Nazi order is seen as a bunch of criminals who somehow took over the legitimate state and through a reign of terror coerced otherwise law-abiding citizens into doing and participating in terrible deeds, in particular the systematic extermination of six million Jews through a quasi-industrial process of incarceration in camps and either being worked to death or exterminated through particular death camps (Auschwitz). The colonial is of course deeply implicated for not only can we see the entire Nazi aim as a form of European colonialism turning upon itself, for unable to expand into new

---

48   Reynolds, *The Law of the Land*, 2nd edn 1992, p. 4.
49   Purdy, 1999, p. 219.

colonies (and having lost theirs as a consequence of WWI) the Nazis created a racial state and attempted the entire biological reorganisation of Europe. Not only would the Jews (and Gypsies and Gays) be exterminated, but whole subject races (the Poles and the Slavs) would be rendered into slave labour and many millions allowed to starve to death freeing up living space for a revitalised Aryan race (revitalised since weaker members would have been medically put to death or sterilised). The purity of the race/blood was the key principle in the making of a new utopia – combined with the technology of eugenics. In addition of course the camps themselves came from the colonial; in 1896 the Spaniards in Cuba created the *campos de concentraciones* to repress the insurrection of colonies population, and the beginning of the 20th century the English herded the Boers into concentration camps. In both situations the context was a colonial war, and an extension to a possible entire civilian population of a state of exception. But is the state of exception, the declaration of martial law, declaration of a state of emergency, a departure from the law or somehow internal to law? There is no doubt that the Nazis perpetrated such outrages that the events stand for an abyss of evil, but could law cope with them? Many consider that the events go far beyond the concept of crime or the ability of law to respond. The British Foreign Secretary, Anthony Eden, considered that: 'The guilt of such individuals is so black that they fall outside and go beyond the scope of any judicial process.'[50] Winston Churchill, Britain's wartime prime minister, considered them 'outlaws', and proposed that enemy leaders should simply be executed when they were caught. Summary execution (at six hours' notice, following identification of the prisoner by a senior military officer) became the policy of the British government from 1943. Yet, as war ended it was agreed to set up a Tribunal of the Allied nations (called the United Nations) and use the Common law (instead of the Civil Law 'Roman' tradition) as the working module of jurisprudence and trial procedures (in particular due process) that could cope. In his opening speech the lead prosecutor, Jackson, contends that Germany, prior to the rise of the Nazi regime, had entered into numerous treaties with other nations regarding the rules of warfare. These included agreements prohibiting 'aggressive war' and the mistreatment of captives (either prisoners of war or civilian populations), among other actions that the Nazis were charged with violating. It is asserted that Germany was still operating under the obligation to abide by those agreements, and so their wilful disregard was cause for legal action taken by the other countries with whom the treaties were signed. In evidence for this, Jackson cites the Weimar Constitution's provision that 'The generally accepted rules of international law are to be considered as binding integral parts of the law', and that the treaties signed were part of those 'generally accepted rules'. In addition there is pressing need for the future of civilisation that trial take place owing to the 'abnormal and inhuman' acts perpetrated by these formerly-powerful men. Moreover we must recognise the 'faith' that the law applies to all men, including rulers, as they are all 'under God and the law'. Thus there can be no denying that the 'mass killings of countless human beings in cold blood' is murder, a criminal offence, even though the individuals who did the actual

---

50   PRO, PREM 4/100/10, minute by the Foreign Secretary, 'Treatment of War Criminals', 22 June 1942, pp. 2–3.

killing considered that they were following orders, the lawful orders of a legitimate Government acting in accordance with the then accepted form of jurisprudence (or what Hart would say, following the rule of recognition). In the absence of any clearly stated legal code Jackson turns to the Common Law tradition to integrate the appeal to International Law and the general concepts of justice by saying that International Law can grow as the Common Law grows. To Jackson, International Law 'grows . . . through decisions reached from time to time in adapting settled principles to new situations' (emphasis mine) just as is done with the evolution of Common Law.' These 'settled principles' provide the background (legal/spiritual) notions of justice. Since International Law by its very nature is not subject to 'development by normal processes of legislative authority', Common Law techniques allow us to accept the existence of International Law even when it is not expressly written (this is the classical Declaratory theory of the Common Law where the written law is evidence of, but not the actual limits of the law). We can thus make appeals to common justice and to timeless principles from within the context of an International Law Tribunal. The legitimacy of the trials must be a practical matter of due process also: the trial must be exemplary, including the 'presumption of innocence', 'fair and dispassionate hearings', and 'undeniable proof' of the claimed criminal acts. The simple fact that the trial is composed of 'victor nations over vanquished foes' presents practical difficulties but the court must not give in to unjust impulses.

What of the Nazi perspective? We should remember that the Hitler and the Nazi party came legally to power in 1933. The Weimar constitution contained a clause, article 48, which allowed the president to take extreme measures to preserve security in the face of emergency. Taking advantage of the Reichstag fire, Hitler persuaded the then president to use that article to ban opposition and after a new election parliament, the Reichstag, passed an enabling act which thenceforth gave virtual dictatorial powers to Hitler and the Reich Cabinet. In this way a legal dictatorship was created. The primary enemy that Hitler identified – against the backdrop of the humiliation of Germany after the First World War and the Treaty of Versailles – was the Jew. 1935 saw the passing of the Nuremberg laws, this was the essential first step to the stripping of Jews of their citizenship rights, of the transformation from rights bearing citizens to entities of administrative direction.

The Constitution of the Weimar Republic was never formally abolished but in effect after the Enabling Act the Nazis ruled in a permanent state of emergency (state of exception). We should remember that very intelligent jurisprudential scholars were enemies of the Weimar Republic and the liberal legalism that underlay it. As Carl Schmitt – one of the foremost legal scholars of the twentieth century – identified it, the constitution of the German Reich, the element in the new democracy of a state based on the liberal rule of law that could not create for itself 'any vivid presence in the mind of the German citizen'. It was 'empty and unsatisfying'. For Schmitt the new constitution was not part of the spirit of the people, as many would say the common law is part of the spirit of the Anglo-Saxons. Moreover for Schmitt, the Weimar constitution was an English suit of clothes put on the German Reich in 1919. This could only be temporary, new Clothes were required; clothing that fitted the pure body of the German Volk, the demos (people) that fitted German soil. For Schmitt, every democracy requires complete homogeneity of its people. Only such a unity can assume political

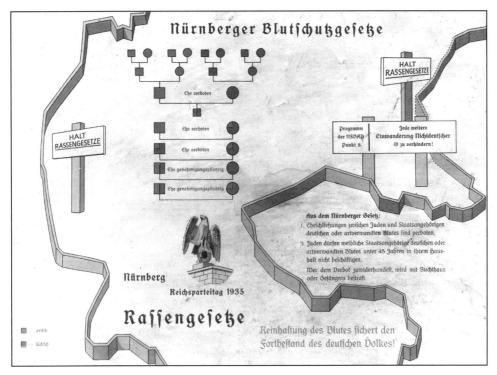

Figure 5.5 United States Holocaust Memorial Museum, courtesy of Hans Pauli. © United States Holocaust Memorial Museum.

Eugenics poster entitled 'The Nuremberg Law for the Protection of Blood and German Honor'. The illustration is a stylised map of the borders of central Germany on which is imposed a schematic of the forbidden degrees of marriage between Aryans and non-Aryans, point 8 of the Nazi party platform (against the immigration of non-Ayrans into Germany), and the text of the Law for the Protection of German Blood. The German text at the bottom reads, 'Maintaining the purity of blood insures the survival of the German people.'

This poster is no.70 in a series entitled, 'Erblehre und Rassenkunde' (Theory of Inheritance and Racial Hygiene), published by the Verlag für nationale Literatur (Publisher for National Literature), Stuttgart.

Note how the poster works: it creates a bounded territory and makes reference to the processes by which the people of that territory may be destroyed; outside lies a (mythical) enemy. Note issues of identity: the claim seems to be of a group identity (essentialist) that is being undercut, but in fact the poster unwittingly shows it is relational. The resultant identity – the pure German – is constituted in relation to the outside, the 'negated other'. Without this radical other, located in the threatening surrounds, it is not possible to define one's particularity.

responsibility.'[51] Against liberalism, Schmitt seeks concrete reality, liberalism gives us the emptiness of abstract individuals valuable as a human being; the zone concerned is thus humanity, humanity as a whole. For Schmitt this is absurd, politics is the art of distinguishing the friend and the enemy and how can one do this if humanity as a whole is your concern?

Liberalism has stripped the state of the particular contents giving it a pluralism (and thus politics was wrongly conceived as compromises, discussion, negotiation),

---

51   References to Schmitt are to extracts of his writings included in Jacobson & Schlink (eds.), 2000. Above quotes from 1928 article, p. 299 of the text.

but the governing idea of humanity constituted *nothing*, gave no distinguishable community.

If the people could not internalise the world view disaster would strike: 'If a state unity becomes problematic in the reality of social life, this leads to a condition unbearable for every citizen, for because of this the normal situation vanishes and with it the presumption of every ethical and legal norm.'[52]

What did this appeal to concrete reality mean in real cases? After the passing of the Nuremberg laws Schmitt stated that the German Reichstag had met under the 'motto of freedom'. The assembly and the great Nuremberg rally (see the film *Triumph of the Will*) was the German people itself, led by the National Socialist movement and following the Fuhrer, Adolf Hitler; its 'laws embody the first German constitution of freedom in centuries'. Whereas before the liberal constitution had offered equality before the law; it was now to be only Germans who could be equal before the law as Germans. Whereas before the nation was the sum of its citizens, and the state an invisible legal person, now the German people had in a legal sense become the German people again. 'German blood and German honour were now the main concepts of our laws, and the state the people's strength and unity' (paraphrasing Hobbes but giving it a bio-political 'reality'). Chillingly Schmitt warned that if

> the current regulation of the situation of the Jews not lead to its goal, the Fuhrer has mentioned the possibility of fresh scrutiny and suggested that resolution of the question would then be transferred by law to the party. This is a serious warning. It declares the Nazi party the Guardian the sanctuary of the people, the Guardian of the constitution.

Moreover Schmitt ends with a grand rhetorical flourish:

> These statutes income pass and pervade our entire law. They determine what we may call morality and public order, decency and good practice. They are the constitution of freedom, the core of our German law today. Everything that we German lawyers do gains its meaning and honour from them.[53]

The response to the Nazi atrocities meant that such writing had to be put in the category of propaganda and Nazi law as failed law, corrupted law. And so we are told it can be put in the past: post-Auschwitz law is different to pre-Auschwitz. This is a gross oversimplification. We should take from Schmitt a firm warning: Schmitt correctly sees modern societies as disenchanted (following Weber) and unable to articulate a meaningful set of values. His catholic theo-jurisprudence led him to look for a strong figure that would be a concrete representative of the otherwise 'invisible' spirit and place the state of exception as the absolute foundation of the normal order. We have much to be vigilant: such thinking is implicit in a great deal globally today.

---

52   Ibid, at p. 312, a 1930 article.
53   Ibid., pp. 323–325, a 1935 article.

CONCLUSION: LAW'S PAUSE IN THE POST-COLONIAL?

Whether or not one accepts that the global was first understood practically through the practices of colonialism the post-colonial and the global interact. Europe attempts to defend its 'civilised space' through strategies of boundary drawing, creating a common space which demarcates itself from the other, but it is constituted by relationship with the other and the colonial violence that has shaped so much of modern law. What of justice? In her review Tuitt seems to hope that our intellectual work of rewriting histories and identities may provide for 'law's pause, and . . . hesitation', offering some place 'for justice' precisely where 'the law sees the terror of its own force'[54] Yet we may suspect that there are many forces preventing the interconnections – and racism of the global order – being in view. To end: the current war on terror, presented in a iconic image by the *Economist* magazine as the globe in the shape of a human skull,[55] may be itself read as a continuation of the strategies of allowing some narratives of cause and effect and not others. If September 11 2001 brought images of terror, fear, mistrust and death, as part of normal reality to the west, to others these images, however, were only a realisation by the powerful of the terror that many in the world already lived with on a daily basis.[56] What then is the figure of law we could see? For some the challenges are so great that power will have to work in the shadows, a permanent state of exception, with detention camps, rendition, and the always present mythical enemy. Against which who are we and what – legal – clothes do we wear? Perhaps Schmitt is useful for he could only believe in a metaphysics of presence, there had to be some real transcendental, demiurgic, collective entity, behind law, making decisions. But law requires people and humans are the subjects of rights. A more surreal image may be required – see our front cover.[57]

....

54   Tuitt, 2004, p. 114.
55   The front cover of the *Economist*, Nov 30–Dec 6 2002 edition, under the heading of *Preparing for Terror*, made the globe as now one human skull. The cover of the October 19–25 2002 edition, under the heading *A World of Terror*, was of a small figure standing before a forest of tall sticks of dynamite with their fuses lit.
56   In 1994 Rwanda, experienced perhaps the easiest of the great massacres of the twentieth century to have stopped, resulted in over 880,000 deaths. This was a state sponsored massacre that was planned and with considerable measures taken to achieve it (such as buying and distributing machetes to about one third of the population). If, in the years immediately afterwards the stories were confusing and contested, we now know that the power elites of the west (the White nations) knew of the plans and the event and deliberately decided to do nothing. See, for example, Melvern, 2004.
57   Or to give the Jewish legal scholar dismissed by the Nazis Hans Kelsen a deconstructive word: 'If we take the actors who play out the religious or social drama on the political stage, and strip the masks from their faces, then we no longer have God rewarding and punishing, or the state condemning and making war, but men putting coercion on other men, whether it be Mr X triumphant over Mr Y, or a wild animal slaking its reawakened thirst for blood.' ([1922] 1973, p. 67).

6

INSTITUTIONALISING JUDICIAL DECISION MAKING: PUBLIC REASON AND THE DOCTRINE OF PRECEDENT

The law of England would be a strange science if indeed it were decided by precedents only. Precedents serve to illustrate principles and to give them a fixed certainty. But the law of England, which is exclusive of positive law, enacted by statute [i.e. Mansfield specifies he is referring to case law developed by the courts], depends upon principles, and these principles run through all the cases according as the particular circumstances of each have been found to fall within the one or the other of them.[1]

If a group of cases involves the same point, the parties expect the same decision. It would be a gross injustice to decide alternate cases on opposite principles. If a case was decided against me yesterday when I was a defendant, I shall look for the same judgment today if I am plaintiff. To decide differently would raise a feeling of resentment and wrong in my breast; it would be an infringement, material and moral, of my rights . . . . Adherence to precedent must then be the rule rather than the exception if litigants are to have faith in the even-handed administration of justice in the courts.[2]

The paradigm case of injustice is that in which there are two similar individuals in similar circumstances and one of them is treated better or worse than the other. In this case, the cry of injustice rightly goes up against the responsible agent or group; and unless that agent or group can establish that there is some relevant dissimilarity after all between the individuals concerned and their circumstances, he or they will be guilty as charged.[3]

If lawyers hold to their precedents too closely, forgetful of the fundamental principles of truth and justice which they should serve, they may find the whole edifice comes tumbling down about them. Just as the scientist seeks for truth, so the lawyer should seek for justice. Just as the scientist takes his instances and from them builds up his general propositions, so the lawyer should take his precedents and from them build up his general principles. Just as the propositions of the scientist fail to be modified when shown not to fit all instances, or even discarded when shown in error, so the principles of the lawyer should be modified when found to be unsuited to the times or discarded when found to work injustice.[4]

---

1   Ld. Mansfield, *Jones v. Randall*, [1774] 1 Cowp. 37
2   Cardozo, 1921, pp. 33–4.
3   Frankena, 1973, p. 49.
4   Lord Denning, former Master of the Rolls, 1979, p. 292.

INTRODUCTION

After the historical approach of the previous chapter, we now want to turn to one of the fundamental, defining features of common law: the doctrine of binding precedent. The first part of the chapter considers the roots of the doctrine and the argument that judges do not make law. We want to place our understanding of precedent on a more contemporary foundation. We will argue that the doctrine of precedent can be understood as an institutional form of public reason that operates in a democratic context: legitimate judicial law making in a democracy is characterised by judicial restraint, and by the public reasons judges give for reaching the conclusions that they have. We will go on to outline a theory of precedent as a judicial practice that we will develop in more detail in the following chapter.[5]

THE JUDGE AND THE COMMON LAW

Judges are the central figures in common law systems. Case law is the product of judicial determination and it is sometimes referred to as judge-made law. Yet common law systems claim they operate the rule of law, not of men (and traditionally, and in large part continuing today, appellant courts are staffed by male judges). The human element to law's operation appears inescapable; how is case law justified, legitimised and rescued from claims of arbitrariness and rampant subjectivity? At one time, a progressive view was that codification was the solution to the problem of a perceived chaos of competing cases and seemingly ad hoc, if not retrospective judicial 'law making'.[6] With limited (if sometimes, as in India, notable) exceptions this did not occur. Most large scale schemes of converting case law into statutes consisted mainly of consolidating legislation with the aim of preserving the existing structure of principles and rules developed over time by the common law judges.

In addition, common law systems with their variety of formal sources of law[7] specify that certainty and recognisibility of law are features of their systems. The statements of the judge(s) are in Blackstone's classic words of 1765 (the peak of the 'declaratory' theory of the common law) but 'evidence of what is the common law', they are not themselves the final word. Apologists of the declaratory theory would hold that judicial fidelity is not owed to the articulations of previous judges, but to the law.

It is hard to know exactly what this means. The modern practice of precedent challenges the declaratory theory with the argument that judges do make law. How

---

5   'Underlying precedent is an emphasis on stability, permanence and the wisdom of the past – the common law being conceived as an accumulation of such wisdom – combined with reverence for the higher courts as the "elders and betters" of the lower courts. Precedent reflected the vision of law as an undertaking based on learning, acquired skills and experience. At the same time, since precedents exist in order to be applied, the system essentially empowered the higher courts to legislate. Presented as a restraint, precedent camouflaged law-making whilst in reality constituting law-making.' (Nicol, 2006).

6   The reference to case law and 'judge-made' law began with Bentham, who so defined it in the hope of destroying its legitimacy.

7   Historically, these were custom, case law, national statutes, transnational agreements and institutional links and academic commentary.

can we understand judicial law making? Evolving historical conditions, not some analytical set of logical related and clearly specified concepts and ideas, provides our first point of reference. We want to focus on two interrelated issues, the development of modern case reporting, and the formalization of techniques of legal argument.

A characteristic and vital concern in the common law world is the determination of the authority of propositions found in the law reports to be considered to be accurate statements of the law, i.e. strategies of reading and giving weight and according substance to the recorded statements by the judges in making judgment in deciding cases. Put simply, what is the status of the words therein contained? As generations of introductory books state the most important method of ranking and weighing judgments is adherence to the 'doctrine' or 'rule' of precedent (in modern form a tightening of the older principle guiding judicial determination called 'stare decisis'). The doctrine may be relatively easily stated in crude terms but it soon becomes more complex when we perceive the multifaceted calls a lawyer makes in work on a hard case. Reading case reports to find relevant propositions 'of law', negotiating between 'leading' and 'dissenting' judgments, weighting up whether statements are 'ratio' or 'obiter' is not mechanical process. Statements are given differing weight to statements depending on how they contribute to developing an answer to a legal question and as material to evaluate the arguments of the opponent or formulate legal arguments that best fit with his or her sense of the case 'for' his or her client.

A term that is often used is 'authority': what is the authority *for*, or *against*, the argument? This is not an abstract consideration but deeply practical. Put another way: one part of legal research is about the technical problems of how to find or look up 'the law'; but faced with one set of concrete results of those searches – i.e. a range of decisions and judgments – how should the lawyer rank and differentiate the material that he or she finds? One answer is by following the doctrine of precedent.

It is relatively easy to paraphrase scholarly descriptions of precedent; it is usually explained by reference to the English translation of the Latin phrase 'stare decisis', which literally translates as 'to stand by decided matters'. The phrase stare decisis is itself a shortened version of the Latin phrase 'stare decisis et non quieta movere', 'to stand by decisions and not to disturb settled matters'. In student books it is common to run together stare decisis and the modern doctrine of precedent as if they were the same, but technically, stare decisis is the older term referring to the practice before the modern doctrine of 'binding precedent'; it appears to have given judges flexibility, one stood by previous decisions but weighed up their effects and their meaning in the overall understanding of the common laws' conception of the just state of affairs for the community.

Precedent, in its modern form, i.e. binding precedent, developed from the looser stare decisis in the course of the nineteenth century and took on more of the character of a binding set of rules, whereby the decision of a higher court within the same national or provincial, state or district jurisdiction acts as *binding* authority on a lower court within that same jurisdiction. The decision of a court of another jurisdiction only acts as *persuasive* authority. The degree of persuasiveness is dependent upon various factors, including, first, the nature of the other jurisdiction and second, the level of court which decided the precedent case in the other jurisdiction. Other factors include the date of the precedent case, on the assumption that the more recent the case, the more reliable it will be as authority for a given proposition, although this is not necessarily so. And on some occasions, the judge's reputation may affect the degree of persuasiveness of the authority.

If things seem simple at this level of generality they get complex when we realise that all cases are an intermixing of procedure, facts and 'law', and that it is only particular parts of a decision that are called upon as authority, but often it is not easy to differentiate between the different parts. Glanville Williams described it for generations of law students thus:

> [w]hat the doctrine of precedent declares is that cases must be decided the same way when their material facts are the same. Obviously it does not require that all the facts should be the same. We know that in the flux of life all the facts of a case will never recur, but the legally material facts may recur and it is with these that the doctrine is concerned. The ratio decidendi [reason of deciding] of a case can be defined as the material facts of the case plus the decision thereon. The same learned author who advanced this definition went on to suggest a helpful formula. Suppose that in a certain case facts A, B and C exist, and suppose that the court finds that facts B and C are material and fact A immaterial, and then reaches conclusion X (e.g. judgment for the plaintiff, or judgment for the defendant). Then the doctrine of precedent enables us to say that in any future case in which facts B and C exist, or in which facts A and B and C exist the conclusion must be X. If in a future case A, B, C, and D exist, and the fact D is held to be material, the first case will not be a direct authority, though it may be of value as an analogy.

It follows from William's analysis, however, that the addition of fact D to a future case means that conclusion X may or may not follow. In other words, the presence of a new fact D may have the effect of distinguishing the future case from the precedent or conversely the precedent may be extended to apply to the future case.[8]

There has been considerable writing on whether the doctrine of binding precedent is a good or bad one but the doctrine is usually justified by arguments which focus on the desirability of stability and certainty in the law and also by notions of justice and fairness.

Reliance upon precedent also promotes the expectation that the law is just. The idea that like cases should be treated alike is anchored in the assumption that one person is the legal equal of any other. Thus, persons in similar situations should not be treated differently except for legally relevant and clearly justifiable reasons. Precedent promotes judicial restraint and limits a judge's ability to determine the outcome of a case in a way that he or she might choose if there were no precedent. This function of precedent gives it its normative force.

----

8   References to Williams are to his *Learning the Law*, 9th edn 1973 (my student copy WM). In this account, legal rules, embodied in precedents, are generalisations that accentuate the importance of certain facts and discount or ignore others. The application of precedent relies on reasoning by analogy. Analogies can be neither correct nor incorrect but only more or less persuasive. Reasonable persons may come to different yet defensible conclusions about what rule should prevail.

Precedent also enhances efficiency. Reliance on the accumulation of legal rules helps guide judges in their resolution of legal disputes. If judges had to begin the law anew in each case, they would add more time to the adjudicative process and would duplicate their efforts.

The use of precedent is related to and dependent upon the publication of law reports that contain case decisions and the articulated rationale of judges. The paucity of law reports until their reorganisation under the Council of Law Reporters and the adoption of 'official' series meant that uncertainty existed as to the actual words that justified early decisions (many early reports were more reporting the procedure or the argument used, often the decision was not included!).

We could say, then, that there are at least three audiences listening to and watching contemporary judicial argument: the parties to the dispute, the public, and other legal professionals. The latter include fellow judges and in particular the judges who are likely to hear the case again if the legal issues go on appeal as well as legal academics eager to write case notes or articles and books in which particular cases are described as correct, others 'wrong', certain judgments as incisive, others as not particularly well reasoned and so forth. The process of interpretation and pronouncement on the law is no mechanical process; if it were then the issue should not have reached court. We now want to develop these points.

PRECEDENT, ADJUDICATION AND PUBLIC REASON

The section above has examined the basic themes that define judicial reasoning. Some of these are historical, such as the development of stare decisis or of the system of reporting judicial decisions; others are structural and concern how form is given to judicial argument. We also drew attention to various terms, for the most part Latinate, that are used to describe various features of the judicial art. We now want to draw together these diverse themes to give us a clear sense of the dynamic nature of the contemporary doctrine and practice of precedent.

Our focus is the idea that judicial reasoning, and the structures that define it, articulate a particular form of public reason that is essential to a functioning democracy. To develop this argument, we need to define a key term which we will then link back to the justification of judicial law making: adjudication. Fuller made the following comments on adjudication:

> It is customary to think of adjudication as a means of settling disputes or controversies. . . . . More fundamentally, however, adjudication should be viewed as a form of social ordering, as a way in which the relations of men to one another are governed and regulated. Even in the absence of any formalized doctrine of stare decisis or res judicata, an adjudicative determination will normally enter in some degree into the litigants' future relations and into the future relations of other parties who see themselves as possible litigants before the same tribunal. Even if there is no statement by the tribunal of the reasons for its decision, some reason will be perceived or guessed at, and the parties will tend to govern their conduct accordingly.[9]

The important point for Fuller is that adjudication is a way of resolving disputes over the terms in which social relations are 'regulated'. Adjudication influences future legal relationships by determining the existence or extent of duties, rights and obligations. The adjudicator will have reasons for the decision that s/he has given. In a formalised system of adjudication, these reasons will be made clear. Indeed, the whole point of the first part of this chapter was to look at those historical and logical structures that define the British common law system of adjudication. However, what still remains vague is the link between judicial reasoning in adjudication and public reason. We now want to clarify this relationship.

In the contemporary doctrine of precedent a judge gives reasons for the decision that s/he has made. Why? Let's revisit some of the key points that we made in our argument above. We asserted that judicial reliance on precedent 'promotes the expectation that the law is just'; moreover, precedent 'promotes judicial restraint' and 'limits the judge's ability to determine the outcome' of a case in an arbitrary manner. To elaborate: our notions of justice and fairness are linked to the sense that, in the doctrine of precedent 'like cases are decided alike' and (to echo Hart's clarification of this principle of justice) unlike cases are not decided in the same way. So, our first point is that precedent is an institutionalised system of reasoning where patterns of likeness are asserted or denied. This relates to the second point. These interpretative rules of practice impose restraints on what a judge can and cannot 'do with the law' in a case. We will return to this point in later chapters: the art of the judge is very much one of deference or restraint: of working within limits. In other words, to elaborate a point that we made above, judicial law making is legitimate because it is restrained: it operates within certain boundaries (the boundaries are themselves defined by the institutional location of the democratic judge). There is still more that we want to say.

The hierarchy of the courts provides the under-arching foundation for judicial public reason. Recall Fuller's argument above that: 'adjudicative determination will . . . enter in some degree into the litigants' future relations and into the future relations of other parties . . .' This is a way of thinking about the thesis that the law needs to be stable and certain. Fuller has himself stressed that this is one of the conditions for the legitimacy of a legal system. We should therefore not be surprised to find that the hierarchy of the courts and the notion of binding precedent ensure that judicial law making is, to a large extent, controlled and predictable. As we will see in the next chapter, there are perturbations in judicial practices, but, they do not jeopardise the fundamental structures of the doctrine which assert the predominant values of stability and hierarchy over flexibility and 'justice' in an individual case.

But it is not just the hierarchy of the courts that is important. To return to the point we made above: underlying the notion of the legitimacy of judicial law making is the fact that a judge must give reasons for his or her decision. This 'duty' assumes particular importance in a modern democracy. The following argument helps us to develop

---

9   Fuller, (1978: 409).

this point: '[w]e must give public reasons if our justifications for the law are to inform or persuade our fellow citizens in general and the legal community in particular'.[10] Explaining this point requires us to elaborate another argument we made in the first part of this chapter. When we were discussing judicial law making we pointed out that there are: 'at least three audiences . . . listening and watching the judicial display: the parties to the dispute, the public, and other legal professionals.' These audiences must be able to understand what the judges are saying and writing. It is this mode of discourse which we are describing as public reason.

Judicial reasons are addressed, first of all, to a professional audience: other judges and lawyers. Whatever a judge asserts in a judgment will be tested by other professional lawyers.[11] The professional audience 'mediates' legal arguments for citizens at large. In part, citizens pay for the services of lawyers in order to have legal reasons explained to them and strategies developed in the light of how the law stands. However, the audience for judicial reasoning is not limited to that of professional lawyers. The reasons that underlie a judicial decision are addressed to the parties to the case itself; and hence to all citizens who are contemplating using the courts to affirm their rights; or find themselves a defendant in a criminal trial. In Chapter 13 these concerns are related to the notion of participation as one of the key normative underpinnings of a civil or criminal trial. A condition of participation is that the parties can understand that their arguments on law and evidence are taken seriously. A judge has to show in detail how his decision is justified.

Judicial reasoning is not limited to the parties to a dispute, or to professional lawyers. As judicial law making relates to the development of the common law, it is of interest to all citizens. Judicial decisions can be read by the public at large but most importantly, decisions are commented on in the media and feature in general political debate. Justice, as we will see, has to be delivered in open court. The fundamental link between freedom of speech and a judge's duty to give reason for a decision both point towards the virtues of democratic culture: everything can be discussed, and everything can be criticised. As Lord Bingham has commented: 'democracies die behind closed doors.'

For us, Lord Bingham's statement has to be understood as recognition of the vital public nature of legal reasoning. A robust culture of argument is central to a democracy. However, public debate has to be, for the most part, well informed and intelligent. Powerful interests must not have undue influence over the dissemination and discussion of matters of public concern. We don't have the space in this book to develop these ideas in detail – but we have profound concerns about the contraction of the spaces and opportunities for all citizens to debate and react to decisions, both legal and political, that affect their interests.

We want to make a final point about public reason: students and academics are important constituents of the audience for legal judgments. The book that you are reading presupposes an educational culture where individuals undertake training to be lawyers, or at least engage with the study of law on the basis that it can be

---

10   Slolum 2004, 230.
11   At one level this relates to the appellate structure of the courts. A decision can be appealed: judge's arguments are either are wrong in relation to evidence or (more rarely) wrong in law.

understood; that reasons can be given for the existence of legal rules and principles. Our arguments throughout this book are reflections on this process. If law is a set of practices, one has to engage in those practices to understand how they work. This means that you, in reading these words, are engaged with a form of public reason. Our concern in writing this book, and (we guess) your concern (dear reader) in reading it, is to understand how underlying structures and practices operate. To further elaborate our arguments above in the light of this fact: if law is not simply addressed to lawyers, but, to the citizens of a democratic culture, then one has to approach it in a very specific way.

Understanding judicial reason must have a critical dimension. The approach is not simply to suggest that a training in law is based on learning 'facts' about the legal system – or is tantamount to learning verbatim legal judgments on the basis that they are somehow 'true', authoritative and beyond criticism. Rather, we need to understand that judges are (of necessity) making arguments about the law. Whilst according the judge and the judgment the necessary respect, we must approach judicial reasoning in a critical way. We need to ask ourselves whether we accept the arguments put before us. Do they persuade us? If not, why not? For us, these are democratic questions; and the proper way in which law should itself be discussed, studied and disseminated in a democracy.

So, to summarise this section of the chapter. Our point is that a judge must give reasons for his/her decision, and that these reasons can be examined by lawyers, and by citizens themselves. One has to study judicial reasoning in the institutional context of the law. Judicial law making operates in the context of a public interested in what judges assert, and if necessary, able to criticise both the reasons for a decision and the impact of that decision on their interests.

There are now a couple of points, implicit in our argument above, that we want to spell out. Judicial reasoning is inherently interpretative and creative. This is why it has to be kept within an institutional framework. In order to explain these issues, we will develop further the concept of judicial practice.[12]

----

12   We can use some ideas developed by the French social theorist Pierre Bourdieu to help us work out what we mean when we assert that precedent (as well as statutory interpretation) is a practice. Our point of reference is to Bourdieu's concept of habitus. A habitus is defined as an understanding of 'systems of durable, transposable dispositions . . . predisposed to function as . . . structures' Bourdieu, (1977: 72). The word habitus in Latin means a condition or a character. It is related to the word habitat. Although this might be used in the natural sciences, we can understand it as relating to an 'environment' which determines both what 'things' exist, and how they relate to each other. It is thus a fundamental 'grounding' concept. To return to Bourdieu: a habitus is 'a durable set of dispositions that are structured (by socialisation and particular historical relations) and structuring (in guiding, but not determining, an individual's actions) (Bourdieu, 1977, 72). In this sense, then, a habitus is a set of historical structures that come out of 'socialisation' and determine how a perceptual "world" is structured. Running throughout this book are meditations on this very theme: those historical and social experiences that define the common law and common lawyers. How is precedent a disposition within the system of law? We can crudely understand a disposition as a way of doing things. Thus, precedent, as a disposition, as a way of deciding cases, is based on a practice of judicial interpretation which relates to other parts of the system – i.e. the interpretation of statutes. So, precedent can be thought of as a structuring disposition because it provides the fundamental means (i.e. the structure) through which the common law operates. The important point to grasp is that this "structure" is not anything as such. It is a way that judges and lawyers do things – i.e. interpret and argue cases. In this sense it is a practice. Clearly it has institutional supports – and an institutional location. For instance, it takes place in courts; it presupposes an adversarial presentation of the case. In a wider sense, it presupposes structure of education, the transmission of legal skills and ideas that constitute the law

PUBLIC REASON AND 'RIGHTS ANSWERS': PRECEDENT AS JUDICIAL PRACTICE

[Precedent understood as a judicial practice allows us to see public reason operating in its institutional context] given shape by those constraints that have developed to guide and define judicial law making. Our account of public reason is not 'thick'. We do not seek to argue that judicial reasoning is moral, or based on clear philosophical grounds.[13] Our account of [public reason has two minimal requirements: that judges give reasons for their decisions and that there are institutional structures that stabilize judicial law making.]

Let's try and clarify the terms of our argument. Law is 'a justificatory enterprise'.[14] This tells us something else about legal argument. An argument that does not cohere with the wider structure of law is likely to be a less persuasive and a weaker justification than an argument that appears to 'fit' with the wider principles of the law. It would be wrong, however, to overstate this coherence of law. Law is animated by tensions and shot through with irresolution. The articulation of a clear rule or principle is a product of the interpreter's 'choice' to assert coherence.[15] The law can be thought of as a 'dough' that can be worked into the desired shape. The shape of the 'dough' will be determined by the coherence of the law, the restraints under which the judge is operating, but also by the ethical or political values of the judge him or herself. Duncan Kennedy has put this point well 'an individual's prejudices will determine their approach to legal interpretation, to the "restraints and possibilities that they find in the law."' Legal argument is a 'project' that takes the interpreter through the law.[16] Rules are 'verbal formulae'[17] that drift in and out of consciousness, or become illuminated in different ways when a project presents itself.

Viewed from the position of a more conventional jurisprudence this exercise is unacceptable. [The judge's job is to apply the rules entirely without prejudice. The point is that this is not a realistic model. Interpretative prejudices are always present.] Although interpretation is constrained in some ways, the 'grey area'[18] of rules can be opened to the discretion and interpretive desires of the judge. Our account of precedent acknowledges that judges are not guided by clear rules and principles in all cases. It is the 'messyness' of law that makes an understanding of public reason so important. [Precisely because the nature or existence of a rule or principle is open to question, a judge must show why and how the articulation of his/her position is justifiable.]

Given space limitations within this book, we cannot develop these themes in the way that they deserve. However, we can briefly consider an illustration of our general idea. Consider Lord Hoffmann's speech from the Belmarsh case:

---

as a broad social practice. There is one final point that we want to stress. The notion of habitus can help us to understand the way in which a legal interpreter is both constrained by the structures of the law but at the same time, able to make certain interpretation choice. It is precisely this argument that we develop in the last section of this chapter.

13   For a counter argument, see Penner (2003) and Waldron (2010).
14   Ernest J. Wienrib (1995) 12.
15   Ibid., at 216.
16   Ibid., at 548.
17   Ibid., at 530.
18   Ibid., at 523.

In proceedings in which the appellant to SIAC may have no knowledge of the evidence against him, it would be absurd to require him to prove that it had been obtained by torture. Article 15 of the Torture Convention, which speaks of the use of torture being 'established', could never have contemplated a procedure in which the person against whom the statement was being used had no idea of what it was or who had made it. It must be for SIAC, if there are reasonable grounds for suspecting that to have been the case (for example, because of evidence of the general practices of the authorities in the country concerned) to make its own inquiries and not to admit the evidence unless it is satisfied that such suspicions have been rebutted. One of the difficulties about the Secretary of State's carefully worded statement that it would not be his policy to rely upon evidence 'where there is a knowledge or belief that torture has taken place' is that it leaves open the question of how much inquiry the Secretary of State is willing to make. It appears to be the practice of the security services, in their dealings with those countries in which torture is most likely to have been used, to refrain, as a matter of diplomatic tact or a preference for not learning the truth, from inquiring into whether this was the case. It may be that in such a case the Secretary of State can say that he has no knowledge or belief that torture has taken place. But a court of law would not regard this as sufficient to rebut real suspicion and in my opinion SIAC should not do so.

Lord Hoffmann was not in the majority on this particular point. In other words, the ratio of the case asserted a different test for torture evidence. In the terms of our argument above, our concern is with the 'fit' of this case into the law as a whole. The majority argued that the correct test was for the person alleging that evidence had been obtained by torture to prove it on the balance on probabilities. This illustrates the point we made above: the law is characterised by tensions between different principles and rules. There were, in the Belmarsh case, two entirely arguable versions of the relevant test. If you read the judgment in its entirety, you will find there are different positions that can be taken; each position closely argued and justified. To return again to the language we used above, each position shapes the 'dough' of the law in a particular way; each Law Lord has a different 'project' or vision of the law. How do we choose between arguments?

This question engages our own interpretative prejudices – just as it does those the Law Lords who decided the case. If, for example, we are so minded to agree with Lord Hoffmann, then we need to produce an interpretation of the favoured version of the test that fits into the wider body of legal rules and principles. Lord Hoffman achieves this end in an accomplished way. He argues that it would be 'absurd' for a person alleging that evidence obtained by torture to bear the burden of proof (in other words, the person alleging that evidence obtained by torture had indeed been so obtained). This would be a misinterpretation of Article 15 of the Torture Convention. Notice how Lord Hoffmann is critical of the practices that have grown up around 'not inquiring' whether or not evidence had been obtained by torture. This leaves the opinion on a masterfully critical note. Without explicitly saying it, Lord Hoffmann has effectively contrasted the integrity of the legal process, with the profoundly compromised nature of the 'political' or diplomatic process that, for whatever reason, are not too squeamish about how evidence might have been obtained.

Who is Lord Hoffmann ultimately addressing? We asked this question above, and suggested that there were at least three kinds of audience for a legal judgment. Lord Hoffmann's argument clearly addresses the other Law Lords who decided the case, the lawyers and parties involved. It is also of relevance to all those who are thinking about torture; and has to be placed in a wider public debate. To further elaborate a point that we made above, we could suggest that Lord Hoffmann's speech ultimately addresses the law itself. What do we mean? To shift metaphors again, from words to music, we could equally ask: who does John Coltrane (or Charlie Parker, or Ornette Coleman, or any musician) play for? Perhaps we could say that it is for the music itself; to show what music can do. We have to be careful with this analogy. Law is not music, but, presumably 'showing what music can do' is showing how notes, rhythms, chords etc can be put together: music addresses music. On this analogy, we can hopefully appreciate what we mean when we assert that Lord Hoffmann addresses the law itself. His judgment 'puts the law together' in a particular way. It is a composition that relates together values, principles and rules. There are other compositions; other arguments in the same way that there can always be another improvisation, another tune.

So, to describe precedent as a practice is to draw attention to the activity of judges interpreting law.[19] Interpretation is not free standing but 'takes place' in the various activities that make up legal systems. Practices are shaped by the legal culture and practices in turn affect legal culture. Moreover, practices are never unitary. They are animated by tensions that reflect disagreements over the precise way in which the practice should be performed. A consensus shared between practitioners over the techniques and performances that constitute a practice reflects the stability of the practice as a whole. We will see that judicial interpretation is a relatively stable practice. However, there have been important disputes over its precise operation and in some important areas, notably human rights, debates are on going.

There are some peculiar consequences of this argument. If practices are essentially ways of acting in given circumstances, any general theory may be too distant from the practice to capture how judges actually interpret cases. Judicial interpretation is always a matter of a specific case and a singular set of facts. To understand why a judge in a particular case comes to the conclusion that s/he does necessitates a study of a precise legal context. In other words, a general account of precedent perhaps can at best provide no more than a 'thin' description of underlying structures. It may be that the best way to understand the practice of judicial interpretation is to see

---

19   Appellate courts create precedents in common law system. The U.S. Supreme Court, settles conflicts over the status of law within a particular constitutional framework laid down at independence. A key factor in the choosing of new Supreme Court judges is their attitude to precedent. Court decisions either reaffirm or create precedents. It is clear that despite it's reliance on precedent, the Court will depart from its prior decisions when either historical conditions change or the philosophy of the court undergoes a major shift. The most famous reversal of precedent is *Brown v. Board of Education*, 347 U.S. 483, 74 S. Ct. 686, 98 L. Ed. 873 (1954), in which the Supreme Court repudiated the 'separate but equal' doctrine of *Plessy v. Ferguson*, 163 U.S. 537, 16 S. Ct. 1138, 41 L. Ed. 256 (1896). This doctrine had legitimated racial segregation for almost 60 years but finally gave way in Brown, when a unanimous court ruled that separate but equal was a denial of equal protection of the laws.

how it proceeds in different doctrinal areas of law. This would indicate that the best way to understand the practice of precedent is to study cases within their specific contexts.[20]

To bring these points together with our arguments above: our study of precedent is bound to be somewhat disappointing. It will outline, in rather bald terms, basic structures and how they inform judicial reasoning. However, in a more meaningful way, it will enable the tyro to get the basics: and to realise that the study of law in its entirety is the study of those precedent cases that define doctrines. As the American poet Ezra Pound suggested: there is no substitution for a lifetime. Get to work.

CONCLUSION

This chapter has focused upon the legitimacy of judicial law making. We started from the understanding that judges make law, and then sought to establish what factors legitimate such an activity. Our answer presupposes that judges work within the context of a democratic society, where their decisions have to be justifiable, foreseeable and coherent. We drew attention to the role that public reason plays in requiring reasoned judgment, and the institutional constraints provided by the doctrine of precedent. We then examined the idea of precedent as an interpretative practice that is driven, at least in part, by the interpreter's prejudices. It is worth stressing that our understanding of judicial practice accepts the inescapable nature of interpretative prejudice as making for good quality decision making; themes we will pick up on in the next three chapters.

CODA: THE LIMITS OF HUMAN RIGHTS

If the doctrine of precedent provides institutional restraints for judicial creativity, what restraints are there within human rights law? It would seem, first of all, that there is far greater lassitude for interpretations of the Convention. The ECtHR sees the treaty as 'a living instrument which . . . must be interpreted in the light of present-day conditions'.[21] This is a dynamic principle that allows the court to update principles so they relate to changing conditions. But, what guides judicial interpretation? There are a number of statements from the Strasbourg court that offer guidelines for the interpreter. Although the ECtHR does not follow a binding doctrine of precedent, the

---

20 English legal education does not contain a formal training in precedent. The study of precedent is restricted (for the most part) to an element of a first year introductory course of the LLB (and was absent from the CPE and the now GDL). To understand the law is to read cases, and to engage in practical arguments about them. Likewise, professional training does not consist of training courses on the interpretation of cases. On the whole this reflects the empirical and practical culture of the common law – and the fact that until relatively recently legal training was more akin to an apprenticeship than a course of university study. The law in general and precedent in particular, are thus essentially ways of 'doing' law that have never seen the usefulness of general or abstract accounts of their operation.

21 *Tyrer v. UK*, No. 5856/72, 25.4.1978, para 31.

Figure 6.1 Dining in common, Middle Temple, 1840s. Credit MEPL

Why put so much emphasis upon the idea of practice? Legal education in the common law until the advent of university education in law in the later nineteenth century, and developing through the twentieth, was a matter of apprenticeship, of learning in practice and for those who wished to participate in the dealings of the courts of joining one of the four Inns of Court, attending lectures and most importantly living the common life (dining and drinking). One way of understanding the need for modern rules of precedent is proposed by A.W.B. Simpson, namely that historically 'the common law is best understood as a system of customary law, that is, a body of traditional ideas received within a caste of experts'. Practice determines the reality of a rules operation and acceptance, since 'as a system of legal thought the common law . . . is inherently vague' (1973, p. 90). It is not that everything is always in the melting pot 'but that you never quite know what will go in next'. Simpson identifies the common law system as 'a body of practices observed and ideas received by a caste of lawyers, those ideas being used by them as providing guidance in what is conceived to be the rational determination of disputes litigated before them, or by them on behalf of clients and other contexts. These ideas and practices exist only in the sense that they are accepted and acted upon within the legal profession, just as customary practices can be said to exist within a group in the sense that they are observed, accepted as appropriate forms of behaviour and transmitted both by example and precept as membership of the group changes' (p. 94). The modern (positivist) rules of binding precedent and determination of the 'authority' of the statements to be found in the mushrooming sources of law (the vast expansion of law reports) is a response to the breakdown of the previous largely un-stated techniques of acceptance on the corpus of ideas and processes and requires new mechanisms for the transmission of the traditional ideas and the encouragement of orthodoxy, new forms of learning the processes of deference, of when to innovate when to follow almost mechanically. In a time when the legal profession was small 'the law was the peculiar possession of a small, tightly organised group comprising those who were concerned in the operation of the Royal courts', and within this group the judges and senior barristers were crucial. 'Orthodox ideas were transmitted largely orally, and even the available literary sources were written in a private language as late as the seventeenth century. A wide variety of institutional arrangements tended to produce cohesion of thought. These have changed and diversity now is sought, the common law is no longer able to be confined as a system of customary law and arrangements, but the basic point remains that 'to argue that this or that is the correct view, as academics, judges, and counsel do, is to *participate* in the system, not simply to study it scientifically. (p. 97)

This is also the rise of the textbook. As Birks puts it: 'it ought to be possible to take any legal subject and to cut away its detail so as to reveal the skeleton of principle which holds it together', and then keep that elementary structure under constant review. This skeleton of principle is a particular organisation, 'a version chosen from a number of possibilities'. The choice is made, not in the cases themselves but found outside the adversary institutions in the production of the 'textbook'. Since the late nineteenth century, 'textbooks have borne the responsibility for restraining the centrifugal tendencies of case-law. If subjects such as contract or tort now are accepted as having a settled structure it is not because of some pure structure that the subject rationally follows, but 'because generations of textbooks, from different hands and going through successive editions, have selected and evolved a structure which for the moment seems best fitted to the matter' (Birks, 1985, pp. 1–2).

Grand Chamber has stated that 'it is in the interests of legal certainty, foreseeability and equality before the law that it should not depart, without good reason, from precedents laid down in previous cases'.[22] As far as interpretations of the Convention rights themselves are concerned, the court asserted in *Wemhoff* v. *Germany*, that it will 'seek the interpretation that is most appropriate in order to realise the aim and achieve the object of the treaty' in order to elaborate human rights principles, and will refrain from following an interpretation 'which would restrict to the greatest possible degree the obligations undertaken by the Parties'.[23] The object of the treaty is to 'maintain and promote the ideals and values of a democratic society' – or – to further 'the protection of individual human beings' and ensure that the rights provided are 'practical and effective'.[24] The Convention must also be interpreted in such a way as to 'promote internal consistency and harmony between its various provisions' and so as to be coherent with the 'relevant rules and principles of international law'.[25]

As we will see in Chapter 8, these principles can lead to tensions between the interpretations offered by domestic courts, and those favoured by Strasbourg. However, we need, for the moment, to deal with a question of the legitimacy of human rights law, given the interpretative freedom that it appears to give judges. Certainly critics of human rights have seized on this problem. Human rights are not properly 'legal'; they are somehow 'too' indeterminate. Rulings on human rights are not sufficiently guided or restrained by principle. Furthermore, Strasbourg decisions are essentially political interpretations of matters best left to national Parliaments. We can deal with these points in order. As we will show below, all legal interpretation involves a set of interpretative choices. It is difficult to prove that human rights are either more or less indeterminate than other areas of legal doctrine. Detailed study of human rights doctrines would, no doubt, show that developments within human rights law are as predictable as those in other areas of law. In other words, Strasbourg's commitment to

---

22 *Christine Goodwin* v. *UK*, No. 28957/95 [GC], 11.7.2002, para 74.
23 *Wemhoff* v. *Germany*, No. 2122/64, 27.6.1968, para 8.
24 *Kjeldsen, Busk Madsen and Pedersen* v. *Denmark*, Nos. 5095/71, 5920/72 and 5926/72, 7.12.1976, para 53;
25 *Soering* v. *UK*, No. 14038/88, 7.7.1989, para 87; see also *Saadi* v. *UK*, No. 13229/03 [GC], 29.1.2008, para 62.

'certainty' and 'foreseeability', and the principles underlying human rights law, provide institutional and structural restraints that allow more or less coherent development of doctrine.

How can we deal with the other criticism? Those who object to the political elements of human rights do not perceive the political elements inherent in legal decisions. All legal decisions offer a 'template for . . . human life' in one way or another. If politics cannot be 'stripped out' of law, then we must acknowledge that law is a way of doing politics by other means. This underlies the law of human rights. Judicial development of human rights principles is a way of understanding a compelling idea of the rule of law: there should be limits on the power of government.

7

WHAT WE TALK ABOUT WHEN WE TALK ABOUT COMMON LAW: THE PRACTICE OF PRECEDENT

INTRODUCTION

The contention of this chapter is that the doctrine of precedent is best seen as a practice through which many competing pressures are, if not reconciled, at least kept in a workable equilibrium. Our study of precedent will begin with an overview of the tension between hierarchy and flexibility. We will then look specifically at the relationship between the House of Lords and the Court of Appeal, and the possible development of an alternative practice of judicial interpretation. The final sections will engage specifically with judicial law making and human rights.

We will see that it is difficult to produce any clear overarching theory of judicial law making, as it relies on the discretion and sense of a judge to 'do the right thing'. Rather like a Raymond Carver story, the unsaid is as important as the said. This theme points back at the practice of precedent: it is a way of reading, interpreting and justifying arguments within institutional constraints. The chapter will conclude with some final reflections on substantive justice and procedural legitimacy.

THE HIERARCHY OF COURTS AND BINDING PRECEDENT

⌐The practice of precedent works within the context of the court structure; the hierarchy of the courts provide the fundamental institutional structure.⌐ ⌐The doctrine asserts that decisions of the Appellant Committee of the House of Lords bind all the courts below it in the hierarchy.[2]⌐ *London Tramways* v. *London City Council* (1898)

----

1 This can be seen as having three distinct elements: 'These are the respect paid to a single decision of a superior court, the fact that a decision of such a court is a persuasive precedent even as far as the courts above that from which it emanates are concerned, and the fact that a single decision is always a binding precedent as regards courts below that from which it emanated.' Cross and Harris, 1991, p.3. ⌐The hierarchy of the courts is based on the 'respect' given to the decisions of superior courts. The 'binding' nature of precedent applies to the inferior courts.⌐ However, as the persuasive nature of an inferior court on a superior court has not been a particularly contentious issue, we will not consider it in this chapter. However, note that these distinctive features of precedent are introduced as being an accurate description '[a]t present' (5). This is somewhat peculiar. It suggests that the doctrine itself is developing and changing over time. Any global definition has to be sensitive to this particular problem; a problem that corresponds with the idea that precedent is a practice, and that practices themselves develop.

2 This could be linked to the dominance of the declaratory theory of common law interpretation.

was central to the foundation of what was to become the conventional form of the doctrine. In *London Tramways*, the House of Lords decided that it was bound by its own previous decisions:

> Of course, I do not deny that cases of individual hardship may arise, and there may be a current of opinion in the profession that such and such a judgment was erroneous; but what is that occasional interference with what is perhaps abstract justice, as compared with the inconvenience ... of having each question subject to being rearguarded and the dealings of mankind rendered doubtful by reason of different decisions, so that in truth there is no final court of appeal. My Lords, 'interest rei publicae' is that there should be '*finis litium*' sometime and there can be no *finis litium* if it were possible to suggest in each case that it might be reargued because it is 'not an ordinary case' whatever that may mean.[3]

Lord Halsbury acknowledges that cases of individual hardship may result from the House of Lords being bound by its own decisions. However, the need for clear general principles over-rides the hardship caused in individual instances. Does the need for general principles also over-ride the requirement that the court make just judgments? Lord Halsbury rules that justice is of little consequence in comparison with the need for finality in litigation. His argument denies that there could be such a thing as an extraordinary case where justice may demand a departure from general principles.

London Tramways lays down the parameters of modern practice demonstrating a preference for a clear, unambiguous statement of the binding nature of precedent. Very little allowance is made for a departure from the hierarchical ordering of the courts.[4] Sixty-eight years later the Practice Statement of 1966 stressed the need for the flexible development of the law:

> Their Lordships regard the use of precedent as an indispensable foundation upon which to decide what is the law and its application to individual cases. It provides at least some certainty upon which individuals can rely in the conduct of their affairs, as well as a basis for the development of legal rules.[5]

What does this tell us about the re-shaping of the practice? Precedent is now described as fulfilling a dual function: it has a doctrinal aspect – the development of legal rules, and a social function as well. We find a different argument from that of Lord Halsbury:

> Their Lordships nevertheless recognise that too rigid adherence to precedent may lead to injustice in a particular case and also unduly restrict the proper development of the law.[6]

The Practice Statement reclaims the concern for the individual case; it asserts that there is no point having general rules, if these lead to injustice in individual instances. What

3   *London Tramways v. London City Council* [1898] AC 375.
4   *Rookes v. Barnard* [1964] AC 1129.
5   Practice Statement (Judicial Precedent) [1966] 1 WLR 1234, at 1234.
6   Ibid., 1234.

is to be done? Their Lordships resolve to 'modify' the way they approach precedent: they will consider that they are normally bound by their previous decisions, but, in certain cases they will depart from previous decisions when 'it is right to do so'.[7] How are we to know when the time is right? Their Lordships will consider:

> the danger of disturbing the basis on which contracts, settlements of property and fiscal arrangements have been entered into and also the especial need for certainty as to the criminal law.[8]

This gives some general guidelines as to how the judges will understand the institutional legitimacy of their practice. The law would be illegitimate if it simply asserted the need for general rules, and ignored the fact that justice required general rules to be changed. However, the law would also become illegitimate if it simply treated each case as exceptional and failed to develop general rules. Law fulfills a social function: there is a social interest in settled general principles of law. If there is an implicit acknowledgement of judicial law making in the Practice Statement, there is also an understanding that the power should be used sparingly and that stability would ultimately be preferred to creativity.

In the years after 1966, it indeed became clear that departing from precedent decisions would only take place in very rare circumstances. We can develop this point by examining some important decisions. In *Miliangos* v. *George Frank*[10] the House of Lords departed from a previous decision, arguing that changing the law would enable the courts to 'keep step with commercial needs' and, furthermore, would not lead to 'practical and procedural difficulties'. The following passage from Lord Wilberforce's judgment is worth considering in detail:

> The law on this topic is judge-made: it has been built up over the years from case to case. It is entirely within this House's duty, in the course of administering justice, to give the law a new direction in a particular case where, on principle and in reason, it appears right to do so. I cannot accept the suggestion that because a rule is long established only legislation can change it – that may be so when the rule is so deeply entrenched that it has infected the whole legal system, or the choice of a new rule involves more far-reaching research than courts can carry out. Indeed, from some experience in the matter, I am led to doubt whether legislative reform, at least prompt and

....

7   Later in this chapter, we will see that this claim coordinates with one about the need to do justice in individual cases.

8   Supra n. 5, at 1234.

9   Some indications are given in *Jones* v. *Secretary of State for Social Services* [1972] 1 AC 944. It is insufficient that the case was wrongly decided. Lord Reid refused to give precise criteria – arguing only that experience would prove to be a guide for discretion. He indicated that it would involve 'broad issues' – of both justice and legal principle – and that in the instant case neither of these criteria were present. Lord Wilberforce argued on slightly different grounds that if an interpretation of a statute had been given, then, unless Parliament was to change that statute, the interpretation was to stand. Lord Pearson's argument stressed the idea of 'finality of decision' supported by arguments with which we are already familiar. Of all the judgments, Lord Simon's is perhaps the most interesting, because he provides a list of reasons for not departing from the earlier case. Alongside reasons with which we are already familiar, he added a consideration of the nature of the parties and the litigation in issue – it was a revenue case with frequent litigants.

10   *Miliangos* v. *George Frank* [1975] 3 WLR 758.

comprehensive reform, in this field of foreign currency obligation, is practicable. Questions as to the recovery of debts or of damages depend so much upon individual mixtures of facts and merits as to make them more suitable for progressive solutions in the courts. I think that we have an opportunity to reach such a solution here. I would accordingly depart from the Havana Railways case and dismiss this appeal.[11]

Lord Wilberforce argues that because the law in this area is judge made, it is legitimate to alter it provided that 'on principle and in reason, it appears right to do so'. The sterling principle for the award of damages had become anachronistic. The law of damages has to keep pace with modern developments. There is thus a strong argument for change. However, it is also important to note that the rule can be changed without upsetting other deep-seated principles. Miliangos thus refers to a set of rules that may be of ancient providence, but, because they are in an area of judge-made law, it would not be necessary to defer to Parliament. The particular mixture of 'facts and merits' makes this pre-eminently an area for judicial law making.[12]

Miliangos indicates the factors that legitimise judicial law making in civil law. Are there similar considerations in criminal law? Given limitations of space, we will look in detail at two important cases: Shivpuri and Howe. In R. v. Shivpuri,[13] the House of Lords overruled itself. The case concerned the construction of s.1 of the Criminal Attempts Act 1981.[14] In an earlier case, Anderton v. Ryan,[15] the House of Lords had argued that the section could be approached on the basis of a distinction between acts that were 'objectively innocent', and those that were not so considered. However, in Shivpuri they were of the opinion that Anderton had been wrongly decided.

Lord Bridge's judgment in Shivpuri is worth looking at in detail, in particular his criticisms of the notion of objective innocence. He argues that the concept is 'incapable of sensible application' in criminal law. This is very emphatic language. The concept of objective innocence makes little sense because it avoids the central concept of the actor's intention. This is the essential ingredient in the law of attempt. Thus, if a person attempts to buy drugs, but is sold a harmless substitute, the criminal law must approach the attempted offence from the viewpoint of the actor's criminal intention. It would be wrong to argue that 'objectively' the act is innocent because the drugs did not

---

11   Ibid., at 470.
12   A close reading of the relevant cases might suggest the presence, or variation, of some of Lord Wilberforce's concerns in Jones. Arguments about social change lie behind *Herrington v. British Railways Board* [1972] AC 877. It is no longer acceptable that a property owner should have limited responsibilities to trespassers, and the law must be amended accordingly. However, in *Knuller v. D.P.P.* [1973] AC 435 the House of Lords refused to overrule *Shaw v. D.P.P.* [1962] AC 220. Does this suggest that there are slightly different considerations in criminal law? In *Shaw*, the court made the claim that it had a jurisdiction to try offences against good morals, even though Parliament had not legislated to cover such behaviour, or the existing law was either ambiguous or silent. In *Knuller*, the court refused to overrule the earlier case even though it was wrong. Does this suggest that their Lordships are willing to go munch further in the area of social control, than they are in commercial law or tort?
13   *R. v. Shivpuri* [1986] 2 WLR 988.
14   The section provided that a person is guilty of an offence if s/he does an act which is 'more than merely preparatory'. 1(2) goes on to state that even if 'the facts are such that the commission of the offence is impossible', a person may still be found guilty of an attempt to commit an offence.
15   *Anderton v. Ryan* [1985] AC 560.

exist. Acts cannot be considered 'independently' of the state of mind of the actor.[16] Lord Bridge also stressed his own 'conviction' as a 'party to the decision' that *Anderton* was 'wrong'.[17]

If *Anderton* was so clearly flawed, what course of action was open to the House of Lords? It was not possible to distinguish *Anderton* from *Shivpuri*. If their Lordships were bound by the unworkable test, the law of attempt would be based on flawed concepts. The only alternative would be to invoke the Practice Statement. Was this a justifiable course of action? Departing from a precedent case would lead to uncertainty in the law. However, in *Shivpuri* this was justifiable. As *Anderton* was a recent decision, settled law had not yet developed. However, this is not the determining factor. The most pressing factor is the need to correct a 'serious error', 'a distor(tion)' in the law.[18]

It might appear, then, that any understanding of the interpretation of *Shivpuri* is rooted in the context of the criminal law, and the serious error in which the House of Lords had fallen into in *Anderton*. Can we observe a similar pattern if we turn our attention to a *R. v. Howe*?[19]

In *Lynch*[20] the House of Lords had held that the defence of duress was available to someone who had been charged with aiding or abetting murder.[21] In *R. v. Howe*[22] the House of Lords over-ruled this decision. As with *Shivpuri*, we encounter very strong language. Lord Bridge asserted 'I can find nothing whatever to be said for leaving the law as it presently stands'.[23] He went on to argue that an 'odd quirk of the system' had allowed the decision in *Lynch* to stand, despite the fact that four out of the seven presiding law lords (in the appellate courts in Northern Ireland and England) had rejected the reasoning in the case.[24]

Lord Hailsham argued that *R. v. Howe* afforded an 'ideal and never to be repeated opportunity' to re-consider the issue from the standpoint of 'authority'.[25] A review of the law of homicide stretching back to Hale and Blackstone showed that duress had never been available for murder. It was possible to invoke the Practice Statement

16   Ibid., at 22. An alternative ground to justify the decision in *Anderton* was to analyse attempts in terms of the actor's 'dominant intention'. However, this test also runs into difficulties, because it is very difficult to distinguish between dominant intention and incidental beliefs; there are also problems in devising any way of articulating a meaningful test that would be helpful to a jury.
17   Ibid., 22.
18   Ibid., 12.
19   *R. v. Howe* [1987] 2 WLR 568.
20   *DPP for Northern Ireland v. Lynch* [1975] 2 WLR 641.
21   Per Lord Bridge: in the law established by *Lynch* and *Abbott*, duress is a complete defence to a murderer otherwise guilty as a principal in the second degree, it is no defence to a murderer guilty as a principal in the first degree.
22   *R. v. Howe* [1987] 2 WLR 417.
23   Ibid., at 437.
24   Ibid., at 436. Lord Bridge is discussing the two cases that establish the present law: *Lynch* and the Privy Council case, *Abbott v. The Queen* [1977] AC 755. Although the two cases come from 'two distinct jurisdiction', three Lords of Appeal sat in both cases. The 'odd quirk of the system' is that 'the two decisions should have had the "combined effect of affirming a distinction which four out of the seven participants in the decisions rejected".
25   Ibid., at 427.

because *Lynch* could not 'be justified on authority'.[26] Furthermore, 'judicial legislation [had] proved to be an excessive and perhaps improvident use of the undoubted power of the courts to create new law by creating precedents in individual cases'.[27] The improvident use of judicial legislation in *Lynch* was also indicated by Parliament's refusal to legislate on the issue. Lord Bridge pointed out that Parliament had not acted on the Report of the Law Commission's recommendation to allow a defence of duress.[28] Parliament's refusal to legislate suggests that the judges should not have taken upon themselves the reform of the law.

Lynch was fundamentally wrong in principle. Lord Hailsham justified this criticism by referring to the overriding objects of the criminal law to set standards of conduct that are clear in specifying how people are to 'avoid criminal responsibility'.[29] This means that the duress defence must not blur the offence of murder. The law must be based on the principle that it is never justifiable to commit murder, even to save one's own life. Does this mean, though, that as other offences allow a duress defence, the criminal law is inconsistent? This criticism is met with an argument from principle: 'consistency and logic . . . are not always prime characteristics of a penal code based like the common law on custom and precedent'.[30] Indeed, if law is an art, rather than 'an exact science',[31] a pragmatic response to problems is more important than a consistent development of abstract principles.[32]

What, then, can *Howe* and *Shivpuri* tell us about the practice of precedent within criminal law? The Law Lords in both cases approach the law from the perspective that there has to be very compelling arguments for change. The House of Lords will overrule itself when it has fallen into serious error, and when the circumstances of the case are such that it is practical to overrule an earlier decision. These narrow guidelines preserve the legitimacy of judicial law making. The House of Lords is ensuring the consistent development of principles. Criminal law is legitimised as the courts dispel the errors into which they have fallen. It is not necessary to depart from the hierarchical organisation of the courts to achieve this end. However, in turning to the question of the Court of Appeal's jurisdiction, we now have to grapple with this very problem. How does this raise the problem of institutional legitimacy in a slightly different context?

THE HOUSE OF LORDS AND THE COURT OF APPEAL: PRECEDENT AND JUSTICE

Perhaps one of the most fraught questions in the area of precedent relates to the right of the Court of Appeal to depart from a judgment of the House of Lords. This is linked to the question of whether the Court of Appeal was bound to follow its own decisions.

26 Ibid., at 429.
27 Ibid., at 430.
28 Ibid., at 437.
29 Ibid.
30 Ibid., at 423.
31 Ibid.
32 Ibid., at 434.

Tensions between the Court of Appeal and the House of Lords had developed in *Schorsch Meier*. The Court of Appeal had argued that circumstances had changed so much since the House of Lords ruling in *Havana Railways*[33] that 'the sterling judgment rule' principle should no longer apply. Denning MR stated that the underlying reason for damages being given in sterling was essentially 'practical'.[34] He went on to invoke the principle *cessante ratione legis cessat ipsa lex*[35] or – as he pithily put it '[s]eeing that the reasons no longer exist, we are at liberty to discard the rule itself'.[36] Lord Denning justified this principle by arguing that it would be wrong to abrogate substantive rights by reference to procedural concerns.[37] Furthermore, he pointed out (and Lawton LJ agreed) that Article 106 of the Treaty of Rome required that judgment should be given in the currency of the member state in which the creditor resided.[38]

This suggests the development of an alternative practice of interpretation that departs from the conventional understanding of the doctrine of the hierarchy of the courts.[39] The response of the House of Lords to the Court of Appeal in *Schorsch Meier* came in *Miliangos*. Lord Simon, with the explicit agreement of Lord Wilberforce, rejected Lord Denning's use of the *cessante ratione legis cesset ipsa lex* principle. The wide meaning of the principle would mean that any court could 'disclaim any authority of any higher court on the ground that the reason which had led to such higher court's formulation of the rule of law was no longer relevant'. Application of the principle would mean that the court could even overrule Acts of Parliament, if it judged that the reasons for the rule no longer applied; as such, the rule has 'no place in our own modern constitution'.[40]

This re-assertion of the conventional understanding of the practice did not prevent another deviation arising on a later occasion. However, the matter now concerned the question of whether the Court of Appeal could depart from its own previous decisions. The conventional position, as stated in *Young* v. *Bristol Aeroplane Co.* asserted that even if the Court of Appeal regretted a previous decision, it was obliged to follow it and recommend an appeal to the House of Lords.[41] As the Court of Appeal was

---

33   In Re United Railways of Havana [1961] A.C 1007.

34   *Schorsch Meier* v. *Henin* [1975] QB 416., at 428. It was outside the competence of the court to determine the value of a currency other than sterling; besides, it was 'appropriate to trading conditions' in a time before instantaneous communications (ibid.).

35   Ibid., at 425.

36   Ibid., at 425.

37   However, it would appear that there are at least two factors that justify the use of the principle. In a prior case, *Jugoslavenska Oceanska Plovidba* v. *Castle Investment Co. Inc.* [1974] QB 292, the court had allowed arbitrators to make awards in foreign currency. Denning MR also made reference to this principle in the Court of Appeal's hearing of *Miliangos*.

38   Supra, n. 34, at 431.

39   See also *Broome* v. *Cassell* [1972] AC 1027. The Court of Appeal had attempted to show that the House of Lords had acted *per incuriam*, or incorrectly in the case *Rookes* v. *Barnard* [1964] AC 1129. The case concerned the issue of damages. Lord Hailsham articulated the conventional position clearly: 'In the hierarchical system of courts which exist in this country, it is necessary for each lower tier, including the Court of Appeal, to accept loyally the decisions of the higher tiers.' Lord Hailsham's words return to the notion that far worse than individual injustice is the compromise of general principles.

40   Supra n. 10, at 476.

41   *Young* v. *Bristol Aeroplane Co.* [1944] KB 718, at 725. This would also apply whether the Court of Appeal was sitting as a 'full court' or as a division with only three members present.

created by statute, it had to adhere to its statutory powers, and could not exceed its limited role.[42]

Lord Denning attempted to avoid this rule in *Davis v. Johnson*.[43] In *Davis v. Johnson*, the Court of Appeal considered the case of a victim of domestic violence. Ms Davis had unsuccessfully asked the court for an order to compel her abusive partner to leave the flat that they had been sharing. To allow her appeal, the Court of Appeal would need to depart from previous decisions where injunctions had not been awarded in similar situations.[44] Lord Denning made a strong argument from principle. He began by admitting that, in normal cases, the Court of Appeal was bound by its own previous decisions. He went on to criticise the consequences of this argument. It may be that an appeal is never made to the House of Lords, or that there is a long delay before the House of Lords has an opportunity to over turn an incorrect decision.[45] It may also be that an individual lacks the financial means to bring the appeal to the House of Lords. This problem is compounded by the fact that wealthy litigants can 'pay off' appellants, and so perpetuate a decision erroneous in law. Moreover, in the present case, the delay that an appeal would cause would add to Ms Davis' hardship. She was resident in a battered women's refuge in 'appallingly' overcrowded conditions:

> In order to avoid all the delay – and the injustice consequent upon it – it seems to me that this court, being convinced that the two previous decisions were wrong, should have the power to correct them and give these women the protection which Parliament intended they should have.[46]

There is a compelling case for the avoidance of delay. However, what are the consequences of allowing the Court of Appeal to overrule itself? Would the lower courts be left in confusion? For instance, a judge in a county court would not know which Court of Appeal case stated the correct law. Lord Denning argues that the lower court would simply follow the later decision, based on the principle that as long as the later case contains a 'full consideration' of the earlier cases, it was the preferable authority.[47]

This is a good illustration of the conflict between general procedural principles and individual injustice. But, how, as a question of law, would it be possible to get around

---

42   Lord Greene concludes: 'On a careful examination of the whole matter we have come to the clear conclusion that this court is bound to follow previous decisions of its own as well as those of courts of co-ordinate jurisdiction. The only exceptions to this rule (two of them apparent only) are those already mentioned which for convenience we here summarise: (1) The court is entitled and bound to decide which of two conflicting decisions of its own it will follow. (2) The court is bound to refuse to follow a decision of its own which, though not expressly overruled, cannot, in its opinion, stand with a decision of the House of Lords. (3) The court is not bound to follow a decision of its own if it is satisfied that the decision was given per incuriam.'

43   *Davis v. Johnson* [1974] AC264.

44   In *B v. B* [1978] 1 All ER 821 and *Cantliff v. Jenkins* [1978] 2 WLR, it was held that the county court did not in fact have the power that it claimed under the Act. The task of the court in *Davis v. Johnson* is to 'review' the decisions – and if they are wrong, to articulate correct principles. Clearly, against this position is the conventional argument that the Court of Appeal is bound to follow its own previous cases in the area, and if the law is incorrect, it must be altered by an appeal to the House of Lords.

45   The example is the 60 year period before the wrong decision in *Carlisle and Cumberland Banking Co. Ltd. v. Bragg* [1911] 1 KB 489 was corrected in *Gallie v. Lee* [1971] AC 1004.

46   Supra, n. 43, at 280.

47   *Minister of Pensions v. Higham* [1948] 2 KB 153, 155.

Bristol Aeroplane Co.? Lord Denning showed that *Bristol Aeroplane Co.* was not an accurate statement of the law. This argument returns to roots of the jurisdiction of the Court of Appeal. When the Court was set up in 1873, it was the final appellate court, as the jurisdiction of the House of Lords was not established until 1875. The Court 'inherited' the jurisdiction of the Exchequer Chamber and the Court of Appeal in Chancery. As these courts were always considered to have the power to review their own decisions, it would be fair to assume that the new court had inherited this jurisdiction.[48] The argument also returns to *Hutton* v. *Bright*[49] which held that 'every court of justice possesses an inherent power to correct an error in which it had fallen'. What conclusion can be drawn from this argument? As Lord Denning succinctly puts it, *Young* v. *Bristol Aeroplane Co* 'overruled the practice of a century'.[50] The Court of Appeal is not, as a matter of law, bound to follow its previous decisions. It does so as a 'matter of judicial comity'.[51] Arguing that the 1966 Practice Statement effectively overturns the *London Tramways* case, Lord Denning concludes:

> a rule as to precedent (which any court lays down for itself) is not a rule of law at all. It is simply a practice or usage laid down by the court itself for its own guidance: and, as such, the successors of that court can alter that practice or amend it or set up other guide lines, just as the House of Lords did in 1966.[52]

We are compelled to the conclusion that the Court of Appeal can follow the 1966 Practice Statement and depart from its own decisions if it considers them wrongly decided.

These arguments were not ultimately successful. The conventional form of the doctrine was re-asserted by the House of Lords.[53] The court considered the alternative approach to the problem articulated by Sir George Barker P and Shaw LJ in the Court of Appeal.[54] The latter had argued that '*stare decisis* should be relaxed' only when applying a precedent would mean that 'actual and potential victims of violence' would be deprived of the protection afforded them by an Act of Parliament. It was stressed that this situation would be very rare. However, Lord Diplock preferred that the House of Lords should 're-affirm expressly, unequivocally and unanimously' the rule in *Bristol Aeroplane Co.*[55]

Viscount Dilhorne elaborated this argument. It had to be the case that the 1966 Practice Statement applied only to the House of Lords. If it did not, any court could argue that it was not bound by its previous decisions. Lord Denning's argument ignored 'the unique character of the House of Lords sitting judicially'.[56] As the Practice

---

48   Supra, n. 43, at 195.
49   *Hutton* v. *Bright* (1852) 3 HL Case 341.
50   Supra, n. 43 at 196.
51   Ibid.
52   Ibid., at 197.
53   The House of Lords rejected the argument that the CA could depart from its own decisions if it considered itself to be in error, and affirmed the doctrine with which we are familiar. The CA is bound by its own decisions, except in the exceptions laid down in *Bristol Aeroplane*.
54   Supra, n. at 43.
55   Ibid., at 328.
56   Ibid., at 336.

Statement was based on this feature of the House of Lords, it could not be extended to another court. Lord Salmon and Lord Diplock elaborated this point by citing the concluding words of the 1966 Statement: 'This announcement is not intended to affect the use of precedent elsewhere than in this House.'[57] Furthermore, the fact that there are up to 17 Lord Justice in the Court of Appeal meant that, if Lord Denning's arguments were followed to their conclusion, there was the risk that there would be a 'plethora of conflicting decisions' which would lead to great confusion in the law. Lord Salmon's argument goes some way to countering some of Lord Denning's points about the denial of justice, by proposing that the Court of Appeal could be given a power to grant, when circumstance dictated, the payment of costs out of public funds.

Davis v. *Johnson* is a unique case. Although Lord Denning's arguments make a compelling case for the Court of Appeal to respond to the demand for justice, the House of Lords effectively asserted that there are no exceptions to the priority of general procedural rules. The case shows judicial law making at its most dramatic. Perhaps this is precisely the problem. Lord Denning has an eccentric appreciation of the boundaries of institutional legitimacy. He raises the protection of substantive rights over the general understanding of the limits of judicial creativity. For the purposes of our argument, we need to locate a more modest understanding of the legitimate parameters of judicial legislation. However – as we will see towards the end of the chapter – substantive issues of justice cannot be entirely expelled from judicial practice.

JUDICIAL LAW MAKING

Determining the boundaries of judicial law making is partly a doctrinal and partly a constitutional question. If we require some broad guidelines, a useful place to start is Lord Scarman's speech in *McLoughlin Appellant* v. *O'Brian*.[58] The appeal in this case raised the very question of the relationship between the legislature and the judiciary. Lord Scarman argued that the judge had a jurisdiction over a common law that 'knows no gaps' and no '*casus omissus*'. If this is the case, the task of the common law judge is to adapt the principles of the law to allow a decision to be made on the facts in hand. This may involve the creation of new law. Whatever the case, judicial reasoning begins from 'a baseline of existing principle'. The judge works towards a solution that can be seen as an extension of principle by process of analogy. For Lord Scarman, this is the 'distinguishing feature of the common law': the judicial creation of new law, as the justice of the case demands. This process may involve policy considerations, but, the judge can legitimately involve him/herself in this activity, provided that the primary outcome is the formation of new legal principles. In those cases where the formation of principle involves too great an intrusion into the field of policy, the judge must defer to Parliament:

---

57   Ibid., at 344.
58   *McLoughlin* v. *O'Brian* [1983] 1 AC 410.

Here lies the true role of the two law-making institutions in our constitution. By concentrating on principle the judges can keep the common law alive, flexible and consistent, and can keep the legal system clear of policy problems which neither they, nor the forensic process which it is their duty to operate, are equipped to resolve. If principle leads to results which are thought to be socially unacceptable, Parliament can legislate to draw a line or map out a new path.[59]

This argument demarcates quite clearly the role of judge and Parliament. Judicial interpretation keeps the common law 'flexible' and responsive to change, and defers to Parliament on those issues with which the courts are not well equipped to deal. Parliament also acts as a final adjudicator. If the courts make mistakes, they can be corrected by legislation. Whilst this argument is compelling, it is hard to see precisely where the dividing line lies between principle and policy. We will examine this issue below, but it is perhaps worth bearing in mind that where this line falls is a rather complex issue that cannot be precisely determined by some general theory. Before we examine this issue, however, it is worth looking at another aspect of Lord Scarman's argument:

The real risk to the common law is not its movement to cover new situations and new knowledge but lest it should stand still, halted by a conservative judicial approach. If that should happen, and since the 1966 practice direction of the House it has become less likely, there would be a danger of the law becoming irrelevant to the consideration, and inept in its treatment, of modern social problems. Justice would be defeated. The common law has, however, avoided this catastrophe by the flexibility given it by generations of judges.[60]

This is the second reference to justice in this passage – and it might suggest that Lord Scarman's account of judicial creativity is indeed underpinned by such a concept. It is a description of the common law judge as the guardian of the conscience of the common law. The judge is charged with the development of the law in such a way that its principles remain coherent as it develops and adapts itself to changing social conditions. Thus the flexibility of the common law is an element of what makes it just.

However, things are somewhat more complicated. Flexibility is inseparable from the 'risk' of 'uncertainty in the law'. This risk varies with the context of the legal problem under consideration. In other words, problems of uncertainty take a different form in areas of 'commercial transaction' and 'tortious liability for personal injuries'. Returning to the issue of justice, Lord Scarman argues that justice can demand a degree of loss of certainty in the law ('the search for certainty can obstruct the law's pursuit of justice, and can become the enemy of the good'). In the area of damages for nervous shock, certainty could have been achieved by leaving the law as it stood as stated by authorities in the early 1900s.[61] However, the law has had to respond to advances in

---

59   Ibid., at 430.
60   Ibid.
61   *Victorian Railways Commissioners v. Coultas*, 13 AC 222, *Dulieu v. White & Sons* [1901] 2 KB 669 or in *Hinz v. Berry* [1970] 2 QB 40.

'medical science' and technology, and adapt the relevant test for foreseeability. The extent of these developments means that the problem has now become one for Parliament. Arguments of principle have become over-determined by arguments of policy. We could say, then, that one important element of this theory of interpretative justice is that the judge should know when it is necessary for Parliament to intervene.

What do we make of Lord Scarman's presentation of the role of the judge? It would be too bold to argue that all judicial accounts of their task make use of a theory of interpretative justice. However, in looking at some other important cases in which the role of judicial law making has been considered, we can pick up and develop the concern with judicial development of the common law. We will examine a sample of cases from different areas of law.

Regina v. *R.*[62] is perhaps one of the best examples of judicial creativity. The House of Lords determined that a husband could be held guilty of raping his wife. This involved a particularly bold interpretation of the Sexual Offences (Amendment) Act 1976, which would otherwise seem to perpetuate the husband's exemption to a charge of rape. Indeed, Lord Lane asserted that this was precisely the conclusion to which a literal interpretation of the Act would come. He proposed a 'radical' solution.[63] It was necessary to:

> disregard the statutory provisions of the Act of 1976 and [thus] . . . it is said that it goes beyond the legitimate bounds of judge-made law and trespasses on the province of Parliament. In other words the abolition of a rule of such long standing, despite its emasculation by later decisions, is a task for the legislature and not the courts. There are social considerations to be taken into account, the privacy of marriage to be preserved and questions of potential reconciliation to be weighed which make it an inappropriate area for judicial intervention.[64]

Lord Lane's interpretation of the Act is creative enough to amount to judicial legislation. However, against these 'formidable objections' is the authority of the judge to update the common law to 'changing social attitudes'. Furthermore, the powerful authority *S.* v. *H.M. Advocate*[65] would appear to be on Lord Lane's side. In the wake of this case, the exception is revealed as 'a fiction'; and 'fiction is a poor basis for the criminal law'. The conclusion of the argument is compelling:

> It seems to us that where the common law rule no longer even remotely represents what is the true position of a wife in present day society, the duty of the court is to take steps to alter the rule if it can legitimately do so in the light of any relevant Parliamentary enactment.[66]

The legitimacy of the court's action is further justified by the fact that it is not creating a new criminal offence, but removing from the 'common law an anachronism that is

---

62   *Regina* v. *R.* [1991] 3 WLR 767.
63   Ibid., at 609.
64   Ibid.
65   *S.* v. *H.M. Advocate* 1989 SLT 469.
66   *Regina* v. *R.* at 610.

"offensive" to contemporary social attitudes and standards of behaviour'. *R. v. Clegg*[67] suggests the kind of situation in which a judge will not legislate. The House of Lords refused to change the law in relation to the reduction of murder to manslaughter when excessive force was used in crime prevention. Why, in this instance, did their lordships refuse to alter the law? Lord Lloyd's speech is instructive, in particular his reference to Lord Simon's dissenting speech in Lynch.[68] Although Lord Simon acknowledges that judges do make law, they have to refrain from so doing when policy matters are involved. Picking up on Lord Simon's principle, Lord Lloyd argues that in distinction to *Regina v. R.*[69] where the House of Lords did change the common law without waiting for Parliament to legislate, the present issue is indeed one for the legislature.

A variation on this theme can be found in *C. v. DPP*.[70] The case concerned the concept of *doli incapax*, or the presumption that a child between 10 and 14 was incapable of committing a crime. The House of Lords refused to abolish the rule, arguing that although it was not consistently applied, it was necessary for Parliament to legislate. A number of Acts showed a definite legislative position on the presumption of *doli incapax*. Legislation stressed that it was still necessary for the prosecution to show that the child knew that what s/he was doing was 'seriously wrong'.[71] Although this policy had met with objections and criticism, this was not enough to justify judicial legislation. Again, though, this begs the question of where the line between judicial intervention and the correct province of Parliament lies. Lord Lowry is careful to point out that this is indeed a difficult line to draw. He draws support for the refusal to overturn the presumption from *R. v. Kearley*[72] where the House of Lords refused to alter the hearsay rule. This allows certain guidelines to be posited:

> (1) If the solution is doubtful, the judges should beware of imposing their own remedy. (2) Caution should prevail if Parliament has rejected opportunities of clearing up a known difficulty or has legislated, while leaving the difficulty untouched. (3) Disputed matters of social policy are less suitable areas for judicial intervention than purely legal problems. (4) Fundamental legal doctrines should not be lightly set aside. (5) Judges should not make a change unless they can achieve finality and certainty.[73]

It is hard to know what the status of these guidelines is. Although *C. v. DPP* has been an influential decision in the area of criminal responsibility, Lord Lowry's thoughts on judicial activism do not appear to have been cited. However, these principles go some way to articulating the areas where judges can safely legislate. The grounding

---

67   *R. v. Clegg* [1995] 1 All ER 334.
68   Ibid., at 684–685. In *Lynch* the court justified its activity because, despite having a Law Commission report, Parliament had not acted, thus opening an opportunity for the court; an opportunity which in retrospect, it had not been wise to take. In *Clegg*, Lord Lloyd pointed out that despite the recommendation of the House of Lords (Report of the Select Committee on Murder and Life Imprisonment (Session 1988–89) (HL 78-I)) that 'a qualified defence of using excessive force in self-defence [was] convincing', Parliament had chosen not to change the law. The court should not pre-empt Parliament in cases where broad policy issues are involved.
69   *Regina v. R.* [1992] 1 AC 599.
70   *C. v. DPP* [1995] 2 WLR 383.
71   White Paper entitled Crime, Justice and Protecting the Public (1990) (cited by Lord Lowry) p. 26.
72   *R. v. Kearley* [1992] 2 AC 228.
73   Supra, n. 75, at 228.

idea appears to be deference to Parliament when the 'solution is doubtful' – or – Parliament has already considered the issue and refused to legislate. There is also a presumption against changing the law; and change should only come when it brings with it 'finality and certainty'. Lord Lowry's guidelines are congruent with those of Lord Lloyd in *Clegg*.

In case it seems like all the examples that we have chosen come from criminal law, consider *Airedale NHS v. Bland*[74] – a case that raised difficult moral, ethical and legal issues about the role to be played by medicine in keeping alive someone in a persistent vegetative state (P.V.S.). On the facts of this case, the court had to determine whether or not the patient's treatment could be continued. Medical opinion was unanimous that there was no hope of recovery. The court found that there could be no further benefit to the patient of continuing medical treatment; and held the medical staff no longer under a duty to continue treatment sustaining the patient's life.

Lord Browne-Wilkinson took the opportunity to consider the correct role of the courts in such a fraught area. Precisely because there was no consensus in society about the correct values that should inform this area of medical ethics, it was not fitting for the judges to 'develop new, all embracing, principles of law' that only reflect 'individual judges' moral stance'. A judge thus must work with the 'existing law'. Although this is in itself 'unsatisfactory' – a judge was unsuited to consider the wider issues that were attendant on the decision in this given case. Given these circumstances, Lord Browne-Wilkinson considered that it was 'imperative that the moral, social and legal issues raised by this case should be considered by Parliament'. It was up to Parliament, and the 'democratic process' to give voice to principles that reflected a consensus.

Clearly the legitimate boundaries of judicial law making are difficult to draw precisely. Lord Lowry's guidelines suggest some of the factors that a judge would take into account, however, how these factors are weighed, or, the extent to which other factors may be influential, is impossible to determine in abstraction. That common law interpretation proceeds for the most part without such guidelines being absolutely explicit, suggests they may be embedded within judicial culture in such ways that many elements remain obscure to observers and commentators. A general statement about institutional legitimacy may allow us to glimpse the contours of the practice, but it will never allow us to get 'inside' its operation. We are able, however, to further explore the way in which the practice is transforming itself – and the parameters of institutional legitimacy are being re-negotiated.

JUDICIAL LAW MAKING AND THE HUMAN RIGHTS ACT

After the HRA became law, there were a number of important cases where the judges took a particularly creative approach to realising Convention rights in British law. As

---

74   *Airedale NHS v. Bland* [1993] 1 All ER 821.

this is a complex area, we will deal with two outstanding examples. The first case, *Venables and Thompson* v. *Newsgroup Newspapers*[75] concerned two children who were convicted of the murder of another child. *Venables and Thompson* won the continuation of injunctions preventing newspapers publishing information about them. In granting the injunctions, the court argued that it could protect confidential information in 'exceptional cases where it was strictly necessary'. Given the notoriety of *Venables and Thompson*, it was very likely that they would be seriously injured if the press did reveal their identities or whereabouts on their release from custody. Most interestingly, the court argued that:

> the ECtHR applied in this case via the obligation on the courts in the Human Rights Act, even though the defendant newspapers were not a public authority and the dispute was one between private parties. The claimants' rights under Articles 2, 3 and 8 of the ECtHR were at risk, and had to be balanced against Article 10.

What can we summarise from this argument? It would appear that the court will utilise the HRA in disputes between private parties only in exceptional circumstances, and where there were significant human rights issues at stake. This probably means that the courts will refrain from employing the HRA in all but the most extreme cases.

This authority can be placed against *Douglas* v. *Hello*.[76] On very different facts, the court showed that it was willing to protect the privacy of celebrities against journalists using particularly intrusive methods of photography. Consider Sedley LJ's argument that the courts should recognise a right of privacy. Sedley LJ begins by pointing out that the common law and equity have developed slowly and 'by uneven degrees'; moreover, they have tended to be 'reactive'. Arguably, the time has come for the articulation of 'discrete principles of law' that relate to the protection of privacy. Why is this?

> The reasons are twofold. First, equity and the common law are today in a position to respond to an increasingly invasive social environment by affirming that everybody has a right to some private space. Secondly, and in any event, the Human Rights Act 1998 requires the courts of this country to give appropriate effect to the right to respect for private and family life as set out in Article 8 of the European Convention on Human Rights and Fundamental Freedoms.[77]

So, in *Douglas*, the court felt that it was now necessary to develop a 'positive institutional obligation to respect privacy'. This is a bold decision, and the courts had been struggling with the issue of privacy for a long time prior to this case. What *Douglas* does not suggest is that, in all areas of law, the courts will take upon themselves the obligation to extend the HRA to cover private parties. Nevertheless, *Douglas* does suggest that the courts will take seriously the need, in certain situations, to make sure that a limited interpretation of the Act does not lead to rights abuses.

---

75   *Venables and Thompson* v. *Newsgroup Newspapers* [2001] 2 WLR 1038.
76   *Douglas* v. *Hello* [2001] QB 967.
77   Ibid., at 997.

We will pick up on these themes in later chapters. We can temporarily conclude that the HRA has acted as a catalyst to judicial creativity, but, as we will see in the next section, it has not redefined the institutional constraints in which judicial law making takes place.

THE HUMAN RIGHTS ACT AND PERTURBATIONS IN JUDICIAL PRACTICE

Has the Human Rights Act impacted on the judge's perception of the boundaries of their law making powers? Despite the differences of opinion shown in the approach to the retrospective effect of the HRA[78] perhaps the most interesting factor is the assertion of the importance of a coherent practice of precedent in a time of doubt. It is perhaps not so much motivated by a political conservatism, but an inbuilt appreciation that a practice takes its primary orientating points from what has been; from the way in which people have behaved in the past. *Leeds City Council* v. *Price* and *Kay* v. *London Borough of Lambeth* are the key cases.[79] Lord Bingham outlined the fundamental point. The issue was:

> whether a court which would ordinarily be bound to follow the decisions of another court higher in the domestic curial hierarchy is, or should be, no longer bound to follow that decision if it appears to be inconsistent with a later ruling of the court in Strasbourg.[80]

To understand this question, we have to reconstruct the context – and this takes us to a line of cases that considered Article 8 in the light of fundamental principles of the law of property. In *Harrow LBC* v. *Qazi* the plaintiff had attempted to use an argument based on Article 8 to defeat possession proceedings brought against him by the local authority. Despite the dissent of Lords Bingham and Steyn, The House asserted that property law rights could not be limited by Article 8. In *Connor* v. *UK*[81] the ECtHR found that there had been a breach of Article 8 on similar facts relating to the eviction of travellers from local authority land. Strasbourg held that the council had to establish that there was a compelling reason for the interference with Article 8 rights. In *Leeds City Council* v. *Price/Kay* v. *London Borough of Lambeth* a specially convened House of seven had to reconcile *Qazi* and *Connor*. They did so by arguing that someone who claimed that his or her Article 8 rights had been breached must be

---

78   That the HRA introduced a disturbance or a perturbation into the judicial practice of precedent is evidenced by the cases *R.* v. *Lambert* [2001] HRLR 55 and *R.* v. *Kansal* [2001] UKHL 62. In *Lambert* the House of Lords held that the HRA should not have retrospective effect. The same question was raised in *Kansal*, and their Lordships felt that, although *Lambert* was a doubtful authority, it should be followed. Thus *Kansal* shows the judges feeling their way into a new jurisprudence of the Human Rights Act; their different approaches all suggest the various orientating points that a new interpretative practice might take.
79   *Leeds City Council* v. *Price/Kay* v. *London Borough of Lambeth* [2006] UKHL 10.
80   Ibid., para 40.
81   *Connor* v. *UK* [2004] 40 EHRR 9.

given an opportunity to show that Article 8 did apply. However, there was no obligation on the party seeking to assert their property law rights to show that their argument was justified.

Having reconstructed the context, we can turn to the issue of precedent. The Court of Appeal had considered themselves bound by *Qazi* – but this case was out of line with *Connor*. What was the correct course of action? The civil liberties groups who had intervened in the case urged that a lower court should be entitled to follow ECtHR rulings clearly inconsistent with earlier domestic authorities. This course of action would be open to a court when a Strasbourg case laid down a clear principle that comprehended both Convention law and domestic law and was not inconsistent with any relevant statute. The House of Lords did not agree. Lord Bingham's leading judgment began by stressing the centrality of the doctrine of precedent to the development of English law. He quoted the 1966 Practice Statement, and returned to the words with which we are now familiar: precedent is 'an indispensable foundation' to the common law.[82] An integral part of the jurisprudence of the 1966 Practice Statement is that it only applies to the House of Lords. Lord Hailsham's argument in *Broome* v. *Cassell & Co Ltd*[83] is not cited because it is 'too well known to call for repetition'.[84] If Lord Denning was unable to disturb this principle, it is unlikely that human rights will upset the fundamental terms of judicial practice.

The House had been presented with arguments that called for a modification of the rules of precedent. They rested on assertions that a lower court could follow a Strasbourg ruling in preference to one of the House of Lords where there is clear inconsistency between the ECtHR and the English authority. However, as Lord Bingham argued, the present appeal shows that inconsistency is itself difficult to determine. The appellants and the Court of Appeal in *Leeds* v. *Price* had argued that there was a clear inconsistency between *Qazi* and *Connor*; the respondents and the Court of Appeal had taken the opposite position. Echoing the criticisms made of Lord Denning's attempts to apply the Practice Statement to the Court of Appeal, Lord Bingham invoked the spectre of confusion that would haunt the common law if the settled arrangements for the creation of authorities were disturbed. The appellant's argument suggested that 'different county court and High Court judges, and even different divisions of the Court of Appeal' might take 'differing views of the same issue'.[85] Faced by the challenge of human rights law, then, we fall back on our trusted institutions. The certainty of the common law is achieved by 'adhering, even in the Convention context, to our rules of precedent'.[86] If an authority is inconsistent with a Strasbourg ruling, then it is best dealt with as an appeal – and the House of Lords given the opportunity to produce a definitive statement of the law.

Lord Bingham supports his position with a second argument. The Convention requires a constructive dialogue between national courts and the ECtHR. The ECtHR has the authority to pronounce on the Convention and the correct interpretation of its

---

82 Supra, n.110, at para 42.
83 *Broome* v. *Cassell & Co Ltd.* [1972] AC 1027 at 1053–1055.
84 Supra, n. 100, at para 42.
85 Ibid., para 43.
86 Ibid.

principles. However, in its 'decisions on particular cases'[87] the ECtHR allows a significant 'margin of appreciation'[88] to national courts – and in particular to their understanding of the facts of the case. This means that the national court must decide precisely how the Convention applies and 'how the principles expounded in Strasbourg should be applied in the special context of national legislation'.[89] If the national courts have to apply Convention jurisprudence, then they must do so in the prevalent terms of a national legal system: thus, as far as the UK is concerned: 'the ordinary rules of precedent should apply.'[90]

There is one 'partial exception' to this principle. In *D. v. East Berkshire Community NHS Trust*[91] the Court of Appeal had argued that the House of Lords in *X (Minors) v. Bedfordshire CC*[92] should not be followed. The decision in *X v. Bedfordshire CC* was prior to the Human Rights Act and based on reasoning and 'policy considerations' that were inconsistent with the Act.[93] The House of Lords in *D.* had agreed with the Court of Appeal.[94] Note, however, the special considerations that applied in this case. The 1995 ruling of the House of Lords had contained no reference to the Convention. Furthermore, the applicants in *D.* had successfully argued a breach of Article 3 in Strasbourg, and obtained significant damages. Lord Bingham notes: 'such a course is not permissible save where the facts are of that extreme character.'[95]

What do we make of this? Could the case be seen as a failed opportunity to re-invent both the doctrine and judicial practice? Harris has suggested, albeit in a different context, that the principle of overruling needs to be re-considered.[96] He argues that the present practice of allowing wrong precedents to stand stresses the value of certainty at the cost of the 'quality of justice'. He argues that the better approach would be for the final appellate court to 'depart from precedent after systematically weighing up all the competing considerations'.[97] In some cases there may be compelling reasons for the decision to stand, in others the weight of the argument may be to overrule and re-state the correct principles. The doubts expressed by the Lords suggest that the issues raised in *Leeds City Council v. Price/Kay v. London Borough of Lambeth* were not crisp enough to make this case a clear authority for the need to re-define precedent in such a dramatic way. In a later chapter, we will see that *Leeds City Council v. Price/Kay v. London Borough of Lambeth* raised issues with the so-called mirror principle that should guide the relationship between domestic courts and Strasbourg. We will pick up on these themes in Chapter 8, but, we need to point out that since the ruling of the Supreme Court in *Pinnock*, the issues that arose in *Price/Kay* have effectively been resolved.

87   Ibid., para. 44.
88   Ibid.
89   Ibid.
90   Ibid.
91   *D. v. East Berkshire Community NHS Trust* [2004] QB 558.
92   *X (Minors) v. Bedfordshire CC* [1995] 2 AC 633.
93   Ibid., at para 45.
94   *X (Minors) v. Bedfordshire CC* [2005] UKHL 23.
95   Supra, n. 112, at para 45.
96   B.V. Harris, Final Appellate Courts Overruling their own 'wrong' Precedents: The Ongoing Search for Principle, LQR 2002, 118(JUL), 408–427.
97   Ibid., at 427.

Other perturbations in the doctrine of precedent take us to the relationships between the domestic courts. We need to make a brief reference to s.6 of the HRA. A judge is considered to be a public body for the purposes of this section of the Act. As a public body, a judge must issue rulings that are Convention compliant. The following question thus arises: if a judge is faced with a binding decision from a superior court, which is in conflict with the Convention, should s/he follow the Convention or the decision of the national court? This was the dilemma facing Eady J in the High Court. *Culane* v. *Morris*[98] concerned s.10 of the Defamation Act 1952 and the defence of qualified privilege. The CA had determined in *Plummer* v. *Charman*[99] that there were limitations on the defence during a period in which an election was taking place. This interpretation of the Act was arguably out of line with the Convention; and Eady J was compelled by the HRA to construe the Defamation Act as Convention compliant and depart from the ruling of the Court of Appeal.

Culane v. *Morris* has to be distinguished from the issues that arose in *Miller* v. *Bull*.[100] *Miller* v. *Bull* raised complex technical issues in relation to the Election Petition Rules 1960. The Court of Appeal had decided in *Ahmed* v. *Kennedy*[101] that it was not possible to extend certain time limits relating to security for costs; with the consequence that the 'election petition' failed. This case had been decided after the HRA, but no arguments had been made which addressed the human rights concerns, in particular about a potential breach of Article 6. In *Miller*, a breach of Article 6 was pleaded – and Tugendhat J decided that he was not bound by *Ahmed* v. *Kennedy*, preferring an approach to the election petition that was in accordance with Article 6.

CONCLUSION

It is hard to think about the impact of human rights on judicial practice in terms of the old debates centring on *Schorsh Meier* and *Davis* v. *Johnson*. Whilst *Kay* shows that the courts are not suddenly going to depart from the hierarchic structure of the common law, human rights law has, in certain areas, been the spur to the creation of new law. It would be presumptuous to see this as a constitutional revolution. After the Human Rights Act, judges are doing precisely what they did before the Act came into force: making law. It may be that the mechanisms of the Human Rights Act lead to a re-working of judicial practice – subtly shifting the sense of where the legitimate boundaries of judicial legislation lie. Ultimately, this is what makes it difficult to offer any final conclusion. Practices take time to develop. It will be interesting to see the precise form that the judicial practice of precedent will assume.

---

98   *Culane* v. *Morris* [2005] EWHC 2438.
99   *Plummer* v. *Charman* [1962] 1 WLR 1469.
100 *Miller* v. *Bull* [2009] EWHC 2640 (QB).
101 *Ahmed* v. *Kennedy* [2002] EWCA Civ 1793.

8

THE MIRROR AND THE DIALOGUE: THE COMMON LAW, STRASBOURG AND HUMAN RIGHTS

Two metaphors have developed as ways of thinking about the relationship between British courts and Strasbourg. In this chapter, we want to examine them in some detail.

The mirror principle determines that the rulings of the Supreme Court (SC) (and the House of Lords) must reflect the jurisprudence of the ECtHR. The idea of the dialogue is a way of thinking about this relationship in a more nuanced way. Domestic courts may have to follow the rulings of Strasbourg to enable the coherent development of international human rights, but this principle does not mean unquestioning obedience. Whilst there have been tensions between the domestic courts and Strasbourg, the role that the British courts have played in the development of human rights law suggests that there is indeed a developing relationship that is slowly helping to create a continent-wide human rights culture.

But, all is not well. As Sir Nicolas Bratza has commented: '[t]he vitriolic . . . fury directed against the judges of my Court is unprecedented in my experience, as someone who has been involved with the Convention system for over 40 years'.[1] Why should this be the case? We will look at the relationship between British politics and human rights to analyse why the complex relationship between Strasbourg and the domestic courts have been 'flattened out' and seen in terms of crisis. We will argue that we need a more sober assessment of human rights in British politics.

Our argument will develop as follows. As the question of the relationship between Strasbourg and the common law has to be addressed in the terms of the Human Rights Act, the first section of the chapter will outline the Act's key provisions. We will then turn to examine in detail the relationship between European human rights and the common law; assessing both the key cases and scholarly and judicial commentaries. Although the mirror principle is under strain, we have to appreciate that it continues to play an important role. We will then turn to our analysis of the dialogue between the domestic courts and Strasbourg, before concluding with our discussion of the tensions between law, politics and democracy.

---

1   Bratza (2011: 505).

EUROPEAN HUMAN RIGHTS AND
THE COMMON LAW

Our discussion of the mirror principle begins with the key sections of the HRA that articulate the relationship between common law and European Human Rights Law. We have already outlined the key provisions of the Act, but it is useful to recall the sections relevant to our discussion in this chapter. Section 2(1) of the HRA specifies that in the interpretation of Convention rights,[2] a court or tribunal must take into account a number of sources of European human rights law[3] if 'in the opinion of the court or tribunal, it is relevant to the proceedings in which that question has arisen'. The court thus has discretion to determine whether or not the authorities are relevant to the proceedings in question; even if they pre-date the Act.[4] The Act then goes on to state at s.3(1), that as far as the interpretation of legislation is concerned, primary legislation and subordinate or delegated legislation must be read and given effect so that they are compatible with Convention rights, 'so far as it is possible to do so'. Once again, the court has a wide discretion to determine whether or not legislation is Convention compliant. Section 3(2) concerns the extent of this section's operation. It applies, first of all, to primary legislation and subordinate legislation whenever enacted. Bear in mind that incompatibility does not affect the validity or continuing operation of any provision, or the validity or continued operation of incompatible subordinate legislation, if the primary legislation from which it is derived prevents the removal of that incompatibility.[5]

In *Re McKerr*[6] Lord Nicholls pointed out that the scope of Convention rights in common law depends on the 'proper interpretation of that HRA'. This takes us back to s.2(1) of the Act. But, how is this section to be interpreted? Lord Slynn's speech in *R. (Alconbury)* v. *Secretary of State for the Environment, Transport and the Regions*[7] is seen as the origin of a particular interpretation of s.2(1). Lord Slynn pointed out that

---

2   That is, those under the European Convention on Human Rights – ECHR.
3   These are:

   (a) judgment, decision, declaration or advisory opinion of the European Court of Human Rights;
   (b) opinion of the Commission given in a report adopted under Article 31 of the Convention;
   (c) certain decisions of the Commission in connection with Articles 26 and 27 of the Convention; or
   (d) decisions of the Committee of Ministers taken under Article 46 of the Convention.

4   Section 2(1) states that the relevant source can be taken into account 'whenever made or given'.
5   Lewis contrasts s.2 of the HRA with s.3(1) of the EC Act 1972, which states that UK courts are bound by the decisions of the ECJ, 729. Later, he cites Masterman's rationale for the structure of the HRA, which in turn (at least for the first three points), are taken from statements of Lord Irvine during Parliamentary debate. Domestic courts are not bound to follow the ECtHR because: (a) the Convention is the 'ultimate' source of law; but has 'no strict rule of precedent' (731); (b) the Convention states that the UK is bound only by rulings in cases in which it was a party; (c) [from the White Paper], the common law courts must be free to develop Convention law; (d) as the judgments of the ECtHR are 'declaratory' in nature, it is difficult to follow them as precedent decisions. Lewis cites Clayton's (below) argument that there is a difference between the way in which the ECtHR and common law courts produce their decisions. This makes it all the more necessary to qualify strict adherence to the mirror principle and to develop indigenous interpretations of the Convention.
6   *Re McKerr* [2004] 1 WLR 807, 25, 62–65.
7   *R. (Alconbury)* v. *Secretary of State for the Environment, Transport and the Regions* [2003] 2 AC 295, at para 26.

whilst a court was not bound by decision of the ECtHR, it was 'obliged to take account of them so far as they are relevant'. He went on to assert that unless there were 'special circumstances', a domestic court had to follow 'clear and constant jurisprudence of the European Court of Human Rights'. If a domestic court failed to follow consistent Strasbourg case law, then there was the likelihood that the case would be heard by the ECtHR, and the outcome would presumably be that the court had failed to apply the *'constant jurisprudence'* and rule against the domestic court.

Lord Bingham developed these arguments in *Ullah*:

> It is of course open to member states to provide for rights more generous than those guaranteed by the Convention, but such provision should not be the product of inter-pretation of the Convention by national courts, since the meaning of the Convention should be uniform throughout the states party to it. The duty of national courts is to keep pace with the Strasbourg jurisprudence as it evolves over time: no more but certainly no less.[8]

Lord Bingham is drawing attention to the central role of the ECtHR: the uniform development of European human rights law. Whilst national legislatures could supplement Convention rights if they so chose, courts have to be mindful of the need not to move too far ahead of Strasbourg, or fall too far behind. The national courts need to keep 'pace' with the evolution of international human rights law: 'no more, or no less'.[9]

Whilst this view of the relationship between national courts and Strasbourg makes general sense, it leaves certain matters of detail unresolved. What does it mean, for example, to 'keep pace' with Strasbourg? Lord Bingham had argued that national courts 'should not without strong reason dilute or weaken the effect of the Strasbourg case law'. Does this suggest that, provided strong reasons exist, there might be room for a national court to offer a narrower or more restricted interpretation of Convention rights than Strasbourg? It may also suggest that a court could, if it had strong reasons, develop Strasbourg case law. However, it tells us very little about how a domestic court should respond to Strasbourg if the latter misunderstood a fundamental principle of national law.

We need to think about these general guidelines in the light of key recent decisions. We will analyse these decisions in five groups. The first group contains those cases in which Strasbourg has overruled decisions of the House of Lords (*Marper*, *Gillan*, *Othmann*; and *Hirst*). In the second group are cases where the SC has followed Strasbourg, but expressed doubts about the principles of law concerned (*AF*). We will also examine those cases where the SC has refused to follow Strasbourg (*Horncastle*, *and Animal Defenders*) or otherwise asserted itself in a more 'nuanced' way[10] (*Pinnock*). The fourth group consists of those cases where the national court has preferred not to develop human rights principles because so doing would go beyond the position of the ECtHR (*Ambrose*). Finally, we will consider a fifth group of cases where the House of

---

8   R. v. *Special Adjudicator, ex parte Ullah* [2004] UKHL 26, para 20.
9   *Ullah*, para 21.
10   Lord Irvine (2012: 5).

Lords pushed human rights jurisprudence in such a way as to broaden the principles involved (*R.* (*Limbuela*); *EM* (*Lebanon*); *R.* (*G*).)

FIGHTING TERMS? OVERRULING THE HOUSE OF LORDS

The first two cases that we will examine are examples of the House of Lords being overruled by the ECtHR. In *R. (on the application of Marper) v. Chief Constable of South Yorkshire*[11] the House of Lords determined that there was no breach of Article 8 rights when the Police retained DNA and fingerprint evidence after an acquittal or discontinuance of a prosecution. However, in *S. v. United Kingdom*[12] the ECtHR unanimously held that there had been a breach of Article 8. One of the essential grounds of the argument was that UK law was unclear on a number of important points relating to the storage and use of such personal information. The ECtHR argued that it was 'essential' that 'telephone tapping, secret surveillance and covert intelligence-gathering' were defined by 'clear, detailed rules' that governed 'the scope and application of measures' and also provided 'minimum safeguards' that provided 'sufficient guarantees against the risk of abuse and arbitrariness'.[13]

In *R. (on the application of Gillan) v. Commissioner of Police of the Metropolis*[14] the House of Lords upheld the legality of searches under the Prevention of Terrorism Act 2000 on two individuals who had been stopped near an arms fair in East London. The powers that enabled the Police to undertake such searches had been continually renewed since the Act entered into force. The applicants argued that this amounted to 'a continuous ban throughout the London area'. The applicants also asserted that their rights under Articles 5 and 8 had been breached by the searches to which they were subjected. In *Gillan and Quinton v. United Kingdom*[15] the ECtHR found that there had been a breach of Article 8 and was particularly critical of the broad and arbitrary nature of the powers under the Act. Given the evidence of the disproportionate use of such powers on black and Asian 'suspects'[16] the court found that 'the risks of the discriminatory use of the powers against such persons is a very real consideration'.[17]

The notorious case of *Abu Qatada v. UK*[18] saw the ECtHR overrule the House of Lords on a point relating to Article 6 and torture. Abu Qatada, an Islamic fundamentalist, had been detained under the 2001 Anti-Terrorism, Crime and Security Bill, and then subject to control orders under PTA 2005. The Secretary of State sought to deport Qatada on the ground of national security to Jordan. Qatada appealed to the Special Immigration Appeals Commission (SIAC). His argument was based on Article 3. He

11 *R. (on the application of Marper) v. Chief Constable of South Yorkshire* ([2002] EWHC 478).
12 *S. v. United Kingdom* (Application Nos 30562/04 and 30566/04).
13 Ibid., at para 99.
14 *R. (on the application of Gillan) v. Commissioner of Police of the Metropolis* [2006] UKHL 12.
15 *Gillan and Quinton v. United Kingdom* (Application No. 4158/05).
16 Ibid., para 84.
17 Ibid., para 85.
18 *Othman (Abu Qatada) v. UK* No. 8139/09, 17.1.2012.

had been tried in his absence, and found guilty by the Jordanian authorities for terrorism related offences. Qatada's case was that, if he was returned to Jordan, he would be retried, put at risk of being tortured, and evidence obtained by the torture of a third party would be used against him. SIAC dismissed his appeal on the grounds that the UK government had sought diplomatic assurances that torture evidence would not be used and he would not be mistreated. We will deal in depth with the argument around Article 6 in another chapter. Suffice to say for our purposes in this chapter, that whilst the Court of Appeal held that the use of torture evidence would amount to a flagrant abuse of Qatada's Article 6 rights, the House of Lords held[19] on the contrary, that the diplomatic assurances were sufficient, and that there was no 'rule that in the context of a trial in a foreign state the risk of the use of evidence obtained by torture necessarily amounted to a flagrant denial of justice'.

The ECtHR[20] agreed with the House of Lords on the Article 3 point: diplomatic assurances, in the context of the UK's relationship with Jordan, were sufficient to ensure that Qatada would not be ill treated. However, they disagreed with the House of Lords in relation to the use of torture evidence. Citing the Belmarsh case, and Lord Bingham's strong condemnation of torture evidence, Strasbourg asserted that torture evidence was inherently unfair. The court also relied on evidence that torture was widespread in Jordan, and that Qatada's co-accused had indeed been tortured. The Jordanian court had taken no action on the allegation that torture had been used.

This is a controversial ruling, but we will defer any analysis until we have reviewed the other groups of cases that we described above. So, we now move to the second category of cases: where the SC has expressed doubt about Strasbourg's interpretation of the law, but nevertheless followed the ECtHR's ruling.

RELUCTANT PARTNERS?

To understand the main case, *AF*, we need to briefly reconstruct the context. In *MB* the House of Lords had held that, for the most part, failure to disclose closed procedure material was compatible with Article 6, although there would be 'rare' occasions when failure to disclose did breach the Article. Failure of clarity over the precise terms of the ruling in *MB* provided ground for the CA to order an appeal in *AF*. However, just after the House of Lords had begin its hearing of the case, Strasbourg published its judgment in *A. and others* v. *United Kingdom*.[21] How did the House of Lords understand this ruling?

Lord Phillips argued that *A.* meant that closed material could not be relied upon when it contains the major evidence against the applicant that was not available in the open material. Lord Hoffmann gave a powerful dissenting judgment. He asserted that although the ECtHR should be followed, the court's decision on closed procedure material was 'wrong' and that it would compromise the system of control orders. The

19   *RB (Algeria) v. Secretary of State for the Home Department* [2009] WLR 512.
20   *Othman (Abu Qatada) v. UK*, No. 8139/09, 17.1.2012.
21   *A. and others v. United Kingdom* (Application No 3455/05).

House of Lords had no choice but to 'submit' to Strasbourg. This argument took Lord Hoffmann to the interpretation of 2(1)(a). Although it only requires the court to 'take into account' the ECtHR, and therefore, in principle the House of Lords could still prefer not to follow a Strasbourg ruling, such a course of action would risk putting the UK in breach of the ECtHR.[22]

MB and *AF* were exercises in 'reading down' the PTA under s.3 of the HRA. In *MB* the House of Lords read down para 4 of the schedule to the 2005 Act to ensure that an 'irreducible minimum of procedural protection' was accorded to the 'controlled person'. In *AF* para 4 was again read down so as to be coherent with Article 6 protection. Lord Phillips commented that the approach in *MB* marked a departure from 'the apparently absolute requirements of the relevant statutory provisions'; indeed, the approach of the court raised questions about the extent to which the statute could be made compatible with the Convention. However, as a declaration of incompatibility was not suggested by either party to the case, 'there is good reason to let the reading down stand'.[23]

TAKING A STAND?

In contrast with *AF*, there are cases where SC has explicitly refused to follow Strasbourg. Our starting point is *R. (Animal Defenders)* v. *Secretary of State for Culture, Media and Sport*.[24] The House of Lords decided not to follow Strasbourg case law that would require them to depart from a fundamental principle of media neutrality before an election. Lord Bingham pointed out the compelling reasons that justified this departure from human rights principles. Parliament had considered that the ban on political advertising might be in breach of Article 10, but had still chosen to 'maintain the prohibition' in order to 'to safeguard the integrity of our democracy'. Lord Bingham's language suggests that this case raises a profound and fundamental point; and, as such, provides a clear rationale for the House of Lord's decision.

The second major authority, *R.* v. *Horncastle*,[25] also reflects a very specific issue. To understand *Horncastle*, we need to begin with *Al-Khawaja and Tahery* v. *United Kingdom*.[26] In *Al-Khawaja and Tahery* Strasbourg held that there had been violations of Article 6 when the applicants were convicted on the basis of hearsay evidence. In *Horncastle*, the SC refused to follow this ruling. Lord Phillips argued that 'the jurisprudence of the Strasbourg Court in relation to article 6(3)(d) has developed largely in cases relating to civil law rather than common law jurisdictions'.[27] He went on to boldly state that there would be 'rare occasions' when the domestic court has doubts over 'whether a decision of the Strasbourg Court sufficiently appreciates or

....

22   *AF*, para 70.
23   *AF*, para 67.
24   *R. (Animal Defenders)* v. *Secretary of State for Culture, Media and Sport* [2008] UKHL 15.
25   *R.* v. *Horncastle* [2009] UKSC 14.
26   *Al-Khawaja and Tahery* v. *United Kingdom* (2009) 49 EHRR 1.
27   Supra, n. 23, at para 107.

accommodates' principles of common law. It would therefore be acceptable for the domestic court not to follow the ruling and to give 'the Strasbourg Court the opportunity to reconsider the particular aspect of the decision that is in issue'.

Strasbourg did indeed reconsider their ruling. In *Al-Khawaja and Tahery v. United Kingdom*[28] they decided that the SC was right on this occasion. As far as the exclusion of hearsay evidence rule was concerned, the ECtHR accepted that they had ignored 'the specificities' of the common law when it came to hearsay evidence. The common law had developed its own principles of 'weighing' 'the competing interests of those involved in a trial', and ensuring that there were checks and safeguards on the administration of hearsay evidence.[29]

MANCHESTER: SO MUCH TO ANSWER FOR

Horncastle suggests that the SC is willing to assert itself against Strasbourg. *Pinnock*[30] is a less dramatic case. It shows that the SC will follow Strasbourg, but retain a critical eye on its decisions. In *Pinnock*, the SC provided a definitive conclusion to a long running argument over Article 8. The question to be resolved was whether or not a tenant facing eviction from public housing could rely on Article 8. Article 8 requires the judge to consider the proportionality of the eviction. There were dissenting judgments in the House of Lords (*Doherty*, *Harrow* and *Kay*) suggesting such an argument could be made. *Pinnock*'s case before the Supreme Court was that this dissenting line should be followed as it would be consistent with rulings by the Strasbourg court.

The Supreme Court's approach to the issue indeed stressed that Strasbourg now had an 'unambiguous and consistent approach' that must be taken into account in determining whether or not it was 'appropriate for this Court to depart from the three decisions of the House of Lords'.[31] Citing *Horncastle*, the SC argued that it was 'not bound to follow every decision of the ECtHR'. It would be both 'impractical' and 'inappropriate' for the SC to be bound by every decision of the ECtHR. It was necessary to preserve the 'ability of the Court to engage in the constructive dialogue with the ECtHR' as this 'is of value to the development of Convention law'.[32] However, it would 'usually' be the case that they would follow 'a clear and constant line of decisions' by Strasbourg. This argument rested ultimately on the authority of s.2 of the HRA. Strasbourg should be followed when there is a 'clear and constant line of decisions' that are 'not inconsistent with some fundamental . . . aspect' of common law, and when Strasbourg's reasoning 'does not appear to overlook or misunderstand some argument or point of principle . . . .'[33]

---

28   *Al-Khawaja and Tahery v. United Kingdom* [2011] ECHR 2127.
29   Ibid., at para 146.
30   *Pinnock v. Manchester City Council* [2010] UKSC 45.
31   Ibid., at para 45.
32   Ibid., at para 48.
33   Ibid.

So, how would this principle apply to *Pinnock*'s eviction? The ECtHR case law certainly considered the relevant principles of domestic law. British law, as evidenced by the ruling in *Doherty* was 'already moving in the direction' of Strasbourg jurisprudence. Lord Neuberger also pointed out that had the British courts ruled on the Article 8 point, they would have followed the dissenting judgments in *Harrow* and *Kay*. Thus, to make British law consistent with the ECtHR's position on Article 8, the matter of proportionality would have to be taken into account.

JUMPING AHEAD OF STRASBOURG

This brings us to the fourth group of cases. Is it justifiable for a domestic court to 'jump ahead'[34] of Strasbourg jurisprudence? This happened in *Ghaidan*,[35] where the CA anticipated the outcome of *Karner* v. *Austria*[36] More recently, this issue has appeared in *Ambrose* v. *Harris*.[37] The issue in *Ambrose* was whether Article 6 should be interpreted to provide legal advice before interrogation took place in a police station. The Supreme Court held that because this point had not yet been determined by the ECtHR, the SC could not make a ruling that anticipated developments in Article 6 jurisprudence. Lord Hope's speech made the crucial issue clear: '[i]It is not for this court to expand the scope of the Convention right further than the jurisprudence of the Strasbourg court justifies'.[38] However, Lord Kerr's dissenting judgment denounced the '*Ullah*-type reticence' which 'considered wrong' an 'attempt to anticipate developments at the supra national level of the Strasbourg court'.[39] He suggested that although Strasbourg had not ruled on a particular point, national courts should not 'refrain from recognising such a right simply because Strasbourg has not spoken'.[40] It would be impractical for national courts to wait for Strasbourg rulings. Furthermore, 'as a matter of elementary principle, it is the court's duty to address those issues when they arise, whether or not authoritative guidance from Strasbourg is available'.[41] Lord Kerr's speech supports this line of argument. He asserted that if the 'much vaunted dialogue between national courts and Strasbourg is to mean anything' that the SC must ' "assert" itself and indicate how it believes the law should develop'.[42]

---

34 Baroness Hale, cited in Equality and Human Rights Report (2012: 136).
35 [2002] EWCA Civ 1533.
36 Cited in Equality and Human Rights Report (2012: 136). *Karner* v. *Austria* No. 40016/98, 24.7.2003.
37 *Ambrose* v. *Harris (Procurator Fiscal)* [2011] 1 WLR 2435.
38 See also in *R. (on the application of Clift)* v. *Secretary of State for the Home Department* [2006] UKHL 54, the court refused to extend the protection offered by Article 14, as it was necessary to work within the limits imposed by the ECtHR; similar approaches have been taken to Article 5 in *Secretary of State for the Home Department* v. *JJ* 2006 EWCA Civ 1141 and Article 9 in *R. (on the application of SB)* v. *Denbigh High School* [2006] UKHL 15. Lord Bingham was clear in *Begum*'s case that the HRA was not to allow the courts to expand the protection offered by the Convention but to ensure that Convention rights were available in English law.
39 Supra, n. 35 at 126.
40 Ibid., at 129.
41 Ibid.
42 Ibid., at 130.

THE HL TAKES THE LEAD: DEVELOPING HUMAN RIGHTS PRINCIPLES

We now turn to our final group cases: three instances in which the House of Lords has suggested developments of Convention jurisprudence that enhance the protection of human rights. *EM (Lebanon) v. Secretary of State for the Home Department*[43] concerned an asylum seeker who argued that her removal to Lebanon would breach her rights under Article 8. Under Sharia law, she would be forced to give custody of her son to her abusive and violent partner. As Lord Hope pointed out, there was a 'real risk ... that the very essence of the family life that mother and child have shared together up to that date will be destroyed or nullified'.[44] (para 5). The pressing issue was how to interpret Convention jurisprudence. Strasbourg had indicated that 'in the absence of very exceptional circumstances, aliens cannot claim any entitlement under the Convention to remain [in a country] to escape from the discriminatory effects of the system of family law in their country of origin'. In other words, removing *EM* to Lebanon would not necessarily violate her Article 8 rights. Strasbourg allows: 'limits [to be] set on the extent to which [nations] can be held responsible outside the areas that are prescribed by articles 2 and 3 and by the fundamental right under article 6 to a fair trial'. Nevertheless, the House of Lords went on to hold that a 'flagrant viola-tion' of *EM*'s rights would take place if she was returned to Lebanon: 'the evidence made plain that the bond between' *EM* and her son 'was one of deep love and mutual dependence' and their family life would be 'destroyed' if custody passed to a man who had 'inflicted physical violence and psychological injury' on *EM*.

In *Re G*[45] 76, an unmarried couple, who were living together, wished to apply for adoption of the woman's child. The woman's partner was not the child's biological father. Article 14 of the Adoption (Northern Ireland) Order 1987 prevented their appli-cation for adoption because they were not married. The couple argued that article 14 of the Order breached articles 8 and 14 of the ECtHR. The House of Lords held that their rights had been breached as it was wrong for the law to be based on an 'irrebuttable presumption that no unmarried couple could make suitable adoptive parents'. Importantly from our perspective, Lord Hoffmann, Lord Hope and Lord Mance argued that the 'developing jurisprudence' of the ECtHR was such that: 'it was likely that the European Court of Human Rights would hold that discrimination against a couple wishing to adopt a child on the ground that they were not married would violate article 14 of the Convention'. They also asserted that the 'margin of appreciation' that was accorded to national authorities applied to the courts as well as the legislature. As such the House of Lords could give 'what it considered to be a principled and rational inter-pretation to the concept of discrimination on grounds of marital status'.

R. (on the application of Limbuela) v. Secretary of State for the Home Department[46] concerned three asylum seekers who, although destitute, had been refused support

---

43 *EM (Lebanon) v. Secretary of State for the Home Department* [2008] UKHL 64.
44 Ibid., para 7.
45 *Re G* (Adoption: Unmarried Couple) [2008] 3 W.L.R. 76.
46 *R. (on the application of Limbuela) v. Secretary of State for the Home Department* 2005 3 WLR 1014.

under the Immigration and Asylum Act 1999 as they had not claimed asylum 'as soon as reasonably practicable' under the Nationality, Immigration and Asylum Act 2002. The applicants were in desperate circumstances, one of them 'sleeping in the open'. They were prevented from working and, other than relying on charity, had no means of supporting themselves. They argued that 'their suffering was so severe' as to constitute a breach of Article 3 of the Convention. The Secretary of State appealed against the order of the judges who granted the claimants application, and also sought clarification of the relevant test. The House of Lords upheld the original applications and further determined that the correct test to assess 'inhuman or degrading treatment' under Article 3 related to the severity of the 'entire package of work restrictions and deprivations'. They went on to hold that: 'the threshold of severity would, in the ordinary way, be crossed where a person deprived of support. . . . was obliged to sleep in the street, or was seriously hungry or unable to satisfy the most basic requirements of hygiene'.

Lord Bingham – stressing Lord Hope's argument – showed that Convention jurisprudence could be pushed in a specific direction: Article 3 cases required a 'minimum standard of severity' and, in the 'context' of the present case precisely because 'deliberate infliction of pain or suffering' was not at stake, 'the threshold is a high one'. It would not be possible to interpret Article 3 in a very broad way, and derive 'a general public duty to house the homeless or provide for the destitute', but, the threshold of severity 'may be crossed if [an applicant] with no means and no alternative sources of support, unable to support himself, is, by the deliberate action of the state, denied shelter, food or the most basic necessities of life'.[47]

STRASBOURG, THE HOUSE OF LORDS AND THE SUPREME COURT: A WORK IN PROGRESS?

How can we weigh up these claims? The first group of cases are, of course, entirely consistent with the mirror principle. If the domestic courts have failed to understand the scope of rights, then it would follow that there is a risk that they will be overruled by Strasbourg. Is this justifiable? As Sir Nicolas Bratza has pointed out 'at the heart' of *Marper* and *Gillan* were 'disagreement[s]' as to 'the seriousness of the interference with the right to respect for private life involved'.[48] The ruling of the Strasbourg court should be preferred, as it was 'able to examine the law and practice in other Member States' and concludes: 'England and Wales [was] the only European jurisdiction expressly to permit the systematic and indefinite retention of DNA profiles and cellular samples of persons who had been acquitted or in respect of whom criminal proceedings had been discontinued'. In this instance, then, the

---

47 See also *Rabone and another v. Pennine Care NHS Foundation Trust* [2012] UKSC 2. In *Rabone* the SC developed an interpretation of Article 2 that went further than the Strasbourg court in asserting that employees of the NHS trust had duties to protect a patient voluntarily detained for mental health reasons from threats to his life, including suicide.
48 Supra, n. 1, at 509.

mirror principle is preserving the coherent development of human rights law across Europe.

Most controversially, *Qatada* shows a clear disagreement between the House of Lords and Strasbourg. We need to avoid any easy argument that *Qatada* is somehow escaping justice. The point is not that he should not face trial, but that his trial would be compromised by the use of torture evidence. Indeed, Strasbourg cited the Belmarsh case on the inherent unreliability of torture evidence. We could also argue that the decision of the ECtHR in *Qatada* ensured the principled coherence of human rights law. If one is committed to the rule of law, then a trial process cannot be compromised through qualifications to the prohibition on torture evidence. Furthermore, as the Strasbourg decision is consistent with United Nations Convention Against Torture (UNCAT), of which the UK is a signatory, it would appear that there are strong arguments to support Strasbourg's interpretation of Article 6.

The effect of these rulings might play into the hands of those claiming that the SC should be more assertive. As we will see in the section below, Lord Irvine has argued that it is 'the constitutional duty of judges to reject Strasbourg decisions they feel are flawed in favour of their own judgments'.[49] However, we have to be aware that the coherence of European human rights law would be compromised if the SC began to depart radically from the ECtHR's rulings. This point was perhaps appreciated in *AF*. Lord Hoffmann's dissent shows that although senior judges were uncomfortable with Strabourg's decision in *A*.[50] they nevertheless followed the ruling.[51] This is entirely consistent with *Horncastle*. This case showed that the Chamber had seriously misunderstood fundamental common law principles. There was a compelling reason to depart from Strasbourg case law. Although the SC followed the ECtHR in *Pinnock*, its critical comments on the nature of a 'constructive dialogue' appears to be consistent with the position outlined in *Horncastle*.

How can we sum up on those cases that show national courts moving ahead of Strasbourg? A consistent development of Convention jurisprudence requires national courts to be careful in this area. In *Ambrose*, the Supreme Court was reluctant to move forward on an Article 6 point because Strasbourg had not yet made a definitive ruling. *Ambrose* can perhaps be distinguished from the cases in the fifth group because the state of Convention jurisprudence was such that the national courts were able to interpret principles broadly without going beyond Strasbourg's position. The House of Lords approach in *EM*, *Limbuela* and *Re G* suggests that there is room for a domestic court to indicate how human rights law should develop. The domestic court has room for manoeuvre where: 'Strasbourg has deliberately declined to lay down an interpretation for all member states, as it does when it says that the question

---

49   *The Guardian*, 14/12/11, at http://www.guardian.co.uk/law/2011/dec/14/lord-irvine-human-rights-law? intcmp=239.

50   See also *Anderson*, where Buxton LJ felt compelled to follow Strasbourg, even though it prevented him from coming to a more appropriate conclusion. The notion that the mirror principle is based on ensuring consistency in the development of European human rights law has been criticised by Lewis. In *M. v. Secretary of State for Work and Pensions* [2006] UKHL 11 the House of Lords had the opportunity to expand the protection offered by Article 14 but refused to take the lead, arguing that any development would have to await a Strasbourg ruling to ensure the uniform interpretation of the Convention.

51   *Supra*, n. 99 at 731.

is within the margin of appreciation'. This is why, in *EM*, the House of Lords saw itself as 'free to give, in the interpretation of the 1998 Act, what it considers to be a principled and rational interpretation to the concept of discrimination on grounds of marital status'.

Sir Nicolas Bratza has commented that this approach is correct. He has been careful to also show that the relationship between the ECtHR and the British courts is indeed one of dialogue. There are numerous occasions when Strasbourg has either deferred to the House of Lords, or followed House of Lords or SC rulings in developing human rights principles. We cannot, for limitations of space, consider all these cases: but there are a couple of key points to focus upon. Consider *Friend* v. *UK*.[52] Precisely because this case was so contentious, with English and Scottish courts coming to different interpretations of Articles 8 and 11, the ECtHR deferred to the UK Parliament.[53] We have also seen how important Lord Bingham's interpretation of the prohibition of torture was for the development of European human rights principles. Perhaps we could conclude that there is indeed evidence that the ECtHR 'has demonstrated a willingness to engage in a "judicial dialogue" with the superior courts of the UK'.[54]

BETWEEN STRASBOURG AND WESTMINSTER: THE POLITICS OF HUMAN RIGHTS

Is it possible to approach the relationship between Strasbourg and the British courts in a principled way? The mirror principle certainly seems to be necessary and justifiable in terms of the development of coherent international human rights law. There are however, certain tensions. Lord Irvine, for one, has attempted to return to 'the jurisdiction under the HRA that Parliament intended' and, in so doing, encourage the SC to strike the correct balance between respecting the decisions of the ECtHR and not limiting its own creativity. The SC should only depart from the ECtHR 'on the basis that the resolution of the resultant conflict must take effect at State, not judicial, level'. Influencing this argument is the desire to 'enhance public respect for our British HRA and the development and protection of human rights by our own Courts in Britain'. Accompanying this claim is a powerful statement of the cultural autonomy of the common law judge:

> It is our own Judges who are embedded in our culture and society and so are best placed to strike the types of balance between the often competing rights and interests which adjudication under the HRA requires. Put shortly, more often than not we should trust our own judges to reach a 'better' answer.[55]

---

52   *Friend and Others* v. *UK* Nos. 16072/06 and 27809/08, 24.11.2009.
53   Supra, n. 1, at 508.
54   Equality and Human Rights Commission Research Report (2012: x).
55   Supra, n. 10, at 9.

But what is a 'better' answer? This is a slippery expression (as the quotation marks around the word suggest). Does the better answer relate to the terms of the 'dialogue'? Certainly a '[c]ourt which subordinates itself to follow another's rulings cannot enter into a dialogue with its superior in any meaningful sense'.[56] This, as a strategic point, may be true: however, it does beg the question of the values that inform the dialogue. The question can perhaps only be resolved at the level of principle: but, are the principles crisp enough to allow a determination?

Sales has provided a defence of the mirror principle that takes on Lord Irvine's position. He allows that '[t]here is certainly scope for argument in many cases about how to identify the proper interpretation of Convention rights' – even though this is not a dispute over the mirror principle itself.[57] He accuses Lord Irvine of misunderstanding the way in which the judges have developed a 'critical space' where they will only follow Strasbourg if it has established a 'clear and constant' line to be followed; a point supported by Lord Hoffmann's argument that the SC would not follow a ruling 'fundamentally at odds with the distribution of powers under British constitution'.[58]

So, we should probably avoid the extremes of the argument. The relationship between Strasbourg and the domestic courts is not one of the latter slavishly following the rulings of the former. We can see the dialogue between the domestic courts and the ECtHR as work in progress over the precise terms in which the mirror principle operates; or, to put this in slightly different terms, over the relationship between the domestic courts and an international court whose role is to ensure the coherent development of international law. In the final section of this chapter, we want to turn to a broader set of problems and issues that are impacted in the discussion of this area: the problem of democracy and human rights.

Criticisms of the ECtHR have come from both sides of the party political divide. In Parliamentary debate, Jack Straw, former New Labour minister, accused the court of 'judicial activism'. David Cameron has also shown himself to be a critic of the ECtHR.[59] These arguments have been taken up, in a somewhat different form, by Lord Sumption, who has tried to articulate the issue in terms of judicial encroachment on political decision making. He has argued that the whole idea of a 'a common legal standard' that underlies the law of human rights, 'breaks down when it is sought to apply it to all collective activity or political and administrative decision-making'. This is because 'the consensus necessary to support it at this level of detail simply does not exist'.[60] We might suggest then, that there are two variations on a theme in the

---

56   Ibid.
57   Sales (2012: 254).
58   Cited in Sales (2012: 255). There are two other fundamental moves in Sales' argument: first, that, as the problems concern statutory interpretation, that 'subjective views' of an Act's promoter are not definitive (255). Indeed, this can be understood as suggesting that public promulgation of legal principles is a task for the court who establish coherence using the 'fiction' of parliamentary intention. Thus: 'It is the objective interpretation of an Act, produced in line with a settled tradition and generally accepted standards of construction, which governs' (255).
59   Cited in Equality and Human Rights Report, 2012; Jack Straw MP, *Hansard*, HC Vol. 523, Col. 502, 10 February 2011.
60   Sumption (2011: 14).

criticisms of Strasbourg: the court has somehow 'encroached' on the power of politicians, and that human rights adjudication is increasingly political, and therefore, illegitimate.

What do we make of these arguments? Perhaps human rights have come to fill something of a void in British democracy. In the wake of the HRA, and as the very idea of a dialogue between the courts and Parliament assumes, judges are acting differently and, in certain instances, standing up to ministers. Is this a bad thing? The politicians who take anti-Strasbourg positions are perhaps responding to their sense in which their own power has somehow been questioned. As Nicol has argued 'the European Court of Human Rights' appears to have 'assume[d] a decisive role' because 'the guidance of rationally developed human rights law' is 'seen as more reliable than electorates: rational technocrats would not be swung by the vagaries of party-political ideology'.[61] Human rights – a discourse of 'rational technocrats' – leads to a clearer and less irrational development of principles to regulate public life. Politics is too emotive; driven by an irresponsible and unaccountable press and media. However, this argument is also problematic. It suggests a lack of faith in political processes.

The risk is the whole debate becomes distorted. If one examines the figure, then one finds that in 2011 only 3 per cent of the total number of cases against the UK considered by Strasbourg 'resulted in a judgment of the Court, several of which ended in findings of no violation'.[62] This hardly suggests that politicians are losing control, or that Strasbourg has taken over political and legal decision making. If we leave to one side the frustrations with certain elements of British politics, then we have to suggest that human rights law provides an important element in both political and legal decision making. We cannot allow hard cases and extreme political rhetoric to distract us from the facts. The HRA has led to changes in law and politics, changes that are arguably better for a realisation of a contemporary rule of law culture which means that, in certain cases, human rights places limits on what the executive can do.

Think again about cases like *EM*, *Limbuela*, *Re G* and *Abu Qatada*. Surely is it a good thing that asylum seekers are not left destitute, sleeping in car parks; that violent, abusive men do not get custody of children; that married and unmarried people have the same right to adopt, and that individuals, no matter how unpleasant they seem, and no matter how much we disagree with their ideas, are not tried on torture evidence.

CONCLUSION

This chapter has considered the relationship between Strasbourg and the common law courts. Since the HRA, human rights law has begun to play a more and more central role in the development of the common law. The common law courts are meant to be guided by the mirror principle, in ensuring that common law principles are coherent with those of human rights law. We have examined the developing jurisprudence around this issue reviewing a set of key authorities that concern various points of conflict and

---

61   Nicol (2010: 276).
62   Supra, n. 1.

collaboration between the ECtHR, the SC and the House of Lords. We have argued that – although there are points of tension – one needs to see the relationship as a work in progress. Whilst the idea of a dialogue remains a little vague, it can be used in a qualified sense to sketch out the dynamics of the relationship between the common law courts and Strasbourg. Our final points related to the ongoing debate about human rights law. We suggested that – while these issues are inseparable from our thinking of human rights – it is necessary to avoid the more extreme rhetoric, and to appreciate the key role that human rights plays in affirming the central values of a democratic polity.

CODA: PRISONER'S RIGHTS

In 2005, Strasbourg ruled that the blanket ban on prisoner's voting rights was a breach of Article 3 of Protocol No 1 of the European Convention on Human Rights. The Labour government failed to develop policy on this issue before defeat in the election of 2010. Coalition policy, founded on a compromise of granting a limited class of prisoners voting rights, was rejected by Parliament, and the blanket ban continued in force. The ECtHR responded by re-affirming its original decision, and giving the government a six-month deadline for reform; a deadline that was subsequently extended.[63]

While the Coalition government vacillates in its approach to prisoner's rights, critics of Strasbourg have seized upon the court's rulings to argue that its interference in policy making has gone too far. The time has come, so the argument goes, to 'stand up to' Strasbourg and assert the sovereignty of Parliament, even if this means that the UK is in breach of its international obligations. The European commissioner for human rights, Thomas Hammarberg, has countered this argument. He has asserted that:

> Any weakening of the human rights protections in the act would be noted outside the UK, and welcomed by less democratic states as tacit encouragement to weaken their own human rights protections. . . . What the UK does today will send a powerful signal to other states about what they can do tomorrow.

Hammarberg has criticised the general lack of knowledge and the tone of debate in the UK about the Convention:

> I must say that I find some of the criticism here in the UK against the Strasbourg system surprisingly ill-informed, and I have hoped that the politicians who know better would stand up stronger against this populist and xenophobic discourse.

The following point is worth pondering:

> Universal suffrage is a fundamental principle in a democracy. My position is that a blanket, automatic ban does indeed violate basic principles. If deprivation of the right

---

63 http://www.parliament.uk/documents/commons/lib/research/briefings/snpc-01764.pdf.

to vote is to be a punishment, then this should be expressly spelled out in each individual case by a judicial authority.

Hammarberg is not arguing that prisoners should – without question – have the right to vote. His argument is that a 'blanket ban' is a violation of human rights principles. Such principles are entirely coherent with the argument that prisoners should be deprived of the right to vote as a punishment. Depriving a prisoner of the right to vote, would, however, have to be 'expressly spelled out'. Surely this general approach is a development of rule of law principles that are meant to be central to the English legal system and the constitution. Where the state has the power to deprive an individual of a right, such a power should be carefully circumscribed by the law. Hammarberg's point is well made. Criticisms of the Convention and the ECtHR appear to be driven by xenophobia and ignorance, rather than an understanding of human rights.[64]

---

64   *The Guardian* 10/12/11, at http://www.guardian.co.uk/law/2011/dec/10/human-rights-uk-laws.

9

THE JUDICIAL PRACTICE OF STATUTORY INTERPRETATION

—————————•◦•—————————

An act of parliament is the exercise of the highest authority that this kingdom acknowledges upon earth. It hath power to bind every subject in the land, and the dominions thereunto belonging; nay, even the King himself, if particularly named therein. And it can not be altered, amended, dispensed with, suspended or repealed, but in the same forms and by the same authority of parliament.[1]

Parliament generally changes law for the worse, and . . . the business of the judges is to keep the mischief of its interference within the narrowest bounds.[2]

I shall . . . state, as precisely as I can, what I understand from the decided cases to be the principles on which the Courts of Law act in construing instruments in writing; and a statute is an instrument in writing. In all cases the object is to see what is the intention expressed by the words used. But, from the imperfection of language, it is impossible to know what that intention is without inquiring farther, and seeing what the circumstances were with reference to which the words were used, and what was the object, appearing from those circumstances, which the person using them had in view; for the meaning of words varies according to the circumstances with respect to which they were used.[3]

I remember only too well my first intervention as a new Minister at the Treasury on the Finance Bill in the very early hours of the morning on a subject about which I knew absolutely nothing but on which I had a marvellously thick book of briefing from the Inland Revenue. I appropriately read out the response to some detailed points that had been made by one of the Opposition spokesmen who stood up afterwards to say how well I had dealt with the point he had raised and welcomed my first intervention in Finance Bill Committees. However, I discovered from my private office afterwards that I had read out the wrong reply to the amendment. Clearly, it made not the slightest bit of difference.[4]

----

1   Blackstone, *Commentaries*, Vol. I, p. 185*.
2   Pollock (1882: 85).
3   Lord Blackburn in *River Wear Commissioners* v. *Adamson* [1877] 2 AC 743 at 763.
4   Lord Hayhoe, as reported in *Hansard*, 27 March 1996, reflecting upon the circumstances in which 'explanations' on proposed legislation are given in parliament. In the Westminster Parliament, exchanges sometimes take place late at night in nearly empty chambers while members have dinner, drink and discuss in places often away from the actual building but are called back to vote. Often a bill reflects a party political debate with party 'whips' ensuring that party members vote on one side or the other. The questions are often difficult but political warfare sometimes leaves little time for reflection. These are not ideal conditions for the making of authoritative statements about the meaning of a clause in a bill.

INTRODUCTION

We begin with a mixture of views on constitutionalism, political reality and separation of powers therein expressed. Statutory interpretation as performed by the judiciary is a subset of constitutional practice. The first, from Blackstone, can be seen as a representative statement of the doctrine of parliamentary supremacy. The second, from Pollock, may be seen as a more or less accurate description of the judicial mindset in Victorian times. While the common law could be presumed to be the repository of the community's collective wisdom as expressed through its judiciary, legislation was the imposition of a political will for reform. This could, and was perhaps best presumed to be, partisan and unreflective of the nuances of social life. This approach led to restrictive interpretation by literalist methods which sometimes blocked social progress. It remained the approach of English judges until some time after World War II, yet Lord Blackburn's comments show that it is not correct to hold that one approach dominated.

The first part of this chapter outlines the concept of the contemporary practice of statutory interpretation. Understanding statutory interpretation has not been helped by references – in decades of student orientated texts at least – to a model of 'rules' of interpretation, which, if they ever did convey any feel of what went on, were a relatively constrained account of options in practice. Instead we need to see it as a dynamic engagement with legal texts. We will not in this chapter present a guide to interpretation; instead, after setting the scene, we will concentrate upon certain recent developments, namely the impact of *Pepper* v. *Hart*, European methods of interpretation and the interpretative provisions of the Human Rights Act (HRA)1998. Our stance is to focus on the parameters, or limits, of judicial interpretation. Although the vast bulk of everyday practices of interpretation seem to pose few constitutional issues, we argue that the general practice operates within constraints of institutional legitimacy; any act of statutory interpretation involves matters of constitutional propriety. Indeed, writing in 1999 about the Human Rights Act, Lord Irvine spoke of the judiciary as 'an integral component in a constitutional machinery that seeks to secure accountable government'. Similarly, Lord Steyn has argued: 'The language used by Parliament does not interpret itself. Somebody must interpret and apply it. A democracy may, and almost invariably does, entrust the task of interpretation to the neutral decision-making of the judiciary'.[5] What are the current limits of this interpretive role? We will suggest that contemporary practice can be seen as evolving, informed by a democratic vision where the courts and Parliament operate in dialogue about the relationship of legislation and human rights.

STATUTORY INTERPRETATION AND INSTITUTIONAL LEGITIMACY

Statutory interpretation has very little to do with so-called 'rules' of interpretation. Whether or not these rules accurately reflect the approach of the courts in the past,

---

5   Lord Steyn (2004: 248).

they are largely irrelevant to the contemporary practice. At best, the priority of the literal approach stressed a general problematic: interpretation needs to be kept within certain constitutional constraints.[6] The main question in this chapter is thus a variation on one of the key points of the previous chapter: what picture can be drawn of the constitutional arrangements in which interpretation takes place? To what extent can interpretation be seen as law making, and, if so, what are the acceptable constraints of judicial legislation? This is, of course, a question of institutional legitimacy. Again we may have settled on a practice wherein interpretation takes place on a daily basis in such a fashion that the majority of cases do not appear to raise this problem of where the boundaries of interpretation lie. If the language of a statute is clear then interpretation is presumably entirely secondary to the application of the statute to the facts. While all interpretation occurs within an interpretative community and there are interesting issues in explaining interpretation in an increasingly pluralist social body, we are more concerned in this text with the constitutional propriety of interpretation in those instances where statutory language is ambiguous or capable of carrying different meanings, or where the law places on judges a particular set of interpretative demands stemming either from European law or the interpretative provisions of the Human Rights Act. The choice of one meaning rather than another may amount to law making. As the courts cannot be seen to overstep the boundaries in their legislative role, and intrude upon the province of Parliament, the real issue, in terms of the constitution of the practice, is where this boundary lies.

In elaborating this issue, we need to remind ourselves of some important arguments from the previous chapter. One should be careful when discussing rules of statutory interpretation not to impose too great a degree of rigidity or level of generality that fails to reflect what the judges are actually doing when they interpret statute. There are a couple of points to bear in mind. Any discussion of these 'techniques' as 'rules' is problematic, not least because we will be concerned with a practice as a rule in a non-legal sense: a rule as a guide to action. Future references of the rules of statutory interpretation will be understood as referring to the techniques that compose judicial practice. There is a second problem. Statements of practice in one case may or may not be understandable as general theories of interpretation. Judges tend not to give methodological statements that reflect in a general sense what they are doing. This begs another question: if judges practice statutory interpretation without a textbook, then why do textbooks have chapters on statutory interpretation?

This chapter offers an engagement with a number of key cases in order to try and determine how different judges in different areas of law deploy the techniques of interpretation. It is only at this level that anything useful or relevant can be said about statutory interpretation.

---

6   In *Duport Steels Ltd* v. *Sirs* [1980] 1 WLR 142, Lord Scarman stressed: 'In the field of statute law the judge must be obedient to the will of Parliament as expressed in the enactments. In this field Parliament makes and unmakes the law, the judge's duty is to interpret and to apply the law, not to change it to meet the judge's idea of what justice requires. Interpretation does, of course, imply in the interpreter a power of choice where differing constructions are possible. But our law requires the judge to choose the construction which in his judgment best meets the legislative purpose of the enactment' (p. 169).

It is worth considering another point that will run through this chapter. If we were trying to describe contemporary judicial practice, then we would have to take into account European 'purposive' methods of interpretation. The rules of interpretation have the virtue of reminding us that – at least in a historical perspective – purposive interpretation was always part of the common law.[7] Indeed, Twining has argued that purposive interpretation by British judges is justified not by references to European law, but to common sense.[8] Twining argues that interpretation of statutes can be analysed as falling into two stages. The first stage is to acquire a general sense of both the legal and factual context and the intention of the legislature; the next stage is to read the particular words in their primary and natural meaning, if they are ordinary words, or according to their technical meaning. If this leads to an absurd interpretation, the interpreter may put forward an interpretation that avoids the absurdity. With reference to this second stage, there are limits to the kind of materials to which the interpreter can make use. Another misleading aspect of statutory interpretation is that it suggests that there may be more of a clear distinction between literal and purposive interpretation than there in fact is in practice. It suggests a rather artificial approach that imagines a judge asking first about whether the words are unambiguous and if not, then how can they be read so as to give effect to the intention of Parliament.[9]

Twining is describing modern judicial practice. It is largely determined by pragmatism, and an engagement with the language of the Act in question in its legal context. This goes a long way to suggesting how judges approach statutory interpretation in those cases where no European or human rights issues might impinge; or, indeed, where no reference to *Pepper* v. *Hart* is necessary. We need, therefore, to move towards an engagement with these problematic and developing areas. However, for the moment we can ask some further questions about the suppositions that inform modern practice, and examine the role of the presuppositions of statutory interpretation.[10] The presumptions reflect the cast of the common law and the orientation of practice towards pragmatic questions of context and sense. A review of the presumptions may develop this argument.

....

7   The literal approach reflects the relatively recent dominance of Parliament over the courts.

8   Twining (1992: 368). We also need to be careful with the argument that community or civilian manners of interpretation should be adopted, or are being adopted by English judges. The problem is in part definitional. It is not entirely clear what is meant by continental ways of interpretation, other than stating that they are purposive. (As the mischief rule is purposive, English judges have always had recourse to purposive interpretation; *Re Marr* would also suggest that the judges themselves do not necessarily see purposive interpretation as European). It is a question more of preserving the idea that the court defers to Parliament. In European law purposive interpretation may be legitimate, but there is the risk that if followed too far, it would involve the courts in making rather than interpreting the law. Besides, as Twining writes: 'the pragmatism of English judges makes discussion of the proposition that they ought in general to adopt a purposive approach a little unrealistic'.

9   Glanville Williams has suggested that a more accurate description of the judge's practice would read as follows: 'What was the statute trying to do? Will the proposed interpretation [be] ruled out by the language of the statute?' What does this mean? He explains: 'literal and purposive interpretation may be seen to represent varying emphases on how these questions are to be answered; in particular, on how far a judge is prepared to go in deciding whether a proposed interpretation is or is not sustained by the language of the statute. In short, context, language and purpose are all relevant, but there is still no settled priority rules for weighting these factors'. Cited in Twining (1992: 369).

10   The presumptions are: against the alteration of the common law; that *mens rea* should be an element in criminal offences; against the retrospective application of statute; against the deprivation of individual's liberty, property or rights; a presumption that legislation does not apply to the Crown; a presumption against breach of international law and a presumption that words take their meaning from their context.

The first presumption, against the alteration of the common law, suggests that interpretation is inherently conservative; the law appears as a repository of meanings that are authorised by its history. Thus, rather than presuming a change in the law, a judge will presume that the law is coherent and without gaps. There are also presumptions that have a particular slant towards rights or liberties.[11] That the HRA contains an interpretative provision suggests that these presumptions may not have been as effective as they might have been in protecting rights and liberties. Nevertheless, we could say that common law interpretation appears to have always had a commitment to preserving these values. The presumptions against breach of international law can be seen as informing a notion that common law is coherent with international law, unless Parliament has stated otherwise. It suggests some interesting points about the relationship of national and international legal norms, but we cannot engage with this material in this chapter. The presumption that legislation does not apply to the Crown is historic and suggests the privileges accorded to the Crown. The seventh presumption reflects on the aids to construction that can be utilised. Within this catalogue, there is a basic distinction between intrinsic and extrinsic evidence, and a grouping of rules that relate to presumptions about how certain verbal formulations are to be understood. We could say that this represents the legal employment of certain grammatical rules. These rules reflect more upon the micro-economic level of interpretation, and stress that statutory interpretation is inherently a form of textual close reading. It is as much about resolving grammatical and syntactical problems as it is about the operation of specifically legal principles of interpretation. The presumptions remind us that statutory interpretation is about rules that are necessarily involved in acts of reading that operate within a specifically legal context.

PEPPER V. HART[12]

To return to our principle of analysis: we will examine statutory interpretation through a close reading of some central cases. One of the most important cases defining contemporary practice is *Pepper* v. *Hart*. Here the Judicial Committee of the House of Lords sat nine strong (over half of the total membership of the Judicial Committee) to hear an appeal in which the plaintiff claimed that the advocates of the bill had a quite different intention for the Act than the one put forward by the Inland Revenue. The minister had actually said on the floor of the House of Commons that teachers in private schools who had their children take up spare places at discounted fees would not be taxed on the difference as if this was a financial benefit in kind, whereas the Inland Revenue wanted to tax the teachers as if the teachers had received the benefit of the discounted school fees (as the clear words of the Act seemed to indicate). The Lords took the opportunity to consider whether when applying a statute the judges should consider only the words of the Act or whether they could look at *Hansard* to

---

11   The requirement that criminal offences have *mens rea*; that statute does not apply retrospectively; that people are not to be deprived of rights and liberties.
12   *Pepper* v. *Hart* [1993] 1 All ER, 42.

see evidence of the clear intention of the progenitors. They decided in favour of the teachers.

To what extent did *Pepper* v. *Hart* revolutionise methods of interpretation by allowing judges access to Parliamentary materials to which they would not otherwise have access? The case shows that defining the parameters of judicial interpretative practice involves questions of constitutional propriety and the very function of the forensic process. Indeed, the subsequent case law attempts to define a line between the political and the judicial that may be very difficult to hold.

Prior to *Pepper* v. *Hart*, the courts had not been able to look at the *Hansard* debates[13] as an aid to interpreting statute. Although the case changed this rule, it went on to narrowly define the occasions when a court could make reference to *Hansard*. To enable a reference to *Hansard*, legislation must be ambiguous. To resolve the ambiguities, the court can make use of ministerial statements. This clearly means that the courts cannot make use of statements made by MPs in debate or argument, and the statements themselves have to be clear.

How can this approach be justified? Why should the rule that had always structured judicial practice be relaxed? Lord Browne-Wilkinson began the leading speech in *Pepper* v. *Hart* by reviewing the arguments as to why references to *Hansard* should still be prohibited. The primary reason was constitutional. The courts must look only to the words used in the Act, as otherwise there is a risk of judicial legislation. Lord Browne-Wilkinson then touched upon a related issue. *Hansard* material may not be forensically suitable, as it may have been said in the heat of debate, or from a politically partisan position. Difficulties in providing access to definitive text of debates, and cost implications, had also militated against the use of *Hansard* in the court.[14]

If these are the arguments for preserving the existing practice, what are the issues that compel change? It would appear that practice itself has already moved beyond the constraints of the old approach: the courts have departed from the old literal approach of statutory construction and now adopt a purposive approach, seeking to discover the Parliamentary intention lying behind the words used and construing the legislation so as to give effect to, rather than thwart, the intentions of Parliament. Where the words used by Parliament are obscure or ambiguous, the Parliamentary material may throw considerable light not only on the mischief which the Act was designed to remedy, but also on the purpose of the legislation and its anticipated effect.[15]

This speech stresses that there is a historical shift in judicial interpretation. This is, in part, due to the impact of purposive styles of European interpretation; it is no wonder that *Pepper* builds on *Pickstone* v. *Freemans*.[16] Note that a difference has to be observed in the interpretation of domestic and European legislation. It is with the latter that the court can be 'more flexible'.[17] However, there is another factor in the

---

13   The official record of debates in Parliament.
14   Against this position, the Law Commission reporting in 1969 and the Renton Committee had recommended that the rule outlawing the use of *Hansard* be reconsidered.
15   *Supra* n12, at 633.
16   *Pickstone* v. *Freemans* [1988] 3 WLR 265.
17   The precise parameters of this flexibility will have to be defined by subsequent case law.

argument that suggests that purposive interpretation cannot be so neatly limited to European law. Lord Griffith's speech elaborates this point. He argued that the increasing volume of legislation carries with it the risk that 'ambiguities in statutory language' are not apparent at the time the bill is drafted.

How should the new approach be defined? It is necessary to return to fundamental principles. The task of the court is to interpret the intention of Parliament. If the court cannot use *Hansard* to interpret ambiguous language then it may become frustrated in this task.[18]

What does this mean? How is the purposive approach to be defined? It is a question of carefully plotting the parameters that are discoverable in the cases where *Pepper* v. *Hart* has been applied.[19] In *R. (on the application of Spath Holme Ltd)* v. *Secretary of State for the Environment, Transport and the Regions*,[20] the House of Lords considered an argument that it was necessary to make a reference to *Hansard*. The reference would show that the powers of a minister granted by the Landlord and Tenants Act 1985 to restrict rent increases were narrow and applied only to the restriction of inflation in the economy. Rejecting this approach the court stressed the importance of the first limb of the ratio of *Pepper* v. *Hart*. Unless this first condition was satisfied, there was a danger that any case that raised an issue of statutory construction would necessitate disproportionate costs as lawyers researched the relevance of Parliamentary statements. However, there is also a constitutional element to the House of Lord's argument that returns us to one of the structuring concerns of statutory interpretation. Whereas it may be acceptable to rely on the statements of the minister sponsoring the bill, the court cannot consider Parliamentary exchanges in debate. Such matters are

----

18   *Pepper*, at 617. In summary: Lord Browne-Wilkinson's guidelines show that a reference to *Hansard* is only acceptable when three conditions applied. First, the legislation in question was 'ambiguous or obscure, or led to an absurdity'. Second, that the material to which reference would be made were 'statements by a minister or other promoter of the Bill' with material that might support these statements which, third, had to themselves amount to a clear statement.

19   *Melluish (Inspector of Taxes) Appellant* v. *B.M.I. No. 3* [1996] AC 454 affirmed that the rule in *Pepper* was narrow; the case should not be seen as an opportunity to begin to 'widen' the kinds of materials that could be considered to interpret legislation. This rule was clarified still further in *Three Rivers DC* v. *Bank of England No. 2* [1996] 2 All ER 363. The court asserted that speeches made in Parliament could be used by a court to ascertain both the true meaning of statutory language and the intention of Parliament in passing a particular Act. More recently, the issue of the correct use of *Hansard* has arisen with respect to construing the Human Fertilisation and Embryology Act 1990 s. 28(3). The question facing the court in *U* v. *W (Attorney General Intervening) No. 1* [1997] Eu. LR 342 was whether a licence was required for certain forms of fertility treatment. The court held that *Hansard* could be used to resolve the issue of whether or not the restriction on licences was justifiable. This was because relevant issues arose in the discussion of the bill in the House of Lords. The second and third parts of the *Pepper* v. *Hart* conditions also applied. However, in an interesting adaptation of the test, it was held that *Hansard* could be referred to even though the first part of the *Pepper* v. *Hart* conditions did not apply.

20   *R. (on the application of Spath Holme Ltd)* v. *Secretary of State for the Environment, Transport and the Regions* [2001] 1 All ER 195. It is worth briefly examining two recent cases to see how *Pepper* v. *Hart* continues to be used. In *Chilcott* v. *Revenue and Customs Commissioners* [2009] EWHC 3287 (Ch). The Court of Chancery considered – and rejected – the argument that in order to prevent an 'injustice produced by a literal interpretation' Parliamentary materials should be considered, and the court should read the relevant section of the Income and Corporation Taxes Act 'as if the unjust provision were not incorporated'. The court could resolve ambiguities in an Act, but it could not re-write legislation. *Morgan* v. *Fletcher* [2009] UKUT 186 (LC) also concerned an issue of fairness, but is a very different case from *Chilcott*. *Morgan* involved arguments over the meaning of service charges under the Landlord and Tenants Act 1985. The relevant section was ambiguous and a report and ministerial statements were used to clarify the relevant words. The court decided that the tribunal had acted in error in changing the proportions in which different tenants paid service charges.

unsuited for the forensic process. Furthermore, such scrutiny comes close to breaching Article 9 of the Bill of Rights. This prohibits the court from questioning proceedings in Parliament. The case concluded with the court asserting that as the meaning of the relevant section was not ambiguous, there was no need to make use of *Hansard*.[21] *Spath Holme Ltd* thus goes some way to determining the form of the post-*Pepper v. Hart* practice. We can see that, while *Pepper v. Hart* acknowledges that a new practice is necessary, this practice has to be informed by a conventional understanding of the role of the courts. The techniques of purposive interpretation are thus 'revolutionary' only to a degree. They work within the existing constitutional settlement. It is worth clarifying this point still further. Just because a new practice is under development, this does not mean that the institutional or doctrinal structure of law is also being transformed. A significant development in a practice is thus entirely consistent with the continuity of other institutions. Furthermore, the fundamental 'shape' of the practice remains continuous with its general orientation, despite its own transformation. Purposive interpretation might thus realign, but it does not fundamentally alter the relationship between Parliament and the courts.

PURPOSIVE INTERPRETATION

So, might it be the case that the judicial practice of statutory interpretation is increasingly purposive? It is interesting, in this respect, to consider an American authority from 1945. Learned Hand J, explained in *Cabell v. Markham*[22] that the 'literal sense' remains the 'most reliable' way of interpreting words; but 'a mature and developed jurisprudence' also 'remember[s] that statutes always have some purpose or object to accomplish, whose sympathetic and imaginative discovery is the surest guide to their meaning'. Purposive interpretation has always been a technique of common law judges.[23] Lord Bingham, who cited this case in *R. (on the application of Quintavalle) v. Secretary of State for Health*[24] suggested that – in contemporary judicial practice – the 'pendulum has swung towards purposive methods of construction'. These interpretative tendencies have been encouraged by 'the teleological approach of European Community jurisprudence, and the influence of European legal culture generally'. But, how purposive should a court be? Lord Bingham argued that: 'the degree of liberality permitted is influenced by the context, e.g. social welfare legislation and tax statutes may have to be approached somewhat differently.' So, we might think that the extent to which a court will use a purposive method relates to the area of law under consideration.

This point appears to be confirmed by the main authorities. *Quintavalle*, and an important earlier case, *Royal College of Nursing v. DHSS*, concerned advances in

---

21   Also relevant to the argument in this case was the status of the 1985 Act as a consolidating statute. The normal rule for the interpretation of this kind of statute is that it is not permitted to look at the law that it replaced as an aid to its interpretation. It was only possible to make use of the old law when the Act itself was ambiguous.
22   *Cabell v. Markham* (1945) 148 F 2d 737, at 739.
23   See Lord Blackburn in *River Wear Comrs v. Adamson* (1877) 2 App Case 743, 763.
24   *R. (on the application of Quintavalle) v. Secretary of State for Health* [2003] 2 AC 687.

medical technology and techniques. Could the relevant statutes be interpreted purposively so that they covered new concerns? In *Royal College of Nursing v. DHSS*,[25] Lord Wilberforce (dissenting) pointed out that the starting point is to 'have regard to the state of affairs existing, and known by Parliament to be existing, at the time' that the Act became law. The courts then have to consider whether a 'fresh set of facts . . . fall within the parliamentary intention'. Lord Wilberforce proposed a test. A new set of facts could be held to fall within Parliament's intention if the facts cover 'the same genus of facts as those to which the expressed policy has been formulated'. This is, of course, a rule of thumb. Further guidance can be obtained by reference to 'the nature of the enactment, and the strictness or otherwise of the words in which it has been expressed'. Thus, judges would be 'less willing' to 'extend' the meaning of a statute if 'it is clear that the Act in question was designed to be restrictive or circumscribed in its operation rather than liberal or permissive'. Extending the meaning of the Act would be even less permissible if 'the subject matter is different in kind or dimension from that for which the legislation was passed'. The key point is that judges 'cannot fill gaps'.

Remember that we are not concerned with HRA or European Union law. We are attempting to determine the acceptable degree of purposive interpretation outside of these areas. Lord Bingham in *Quintavalle* provided an updating of Lord Wilberforce's argument that the court could not fill in gaps. He pointed out that a narrow adherence to the literal rule may even lead to the 'frustration of the will of Parliament' because 'undue concentration on the minutiae of the enactment may lead the court to neglect the purpose which Parliament intended to achieve when it enacted the statute'. Context, for Lord Bingham as for Lord Wilberforce, is the guide: 'the controversial provisions should be read in the context of the statute as a whole, and the statute as a whole should be read in the historical context of the situation which led to its enactment'.

Whilst the key points are clear, these are still very general guidelines. How could they be applied? We can take up this question in our analysis of *R. v. Human Fertilisation and Embryology Authority, ex parte Blood*.[26] This case concerned Mrs Blood's argument that sperm from her terminally ill and unconscious husband could be used for her posthumous insemination. The Court of Appeal refused to interpret the Human Fertilisation and Embryology Act 1990 in such a way as to obviate the need for written consent from Mr Blood for the 'cryopreservation' of the sperm. The applicant's argument was that – given the context of their loving relationship, desire for a family, and her husband's family's consent – the relevant part of the statute could be interpreted as allowing an exception to cover those couples in a 'common joint enterprise'. Sir Stephen Brown did not accept this argument. Why? Perhaps his reluctance to interpret the statute broadly was to do with the evidence that the court had heard: he stressed that taking the samples were Mrs Blood's 'unilateral' decision. However, Sir Stephen Brown was also reluctant to interpret purposively in such a 'highly sensitive and ethically controversial' area. This would seem a little strange, given that in

25   *Royal College of Nursing v. DHSS* [1981] AC 800.
26   *R. v. Human Fertilisation and Embryology Authority, ex parte Blood* [1999] Fam. 151.

Quintavalle, the court chose to interpret purposively in an area that was just as controversial: regulations relating to embryo experiments. Likewise, in *Royal College of Nursing* v. *DHSS*, the court held that nurses could take part in a medical procedure not envisaged by the Abortion Act 1967.

A great deal may depend on the actual wording of the statutes concerned; but, other factors are important as well. We can examine another authority. In an unrelated area of law, the House of Lords held in *R*. v. *Z*.[27] that the reference to the IRA as a prescribed organisation under the Terrorism Act 2000 could be interpreted to cover a breakaway organisation, the real IRA. So, we have to ask questions of context. As Lord Carswell put it:

> If the words of a statutory provision, when construed in a literalist fashion, produce a meaning which is manifestly contrary to the intention which one may readily impute to Parliament, when having regard to the historical context and the mischief, then it is not merely legitimate but desirable that they should be construed in the light of the purpose of the legislature in enacting the provision.[28]

Lord Carswell's reference to 'the mischief' which the statute chooses to engage is not a reference to the mischief rule. Rather, he is identifying the 'purpose or mischief' – that of combating terrorism – that allows the Act to be legitimately interpreted in a broad manner. To read back from this case to *Regina* v. *Human Fertilization and Embryology Authority*, the decision to interpret purposively in one case and not in the other seems somewhat arbitrary; surely it would be possible to have argued in the earlier case that the facts were such that they fell outside of the mischief that Parliament sought to resolve; and that it was indeed possible to argue that – on the facts – consent could have been deemed to those in a joint enterprise. The general conclusion is that, whilst the general boundaries of the practice of purposive interpretation can be sketched with reasonable precision, there are too many subjective factors in play to say with great certainty whether or not any given statute will be interpreted narrowly or broadly.

EUROPEAN INTERPRETATION

To what extent has the court's interpretation of European law influenced the forms that judicial practice is taking? Lord Denning provides a starting point:

> No longer must they [the judges] examine the words in meticulous detail. No longer must they argue about the precise grammatical sense. They must look to purpose or intent. To quote the words of the European Court in the Da Coasta case they must deduce from the wording and the spirit of the Treaty the meaning of the Community rules . . . They must divine the spirit of the Treaty and gain inspiration from it. If they

---

27 *R*. v. *Z* [2005] UKHL 2005.
28 Ibid., para 49.

fill a gap, they must fill it as best they can. They must do what the framers of the instrument would have done if they had thought about it. So we must do the same.[29]

[The impact of European methods of interpretation is undoubtedly having an important impact on the practice of statutory interpretation] But think about what Lord Denning is saying. The claim about 'no longer' needing to examine words in meticulous detail are somewhat misleading. We have seen above that[common law judges always made use of a form of purposive interpretation][The need to interpret European law lifts this into a new context; it may even be that this means that the courts have to follow European law rather than English law if there is a conflict] We will deal with this matter presently. For the moment, let us focus on one of our key concerns: how do European methods of interpretation shape or reshape the constitutional parameters of interpretative practice. We need to return to the principle of the supremacy of European law. Lord Denning outlined this doctrine in *Macarthys* v. *Smith*:

> It is important now to declare – and it must be made plain – that the provisions of Article 119 of the Treaty of Rome take priority over anything in our English statute on equal pay which is inconsistent with Article 119. That priority is given by our own law. It is given by the European Communities Act 1972 itself. Community law is now part of our law: and, whenever there is any inconsistency, Community law has priority. It is not supplanting English law. It is part of our law which overrides any other part which is inconsistent with it.[30]

[European law takes priority over English statutes because Parliament has so provided] How does the doctrine of sovereignty relate to judicial interpretation? Our concern could be phrased as follows: in understanding the judicial interpretation of community law and the extent to which it allows a distortion of the literal meaning of statute, to what extent is judicial creativity limited by their perception of constitutional boundaries?

FIRST STEPS: [*GARLAND* V. *BRITISH RAIL ENGINEERING LTD*]

Once again, answering this question means looking at the development of the judicial practice.[In *Garland* v. *British Rail Engineering Ltd*[31] the House of Lords held that s.6 (4) of the Sexual Discrimination Act should be interpreted in such a way as to make it consistent with Article 119 of the EEC Treaty][The problem was that the words of the relevant section were capable of two different and opposed interpretations: one that suited the applicants and one that suited the respondents][Lord Diplock argued, and

---

29   *Bulmer v. Bollinger* [1974] Ch 401, at 426.
30   *Macarthys v. Smith* [1979] 3 All ER 32, at 218.
31   *Garland v. British Rail Engineering Ltd* [1982] 2 WLR 918.

the rest of the House concurred, that the meaning of the section which was consistent with Article 119 had to be preferred. Lord Diplock also made use of a principle of interpretation 'too well established to call for citation of authority' that a statute passed after an international treaty had to be interpreted as consistent with the obligations that the country had undertaken. Interestingly, he avoided the question of whether or not a provision expressly intended by Parliament to contravene European obligations would be so interpreted by the court.

THE FORKING PATH: *DUKE V. GEC RELIANCE*

The parameters of this mode of interpretation can be seen in the later case *Duke* v. *GEC Reliance*.[32] In this case the House of Lords interpreted sections 2(4) and 2(6) of the Sexual Discrimination Act. It was asserted that the 1975 Act was not meant to give effect to the Directive on Equal Treatment issued in 1976. As s.2 (4) of the EC Act did not allow a court to 'distort' the meaning of the statute, European employment rights should not be available in English law. This is surprising. One would expect that the court would have to construe the British statute in such a way as to make it harmonise with Community law. However, the court followed an earlier precedent. *Marshall*[33] promoted a much narrower approach to the interpretation of statute; stressing that if the domestic statute had not been 'intended'[34] to give effect to European obligations, then the court was limited by the words of the Act. On the facts of the present case, as the provisions of the 1976 Act could not carry the interpretation urged by the appellants, the court had to give effect to the literal meaning of the Act. The 1986 Sex Discrimination Act was passed to bring retirement ages into line with European law, but, as this Act was not retrospective, it did not help the appellant's case. What conclusions can we draw from these two cases? Although the issues raised are similar, and the same sections of the 1975 Act are interpreted in both cases, it would seem that the central difference relates to the court's understanding of the 1976 directive and its effect in English law. As the 1986 Act did not have retrospective effect, it was not possible to apply a strained interpretation to the 1975 Act to make it consistent with the directive. Some commentators have argued that *Duke* was wrongly decided.[35] *Marshall* had held that a directive could not create obligations between individuals. In *Marleasing*, the European Court of Justice (ECJ) had relied on an earlier authority, *Van Colson*, to assert that a court had to interpret national law as consistent with European obligations whether or not the national law pre- or post-dated a directive.[36] From this perspective, it would appear that the courts have a much bolder role to play

---

32   *Duke v. GEC Reliance* [1988] 2 WLR 359.
33   Case 152/84, *Marshall v. Southampton and South West Hampshire Area Health Authority* [1986] ECR 723; [1986] 1 CMLR 688; [1986] QB 401.
34   *Marshall v. Southampton and South West Hampshire Area Health Authority* [1986] 2 All ER 584, cited in Duke at 639.
35   Mead (1991).
36   The ECJ argued that the obligation to enforce directives was a duty under Article 5 and Article 189 of the Treaty of Rome.

in the interpretation of national legislation, and that judicial practice could make use of the *Van Colson* doctrine to assert, against *Duke*, that there was an overriding objective to ensure judicial protection of European rights.[37]

THE PATH REGAINED: *PICKSTONE V. FREEMANS*

Pickstone v. Freemans[38] (shows the court approaching the interpretation of national legislation far more robustly than they had in *Duke*. In this case, the House of Lords had to interpret s.1 (2) of the Equal Pay Act 1970. The Act had been amended to make it coherent with obligations arising under Article 119 of the Treaty of Rome. The key question was whether the amendment of the Act actually did give effect to the obligations under the treaty. In approaching the interpretation of the Act, their lordships began from a purposive position. Lord Nicholls, for instance, determined that the purpose of the Article was twofold: to ensure consistency in the legal systems of member states across the community, and to improve working conditions. These objectives are furthered by a directive, and by ECJ cases that clarify the precise terms of community law. A problem arose because on at least one interpretation of the relevant sections of the UK Act, it did not accord with European law. Furthermore, the 'broad' interpretation of the section that would have made the law coherent was difficult to square with the wording of the Act.

What, then, should be the correct approach? Lord Diplock's argument in *Garland* provided a point of reference. Only express wording in an Act passed prior to the date that the UK had joined the Community would allow a court to conclude that it was not intended to be consistent with European law. The court was thus justified in particularly 'wide' departures from the wording of the Act 'in order to achieve consistency'. Argument focused on whether 'exclusionary' words in the Act had the effect of limiting the section in such a way as to not give full effect to Convention Rights.[39]

What are the consequences of this argument? The literal interpretation would compel the conclusion that the Act was in breach of European law; furthermore, it would not be consistent with the principle articulated by Lord Diplock. In Lord Oliver's opinion, the Act was reasonably capable of bearing the interpretation that would make it consistent with European law. Ultimately, it was held that a purposive interpretation allowed the appellant's case to succeed. Their argument was helped by

---

37   See *Marleasing SA v. La Commercial Internacional de Alimentacion SA* [1992] 1 CMLR 305. The issue in these cases is also the extent to which European law is enforceable against private parties as well as the state. *Marleasing* went beyond *Marshall*, and extended European law rights to private parties.
38   *Pickstone v. Freemans* [1988] 3 WLR 265.
39   This impacts on interpretative techniques. Lord Keith argued that it was 'plain' that Parliament could not have 'intended' to depart from its European law obligations. Under the circumstances of the case, he felt it was entirely legitimate that the court should consider the draft regulations. Lord Oliver was concerned that the case did indeed raise issues that made for a 'departure' from the normal rules of statutory interpretation. It would not normally be open to a court to depart from a literal interpretation of an Act simply because the Act was passed to give effect to an international treaty. Furthermore, parliamentary materials cannot normally be relied upon as aids to construction. However, European law was different. Parliament had in s.2 (1) of the EC Act, incorporated European law into domestic law.

the fact that the court took into account the Equal Pay Regulations of 1983 that had brought the statute in line with Community law. Although these draft regulations had not been subjected to the same Parliamentary process as a bill, they had been passed to give effect to a decision of the ECJ. It was thus legitimate to take into account Parliament's purpose in interpreting the draft regulations.

ON THE ROAD: *LITSTER V. FORTH DRY DOCK & ENGINEERING CO. LTD*

In *Litster v. Forth Dry Dock & Engineering Co. Ltd*[40] the House of Lords went even further than *Pickstone.* The court gave a purposive interpretation to a statutory instrument that concerned rules relating to the transfer of employees' rights in the event of the sale of a business. The court 'implied' words into the terms of the regulation so as to make it compatible with obligations under European law. Lord Oliver provided a useful summary of the court's approach in *Litster*. The court must first of all determine the precise nature of the obligations concerned by construing the wording of both the relevant directive, and the interpretation given to that directive by the ECJ. If it can be 'reasonably construed' in such a manner, UK legislation must then be purposively interpreted so as to give effect to European law. This approach can allow the courts to depart from the literal meaning of the words used.

OFF THE MAP? *WEBB V. EMO AIR CARGO* AND *GRANT V. SOUTH WESTERN TRAINS*

Pickstone v. Freemans and *Litster* certainly seem to show the development of a new judicial practice that moves beyond the restraints on statutory interpretation prior to 1972. However, it would be wrong to assume from these cases that practice has so moved on that literal interpretation is 'dead'. The starting point remains a literal reading of the statute. Thus, in *Carole Louise Webb v. EMO Air Cargo (UK) Limited No.2*[41] the 1975 Sex Discrimination Act was again subject to interpretation. As the House of Lords could interpret the relevant sections of the Act in such a way, there was no need to distort the language of the statute or to otherwise alter the literal sense. It is also worth remembering that the law of the EU itself limits the purposive approach.

This can be seen in *Grant v. South Western Trains*.[42] The ECJ refused to prohibit discrimination based on sexual orientation. In theory, they might have been able to

40   *Litster and Others Appellants v. Forth Dry Dock & Engineering Co. Ltd* [1989] 2 WLR 634.
41   *Carole Louise Webb v. EMO Air Cargo (UK) Limited No. 2* [1995] 1 WLR 1454.
42   *Grant v. South Western Trains* (Case 249/96) (1998) *The Times*, 23 February.

broaden the terms of Article 119 and the relevant directives.[43] However, the court felt that as community law did not recognise homosexual marriages, this issue could only be dealt with at a national level. *Grant* indicates one extreme constitutional line that Community law will not cross. It is interesting that this raises a question of sexual morality. The consequence of this means that while issues of sexual discrimination have frequently formed the context for tensions between UK and Community law that have occasioned debates on the acceptable boundaries of judicial discretion, the resistance to equal rights for gays and lesbians means that it is unlikely to give rise to acts of bold interpretation.[44]

Recent cases have further clarified the terms of the interpretative powers of the court. *Pfeiffer* v. *Deutsches Rotes Kreuz*[45] stressed this point: 'the principle of interpretation in conformity with Community law requires the referring court to do whatever lies within its jurisdiction, having regard to the whole body of rules of national law, to ensure that [a Directive] is fully effective'. An elaboration of this principle can be seen in *Revenue and Customs* v. *IDT Card Services Ireland Ltd.*[46] In interpreting a tax directive, the Court of Appeal applied *Ghaidan* (see below) even though the case did not raise a human rights point. In interpreting European Union law, the court asserted that the correct approach was to ensure that the court kept within the fundamental terms of the legislation in question. In so doing, a wide power of interpretation did not breach the principle of legal certainty.

THE POLITICS OF INTERPRETATION UNDER THE HUMAN RIGHTS ACT

The interpretative provisions of the Human Rights Act have had a major impact in judicial interpretative practices. Our consideration of the new practices has to begin by

---

43   *Webb* was followed in *Alabaster* v. *Woolwich* [2005] EWCA Civ 508 by the Court of Appeal, when they dis-applied the requirement for a male comparator under the Equal Pay Act 1970 to allow an increase in maternity payments under the relevant EC law. *Webb* was also followed in *Hardman* v. *Mallon* [2002] IRLR 516. In *AC* v. *Berkshire West Primary Care Trust* [2010] EWHC 1162 (Admin) the QBD held that the policy of a care trust to consider requests for breast augmentation from transsexual patients as 'non core' procedures was not discriminatory. The Equality and Human Rights Commission had intervened relying on *Webb*, but the court did not accept their argument and distinguished *Webb*. They pointed out that, whilst a transsexual 'seeking genital reconstruction surgery' might be able to 'rely on *Webb* for breast augmentation' it was necessary to take into account limitations on NHS budgets and the fact that some requests for surgery from transsexual patients could be legitimately refused. In *R.* v. *South Bank University* v. *Coggeran* [2000] ICR 1342 *Webb* was also distinguished. The case concerned the exclusion of a student from her University course. The Court of Appeal held that although the Board of examiners should reconsider Coggeran's dismissal from the course, the trial judge had mistakenly compared 'the dismissal of pregnant women from employment and the exclusion of a woman from an educational establishment' for a pregnancy related illness. This approach broadened the relevant Directive to too great an extent.
44   For other limitations on European law, see *R.* v. *Immigration Appeal Tribunal Ex p. Bernstein* [1988] 3 C.M.L.R. 445. Bernstein was refused a work permit on the basis that the job she sought was 'modestly paid' and 'did not justify recourse to a foreign worker'. On appeal, the applicant argued that the Treaty of Rome and Council Directive 76/207 required the Sex Discrimination Act 1975 to be interpreted in such a way as to apply to immigration proceedings. The Court of Appeal did not agree. Bingham LJ succinctly summarised the position: the Directive did not 'oblige member-States to observe the principle of equal treatment in granting permits to non-Community nationals outside the Community seeking leave to enter and work in a member-state [.]' (33).
45   *Pfeiffer* v. *Deutsches Rotes Kreuz* [2005] 1 CMLR 44.
46   *Revenue and Customs* v. *IDT Card Services Ireland Ltd* [2006] EWCA Civ 29.

looking at section 3 of the Act. Note first of all that the range of this provision – it applies to primary and secondary legislation 'whenever enacted' – before or after the Act. The effect of s.3 (2) b, however, is that the incompatibility of a piece of primary legislation with the HRA does not mean that this legislation is held to be void.[47] In other words, parliamentary sovereignty is left in place. We are thus concerned with the realignment of a judicial practice rather than its complete redefinition. The pressing question is: how will the courts interpret legislation in the light of s.3? The government White Paper, 'Rights Brought Home' stated that s.3 would go 'far beyond' the rules prior to the HRA which had allowed the court to take into account the ECHR in interpreting legislation and clarifying ambiguity: 'The courts will be required to interpret legislation so as to uphold convention rights unless the legislation itself is so clearly incompatible with the Convention that it is impossible to do so'.[48] While this clearly articulates a rule of interpretation, it leaves a great deal of discretion in the hands of the interpreter to determine whether or not it is impossible to interpret legislation as compatible with the Convention. We are concerned once again with the constitutional boundaries of the judicial practice.

One of the first key authorities is *Wilson v. First County Trust*.[49] Let us consider Lord Nicholls' argument. He addressed the idea that the courts are themselves public authorities, and therefore bound by the HRA. Would this mean that as the courts are bound by the Act, they would be compelled to discount an Act of Parliament that was inconsistent with the Act? This would clearly be a very broad interpretation of the Human Rights Act. Indeed, it would effectively make the Human Rights Act itself sovereign, and bring to an end the sovereignty of Parliament. As this was never the intended effect of the Act, it could not be a valid interpretation. In interpreting a statute in the light of the HRA, it was necessary to abide by constitutional principles and give effect to the will of Parliament; however, the court could consider the 'proportionality of legislation'. In approaching the issue of proportionality, the court was fulfilling a reviewing role. Parliament retained the primary responsibility for deciding the appropriate form of legislation. The court would reach a different conclusion from the legislature only when it was apparent that the legislature had attached insufficient importance to a person's Convention right. The readiness of the court to depart from the views of the legislature depended on the circumstances, one of which was the

47 Moreover, it does not allow a court to hold subordinate or secondary legislation to be invalid if the primary legislation does not allow the incompatibility with the HRA to be remedied.
48 Rights Brought Home: The Human Rights Bill, Command Paper No. Cm 3782, para 2.7.
49 *Wilson v. First County Trust* [2003] HRLR 33. Mrs Wilson had argued that a loan that she had taken from a pawnbroker and not repaid was unenforceable, because the agreement did not contain all the prescribed terms, contrary to the Consumer Credit Act of 1974. In particular Mrs Wilson was objecting to a fee for preparation of documents that she had been charged and which was not mentioned in the loan agreement. Her argument was that the 1974 Act made the agreement unenforceable. The County Court held that the agreement was enforceable, and Mrs Wilson had appealed to the Court of Appeal, which reversed the County Court's judgment. The Court of Appeal also made a declaration under s.4 of the HRA. The Court of Appeal argued that the 1974 Act was incompatible with the rights guaranteed to the creditor by Article 6(1) of the European Convention on Human Rights ('the Convention'). The Secretary of State, who had been added to the proceedings, appealed, and the House of Lords allowed the appeal.

subject matter of the legislation. The more the legislation concerned matters of broad social policy, the less ready a court would be to intervene.[50]

The interpretation of sections 3 and 4 has shown itself to be one of the sites where the scope of the Act has been fought out. As Nicol has observed,[51] those judges 'who wish the HRA to ensure that the Convention rights as interpreted by the European Court of Human Rights become the supreme law of the land' take a broad approach to section 3 that enables the court to strain the literal meaning of an Act to find a Convention compliant interpretation.[52] Nicol opposes this interpretative faction to those who understand the Act as 'a unique participatory instrument', which must involve the courts and Parliament in a dialogue over the extent of human rights in common law. This tendency prefers narrower interpretations of section 3, with the concomitant reliance on declarations under section 4. Thus, underlying the disagreements over the scope of the Act are different understandings of 'constitutional fundamentals'.[53] Has this argument been resolved in the wake of *Anderson* in favour of the narrow interpretation of section 3? We will examine this claim, and Kavanagh's counter argument[54] in the following section.[55]

OPENING THE FIELD: *R V. A*

In *R. v. A.*,[56] the House of Lords interpreted Section 41 of the Criminal Evidence Act 1999 in the light of Article 6. Section 41 prevented evidence being given about the complainant's sexual history without the leave of the court. The instances where the court could allow this kind of evidence were narrowly drawn. Despite the clarity of the wording of the section, the House of Lords interpreted the Act so as to make it compatible with Article 6. In Lord Steyn's judgment, the interpretative powers given to the court under section 3 were broad enough to allow a 'linguistically strained interpretation', even when there was no ambiguity in the Act. Can *Re S.* be seen as a reaction to the 'judicial overkill' of *R. v. A.*? The Court of Appeal interpreted the Children's Act 1989 in such a way as to make it compatible with Articles 8 and 6. The House of Lords disagreed with this approach, asserting that section 3 did not allow a court to read a statute in such a way as to depart from 'a fundamental feature of the Act':

---

50   Ibid., H17. These are nuanced arguments. Insofar as it is possible to draw a conclusion, the House of Lords might be suggesting that legislation would be interpreted to protect Convention rights if the court thought it necessary when considering the 'proportionality of legislation'. In so doing, the Court would defer to Parliament, but would reserve for itself the power to 'reach a different conclusion from the legislature' if 'the legislature had attached insufficient importance to a person's Convention right'.

51   D. Nicol, 'Statutory interpretation and human rights after Anderson' [2004] PL 273.

52   This approach obviates the need to issue a declaration of incompatibility, and the tension that might result if Parliament does not agree.

53   Ibid., 274.

54   Kavanagh, (2004: 274–282).

55   Kavanagh, ibid.

56   R. v. A. [2001] UKHL 25.

[A] meaning which departs substantially from a fundamental feature of an Act of Parliament is likely to have crossed the boundary between interpretation and amendment. This is especially so where the departure has practical repercussions which the court is not equipped to evaluate.[57]

[This argument rests on the distinction between the functions of the executive and the courts. The former are far more able to create policy and assess its impact, as the court is fundamentally passive and limited to responding to the evidence given by parties to a dispute. Judges must therefore restrain the uses that they make of section 3.] Lord Nicholls was especially critical of Lord Steyn's position. It was not the case that the court's interpretative duty would only be limited by express words indicating that Parliament intended that an Act was incompatible with the Convention. There thus appears to be a departure from *R. v. A* in *Re S.* – a line of reasoning that was confirmed in *Anderson*.[58]

PLOUGHING A NEW FURROW? [R. (ON THE APPLICATION OF ANDERSON) V. SECRETARY OF STATE FOR THE HOME DEPARTMENT]

[The argument pressed upon the House of Lords in *Anderson* was that as the sentencing powers of the Home Secretary in section 29 of the Criminal (Sentences) Act 1997 were incompatible with Article 6, their Lordships should read into this section a requirement for the Home Secretary's power to be limited by the recommendation of the trial judge and the Lord Chief Justice. [The House of Lords refused to accept this position, and were unanimous in their agreement that reading section 29 in this way would exceed the interpretative powers of section 3.] Lords Bingham, Steyn and Hutton agreed with Lord Nicholl's speech in *Re S.*

Nicol observes that even Lord Steyn performed a '*volte face*' and appeared to retreat from the arguments made in *R. v. A.* [Precisely because a panel of seven Law Lords decided *Anderson*, it represents a resolution of the argument about the scope of the court's interpretative powers in the understanding of the position of the court] articulated by Lord Nicholls. Later cases, such as *Bellinger* v. *Bellinger*[59] are coherent with Anderson. In the former, Lord Steyn referred to Lord Nicholl's speech and, in the latter, a certificate of incompatibility was issued, rather than subject the Matrimonial Causes Act 1973 to a strained reading.

Are we therefore to accept that *Re S.* and *Anderson* represent the correct statement of the limits of section 3? Kavanagh argues that [the significant differences of fact between *R. v. A.* and *Re S.* mean that *Re S.* cannot be given the status accorded to it by *Nicol.* [R. v. A.* concerned judicial interpretation of a specific section of the 1999

57   *Re S.* [2002] UKHL 10, at 41.
58   *R. (on the application of Anderson)* v. *Secretary of State for the Home Department* [2002] UKHL 46.
59   *Bellinger* v. *Bellinger* [2002] 1 All ER 311.

Act. In *Re S.*, there were no sections of the Children's Act 1989 that could be singled out. The Court of Appeal was thus forced to consider (in Hale LJ's words), not so much what the Act said, but what it did not say.[60] *Re S.* cannot, therefore, be seen as dealing with the same issue as *R. v. A.* Furthermore, whereas the consequences of the Court of Appeal's decision in *Re S.* would have had significant cost implications for local authorities, *R. v. A.* concerned an area in which the courts have much greater competence: the regulation of the forensic process. *Re S.* cannot be read as a more general statement of a correct judicial attitude to section 3. As Kavanagh puts it:

> Section 3(1) should not be used as a way of radically reforming a whole statute or writing a quasi legislative code granting new powers and setting out new procedures to replace that statute. However, that does not necessarily mean that the decision rules out the type of 'reading in' which was adopted in *R. v. A.*[61]

If this argument is correct, then cases such as *Anderson* must be seen as specific responses to statutes, rather than as evidence of a coherent judicial attitude adopted to section 3. The refusal of the House of Lords in *Anderson* to read limitations into the power of the Home Secretary under section 29 of the 1997 Act can be explained by reference to the context in which the case was heard. The ECtHR had just issued two rulings against the UK holding that section 29 was in breach of Article 6. As the government was thus 'legally obliged'[62] to change the law, there would have been no point in making a strained interpretation of section 29 and, thus, the better course of action was to issue a certificate of incompatibility. *Bellinger* shows that the 'case by case' or 'limited' law making powers of the court were not suitable to interpret the Matrimonial Causes Act in a radical way; it was correct to issue a declaration of incompatibility so that Parliament could assess the policy implications of changes in the law.

What do we make of these two positions? Perhaps the precise scope of section 3 is still open and that (for the most part) the Law Lords are seeking a working relation, rather than a confrontation with Parliament. Klug[63] has specifically taken the notion of dialogue as the key to understanding the operation of the Act:

> Behind the construction of ss.3 and 4 was a carefully thought-out constitutional arrangement that sought to inject principles of parliamentary accountability and transparency into judicial proceedings without removing whole policy areas to judicial determination. In other words it sought to create a new dynamic between the two branches of the State.[64]

Klug argues that Lord Hope's approach in *R. v. A* is much closer to the spirit of the Act than that of Lord Steyn. The 'dialogic' relationship envisaged by the Act requires the

---

60   Supra, n. 11, at 538.
61   Ibid., 540.
62   Ibid., 542.
63   Klug (2003: 125–133).
64   Ibid., at 130.

judges to have the 'courage' to issue declarations, and to actively engage the dialogue with the executive, rather than to see them as a last ditch measure. Declarations cannot therefore be seen as a distortion of the judges' relation to Parliament; rather, they are part of a vision of the legislature, the executive and the judiciary 'influencing' each other. Whether or not this means that *Anderson* correctly states their position is open to question. However, evidence on declarations of incompatibility also suggests that the Act is opening up a dialogue between the courts and the executive.

MENDING FENCES? *GHAIDAN* V. *GODIN-MENDOZA*

A good example of a broad interpretation of an Act under the HRA is *Ghaidan* v. *Godin-Mendoza*.[65] The case saw the House of Lords dealing with a question of property law that related to succession to a tenancy under paragraph 2 of schedule 1 to the Rent Act 1977. The defendant was contending that the Rent Act discriminated against him as a homosexual in depriving him of rights over the flat of his deceased partner. What precisely was the issue in *Ghaidan*? Paragraph 2(2) makes a distinction between a heterosexual and a homosexual couple who are living together. For the former, the survivor can take over the tenancy if the property was in the name of the deceased, whereas for the latter, the survivor cannot. The survivor in a gay relationship is not deprived of all rights over the property. He/she is entitled to an assured tenancy. However, in terms of both rent protection and rights against eviction, the survivor of the homosexual relationship is clearly not in as beneficial a situation as the survivor of the heterosexual relationship.

The Court of Appeal had held that the Act amounted to an infringement of the defendant's rights under Articles 8 and 14 of the Convention. The Court of Appeal had used s.3 of the HRA to read the Act in a broad way, thus allowing the defendant to take over the tenancy of the flat. The House of Lords dismissed the appeal against this ruling, and confirmed the approach of the Court of Appeal. It was thus not necessary to issue a declaration of incompatibility, as the Act could be read in such a way as to make it Convention compliant. The House of Lords did note, however, that the new meaning of the Act must be 'consistent with the fundamental features of the legislative scheme'.[66] We need to investigate this argument in a little more detail.

Lord Nicholls pointed out that there are a number of ways of reading s.3 as there is a certain degree of ambiguity in the word 'possible'. A narrow reading would hold that s.3 only allowed courts to resolve ambiguities in statutory language in favour of Convention-compliant interpretations. A much broader interpretation of the section has been preferred, which allows the courts to give a different meaning to the language of the statute in order to make its meaning consistent with the Convention. This could involve reading in words, as in *R. v. A.* There is no need for the language of the Act to be ambiguous for the Court to take this course of action.[67] This means that the court

....
65   *Ghaidan* v. *Godin-Mendoza* [2004] UKHL 30.
66   Ibid., 558.
67   Ibid., 570–1.

can 'depart from the unambiguous meaning the legislation would otherwise bear'. Normally, the court would have to determine the intention of Parliament by using the language in the Act. However, s.3 means that the court may have to 'depart from the intention of the enacting Parliament'.[68]

We can begin to appreciate how the Human Rights Act makes for a potentially radical departure from conventional methods of interpretation. However, this does not extend to the idea that the court is now an equal partner with Parliament when it comes to legislation. The fundamental requirement is that the courts should follow Parliamentary intention in interpreting an Act. The question becomes: how would a court know that it is legitimate to depart from Parliamentary intention? The answer to this question depends on the degree to which Parliament intended that the 'actual' words of a statute, as opposed to the concept that those words express, is to be 'determinative' of the Act's meaning. What does this mean? Lord Nicholls argues that the determinative factor cannot be the word of the Act, since the HRA allows them to be interpreted against their obvious sense. It would be possible, therefore, for a court to read words into an Act. This would be consistent with the fact that s.3 'requires' that courts read in words to make an Act compliant with the Convention.[69] There is a limit to this process. Although the court can read in words, Parliament could never have intended that 'the courts should adopt a meaning inconsistent with a fundamental feature of legislation' (ibid.). This would cross the line, and show the courts interfering with the sovereign rights of Parliament.[70]

DEFINING THE PARAMETERS OF THE NEW PRACTICE

The sample of cases that we have been examining suggests that we are at the cutting edge of a new kind of judicial practice. Perhaps we can think of the practice of

----

68   R. (on the application of Wilson) v. Wychavon DC [2007] EWCA Civ 52 saw the Court of Appeal attempt to define the 'range' of the Ghaidan principles. Reference was made to Lord Nicholls' speech. Lord Nicholls pointed out that Parliament was charged with 'the primary responsibility for deciding the best way of dealing with social problems' and the court's role was one of review. The only legitimate grounds on which the court could reach 'a different conclusion from the legislature' is 'when it is apparent that the legislature has attached insufficient importance to a person's Convention rights'. The court's willingness to undertake a review depends on context. For instance, the court will only rarely consider matters of '[n]ational housing policy' – as it is up to Parliament to determine where 'a fair balance' lies 'between competing interests'. However, the court will be more willing to consider 'alleged violations' of convention rights based on race, gender or sexual orientation. In such instances, 'the court will scrutinise with intensity any reasons said to constitute justification' and reasons given must be 'cogent' to justify 'differential treatment'. 'Stop notices' under the Town and Country Planning Act could be used to prevent gypsies developing land on which they had settled without planning permission. As the legislation did not apply to normal dwellings, the applicants were arguing that the provisions were discriminatory and in breach of their Convention rights. However, the court considered that the legislation was proportionate on grounds of environmental protection. In considering whether or not legislation was proportionate, the court had to accord a large measure of discretion to Parliament. This authority can be contrasted with R. v. Webster [2010] EWCA Crim 2819. The Court of Appeal used Ghaidan to justify 'reading down' s1(2) of the Public Bodies and Corrupt Practices Act 1889, and the Prevention of Corruption Act 1916 s.2 so as to make them compatible with Article 6 of the Convention. This effectively changed the meaning of the statutes – as they had originally placed a 'reverse burden of proof' on the defendant in breach of the presumption of innocence.
69   Ibid., 572.
70   Ibid.

statutory interpretation as the judges entering into some form of dialogue with Parliament. This would certainly have the authority of Jack Straw, who, in a Parliamentary debate, argued that:

> Parliament and the judiciary must engage in a serious dialogue about the operation and development of the rights in the Bill . . . this dialogue is the only way in which we can ensure the legislation is a living development that assists our citizens.[71]

If we accept that the idea of dialogue is useful then it is necessary to determine the precise terms in which it operates. If this is a democratic dialogue, then it cannot simply be a judicial usurpation of legislative power in the name of human rights. As Lord Irvine's words quoted in the introduction suggest, the dialogue must take place within a constitutional settlement that stresses separation of powers. However, it is necessary to accept that the dialogue does open up a new judicial vocabulary. Does this take us back to the proportionality test? The proportionality test is a powerful mechanism that can allow either the broad interpretation of statutory language or the reading in of words in order to make legislation Convention compliant. However, the test, as shown by *Ghaidan* v. *Godin-Mendoza*, must itself be subject to some constraints, otherwise the courts would be moving far beyond the powers given to them by the Human Rights Act, as the intention of the Act was to preserve parliamentary sovereignty. The approach in *Ghaidan* was legitimate because the interpretation proposed by the House of Lords was consistent with the fundamental policy objectives of the legislation, which were to provide security of tenure. Clearly, where a judicial interpretation moved beyond the policy of legislation, the courts could not effectively legislate in Parliament's place. It could thus hesitatingly be suggested that after the Human Rights Act judicial practice is changing to such an extent that judges now have an acknowledged legislative power. This allows them to make legislation Convention compliant. Compared to the legislative power of Parliament it is limited, but the interpretative provisions of the 1998 Act effectively makes judges the legislators of human rights.

This is perhaps coherent in some way with Klug's interpretation of the Act.[72] She argues that sections 3 and 4 bring an end to 'judicial deference to the legislature'; in particular, judges need to appreciate that s.4 allows them to enter into a dialogue with Parliament. It would be a mistake to see s.4 as mandating a change of law, rather the Act 'was specifically structured to allow the courts to uphold rights while also retaining parliamentary authority'. Klug suggests that the HRA was intended to 'inject principles of parliamentary accountability and transparency into judicial proceedings without removing whole policy areas to judicial determination'. Changes in judicial practice would have to be seen as driven by the 'new dynamic' that the Act attempts to create.[73]

This would suggest that the precise terms of the practice or dialogue of statutory interpretation in the wake of the HRA are focused on sections 3 and 4. Kavanagh has

---

71   Jack Straw, 314 HC 1141, June 24. Cited in Klug (2003: 131).
72   Klug (2003).
73   Ibid., 130.

made similar points. We can consider her response to the criticisms of *R. v. A.*[74] The critical issue is of the nature of the obligation under s.3(1), and whether it allows or requires the court to depart from the intention of Parliament expressed in the words of the statute. Placing *R. v. A.* in the context of *Lambert*, Kavanagh asks why this authority has been singled out for criticism, when in *Lambert* the court went against the clear intention of Parliament. This begs the question about how parliamentary intention is understood. Recent authorities[75] on s.3(1) suggest that there are two legislative intentions at play, namely that which is underlying the statute in question, and that which is 'expressed' in s.3(1). Section 3(1) only becomes relevant when there is a 'conflict' between these two intentions. How should this conflict be resolved? If one applies the doctrine of implied repeal, the later Act would repeal the earlier, but as the HRA applies to legislation 'whenever enacted', then it would apply to legislation after 1998. The 'effect' of s.3(1) is thus quite specific:

> Ordinarily, Parliament intends its legislation to be understood in accordance with its ordinary meaning. By empowering judges to go beyond the ordinary meaning, s.3(1) instructs judges to go against that legislative intention.

This is supported by the AG reference 4 of 2002[76] which describes s.3(1) as 'very strong and far reaching' and can require a departure from the 'intention of Parliament'. This would justify the approach of Lord Steyn in *R. v. A.*, but also in his wider reflections on the justification for a more expanded role for the judiciary. Elaborating these arguments is best left for Chapters 10 and 11 but we need to move away from static understandings of the court somehow mechanically trying to discover the intention of Parliament through a literal reading of an Act. We also need to understand the practice of statutory interpretation as a dialogue. In this dialogue the courts do not usurp the legislative power of Parliament, but on a mandate given to them by Parliament itself, engage in articulating legislation that is compliant with human rights.

CONCLUSION

Statutory interpretation is a pragmatic practice within constitutional limits. In attempting to define the parameters of the contemporary practice of statutory interpretation we have avoided any approach that stressed the centrality of the rules of interpretation and have attempted instead to see how, in important cases, judges

---

74   Commentators have been critical of Lord Steyn in *R. v. A.* Ekins (2003) argues that approaches such as that of Lord Steyn subvert the fact that the judges are trying to determine Parliament's intention: 'Thus, statutory interpretation in a rights-conscious era remains a search for legislative intent and judgment and s.3 should therefore be understood simply as a rule that stipulates defeasible presumptions of legislative intent and which acts as a tiebreaker in the event of genuine interpretative uncertainty . . . Given the indeterminacy of rights adjudication and the democratic unaccountability of the judiciary, we would do well to be grateful for that fact' (p. 650).

75   Kavanagh (2003) relies on Lord Nicholls' and Lord Steyn's speeches in *Ghaidan* [2004] UKHL 30; [2004] 2 AC 557 at [30] (Lord Nicholls), [40] (Lord Steyn).

76   Attorney General's Reference (No. 4 of 2002) [2004] UKHL 43 [2004].

actually interpret the statutory language with which they have been presented. We have hazarded a general thesis. Alongside the presumptions of interpretations, which describe the concern with the general structure of the law as meaningful language, there is a structuring concern with the parameters of the practice. This can only be described in constitutional terms. Where does the boundary lie between interpreting a statute and creating new law? This raises the issue of institutional legitimacy. For us the development of the practice is itself bound up with three important recent developments: the ruling in *Pepper* v. *Hart*, the impact of European interpretative methods, and the powers of interpretation created by the Human Rights Act. As a general point, describing judicial practice requires an engagement with specific legal issues, the tensions in approach that show an interaction between different judicial understandings of practice, and the spaces in the law that allow these arguments to be made.

Building on the previous chapter, we could say that practices always allow for a degree of dispute over their central terms and suppositions. Over time, these disputes may become resolved, or at least less 'hot', and the practice assumes a conventional form. Given the impact of so many recent legal developments in statutory interpretation, it would not be surprising to find some degree of dispute over the precise constitution of legitimate techniques. However, this can exist alongside a more or less settled understanding of the fundamental orientation of the practice. What we find in recent statutory interpretation is just this mixture of coherence and dispute. Thus a central strand in the emerging practice of statutory interpretation can be seen as an ongoing dialogue with Parliament over the relationship between domestic legislation and human rights.

10

THE POLITICS OF THE JUDICIARY REVISITED: RIGHTS, DEMOCRACY, LAW

INTRODUCTION

A great deal has changed since Griffith published his seminal text on the inherently conservative nature of the judiciary.[1] In this chapter, we will argue that we need a new understanding of the politics of the judiciary. Consider the following paragraph:

> [I]f in our own society the rule of law is to mean much, it must at least mean that it is the obligation of the courts to articulate and uphold the ground rules of ethical social existence which we dignify as fundamental human rights . . .[2]

This kind of statement would have been unimaginable in the 1950s, and remains controversial today.[3] However, what is clear is that, at least since 1998, there has been a significant shift in judicial understanding of the role that they play in a democratic state. These themes are complicated and we will develop them over the course of this and the following chapter. Our focus for the moment is a study of the transformation of the judicial role, and the judge's perception of their role. This argument requires that we acknowledge that the politics of the judiciary are not simplistic or party political, but raise complex arguments over the relationship between rights and democracy.

After a historical introduction, we will engage with a number of important authorities that raise issues about the relationship of the courts to Parliament. One particular area of concern will be the famous Belmarsh case on torture evidence. We will go on to argue that the politics of the judiciary can now be understood as a form of dialogue between the judges and Parliament, animated by tensions over the correct balance between judicial and governmental power.[4] The dialogue is not based on deference to Parliament. Whilst acknowledging their constitutional subordination to Parliament, the courts have shown themselves willing to uphold human rights and the rule of law against the executive. This raises complex issues. Those commentators who have objected to the idea of dialogue from various republican premises have articulated

---

1 First edition 1977, the text soon provided a point of writing from which to analyse notions of bias, competence and impartiality. For the debate between Sir Stephen Sedley and J.A.G Griffith, see Sedley, 2001, pp. 68–70.
2 Sedley (1995: 386–340).
3 We should also not be too hasty in thinking that the judges are not all strong advocates of human rights. See Tomkins, 'In Defence of the Political Constitution', 22 *Oxford Journal of Legal Studies* 157.
4 Cohn (2007). The judge is as an 'actor in a continuous multi-participant process or network of decision-making'.

valid criticisms of the term.[5] It is still necessary to be critical of the constitutional propriety of unelected, unaccountable and unrepresentative judges. However, any scepticism directed towards the judges has to be tempered by criticism of 'executive dictatorship'. With radical democratic reform off the political agenda, it would appear that a rather skewed dialogue between the courts and Parliament is the best for which one might hope. It still remains to be seen whether the British constitution can move from its tendencies towards centralisation of power to meaningful democratic accountability.

THE POLITICS OF THE JUDICIARY

The contents page of Griffith's text shows the study split into a number of engagements with judicial activity. The book concerns itself with industrial relations, personal rights, property rights, government secrecy and students and trade unions. It reflects areas of importance at the time of writing in 1977. In brief, Griffith discussed the political problems of his day: concerns over the power of trade unions and the parlous state of industrial relations, student demonstrations, the early years of race relations, the tensions that resulted from economic recession and the impact of the equality agenda. We are in a time prior to the reforms of the Thatcher governments in the 1980s that changed the face of British politics. What conclusions are drawn about the role of the judges in this period?

> My thesis is that the judges in the UK cannot be politically neutral because they are placed in positions where they are required to make political choices which are sometimes presented to them, and often presented by them, as determinations of where the public interest lies; that their interpretation of what is in the public interest and therefore politically desirable is determined by the kind of people they are and the position they hold in society; that his position is part of established authority and so is necessarily conservative and illiberal. From all this flows that view of the public interest which is shown in judicial attitudes such as tenderness towards private property and dislike of trade unions, strong adherence to the maintenance of order, distaste for minority opinions, demonstrations and protests, the avoidance of conflict with Government policy even where it is manifestly oppressive of the most vulnerable, support of government secrecy, concern for the preservation of the moral and social behaviour to which it is accustomed, and the rest.[6]

Griffith stressed that, contrary to conventional opinion, judges are political, and their politics are essentially those of an illiberal clique dedicated to frustrating progressive government policies. This was, of course, a bold and shocking statement for the time. Judges are meant to be neutral and impartial. Griffith demonstrated that, in the areas of decision-making he examined, this was far from the truth. Whilst this suggests that

---

5 Tomkins (2005).
6 Griffith (1977 edition).

in other areas of decision-making, judges retained their impartiality, it did suggest that, in those areas of contentious policy, a right wing bias was manifest. What do we make of this?

The evidence suggests that Griffith was correct, and an examination of recent history shows that judges conceived their role in conservative political terms. Progressive administrations explicitly took into account this reality in pushing through the creation of the welfare state and its institutions. However, in more recent years there has been something of a shift in the politics of the judiciary. Indeed, whilst Griffith's point about the composition of the appellate courts remains accurate, it would appear that important senior members of the judiciary have begun to champion and support human rights in such a way that brings them into conflict with the executive. This has also produced tensions within the judiciary itself. Understanding these developments requires us to carry forward Griffith's essential thesis on the politics of the judiciary, but to appreciate that these politics are now articulated over the meaning of human rights within a democratic polity.

If one considers the judiciary from the perspective of a time frame broader than that of Griffith, one realises that their 'politicisation' began well before the 1970s. Stevens seeks to analyse the politics of the judiciary in the context of modern British history. Although the identification and division of historical periods is always rather arbitrary, this approach does allow us to identify certain overarching themes. The period 1900–1960 covers two world wars, and significant social, economic and political changes. To what extent do these broader concerns affect the composition of the judiciary and their awareness of their role? At the end of the 1800s, the conservative Prime Minister, Lord Salisbury, appointed Lord Halsbury as Lord Chancellor. Lord Halsbury immediately began to staff the junior and senior ranks of the judiciary with his political allies. Whilst these appointments did not always meet with the approval of the legal profession, they reflected what Salisbury saw as an unwritten rule of the constitution: the ruling party could explicitly influence the composition of the bar on ideological lines. Indeed, in the 1870s, with the establishment of the House of Lords as the final court of appeal, Salisbury had observed that it merely made judicial law making more explicit.

However, although momentarily in the ascendant, Conservative political philosophy did not go unopposed. There were strong currents of reform in British politics. The extension of the franchise in 1832 had changed the political landscape significantly. Government was now to be increasingly accountable to a Parliament elected on a broad franchise. Influential ideas of law reform stressed the need for clear principles, downplaying the role of judicial creativity and privileging the authority of Parliament.[7]

Nevertheless, Lord Halsbury presided over a number of important decisions that reflected his biases – although these cannot perhaps always be explained in party political terms. In *London Tramways* v. *London City Council*,[8] Lord Halsbury's ruling was a way of preserving the political influence of the Conservative House of Lords. However, he was also capable of affirming that the balance of power between

---

7   Stevens (2002) who sees this as the legacy of utilitarian thought, which drew on Bentham's hostility to the obfuscations of the judges and Blackstone's defence of the common law.

8   *London Tramways* v. *London City Council* [1898] AC 375.

legislature and executive lay firmly with the latter in the *Earldom of Norfolk Peerage Case*.[9] There were also a number of cases that sought to limit the power and influence of the trade unions. After suffering a reverse in *Allen v. Flood*,[10] Halsbury managed to carry the day in *Quinn v. Leatham*.[11] This anti-union decision depended as much on Halsbury's political manoeuvring as the legal reasoning of the court; a strategy repeated in the notorious *Taff Vale* decision.[12]

The political repercussions of this case helped lead to the Tory defeat in the elections of 1906. The Lord Chancellor in the new Liberal government, Lord Loreburn, made a number of new appointments. Although those to the High Court were not party political, the more senior appointments continued the 'tacit assumptions' that the new government shared with the Tories. At the same time, Lord Loreburn understood that judges had to be kept away from trade union cases, and also prevented from sabotaging the government's project: the construction of the welfare state. It was necessary to stress the neutral nature of judicial decision making – and where the Liberal government was rebuffed by the courts, to legislate. The 1913 Trade Union Act thus reversed the decision of the Lords in *Amalgamated Society of Railway Servants v. Osborne*.[13] Thus, it would be possible to observe a change in judicial appointments that went alongside the pushing through of the political reforms of the Liberal, and later on, Labour governments. The legal regulation of the welfare state was to be achieved by a system of tribunals and administrative law that bypassed the formal court system, where the Conservative Law Lords had entrenched their position. Stevens points out that the move to appointment by merit rather than patronage in this period reflects this broader project.

We cannot dwell upon the appointments made by the Liberal Prime Minister, Lloyd George and Loreburn's replacement, Lord Haldane, other than to note that appointments to the Law Lords, and in particular to the office of Lord Chief Justice, were made on political grounds, and also reflected the alliances and falls from favour of ministers and their allies within the party. By the 1930s, the system of legal regulation of the institutions of the welfare state was such that the role of the courts was increasingly sidelined through statutory clauses that protected legislation from challenge in the courts. Courts also refrained from examining executive acts done under prerogative powers and the decisions of administrative bodies. Following the report of the Committee on Ministers Powers in 1928, an 'official' understanding of the relationship between the courts and administrative tribunals stressed the distinct and separate spheres in which the institutions operated. Whilst the former dealt with disputes by ruling on the facts with reference to objective rules, the latter dealt with administrative matters through the use of discretion, which was not the proper province of the judge. As Stevens points out, this presupposed the 'objectivity of legal rules and the feasibility of interpreting statutes "impartially" '.[14] Underpinning this position

---

9   *Earldom of Norfolk Peerage Case* [1898] AC 375.
10   *Allen v. Flood* [1898] AC 1.
11   *Quinn v. Leatham* [1907] AC 10.
12   *Taff Vale Railway Company v. Amalgamated Society of Railway Servants* [1901] AC 426.
13   *Amalgamated Society of Railway Servants v. Osborne* [1910] AC 87.
14   Stevens (2002: 23).

was the declaratory theory of law, which further sought to stress the formalism of common law decision-making and reject any emphasis on creativity.

It was in this environment that the perception of the class bias of the Law Lords became increasingly apparent. It was as if the Law Lords revenged themselves on the executive, by using what powers they had to limit or undo progressive legislation. Thus, in *Roberts v. Hopwood*[15] minimum wage policy was effectively 'struck down'. This showed their class bias, to the extent that they privileged the protection of propertied interests over the funding of the welfare state. Stevens argues that the courts, and in particular, the House of Lords and the Court of Appeal, made themselves increasingly irrelevant in the period from 1939–1960. This can be shown by the number of cases these courts heard. In 1953 half as many cases were heard as in 1939.[16]

The 1945 election returned a Labour government committed to the economic and social reconstruction of the country. This added to the sense in which the defence of privilege by the courts was out of step with the will of the country. However, the reluctance or refusal of the courts to engage in any meaningful collaboration with the executive arguably resulted in a public law characterised by the failure to develop notions of both substantive and procedural due process. Furthermore, the commitment of the 1945 Labour government to radical reform might have led to reforms of the judiciary and the legal profession itself. Proposals were made at a Cabinet level for a new system of courts, and a movement towards continental styles of litigation and procedure. The Labour Lord Chancellor, William Jowitt was not of a radical cast of mind. He managed to limit proposals for reform, and preserve the structure and institutions of the profession.[17] The civil courts continued working on private disputes, in the 'most formalistic manner'[18] and eschewed the development of public law.

It would be simplistic, however, to think of the immediate post-war period as entirely characterised by the irrelevance of the courts to constitutional development broadly conceived. Voices within the Labour government spoke of the need to involve the law in the management of the state, and more independently minded judges began to make their influence felt. The career of Lord Denning prompted a reappraisal of formalistic methods of interpretation, and suggested that the common law might be open to creative development by judges. Alongside Lord Denning, other important figures such as Lord Gardiner also opened up new possibilities. Although Lord Gardiner was more of a formalist than Lord Denning, he played an important role in arguing that the House of Lords could over-rule itself, asserting that it would lead to a more coherent development of the law. When the House of Lords began to feel the influence of Lord Reid, public law was also re-invigorated, with a series of important judicial review decisions that developed notions of due process. Labour relations remained troubled, and led to tensions between the courts and Parliament. As a response to

---

15   *Roberts v. Hopwood* [1925] AC 578.
16   Stevens (2002: 26–7).
17   Stevens (2002: 31), suggests that the 'conservative provenance' of the Evershed Committee, who had been tasked to report on the courts, cast its shadow on developments 'for the remainder of the century'.
18   Stevens (2002: 31).

House of Lords rulings in *Rooks* v. *Barnard*[19] and *Stratford* v. *Lindley*[20] the Labour government proposed that labour relations be regulated by an administrative board. Failure to resolve these issues prompted the Conservative government to introduce the Judges Industrial Relations Court in 1971. With the change from a Conservative to a Labour government in 1974, the court was disbanded – but not before its president, Sir John Donaldson had nearly been impeached for his political prejudice. This might show nothing more than the repetition of old patterns; a suspicion confirmed by Lord Diplock's statement that the task of the judge was to stick to the interpretation of the law made by Parliament – especially in politically contentious issues.

Although judges appeared to be playing a more prominent role in politics, their work in the courts was characterised by formalistic interpretations of the law that confirmed some opinions that the Law Lords were establishment figures incapable of criticising government. The succession of senior judges who presided over reports on the situation in Northern Ireland also 'threw doubt on the impartiality and independence of the British judiciary'.[21]

Whilst these concerns suggest the right-wing prejudice of the Law Lords, developments throughout the 1980s and the 1990s indicated that an activist judiciary were inventing themselves around a new set of challenges. Other factors that led to a reinvention of the judiciary and their increasing involvement in politics were the accession of the UK to the EEC in 1972, and the shift in the political landscape with the election victory of Margaret Thatcher's Conservative party in 1979. The judges were propelled into the centre of British politics; a space that was created by a populist 'right' government, intent on pushing through a package of reforms, and a Labour party that turned sharply to the left. Whilst the Conservative government remained somewhat sceptical towards Europe, and insisted on the 'sacrosanct' nature of Parliamentary sovereignty, the House of Lords enthusiastically applied European Community law, most notably suspending the operation of a UK statute in ex parte Factortame.[22] The House of Lords also showed itself willing to take a stand against the executive in *M.* v. *The Home Office*[23] and *Woolwich* v. *IRC.*[24] Whilst the European Convention was not part of UK law, influential judicial voices argued for its incorporation. The old stereotypes of a politically quiescent or pro status quo judiciary appeared to be breaking down. Indeed, in the 1990s, there were frequent clashes between the courts and the Conservative administration over immigration, sentencing policy, criminal justice and international development.[25] The

---

19   *Rooks* v. *Barnard* [1964] AC 1129.
20   *Stratford* v. *Lindley* [1965] AC 269.
21   *Stevens* (2002: 43).
22   *R* v. *Secretary of State for Transport, ex parte Factortame* [1989] 2 CMLR 353.
23   *M* v. *Secretary of State for the Home Office* [2006] EWCA Civ. 515.
24   *Woolwich* v. *IRC* [1993] AC 70.
25   For instance, in *R.* v. *Sec of State Ex parte World Development Movement*, a successful challenge was launched to the Foreign Secretary's decision to go ahead with a decision to support a hydroelectric scheme in Malaysia despite the findings of the Overseas Development Administration that it was uneconomical. The Foreign Secretary had argued that the World Development Movement did not have locus standi to challenge his decision. The courts held otherwise. They held that having regard to the merits of the challenge and the importance of vindicating the rule of law, the applicants could make the application. Moreover, they held that the Foreign Secretary's decision was not within the terms of the statute which empowered him, the Overseas Development and Co-operation Act, as he should be promoting economically sound development.

invigorated approach to the development of the common law was strikingly evidenced when Lord Bingham and Lord Hoffmann argued that the right to privacy should be created by judges if Parliament refused to legislate.[26] Furthermore, with the ruling in *Pepper* v. *Hart* 'judicial power was dramatically extended'.[27]

Can we hazard any general conclusions? Reflecting on the recent history of public law, Sir Stephen Sedley, writing extra-judicially, argued that:

> ... the subsequent reassertion of judicial oversight of government which has been the achievement of the 1970s and 1980s in this country has been replicated all over the common law world as judiciaries have moved to fill lacunae of legitimacy in the functioning of democratic polities . . . .[28]

The re-assertion of the judicial scrutiny of the executive represents an important reinvention of democratic politics. Lord Woolf has articulated a sense of the courts as central to maintaining 'the delicate balance of a democratic society'.[29] This did not mean loyally accepting the will of Parliament, but asserting such values as due process and human rights. In one public address, he referred to the 'limits on the supremacy of Parliament' that were linked to the operation of judicial review. Stevens suggests that certain judges began to see themselves, albeit in an undeveloped way, as a 'separate branch of Government' – along the lines of the American judiciary.[30] The sense in which judges are working towards a more enhanced understanding of their role can also be seen in the extra judicial writings of Sir John Laws. His understanding that the 'doctrine of Parliamentary sovereignty' was itself dependent on, and limited by, a 'higher order law'[31] can be seen as paralleling the jurisprudence of Ronald Dworkin, and suggesting a sympathy for a notion of fundamental human rights. The Human Rights Act 1998 encouraged these tendencies within the judiciary.[32]

In order to study the way in which some important and influential judges now understand their role, it is worth looking in some detail at a recent lecture by Lord Steyn.[33] Although some of the points that he considered are perhaps original to him, we may be able to appreciate that it resonates with the approach suggested by the statements of the other senior figures we briefly reviewed. Lord Steyn locates the judiciary within the 'two strands' of democracy in the UK. The 'principle of majority rule' translates itself into the supreme law making power of Parliament, and the function of the executive, which is to carry on 'the business of the country'. Lord Steyn is primarily concerned with the Cabinet. The Cabinet is composed of Ministers drawn from the

---

26   Stevens (2002: 54).
27   Ibid.
28   Sedley (1995: 386–400).
29   Stevens (2002).
30   Ibid.
31   Ibid., 60.
32   To understand the origins of the Human Rights Act, we need to turn to the white paper *Rights Brought Home*. It is necessary to appreciate the political context: John Major's Conservative government had just been removed from office by an overwhelming Labour majority in 1997. Conservative governments had always been reluctant to incorporate the Convention into domestic law, and had not appreciated the need for legislation on human rights.
33   Lord Steyn (2006: 243–253).

ruling party. To the extent that it is in charge of policy execution, and to the extent that it is executing the political programme of a democratically elected party, the Cabinet represents the way in which the 'will of the people' expresses itself in party political terms.

In distinction to the executive, the judiciary is not elected, and has no popular mandate; it 'adjudicates disputes between the state and individuals, and between individuals and corporations'.[34] From what source, then, does the judiciary draw its legitimacy? We could say that it is rooted in a broad set of values: firstly, those of 'liberty and justice for all'[35] This is precisely linked to 'fundamental freedoms'[36] as stated in the Human Rights Act 1998; secondly, the legitimacy of the judiciary is founded on the extent to which they are 'independent, neutral, and impartial'.[37] None of these values are necessarily based on the idea of a political majority. Indeed, some human rights, the rights of immigrants for example, are particularly unpopular. Lord Steyn defines liberty, the spirit of the common law, in traditional terms. An individual can do anything that the law does not explicitly prohibit. Note, however, that this definition is much narrower when applied to the state and its agencies, who 'may only do what the law permits'[38] This is because 'what is done in the name of the people requires constant examination and justification'.[39] It would thus seem that the courts also obtain their legitimacy from their ability to scrutinise the executive, and demand that they justify their actions. How does this argument develop?

Lord Steyn's examples are interesting. The Hunting Act 2004 shows that 'even ancient liberties are not immune from abolition by a government set on doing so for party political reasons'. Whilst it is only perhaps a vocal minority who engage in hunting or would even be particularly concerned about the 'ancient liberty' to kill animals, the point is somewhat broader. It recalls Lord Hailsham's warning that the British political system does not offer sufficient restraints on an executive with a large majority.[40] Parliamentary government is effectively 'an elected dictatorship'.[41] However, this legitimacy gap is to be filled by a newly empowered judiciary who can rise to the challenge of protecting minority rights and articulate the democratic nature of a 'multi cultural society'. Lord Steyn goes on to argue that:

> The public is now increasingly looking not to Parliament, but to the judges to protect their rights. In this new world, judges nowadays accept more readily than before that it is their democratic and constitutional duty to stand up where necessary for individuals against the government. The greater the arrogation of power by a seemingly all-powerful executive which dominates the House of Commons, the greater the incentive and need for judges to protect the rule of law.[42]

....

34   Ibid., 246.
35   Ibid.
36   Ibid.
37   Ibid.
38   Ibid.
39   Ibid.
40   Lord Hailsham (1978: 126).
41   Lord Steyn (2006).
42   Lord Steyn (2006: 247).

It is now the judges, not Parliament, who can give an authentic voice to a human rights culture. This is evidenced by a number of recent decisions. *Director of Public Prosecutions of Jamaica* v. *Mollison*[43] show that the independence of the judiciary is a 'constitutional fundamental' and cannot be trespassed upon by other branches of government. In *Anufrijeva*,[44] the House of Lords held that the executive could not make unilateral determinations of people's rights which bypassed the scrutiny of the courts. This right of 'access to justice' could also be considered a 'fundamental' constitutional principle. In the Belmarsh case,[45] the House of Lords stated that indefinite detention of foreign terrorism suspects was in breach of the ECtHR. In so doing, the House of Lords was giving effect to section 6 of the HRA. It would thus be hard to say that this decision lacked any kind of democratic legitimacy.

Lord Steyn's notion of the legitimacy of the court is thus twofold. There does appear to be something of a democratic justification, to the extent that the court acts 'in the name of the people' and has enabled Britain to become a 'constitutional state'. Support for this vision of the politics of the judiciary can be found in Lord Hope's speech in *Jackson*. Lord Hope points out that the rule of Parliamentary sovereignty might rest on a 'political reality' – but this in turn requires that the 'legislature [maintain] the trust of the electorate'. Bringing together Lord Hope and Lord Steyn's views, we could suggest that the court is precisely the body that inculcates and preserves this trust by ensuring that government remains within the law. If we assert, as Lord Hope does, that the sovereignty of Parliament was 'created by the Common law', and Parliament 'represents the people whom it exists to serve',[46] then we can appreciate that these arguments envisage a far more central role for the court in preserving the constitutional legitimacy of the state. Lord Hope also said:

> The rule of law enforced by the courts is the ultimate controlling factor on which our constitution is based. . . . Parliamentary sovereignty is an empty principle if legislation is passed which is so absurd or so unacceptable that the populace at large refused to recognise it as law.[47]

Regina (Jackson and others) v. *Attorney General*[48] is a key case for understanding the judge's perception of their role. Lord Bingham pointed out that the constitutional balance has been thrown and the 'Commons, dominated by the executive, [has become] the ultimately unconstrained power in the state'.[49] However, his speech is also noteworthy for stressing an important constitutional convention. It is 'inappropriate for the House in its judicial capacity'[50] to elaborate political criticisms of the Executive. The point made, though, corresponds with the arguments made by Lord Steyn extra judicially. As far as his speech in Jackson is concerned, and acknowledging that there

---

43   *Director of Public Prosecutions of Jamaica* v. *Mollison* [2003] 2 AC 411.
44   *R. (Anufrijeva)* v. *Secretary of State for the Home Department* [2003] UKHL 36.
45   *A.* v. *Secretary of the State for the Home Department* [2004] UKHL 56.
46   *Regina (Jackson and others)* v. *Attorney General* [2005] UKHL 56, at para 126.
47   Ibid.
48   Ibid.
49   Ibid., at para 41.
50   Ibid.

is a certain circumspection to what can be said in the House of Lords, the comment that the HRA 'created a new legal order' and the 'pure and absolute doctrine' of Parliamentary sovereignty is 'out of place', must be considered radical statements.[51]

Central, then, to the new politics of the judiciary is the development of a body of human rights law. This uses the inspiration and resources of the HRA and the Strasbourg court, to adapt European rights jurisprudence to a common law context.[52] The main thrust of the different judicial statements and writings suggest that the intention of the judges is to use the powers that Parliament has given them to remake the checks and balances of the constitution. What this might mean in terms of concrete adjudication can be glimpsed in *R. (on the application of ProLife Alliance) v. BBC.*[53]

The case was argued in relation to freedom of expression under Article 10. The ProLife Alliance, an anti-abortion group, had fielded enough candidates in the 2002 General Election to entitle them to a short public broadcast to be shown in Wales. The BBC refused to show the film that they produced, on the grounds that it would be offensive to public feeling under 6(1)(a) of the Broadcasting Act 1990. The ProLife Alliance sought judicial review of this decision. Although they were successful in the Court of Appeal, the House of Lords affirmed the decision of the Court of First Instance that the refusal to transmit the film was not a breach of their freedom of expression.

We are not so much concerned with the technical arguments about judicial review or Article 10, as with the broader constitutional issues that this case raised. How could the decision of the court be justified? It would be possible to argue that this was an interference in the democratic process; that the imposition of standards of taste on party political broadcasting was inappropriate in a mature democracy. A variation on this argument would assert that the courts were not taking their human rights obligations seriously enough, and should have affirmed that the right to freedom of expression against any limitations in the 1990 Act. Counter arguments would stress that even after the HRA, the courts are bound to follow statutes, and not to substitute their own decisions in place of laws passed by a democratically elected Parliament. But, does such an argument suggest that the HRA changes nothing? That human rights are entirely subordinate to the will of Parliament?

The starting point of our discussion is the bold statement of Laws LJ. He argues that the authority of the court 'rests in its constitutional duty to protect and enhance the democratic process, irrespective of the wisdom or the rightness of any or all the diverse political opinions which in the course of that process are paraded before the people'.[54] The court has to hold the line between various opinions, and, in so doing, may contribute to the development of a democratic culture by allowing a public domain in which all shades of opinion can be articulated. In such a culture there should only be minimum restrictions on freedom of speech – a position which Article 10 itself acknowledges. The pressing question is how the court's obligation to give effect to Article 10 affects their relationship with Parliament. Should the House of Lords

---

51   Ibid., at para 102.
52   We return to this theme in the chapter on the general jurisprudence of the HRA. It is a little more complex than this sentence allows.
53   *R. (on the application of ProLife Alliance) v. BBC* [2003] UKHL 23.
54   Ibid., para 5.

have been bold in this case, and argued that the ban on transmission went beyond a minimal restriction on freedom of speech? How can the judges understand the correct role of human rights in the democratic process?

Lord Hoffmann considered the argument that the courts should show 'deference' to Parliament and asserted that, if the word carried the meaning of subservience, then it was not an accurate description. The question of the precise powers of the different branches of government, and their relationship to each other, was a matter for the 'rule of law and the separation of powers': in every instance, it had to be determined where supreme decision making power lay, and the limits on that power. As a question of law, this was a matter for the courts.[55] This of course means that the 'courts themselves often have to decide the limits of their own decision-making power' – but – it does not follow that these limits are out of deference. Respective powers rest on a differentiation of the tasks of the courts and Parliament: 'independence makes the courts more suited to deciding some kinds of questions and being elected makes the legislature or executive more suited to deciding others.'[56] Underlying this distinction are principles:

> The principle that the independence of the courts is necessary for a proper decision of disputed legal rights or claims of violation of human rights is a legal principle. It is reflected in article 6 of the Convention. On the other hand, the principle that majority approval is necessary for a proper decision on policy or allocation of resources is also a legal principle. Likewise, when a court decides that a decision is within the proper competence of the legislature or executive, it is not showing deference. It is deciding the law.[57]

This is a powerful statement of the rule of law, and its relationship to human rights. Underlying the constitution are legal principles that assign the executive, the legislature and the judiciary to their respective sphere of competence. This is 'reflected' in Article 6. In other words, European human rights are entirely coherent with the common law on this particular principle. The relationship of the courts to Parliament is thus based on the law of human rights to the extent that it is not based on deference, but, is a matter of principle. On the facts of the present case, the decency requirements for political broadcasts reflects the view of Parliament, and is based on the finding of the Annan Committee who stated that public opinion cannot be totally disregarded in the pursuit of liberty.[58] To the extent that this is an argument of principle, it was said to involve no arbitrary or unreasonable restriction on the right of free speech.

Lord Hoffmann's arguments address broad matters of principle. Lord Walker considered a more technical issue. How should the courts review legislation and executive decisions in the light of the Human Rights Act? Prior to the HRA, the test was based on the principle of *Wednesbury* irrationality.[59] After the HRA, the courts felt

---

55   Ibid., para 75.
56   Ibid., para 76.
57   Ibid.
58   Report of the Annan Committee, Cmnd 6753, 1977.
59   After the decision *Associated Provincial Picture Houses Ltd v. Wednesbury Corporation* [1948] 1 KB 223.

that a more exacting standard was required – and looked increasingly towards the concept of proportionality: in other words, in considering human rights, the court had to ask itself not was the executive decision irrational, but, was it proportionate to the end to be achieved, taking into account the human rights obligation of the 1998 Act. In applying this test, the courts determined that they would have to show a certain degree of deference to Parliament. Lord Steyn's guidelines in *R. (Daly) v. Secretary of State for the Home Department*[60] outline the path the court must tread. In order to determine whether a limitation imposed by either a statutory rule or an executive decision is 'arbitrary or excessive' the court had to ask three questions. Firstly, whether or not the objective of the Act is important enough to justify a limit on human rights; secondly, whether or not the precise measures in the Act are 'rationally connected' to the restriction on a right(s) and thirdly whether the 'means' put in place to 'impair' the right are 'more than is necessary to accomplish the objective'.[61]

This new test does not mean that the courts are reviewing the merits of a decision; but, nor does it mean that the old *Wednesbury* test is still in place. This is because the 'intensity' of the proportionality review is much greater. Thus, the court does not ask whether or not the decision made was within 'the range of rational or reasonable decision'. The court has to 'assess' whether the decision maker has unduly limited fundamental rights. This court must consider whether or not the 'limitation of the right was necessary in a democratic society, in the sense of meeting a pressing social need'.[62]

To return to a broader constitutional argument, this does not suggest that there has been a blurring of judicial and executive functions – but it does mean that the HRA requires the courts to carefully scrutinise both legislation and executive decisions stemming from statutory powers[63] Lord Justice Laws' guidelines in *International Transport Roth Gmbh v. Secretary of State for the Home Department*[64] are definitional of this new understanding. Laws LJ argues that: 'greater deference is to be paid to an Act of Parliament than to a decision of the executive or subordinate measure.' There will be a greater scope for deference when the Convention requires it. The courts must also afford greater deference to democratic powers acting within the sphere of their constitutional competence, and the courts must observe that, within the constitutional settlement, they are entitled to pay less deference to a matter that falls within their area of 'expertise'. Lord Walker singled out the first of the guidelines as of particular relevance not only to the case in hand, but, also as an interpretation of the underlying foundation of the Convention: to strike a 'fair balance between individual rights and the general interest of the community'.

60   *R. (Daly) v. Secretary of State for the Home Department* [2001] 2 AC 532.
61   Cited in Pro Life Alliance, at para 133.
62   Ibid., para 135.
63   See *R. (Mahmood) v. Secretary of State for the Home Department* [2001] 1 WLR 840.
64   *International Transport Roth Gmbh v. Secretary of State for the Home Department* [2003] QB 728, 765–767.

THE JUDGES, THE EXECUTIVE AND THE RESPONSE TO TERRORISM

Tensions over the application of human rights continue into one of the most important and pressing areas where conflict has developed between the executive and the judiciary: the legislative response to terrorism. To develop themes from the analysis above, we need to appreciate that the judicial response to the Anti-Terrorism Acts is not of a piece. Some judges have shown themselves willing to follow the executive, and not to challenge legislation in the courts; others have attempted to stress the importance of human rights values, and courts' scrutiny of executive actions.[65] Nicol argues that the issue of 'who has ultimate authority to determine the dividing line between the state's judicial and elective officers . . . is contested and will remain so'.[66]

The response of the government to the terrorist attacks of September 2001 had two main aspects: the enactment of Part 4 of the Anti-Terrorism, Crime and Security Act 2001, and the passing of a statutory instrument, the (Designated Derogation) Order 2001[67] derogating from certain Articles of the ECtHR. Section 23 of the 2001 Act allowed the Home Secretary to detain foreign nationals under suspicion of involvement in terrorism, if they are believed to be a risk to national security. The detention of foreign nationals must be under such circumstances that they cannot be deported from the UK if this would expose them to the possibility of torture. This would put the UK in breach of both Article 3 of the Convention Against Torture (CAT) and Article 3 of the ECtHR. However, it was still necessary to derogate from Article 5 of the ECtHR to constitute these detention powers. This is because immigration detention powers are limited to the period that is required to deport the person in question. If there is no possibility that the individual will be removed from the UK in a reasonable time, then that individual cannot be lawfully detained. Thus, to make sure that the UK was not in breach of the ECtHR, the government used the power allowed by Article 15 to derogate from Article 5 (and also Article 9 of the ICCPR).

The legislation thus shows a desire to remain human rights compliant with Article 3 of the CAT and the ECtHR, whilst using derogations to strengthen the Home Secretary's power to detain terrorist suspects. It would therefore be wrong to see the

---

65   Answering these questions demands that we look at the general legal context. The UK ratified the Convention Against Torture in 1988, and it entered into force in January 1989. The European Convention, which also came into force in January 1989, also supplements the protection offered by the Convention for the Prevention of Torture. However, opposition to torture in English law existed prior to the undertaking of these international commitments. The common law has had its face set against torture since the seventeenth century (CAT Report November 2004, p. 3). The Treason Act 1709 definitively stated that no one accused of crime could be tortured, and, alongside this Act, both the common law, and the Offences Against the Person Act 1861 criminalised the act of torture. The law against torture was updated at the time the UK acceded to the Convention with s.134 of the Criminal Justice Act 1988. This made it an offence for a public official, or someone acting in a public capacity to commit torture or engage in cruel, inhuman or degrading treatment or punishment. Criminal liability attaches to the act of torture under this section irrespective of the nationality of the alleged torturer, or where in the world the offence was committed. (CAT Report November 2004, p. 3). The commitment outlawing torture in domestic law and honouring international obligations must be seen in the light of recent legal reforms as part of the ongoing response to international terrorism.
66   Nicol (2006: 741).
67   SI 2001/3644.

struggle between the judges and the courts over the response to terrorism as simply that of an anti-rights executive and a pro-rights judiciary. The legislation itself shows an intent to realise human rights standards. The issues that we must examine lie within this general context.

We will be concerned with the House of Lord's ruling in the *A.* case.[68] It focuses attention on the nature of the Home Secretary's power to make political decisions that are outside the province of the courts. The House of Lords held, first of all, that although there was not a specific terrorist threat, this did not invalidate the judgement that there was a real risk of a terrorist attack at some point in the future. This assessment of risk was a political judgment. Great weight must be accorded to the decision by the court. Despite Lord Hoffmann's dissent, the court believed that the Home Secretary had made an accurate assessment that the nation was facing a public emergency. However, the House of Lords also held that the deference that the court owed to Parliament did not prevent the court from considering the proportionality of measures made by the executive to restrict rights. On this ground, s.23 was a disproportionate response to the terrorist threat.[69]

On these grounds the measure was illogical, disproportionate to the threat faced and the limitation on the right to liberty was therefore not justifiable. The House of Lords was also concerned that there had been no derogation from Article 14 and the effect of the section was discriminatory. Finally the House held that the measures were not coherent with international human rights obligations, citing the Refugee Convention and the Convention on the Elimination of All Forms of Discrimination, to protect the rights of those in a national territory and secure equality before the law.

How are we to understand this decision? The courts affirm that they respect the political nature of the Home Secretary's decision and accord 'great weight' to his conclusions. However, this deference to the Home Secretary does not prevent judicial assessment of the proportionality of the legislation that Parliament has passed. From this perspective, it would appear that the courts are political actors, assuming the power to assess executive decisions, and not to defer to them. How acceptable is it for judges to proceed in this way? This is a difficult question to answer. How one approaches the issue depends on where one feels ultimate authority lies in the constitution. Does it rest with the protection of human rights, or the executive's 'right' to protect national security, even if this means restricting human rights protection? The real answer to this question probably rests in a dialogue around the values of national security and human rights where both the courts and Parliament contribute to a meaningful articulation of democratic values. Whether or not the *A.* case, and the cases that we will now examine establish this dialogue, remains open to question.[70]

....

68 *A. and others v. Secretary of State for the Home Department* [2005] 2 WLR 87.
69 This was because, *inter alia*, the section applied to non-nationals, but not to nationals; moreover it permitted non-nationals to leave the UK, and did not assess the threat from British nationals. Finally, the court argued that s.23 could also apply to those who did not present a threat.
70 The government responded to the House of Lords' ruling in *A.* with the Prevention of Terrorism Act 2005 (PTA). Amnesty International has argued that this 'broke the spirit, if not the letter, of the Law Lords' ruling'. This is because the 2005 Act gives a government minister 'unprecedented powers' to issue control orders to those suspected of terrorism. These orders can be made on the basis of 'secret evidence'.

The issue of torture is certainly one where differences of opinion between judges and between the courts and Parliament, has emerged. The key case is *A. and others* v. *Secretary of State for the Home Department (No. 2)*.[71] The case also concerns emergency powers enacted in Part 4 of the 2001 Act. One of the points of the appeal addressed rule 44(3) of the Special Immigration Appeals Commission (Procedure) Rules 2003. This rule allowed the Commission to receive evidence that would not be admissible in a court of law. This could include evidence obtained by torture by officials acting for foreign governments. The Court of Appeal stated that provided that the Home Secretary had neither procured or connived in torture, and provided that he was acting in good faith, he could use evidence 'which had or might have been obtained through torture by agencies of other states over which he had no power'.

The Court of Appeal thus shows less willingness than the House of Lords in the previous *A.* case to question the executive's actions in defence of national security. How is this justified? No doubt it would be correct to say that the courts must follow the legislature; but, is one then compelled to agree that if the legislature makes a law that condones or authorises torture, the courts must follow it? From the viewpoint of the CAT, such laws would be in immediate violation of the Convention, and hence a nation's international human rights commitments.

In 2005, the House of Lords[72] reversed the Court of Appeal. The House of Lords held that evidence obtained by torture was unreliable and 'incompatible' with a principled administration of justice. As such, evidence obtained by torture, no matter whether or not this was by a third party outside of the UK, was inadmissible in court. The House of Lords also went on to consider the use of such information in the detention or arrest of a person ordered by the Home Secretary. Although the Home Secretary did not act 'unlawfully' in making use of 'tainted' information in these decisions, the Commission reviewing the reasonableness of the Home Secretary's suspicion could not admit evidence obtained by torture. However, the Commission was entitled to admit 'a wide range of material' that would not be inadmissible in 'judicial proceedings'. Furthermore, as those detained pursuant to the Home Secretary's decision had 'only limited access' to the evidence that was being used against them, it was necessary to use a specific approach to the issue of whether or not a statement had been obtained by torture. The correct approach was to be found in Article 15 of the Torture Convention. If, on the balance of probabilities, evidence has been obtained by torture, it should not be admitted. However, if the Commission was in doubt as to whether evidence had been so obtained, the evidence should be admitted. If a detainee was able to show a 'plausible reason' that evidence was obtained by torture, then the Commission had to 'initiate relevant inquiries'.

What sense do we make of this decision? Does it show the House of Lords championing human rights against a pusillanimous Court of Appeal? It would perhaps be more accurate to read this ruling as indicative, albeit in a rather limited form, of the dialogue that we have been describing in the section above. Although the House of Lords does over-rule the Court of Appeal with a bold statement of principle, and asserts that such evidence cannot be used in court, they assert that it is the Commission

---

71   *A. and others* v. *Secretary of State for the Home Department (No. 2)* [2005] UKHL 71.
72   Ibid.

reviewing the Home Secretary's decision that cannot make use of torture evidence, and that the Home Secretary himself would not be acting unlawfully in making use of such evidence. The Commission might also be able to make use of torture evidence given the nature of the test under Article 15 of the CAT. If there is a dialogue taking place between the executive and the judiciary in this case, it suggests that the courts will police the due process and integrity of forensic processes – to the extent that torture evidence cannot be used. However, at the same time, they appear to acknowledge that such evidence may be used by the Home Secretary, and that, given the terms of the relevant test, torture evidence might be used in court. This suggests a subtle and shifting alliance between the court and the executive. Although the Court of Appeal was in error in *A.* in suggesting a broad discretion to use torture evidence, the House of Lords do not go as far as asserting a general ban.

A note on the common law tradition and the independence of the Judiciary

In this chapter, we are concerned with the role that Judges can play in articulating the values of contemporary British democracy. In this they often self-consciously position themselves in terms of an imagined and reconstituted tradition of the common law. For example, in *A. and others* v. *The Secretary of the State for the Home Office (No. 2)*, Lord Bingham began his judgment looking back at the views of Jurists expressed from the 'earliest days the common law of England'. Writers such as Sir John Fortescue (*De Laudibus Legumback Angliae*, c. 1460–1470, ed. S. B. Chrimes (1942), Ch. 22, pp. 47–53), Sir Edward Coke (*Institutes of the Laws of England* (1644), Part III, Ch. 2, pp. 34–36), and Sir William Blackstone (*Commentaries on the Laws of England* (1769) Vol. IV, Ch. 25, pp. 320–321) had set their face firmly against torture (although they acknowledge that torture had been used under Royal Prerogative). But the claim was that common lawyers regarded torture as 'totally repugnant to the fundamental principles of English law' and 'repugnant to reason, justice, and humanity'. The design of the new Supreme Court building incorporates reminders of that tradition. In a recent speech, Baroness Hale (2010) ended by quoting one of the phrases on the rule of law that are engraved into the wood and glass balustrade of the library ('Injustice anywhere is injustice everywhere', Martin Luther King). Opposite the main entrance to the Court is a set of semi-circular stone benches inscribed with the lines of the 'Supreme Court Poem', composed for the opening of the court and reading in part: '. . . . Here Justice sits and lifts her steady scales, Within the Abbey's sight and Parliaments, But independent of them both. And bound by truth of principle and argument, A thousand years of judgment stretch behind – The weight of rights and freedoms balancing, With fairness and with duty to the world: The clarity time-honoured thinking brings, New structures but an old foundation stone: The mind of Justice still at liberty . . .' The Court library contains a facsimile copy of Bracton, *De legibus et consuetudinibus Angliae*, fols, 1b and 2 [c. 1235, *On the laws and customs of England*] where Bracton states: 'The seat of judgment is like the throne of God. Let the unwise and unlearned not presume to ascend it, lest he should confound darkness with light and light with darkness, lest with a sword in the hand, as it were, of a madman he should slay the innocent and set free the guilty, and lest he should tumble down from on high, as from the throne of God, in attempting to fly before he has acquired wings . . . .'

Whereas the Supreme Court poem refers to 'duty to the world', writing in the thirteenth century Bracton used the image of a severe Divine judge to warn human judges against corruption, prejudice, rashness and ignorance. In Bracton's world view, the eschatological teachings of Christianity provided final accountability. He wrote before notions of human sovereignty, or the rise of the legal positivist philosophy that defined law as something totally and wholly posited by man; instead, he held broad and encompassing notions of humanity's place in the cosmos and considered virtue and prudence to be guides to decision making. Importantly, all were to be subject to the law: 'The King himself, however, ought not to be under man but under God, and under the Law, for the Law makes the King. Therefore, let the King render back to the Law what the Law gives to him, namely dominion and power; for there is no King where will, and not Law, wields dominion.'

In the late sixteenth and early seventeenth century Edward Coke, sometime Chief Justice and member of Parliament (who personally was an arrogant and scheming individual but who had the courage to take stands against power), put forth the common law as the boundary, not the instrument of royal prerogative, and opposing his rival – Francis Bacon – declared that judges were not 'lions under the throne', but 'umpires between King and subject'. He opposed the practice of the King conferring with Judges before trials and swaying their judgments, stating that law was 'an artificial reason' which required 'long study and experience'. In Bonham's Case, Coke ruled that Judges could look to fundamental principles to control the Act of Parliament: 'when an Act of Parliament is against common right and reason, or repugnant, or impossible to be performed, the common law will control it and adjudge such Act to be void.' While in England the doctrine of Parliamentary supremacy overtook this opinion, it became (at least mythically) the foundation of the United State's Supreme Court's declaration that they had the power to judge the constitutionality of statutes. Later in Parliament, in the early years of the disastrous reign of Charles I (later tried and beheaded), Coke responded to the declaration of martial law by preparing the Resolutions (the basis later of the Habeas Corpus Act 1679). These stated that Magna Carta was still applicable, thus: 'no freeman is to be committed or detained in prison, or otherwise restrained by command of the King or the Privy Council or any other unless some lawful cause be shown . . . the writ of habeas corpus cannot be denied, but should be granted to every man who is committed or detained in prison or otherwise restrained by the command of the King, the Privy Council or any other. . . Any freeman so committed or detained in prison without cause being stated should be entitled to bail or be freed.'

THE JUDGES, PARLIAMENT AND 'THE DIALOGUE'

In this section, we want to draw out a clearer sense of the tensions that have developed between the judges and Parliament (it is worth also referring to the issues around fair trials and closed procedure material in Chapter 14), and return to consider the notion of the dialogue between the courts and Parliament. First of all, then, we want to look at the way in which the Law Lords themselves have understood the issues raised by the terrorism cases.

Lord Justice Hale draws attention to the dilemma that judges confront: they are 'janus faced' – both implementing executive power, and attempting to hold government to account and to keep executive power within the law. There are compelling reasons for the protection of national security. However, the prevention of terrorism cannot be achieved by 'compromising the rule of law'.[73] The courts have thus resisted the government's attempts to impose executive detention (the first Belmarsh case). The government responded by increasing the period in which a person could be detained without trial. This form of detention is clearly problematic in a democracy. As we have seen, the courts asserted in the second Belmarsh case that torture evidence would never be admissible as evidence; a powerful defence of the rule of law (even though the majority went on to hold that a person alleging that evidence was obtained by torture carried the burden of proof; a difficult, if not impossible task). The judges have attempted to maintain the standards of a fair trial against the executive creation of a regime of closed order proceedings and closed evidence. Would it not be better to deal with alleged terrorist offences through the criminal courts, adapting procedures (especially those around Public Interest Immunity (PII) certificates to take account of national security concerns) 'rather than by way of executive control on the grounds of mere suspicion rather than proof?'[74] We will return to these questions in detail presently (see Chapter 14).

These concerns suggest that the judges have attempted to assert rule of law values in a troubling period where Parliament and the executive are under immense public pressure to take action against terrorist threats. The risk is that extraordinary powers are normalised and the very values which are worth preserving against terrorist violence are compromised. The judicial response to terrorism can thus be linked to arguments that judges have used human rights to define and limit legislative and executive power. We will now turn to examine these claims.

Lord Hope has stressed the 'dangerous doctrine' that lies beneath the supremacy of Parliament: an 'increasingly powerful executive' can 'abuse the legislative authority of a Parliament which, *ex hypothesi*, it controls because of the absolute majority that it enjoys in the House of Commons'.[75] Although Parliamentary supremacy rests on the democratic idea that it reflects the will of the people, it is an 'uncomfortable fact' that tensions can develop between 'Parliamentary sovereignty and the rule of law'. The fundamental problem is that 'the rule of law' can be 'subordinated to the will of the government'.[76] Lord Hope's words reflect the kind of concerns that we studied above in Jackson, but in the context of the judicial and legislative response to terrorism. To return to Hale LJ's argument, the judges appear to be asserting the rule of law against the 'will of the government'. This takes us towards a more sustained reflection on the claim that there is a dialogue between the courts and Parliament.

The notion of dialogue is based on a distinction between judicial and legislative functions. How can we distinguish between these two functions? The rule of law

---

73   Baroness Hale, 2010: 1.
74   Baroness Hale, 9.
75   Lord Hope, 12.
76   Ibid., 14.

requires judges and Parliament to restrict themselves to one or other of these two roles as far as possible. Young, an apologist for the notion of dialogue, develops this argument by distinguishing between contestable and non-contestable 'rights issues'. The terms 'contestable' and 'non-contestable' needs to be clarified a little.[77] A contestable right is a 'watershed' issue best left to the legislature to resolve. Non-contestable rights are the proper province of the courts. A non-contestable right can be argued about in legal terms; it is possible for the courts to rule on whether the right exists or not; or, if it does exist, the precise nature of the right. In other words, Young is trying to draw a line between the kinds of argument that are best suited to the courts, and those that are best dealt with by Parliament.[78]

The line needs to be held, as it demarcates the proper province of judge and politician. Take, for instance, Tomkins' objections to some human rights arguments. He argues that human rights (other than absolute rights, such as the prohibition against torture, or process rights, that are the proper province of the judiciary) are most properly political arguments, not legal ones, and should be resolved through political debate: 'enlightened parliamentary democracies such as the United Kingdom shows that these are tools that intelligent and responsive policy makers are perfectly capable of using and, sometimes, of using well.'[79]

Although these are insightful arguments, we want to be critical of their terms. Whilst it is important to distinguish between legal and political decision making, it is more difficult to show exactly where the line lies. To talk in terms of contestable and non-contestable is also problematic. Whilst, for example, Jackson shows the Law Lords keeping to constitutional proprieties, their obiter statements suggest that the significance of the case goes beyond a distinction between contestable and non-contestable rights. Likewise, the Belmarsh case is difficult to analyse in terms of the contestable/non-contestable distinction. Whilst the decision is clearly an interpretation of the law, it has profound political consequences. The extra judicial speeches of the Law Lords that we examined above, also suggests a more acute sense of the fault lines of the constitution than the contestable/non-contestable distinction would allow.

However, none of our arguments suggest that the dialogue idea should be rejected. Rather, it draws our attention to the ongoing transformation of judicial and constitutional practices; a 'messy' debate over the balance of power in the constitution. Perhaps this sense of dialogue is captured best by Nicol's notion of both courts and Parliament putting forward rival interpretations of rights. Parliament can 'substitute . . . its own favoured interpretation [to that of the courts] provided it is willing to pay the political price'. In this idea of dialogue '[e]lucidating the meaning of the Convention rights should therefore be seen as a shared responsibility between judiciary and legislature'.[80] This shared responsibility means that judicial decision making is never free of politics, never entirely 'non-contestable'. The judiciary remain, in this sense, irreducibly

77   The terms are borrowed from Waldron (2010).
78   This is a theory of judicial restraint: 'the courts ought to adopt a cautious and restrained approach to the choices presented to them in their adjudicative function' (Kavanagh, 2010). As far as the HRA is concerned, the court should approach non-contestable rights through s.2/3, and contestable rights through s.4.
79   Tomkins (2010: 22).
80   Nicol (1996: 744).

political – with a small 'p'. The politics of the judiciary, as we hope to elaborate, are not simplistic party politics: rather, to the extent that the judges are upholding the rule of law, they are asserting the values of a democratic culture where government is in accordance with human rights. We want to follow the consequences of this argument into the next chapter.

CONCLUSION

In this chapter we have argued that the senior judiciary are playing a distinct role in the articulation of the values of British democracy. We have argued that – at least since 1998 – there has been a transformation of judicial attitudes. We engaged with a number of cases, including the recent House of Lords cases on terrorism and torture that provide evidence for a new expression of judicial politics. We have described this relationship as a dialogue with Parliament. Extra-judicial writings by Supreme Court justices also suggest that there is a willingness to criticise Parliament and affirm rule of law values against the executive. This begs a number of serious questions. Human rights are themselves indeterminate; decisions on human rights are as much political as legal. We need to consider how the law-making power of the court is legitimate. The next chapter develops this important theme.

11

JUDGES AND DEMOCRACY

———·•·———

Even when a man is obliged to decide cases and to be a judge, still let him beware of the dangers to himself, lest by judging perversely and against the laws, through entreaties or for a price, he should purchase for himself the measureless sorrows of eternal damnation for the momentary enjoyment of a paltry gain.[1]

. . . all the judges, without exception, are members of the Athaneum [a private club], and I presume that you will wish to be a member.[2]

The English judiciary includes few women, even fewer blacks and nobody under the age of 40. English judges tend to be elderly gentlemen most of whom have had a public school education. It is disturbing that our judges come from such a narrow range of the community. To adjudicate cases is to exercise discretion in fact finding, sentencing, applying the law and awarding costs. Such powers should be exercised by judges of different backgrounds, ages, races and sexes. This is for two main reasons. First, it is inequitable in a democratic society that one set of values should predominate on the Bench. Second, there is a danger that minority groups and women faced by a Bench on which they see few, if any, of their number will lose respect for the law. A more diverse judiciary is unlikely to be attained while appointment is confined to practising barristers. There are few blacks, women and Labour Party supporters among the ranks of senior barristers.[3]

INTRODUCTION

In this chapter we will continue our analysis of the politics of the judiciary. We will argue that the judiciary has to be understood as an essential element of a democratic political order. Our conception of the democratic judge requires us to acknowledge that his/her powers to 'rule' are limited by the law. Our argument will develop as follows. After a broad overview to orientate our arguments, we will outline a theory of judicial restraint that legitimately limits judicial law making. Acknowledging judicial law making power requires us to think critically about the system of judicial appointments. We will engage with the seeming failure to achieve diversity; a problem which, if not tackled, raises questions about the responsiveness of the judges to the communities they serve.

---

1   Bracton, *De legibus et consuetudinibus Angliae*, fols, 1b and 2. [c. 1235, *On the laws and customs of England*].
2   The Master of the Rolls, Cozens–Hardy, writing to Lord Buckmaster when Lord Buckmaster was appointed to the Lord Chancellorship in the early twentieth century, quoted Pannick (1989: 50).
3   Pannick (1989), making the argument for a more representative judiciary.

THE JUDGE AND THE LIMITS OF THE LAW

How can we think about the present role of the judge within a democratic polity? As we saw in Chapter 10, the role of the judge has changed markedly over the last fifty or so years. We explored the notion of dialogue between the courts and Parliament. We could also, at this stage, recall our arguments from Chapter 6 about law and public reason. We can now develop these ideas by referring to American scholarship (with appropriate adaptations) on the role of the judge. Owen Fiss has argued that:

> [the] [j]udges' capacity to make a special contribution to our social life derives not from any personal traits or knowledge, but from the definition of the office in which they find themselves and through which they exercise power. That office is structured by both ideological and institutional factors that enable and perhaps even force the judge to be objective – not to express his preferences or personal beliefs, or those of the citizenry, as to what is right or just, but constantly to strive for the true meaning of the constitutional value. Two aspects of the judicial office give it this special cast: one is the judge's obligation to participate in a dialogue, and the second is his independence.[4]

Fiss means that the 'office' of the judge defines the role and function of judging. In other words, a judge is constrained in his/her decision making by the constitutional position that defines his/her powers. Note, however, that this is not a description of a narrow institutional position: a judge contributes to the meaning of 'our social life'. We want to develop these points in more depth.

We are not denying that the law making power of judges is linked to their discretion. As we have seen, there is a large measure of discretion in judicial interpretation. This does not mean that the law is completely indeterminate, or that the 'politics of the judiciary' are illegitimate. In Fiss' terms they can perhaps be seen as arguments over the terms of our 'social life'. Judicial argument over the nature of rights takes place in a 'space' where different interpretations of the law are possible and different values compete. We will repeatedly return to the different interpretations of the law that senior Law Lords make. However, our main point is that – whatever the interpretation, and, indeed, whatever the values that inform interpretation, they are to a significant extent defined and limited by the institutional requirements that law itself is rational and structured. This does not prevent 'play' or argument over the meaning of the law; it merely keeps it within the limits that are themselves defined by the legal system itself. So law is not completely delinked from politics; rather, law is politics by other means: ongoing arguments over the meanings of democracy and the rule of law.[5]

We can return to Fiss' analysis to clarify these points. The limits under which the judge operates are many and various. Fiss does indeed refer to a 'dialogue' – but in a sense slightly different from the one that we have deployed in this book. Fiss' understanding of dialogue is closer to our notion of the limits or institutional context in and

---

4   Fiss (1979: 13).
5   Our point would correspond, at least in some ways, with Griffith's argument about the 'political constitution'. See Griffith (1979: 14).

under which the judge decides a case. These are, in Fiss' sense, a prerequisite for the judicial exercise of power. The institutional constraints are:

(a) Judges are not in control of their agenda, but are compelled to confront grievances or claims they would otherwise prefer to ignore. (b) Judges do not have full control over whom they must listen to. They are bound by rules requiring them to listen to a broad range of persons or spokesmen. (c) Judges are compelled to speak back, to respond to the grievance or the claim, and to assume individual responsibility for that response. (d) Judges must also justify their decisions.

Points (a) to (d) outline the terms which define judicial decision making. Judges are limited in the extent to which they can consider the broader issues raised by the dispute which they are adjudicating. They are responding to a specific dispute (a), and can only engage with parties to that dispute (b). Perhaps most importantly (c and d) they must issue a written and reasoned response: they must justify the decision that they have reached.

To assert the conventional position: judges are not, and should not be, legislators: they cannot take into account the range of materials that lawmakers can – they have no mandate to claim a general law making power, and are not accountable in the way that lawmakers are to the electorate. Judicial law making is necessarily interstitial and limited. Ultimately, there is no clear line to draw between judicial law making and legislation. At best, we can say that tracing the boundary is a matter of practice and relies on a diffidence on the part of the judiciary: a legal/cultural sensitivity to those instances when law making is acceptable, and those when it is not. To elaborate further – as Kavanagh writes – there is no easy answer to the question 'How can judges uphold human rights, without straying beyond the limits of their constitutional

THE ROLL CALL

Figure 11.1 Being 'called' to the bar, Middle Temple, 1840s. Credit: MEPL

Figure 11.1 Continued

This image captures the traditional process of joining the professional elite, along with its rituals and ideologies that many believe protect members of the Bar and the Judiciary from undue influence. The argument of this chapter holds that judges are political and that it is better to have openness about the politics of their role than hold to some version of an apolitical rule of law. This will appear strange to some people who will prefer an ideal of judicial neutrality and may argue that judicial espousal of a political position goes against their professional ethics. Traditionally judges in the UK were appointed from the ranks of senior barristers. The background of their role and politics was the culture of the Bar and the Oath of office. Barristers are Officers of the Court, and in most countries judges on appointment take an oath to uphold the constitution and/or support the rule of law.

There are numerous instances however, when judges have supported legal or quasi-legal orders to produce clearly (to an outsider) unjust processes and decisions. In the cases, for example, of the American judges who applied the Fugitive Slave Laws, German judges who implemented Nazi law, or South African judges who imparted legal legitimacy to apartheid, professionals charged with administering justice provided institutional support passively and sometimes directly for state-sponsored (and often arbitrary) degradation, repression, and brutality. Should judges bear a particular moral expectation? Clearly, in rule of law societies judges are central. Camenisch in his classical work on ethics and professionals in society put it as follows: judges are the 'bearers of a public trust, bestowed upon them in the form of a professional degree and title, and endowing them with a monopoly in the provision of a service which is crucial to society'. Their role provides them with a power that can be used either 'for great societal benefit or to considerable societal harm', and thus 'they can rightly be accused of failure not only when they use their power, influence and expertise for the wrong purposes, purposes which are positively harmful, but also when they fail to use them for the proper purposes, or even fail to do so with sufficient energy and perseverance' (Camenisch (1983: 15 and 17). Judges are subject to particular scrutiny because they are trained and take oaths to administer justice, or at least to uphold the constitution and the laws, which contain principles of justice.

In one interesting study, Hilbink (2007) analyses the submissive role that the judges in Chile played under the Military Dictatorship of General Pinochet even though they had been trained and appointed under a democratic regime and had taken an oath to uphold the constitution of that regime, which provided a host of liberal and democratic protections. Their support for the illiberal, antidemocratic, and anti-legal agenda of the military government (for example, of more than 5,400 *habeas corpus* petitions filed by human rights lawyers between 1973 and 1983, the courts rejected all but ten) is explained institutionally. In common with some who have sought to explain the behaviour of the judges who supported the Nazi regime, Hilbink first finds the ideology of legal positivism, as making morality irrelevant to law and thus as consigning judges to be 'slaves of the law' (this is actually a misunderstanding of positivism). This view developed into an 'antipolitical' conception of the judicial role amongst judges. Judges believed 'law' and 'politics' were two entirely distinct and unrelated pursuits. They considered the goals of judges and legislators to be completely separate and divergent; thus, the less 'political' judges were, the more 'legal' they would be. This understanding was strengthened and reproduced by the institutional structure that was established in the 1920s, when reformers sought to end executive manipulation of the courts and professionalise the judicial career. A formal judicial hierarchy was established and the Supreme Court was given control over discipline and promotion within the legal profession, even controlling nominations to its own ranks. Although this structure successfully increased judicial independence from executive control, it provided incentives for judges to look primarily to their superiors – rather than to any other audience or reference group – for cues on how to decide cases. Judges thus learned that to succeed professionally, the best strategy was to eschew independent or innovative interpretation in favour of conservative rulings that would please the high-court justices. In this way, conservatism and conformity were continually reproduced within the inward-looking judicial ranks.

Thus after the 1973 military coup in Chile even judges personally at odds with the laws and practices of the military regime were professionally unwilling or unable to defend liberal democratic principles and practices. Publicly challenging the validity of the regime's laws and policies in the name of liberal-democratic values and principles was viewed as unprofessional 'political' behaviour, which threatened the integrity of the judiciary and the rule of law. Under the watchful eye of the Supreme Court, any judge who aspired to rise in the ranks of the judiciary learned not to take such stands. Hilbink offers several lessons:

> First, formal judicial independence, even when achieved and respected, is not sufficient to produce a judicial defence of rights and the rule of law. Indeed, institutional variables appear to impact significantly on whether or not judges will be willing and able to assert themselves in defence of rights and the rule of law. Second, it is important to understand not only the way institutions constrain the expression of judges' pre-existing attitudes but also as to how they constitute judges' professional identities and goals. Judicial role conceptions matter, and we need to understand better how they are formed, maintained, or altered. Third, 'apoliticism' appears to be the wrong ideal around which to construct a judiciary in service of liberal democracy. Although judicial independence and professionalism are desirable for any polity committed to the rule of law, it is neither possible nor desirable to construct a judiciary beyond politics. When judges are prohibited by institutional structure and/or ideology from engaging with the wider polity, they are unlikely to cultivate the professional attributes necessary for them to defend and promote liberal-democratic constitutionalism.

Hilbink concludes that an 'apolitical' judiciary is thus far better suited to authoritarianism than to democracy.

role?'[6] These considerations make it all the more important to approach the issue of the appointment and accountability of the judiciary.

JUDGES, ACCOUNTABILITY AND THE RULE OF LAW

If, as we have argued above, judges are fundamentally political creatures, then to what extent are they 'democratically accountable'.[7] Precisely because the HRA has empowered judges, it may be necessary to reassess the checks and balances that exist over the judiciary. With the creation of a Supreme Court, these matters are brought to a head. As the issue of the democratic accountability of judges is quite broad, we will examine one particular aspect of this problem: the reforms in the area of judicial appointment. To what extent do they open judicial appointments to democratic scrutiny? Why should this be important? Baroness Hale has argued, and most would agree, that it is a matter of principle:

> In a democratic society, in which we are all equal citizens, it is wrong in principle for that authority to be wielded by such a very unrepresentative section of the population.[8]

That the composition of the judiciary should reflect that of society is a claim about the composition, rather than the function of the body. The argument for a representative judiciary is founded on the assertion that institutions should reflect the nature of the society in which they are embedded. This can be justified by principles of democratic pluralism, or equality of opportunity. Arguments for a representative judiciary are not the same as arguments for a representative legislature. Parliament is elected on a broad democratic franchise. Its function is to represent the interests of the electorate as a whole. Whilst judges should be more representative of the society from which they are drawn, their predominant function is that of neutral adjudication. Indeed, the first report of the Select Committee on Constitutional Affairs stressed that reforms in judicial appointments should be driven by a notion of 'democratic accountability' that sought to achieve a balance between the need to secure the transparency of the appointments procedure, and the requirement of judicial independence within both the domestic and European contexts of the British state.[9] It was becoming increasingly clear that the old system was lacking in democratic credibility.

---

6   Kavanagh (2010: 24).
7   Gearty (2004: 209).
8   Hale (2001: 502).
9   The government was also keen to promote a diversity agenda – but within the context of cost and efficiency. There were some arguments that the creation of a Judicial Appointments Committee would simply be too expensive; or would take up too large a part of a budget that had to be shared between the Court Service and the provision of legal aid. Indeed, there were misgivings about the time scale in which reforms could be worked out and then implemented. The reason for haste was seen as 'primarily political' – although it is hard to understand this point. Is this a criticism of the party political agenda that lay behind the reforms, or an acknowledgement that reforms are necessary to make British institutions human rights compliant? See (http://www.parliament.the-stationery-office. co.uk/pa/cm200304/cmselect/cmconst/48/4803.htm#a2).

Prior to the 2005 Act, the Lord Chancellor's 'power' to appoint judges[10] meant that the process was secretive and headed by a person who held political office. The pool of possible appointments was small and almost entirely composed of senior barristers, or, in the case of most appointments to the office of High Court judge, those who were currently practising as recorders. It became increasingly difficult to justify this unaccountable and un-transparent system of 'secret soundings'.[11] Furthermore, the blurring of judicial and executive functions in the office of Lord Chancellor appeared to be in breach of democratic principles. The Human Rights Act 1998 signalled the reform of the system. Proposals focused on the need for a judicial appointments body that would bring to an end obscure methods of appointment and limit the power of the Lord Chancellor.[12]

The government's preference for a recommending body[13] was ultimately successful, and suggests that the major ways in which transparency will be maintained is through the traditional constitutional mechanism of accountability to Parliament. While this stresses the element of political accountability in appointments, it does beg the question of the terms of this constitutional convention. There is an argument that should a sufficiently strong government choose to support a minister's decision, then he or she would be unlikely to resign. Such criticisms of Parliament's weakness in the face of the resolve of governmental power suggest wider concerns about the 'democratic deficit' in British politics. Whilst we cannot consider them in detail in this chapter, we could suggest that the weaknesses of the present reforms to achieve a transparent and democratic system of appointments are inseparable from wider concerns about the

....

10   Appointments to higher judicial positions, to the Court of Appeal, the appellate Committee of the House of Lords and to offices of Lord Chief Justice and President of the Family Division were made by the Queen, on the advice of the Prime Minister after consultation with the Lord Chancellor, who had himself consulted with senior members of the judiciary. High court judges, circuit judges, recorders and stipendiary and lay magistrates were appointed by the Queen on the advice of the Lord Chancellor.

11   Although solicitors were allowed for some posts in the early 1990s in the mid-1990s it was still the case that information on potential judges was kept in the Lord Chancellor's department in closed files (written for barristers on pink cards and for solicitors on yellow cards) consisting of a range of appreciative and not so favourable comments, some related to much earlier stages in a person's career. A person's reputation could be made or unmade by comments, phrases and allegations that were never fully scrutinised.

12   At http://www.dca.gov.uk/consult/jacommission/index.htm#ch2.

13   The different forms that the body might take reflect different understandings of where the balance of power should lie between Ministers, lay members, the legal profession and judges themselves. An Appointing Committee, at least in the form presented in the government's consultation paper, would take over the appointment powers of the Lord Chancellor and the Prime Minister. Power to appoint judges would effectively be removed from the hands of ministers. This would have the virtue of independence from the political process, but it would also be necessary to make sure that the Commission was not biased with views from the profession or other sources. Although there are regulatory bodies that have no ministerial presence, and this model removes whatever political influence a Minister might bring to bear on judicial appointments, it raises a serious constitutional issue. The removal of Ministerial input also compromises the element of Parliamentary scrutiny, because a Minister is responsible to Parliament. A recommending Commission reflects a different understanding of the balance of power. This model retains the involvement of Ministers, and hence the element of responsibility to Parliament. The Commission itself makes the recommendation, and the Minister rejects or accepts the recommendation. The model requires a precise demarcation of responsibilities between Commission and Minister to be worked out – as otherwise a Minister might find him or herself in the position of responsibility for appointments in which he or she had little or no input. A hybrid Commission represents a variation on this theme: the power to make junior appointments would rest with an Appointing Commission, but appointing to senior positions would require Ministerial input. A hybrid Commission would allow Ministerial responsibility to Parliament, while also creating an independent body.

unrestrained power of the executive – and the ongoing need for general constitutional reform.

How does the Constitutional Reform Act structure the operation of a recommending commission? The Act begins by re-affirming the independence of the judiciary. This is the first time in British history that a statement of this value has taken a statutory form. Give the absence of a fundamental document that describes the relationship between the executive, the legislature and the judiciary, this particular statement of judicial independence reflects the need to define a constitutional settlement without committing to a written constitution. It thus needs to be read in the context of 'constitutional' statutes such as the Human Rights Act 1998 and the European Communities Act 1972 that are seen as structural to the legal form of the British state. The other point that needs to be borne in mind is the sense in which the Constitutional Reform Act is driven by the political need to ensure that British institutions are compliant with the European Convention on Human Rights.

The Constitutional Reform Act makes a number of changes to the office of the Lord Chancellor – but – most importantly for our purposes, we need to realise that the Lord Chancellor retains an important set of powers to affect and influence the appointment of judges. Although these powers are offset by those of the Appointments Committee, it would be wrong to see the new system as bringing to an abrupt end the influence of the executive in the appointment of judges.

Section 3(1) of the 2005 Act thus places a duty on the Lord Chancellor and other Ministers with responsibility for the 'administration of justice' to 'uphold' the 'independence of the judiciary'. This section of the Act also contains provisions in relation to the independence of the judiciary in Scotland and Northern Ireland, but we do not have the space to consider these in detail. This is not too problematic, as they follow the general schema of the Act outlined below.

The general duty at s.3(1) is elaborated in a number of more specific responsibilities. Section 3(5) prohibits the Lord Chancellor and other Ministers from influencing judicial decisions 'through any special access to the judiciary'. It is hard to know precisely what this notion of 'special access' covers. The notes for guidance put it in the following way: "'special access" is intended to refer to any access over and above that which might be exercised by a member of the general public'.[14] It is hard to believe that Ministers will be prevented by the Act from influencing decisions through subtle forms of political pressure. It is also difficult to see how a member of the general public may be able to question any particular decisions. Despite these criticisms, s.3(1) has the virtue of a clear statement of the broader constitutional principle of the division of power. Ministers must leave the judiciary to their own sphere of competence. Likewise, judges must not trespass on executive or legislative functions. Given the cult of secrecy in much of central government, and our general ignorance of how judges make decisions, it is hard to know whether or not the branches of the state keep to their respective fields of competence. The Lord Chancellor is given specific duties to ensure the defence of judicial independence and the reflection of the 'public interest' in matters relating to judges and the administration of justice.

---

14   At http://www.opsi.gov.uk/acts/en2005/2005en04.htm.

The main structural provisions are provided for by s.61 of the Act, which sets up the Judicial Appointments Commission. The Act goes on to specify that appointments must be solely on merit[15] and the Commission must be certain that the appointee is of 'good character'.[16] There is also a statutory duty to ensure that appointments are made in such a way as to achieve diversity in the composition of the judiciary – although such a duty is subject to the requirements of the sections described above. The Lord Chancellor retains an advisory role with respect to both procedure and the selection of candidates – and the Commission is under a duty to take into account the advice that may be given. However, given the importance of this guidance for the operation of the Commission, the Act does specify that the Lord Chancellor must consult with the Lord Chief Justice and bring the advice to the attention of the Commons for its approval. We could see this mechanism as the way in which the system of 'secret soundings' is opened to the democratic process.

The appointment powers of the Commission are also defined by the Act. The Act effectively divides judicial appointments in terms of the hierarchy of seniority. As far as appointments to senior positions[17] are concerned, the Lord Chancellor must first request the Commission to select a person if a vacancy arises in one of these offices. Once the selection has been made, the Commission must submit a report to the Lord Chancellor. When he is in receipt of the report, the Lord Chancellor may accept or reject the selection; he also has the power to require the Commission to reconsider its choice of person. The procedure laid down by the Act is rather complicated, but the Lord Chancellor can refuse a selection on the basis that the person is not suitable or that the person is not the best candidate on merit. The Act requires the Lord Chancellor to put his decision in writing.[18]

The Judicial Appointments Commission [JAC] consists of a chairman and 14 other members who are appointed by the Queen on the recommendation of the Lord Chancellor. The composition of the Commission is crucial as it must achieve a balance between those who represent the legal profession, and those who are drawn from a non-legal background. As the Select Committee report argued, there was a fear that if judicial members of the Commission predominated, they would recruit 'in their own image'. Indeed, it was pointed out that the Appointments Commission in Scotland was considered successful despite the fact that judges and lawyers were in the minority. The structure of the Act reflects a partial triumph of this position. The chairman has to be a 'lay member' rather than a judge. Of the other Commissioners, five must be judicial. The five judicial members must reflect a cross section of judicial ranks, from Lord

15   Constitutional Reform Act 2005, 63(2).
16   Ibid., 63(3).
17   This group includes: the Lord Chief Justice, who, amongst other offices and duties is the head of the judiciary and President of the Criminal Division of the Court of Appeal; the Master of the Rolls, who presides over the Civil Division of the Court of Appeal, and the three Division Heads of the High Court: the President of the Queen's Bench Division, the President of the Family Division, and the Chancellor of the High Court.
18   The next group of judicial offices, as defined by s.85 of the Act includes puisne judges or the High Court Judges, Circuit Judges, who sit in the regional Crown and County Courts, and Recorders, who also sit in the Crown or County Court and hear less complex matters than Circuit Judges and District Judges, who preside over County Courts and Justices of the Peace. The rules in relation to consultation and selection are similar to the group of senior judges.

Justice of Appeal to district judge. Two members must be professional, representing the bar and the solicitors' branch of the profession. The five lay members are defined as those who are not practising lawyers, and have not held judicial office.[19]

Criticisms have been made of the composition of the JAC. The Law Society has argued that the government still has too much control, as it appoints the Commission's staff, 82 per cent of which are seconded from the Ministry of Justice. They have also argued that the members of the Commission are 'selected primarily by the Lord Chancellor and the Lord Chief Justice'; the latter retaining a great deal of control over final appointments. Within the Commission, there are fears that the view of the judiciary predominate: five of the 15 JAC members must be judges, while at present three others happen to be current or former judges. Judicial influence is also cemented by the practice of obtaining references before interview – as this operates as a kind of filter. The JAC is also slowed down by cumbersome bureaucracy – a vice that the old system did not suffer from (at least in the opinions of some judges).[20]

Will the JAC create a more diverse judiciary? In January 2008, with the appointment of the first ten high court judges, many people began to think otherwise. Of a group of 21 candidates who have been approved, the first ten to obtain appointments 'are white male former barristers and six of the nine educated in Britain went to leading independent schools'. The group of approved candidates consists of three women, none of whom are ethnic minority appointments.[21] The Commons Inquiry into Judicial Appointments found that although some progress had been made at lower judicial levels, there was a 'glass ceiling' at recorder level. As the position of recorder was the 'bridge' to more senior appointments, it would appear that whilst the lower courts and tribunals are becoming more diverse, the higher courts remain the preserve of white males.

To some extent it is unfair to criticise the JAC for this problem as the last two rounds of appointments to Recorder were made by the Ministry of Justice. Complaints were also made over the advertisements for specialist circuit judges that appeared to exclude applications from district judges. Whilst there is a degree of diversity amongst district judges, there is very little amongst circuit judges. This would also suggest that there is another failure to push through a coherent agenda.

---

19 The Act also sets up a Judicial Appointments and Conduct Ombudsman s.62(1). It also creates a set of disciplinary procedures. Based on s.108, these allow the Lord Chancellor to remove holders of judicial office and sit alongside the powers of the Lord Chief Justice that are also subject to statuary procedures. The Lord Chief Justice, with the agreement of the Lord Chancellor, may formally reprimand or suspend from office a judicial officer holder who is, amongst other concerns, subject to criminal proceedings or convicted in criminal proceedings. The objective of this disciplinary code is to preserve public confidence in the judiciary. These disciplinary powers themselves sit within a system of checks and balances. Section 110 empowers the Ombudsman to review disciplinary cases in certain circumstances, but, it is worth remembering that this is a review of procedure, rather than the substance of the claim made against the judicial office holder. Under s.111, the Ombudsman has the power to set aside a decision, and to order that the matter be reconsidered.

20 See http://business.timesonline.co.uk/tol/business/law/columnists/article3283286.ece.

21 Reported in *The Guardian*, 28 January 2008. See http://www.guardian.co.uk/uk_news/story/0,2247993,00.html.

More recent figures on judicial diversity remain discouraging:

> . . . only 4% of our judges are from ethnic minorities (who make up about 8% of the
> population) compared with the US's 16% (where they make up about 25%). There are
> only three senior judges, and no law lords, from minority backgrounds in this country.
> Any praise for the UK's commitment to diversity in the judiciary – of which much is
> said but little evidence can yet be seen – must be placed in this context.[22]

As of December 2011, Lady Justice Hale is the only one of the ten Justices of the
Supreme Court who is female. Data published by the JAC on selection exercises
completed since 1 April 2008 shows that: 'five of the 22 High Court judges recommended for appointment by the JAC this year are women, which will raise the number
of women High Court judges to 17, the highest number ever.'[23] Comparative data
shows just how poor these figures are. A recent report published by the Council of
Europe drew attention to the increasing 'feminisation of the judiciary' across Europe,
so that one could speak of 'near gender equality'. In 2012, only 23 per cent of judges
in England and Wales, and 21 per cent in Scotland, were women. It is clear that the
British judiciary are perhaps the least diverse in Europe (indeed the CoE report shows
that only Azerbaijan and Armenia have fewer female judges).

It is not as if there is an official failure to appreciate the problem. In May 2011 the
House of Lords Constitution Committee began its inquiry into judicial appointments.
The fundamental problem is that, despite the operation of the JAC, the pattern of
appointments does not seem to have changed, and, as far as the public is concerned, the
process appears difficult to scrutinise. Furthermore, the pressing question is: to what
extent have the relevant sections of the Constitutional Reform Act been 'clarified' by the
Equality Act 2010? Section 159 of the Act contains a 'tie break' provision, that allows
the selecting body to choose the candidate from 'the underrepresented group'. Lord
Pannick, in particular, expressed his doubts over the effectiveness of these provisions.

If the official position is that the system promotes by merit, and given time, those
female and non-white candidates with merit will be appointed, then there will
always be a 'wait and see' argument. There are, however, significant problems with
this gradualist approach:

> Once enough women, members of ethnic and religious minorities, gays, and other non-
> standard issue have been at Bar for long enough, they are bound to come through to
> the higher positions. Most serious outside observers know that it is not so simple. . . .
> There are also systemic obstacles to making sufficient progress to be regarded as a
> serious candidate.[24]

It is not simply a question of believing that the most able candidates will come to the
top. It would appear that despite the reforms and protestations to the contrary, a

22   Afua Hirsch, *The Guardian*, 27/7/09 at http://www.guardian.co.uk/commentisfree/2009/jul/27/race-
judiciary-supreme-court.
23   http://jac.judiciary.gov.uk/about-jac/172.htm.
24   Hale (2001: 492).

tightly knit social group still recruits in its own image. This has been commented on by Mrs Justice Dobbs, one of the ten female High Court judges, and the only one from an ethnic minority. She cites Lady Justice Arden on the:

> notable lack of progress for women at a time when there is considerable pressure for diversity in the profession and on the bench.[25]

It would seem that, at least for now, the old order remains in control of appointments to the judiciary.

Of late, a sophisticated set of arguments have emerged that show how 'the quality' of judicial decision making can be improved by broadening the pool of 'talent' available for promotion to judicial office. In particular Lord Justice Etherton's arguments, backed up by those of Moran and Rackley, have refuted Genn's research argument that there is little or no evidence to suggest that female judges, or those from ethnic minority backgrounds, will make a significant difference to judicial decision making. These arguments address the sense in which judges can engage with different experiences in a meaningful way – and avoid the stridency of Justice Sotomayer's assertion that 'a wise Latina woman with the richness of her experiences would more often than not reach a better conclusion than a white man' (Horne (2010: 32) citing Malleson 33). What conclusions can we draw from these arguments? Given that there is little or no enthusiasm for judicial confirmation hearings[26] and arguments for positive discrimination are not being seriously mooted, the way forward may be to examine again the structures of the profession itself. If we are forced to accept a 'wait and see' argument, how is it possible to open up the professions to those who would otherwise suffer systemic obstacles to promotion to high office?

CONCLUSION

Within a democratic constitution judicial law making is legitimate to the extent that it is subordinate to an institution that has something like a general electoral mandate for its supremacy. However, simply asserting the democratic mandate of Parliament is no longer a convincing justification for its sovereignty. The defence of human rights and the rule of law is also a legitimate task for a judge – even if this creates a tension between the courts and Parliament. Judicial law making requires us to revisit the problematic issue of judicial appointments. We have argued that the debate has reached

----

25   See http://business.timesonline.co.uk/tol/business/law/article1984466.ece.

26   Confirmation hearings would provide an opportunity to examine an individual candidate's politics before they were invited to take judicial office. Such a practice is an accepted part of politics in the United States. However, proposals for confirmation hearings have not found acceptance in British politics. The Commons Committee that considered the issue did not accept that confirmation hearings would 'ensure confidence in the judiciary'. Moreover, they would be inconsistent with the objective of taking the Supreme Court out of the political arena. (29) The Ministry of Justice's Green Paper on The Governance of Britain also considered a more enhanced role for Parliament in judicial appointments. Although the government rejected both confirmation hearings and Parliamentary input in appointments, there was a proposal that a 'meeting of the Commons Justice Committee and the Lords Constitution Committee' could 'hold the system to account on an annual basis'. (30).

something of an impasse; and that the creation of a diverse pool of talent for high office requires a much broader consideration of the structures of the profession that still appears to recruit and promote in its own image.

POSTCRIPT: THE POLITICS OF THE NEW LEGAL OFFICIALS IN A GLOBALISED LEGAL ORDER

In this chapter we have been concerned with conceptions of the judging within a national context. Some would consider this too narrowly focussed. We may also be open to the charge that we are assuming that judges matter, and that the adjudicative system in which they appear as the apex is a vital place for the resolution of disputes.

From one side the critique would be that within the modern common law nation-state, as represented by the UK, the US, Canada (and increasingly other countries such as New Zealand, Australia and Singapore), judges are not, apart from in textbooks, the figures in charge of the law-in-operation. Other officials and controllers of access are far more important than judges. It is also undeniable that in large part legal special-ists are moving from the litigation model to a dispute-management model, organised so as to settle disputes far from the courts. The dispute resolution function has shifted elsewhere including 'into the law firms themselves'. 'If lawyers once followed judges and clustered around courts, now increasingly lawyers follow the client.'[27] These lawyers or service providers are located in a vast diversity of firms, but with consider-able power and prestige in large groupings; the international law firm.

The international law firm increasingly operates in a globalised legal world that seems above democratic accountability. Globalisation renders problematic the bound-aries of the nation-state. The important sources of lawmaking are international agen-cies like the World Bank, the IMF and the WTO. Furthermore, commercial rules, like the *lex mercatoria*, are generated by actors not accountable to nation states. We have returned to the ways in which legal actors such as Lord Mansfield fashioned the commercial elements of common law from the customs and understandings of economic actors. But who holds Lord Mansfield's contemporary equivalents account-able? Whose ethics, rights, and claims to process hold sway? To what legal order, to what system of scrutiny do the new legal officials belong? Other examples are the legal, political, and economic reforms routinely forced upon countries seeking economic aid from international lenders and relief agencies. More examples exist, varying in degree as to their 'voluntary' nature; consider the legal reforms necessary for membership in the GATT of the European Union, or the adoption of child and sweatshop labour regulations to satisfy consumer groups from abroad. The norms and ethics of those responsible for implementation may or may not be resonant with those of local officials.

---

27   Murphy (1997: 192).

Whatever the impact on democratic accountability, globalisation is already affecting the culture and ethics of judges in national context. As Slaughter put it:

> Judges are building a global community of law. They share values and interests based upon their belief in law as distinct but not divorced from politics and their view of themselves as professionals who must be insulated from direct political influence . . . National and international judges are networking, becoming increasingly aware of one another and of their stake in a common enterprise. The most informal level of transnational judicial contact is knowledge of foreign and international judicial decisions and a corresponding willingness to cite them.[28]

The movement of students from one jurisdiction to another, for LLM studies in particular, offers one piece of the picture of an emerging legal culture that might allow the development and solidification of a transnational legal culture. However, the emergence of a transnational, global practice is far from certain.

What ideal, or set of understandings, could guide this new reality? Perhaps we can see an emerging global code of legality (undoubtedly with human rights central to it), but who is to judge the judges, where will accountability lie?

The chapter began with an epigram from Bracton, an appeal to the judges to remember that they would be held accountable in a day of final judgment. Tim Murphy explains that the common law has a particular claim to be 'the oldest social science' dating from its early days when judges were a feature of the (Royal) court and the court practised 'adjudicative government'.[29] Decisions were made in accordance with a way of looking at things, in accordance with the manner in which things looked if you sat behind a bench – or a table – and listened to an argument before giving judgment. 'In Occidental culture, such a tableau unfolded, of course, at the very end of time itself, in the Last Judgment.' This was not a version of natural law where one was meant to follow God's will for a 'greater weight is carried by the image of God as judge than by that of God as Lawgiver. The Laws, as given, are given'. The image of God as judge is not mechanical jurisprudence, it is not a matter of applying what is laid down in some simple allocation of facts to clear law: once we put an emphasis on the seat of judgment the central question becomes how the king of heaven or his regent on earth should judge. This in the end means: 'how to weigh in the balance good and evil, or how to determine what is good and what is evil. This is the character of the question of truth, which is not really imaginable outside the setting of power and judgment.' Yet if we are to conceive of a politics of judging transnationally – given that we are in an era where it is clear that forces prevent knowledge of global interconnectedness, and 'realistic' notions seem akin to announcing that one is too exhausted to care for more than a sympathetic moment – it will need great powers of judgment to link law, democracy and truth.

---

28   Slaughter (1997: 186).
29   Murphy (1997), see Chapter 5.

12

THE INTEGRITY OF THE COURT: JUDGMENT AND THE PROHIBITION ON BIAS

—·◆·—

We outlined in the Introduction our normative account of the trial. In this chapter we want to elaborate the principle of integrity. The principle of integrity gives the court the moral authority to either punish or determine the civil liability of citizens. Our argument is that the jurisprudence of Article 6 allows us to make a more detailed investigation of these key concerns. We will first examine the central doctrine of Article 6: the independence and impartiality of the court. We will then turn to the related issue of bias. We will consider how the law on judicial bias has developed, before turning our attention to the question of biased juries.

Appreciating the fundamental importance of the principle of integrity is perhaps fairly straightforward. If a court or a judge is biased, one would conclude that a fair trial has not taken place, and that any decision that the court issues is compromised. The common law and the Convention take this principle seriously. However, in assessing the impact of Article 6 jurisprudence on the common law, we will see that the common law has been forced to redefine itself to remain compatible with human rights standards. We will also argue that there are tensions between common law understandings of due process, and those developed by Strasbourg with reference to the jury. If nothing else, these tensions allow us to study the peculiar insistence that the common law places on the role of citizens in a criminal trial.

INDEPENDENT AND IMPARTIAL TRIBUNAL

By far the most important guarantee enshrined in Article 6 is that to an independent and impartial tribunal established by law. It is probably also one of the most important guarantees of the whole Convention. In fact, there are two aspects to this guarantee. On the one hand it is an individual human right which ensures that disputes in which the individual is involved are decided by a neutral authority. On the other hand, however, it also has an institutional aspect of constitutional importance: it lays the foundation for what has been labelled . . . the third power in a state after the legislative and the executive. While the right to free elections under Article 3 of the First Protocol protects the foundations of democracy, the guarantee to an independent and impartial tribunal lays the foundations necessary for the rule of law.[1]

....

1   Trechsel (2005: 46).

This passage places Article 6 in the context of the politics of the Convention. It stresses that the Article is central to the very idea of the rule of law, as it guarantees the impartiality of the courts. Indeed, we could even talk about the constitutionalisation of procedure to the extent that the Article provides a foundation for a value that is often enshrined in constitutional documents. This reminds us that procedural law is an essential feature of the politics of democracy. The rule of law requires that the body that adjudicates disputes is not subject to the executive or, at the very least, that the executive and the judiciary respect their mutual spheres of competence. In this chapter we will outline the jurisprudence of Article 6 and its impact on the common law.

The key theme that underlies Article 6 jurisprudence is the elaboration of principles that define the impartiality of the court or tribunal. Should a court be partial, the ECtHR will hold that proceedings are not fair.[2] This reflects the need to affirm the democratic order of the courts against that of 'military' or 'special' courts that retain a right to try civilians, although, as we will see, it also covers the operation of welfare tribunals and professional disciplinary bodies. To cover the range of judicial and quasi-judicial bodies, the jurisprudence of the ECtHR stresses that irrespective of the name given to a body in national law, a court or tribunal must be independent 'in particular of the executive', and 'impartial'. A tribunal must also have in place the procedural guarantees that are provided by the Article.[3] What sense, then, can be made of the particular wording of Article 6; that the tribunal must be 'independent, impartial' and 'established by law'? Are these terms merely amplificatory of the core sense that the court must be independent or do they add distinct substantive requirements?

Arguably, the court sees the requirement that the tribunal is 'established by law' as part of the criteria of impartiality.[4] An impartial body is one established by law and not beholden to a superior body.[5] This does raise issues of definition: to what extent must law regulate every element of the tribunal? Does it leave no room at all for discretion? The consensus appears to be that the 'organisational set up'[6] of the court, including the definition of its jurisdiction and its proceedings, must be determined by law, but there can be some discretion in the hands of the executive, provided that it does not compromise judicial independence. This is perhaps a difficult line to draw. What does seem clear is the sense in which the requirement that a tribunal should be established by law shades into the idea of independence. The case law of the Convention[7] establishes that a tribunal's independence must be judged with reference to the appointment of its members, the 'safeguards' that exist to protect it from pressure to determine a case in a particular manner, and that it actually appears to be independent to the parties concerned.

Thus, independence describes the constitutional position of the court and does not mean that a hierarchical relationship cannot exist between courts, or that a higher court cannot have a supervisory or appellate relationship to a lower court, provided

2   Ibid., 47.
3   *Belios v. Switzerland* [1988] ECHR 4.
4   Trechsel, supra n. 1, citing *Oberschlick v. Austria*, 19 EHRR 389.
5   *Zand v. Austria* Application 7360/76.
6   Ibid., para 51.
7   *Le Compte and other v. Belgium* [1981] ECHR 3, *Incal v. Turkey* [1998] ECHR 48.

that the impartiality of the tribunal as to the determination of matters of fact and law is ensured. Clearly, impartiality extends to cover the lack of bias of the judge towards either party to the proceedings. In *Inçal*, one of the major rulings of the ECtHR, the court articulated the broader principle at stake in issues of independence and bias: '[w]hat is at stake is the confidence which the courts in a democratic society must inspire in the public and above all . . . in the accused.'[8] The presence of a military judge in the Turkish National Security Court meant that 'the applicant could legitimately fear' that the court 'might allow itself to be unduly influenced by considerations which had nothing to do with the nature of the case'.[9] This amounted to a breach of Article 6(1). The ECtHR thus links together impartiality and independence as closely related concepts that are fundamental to the notion of the fair trial.

How can we think about the British courts from the perspective of Article 6? As we do not have the space to examine all the aspects of Article 6 considered above, we will turn to one particular area: military discipline. A great deal of the cases brought against the UK concern the operation of military tribunals. The key authority is *Findlay v. UK*.[10] The appellant, a veteran of the Falklands war, suffered from Post Traumatic Stress Disorder, which was exacerbated by an accident suffered shortly after his posting to active duty in Northern Ireland. The appellant 'snapped' and held a number of his colleagues at gunpoint, threatening to kill them and himself. He fired two shots, which were not aimed at anyone, then surrendered the pistol and was arrested. Charged with assault, threatening to kill, and with offences against military discipline, Findlay was tried by a court martial. At the time of his trial, the powers and constitution of court martials derived from the Army Act 1955. The case drew attention to the composition of the tribunal, in particular the role of the convening officer, who was responsible for calling the body together, and its procedural correctness. The tribunal was staffed by a president and four other serving officers, all of whom were subordinate in rank to the convening officer. None of them had any legal training. The prosecuting and defending officers were also, at least in theory, subordinate in rank to the convening officer. The court martial was advised on points of law by a Judge Advocate, who was an assistant judge. As well as advising the tribunal on points of law, the Judge Advocate (and the president) had to ensure that the defendant did not suffer any disadvantages during his or her trial, and understood the charges and the relevant law.

Findlay pleaded guilty. However, despite convincing medical evidence and the urging of his solicitor that he should be given a lenient punishment, the tribunal ordered a period of imprisonment, a reduction in rank, a dismissal from the army and a reduction in pension entitlement. The applicant then made a number of appeals against his sentence, all of which were rejected by officials who were not legally qualified, although they did receive advice from the Judge Advocate General's office. Neither the nature of this advice, nor the reasons for refusal were revealed to the applicant.

After the failure of an application for judicial review, Findlay applied to the Commission alleging that he had not received a fair trial by an impartial and

8   Supra n. 1, at para 56.
9   Ibid., para 72.
10   Supra n. 8.

independent tribunal. The essence of his argument was that the subordinate position of the members of the tribunal to the convening officer, and their lack of legal training, rendered the tribunal incapable of making a fair decision. He also argued that the decisions on the appeal had been made in private and with no rules of procedure. Findlay's arguments also drew attention to the fact that the relevant statute contained no rules on the appointment of the convening officer and reviewing authorities; the tribunal was thus not established by law. The British Government did not reply to these allegations, but submitted both to the Commission and the Court that the Army Act was being amended in the light of these failures of due process.[11] However, these changes did not apply to the present case, which was dealt with entirely under the old procedures.

Both the ECtHR and the Commission agreed with the applicant's argument. The ECtHR's decision in Findlay is consistent with the general jurisprudence on this point, as it asserts the close relationship of the concepts of independence and impartiality. They also stressed that the presence of the Judge Advocate in the court martial, and the availability of advice for the authorities that reviewed the tribunal's decision, were not sufficient enough to dispel the serious doubts about the tribunal's impartiality. Relying on *Pullar* v. *UK*,[12] the court asserted that the tribunal had to be free of both 'personal prejudice' and objectively free of bias.

The court's decision in Findlay opened the floodgates. The number of cases received in its wake suggests that there had been major failures in the due process requirements of military justice[13] and that these remained even after reforms of the system.[14] Indeed, *Morris* v. *UK*[15] went even further, casting doubt on the entire structure of the court martial system. The applicant argued that a court martial had to be 'independent of the army as an institution, particularly of senior army command'. The problem was that this was clearly not the case: 'at all key stages of the applicant's court martial, including the bringing of charges, the appointment of the members of the court, the reaching of a decision on verdict and sentence, and the review of such verdict and sentence, army institutions were involved.'[16] His argument also showed that there

---

11   In *Morris* the court noted the changes that the British Government had made to the system of military justice in the 1996 Act: 'The posts of convening officer and "confirming officer" have been abolished, and the roles previously played by those officers have been separated. The convening officer's responsibilities in relation to the bringing of charges and progress of the prosecution are now split between the higher authority and the prosecuting authority. His duties concerning the convening of the court martial, appointment of its members, arrangement of venue and summoning of witnesses have been entrusted to the Army Court Service (formerly the Court–Martial Administration Office), whose staff are independent of both the higher and prosecuting authorities. The convening officer's powers to dissolve the court martial have been invested, prior to a hearing, in the Army Court Service and thereafter in the judge advocate, who is now a formal member of the court martial, delivers his summing-up in open court and has a vote on sentence.'

12   *Pullar* v. *UK*, 10 June 1996, at para 30.

13   Cases drew attention not just to these problems in relation to army tribunals, but also to similar bodies presiding over discipline in the RAF (*Cooper* v. *UK* Application no. 48843/99) and the Royal Navy (*G.W.* v. *UK* Application no. 34155/96).

14   See *Hood* v. *UK* (Application no. 27267/95); *le Petit* (Application no. 35574/97); *Thompson* v. *UK* (Application no. 36256/97); *Miller and others* (Applications nos. 45825/99, 45826/99 and 45827/99), *Whitfield and others* (Applications nos. 46387/99, 48906/99, 57410/00 and 57419/00); and *Martin* v. *UK* (Application no. 40426/98).

15   *Morris* v. *UK*, 26 February 2002.

16   Ibid., para 40.

were no statutory guidelines to regulate the appointment of court martial personnel, and the lack of security of tenure of the permanent presidents of the tribunals meant that they were vulnerable to pressure from more senior officers. A related problem was the fact that there could be a difference in rank and seniority between the president and the other members of the court martial, also suggesting that a senior officer might be able to pressure or influence the opinion of a more junior colleague. The 'strong officer corps ethos', which privileged 'discipline' and the need to create examples to deter others, further compromised the independent nature of the court martial.[17]

Whilst not accepting the applicant's point about the role of the Defence Council and the Adjutant General, the court relied on *Inçal* v. *Turkey* to find breaches of Article 6 in relation to both the permanent president and the officers who served on the tribunal, and the failure of judicial supervision in relation to appeals from the decision of court martial.[18]

THE TESTS FOR BIAS

The notion of the independence and impartiality of the tribunal is bound up with the issue of the test for bias. We now need to turn our attention to this essential concern. How does the ECtHR understand bias? Impartiality is compromised by bias. Bias, in this sense, would be one of the fundamental breaches of the right to a fair trial. As the court stated in *Piersack* v. *Belgium*,[19] underlying Article 6 is 'the confidence which the courts must inspire in the public in a democratic society'. Given the importance of the concept, the issue that has occupied the courts has been the correct test for bias. In *Piersack* the court pointed out that there are different ways in which bias shows itself. The fundamental distinction is between subjective and objective forms of bias:

> A distinction can be drawn . . . between a subjective approach, that is endeavouring to ascertain the personal conviction of a given judge in a given case, and an objective approach, that is determining whether he offered guarantees sufficient to exclude any legitimate doubt in this respect.[20]

At the core of the distinction is the difference between the actual biases of a judge, and the perception of bias that would be justified if there were not ways of showing that the court was operating impartially. However, the ECtHR went on to suggest that

---

17   Ibid., para 43.
18   The system of military justice was brought into question in two later cases *Cooper* v. *the United Kingdom* and *Grieves* v. *UK* 57067/00 16/12/2003. In *Cooper*, the applicant was unsuccessful before the ECtHR in his challenge to the composition of the Air Force Court Martial Panel as it was constituted under the Army Act of 1996. However, in *Grieves* the applicant's complaint against the composition of a Navy Court Martial was upheld. This was largely to do with the office of the Judge Advocate in a naval court-martial. The Judge Advocate is also a 'serving naval officer who, when not sitting in a court martial, carries out regular naval duties'. In comparison, the Judge Advocate in the air force court martial is civilian (para 82). Precisely because the Judge Advocate was a serving officer, his independence was potentially compromised.
19   *Piersack* v. *Belgium*, 1 October 1982.
20   Ibid., para 30.

it might be difficult to separate the two forms of bias. Citing *Delcourt* v. *Belgium*,[21] the ECtHR argued that if a judge is subjectively biased, then there would be a 'legitimate' reason to doubt the neutrality of the court and, therefore, unless the judge withdrew, there would also be objective bias. On the facts of *Piersack*, the ECtHR had to determine whether the presence of a former public prosecutor, who was now a judge in the same case that he had been prosecuting, breached the test for bias. While it would be 'going to the extreme' to hold that no public prosecutor could ever act as a judge, the facts suggested that there had indeed been bias. The ECtHR's argument, to the extent that it covered the composition of the court and the way in which judges were appointed, also suggests the close connection between the finding of bias and the requirement that a court be independent.

The court followed this approach closely in *De Cubber* v. *Belgium*.[22] The applicant was alleging that he had not received a fair trial from an impartial tribunal, because the presiding judge had acted as an 'investigating judge' in the case against him. *De Cubber* thus goes to the heart of the civilian practice of the investigating magistrate, a role that is not a predominant feature of common law courts. The Belgian government stressed that the investigating judge is 'fully independent' as s/he is not party to the proceedings[23] and does not perform a prosecutorial role, helping to establish the guilt of the defendant. The investigating judge must 'strike a balance between prosecution and defence' in assembling evidence, and presenting to the court an 'objective review' of the progress of the case. The ECtHR disagreed with this argument. Examining the legal definition of the powers of the investigating judge, they found that the office is not strictly separate from that of the prosecutor. In particular, the 'preparatory investigation' which is presided over by the judge is 'inquisitorial', 'secret' and 'not conducted in the presence of both parties'. They concluded that:

> One can accordingly understand that an accused might feel some unease should he see on the bench of the court called upon to determine the charge against him the judge who had ordered him to be placed in detention on remand and who had interrogated him on numerous occasions during the preparatory investigation, albeit with questions dictated by a concern to ascertain the truth.[24]

This appeared to amount to a finding of objective bias. There was no reason to doubt the objectivity of the individual judge, but 'his presence on the bench provided grounds for some legitimate misgivings on the applicant's part'. This makes it clear that there is a correspondence between the objective test, and the 'English maxim' that was also cited in the *Delcourt* judgment: 'justice must not only be done: it must also be seen to be done.'[25]

---

21   *Delcourt* v. *Belgium*, 17 January 1970.
22   *De Cubber* v. *Belgium*, 26 October 1984.
23   Ibid., para 29.
24   Ibid.
25   *Delcourt* v. *Belgium*, 17 January 1970.

How has the common law responded to Strasbourg jurisprudence? Before we can properly address this issue, we need to establish the common law approach to bias.[26] We are concerned with the *Gough* test which is an authority on the situation where a 'hypothetical fair-minded and informed observer believes that the judge may be biased'.[27] The *Gough* test asks the court to consider: 'whether, in all the circumstances of the case, there appeared to be a real danger of bias, concerning the member of the tribunal in question so that justice required that the decision should not stand.'[28]

As Lord Goff pointed out in *Gough*, cases of actual bias are 'very rare', and the more pressing issue is 'the degree of possibility of bias'.[29] The law on bias has to negotiate two extremes. If the test were too stringent, it would be too easy to invalidate decisions on the grounds of partiality. An overly lenient test would encourage bad practices. The central idea is that public confidence in the administration of justice requires that the impartiality of the judge be above suspicion. If it is not necessary to prove actual bias, then the fundamental question is how conclusions will be drawn from 'impressions' derived from the circumstances of the case. From the case law, there were two possible ways of thinking about these impressions: one would be from the perspective of the court, the other from that of the reasonable man.[30] However, '[s]ince ... the court investigates the actual circumstances, knowledge of such circumstances as are found by the court must be imputed to the reasonable man', and there should be no real difference between the two perspectives. The related question would be the issue of whether possibility or probability of bias is decided on the standard of the balance of probabilities. This, in Lord Goff's opinion, would be 'too rigorous'. He concludes:

> I am by no means persuaded that, in its original form, the real likelihood test required that any more rigorous criterion should be applied. Furthermore the test as so stated gives sufficient effect, in cases of apparent bias, to the principle that justice must mani-festly be seen to be done, and it is unnecessary, in my opinion, to have recourse to a test based on mere suspicion, or even reasonable suspicion, for that purpose. Finally there is, so far as I can see, no practical distinction between the test as I have stated it, and a test which requires a real danger of bias, as stated in *R. v. Spencer* [1987] A.C. 128.[31]

For the moment we must suspend our judgment about whether or not this approach to bias does balance the competing demands that the test must satisfy. The Gough test was further elaborated in *Ex parte Pinochet No. 2*.[32] Lord Browne-Wilkinson pointed out that the case was about the 'real danger' 'or reasonable apprehension or suspicion' of bias. Returning to the case law, he showed that the test rested on the principles of natural justice: that a man should not be the judge in his own case. However, there are

---

26   Gouldkamp (2008: 32).
27   Ibid.
28   *R. v. Gough* [1993] AC 646, at 647.
29   Ibid., 646.
30   Ibid., 667.
31   Ibid.
32   *Ex parte Pinochet No. 2* [1999] 1 All ER 577.

two ways in which this principle could be understood. It may mean that a judge must not try a case in which he or she is a party or has an interest. The very fact that the judge is a party to the action or has an interest would make for his or her automatic disqualification.[33] The second interpretation is broader. It would apply where a judge is not directly party to a dispute and does not have a financial interest but has some concern with the issue at stake, which may make for a suspicion that s/he is not impartial.

This second interpretation is not, strictly, an application of the principle that a wo/man must not be a judge in his/her own case at all. It is, more properly, an extension of the general sense of the principle: a judge must not be compromised by any direct or indirect interest in the action.

In *Pinochet*, the judges were aware of Article 6(1) and the differences between the Scottish and English courts on the issue of bias. In the former, a judge had been disqualified on the basis that there was reasonable suspicion about her/his impartiality.[34] The reasonable suspicion test was obviously different to the real danger test. Was this a problem? Although Lord Hope would speak of the 'uneasy tension' between the tests in *Porter* v. *Magill*,[35] their Lordships did not seem unduly concerned. They explained that the tests reflected the differences between two legal traditions. The broad principle was the same; the judge must bring to bear 'an unbiased and impartial mind' and '[h]e must be seen to be impartial'.[36] Although the case of *Locabail*[37] went on to provide some guidance on the issue of 'real danger', the common law remained committed to the Gough test and the belief that there was no significant difference between the common and civilian approaches.

Porter v. *Magill*[38] struck a very different note and established that, in the light of Article 6, a new test for bias was necessary. Lord Hope made reference to criticisms of both the real danger and the real likelihood test, as they tended to privilege the view of the court and 'to place inadequate emphasis on the public perception of the irregular incident'.[39] The common law test was out of line with Strasbourg jurisprudence as it lacked the necessary element of objective justification of the fear of bias. Lord Hope went on to look at a passage in *Re Medicaments and Related Classes of Goods*[40] where 'a modest adjustment to the test of *R.* v. *Gough*' was suggested. The new test would involve the court ascertaining 'all the circumstances which have a bearing on the suggestion that the judge was biased', and then asking if 'a fair-minded and informed observer' would come to the conclusion that there was 'a real possibility, or a real danger . . . that the tribunal was biased'. Lord Hope stressed that it was necessary to make some adjustments, and 'delete . . . the reference to "a real danger"' in the test for bias as it 'no longer served a useful purpose'.[41] The fundamental question was

---

33   See *Dimes* v. *Proprietors of the Grand Junction Canal* (1852) 3 House of Lords Case 759.
34   *Bradford* v. *McLeod* 1986 SLT 244 and *Doherty* v. *McGlennan* 1997 SLT 444.
35   *Porter* v. *Magill* [2002] 2 A.C. 359.
36   Supra n. 42, at 595.
37   *Locabail* v. *Bayfield Properties* [2000] 1 All ER 65.
38   *Porter* v. *Magill* [2002] 2 AC 359.
39   Ibid., at 493.
40   *Re Medicaments and Related Classes of Goods* [2002] 2 AC 359.
41   Supra n. 48, at 494.

'whether a fair-minded and informed observer having considered the facts would conclude that there was a real possibility that the tribunal was biased'.[42]

What does this mean? This test was further elaborated in *Jones v. DAS Legal Expenses Insurance Co. Ltd & Ors.*[43] In this case, the Court of Appeal heard an appeal from an employment tribunal that had presided over a sex discrimination case. The appeal was based on the fact that the chairwoman of the Employment Tribunal was married to a barrister whose chambers took work from DAS, the company that employed the appellant. The appeal was dismissed. In *Jones*, the Court of Appeal returned to a point that had been raised in *Re Medicaments*. The task of the court is to scrutinise all the circumstances that are relevant to the allegation that the judge was biased. In *Re Medicaments*, the court stated that this scrutiny would include taking into account any 'explanation' given by the judge, which, if necessary, would be considered from the perspective of the fair-minded observer. The question for the court is whether 'there was a real danger of bias notwithstanding the explanation advanced'. On the facts of the case, it meant that the test should be applied in the following way: the court is not concerned with precisely what the chairwoman of the tribunal knew. Since, following *Locabail*,[44] the presumption is upon disqualification, the fair-minded observer would 'proceed upon a basis that [the chairwoman] knew in general how the system operated and that her husband was to some extent a beneficiary of it even if she did not know all of the detail'. This brings us to a second question: would a fair-minded and informed observer then conclude that there was 'a real possibility that the tribunal was biased'? What qualities must the hypothetical fair-minded and informed observer possess?

Taylor v. Lawrence[45] concerned an appeal before a judge who had made use of the services of the respondent's solicitors the night before he gave judgment. Although the court did not find apparent bias, they offered some reflections on the nature of the test. They stated that judges should be 'circumspect' about 'declaring relationships' where a fair-minded observer would not see it as 'raising a possibility of bias'. Disclosure might itself suggest an 'implication' that the relationship would influence the judge's opinion. In a 'borderline' case the judge should make disclosure and then consider the submissions of either party before making his/her decision about whether or not to withdraw from the case. It had to be stressed that, if disclosure was made, it would have to be full and proper. The court concluded:

> No fair-minded observer would reach the conclusion that a judge would so far forget or disregard the obligations imposed by his judicial oath as to allow himself, consciously or unconsciously, to be influenced by the fact that one of the parties before him was represented by solicitors with whom he was himself dealing on a wholly unrelated matter.[46]

42 Ibid.
43 *Jones v. DAS Legal Expenses Insurance Co. Ltd & Ors.* [2003] WL 21554681.
44 Supra n. 47.
45 *Taylor v. Lawrence* [2003] QB 528.
46 Ibid.

It would seem that the fair-minded observer proceeds on the basis that judges are not biased and that there must be strong evidence to show that there is bias. In other words, the court's interpretation of the test assumes a level of integrity to legal culture in general and to the judiciary in particular. In *Gillies* v. *Secretary of State for Work and Pensions*,[47] Lord Hope suggested that the test demands a consideration of the appearance of the facts, rather than raising a question about 'what is in the mind of the particular judge or tribunal member who is under scrutiny'.[48] It would thus seem that any evidence of the judge's intentions would be irrelevant. Does this suggest that the test grants too much to the judges? *Lawal* v. *Northern Spirit Ltd*[49] suggests otherwise. The fair-minded observer can be seen to be critical of the culture with which he or she is familiar and believe in the necessity of high standards for the administration of justice, and 'may not be wholly uncritical of this culture'.[50]

Where does this leave us? The House of Lords has asserted that the test for bias under Article 6 and the common law test are exactly the same. In applying the fair-minded observer test, it is 'unnecessary to delve into the characteristics to be attributed to the fair-minded and informed observer', and to accept that 'such an observer would adopt a balanced approach'. Importantly, the key reference points return to the common law test: that the observer should be as concerned with the appearance of impartiality as with its actuality. In other words, the impartiality of the decision maker should be assessed to the highest standard, so as not to 'undermine the need for constant vigilance that judges maintain that impartiality'.[51]

---

47   *Gillies* v. *Secretary of State for Work and Pensions* [2006] UKHL 2, 787.
48   Ibid., 787.
49   *Lawal* v. *Northern Spirit Ltd* [2003] UKHL 35.
50   Ibid. *Helow* v. *Secretary of State for the Home Department*, [2008] UKHL 62. An unsuccessful asylum seeker of Palestinian origin alleged that a judge in the Scottish court of session, who had turned down her appeal, was biased against her as the judge was a member of the International Association of Jewish Lawyers and Jurists. The applicant's case was based on speeches by the Association's President, and articles in the Association's journal, showed an 'unbalanced' approach to questions of Israeli–Palestinian affairs; and by virtue of her membership in the association, the judge was apparently biased against her. The House of Lords dismissed the appeal. They held membership of the association did not amount to apparent bias. Most importantly for our purposes, the: 'suggestion that mere membership in an association gave rise in the eyes of a fair-minded observer to a real possibility of unconscious influence, through a form of osmosis, by materials in the relevant association's periodical which would be available to be read by the member was to be rejected.' There are further guidelines that relate to constitution of the 'fair minded observer' in *R.* v. *Oldfield* [2011] EWCA Crim 2910 that return to comments made by Lord Bingham in *Prince Jefri* v *State of Brunei* [2007] UKPC 8, 'The requirement that the observer be informed means that he does not come to the matter as a stranger or complete outsider; he must be taken to have a reasonable working grasp of how things are usually done.' In *Oldfield*, this was elaborated as follows: '[t]his fictional character is neither complacent nor unduly sensitive or suspicious. He or she has access to all facts known by the general public. He or she knows how things are usually done. He or she is aware that judges have years of relevant training and experience. He or she is aware of the terms of the judicial oath.'
51   What is interesting in our context, is the use of the judgment of another court that shares the common law tradition: the Constitutional Court of South Africa, in the case of the *President of the Republic of South Africa & Others* v. *South African Rugby Football Union & Others* [1999] (7) BCLR (CC) 725, 753: 'The reasonableness of the apprehension [for which one must read in our jurisprudence "the real risk"] must be assessed in the light of the oath of office taken by the judges to administer justice without fear or favour, and their ability to carry out that oath by reason of their training and experience. It must be assumed that they can disabuse their minds of any irrelevant personal beliefs or pre-dispositions . . . At the same time, it must never be forgotten that an impartial judge is a fundamental prerequisite for a fair trial . . .' The court came down on one side of the balance: the tribunal was not biased and the court dismissed the appeal.

BIAS, HUMAN RIGHTS AND THE JURY

The essential issues in this area of criminal procedure are focused by Lord Steyn's speech in R. v. *Mirza*.[52] Lord Steyn stressed the context of the problem: the accused is entitled to trial before an 'impartial tribunal'[53] and, should there be allegations that the tribunal showed bias, then there must be a robust way of examining this allegation. How does this 'fundamental'[54] fair trial guarantee sit alongside the common law rule that prevents any examination of the jury's deliberations? What are the risks of this approach? It would appear that the law places the 'efficiency of the jury system' above the possibilities of 'miscarriages of justice'.[55] More specifically, we will see that the law is consistently downplaying the 'corrosive'[56] effect of racism within the jury.[57]

The common law and human rights jurisprudence have not taken this problem of racism seriously enough. It is, of course, easy to argue that a person who has been found guilty of an offence will want to re-open his/her case. However, this does not get to the real issue: the problem of biased jury decisions. To understand this issue, we need to examine the leading cases. In *Gregory* v. *UK*[58] evidence emerged of jury bias. After the jury had retired to consider its verdict a note was passed to the judge which read: 'Jury showing racial overtones. One member to be excused.'[59] The judge went on to show the note to both the prosecution and the defence, and warned the jury that they had to ignore any prejudice and try the case on its facts. The jury found the defendant guilty by a verdict of 10 to 2. The applicant argued before the ECtHR that he had not received a fair trial and his rights under Article 6 and Article 14 had been breached.

What should the judge have done? The relevant test for bias at the time of the trial was R. v. *Gough*.[60] Once the judge became aware of bias on the part of the jurors s/he should have considered whether there was a possibility of actual bias. S/he should have to have asked whether individual jurors could be shown to be biased or, failing that, was it possible to find a 'real danger of bias affecting the mind of the relevant juror or jurors'. This is the so-called objective test. Gregory argued that although the note itself was not evidence of actual bias, the judge should still have discharged the jury or, at very least, put the question to the jury as to whether they were able to continue trying the case, and be able to put bias out of their minds.

---

52   R. v. *Mirza* [2004] HRLR 11.

53   Ibid, para 5.

54   Ibid.

55   Ibid.

56   Ibid, para 151 (Lord Rodger).

57   The sanctity of the jury room and the privacy of its deliberations are to be protected by contempt proceedings by those who publish or otherwise reveal the deliberations that took place during the reaching of a verdict; see *Attorney General* v. *Seckerson* [2009] EWHC 1023 (Admin) and *Attorney General* v. *Scotcher* [2005] UKHL 36. However, the courts have also acted when it is discovered that a jury decision has been influenced by extraneous documents not given in evidence in court. See, for example, R. v. *Karakaya* [2005] EWCA Crim 346.

58   *Gregory* v. *UK*, 25 February 1997.

59   Ibid., para 9.

60   R. v. *Gough*. [199] AC 646.

The ECtHR did not agree with him. They began from the principle that it was of 'fundamental importance' that the criminal courts maintain the confidence of the public, and to this end it was necessary to ensure that they were 'impartial' decision-makers.[61] This returns, in part, to the *Pullar* case,[62] which linked the lack of partiality to the fundamental Article 6 guarantee of a trial before an independent and impartial tribunal. In *Gregory*, the court held that the rule that maintained the secrecy of jury deliberations was 'crucial and legitimate'[63] to the operation of common law courts, as it guaranteed 'open and frank deliberations among the jurors'.[64] They then distinguished Gregory's case from another important authority, *Remli v. France*.[65] In *Remli*, the judge had not taken any action when a member of the jury had been overheard saying that he was a racist. The ambiguous nature of the note that the judge received in Gregory meant that the judge's actions were reasonable.

The dissent of Judge Voegel is interesting, as it suggests one way in which the law could respond to racism in the jury. He pointed out that as the jury is 'the ultimate arbiter of the facts of a case'[66] it is of paramount importance that jurors are made aware of the problem of bias especially as no warning or training is given, and their personal experiences may be a poor substitute for a more structured approach. He argued that, in these circumstances, a speech from a judge would not 'dispel racial prejudice'[67] and the only real remedy would have been to discharge part of the jury or to conduct a more thorough investigation into the note itself. This was not possible because of the rule on jury secrecy.

We could thus suggest that the law is more properly stated by the dissenting judgment in *Gregory*. Does this suggest that, as *Gregory*'s case was distinguished in *Sander v. UK*[68] this latter case is a more desirable statement of the law? Sander had been convicted of conspiracy to defraud but his trial was adjourned because the judge received a complaint from one of the jurors that two other members of the jury had been making racist comments. The judge then received a letter from one of the jurors apologising and a letter from the jury as a whole denying racial prejudice. Rather than discharging the jury, the judge chose to redirect them. The applicant argued that this was a fundamental error that deprived him of a fair trial. As there was a real danger of bias, the jury should have been discharged.

The ECtHR argued that there had been a breach of Article 6. Following *Piersack v. Belgium*,[69] the court held that the impartiality of the decision-maker must be presumed until there is evidence to the contrary and, on these facts, there was evidence that the jury was racially biased. The judge was not sure that there was not actual bias in the jury, and should have made further investigations. On these facts, the applicant

---

61   Supra n. 116, at para 49.
62   *Pullar v. UK* (1996) 22 EHRR 391, at para 32.
63   Supra n. 116, at para 44.
64   Ibid.
65   *Remli v. France* 22 EHRR 253.
66   Supra n. 116, para 18.
67   Ibid, para 40.
68   *Sander v. United Kingdom*, 9 May 2000.
69   *Piersack v. Belgium*, 1 October 1982, Series A no. 53, para 30.

had not received a fair trial. What seems central to the reasoning of the court is that the judge 'had both been informed of a serious allegation and received an indirect admission that racist remarks had been made'.[70] In such a situation, the judge should have discharged the jury. It would appear that the distinction between *Gregory* and *Sander* is one of differences of fact. Indeed, we cannot expect a clear statement of the need to reform the jury from the ECtHR because, given the role and function of the court, it would not take the lead on the issue in such a way. The matter is nuanced. The secrecy rule is not clearly in breach of Article 6. If jury reform is necessary, then it would be up to the English courts to articulate the way forward. In our reading of *R. v. Mirza*[71] we show that this matter has been firmly taken off the agenda.

In *Mirza*, the House of Lords affirmed the centrality of the secrecy rule to the workings of the jury, even if this meant that the partiality of the jury could not be examined:

> The general common law rule was that the court would not investigate, or receive evidence about, anything said in the course of the jury's deliberations while they were considering their verdict in their retiring room. Attempts to soften the rule to serve the interests of those who claimed that they were unfairly convicted should be resisted in the general public interest, if jurors were to continue to perform their vital function of safeguarding the liberty of every individual.[72]

Why, then, is there such a commitment to jury secrecy? What role does it play in the criminal trial? There is a useful consideration of the underlying rationale of the rule in the Canadian case of *Pan*.[73] Secrecy allows jurors to consider the aspects of the case 'without fear of exposure to public ridicule, contempt or hatred'.[74] The virtue of secrecy is that it also allows the jurors a degree of protection from 'harassment' and 'reprisals', an important consideration in the criminal trial.[75] Furthermore, as the case might concern an 'unpopular accused' or someone 'charged with a particularly repulsive crime', this requirement protects the integrity of the decision-making process.[76] Most importantly, though, this has to be taken on faith. Arbour J simply asserts that it is 'sound' and does not need any further justification. The second rationale stresses the 'finality' of the jury's verdict. This is perhaps less convincing in a legal system that allows appeals and reviews of decisions, and should not perhaps 'trump' other due process values.[77]

In *Mirza*, Lord Slynn described the other safeguards that protected both the composition and the integrity of the jury. The principle of random selection means that it is composed of a cross section of the population who are acting on oath. As far as

---

70 Supra n. 117, at para 39.
71 Ibid.
72 Ibid., H5.
73 *R. v. Pan* [2001] 2 SCR 344.
74 Supra n. 117, at para 114.
75 Ibid.
76 Ibid.
77 Ibid.

the operation of the jury in the court is concerned, the fact that the judge gives directions allows irregularities to be dealt with effectively, as does the possibility of an appeal. Indeed, the cases of bias and 'improper behaviour'[78] show the system is sensitive to these matters and that they do come to light. Of course, there are exceptions to the secrecy rule. These exceptions relate to those instances when the jury is allegedly affected by 'extraneous influences'[79] (although this was not an issue in the present case). Another problem was also considered: if it was alleged that 'the jury as a whole declined to deliberate at all, but decided the case by other means such as drawing lots or by the toss of a coin'[80] then the court would intervene, as such behaviour would; 'amount to a complete repudiation by the jury of their only function which, as the juror's oath put it, was to give a true verdict according to the evidence.'[81] The exceptions do not compel the conclusion that there is any profound need to reform jury practices, and that any problems cannot be dealt with by the existing law.

Lord Hobhouse pointed out that since section 17 of the Juries Act 1974 (which requires majority, rather than unanimous verdicts) there will always be situations where the views of one or two jurors have not been followed. While this may be a 'fertile scenario for a dissident juror',[82] the system itself contains sufficient checks to guarantee the legitimacy of the result. Besides, without definite evidence of 'actual bias', the bias of an individual cannot affect the decision. Furthermore, the trial judge supervises the trial and can give jurors directions and guidance; prejudicial evidence can be excluded. Most importantly, the jury trial represents a particularly common law approach to human rights;[83] 'a bastion of the criminal justice system against domination of the state and a safeguard of the liberty of its citizens'. While this does indeed stress the foundational values of due process, it is interesting that Lord Hobhouse distinguishes the jury system in the US, with its 'very thorough and public procedure of jury vetting which precedes the empanelling of the jury' and allows 'an investigation of their prejudices' from that of the UK.[84] He appears to be arguing that the US approach is not necessary; if the confidentiality rule was rejected there would be 'no stopping point in the other changes which would consequentially have to be made short of introducing a full-blown pre-trial procedure of jury vetting in order to maintain an acceptable minimum level of finality and public confidence in the jury verdict'.

This may be the case, but, it is absolutely necessary to preserve public confidence in the jury:

> . . . it is difficult to see how it would promote public confidence in the criminal justice system for the public to be informed that our appellate courts observe a self denying rule never to admit evidence of the deliberations of a jury even if such evidence strongly suggests that the jury was not impartial. In cases where there is cogent evidence

78   Ibid., para 50.
79   Ibid., para 102.
80   Ibid., H 55.
81   Ibid., para 123.
82   Ibid., para 135.
83   Ibid., para 144.
84   Ibid.

demonstrating a real risk that the jury was not impartial and that the general confidence in jury verdicts was in the particular case ill reposed, what possible public interest can there be in maintaining a dubious conviction?[85]

Lord Hobhouse's approach suggests that there is a failure to appreciate the nature of racism. As it is a social problem and an issue of people's prejudices, arguments about the jury as a defence against the state miss the point. Likewise, arguments stressing the liberty of the individual do not necessarily deal with racism. A defendant who alleges jury bias is not making an argument about liberty, but about distorted perceptions that make objective judgments impossible.

Questions about bias in the jury will not go away. Indeed, changes in the composition of the jury have raised new issues[86] about the relationship between Article 6 and this common law institution.[87] As well as issues of racism, recent cases on irregularities in jury deliberations have concerned the nature of collective responsibility for the jury verdict, and the issue of improper pressure or stress that may influence jurors to come to decisions that they later regret. However, the Court of Appeal appears committed to defending the centrality of the jury to the criminal trial. In *R. v. Thompson*[88] the court acknowledged that '[j]ury service is not easy' but that:

Our confidence in the jury system ultimately depends on the belief that, whatever the difficulties involved in the process, after reflecting on the views expressed by the other members of the jury, each juror will be faithful to the dictates of his or her conscience

....

85   Ibid., para 16.

86   The Criminal Justice Act 2003 brought to an end the automatic disqualification of certain classes of people from jury service. Police officers could now serve on juries. This point was directly at issue in *R v. Abdroikof and others* [2007] UKHL 37. The court held that that, as far as Article 6 was concerned, a police officer sitting on a jury did not compromise the independence of the panel. It would indeed be hard to hold that the presence of a police officer was unfair, as Parliament had itself changed the law. Significantly for the first appeal 'it was not a case which turned on a contest between the evidence of the police and that of the appellant' and it 'would have been hard to suggest that the case was one in which unconscious prejudice, even if present, would have been likely to operate to the disadvantage of the appellant . . .' (per Lord Bingham para 25). However, where (as on the facts of the second appeal) there was a 'crucial dispute' between the evidence given by a police officer and the accused, even though the officer on the jury had no association with the officer giving evidence, the jury's independence was compromised as: 'the instinct (however unconscious) of a police officer on the jury to prefer the evidence of a brother officer to that of a drug-addicted defendant would be judged by the fair-minded and informed observer to be a real and possible source of unfairness, beyond the reach of standard judicial warnings and directions.' (per Lord Bingham para 26). In the third appeal, the court also held that the independence of the jury had been compromised by the presence of a solicitor who worked for the CPS; and even though he was not involved in the instant case was still 'a full time and salaried member of the prosecuting authority'. Furthermore, the trial judge had not taken into consideration the objections of the defence counsel.

87   *Hanif and Khan v. UK* 52999/08 and 61779/08, 20/12/11. The applicants argued that although the presence of a police officer on a jury was not a violation of Article 6, the case raised two distinct issues. Hanif asserted that there was a breach of 6(1) when a police officer was on the jury and the prosecution case relied on police evidence that was tested during cross examination. Khan's point was a little different: a breach of 6(1) would occur if there was a police officer on the jury and the prosecution's case made use of evidence 'gathered by police officers with whom the police officer juror would have, at the very least, some form of collegiate interest' (para 130). The ECtHR found that there had been breaches of Article 6 in both cases. It is worth stressing that the ECtHR took particular note of conflicts in the evidence given by the police and the fact that the police officer serving on the jury knew the officer giving evidence.

88   *R. v. Thompson and others* [2011] 1 WLR 200.

based on examination and analysis of the evidence, so that those who cannot agree with the views of their colleagues stand firm by their consciences. . . .[89]

This argument shows faith in the intelligence and integrity of individuals. Such a faith might be appealing, but, is it enough to safeguard the integrity of legal procedures? The jury does not just depend on the integrity of its members; it has to be assessed in the context of the checks and balances that ensure that jury verdicts are not in breach of Article 6.[90] Thus, the key questions to be asked in assessing the fairness of the jury's verdict can be outlined as follows. Firstly, it is necessary to establish whether, in the terms of the trial as a whole, the accused was 'aware of the charges against him', the nature of the offence, and the grounds of his conviction.[91] There are other factors that must also taken into account. It is necessary to note that the judge assists the jury to reach its verdict by summing up the evidence, giving directions, and, explaining the relevant law. Furthermore, both prosecution and defence can address the jury and outline the conclusions which they should reach. The defence of the jury system also stresses that the jury deliberates in private, and, if necessary, can ask the judge for further advice.[92]

So, from the viewpoint of Article 6, we need to see the jury as a peculiar institution: a set of procedural safeguards that enable citizens to make difficult decisions under pressure. Lord Rodger in *Abdroikof* made a similar point: 'The reality . . . is that the jury system operates, not because those who serve are free from prejudice, but despite the fact that many of them will harbour prejudices of various kinds when they enter the jury box. . . .' If experience had shown that British juries, made up of people drawn at random from all kinds of backgrounds, could not act impartially, the system would long since have lost all credibility.[93] Perhaps this is an understanding of due process at least as compelling as the most rigorously formal. However, some commentators have suggested that in the wake of *Taxquet*,[94] the ECtHR may be opening up the possibility of further challenges to the jury. This may or may not be the case. At least for the moment, it would seem that the common law jury operates in such a way as to be consistent with the human right to a fair trial.

---

89   Ibid., at para 9.
90   Ibid., at para 72.
91   Ibid., at para 73.
92   Ibid.
93   *R v. Abdroikof and others* [2007] UKHL 37.
94   *Taxquet* v. *Belgium* (2010) is an important recent ruling of the Grand Chamber. Taxquet's application to the ECtHR stated that his conviction by the Assize Court breached Article 6(1) because the jury's guilty verdict did not contain reasoned argument and could not be appealed. The Grand Chamber considered arguments from the Belgian government, and submissions from other jurisdictions that made use of the jury. These submissions stressed that the jury was not inconsistent with the Convention. The UK's submission argued that the obligation to give reasons for decisions was not absolute (71). The Grand Chamber acknowledged that the jury took various different forms in the legal traditions of different nations, and served the important and legitimate function of 'involve[ing] citizens in the administration of justice' (83). The court's sole task was to consider, given the system a nation had adopted, the extent to which it complied with Article 6(84). Indeed, the Grand Chamber's ruling reflects its understanding of the way in which the jury operates in the context of the Belgian assize court, and must be limited to these facts. Thus, the Grand Chamber (check this) found that as the jury 'did not reach its verdict on the basis of the case file but on the evidence it had heard at the trial' it was necessary to 'explain' the verdict 'both to the accused and to the public at large' and 'to highlight the considerations that had persuaded the jury of the accused's guilt or innocence'.

CONCLUSION

In order to sum up on our key points in this chapter, it is necessary to remember one of the main arguments we made in the introduction. We explained that one of the over-arching principles of Article 6 related to the preservation of the integrity of legal proceedings. As we have seen in this chapter, the notion of integrity is based on common sense: a fair trial requires an independent court and an unbiased judge. The prohibition on bias also extends to the jury. In order to assess the fairness of the court, the judge and the jury, we have looked at human rights jurisprudence, and assessed its impact on the common law. It is fairly clear that, as far as the system of military justice is concerned, Article 6 has had a major impact on common law. The way in which the test on bias had to be re-articulated in the light of Article 6 is also evidence that common law rules required re-working to be consistent with international standards. It is perhaps more difficult to sum up on the arguments in relation to the jury. While broadly consistent with fair trial rights, there is a sense that – after *Taxquet* – there will be further challenges to the jury in Strasbourg, and a robust defence of the institution will have to be mounted.

13

THE VALUE OF PARTICIPATION: THE RIGHTS OF THE DEFENCE, EQUALITY OF ARMS AND ACCESS TO JUSTICE

This Chapter examines the importance of participation as an underpinning for a fair trial. The focus is primarily on the criminal trial, although the last section of the chapter will review the principle of access to justice, which is of wider relevance.

Our argument in the Introduction was that participation relates to the idea that the criminal trial is a 'holding to account' of a citizen for an alleged breach of the criminal law. For this holding to account to have moral authority, the trial has to arrive at an accurate reconstruction of the relevant events and the rights of the defendant have to be respected. This is because a criminal trial brings the prosecutorial resources of the state to bear on the individual. To be fairly held to account, the individual must be protected from a greater power. The individual's participation in a trial is thus defined – somewhat paradoxically – by those rights that protect his/her silence or the kind of evidence that might prove prejudicial. We will see that the common law has balanced these defence orientated rights against those which enable the prosecution to secure convictions.

Our argument in this chapter is focused on three fundamental and interconnected Article 6 doctrines: the rights of the defendant, equality of arms and the right of access to the courts. As with Chapter 12, our concern is the relationship between common law principles and human rights norms. Our objective is to assess common law principles against an international standard. In so doing, we will argue that it is necessary to consider dissenting as well as the majority judgments in the ECtHR. This is because we need a broad and critical sense of the criminal trial. In order to assess the extent to which a trial is fair, it may be the case that dissenting judgments provide an alternative vision of the values and structures that constitute a robust understanding of a fair trial.

We will begin with an examination of the presumption of innocence and the privilege against self incrimination. We will then examine the doctrine of equality of arms, and some important recent rulings that draw our attention to issues around hearsay evidence and the right to a solicitor. The final section will engage with the right of access to the courts and legal aid. The right of access relates to both civil and criminal trials, and so broadens out our analysis a little; it does not, however, blur our main points: the common law trial has to be critically assessed from the perspective of human rights principles.

THE PRESUMPTION OF INNOCENCE AND THE PRIVILEGE AGAINST SELF INCRIMINATION

What is the presumption of innocence? Following Roberts and Zuckerman's analysis, this principle could be presented as: 'the right of the innocent not to suffer criminal conviction and punishment.'[1] The presumption of innocence makes most sense as a body of 'rules of evidence' relating to 'the burden and standard of proof'.[2] This point is clearly made in the celebrated speech of Viscount Sankey in *Woolmington* v. *DPP*:[3]

> Throughout the web of the English Criminal Law one golden thread is always to be seen, that it is the duty of the prosecution to prove the prisoner's guilt . . . subject to what I have already said as to the defence of insanity and subject also to any statutory exception. If, at the end of and on the whole of the case, there is a reasonable doubt, created by the evidence given by either the prosecution or the prisoner . . . the prosecution has not made out the case and the prisoner is entitled to an acquittal. No matter what the charge or where the trial, the principle that the prosecution must prove the guilt of the prisoner is part of the common law of England and no attempt to whittle it down can be entertained.[4]

Viscount Sankey's speech shows that the prosecution carry the duty of proving the guilt of the accused. The standard of the credibility of the prosecution evidence must show that the accused is likely to be guilty beyond reasonable doubt. If the prosecution cannot prove their case beyond reasonable doubt then the accused should not be found guilty.[5] It is worth remembering that we are concerned here with a common law court that does not act inquisitorially. In other words, the parties present the evidence and the court acts as a neutral umpire. The standard of proof is effectively the threshold that the prosecution must pass in order for a jury to be very sure that the defendant is guilty of committing a crime.

How has the presumption of innocence become an issue in human rights law? The issue that has arisen is the extent to which it is justifiable that the accused should bear the burden of proof. One of the leading cases is *Salabiaku* v. *France*.[6] Salabiaku had been convicted of offences relating to smuggling goods. He had collected a trunk from Roissy Airport, which he believed had been sent to him by a relative in Zaire. When officials opened the trunk, it was found to contain cannabis seeds. Salabiaku claimed that he had picked up the trunk by mistake. His case before the French court focused on the 'almost irrebuttable' presumption of his guilt. Under the Customs Code, this

1   Roberts and Zuckerman (1994: 329).
2   Ibid., 327.
3   *Woolmington* v. *DPP* [1985] AC 462.
4   Ibid., 481–482.
5   As Roberts and Zuckerman point out, the crucial issue is the status of the presumption itself. Viscount Sankey's speech suggests that the presumption must be a rigorous one and requires the prosecution to prove not simply that the accused had the 'opportunity' to commit the crime, but that the evidence shows that the person in the dock did act in such a way as to satisfy both the mental and the physical elements of the crime.
6   *Salabiaku* v. *France* (Application No. 10519/83).

presumption was based on the mere fact of possession of the trunk. Salabiaku argued that this amounted to a breach of Article 6(2) and 6(1).

The court argued that the problem was not with the presumption of guilt, as all legal systems make presumptions of both fact and law. From the perspective of Article 6, the real issue was the extent to which the presumptions were consistent with the Convention. Certainly, a presumption of guilt could amount to a breach of due process, as it would effectively deprive the court of its 'genuine power of assessment' and make a nonsense of the presumption of innocence.[7] The critical question thus becomes: does the presumption of guilt go beyond 'reasonable limits' to such an extent that it limits the 'rights of the defence'? Under the relevant legislation, the 'possession of smuggled goods' is a finding of fact. However, this finding of fact does not immediately show the guilt of the accused. The court pointed out that the defence of extenuating circumstances was available to Salabiaku. Shifting the burden of proof to the defence is not in itself a breach of the Article, provided that this operates within 'reasonable limits' and acknowledges the fundamental issues in the case and the 'rights of the defence'. *Hoang* v. *France*[8] further elaborates this position. Article 6 is not breached so long as the primary burden for proving guilt case rests with the prosecution.

The presumption of innocence can be linked with the privilege against self-incrimination. The privilege against self-incrimination 'confers a freedom to refuse to answer questions when the reply might incriminate the person to whom the question is addressed'.[9] This privilege is limited to 'suspects and the accused'.[10] Lord Mustill in *ex parte Smith*[11] pointed out that the so-called right to remain silent is, in fact, a cluster of 'immunities', which, despite their different histories and provenance, have been brought together under a single heading. These rights have been limited and redefined by statute. If we take these considerations together, it makes the 'right to silence' appear somewhat high-sounding: a rhetorical claim rather than a legal reality. Is this an accurate judgment? We will begin our analysis by briefly examining the key common law authorities.

The common law has primarily grappled with two related issues: to what extent is pre-trial silence an admission of guilt; and to what extent is it acceptable for the accused's silence to be commented on during their trial?[12] One of the major authorities is *R.* v. *Chandler*.[13] In *Chandler*, Lawton LJ reviewed the law and explained that although the accused had a privilege against self-incrimination, it did not imply that 'the failure to answer an accusation or question when an answer could reasonably be expected' could not 'provide some evidence in support of an accusation'. In other words, the silence of the accused during interrogation was never necessarily sacrosanct and could, in certain circumstances, be used by the prosecution in court.

---

7   Ibid., at para 28.
8   *Hoang* v. *France* [1992] 16 EHRR 53.
9   Supra n. 1, at 392.
10 Ibid., 393.
11 *R.* v. *Director of Serious Fraud Office, ex parte Smith* [1993] AC 1 30–32.
12 Ibid., 473.
13 *R.* v. *Chandler* [1976].

As far as silence during the trial is concerned, the Criminal Evidence Act of 1898 provided that the 'failure' of 'any person charged with an offence to give evidence' could not be made 'the subject of any comment by the prosecution'.[14] This section concerns a person charged with an offence, and so it was necessary to develop case law on the status of the silence of an accused prior to charge. The first thing to note is that although the 1898 Act prevented the prosecution from making comments on the accused's silence, it did not prevent the judge from so doing. There was some confusion about the precise form of the comments that the judge could make. In *Martinez Tobon*,[15] Lord Taylor CJ suggested that it was hard to see where the distinction lay between 'permissible and impermissible comment'.[16] He stressed that the defendant did not have to testify, and the jury were not permitted to assume guilt from his or her silence. The judge could then go on to comment on facts given in evidence by the defence, which contradict prosecution evidence and which the defendant must have known about. The law in this area of criminal evidence has been changed by section 34 of the Criminal Justice and Public Order Act 1994.

Section 34 is controversial. It states that when an accused gives evidence in her/his defence, which, at the time that the offence was charged or when s/he was questioned under caution, s/he 'failed to mention'. The court or the jury may then draw such inferences as 'appear proper'. The section also covers the situation where the accused 'could reasonably have been expected to mention information when s/he was questioned, charged or informed'. In this situation the court or the jury would also be allowed to draw such inferences as appeared appropriate. Section 35(2) and (3) provide something of a safeguard. The accused had to be put on notice that if s/he chooses not to give evidence, then the court or the jury can draw inferences about a refusal 'without good cause . . . to answer any questions'. Section 38(3) goes further: a person cannot be convicted 'solely on an inference' drawn from his or her silence.

The case law relating to this section suggests that the courts have been very careful to stress the narrow meaning of an accused's silence.[17] The judge has to remind the jury that on arrest and at the start of any police interview, the defendant had to be cautioned, and warned about the consequences of refusing to answer questions. In their summing up, the judge must then tell the jury that the accused's defence had relied upon evidence that was not mentioned during police interview. The judge must go on to explain the precise terms of the prosecution case. The judge must then explain that it was for the jury to decide what inferences could be reasonably drawn, stressing that failure to mention information cannot itself establish the accused's guilt. The jury must always bear in mind that the defence may have produced evidence that explains the accused's silence or failure to answer questions and, only if this fails to offer an 'innocent

....
14   Supra n. 1 at 438.
15   *Martinez Tobon* [1994] 1 WLR 388.
16   Ibid., 397.
17   See *R. v. Argent* [1997] Criminal Appeal Reports 27, para 35. See also *R. v. Roble* [1997] Criminal Law Reports, 449 which stressed the importance of making it known to the jury that the defendant had remained silent on the basis of legal advice. Importantly, *R. v. Doldur* (Judgment of 23 November 1999, *The Times*, 7 December 1999) confirmed that inferences can only be drawn by the jury once the prosecution have established a strong *prima facie* case.

explanation', should inferences be drawn against the accused. In *Argent*, the court stressed that whether or not the accused had received legal advice was an important factor to be taken into account by the jury.

Within the scope of this chapter it is difficult to offer any final assessment of the status of the privilege against self incrimination. Whilst the 1994 Act certainly seems to work in favour of the prosecution rather than the defence, it would be premature to conclude that the cases we have examined all privilege prosecution values. The common law has never simply committed itself to protecting the 'right' of the accused not to give evidence, and to refuse to reply to police questions. There have been numerous statutory interventions, and the immunities against self incrimination have been consistently restricted or limited. At the same time, the common law has not abandoned a certain commitment to defence-orientated values. For instance, the concern with the precise words that the judge can use to comment on silence, and the right of appeal if the direction is prejudicial to the defence, suggest that the law is concerned with holding a line between the prosecution and the defence.[18]

SELF INCRIMINATION AND HUMAN RIGHTS

To understand the law of ECtHR on self incrimination, we need to appreciate that the jurisprudence links together the immunity against self incrimination with a related issue: the status of evidence unfairly obtained under compulsion. This kind of evidence would also include confession evidence, which tends to incriminate the accused, and is rendered unreliable because it was obtained by 'oppression'. The relevant provisions of domestic law are contained in the Police and Criminal Evidence Act 1984. In the following section, we will see that, whilst the common law is broadly consistent with international standards of procedural law, we can trace the similar tensions around the status of immunities against self incrimination as we noted in the section above.

A reading of Article 6 reveals that it does not lay down any rules to deal with incriminating evidence. This might suggest the rather startling conclusion that such rules are not part of European human rights jurisprudence. We need to examine three major authorities, starting with *Saunders v. United Kingdom*.[19] Saunders put forward the argument that 'the right not to be compelled to contribute incriminating evidence' was 'implicit' in Article 6[20] and should be 'linked' to the 'presumption of innocence' which was 'expressly guaranteed' by Article 6(2).

Saunders had been convicted on numerous charges including false accounting and theft. He argued that the use of the Department of Trade and Industry [DTI]

---

18   *Adetoro v. UK*, 46834/06, 20/04/2010 is a recent authority on s.34 CJPO 1994 and 6(1) ECHR. Adetoro argued before the ECtHR that the judge had misdirected the jury on the adverse inferences that they could draw from his silence. The ECtHR held that although the judge had misdirected the jury, the applicant had had a fair trial, and that the misdirection had not compromised the jury's understanding of the evidence against the applicant.

19   *Saunders v. United Kingdom*, 9 May 2000, 43/1994/490/572) 17 December 1996.

20   This was recognised by the court in *Funke v. France* (25 February 1993, Series A no. 256-A, p. 22, para 44) and *John Murray v. the United Kingdom* (8 February 1996, Reports of Judgments and Decisions 1996-I, p. 49).

inspector's interviews in the trial had made the proceedings unfair. The ECtHR agreed with Saunders in principle. Although Article 6 did not contain an explicit mention of either the right to silence or the privilege against self-incrimination, both principles are recognised 'international standards' of a fair trial. The 'right' not to self-incriminate is thus 'closely linked to the presumption of innocence contained' in Article 6(2).[21] The court held that there had indeed been a breach of the right not to incriminate oneself. They did not accept the British Government's arguments that the complex nature of crimes of fraud justified 'such a marked departure . . . from one of the basic requirements of fair procedure'.[22]

John Murray v. *United Kingdom*[23] raises a similar point to *Saunders*, but in a different context: the investigation of terrorist offences. Murray had refused to answer any questions either at the time of his arrest or during the 21-hour period of his questioning. It was only towards the end of this period that he was allowed access to a solicitor, although the solicitor was not present during the final hours of the interrogation.

Before the ECtHR, Murray relied on the case law of the Convention to argue that the right to remain silent had to be understood as the refusal to answer police questions and to refuse to testify at trial. Fair trial guarantees would also be breached if adverse inferences could be drawn from either silence in questioning or at trial. These are 'absolute rights which an accused is entitled to enjoy without restriction'.[24] To allow limitations on these rights would 'subvert [. . .] the presumption of innocence and alter the fundamental structure of the trial, where the prosecution have the burden of showing the defendant's guilt'. These arguments were supported by information drawn from Amnesty International, Liberty and Article 14(3)(g) of the United Nations International Covenant on Civil and Political Rights.[25]

The ECtHR refused to give 'an abstract analysis of the scope' of the 'immunities' and refused to comment on the issue of 'improper compulsion'.[26] Instead, they argued that *Murray*'s case required consideration of whether or not the immunities are 'absolute' to the extent that the accused's silence cannot be 'used against him in court' or whether (more precisely) the warning that his silence may be used against him amounts

---

21   See also *Murray* (above) para 68. The court went on to assert that the right to remain silent 'does not extend' to the use of evidence obtained under compulsion that 'has an existence independent of the will of the suspect'. The key examples are 'breath, blood . . . urine' and 'DNA samples'. *Saunders* does not, however, raise concerns with this kind of evidence: the sole question relates to the evidence obtained under DTI interview (para 69).
22   Supra n. 19, at para 74.
23   *John Murray* v. *United Kingdom* (8 February 1996, Reports of Judgments and Decisions 1996-I, p. 49).
24   Ibid., para 41.
25   This explicitly provides that an accused shall 'not be compelled to testify against himself or to confess guilt'. The international context of this principle was also demonstrated by reference to Rule 42(A) of the Rules of Procedure and Evidence of the International Criminal Tribunal for the Former Yugoslavia which also stresses the right of the accused to remain silent. The wording of the Draft Statute for an International Criminal Court further elaborates: the right to silence is not to be limited by 'silence being a consideration in the determination of guilt or innocence'. Cited at para 42. The British Government were not particularly impressed by these arguments. They asserted that the sources used by the applicants 'did not demonstrate any internationally-accepted prohibition on the drawing of common-sense inferences from the silence of an accused whether at trial or pre trial'.
26   Ibid., para 46.

to 'improper compulsion'.[27] There can be no question of solely basing a conviction on silence; but, likewise, the accused should not be able to hide behind his or her silence to frustrate the court.[28] This would suggest that the ECtHR sees the right to silence as limited, and open to qualification. The defendant's silence can therefore have implications at trial. Was there compulsion of the applicant?

The court noted that Murray's silence did not in itself amount to an offence or to contempt of court.[29] If, following the government's case, this silence is not in itself an inference of guilt, then it would be hard to link this to the other cases on compulsion. In *Funke*, charges had been brought in order to compel the defendant to provide evidence of offences that he was suspected of committing. This clearly amounted to a breach of Article 6. However, the case was distinguishable from the facts of *Murray*.

What do we make of these cases? In asserting that the immunity against self incrimination was linked to the presumption of innocence, and that both were implied by Article 6, *Saunders* stressed the centrality of these due process guarantees to European human rights law. The case did not hold that they were absent from the common law; rather, it made a narrower point about reliance on a certain kind of evidence during fraud trials. In this sense, *Saunders* brings the common law into line with international standards and prevents a national government creating different standards of evidence for different criminal offences. *John Murray* also confirms that the common law remains consistent with international standards as far as the status of silence is concerned. The ECtHR argued that:

> Whether the drawing of adverse inferences from an accused's silence infringes Article 6 is a matter to be determined in the light of all the circumstances of the case, having particular regard to the situations where inferences may be drawn, the weight attached to them by the national courts in their assessment of the evidence and the degree of compulsion inherent in the situation.[30]

The use of silence in court must be assessed in the context of the case and the checks and balances that exist in a national legal system. While this might seem much too broad to be a useful clarification of an international standard, it does allow a degree of flexibility to the precise way in which a national court draws inferences on silence. It would not be a breach of international standards to warn an accused that their silence might be used against him or her at trial. The ECtHR's position is probably justifiable as a balancing of defence – and prosecution-orientated values but, before we draw a final conclusion, we should consider one final authority: *Condron v. UK*.[31]

Condron is an authority on section 34 of the Criminal Justice and Public Order Act 1994. The applicants were alleging that the judge's decision to leave to the jury the

27   Ibid.
28   Ibid.
29   Ibid.
30   Ibid., para 47.
31   *Condron v. UK*, 2 May 2000.

question of whether they should draw adverse inferences from the accused's silence had breached Article 6(1). While accepting (on the basis of the *John Murray* judgment) that the right to silence was not absolute, the applicants contended that the necessary safeguards were not in place. In particular, the trial judge had not taken into account the applicants' solicitor's 'honest belief' that the applicants were not fit to be interviewed and were 'vulnerable and confused'.[32] Despite this fact, the judge advised the jury that they could draw negative inferences from their silence in the interview. The judge had not reminded the jury that the applicants' silence may have been due to the fact that they had been so advised, and were suffering from the symptoms of drug withdrawal. Nor had the trial judge reminded the jury that the prosecution had to establish a strong *prima facie* case.

The ECtHR took issue with the judge's advice to the jury. Although he had reminded them of the solicitor's advice, his direction was in such terms as to leave the jury to draw inference 'notwithstanding' that the explanation appeared reasonable:

> In the Court's opinion, as a matter of fairness, the jury should have been directed that it could only draw an adverse inference if satisfied that the applicants' silence at the police interview could only sensibly be attributed to their having no answer or none that would stand up to cross-examination.[33]

In other words, the direction should have been much more precise. The ECtHR found that this was a serious fault, given the fact that the judge's directions to the jury were an important safeguard in the absence of the jury's explanation for its decision. Despite agreeing with the British Government that other safeguards were in place, the ECtHR argued that the nature of the judge's directions were such as to compromise the fairness of the trial. The Strasbourg court held unanimously that there had been a breach of 6(1).

Condron suggests that the checks and balances in the common law only operate in an acceptable way from a human rights perspective if the judge's direction to the jury is precise. The other safeguards in criminal procedure will not offset a mistaken direction. For instance, the ECtHR noted the British Government's arguments that the applicants had been issued with a clearly worded caution, and had indicated that they understood the consequences of remaining silent. Moreover, they had had the advice of a solicitor and the usual safeguards of a criminal trial. It is also interesting that the ECtHR made an important distinction between the Court of Appeal's ruling that the accused's 'convictions' were safe, and the issue of whether or not there had been a fair trial. Even if convictions appear sound, it could be the case that there were issues in the trial that made its procedure unfair. This suggests a more demanding standard than that of the safety of conviction. It is perhaps proper that criminal procedure should be held to this higher threshold, as it poses the power of the state and its resources against the individual. *Condron* suggests that for the jury to be an acceptable institution within

---

32   Ibid., para 44.
33   Ibid., para 61.

a criminal trial, it needs to be carefully advised by the judge, and if this safeguard fails, then it is likely that the trial itself is compromised.[34]

EQUALITY OF ARMS

Although Article 6 does not mention 'equality of arms' explicitly, it has come to be seen as an essential component of fair trial rights. Its definition is a little difficult to pin down. Equality, in this context at least, does not have the sense of a prohibition on discrimination; a meaning that it carries in most human rights law. Trechsel argues that the principle 'implies that each party must be afforded a reasonable opportunity to present his case – including his evidence – under conditions that do not place him at a disadvantage *vis-à-vis* his opponent.'[35] In the jurisprudence of the court, the concept can also be distinguished from the 'right to adversarial proceedings'. Perhaps the most useful statement of the principle comes from *Kaufman v. Belgium*:[36] the defendant in criminal proceedings 'must have a reasonable opportunity of presenting his case under conditions which do not place him at a substantial disadvantage *vis-à-vis* his opponent'.

The principle of equality of arms also applies to civil as well as criminal cases. In *Dombo Beheer v. The Netherlands*,[37] the court made a distinction between the fair trial rights that are relevant in criminal cases and those applicable where civil rights and obligations are at stake. Although contracting states might have a 'greater latitude'[38] in civil cases to determine rules of procedure, there are common concepts shared by both civil and criminal law: most notably that 'the requirement of equality of arms' be understood as making for 'a "fair balance" between the parties'.[39] In relation to litigation between two private parties, this means that each party must have 'a reasonable opportunity to present his case', but national authorities can determine the precise form of the opportunities so afforded. As the majority of the cases concern criminal matters, we will follow this theme.

The leading cases where the principle of equality of arms has been applied to English law have concerned prosecution disclosure of evidence in the criminal trial.

---

34   For a case that falls on the other side of this line, see *Brown* v. *Stott* [2001] HRLR 9. Brown had been under compulsion under s.172(2)(a) of the Road Traffic Act 1988Act to admit that she had been the driver of her car. Could this information be used in a separate prosecution under 5(1)(a) of the same Act? Brown argued that using the evidence of her admission would be in breach of the privilege against self incrimination. The Appeal Court in Scotland accepted this argument, and the Crown appealed to the Privy Council. The basis of their argument was that the privilege was not absolute, and that the relevant sections of the 1988 provided a 'legitimate and proportionate interference'. The Privy Council held that although the 'overall fairness of a criminal trial' could not be 'compromised', the 'constituent rights' could be, provided the limitations were 'legitimate and proportionate'. The court had to achieve a balance between the general interest of the community and the personal rights of the individual. In so deciding, they distinguished *Saunders*. On the facts, the large number of fatalities in road traffic accidents indicted that s.172 was 'legitimate'. It was proportionate because it did not license long and oppressive questioning, and the penalty for refusing to answer was 'moderate and non custodial'.
35   Trechsel (2005: 96).
36   *Kaufman* v. *Belgium*, 50 DR 98, at 355.
37   *Dombo Beheer* v. *The Netherlands*, 27 October 1993.
38   Ibid., para 32.
39   See also the *Feldbrugge* v. *The Netherlands*, 26 May 1986, at para 44.

The authorities determine that although there is coherence between the common law and Article 6 on the duty of the prosecution to disclose evidence, in certain instances there are insufficient safeguards to provide equality of arms. However, there is a vocal minority in the ECtHR who see both rights jurisprudence and English law as failing in its duty to ensure equality of arms. As Judge Zupancic argued, unjust limitations on the right of disclosure can 'affect the whole philosophy of criminal procedure'.[40]

In *Edwards*,[41] the applicant had been sentenced to a long period of imprisonment for burglary. He sought to argue that the police had concocted the evidence against him, and that the use of public interest immunity to prevent his counsel having access to the Police Complaints Authority's investigation into the matter rendered his conviction unsafe. After the Court of Appeal rejected his argument, he unsuccessfully petitioned the Home Secretary. Before the ECtHR, he argued that his trial remained flawed because neither the Court of Appeal, nor the Home Secretary had seen the report, nor examined police witnesses that, he contended, were vital to his case. The ECtHR affirmed that the common law rules on disclosure of evidence recognised the importance of fairness to the criminal trial and there had, indeed, been 'defects'[42] in Edward's case. However, the ECtHR went on to say that fairness must ultimately be assessed in the context of the proceedings as a whole.[43] There had been an independent investigation into the conduct of the police, and the Court of Appeal had considered a typescript of the trial and had rejected the applicant's arguments about the credibility of the police witnesses. Moreover, Edwards had been represented by both junior and senior counsel at the appeal hearing. Edwards alleged before the ECtHR that the failure to disclose the independent report rendered his trial unfair but the court commented that he did not apply to the Court of Appeal for its production.

The dissenting opinion of Judge Pettiti is interesting as it interprets the case through the issue of public interest immunity. He argued that this prevented the disclosure of important evidence at trial, and that the failure of counsel to apply for disclosure before the Court of Appeal was not 'relevant'. He invoked the civilian principle of 'nullity for reasons of public policy'. This doctrine can be employed by the court itself, and thus relieves counsel of the burden of rectifying procedural faults. The principle is justified by 'the fundamental procedural rule that prohibits the concealment of documents or evidence'. Judge Pettiti's concerns are reiterated in his dissenting judgments in *Fitt* and *Rowe and Davis*.

In *Rowe and Davis*,[44] the applicants had been convicted of a number of charges including murder, assault and robbery. They appealed to the Court of Appeal, arguing that there were 'inconsistencies'[45] in the evidence against them. During the appeal hearing, the prosecution made available to the court a document that had not been shown to the defence, arguing that it contained sensitive information. Proceeding *ex parte*, the Court of Appeal held that the document did not have to be disclosed and

....
40   *Edwards* v. *UK*, 16 December 1992.
41   Ibid.
42   Ibid., para 36.
43   Ibid., para 34.
44   *Rowe and Davis*, 16 February 2000.
45   Ibid., para 23.

was protected by public interest immunity. Later, information came to light that the prosecution's case had relied on the evidence of an informer, who had been rewarded for the evidence he provided. The applicants applied to the Criminal Cases Review Commission, who found that the case should be remitted to the Court of Appeal. Whilst the case was waiting to be heard, the ECtHR considered the applicants' argument that they had not had a fair trial. Their argument rested on the understanding that there was no absolute right to disclosure, and that there were legitimate reasons for preventing it; however, 'procedural safeguards' should be in place to ensure the overall fairness of the trial. The *ex parte* hearing by the Court of Appeal was not a sufficient safeguard. They argued that there should be a 'special counsel' who would have access to the information and could test the prosecution's case. The government responded that the special counsel system would involve insuperable procedural difficulties and that the present system, in which the trial judge determined whether or not public interest immunity applied, was the best.

The ECtHR followed the principle in *Edwards*, and asserted that it was necessary to consider the proceedings as a whole. They then invoked the equality of arms argument that the prosecution should not enjoy unfair advantages over the defence, linking it to the very idea of the adversarial trial where 'both prosecution and defence must be given the opportunity to have knowledge of and comment on the observations filed and the evidence adduced by the other party'.[46] Article 6(1), and English law in general, were in agreement on the duty of the prosecution to provide 'all material evidence in their possession for or against the accused'. The court also asserted that this right was not absolute, and it was not for the ECtHR to determine whether any particular refusal of disclosure was legitimate or not, as this fell entirely within the jurisdiction of the national court. However, the problem was that the *ex parte* hearing was not a sufficient safeguard to ensure equality of arms between prosecution and defence.

The case of *Fitt*[47] returns to the approach of *Edwards*. It also concerned an *ex parte* application from the prosecution to the trial judge. The prosecution argued that evidence from a police informer (C.) was protected by public interest immunity and should not be disclosed to the defence. The important point of distinction from *Rowe and Davis* is that the *ex parte* hearing in the case took place during the trial itself, rather than in an appeal hearing. This suggests that the ECtHR found a breach of Article 6 in *Rowe and Davis* because the Court of Appeal should have had more robust safeguards in place. This reasoning did not apply to a trial court.

On the evidence presented by the prosecution, Fitt was found guilty of numerous offences, including conspiracy to rob. In his appeal he argued that the evidence of the informer needed to be examined to show that he had been falsely implicated in the conspiracy to rob. In particular, he was arguing for disclosure of a series of statements made by C. in other cases that would tend to strengthen his case. The Court of Appeal upheld the convictions, and the ECtHR held that the trial had been fair. They stated that:

---

46   See *Brandstetter v. Austria*, 28 August 1991, paras 66–67.
47   *Fitt v. UK*, 16 February 2000.

The Court is satisfied that the defence were kept informed and were permitted to make submissions and participate in the above decision-making process as far as was possible without revealing to them the material which the prosecution sought to keep secret on public interest grounds.[48]

The ECtHR also rejected submissions that there should be a special counsel system to introduce an 'adversarial element' into disclosure hearings. Although there were good reasons for such a system in immigration hearings, there was no argument to extend their operation to criminal trials. The existing law guaranteed equality of arms. For instance, the evidence that was not disclosed in this case never actually formed part of the prosecution's case and was never seen by the jury. This can be distinguished from the kind of non-disclosure issues that lay behind recent major miscarriages of justice, where the 'executive'[49] made use of evidence that the defence never saw. Moreover, the trial judge him or herself provides an important safeguard, as he has a duty to 'monitor . . . the fairness or otherwise of withholding the evidence'.[50] Reviewing the relevant case law, the ECtHR held that English law on the matters to be taken into account on disclosure 'fulfils' the 'conditions' laid down by Article 6.

There were a number of powerful dissenting opinions. We will examine those of Judges Palm, Fischbach, Vajić, Thomassen, Tsatsa-Nikolovska and Traja. They held that the principle of equality of arms was breached by the fact that the prosecution had 'access to the judge' during the *ex parte* hearing, and were thus able to 'participate in the decision making process' without the presence of the defence. The role of the judge as the neutral umpire could not counterbalance this fundamental inequality in the trial process. This was not to impugn the impartiality and independence of the judge but to assert that in order to make a fair decision the judge had to hear arguments from both sides. Judge Hedigan relied on the ruling in *Van Mechelen and others* v. *The Netherlands*.[51] The ECtHR stated that: 'Having regard to the place that the right to a fair administration of justice holds in a democratic society, any measures restricting the rights of the defence should be strictly necessary. If a less restrictive measure can suffice then that measure should be applied.'[52] This suggested that the arguments put forward for a special counsel to operate in criminal trials should have been more carefully considered by the British Government.

We now need to examine three recent authorities on the rights of the defence: *Cadder* v. *Her Majesty's Advocate, Ambrose* v. *Harris* and *R.* v. *Horncastle*.

In *Cadder*[53] the SC held that Article 6(1) normally 'required that . . . access to a lawyer should be provided as from the first interrogation of a suspect'. However, the court went on to say that there was 'room for a certain flexibility' in this principle. Each case would depend on its facts: 'the question . . . was whether, in the light of the entirety of the proceedings . . ., the accused [has been denied] a fair hearing.' It is

---

48   Ibid.
49   Ibid., para 48.
50   Ibid., para 49.
51   *Van Mechelen and others* v. *The Netherlands*, 23 April 1997.
52   Ibid., at para 50.
53   *Cadder* v. *Her Majesty's Advocate* [2010] UKSC 43.

worth stressing, that in *Salduz* v. *Turkey*[54] the ECtHR held that a suspect does not have a right to legal advice at any point prior to 'police custody or pre-trial detention'.[55] Although the general principle appears clear, *Salduz* left questions unanswered. In particular, the critical issue was whether 'the *Cadder* rule' also applies to people charged and questioned before detention at a police station (Lord Brown in *Ambrose*).

This point was considered in *Ambrose* v. *Harris*.[56] The SC chose to stick closely to Convention jurisprudence. According to the ECtHR, the moment when an individual is charged provides a key point of reference. Once a person has been charged, he or she has a right to legal advice. Strasbourg case law understands the point of charge as that moment when 'the situation of the individual [is] substantially affected'.[57] A person's situation is 'substantially affected' if a 'serious investigation' of the alleged offence has begun. Interpreting the position of the ECtHR, the SC held that someone not yet in police custody who was under suspicion for an offence, and being questioned, did not have a right of access to a lawyer. Lord Hope suggested that the definition of 'police interrogation' could include the police putting questions to a suspect at the 'roadside or in the person's home'. These 'initial stages' of an investigation did not engage Article 6. So, on the facts of the case, the statements made by the suspect at the roadside were admissible in court. The SC did stress one point: even if the initial stages of an investigation were not covered by the Article, once 'the police have reason to think that they may well elicit an incriminating response from him' the Article does apply.

So, in *Ambrose* the SC preferred Strasbourg to rule on right of access to a lawyer rather than articulate the terms of the right for themselves. This situation contrasts with the last case we want to examine in this section: *R.* v. *Horncastle*.[58] In *Horncastle*, the SC refused to follow the ECtHR in *Al-Khawaja and Tahery* v. *UK*.[59] *Al-Khawaja* was focused on the admissibility of a written witness statement in court when the witness was absent.[60] More specifically, *Al-Khawaja* raised concerns about the so called 'sole or decisive rule' developed in Convention jurisprudence. This rule held that the rights of the defendant are 'unduly restricted' if a conviction 'is solely or mainly based on evidence provided by witnesses whom the accused is unable to question at any stage of the proceedings'.[61]

The facts and issues raised by *Al-Khawaja and Tahery* can be summarised as follows. Al-Khawaja a surgeon had been convicted for indecent assaults on his patients. One of his patients had given evidence to the police, but had died before the trial took place. The defence acknowledged that the statement from the deceased was crucial evidence, but it would be possible to rebut it through cross examination of other witnesses. The judge reminded the jury in his summing up about the risks of including written witness evidence. Tahery's case was similar to the extent that he was convicted

54   *Salduz* v. *Turkey* (2008) 49 EHRR 421.
55   Ibid., para 12.
56   *Ambrose* v. *Harris* (Procurator Fiscal, Oban) [2011] UKSC 43.
57   Ibid., para 62.
58   *R.* v. *Horncastle* [2009] UKSC 14.
59   *Al-Khawaja and Tahery* v. *United Kingdom* [2011] ECHR 2127.
60   Ibid., at para 126.
61   Ibid., at para 128.

of wounding on the strength of a witness statement read to the court in the absence of the witness. The judge had also given the jury a warning that the evidence had not been tested through cross examination.

Before the ECtHR, Al-Khawaja and Tahery argued that the use of hearsay evidence amounted to a breach of Article 6(3)(d) and the requirement for 'the attendance and examination of witnesses' in court. The Chamber[62] held that Article 6 had indeed been breached. Hearsay evidence in a written form amounted to a breach of Article 6 because the person who made the statement was not present in court and could not be cross examined. However, in *R. v. Horncastle* the Supreme Court refused to follow this ruling. With reference to the relevant UK statutes (the Criminal Justice Act 2003 and the Criminal Evidence (Witness Anonymity) Act 2008), the SC argued that if Strasbourg jurisprudence did lay down such an 'inflexible' and 'unqualified' principle on hearsay evidence, then 'the whole domestic scheme for ensuring fair trials . . . cannot stand and many guilty defendants will have to go free'. It would be hard to countenance that this was the Court's intention; and indeed, that they had properly understood the way in which the law of the UK dealt with hearsay evidence.

It is worth remembering that the ruling in *Al-Khawaja and Tahery* was made by the Chamber. When the Grand Chamber came to rule on the matter in 2011, they came to a different conclusion. In *Al-Khawaja and Tahery v. United Kingdom*[63] the ECtHR concluded that: 'where a hearsay statement is the sole or decisive evidence against a defendant, its admission as evidence will not automatically result in a breach of Article 6(1).'[64] The court asserted that the normal rule was for 'all evidence' to be subjected to 'adversarial argument' in a public hearing. Legitimate exceptions to this principle must not 'infringe the rights of the defence'.[65] Even though the common law had 'abandoned the strict rule against hearsay', statutory safeguards had been put in place which meant that the rights of the defence were not automatically compromised by hearsay evidence.[66]

What do we make of the disagreements between the SC and the ECtHR? As we have argued in Chapter 8, we need to see cases like *Ambrose* and *Horncastle* as part of an ongoing attempt to articulate the proper relationship between the Supreme Court and Strasbourg. From the perspective of this chapter we can comment that *Horncastle* certainly suggests that common law can be misunderstood by the ECtHR. A productive relationship between the two Courts does require the SC to assert itself. However, this relationship has to be understood within the context of European Human Rights law. If national courts depart too far from Strasbourg principles, a consistent law of human rights is compromised. Cases like *Horncastle* are hopefully few and far between; but will arise when Strasbourg falls into a

---

62   Articles 27–30 of the ECHR state that the Court is organised into Committees, Chambers and a Grand Chamber. The divisions of the Court have slightly different powers in relation to declaring cases inadmissible. After a judgment has been delivered, a party can request that the case be considered by the Grand Chamber. The Grand Chamber will hear the case if it raises an important issue of the interpretation of the Convention.
63   *Al-Khawaja and Tahery v. United Kingdom* [2011] ECHR 2127.
64   Ibid., at para 147.
65   Ibid., at para 118.
66   Ibid., at para 130.

serious misunderstanding of the law of the UK. *Ambrose*, on the other hand, is perhaps less extreme, although the decision of the Chamber is certainly surprising in that it limits the reach of Article 6, there were powerful critical voices urging the SC to be more creative. However, there are counter arguments. If the SC departs from Strasbourg rulings, even to extend the scope of rights, the greater the risk that developments in human rights law may bypass the institution that coordinates its continent wide development.

ACCESS TO JUSTICE

As has been pointed out: '[a]ccess to legal advice for those with insufficient resources for their right of access to court to be effective is also recognised as being implicit in the right of access to justice by both the common law and the ECHR.'[67] Article 6(3)(c) provides that a person charged with a criminal offence has the right 'to defend himself in person or through legal assistance of his own choosing or, if he has not sufficient means to pay for legal assistance, to be given it free when the interests of justice so require'. The jurisprudence of Article 6 goes on to further this implicit distinction between criminal and civil proceedings. While criminal proceedings require free legal assistance, there is no equivalent right in civil proceedings. The interpretation of 6(3)(d) also raises complex issues that we cannot deal with in detail. Given the way in which the Article privileges criminal legal aid, the main issue in relation to civil legal aid is the extent to which legal representation is 'indispensable for effective access to court'.[68] This means that the person alleging a breach of Article 6(3)(d) has a difficult argument to make. To obtain criminal legal aid under Article 6, it would be necessary to show that without it effective participation in proceedings was not possible.[69] Provision of legal aid must also be in the interests of justice.[70] Suffice to say, then, that the jurisprudence of Article 6 recognises that a right to legal aid is heavily qualified.

Legal aid is one important aspect of a wider principle: access to the courts. One of the key authorities is *Golder* v. *UK*.[71] We will examine *Golder*, and a second early authority *Airey*, before returning to our discussion of legal aid. The ECtHR argued that the right of access to the courts is 'implicit' given the wording of the Article and

---

67   Human Rights Joint Committee, 22 Report, Legislative Scrutiny: Legal Aid, Sentencing and Punishment of Offenders Bill, 2011, http://www.publications.parliament.uk/pa/jt201012/jtselect/jtrights/237/23702.htm. At para 1.9. In *R.* v. *Secretary of State for the Home Department, ex parte Leech* [1994] QB 198. Lord Steyn stated that the 'principle of our law that every citizen has a right of unimpeded access to a court . . . even in our unwritten constitution . . . must rank as a constitutional right.' In *R. (Daly)* v. *Secretary of State for the Home Department* [2001] 2 AC 532, Lord Bingham held that 'access to a court and the right of access to legal advice may be curtailed only by clear and express words' and even then 'only to the extent reasonably necessary to meet the ends which justify the curtailment' (para 5). (All quotations from http://www.publications.parliament.uk/pa/ld201012/ldselect/ldconst/222/22203.htm#n8.
68   *Airey* v. *Ireland*, Application No. 6289/73, 9 October 1979.
69   *Stanford* v. *UK* A/282 (1994) unreported.
70   *Benham* v. *UK* (1996) 22 EHRR 293.
71   *Golder* v. *UK*, Application No. 4451/70, 21 February 1975.

its context within a Treaty dedicated to preserving the rule of law. The ECtHR went on to locate the right of access within the broader concept of a fair trial right:

> In this way the Article embodies the 'right to a court', of which the right of access, that is the right to institute proceedings before courts in civil matters, constitutes one aspect only. . . . In sum, the whole makes up the right to a fair hearing.[72]

The right of access is understood as the right to 'institute' proceedings. This rejects the British government's argument that the right only applied to proceedings that had been instigated. The ECtHR's interpretation of the Article is much broader. This is not to say, however, that the right of access to the courts cannot be limited. The ECtHR drew an analogy with a ruling on the right to education contained in Article 2 of the 1952 Protocol. The right to education can be limited with respect to available resources, and access to the court must be considered in the same way. However, the important caveat is that the right must not be so limited as to 'injure the substance of the right'.[73] As far as the facts of the present case were concerned, Golder's petition to the Home Secretary for access to a solicitor should not have been refused. Golder intended to initiate legal proceedings against a prison officer, who he accused of libelling him in relation to a matter of prison discipline. The Home Secretary's own determination that Golder's case was not likely to succeed was not a valid limitation on his access to the court.

Golder can be read alongside *Airey v. Ireland*.[74] Mrs Airey was arguing that because legal aid was not available for separation proceedings, the state was effectively denying her access to court in breach of Article 6. The Court asserted that as separation proceedings concerned civil rights and obligations, Article 6 did apply. Furthermore, as judicial separation was only available in the High Court, it involved difficult issues of procedural law making it unlikely that a person could represent themselves; besides a litigant in person would have 'an emotional involvement that is scarcely compatible with the degree of objectivity required by advocacy in court'.[75]

The Irish government attempted to refute the applicant's arguments by distinguishing the case from *Golder*. In *Golder*, a breach of Article 6 was found because of the obstacles that the Home Secretary placed in the way of the applicant's access to court. In the instant case, Airey's inability to initiate proceedings were not a product of an act of the government, but of her own lack of financial resources for which the government could not be held responsible. The ECtHR rejected this argument in forthright terms:

> Although this difference between the facts of the two cases is certainly correct, the Court does not agree with the conclusion which the Government draw therefrom. In the first place, hindrance in fact can contravene the Convention just like a legal impediment . . . Furthermore, fulfilment of a duty under the Convention on occasion

---

72   Ibid.
73   Ibid., para 38.
74   *Airey v. Ireland*, Application No. 6289/73, 9 October 1979.
75   Ibid., 24.

necessitates some positive action on the part of the State; in such circumstances, the State cannot simply remain passive.[76]

The Irish government saw this as asserting that the Convention required a state to provide 'free legal aid' – a position that the Court similarly rejected, noting that 6(3) (c) provided only a qualified right. However, just because the essentially 'civil' and 'political' rights that are contained in the Convention become effectively 'social' and 'economic' rights, as they include commitments for state spending, does not mean that rights such as Article 6 must be interpreted narrowly. The court also stressed that Airey's situation could not be generalised – and that any award of legal aid should not be seen as opening the flood gates, and requiring all determinations of civil rights and obligations to require free legal representation. The court found that there was a breach of 6(1).

What is the impact of this case law on the UK? The key case is *Steel and Morris* v. *United Kingdom*.[77] The applicant's arguments focused on the denial of legal aid. The impact of this on the case is vividly illustrated by the ECtHR:

> At the time of the proceedings in question, McDonald's economic power outstripped that of many small countries (they enjoyed worldwide sales amounting to approximately 30 billion United States dollars in 1995), whereas the first applicant was a part-time bar worker earning a maximum of GBP 65 a week and the second applicant was an unwaged single parent. The inequality of arms could not have been greater.[78]

Against the financial might of McDonald's who employed one of the 'largest firms in England'[79] specialising in libel, the *pro bono* work of largely inexperienced barristers and solicitors would count for very little. Indeed, during the trial, the applicants bore the burden of proof in relation to the allegations that they had made. Without counsel to argue points of law, they also had to cross examine witnesses and lacked means of paying for associated costs of photocopying and expenses for witnesses. The ECtHR sums up their problems well:

> All they could hope to do was keep going: on several occasions during the trial they had to seek adjournments because of physical exhaustion.[80]

The ECtHR framed the Article 6 argument as follows. Central to the notion of the fair trial is the idea that the plaintiff or defendant should be able to present his or her case 'effectively' – and that this required 'equality of arms' – in other words – that there should not be, as there was in this case, an unequal access to legal resources and representation. The legal aid scheme provided just such an equality of arms. However, whether or not legal aid was required had to be determined on the facts of each case.

---

76   Ibid., 25.
77   *Steel and Morris* v. *United Kingdom*, Application No. 68416/01, 15 February 2005.
78   Ibid., para 50.
79   Ibid.
80   Ibid., para 51.

Important determining factors were the complexity of the issues raised, and the extent to which the applicant was able to represent him or herself.[81] This was not to say, of course, that there is an absolute right to legal aid. Any restrictions on this right, however, had to be both legitimate and proportionate. Acceptable factors included chances of success and the financial means of the person applying for legal aid. This meant that it was not necessary that 'complete equality of arms' be maintained – but what was important was that both parties to the action had a 'reasonable opportunity' to present his or her case – in such conditions that one party was not at a 'substantial disadvantage' in relation to the other.[82]

On the facts of the present case, the ECtHR determined that legal assistance would have been necessary to ensure a fair trial. This was because the defendants were defending their right to freedom of expression in an action that raised many complex points of law. Moreover, the financial consequences for the applicants in losing the case were significant. Although the applicants had proved themselves to be articulate, and did receive *pro bono* work from lawyers – this was not sufficient to ensure a fair trial. In other words: 'The disparity between the levels of legal assistance enjoyed by the applicants and McDonald's had been so great that it must have given rise to unfairness.'[83] There was thus a breach of Article 6.

So, *Steel and Morris* determined that whilst absolute equality was not required between the parties to the trial, both sides must be given reasonable opportunity to present their case. As far as the law on Article 6 and legal aid is concerned, it is probably the case that the factors taken into account in finding a breach of the Article, would consider 'what was at stake for the individual, the complexity of the law and procedure and the person's ability to represent themselves'.

In conclusion to this section of the chapter, we want to offer some final comments on the government's Legal Aid, Sentencing and Punishment of Offenders Act 2012. As the House of Lords Constitution Committee reported, the objective of the Bill is to cut the cost of legal aid: 'The annual legal aid budget in England and Wales is £2.1 billion. The Government's proposals are designed to make £350 million of savings (cutting about 16%, or nearly one-sixth, of the budget). The Ministry of Justice has a target of

----

81   See *P., C. and S.* v. *United Kingdom* (2002) 35 EHRR 31 was a case that raised an Article 6 point in relation to removal of children from the parental home. *P.* had been convicted of offences against her son in 1995, and was found to be suffering from Munchhausen's syndrome. In 1996, the relevant authorities began care proceedings against *P.* in relation to her second child, *S.* The judge ordered that the child should be removed from her care. *P.* had represented herself during the care proceedings. The applicant alleged (*inter alia*) to the ECtHR that her rights under Article 6 had been breached, and the court accepted her arguments. The court argued that the key principle underlying the Article was fairness. Even though an individual might be able to conduct him or herself in court without representation, the question may still be asked as to whether the procedure was fair. A key issue was the seriousness of the issues at stake. Within the context of this test, it was not necessary to show that there had actually been prejudice from the failure of legal representation – such a test would be too stringent, and would deprive litigants of Article 6 protection. This decision reflects the facts of the case. At the beginning of the care proceedings, *S.* was represented by a team of lawyers. However, they asked to be removed from the case, as *S.* was asking them to conduct the case in an 'unreasonable manner'. The judge considered that *S.* was capable of conducting the case in their absence, and was also acting on expert evidence that it was necessary to resolve the care issue before *S.*'s first birthday. Against these facts, the ECtHR argued that both the emotive issues involved, the voluminous documentation in the case and *S.*'s own distress at the proceedings required representation in order to make the trial fair.

82   Supra n. 59, at para 62.

83   Ibid.

reducing its overall budget by 23% (approximately £2 billion) by 2014–15.'[84] Amongst its various provisions, the Act amends the Access to Justice Act 1999 to limit the availability of legal aid for civil cases. Kenneth Clarke defined the underlying 'logic' of reform as determining 'which types of cases most urgently merit scarce resources, to encourage people to use non-adversarial solutions to their problems where appropriate, and to speed up and simplify court processes where not'. Thus, legal aid 'must be available where people's life, liberty or home is at stake, where they are at risk of serious physical harm or are victims of domestic violence'. It should also cover cases which involve 'challenge[s] [to] state action' and 'where . . . children may be taken into care'. Availability of legal aid in these cases, requires savings in other areas. Legal Aid is thus no longer 'routine[ly] availability . . . in . . . family disputes' where mediation will be encouraged.[85]

Very real concerns have been expressed about the way in which the Act narrows eligibility for legal aid. Matters of particular concern are the restrictions on the availability of legal aid for victims of domestic violence, and other changes to 'the recoverability' of lawyer's fees that 'will make it virtually impossible for the victims of human rights abuses committed by transnational corporations overseas to bring cases against those corporations in the UK'.[86] Other commentators have predicted that: 'There will be at least 25% fewer claimants and the remaining 75% will lose up to a quarter of their compensation, as the government switches money from individual claimants in favour of the powerful insurance companies' lobby, which stands to gain more than £2.25bn.'[87] It will be interesting to see whether or not it is possible to bring a challenge under Article 6 to these changes in funding civil justice. One thing seems certain: it will be much harder for ordinary people to protect their interests in the courts.

CONCLUSION

The moral authority of the court to hold a citizen to account depends on the balance it can achieve between the rights of the defendant and trial processes that allow the prosecution to secure a fair conviction of those who are guilty of the offences with which they have been charged. Has the common law, in the light of the impact of Article 6, achieved this balance?

We would sum up our answers as follows. Cases like *Saunders* and *Condron* have shown how the common law falls short of international standards. *Edwards, Rowe and Davis* and *Fitt* raised some important issues, especially in relation to the rights of the defence and disclosure of criminal evidence. While breaches were found in *Rowe and Davies*, the three cases taken together do not suggest a major failing of

---

84   http://www.publications.parliament.uk/pa/ld201012/ldselect/ldconst/222/22203.htm#note4. The Constitution Committee is citing figures drawn from the House of Commons Justice Committee, 3rd report of 2010–12, HC 681, paras 11–12.

85   *The Guardian*, 19/12/11, at http://www.guardian.co.uk/commentisfree/2011/dec/19/legal-aid-safe-my-reforms.

86   Human Rights Joint Committee, 22 Report, Legislative Scrutiny: Legal Aid, Sentencing and Punishment of Offenders Bill, 2011, at para 1.44.

87   *The Guardian* 2/1/12, Andrew Dismore, Coordinator of the Access to Justice Action Group.

the common law to protect the rights of the defendant. *Ambrose* and *Horncastle* are 'hard cases' and, as such, hard to fit into a pattern. Certainly, the SC's assertive stance in *Horncastle* shows that common law principles on hearsay are not in breach of human rights standards; *Ambrose*, on the other hand, suggests that an opportunity to elaborate rights to a solicitor may have been missed. *Steel* and *Morris* suggests real failings as far as access to the court is concerned.

14

OPEN JUSTICE, CLOSED PROCEDURES AND TORTURE EVIDENCE

As we argued in Chapter 2, justice in a democracy has to be achieved in open court. The broader dimensions of this principle were articulated in a recent case:[1] '. . . the principle of open justice represents an element of democratic accountability, and the vigorous manifestation of the principle of freedom of expression.' These values are certainly central to democracy, but, we have also argued that the principle of open justice is a critical principle; a principle that, as we will argue below, requires us to object to the 'special regimes' that are growing up around certain forms of evidence and lie behind the Justice and Security Bill. Our argument will take us back to issues of terrorism, and, indeed, to government complicity in torture. Arguments about open justice are thus at the cutting edge of the meaning of a fair trial in contemporary British law.

The first section of this chapter will examine the Article 6 doctrine called the duty to give reasons. Linking the duty to give reasons to the principle of open justice shows how these two essential elements of a fair trial are related. This takes us to a number of issues raised by the regime of control orders and closed material procedures (CMPs) under the 2005 Prevention of Terrorism Act. We will examine the case law on CMPs, and assess the extent to which they are consistent with Article 6. Subsequent sections of the chapter will analyse controversial and 'Kafkaesque'[2] government proposals to extend CMPs to civil cases where issues of national security are at stake. The last section will engage with a related theme: the extent to which Article 6 can be used to prevent extradition to a jurisdiction where there is a risk that torture evidence will be used against the extradited person. We will then weigh up the difficult question of the relationship of human rights and security within a democracy committed to the rule of law.

THE DUTY TO GIVE REASONS

We have already argued that the idea of public reason can be related to the requirement that a court should give reasons for its decisions. We now need to descend to a level of detail, and look at two important authorities that show how the common law courts have interpreted this principle. We will examine *Flannery* v. *Halifax Estate Agencies Ltd*[3] first of all. The case concerned an appeal against a judge's decision that he preferred

---

1   R. *(On the application of Mohammed)* v. *Secretary of State for Foreign and Commonwealth Affairs* [2010] All ER (D) 118 (Feb).
2   Zuckerman (2011: 349–359).
3   *Flannery and Another* v. *Halifax Estate Agencies Ltd. (trading as Colleys Professional Services)* [2000] 1 W.L.R. 377.

the defendant's expert evidence to that given by the plaintiff. The judge had not given any reasons for this preference. The Court of Appeal allowed the plaintiff's appeal, holding that the failure to give reasons breached the principle that the court had to show fairness to both parties. The court began its judgment by affirming the common law duty to give reasons. However, this duty is not absolute or unqualified.[4] The Court of Appeal attempted to clarify these principles by articulating a set of general comments.

The duty to give reasons is part of due process, and its 'rationale'[5] has two elements. Fairness requires that the party that has lost the case knows the reason why; this is to ensure that the court has not 'misdirected itself' and to ascertain whether or not an appeal is possible. Indeed, failure to give reasons may itself constitute grounds of appeal. It could be suggested that fairness is related to 'transparency'.[6] The second principle might be described as a forensic discipline: it encourages good practice as judgments must be soundly reasoned. As mentioned above, this duty must be sensitive to context. The key issue is the 'subject matter' of the case. Once evidence moves beyond the oral, and, in particular, once it is disputed expert evidence, the duty to give a coherent reasoned judgment is triggered.

Flannery was revisited in *English v. Emery Reimbold & Strick Ltd.*[7] Lord Phillips was keen to show the relationship between the Strasbourg case law and common law principles. He argued that Article 6 relates to the procedures, rather than the merits of a case. For a judgment to be compliant with Article 6, it was necessary to show that the 'essential issues' raised by the case have been considered by the court and 'resolved'.[8] In other words, fairness does not require that all elements of a decision are explained.

In Lord Phillips' opinion, the common law has always generally acknowledged that a judgment should be reasoned.[9] His discussion of the relevant authorities largely amplifies the common law understanding of this topic as articulated by *Flannery*. However, he adds some interesting reflections. The common law's commitment to a binding system of precedent cannot in itself explain why there is an acknowledgement of the duty to give reasons, as the fundamental nature of the judgment is that it binds the parties to the case, not that it 'delineate[s]' or 'develop[s]' the law.[10] Lord Phillips also places the duty to give reasons in the context of the appellate system. Given that appeals require permission, it is necessary that a judge sets out the grounds on which s/he made his/her decision. This provides a further measure for the level of detail required. It is not necessary for the judge to deal with every argument given, and refute it on a point by point basis: it is crucial is to show 'issues' which were 'vital' to 'the judge's conclusion' and 'the manner in which [they have been] resolved'.[11]

---

4   See *Regina v. Knightsbridge Crown Court, Ex parte International Sporting Club (London) Ltd.* [1982] QB 304; *Regina v. Harrow Crown Court, Ex parte Dave* [1994] 1 WLR 98. In *Eagil Trust Co. Ltd v. Pigott-Brown* [1985] 3 All ER 119, 122 Griffiths LJ argued that the judge does not have to deal with every argument made by counsel.
5   Supra, n. 3 at 381.
6   Ibid., 382.
7   *English v. Emery Reimbold and Strick Ltd* [2002] EWCA Civ 605.
8   Ibid., 2416.
9   Ibid., 2417.
10   Lord Phillips citing Mahoney JA in *Soulemezis v. Dudley (Holdings) Pty Ltd* (1987) 10 NSWLR 247, 273, at ibid., 2417.
11   Ibid., 2417.

So, the duty to give reasons relates to the appellate structure of the courts and the transparency of judicial making. Although the duty does not apply to all aspects of the trial, it does play a central role in compelling the judge to articulate reasons for key decisions. Interestingly, as Lord Phillips points out above, the doctrine of precedent itself cannot be used to account for the duty to give reasons in common law. We can therefore point to the way in which Article 6 jurisprudence has clarified certain important concerns within common law reasoning. Whether or not the duty is expressed as a human right, it clearly relates to the integrity of the legal system. We will argue in the next section of this chapter that the duty to give reasons is part of a much broader principle of open justice: a principle that tells us something fundamental about the nature of a fair trial.

OPEN JUSTICE

The requirement that judgment be pronounced publicly is a central element of Article 6. In *Pretto* v. *Italy*,[12] the court went some way to articulating the reasons that justified this principle. It protects litigants against the administration of justice in secret where there is no public scrutiny of the decision the court reached.[13] The public pronouncement of judgment also makes for general confidence in the courts. Overall, the objective of Article 6 is to make justice 'visible'. This broader defence of the Article can be linked with the very idea that a publicly pronounced judgment compels the rational defence of the judgment.

In order to get a good grasp of these themes, we need to consider the relationship between the principle of open justice and the common law. *Scott* v. *Scott* is authority for an important point: 'justice should be administered in public' but it should be 'recognised that there may be a departure from that principle where that is necessary in the interests of justice'.[14] When might justice require limitation of the principle of openness? This takes us, first of all, to the matter of public interest immunity (PII). PII certificates are used when the government believes that disclosure of documents is not in the public interest. The modern law rests on the House of Lords decision in *Conway* v. *Rimmer*.[15] This case articulated a 'balance' test which the court has to apply in order to determine whether or not documents should be disclosed. If the 'possible injury' that might result from disclosure was 'so grave that no other interest should be allowed to prevail over it' production of documents should not be ordered. However, 'where the possible injury is substantially less' the court has to balance the risks of disclosure

---

12   *Pretto* v. *Italy*, 8th December 1983.
13   Ibid., 29.
14   *Al Rawi* v. *Security Service* [2011] UKSC 34, at para 26.
15   *Conway* v. *Rimmer* 1986 AC 910. Up until the ruling of the House of Lords in *Duncan* v. *Cammell Laird & Co Ltd (Discovery)* [1942] 1 All ER 587 HL, claims to Crown privilege were used to prevent disclosure of documents. In *Duncan*, for instance, the plaintiffs were seeking to obtain disclosure on the design of a submarine that had sank with large loss of life. The government successfully resisted disclosure on the grounds of national security. The HL overruled *Duncan* v. *Cammell Laird* in *Conway* v. *Rimmer*.

against the risk to a party's interests should the documents not be disclosed.[16] There is an important proviso: when assessing the minister's reasons, the court has to bear in mind that there are certain matters that 'judicial experience is not competent to weigh'. We cannot consider all the case law around the test, but, briefly consider some of the more recent authorities.

In *Carnduff* v. *Rock*[17] a police informer sued the police for payment which he claimed he was owed for providing information on criminal activities. The Court of Appeal struck out the case on the grounds that the trial would require the disclosure of sensitive information, and disclosure was not in the public interest. Laws LJ[18] applying the test from *Conway* v. *Rimmer*, argued that it was 'inevitable' that the court would have to 'hold that the public interest in withholding the evidence . . . outweighed the countervailing public interest in having the claim litigated'.[19] However, it would be wrong to think that *Carnduff* was exemplary of the court's approach. Certainly, in *Al Rawi*, it was the only authority that showed the court deciding that retaining the secrecy of the information 'trump[ed] . . . the administration of justice' and thus depriving the plaintiff of a trial.

The common law has also qualified the principle of open justice when the interests of children are concerned and in cases of sensitive commercial information. These exceptions are justified for different reasons. The former because the 'interests of children are paramount'[20] the latter because 'full disclosure may not be possible if it would render the proceedings futile'.[21] The key point is that both these instances are exceptional – and – any other departures from the principle of openness have to be justified.[22]

As we cannot consider all these issues in detail, we will focus on the ECtHR's approach to cases concerning children. In *B. and P.* v. *UK*,[23] the applicant had argued that an application for a residence order should be heard in open court. The judge had refused, as it was a case concerning children, and had conducted the hearings in chambers, warning the applicant that it would be a contempt of court to publicise anything that had taken place during the hearing. When the case came to be heard by the ECtHR, the government argued that the underlying reason for secrecy in cases concerning children was to protect the children themselves, and to encourage the parties to give 'full and frank' evidence.[24] The judge's discretion to hear cases in public was entirely in keeping with Article 6. Furthermore, the limitations on the right to a public hearing were consistent with Article 6 provided that the restrictions were

---

16   When a Minister certifies that a document 'belongs to a class which ought to be withheld' the court must assess, on the reasons given, 'whether the withholding of a document of that particular class is really necessary for the functioning of the public service'. If, 'on balance', the court thinks that the document should 'probably be produced', then it should go on to 'generally examine the document before ordering . . . production.'

17   *Carnduff* v. *Rock* [2001] 1 WLR 1786.

18   Ibid., at para 36.

19   Cited in *Al-Rawi*, supra n. 14, at para 398.

20   Ibid., at para 63.

21   Ibid., at para 64.

22   Ibid., at para 65.

23   *B. and P.* v. *UK*, 24 April 2001.

24   Ibid., at para 32.

themselves carefully justified. The applicants argued that the presumption of a private hearing was in breach of Article 6. The correct position would be to assert that all cases, even those concerning children, had to take place in open court. This presumption could then be rebutted, in order to allow a case to be heard privately.

The way in which the ECtHR approached this case tells us a great deal about the precise operation of Article 6. The Strasbourg court re-asserted the general principle that the need for a public hearing could be restricted. Most importantly, the court ruled that there was 'an entire class of case' in which there was a compelling argument for closed proceedings. This class would always be subject to the overarching jurisdiction of the court, but on this issue, 'English procedural law' was entirely consistent with European human rights law. In other words, there was no breach of Article 6. The ECtHR's interpretation of 'fairness' thus attempts to balance a number of factors, rather than inflexibly assert a predominant requirement for public pronouncement. Indeed, a 'literal' interpretation of Article 6 would privilege 'public scrutiny' over other values, and effectively 'frustrate' the 'primary aim' of the Article.[25]

Before we sum up on these cases, there is one last case we want to consider: *R. v. Davis*.[26] *Davis* saw the HL consider a ruling of the CA that allowed anonymous evidence to be given in a criminal trial. The House of Lords held that the Court of Appeal had fallen into error in not appreciating that 'the right to be confronted by one's accusers is a right recognised by the common law for centuries'.[27] The HL affirmed that it was a central feature of both criminal and civil trials that evidence was publicly tested. But, surely the Court of Appeal had a good reason for its decision: 'threats of intimidation' would mean that 'the witnesses would not be willing to give their evidence without [anonymity]'.[28] The House of Lords effectively affirmed that the integrity of the trial process was more important than witness anonymity: 'it is not enough if counsel sees the accusers if they are unknown to and unseen by the defendant.'[29]

To summarise: the common law and Article 6 acknowledge that there are limitations to the principle of open justice. The critical question is the nature of those limits. As we saw with the reasoning of both the British courts and the ECtHR, there are strong justifications for closed proceedings when the interests of children are concerned. We have also seen that the PII regime allows the court to attempt to balance competing ideas of the public interest. Whilst problematic, the legality of the PII regime is not at stake. It is as if both the common law and human rights jurisprudence accept that – paradoxically – the principle of open justice is founded on the fact that there are matters which legitimately remain secret. We can read *Davis* in this context. While certain documents may remain secret, even at the expense of the trial itself (*Carnduff*), the House of Lords in *Davis* appeared to assert that the trial itself is founded on a process of examination of evidence whose integrity could not be compromised – even

---

25   Ibid., para 48.
26   *R. v. Davis*, 2008 UKHL 36.
27   Cited in *Al Rawi*, supra n. 14, at para 28.
28   Ibid.
29   Ibid., at para 34.

to the extent that individuals might experience a degree of fear and intimidation in giving evidence against the accused. Although the requirement that some secrets remain secret cannot ultimately be questioned, the courts are still concerned with ensuring the integrity of trial processes.

CLOSED MATERIAL PROCEDURES AND ARTICLE 6

This bring us to our next key concern: any proper assessment of the present state of open justice in the UK has to engage with the system of closed material procedures (CMPs) and control orders that were put in place by the Prevention of Terrorism Act 2005. We need to determine whether or not the law has achieved a balance between the requirements of public scrutiny and national security. It is necessary, first of all, to reconstruct the legal context.

The 2005 Act empowered the Secretary of State to subject individuals suspected of terrorist activity to control orders. A control order placed restrictions on an individual's freedom of movement, residence and communication.[30] The anti-terrorism strategy on which the Act is based focuses on preventative measures. Kavanagh and Fenwick[31] have been critical of the government's 'official' argument that terrorism offences should be punished in criminal courts. Given the difficulties of securing convictions, control orders provide a more immediate way of restricting the activities of those suspected of terrorism.[32]

The 2005 Act created two kinds of control order: derogating and non-derogating. A derogating order imposed such wide restrictions on the controlled person as to require derogation from Article 5. A non-derogating order also imposed stringent conditions, but not to the same degree. The Act excludes from control order hearings the 'relevant party to the proceedings and his legal representative'. In such circumstances a special advocate may be appointed.[33]

Special advocates are solicitors or barristers who represent the interests of 'controlled persons' whose cases are being considered under CMPs. To assess the role of the special advocate from the perspective of open justice, we need to note that the '[c]losed proceedings . . . depart from the paradigm of a fair, adversarial legal hearing of a dispute'. In a normal trial: 'parties are on an equal footing in relation to evidence and cross-examination of identifiable witnesses in full view of the parties and the judge.'[34] In

---

30   Control orders raise serious concerns about breaches of human rights other than Article 6. In *Secretary of State for the Home Department* v. *JJ* [2007] UKHL 45, the House of Lords held that an 18-hour curfew was in breach of Article 5; but see also *Secretary of State for the Home Department* v. *E*; [2007] UKHL 47 a 12-hour curfew was not in breach of Article 5.

31   Kavanagh (2010: 837); Fenwick (2007: 472).

32   The 2005 Act was repealed by the Terrorism Prevention and Investigation Measures Act 2011 (TPIM). Control orders were replaced by TPIM notices.

33   CMPs are a supplement to Public Interest Immunity (PII) Certificates that Ministers could obtain from judges to keep material out of open court. Information could be withheld if it is not in the public interest to disclose it. One of the problems with the PII is that, the government argues, it is impractical and inappropriate to deal with the increasing number of documents concerned. The 1997 Act introduced CMPs in relation to 'immigration deportation decisions' (CMPs are also used in other contexts).

34   Kavanagh (2010: 867).

CMPs, the controlled persons may not know in detail the nature of the evidence against them (see below) and the closed elements of the trial take place without the presence of the controlled person. There are serious doubts about the extent to which a special advocate can effectively protect the interest of the controlled person in such a trial. Suffice to say, then, that the system of closed procedure hearings and special advocates raises controversial issues.[35]

Challenges to control orders under the 2005 Act prompted a series of cases that raised a fundamental issue: were controlled persons to be given any access to the evidence against them? The HL's ruling in MB[36] left unresolved the issue of whether or not it was necessary to disclose a 'core irreducible minimum' of the allegations against a controlee.[37] The Court of Appeal wrestled with this problem in AF.[38] The majority held that the absence of disclosure of an 'irreducible minimum' did not make a hearing unfair. The question of unfairness had to be assessed in context. The key question was whether or not the special advocate had been able to deal 'effectively' with the closed material. Perhaps most importantly, the court held that there were no 'rigid principles' and that the question of fairness was best left to the judge.[39]

The applicants appealed to the House of Lords. Shortly before the hearing of their appeals, the Grand Chamber of the European Court of Human Rights ruled in A. v. UK.[40] The ECtHR was particularly concerned with the role of the special advocate. A unanimous ruling determined that: 'it was essential that as much information about the allegations and evidence against each applicant was disclosed as was possible without compromising national security or the safety of others.'[41] The fundamental principle appears to be that: 'non-disclosure cannot go so far as to deny a party knowledge of the essence of the case against him, at least where he is at risk of consequences as severe as those normally imposed under a control order.'[42]

When the SC came to hear the appeals in AF, they held that they were bound by the decision of the Grand Chamber. The SC asserted that Article 6 required that a person subject to a control order be given 'sufficient information about the allegations against him to enable him to give effective instructions to his special advocate' even where interests of national security were at stake. A fair trial did not require 'detailed disclosure' of the evidence against the controlee, but, when a case was based on 'solely or to a decisive extent on undisclosed materials' the 'sufficient information' rule applied. What do we make of this ratio?

....

35   The government justified the CMP regime on a number of grounds. The CMP regime was meant to: ' "both accommodate legitimate security concerns about the nature and sources of intelligence information" but to "accord the individual a substantial measure of procedural justice" '. (Green Paper 52). The government asserted that CMPs operate in a human rights compliant way to ensure that courts can consider information that 'might otherwise be excluded from consideration altogether by the operation of PII' (Green Paper, 10).

36   MB v. Secretary of State for the Home Department [2007] UKHL 46. MB also concerned a non-derogating control order made under the 2005 Act.

37   Cited in AF v. Secretary of State [2009] UKHL 28, at para 21.

38   Three individuals (AF, AN, AE) who had been made subject to non-derogating control orders argued that their Article 6 rights to a fair trial had been breached as these orders were based on closed hearings.

39   Ibid., para 36.

40   A. v. UK (2009) 26 BHRC 1.

41   Ibid., at para 218.

42   Ibid., at para 65.

Some commentators have argued that *AF* struck a difficult balance between the need to protect national security, and the obligation to do so in a way that protected the human right to a fair trial.[43] Other commentators, however, have argued that the courts should have been much more assertive in defending fair trial rights against the executive.[44] Do we come across a fundamental tension in this area of law? Will issues of national security and secret evidence always 'trump' the values of human rights? Rather than finding an inescapable tension between competing values in this area of law, we could argue that: 'human rights law offers a framework that satisfies both public security concerns, and protects human dignity and the rule of law.'[45] The 'fight' against terrorism rests on 'the rule of law'; most importantly, 'if states' deny 'human rights and the rules of law', they 'create conditions which are conducive to terrorism'.[46] While this is certainly a compelling position, it is hard to see how the courts can ultimately protect human rights against an executive determined to restrict rights in order to counter terrorism. The critical question is: how close does the system of special advocates come to undermining the rule of law itself? There are profound misgivings about the ability of the special advocates to present the interests of the people they represent in closed hearings. Chamberlain, for one, has stressed that human rights law reminds us of the importance of the principles of natural justice, shared by both common law and Article 6, a legacy that should not be abandoned in 'the war against terror'.[47] The debate has become focused on the government's Green Paper that outlines proposals for reform.

THE JUSTICE AND SECURITY GREEN PAPER AND BILL

The government has admitted in the Green Paper on the Justice and Security Bill that there are problems with the role that special advocates play (Justice and Security Green Paper), but, argue that if communications between special advocates and those affected by CMPs are improved, a balance is struck between the interests of national security and the right to a fair trial. Government apologists have stressed the need to protect secret information in order to further collaboration between British security services and those of allied nations. There are indeed examples of occasions when terrorist activity has been frustrated by intelligence shared between the UK and its allies. The defence of British democracy ultimately requires a certain measure of secrecy.[48]

....

43   Kavanagh (2009: 287–304).
44   Ewing (2005: 829); Ewing and Tham (2008: 668).
45   Navi Pillay, UN High Commissioner for Human Rights, at http://www.ohchr.org/Documents/Press/KeynoteStatement.pdf.
46   Ivan Šimonović, Assistant UN Secretary-General for Human Rights, at http://www.ohchr.org/Documents/Press/KeynoteStatement.pdf.
47   Chamberlain (2011).
48   Green Paper, Justice and Security Bill, CM 8194 para 1.6, p. 3. It is worth remembering that although the system of control orders has been replaced with TPIM notices many of the problems and issues of the old system remain in the new regime. An unsuccessful attempt was made to obtain disclosure of closed procedure material in *Secretary of State for the Home Department* v. *CC and CF*, [2012] EWHC 1732 (Admin). The applicants were alleging that their arrest, interrogation and deportation from Somaliland to the UK amounted to abuse of process. Ouseley J ruled that *AF* extended only to the sufficient disclosure of the allegations that the Secretary of State relied upon to impose a control order. As there were no relevant allegations in the abuse claims the applicants could not have access to the closed procedure materials.

Activists groups like Liberty and Reprieve have been vociferous in their criticisms of the system of special advocates and CMPs. Moreover, the Joint Committee on Human Rights Report of 2007 stated that: 'the public should be left in absolutely no doubt that what is happening . . . [CMPs have] absolutely nothing to do with the traditions of adversarial justice as we have come to understand them in the British legal system.' The 2012 Joint Committee on Human Rights Report continued these criticisms. The report found that 'closed material procedures are inherently unfair'.[49] Senior Law Lords have also expressed their concerns. Lord Dyson in *Al Rawi* commented that closed material proceedings are: 'not just offensive to the basic principles of adversarial justice in which lawyers are steeped, but it is very much against the basic notions of fair play as the lay public would understand them.'[50]

One particularly worrying development outlined in the government's Green Paper is the extension of the 'exceptional' regime of closed procedure materials into other areas of law.[51] The extension of CMPs to civil proceedings is justified on a number of grounds. The Minister responsible for the Justice and Security Bill, Ken Clarke, has presented the Bill as extending 'civil justice into the most secret activities of the UK state, bringing our security services further into the light and improving their accountability'.[52] Clarke argues that the new regime will allow courts to consider matters of national security that, under the present system, are expensively settled out of court. This argument is backed up by the claim that CMPs are compatible with Article 6.[53] The Green Paper presents the government as committed to the rule of law and the use of the courts to have matters 'tried fully and fairly'.[54] Above all, however, extending CMPs to civil cases protects the relationship of UK security services with 'our allies'.

TORTURE, NATIONAL SECURITY AND THE COURTS

To examine these issues we need to look at three significant cases which prompted the government to embark on reforms of civil justice: *Al Rawi* v. *Security Services*,[55] *Tariq* v. *Home Office* and *R. (Mohamed)* v. *Secretary of State for Foreign and Commonwealth Affairs*. In *Al Rawi* the claimants argued that British security personnel had connived in their torture and ill treatment in Guantanamo Bay and other secret sites. The government sought to use CMPs (as opposed to public interest immunity certificates) to prevent sensitive information being heard in open court. The case contains some important discussions of the principle of open justice. The ratio of the case may be a

---

49   http://www.parliament.uk/business/committees/committees-a-z/joint-select/human-rights-committee/news/justice-and-security-green-paper-report.

50   Ibid.

51   Outside of the SIAC context, litigation on CMPs had arisen on numerous occasions. For instance, *Carnduff* v. *Rock*, considered above.

52   Ken Clarke 19th September 2012, http://www.guardian.co.uk/commentisfree/2012/sep/19/justice-and-security-bill-on-track.

53   Green Paper, Justice and Security Bill, para 1.29.

54   Ibid., para 1.36.

55   *Al Rawi* v. *Security Service* [2011] UKSC 34.

little unclear[56] but at least four of the Law Lords who heard the case concluded that legislation would be necessary to introduce closed material proceedings into a civil trial.[57]

Lord Dyson stated that open justice is not just a 'mere procedural rule' – it is a 'fundamental common law principle'.[58] The principle of open justice is backed up by the rules of natural justice. This means that a party 'has a right to know the case against him and the evidence on which it is based'. The court must allow a party 'the opportunity to respond' to evidence against him or her and 'any submissions made by the other side'.[59] Open justice requires a party to be allowed to call 'his own witnesses' and to cross examine the witnesses called by the other side.[60] CMPs depart from both these principles.[61] Lord Dyson concluded: 'that the issues of principle raised by the closed material procedure are so fundamental that a closed material procedure should only be introduced in ordinary civil litigation (including judicial review) if Parliament sees fit to do so.'[62] Lord Hope made a similar point; arguing that: 'a line must be drawn between procedural choices which are regulatory only and procedural choices that affect the very substance of the notion of a fair trial.'[63]

Lord Dyson certainly gave a spirited defence of the principle of open justice; Mance and Hale LLJ were, however, a little more circumspect. Lord Clarke was the least critical of such proceedings. On balance, *Al Rawi* suggests that the Supreme Court is reluctant to countenance erosion of common law fundamentals without statutory authority. We could perhaps provisionally conclude that '*Al Rawi* may amount to little more than a small speed-bump in its specific context' if the government's desire in the recent Green Paper becomes law.[64] However, any final analysis of these cases in this chapter must come after our analysis of *Tariq* and *Mohammed*, as we need to remain with *Al Rawi* and link the points we made above to what the case tells us about PII.

It is worth remembering that the claimants in *Al Rawi* actually argued that the information at stake should be considered through conventional public interest immunity proceedings. The government resisted this approach. They drew attention to the fact that there were around 250,000 documents, of which 140,000 would have to be dealt with through PII certificates. If CMPs were adopted, it would be possible to get around these problems. The court would be able to consider the relevant evidence, albeit under the restrictive CMPs regime and through the services of a special advocate. Pondering these points requires us to acknowledge a note of caution in any overly dramatic denunciation of CMPs. The PII system itself has profound flaws. It may be that it is not fit for purpose when large amounts of documents are involved.

---

56   Chamberlain (2011: 360).
57   Ibid., at 360.
58   Supra n. at 11.
59   Ibid., at para 12.
60   Ibid., at para 14.
61   Ibid., at para 15.
62   Ibid., at para 69.
63   Ibid., at para 72.
64   John Ip, 'Al Rawi, Tariq, and the future of closed material procedures and special advocates' MLR, 2012, 75(4), 606–623, at 623.

To return to the ratio of *Al Rawi*. As Zuckerman has pointed out, there were some interesting differences of opinion. The court held that: 'it had no common law jurisdiction to replace the PII procedure with closed material procedure as suggested by the Government.' However, 'only four Supreme Court Justices fully endorsed the Court of Appeal decision that the court had no jurisdiction to order closed material procedure in civil cases' – a decision justified on open justice principles. Two Justices took a different approach; deciding that although the court could not order CMPs, it could allow a claimant CMPs if a PII claim would 'strike out their claim'.[65] As we will see in our analysis at the end of this section of the chapter, the approach to PII by the court in *Al Rawi* and in *Mohammed* led the government to believe that the system of PII certificates was not an effective way of dealing with the problems that were attendant on 'managing' the legal response to terrorism.

In *Tariq v. Home Office*,[66] an immigration officer's security clearance was withdrawn on national security grounds after a closed material procedure under the Employment Tribunals Act 1996 and The Employment Tribunals (Constitution and Rules of Procedure) Regulations 2004. Tariq was represented by a special advocate. The Court of Appeal held that Tariq should at least have been given sufficient details of the case against him to enable him to instruct his representatives. When the Supreme Court considered the case, they argued that although closed material procedures were not in breach of the Convention, questions had to be asked about the sufficiency of the safeguards that protected the rights of the person in CMPs.

Assessing the sufficiency of the safeguards required the Court to begin from the position that: 'the rule of law . . . had to stand for the objective resolution of civil disputes on their merits by a tribunal which had before it material enabling it to do that.' In cases where national security was at stake, a balance had to be struck 'between the interests of claimant and defendant'.[67] The Supreme Court went on to assert that the special advocate system provided just such a balance between the competing interests at stake.

Regina (Mohamed) v. Secretary of State for Foreign and Commonwealth Affairs[68] is a complex piece of litigation but we have to familiarise ourselves with the basic facts. Mohamed was a prisoner at Guantanamo Bay charged with terrorist offences. His lawyers in the UK applied to the Foreign Secretary to release documents that were vital to his defence; in particular, evidence that he had been interrogated by British security personnel and tortured into making false confessions. When the Foreign Secretary refused, Mohamed's lawyers sought judicial review and a court order that would enable the information held by the Foreign Secretary to be sent confidentially to the lawyers defending Mohamed in the United States.

Arrangements were made for both closed and public hearings, and for a special advocate to represent Mohamed. The judge also ruled that before any judgment issued by the court was published, it would be considered by the Foreign Secretary and the

---

65   Zuckerman (2011).
66   *Tariq v. Home Office* [2011] UKSC 35.
67   Ibid.
68   *Regina (Mohamed) v. Secretary of State for Foreign and Commonwealth Affairs* [2010] EWCA Civ. 158.

Security Services to ensure that national security was not compromised. The Divisional Court then went on to hold that security services had indeed been involved in Mohamed's mistreatment and that information would have to be disclosed, provided that it was not covered by a PII certificate. The court also agreed that sections of the open judgment that described Mohamed's detention in Pakistan would be redacted. This information – with the redacted paragraphs – was then made available to Mohamed's American defence team.

The question then arose as to whether or not the redacted paragraphs should be restored to the judgment. The government's case was that restoring the paragraphs would compromise the working relationship between American and British intelligence agencies. When the court came to consider this matter, it held for the government. However, in a subsequent application to the court, Mohamed's lawyers argued that the Foreign Secretary's evidence was flawed. This time the court ordered the sections to be restored.

The ratio of the Court of Appeal is particularly interesting. Dismissing the Foreign Secretary's argument, the court linked the principle of open justice to the rule of law and asserted that the court 'should publish the reasons for its decision' as the case involved 'the mistreatment of detainees' and 'revealed [the] involvement of the United Kingdom intelligence services in the mistreatment of a United Kingdom resident'.[69] Redaction of court judgments should, however, only take place in the rarest possible circumstances; and whilst the utmost regard had to be given to matters of national security, the court would 'override' the Foreign Secretary's 'assessment' when 'the executive were acting unlawfully or it considered the claim for public interest immunity unjustified'. Lord Judge pointed out that: '[h]aving regard to concepts of democratic accountability and the rule of law, it is hard to conceive of a clearer case [than when national security arguments] would partially conceal the reasons "the executive" was "involved in or facilitated wrongdoing in the context of the practice of torture".'[70]

In assessing these cases, we must return to the central question: is there a balance between fair trial rights and national security?

The Green Paper on the Justice and Security Bill cites *Mohamed* as evidence that although the PII system works well in relation to 'marginal or peripheral' material, PII certificates do not give the government the security they need to manage sensitive information. Reflecting on the *Mohamed* case, the government has argued that: 'if we are unable to safeguard material shared by foreign partners . . . we can expect the depth and breadth of sensitive material shared with us to reduce significantly.'[71] This provides a major justification for extending CMPs. Does the need to control sensitive information in the interests of national security justify a new CMPs regime? Hughes has put the issue well: '[p]rocedural fundamental rights are at the heart of the constitutional relationship between the organs of the state and the rights of individuals' and

---

69   Ibid.

70   Lord Neuberger and Sir Anthony May P expressed their strong dissent from this position; but, ultimately held that as the judge in the United States had published the redacted passages in an open judgment, the Foreign Secretary's case was unarguable.

71   Supra, n. at para 122.

the decision in *Tariq*, and the proposed reforms in the Bill 'leave[s] our rights vulnerable. We also need to take seriously the warning about the "slow creep of complacency in relation to secret evidence in closed proceedings."[72] Indeed, the risk with the proposed legislation is that it: "normalis[es] secret evidence and chang[es] our perception of the fundamental requirements of the right to a fair trial."[73] As Lord Hope in *Tariq* pointed out: "[t]here are no hard edges in this area of the law."[74] This makes it even more risky to normalise a regime of secrecy as the norm, rather than the exception.

EXTRADITION AND ARTICLE 6

As we have already overviewed the facts of *Abu Qatada*, we will deal with the Article 6 points that it raises. In *RB (Algeria)* v. *Secretary of State for the Home Department*,[75] the House of Lords argued that Article 6 would only be relevant in an extradition case concerning the legal system of another country when an unfair trial would lead to 'flagrant denial of justice' for the person being extradited. Lord Phillips, Lord Hoffmann, Lord Brown and Lord Mance agreed on this point. Lord Phillips gave the leading judgment on the interpretation of Article 6. He made reference to *Mamatkulov and Askarov* v. *Turkey*[76] a key reference point. The case defined 'flagrant denial' as a breach of Article 6. A flagrant denial was one 'so fundamental [as] to amount to a nullification, or destruction of the very essence' of Article 6.

Lord Phillips admitted that it was not easy to find an 'adequate test' for the application of Article 6 in an extradition case. The case law suggested only 'tentative' principles.[77] However, it would be difficult to accept that 'the complete denial or nullification of the right to a fair trial' meant that 'every aspect' of the trial was flawed.[78] The 'flagrant denial' test pointed towards a fundamental breach in the trial process. One might think that torture evidence would amount to just such a breach. Lord Phillips does not argue this point. Rather, he focused the test on the 'potential consequences' of the breach to the person standing trial. For the test to apply there would have to be a breach of the 'substantive human rights'[79] of the person standing trial. *Bader and Kanbor* v. *Sweden*[80] suggests that the articles to which one should have regard are Articles 2 and 3.

---

72 Kavanagh (2010)
73 Kavanagh (2010: 857). Kavanagh's point is that the court's reluctant acceptance of CMP serves to normalise the exceptional use of secret evidence. Her argument can be extended to suggest that – should the Bill become law, an exceptional practice becomes central to civil justice.
74 Supra, n. 66.
75 *RB (Algeria)* v. *Secretary of State for the Home Department* [2009] WLR 512.
76 *Mamatkulov and Askarov* v. *Turkey* Nos. 46827/99 and 46951/99.
77 Supra, n. 72, at para 137.
78 Ibid., at 59.
79 Ibid., at para 137.
80 *Bader and Kanbor* v. *Sweden* (13284/04).

The relevant test thus had two limbs: it would be necessary to establish that the deportation of an alien would be a 'fundamental breach' of Article 6 and, secondly, that this breach would amount to a 'miscarriage of justice' that was serious enough to 'constitute a flagrant violation of the victim's fundamental rights'. Although the second part of the test was met, Qatada's trial before a military court would not constitute a fundamental or flagrant denial of justice. Whilst the lack of independence of a military court might amount to a breach of Article 6 in a nation that was bound by the ECtHR, the potential breach by a Jordanian court was not itself sufficient to prevent Abu Qatada's deportation.

Lord Phillips also dealt robustly with the finding of the CA that there was a 'real risk' that evidence obtained by torture would be used against Abu Qatada. The CA had required too high a threshold to prove that torture evidence would not be used. The assurances obtained by the British government were in fact sufficient to satisfy the court that torture evidence would not be used in the trial. In order to come to this conclusion Lord Phillips had considered the prohibition on torture evidence. He argued that the principle only applied to state institutions that were seeking to 'adduce such evidence' and did not prevent the extradition of Abu Qatada as the UK had obtained 'a high degree of assurance' that torture evidence would not be used in his trial.[81]

These arguments formed the basis of the British government's case before the ECtHR. To understand how the case developed, we need to make a brief reference to the *Belmarsh* case, as this formed another important plank of the government's argument. Relying on *A. and Others (No. 2)*, the government asserted that the relevant test to assess whether or not evidence had been obtained by torture was the balance of probabilities. In other words, if the defendant could not show – on the balance of probabilities – that evidence was obtained by torture, the court could admit it. We need to go into a little more detail on this point. In *A. No 2*, the House of Lords had in fact divided over the nature of the precise test. Hope, Rodger, Carswell and Brown LJJ adopted the test of balance of probabilities established by UNCAT. However, Lord Bingham, Nicholls and Hoffmann disagreed. They argued that this test was impractical in the circumstances – especially where evidence against a defendant was subject to CMPs. They preferred a test that established the exclusion of evidence if there was a *real risk* it had been obtained by torture.

Relying on the balance of probabilities test, the government asserted that as the evidence could be admitted in a UK court, it would be wrong to hold that Abu Qatada could not be deported to Jordan as the Jordanian court was, in this respect, similar to the British court.

The ECtHR began its judgment on the Article 6 point by declaring that: '[i]nternational law, like the common law before it, has declared its unequivocal opposition to the admission of torture evidence.' There are, moreover, 'powerful legal and moral reasons why it has done so'.[82] Strasbourg agreed with Lord Phillips' point

81 Supra, n. 71, at para 264.
82 *Othman (Abu Qatada) v. United Kingdom* (8139/09) 17 January 2012.

that states had to preserve the integrity of their institutions, but, went further – referencing Lord Bingham's speech in the *Belmarsh* case. Torture evidence is excluded because it is: 'unreliable, unfair, offensive to ordinary standards of humanity and decency and incompatible with the principles which should animate a tribunal seeking to administer justice.' Pithily put: 'experience has all too often shown that the victim of torture will say anything – true or not – as the shortest method of freeing himself from the torment of torture.' It would thus be absolutely inconsistent with the principles that determine the admissibility of evidence in a legal system 'based upon the rule of law' to 'countenance the admission of evidence – however reliable – which has been obtained by such a barbaric practice as torture'. This is because the 'trial process is a cornerstone of the rule of law'. Note the central role that the idea of integrity plays in the ECtHR's argument: '[t]orture evidence . . . substitutes force for the rule of law and taints the reputation of any court that admits it.'[83]

The ECtHR stressed that it preferred the arguments of the CA to the HL. The former court understood that the prohibition on torture evidence is 'fundamental'.[84] International law provides further authority for this principle. UNCAT places 'clear obligations on states' to 'eradicate torture' – an obligation that applies to 'any proceedings, including, for instance, extradition proceedings'. The ECtHR concluded that the use of torture evidence was not just a breach of Article 6, but also 'the most basic international standards of a fair trial'.

Although the ECtHR disagreed with the House of Lords, Strasbourg admitted that the 'flagrant denial of justice' had not yet 'been . . . define[d] . . . in . . . precise terms' and, furthermore, that the court had never found that: 'an expulsion would be in violation of Article 6.'[85] However, it was necessary to take a stand. A flagrant denial of justice would definitely have to 'go beyond mere irregularities'. The House of Lords were right to suggest that 'a fundamental breach of Article 6 was required'. How was this to be assessed? On this point Strasbourg preferred the minority in *A and Others*. The correct standard to assessing whether or not there was a 'real risk' of suffering a flagrant denial of justice. If there was a real risk, the government would then have the task of 'dispelling' those doubts[86]

On the facts of the case, the evidence available to the court suggested that the use of torture in Jordan was 'widespread', 'routine' and 'systematic'.[87] There was 'extensive', 'concrete' and 'compelling' evidence that Qatada's co-accused had been tortured.[88] Although, under Jordanian law, Qatada could challenge torture evidence, there were practical difficulties which made this an unlikely course of action. Qatada had also shown that: 'the Jordanian State Security Court has proved itself to be incapable of properly investigating allegations of torture and excluding torture evidence, as Article 15 of UNCAT requires it to do.'[89]

83   Ibid., at para 264.
84   Ibid., at paras 45–49.
85   Ibid., at 260.
86   Ibid.
87   Ibid., 272.
88   Ibid., 278.
89   Ibid., 285.

Note this final paragraph:

> Torture is uniquely evil both for its barbarity and its corrupting effect on the criminal process. It is practised in secret, often by experienced interrogators who are skilled at ensuring that it leaves no visible signs on the victim. All too frequently, those who are charged with ensuring that torture does not occur – courts, prosecutors and medical personnel – are complicit in its concealment. In a criminal justice system where the courts are independent of the executive, where cases are prosecuted impartially, and where allegations of torture are conscientiously investigated, one might conceivably require a defendant to prove to a high standard that the evidence against him had been obtained by torture. However, in a criminal justice system which is complicit in the very practices which it exists to prevent, such a standard of proof is wholly inappropriate.[90]

The court has to take a stand against torture. Once torture evidence becomes acceptable, a rot spreads through legal and political institutions. This is precisely because it takes place 'in secret' and 'leaves no visible sign' on its victims. There is an inherent risk that governments will turn to torture. Indeed, those who are meant to prevent it are often complicit in its commission. Abu Qatada's case is admittedly difficult: it could be argued that the UK has no real control over how institutions in Jordan operate. However, if human rights are international standards, then a nation committed to the rule of law cannot be seen to compromise itself by deporting individuals when there is a real risk that they will be tortured, or that torture evidence will be used against them. This takes us back to the question of how a democracy should respond to terrorism. Recall the argument we made above that the fight against terrorism rests on the rule of law. Human rights define both the means of the struggle against terrorism, and the very point of the struggle itself.

CONCLUSION

Our analysis in this chapter began with a consideration of the duty to give reasons. This doctrine clearly relates back to our arguments about public reason in earlier chapters. The chapter then turned its attention to Article 6 and CMPs. The development of a regime for dealing with alleged terrorists has led to certain tensions between the courts and the executive; tensions that have resulted in the present government's desire to reform the way in which CMPs operate. Perhaps what lies behind the problems analysed in this chapter are the consequences of an illegal war. The whole issue around CMPs and PII risks furthering the very argument that the terrorists are making: the state is simply unaccountable violence. Unless there is a prohibition on torture evidence, it is hard to sustain the argument that a state committed to the rule of law has a principled basis for asserting its security against those who would seek to subvert and destroy a democratic polity.

....

90   Ibid., 276.

15

IMAGINING CIVIL JUSTICE

Figure 15.1 Signpost at Dale Farm, Oak Lane, Crays Hill, Essex, UK. Photo by Oli Scarff/Getty Images, Copyright 2012 Getty Images

Imagination is more important than knowledge. For while knowledge defines all we currently know and understand, imagination points to all that we might yet consider.

Einstein, as noted by Viereck 1929

This is the Court of Chancery . . . which gives to monied might the means abundantly of wearying out the right; which so exhausts finances, patience, courage, hope; so overthrows the brain and breaks the heart; that there is not an honorable man among its practitioners who would not give – who does not often give – the warning, 'Suffer any wrong that can be done you, rather than come here'.

Charles Dickens, *Bleak House* (1853) (Penguin Classics (1971): 51)

INTRODUCTION: FROM *BLEAK HOUSE* TO THE POST-WOOLF LANDSCAPE

Images of justice help determine the acceptability and success of the processes associated with those images. A system of justice appeals to, and gains acceptance by, parties who believe that a specific injustice has occurred, if the ideal behind and the workings of the system are in line with a clear and compelling vision of fairness, procedurally and substantially. While there is always a difference between vision and reality, when the processes and outcomes seem far removed from the core ideals and images of the enterprise, disillusionment and sense of failure is rife.

There is an image of justice oft repeated, reproduced in pictures and sculptures in courtrooms, offices and books: it is of a blindfolded woman, standing straight and tall, with a stretched-out arm that holds a set of scales. In the traditional court-centred understanding of justice, this represents a place of judgment and since the woman is blindfolded, she cannot be swayed by gender, race, wealth, or other influences or advantages that one party might hold. On her scales, the parties to the dispute place their arguments and recounting of the facts, hoping that their side will have more weight. The matter is weighed on these scales in public view, and the balance resolves the matter. The scales themselves are open in their workings and get more precisely balanced after each weighing, after each case. The weight and moment of precise and particular factors are calibrated, and all understand how much factors weigh, this time and for the future. Should a party suspect that the scales were out of balance or the blindfold had been lifted, he may appeal to higher authorities to test the integrity of the process. This process is accessible to all, rich and poor alike.

When looking at civil justice our journey begins with Charles Dickens' *Bleak House*. *Bleak House*, the ninth novel of Charles Dickens, was published in instalments from March 1852 through September 1853.[1] *Bleak House* presented a compelling and clear set of images of the abject failure of the British Court of Chancery. Dickens had become embroiled in matters of Chancery when he was the plaintiff in five Chancery actions to restrain breaches of copyright. Holdsworth[2] tells us that he was victorious but had failed to recover costs and his experience of the system appears to have had a significant impact on him. At that time there were two main types of courts: the Courts of Common Law applied the precedents, principles and rules developed over time by the judges staffing the common law courts; an alternative court, the Court of Chancery, dealt with cases like property disputes and decided on the principles of equity. Equity, often derided as discretion varying with the length of the Lord Chancellor's foot,

---

1   This is a work that both reflects Dickens' personal life and his desire to fight for a better system (as well as make some money!). Dickens suffered a series of personal difficulties during this time. In 1851 Catherine Dickens, his wife, suffered a nervous collapse. Later Dora Dickens, the youngest daughter of Charles and Catherine, died when she was only eight months old. The father of Charles Dickens also died in 1851. The youngest child of Charles Dickens, Edward, was born in 1852. Dickens had close familiarity with the court system from his time spent as a law clerk. He also had a bad experience with the court in 1844 when he brought a case to Chancery that dealt with the copyright to *A Christmas Carol*. Dickens won the case; however, his opponents declared bankruptcy. Instead of collecting damages Dickens found himself paying court costs – on a case that he won!
2   Holdsworth, W. *Charles Dickens as a Legal Historian* (New Haven: Yale University Press, 1928), p. 80.

Figure 15.2 © Victoria and Albert Museum, London

actually had built up a series of rules and procedures as complex as anything the common law had developed but was even more complicated by the necessity to avoid the set 'forms of action' of the common law procedures and consider each case on its own merits. If this was thought to be an improvement over trying this type of case in the Courts of Common Law, Dickens demonstrated that the Chancery had become as bad, if not worse, as the common law process. The Chancery was ineffective, expensive and technically difficult. The litigants were charged fees at every step of the legal process, fees which went directly to the court officials. The more steps in the justice process, the greater the opportunities to collect fees. The consequence was a bureaucratic nightmare. Sometimes it took years for cases to even come to trial. From that point it could be years before a decision on the case was reached. In the preface of a non-serialised volume of *Bleak House* Dickens writes:

> At the present moment [August, 1853] there is a suit before the court which was commenced nearly twenty years ago, in which from thirty to forty counsel have been known to appear at one time, in which costs have been incurred to the amount of seventy thousand pounds, which is A FRIENDLY SUIT, and which is (I am assured) no nearer to its termination now than when it was begun.

In *Bleak House*, a large group of people, rich and poor (and often made poorer by their involvement in the case), are drawn together by their interest, which is usually financial, in the outcome of the long-running settlement of a disputed inheritance suit. The case is simply known as *Jarndyce* v. *Jarndyce* and Mr Kenge, a lawyer in the story, is astounded when he meets people who have not heard of the case. He says:

> Not heard of Jarndyce – the greatest of Chancery suits known? Not of *Jarndyce* v. *Jarndyce* – the – a – in itself a monument of Chancery practice. In which (I would say) every difficulty, every contingency, every masterly fiction, every form of procedure known in that court, is represented over and over again? It is a cause that could not exist, out of this free and great country.

By the end of the novel the case is settled in favour of one of the hopeful litigants but it becomes apparent that there is no money left for any victor in the case because the long delay has eaten all the profits. The only financial winners in *Bleak House*, it seems, are the lawyers and the Court of Chancery.

Holdsworth[3] makes much of the fact that Dickens' novel opens in physical fog and this fog is indicative of the system at the time. Holdsworth points to four key problems within the system at this time. First, the official machinery of the system was medieval and had been relatively unaltered since that time. Second, the practices of the court had become so technical and so slow and even in uncontested cases the delays were indefensible. Even where new procedures were introduced to attempt to reform the system so the old procedures continued to operate because it was in the officials' interest for them to do so. Finally the court had decided that if it were to act it had to act in entire control of the case. This meant that every time a minute point was raised so the whole procedure had to be undertaken for that point to be resolved. Holdsworth notes that just as Gibbon had commented on the operation of Roman law in much the same way the procedure in the Court of Chancery was 'a mysterious science and a profitable trade'.[4]

Although the two courts were fused in the reforms of the mid-nineteenth century dissatisfaction with civil justice has been widespread and this seems familiar across the common law world. In 1982, US Chief Justice Warren Burger summarised

....

3   Ibid., p. 85.
4   Ibid., p. 87.

dissatisfaction with litigation: 'Our system is too costly, too painful, too destructive, too inefficient for a truly civilized people'.[5]

The message from Dickens was clear. The system was slow, costly and complicated. Reforms did come when the systems were fused as a result of the Judicature Acts 1872–75, so it was hoped that Dickens' criticisms were no longer founded. One hundred and twenty years later and an empirical study, conducted by Professor Dame Hazel Genn, considered what people thought about going to the law.[6] The study did not present a particularly positive portrayal of the civil justice system. One survey respondent said, 'I'd like more access to justice and less access to the courts'.[7] As a quantitative study of the views of 4,125 randomly selected adults, the study offers a valuable insight into how access to justice was often restricted because of the fear of cost and delay associated with use of the courts. The findings of this study confirmed the findings of the National Consumer Council in 1995 who found that the civil justice system was too slow, too complicated and outdated.[8] Given this background the reforms which came in 1997 were apparently timely and necessary if 'access to justice' was ever to become a reality.

The Woolf reforms were implemented by virtue of the Civil Procedure Act 1997 and through the Civil Procedure Rules which followed in 1998. They can be summarised as being concerned with case control, court allocation and tracking and the use of streamlined documentation and procedures.[9] The reforms were meant to simplify the system and speed up the process. This in turn was meant to reduce costs which, although presented as being a marginal concern, were clearly crucial if the reforms were to be seen as a marked improvement on the old system. The use of case control has perhaps seen the most significant change in the process as the progress of cases is far more actively managed by the judge in the case whose task it is to ensure that all avenues of dispute resolution are considered before the case arrives at court and can assess more rigorously, and at a much earlier stage, which evidence needs to be presented if the case is to appear in court. The allocation of cases to a newly organised court tracking system means that cases are allocated to the small claims track, the fast track or the multi track.[10] Each track is used to ensure that the cost and complexity of the claim is dealt with in a more carefully defined arena where expert evidence can be utilised more efficiently in accordance with the case. This track allocation is decided upon via a case allocation questionnaire which, when completed by the disputing parties, will be reviewed and a decision[11] taken as to which court the case should be heard in. This limit to access to the High Court for the purpose of minor claims is thought to ensure that access to justice is rather more 'steered' than it ever had been

5   Burger, W. (1982) 'Isn't there a better way? *Annual Report on the State of the Judiciary, Remarks at the Mid-Year Meeting of the American Bar Association*', American Bar Association Journal.
6   Genn, H., *Paths to Justice* (Oxford: Hart, 1999).
7   Ibid., p 1.
8   Slapper, G. and Kelly, D., *English Legal System* (Oxford: Routledge-Cavendish, 2006) p. 293.
9   For a detailed description of these reforms see Slapper, G. and Kelly, D. *English Legal System* (Oxford: Routledge, 2012) p. 185.
10   Ibid., p. 200.
11   Under Part 26 Civil Procedure Rules.

before. This, coupled with a simplification of the language used[12] in the proceedings, was all geared towards making the system more user-friendly in order to meet those earlier criticisms that Genn referred to.

These reforms have now been in place for over a decade and some assessment has been made as to their success. The changes to the language used and the track allocation system seem to have been successful in making the system more comprehensible to the parties involved and directing the court's time to the particular issues in each case. The case management changes with their greater reliance on an active judge appear to be less successful in that just as one set of problems disappear (in terms of delay later in proceedings) so another emerges. Richard Burns,[13] a recorder from the county court, has argued that this new front-loading for case management simply moves the delay to earlier in proceedings. He comments that the process has been poorly resourced and appears to place too heavy a burden on the parties to the case at an earlier stage in the resolution of the dispute. The one area where the Woolf reforms appear to have had minimal impact is in the reduction of costs. Evidence[14] suggests that 'Lord Woolf's aspiration that case management would achieve his aims in relation to costs has not been achieved'.[15] In fact the front-loading of cases in some instances appears to have meant that costs have increased rather than decreased as was once hoped for. Given the concerns about costs Sir Rupert Jackson, a High Court judge was asked to undertake a year long review of costs in the civil courts with a view to promoting access to justice at proportionate cost. The Jackson Report was presented in 2009 and recommended substantial changes to the ways costs are incurred in the civil justice process.[16] The recommendations of this report were wide ranging and many of them were enacted in the Legal Aid, Sentencing and Punishing of Offenders Act 2012, which overhauls the provision of legal aid in this country. It is too early to tell whether these reforms will allay the critics of the original Woolf reforms but it is clearly an exciting time for monitoring changes to costs in this area.

THE OVERRIDING OBJECTIVE[17]

Much has been made of the Woolf reforms. The reforms are said to have changed the landscape of the civil justice system to the extent that the system now presents itself as being far more in touch with what people require to assist them in resolving their disputes.

---

12   There was a deliberate simplification of terms that took place where arcane terms such as plaintiff were replaced with claimant and formal terms such as particulars of claim were replaced with statement of claim to more clearly indicate what the statement was for.
13   Burns, R. (2000) 'A view from the ranks', *New Law Journal* 150: 1829–30.
14   See discussion in Zander, M., *Cases and Materials on the English Legal System* (Cambridge: Cambridge University Press, 2007).
15   Peysner and Seneviratne, quoted in Zander, M., *Cases and Materials on the English Legal System* (Cambridge: Cambridge University Press, 2007), p. 138.
16   See Jackson, R., 2009 http://www.judiciary.gov.uk/NR/rdonlyres/8EB9F3F3-9C4A-4139-8A93-56F09672EB6A/0/jacksonfinalreport140110.pdf
17   For a useful summary of the application of the overriding objective see Sime, S., *A Practical Approach to Civil Procedure* (Oxford: Oxford University Press, 2011).

The central tenet of these reforms is encapsulated in rule 1.1 of the Civil Procedure Rules, which states: '(1) These rules are a new procedural code with the overriding objective of enabling the court to deal with cases justly'.

This is known as the 'overriding objective' and rather than leaving the term 'just' hanging as a vague and non-specific term, rule 1.1 goes on to explain how a case can be dealt with justly. Given the more active role of judges in the reformed system it is interesting that those who drafted the rules felt the need to explain to judges how to deal with cases 'justly'. After all, this is central to the judicial function. Nevertheless an indicative list is presented to assist the judiciary in their task. To deal with a case justly 'so far as is practicable', it would seem that the judge must:

- ensure that the parties are on an equal footing;
- save expense;
- deal with the case in ways which are proportionate

  - to the amount of money involved,
  - to the importance of the case,
  - to the complexity of the issues, and
  - to the financial position of each party;

- ensure that it is dealt with expeditiously and fairly; and
- allot to it an appropriate share of the court's resources, while taking into account the need to allot resources to other cases.

The list is clear: it tells everyone, including the judge, how cases will be dealt with. But it is also rather mechanical and in some ways it asks more questions than it answers. The reason for this claim is the question of how a judge can ensure that parties are truly on an equal footing. How rapacious must the judge be in attempting to save costs? When dealing with cases proportionately[18] the differences between cases will mean that a starting reference point will be tricky to come by. Will dealing with a case quickly mean the judge runs the risk of not dealing with the case justly? And finally, what share of the courts resources will be 'appropriate'? The list of factors being considered by judges has been considered by the courts[19] but it is not the role of this chapter to go through a host of cases which explain the application of the over-riding objective. The cases, like the list, are perfunctory and would fail to enrich the reader's imagining of civil justice.

----

18   The concept of proportionality has been central to criminal justice since the writings of Beccaria (1767) in Beccaria, C., Bellamy, R. and Davies, R., 'On Crimes and Punishments' and Other Writings (Cambridge: Cambridge University Press, 1995) and for the sentencing exercise it has been critical since the Criminal Justice Act 1991.

19   If you are particularly interested in seeing how the courts have considered these criteria then see the discussion in Sime, S., A Practical Approach to Civil Procedure (Oxford: Oxford University Press, 2011) pp. 26–44 and see Chilton v. Surrey County Council [1999] LTL 24/6/99; Cala Homes (South) Ltd v. Chichester District Council (1999) The Times, 15 October 1999; Maltez v. Lewis [1999] The Times, 4 May 1999; McPhillemy v. Times Newspapers Ltd [1999] 3 All ER 775; Adan v. Securicor Custodial Services Ltd [2005] PIQR P79; Re Hoicrest Ltd [2000] 1 WLR 414; Re Osea Road Camp Sites Ltd [2005] 1 WLR 760; Stephenson (SBJ) Ltd v. Mandy [1999] The Times, 21 July 1999; Adoko v. Jemal [1999] The Times, 8 July 1999; King v. Telegraph Group Ltd [2005] 1 WLR 2282 and Hertsmere Primary Care Trust v. Administrators of Balasubramanium's Estate [2005] 3 All ER 274.

Instead we intend to imagine what judges should be considering when they are ensuring that a case is dealt with justly. What does 'just' mean for these purposes? To begin with, a judge will need to have a sense of what justice is in order to act justly. So what is justice? The idea of justice that is implicit in our arguments so far relates to ideas of the rule of law. However, as we have explained in the introduction, we need to link together formal ideas of justice with a wider appreciation of inequality. Indeed, Freeman[20] tells us that most contemporary scholarship about justice focuses on the idea of 'distributive justice'. That said the foundations of distributive justice can be traced back to the work of Aristotle who argued that goods should be distributed according to an individual's relative claim. This would necessitate a balancing act where competing claims would need to be resolved. Aristotle suggested that the factors affecting the decision to distribute would be desert, or moral virtue or needs.

Contemporary scholarship does have to resolve quite the same dilemmas but it is, according to Freeman,[21] the work of John Rawls which offers a modern take on justice and its concerns. For us, Rawls is important because he offers an approach to the wider issues of justice in a democracy. Rawls stresses that justice must be based on interlinked principles. An account of justice must ensure that within a democratic society there is the:

- Maximisation of liberty, subject only to such constraints as are essential for the protection of liberty itself.
- Equality for all, both in the basic liberties of social life and also in distribution of all other forms of social goods, subject only to the exception that inequalities may be permitted if they produce the greatest possible benefit for those least well off in a given scheme of inequality.
- 'Fair equality of opportunity' and the elimination of all inequalities of opportunity based on birth or wealth.

It is not the aim of this chapter to critically evaluate Rawls' claims.[22] Our purpose is to use this modern framework in an attempt to show what a civil justice system ought to be aiming to achieve if it is to confirm its commitment to dealing with cases 'justly'. An examination of key concerns for those using the civil justice system will be considered alongside Rawls' framework so as to demonstrate why civil justice is important and how fertile the system is for the student imagination.

ALTERNATIVE DISPUTE RESOLUTION[23]

One key aspect of civil justice which has grown in importance in the past 40 years is the emergence of alternative methods for dispute resolution. In civil, as in some

---

20   Freeman, M.D.A., *Lloyd's Introduction to Jurisprudence* (London: Sweet and Maxwell, 2001) p. 522.
21   Ibid., pp. 522–523.
22   See Freeman for a critical evaluation of Rawls' claims.
23   For a pithy consideration of ADR see Zander, M., *Cases and Materials on the English Legal System* (Cambridge: Cambridge University Press, 2007).

criminal,[24] cases the use of these alternatives has become central to resolving disputes before recourse to the courts is deemed necessary. So how does this maximise liberty in accordance with the first criterion for Rawls' *A Theory of Justice*? It would appear that by encouraging a wide range of methods for the resolution of disputes, alternative dispute resolution (ADR) ensures that a claimant and defendant are not necessarily straitjacketed into the court process which, for all its reforms, can still prove to be a costly, lengthy and unrewarding experience. Although judges will have a role to play in the case, the view is that with ADR the parties own the process. This again maximises their liberty.

ADR is the broad name for those methods of dispute resolution that do not involve recourse to the court system. These can include mediation, arbitration, conciliation and early neutral evaluation.[25] Mediation can be both formal and informal and it usually involves an experienced person (mediator) who acts as a facilitator to encourage discussion of the parties' concerns and tries to encourage the parties to reach a solution that they are all happy with. Conciliation is slightly different in that the conciliator is authorised to propose a solution for the parties to consider before they reach a conclusion. Neutral evaluation involves an expert considering all of the evidence and reaching a view which, although not binding, is used in an attempt for all parties to see what the effect could be if the case goes to court. It is hoped that both parties will resolve their disputes if they are confronted by this neutral position. Finally, arbitration tends to be used in commercial cases and a professional arbitrator will determine how the case will be resolved. This is a much more formal process than the previous forms of ADR and it is often seen as an expensive but useful alternative.[26]

Back in 1993 a special edition of the *Modern Law Review*[27] was devoted to ADR and a collection of papers were presented which, prior to the Woolf reforms, did consider how ADR was beginning to make its presence felt in the civil justice system. At this stage Cappelletti[28] considered how far the access to justice movement had succeeded throughout the world in promoting ADR as a real alternative to the adversarial process. Glasser[29] confirmed that the principle of orality, so central to the adversarial system, had been in decline within the civil process for some time. Lastly Lord Hoffmann, writing extrajudicially, commented on the civil process in general and confirmed that change had been afoot. Hoffmann's account is interesting in that as a working judge he does raise some concerns about the changes to the civil process. He also calls on research to be undertaken to consider the impact of these changes to the civil process. What is clear from this collection of papers is that ADR had by 1993

----

24   This is especially true in criminal cases involving young people where restorative justice and the use of mediation are central to the attempt to deal with youth offending at an early age. For a lively critique see Fionda, J., *Devils and Angels* (Oxford: Hart, 2005).

25   To understand the advantages and disadvantages of each method see Sime, S., *A Practical Approach to Civil Procedure* (Oxford: Oxford University Press, 2011) pp. 6–8.

26   Ibid, p. 8.

27   One of the leading law journals in the world.

28   Cappelletti, M. (1993) 'Alternative dispute resolution processes within the framework of the World Wide Access to Justice Movement', *Modern Law Review* 56(3): 282–296.

29   Glasser, C. (1993) 'Civil procedure and the lawyers – the adversary system and the decline of the orality principle', *Modern Law Review* 56(3): 307–324.

been seen as an addition to the process. In 2007, Zander[30] commented that while there has been a significant upsurge in the range of ADR available and the take up by litigants of that ADR, it is not yet directly part of the court system. This is in contrast to the US which has a much more integrated ADR system in place.

Two areas of civil justice which have attempted to embrace ADR, with varying success, have been the construction industry and matrimonial disputes within family law. From 1993 it has been common practice, and the subject of a practice direction,[31] for questions that asked about ADR to be inserted into the pre-trial checklist for both parties to respond to. By 1995 support for ADR came from the Lord Chief Justice and the question was whether solicitors thought ADR would assist in resolving the case. By 1996, judges were prepared, in construction cases, to adjourn the action to see if ADR could, if not already tried, be used to resolve the dispute. At this stage early neutral evaluation may be used as this is likely to be considered positively by both parties. In 1996 the Housing Grants, Construction and Regeneration Act was passed which meant that under s.108 every written construction contract must contain a provision for the right to refer disputes to adjudicators. Parties to the adjudication must provide the adjudicator with evidence of why the dispute has arisen, why the remedy sought is applicable to the party claiming it and all evidence supporting the claim. From this the adjudicator will reach a decision within 28 days. Reasons for the decision must be given and the decision can be court enforced.

Although sometimes proving an expensive option this does appear to be a successful form of ADR. This process, being quite formal, could be seen to be as restrictive as the court which would undermine the maximisation of liberty. That said, its commitment to early intervention does tend to ensure the court is not troubled with these matters which could prove costly. And to refer to adjudicators is a choice not a requirement! This maximises liberty.

Mediation, with its generally informal and flexible approach, was thought to be a useful tool in resolving matrimonial disputes. There was so much confidence in it as a form of ADR that it was announced in 1995 that a new no-fault divorce would be introduced which involved a formal role for mediation. This became law with Part II of the Family Law Act 1996. The thrust of the 1996 Act was to facilitate agreements about the future, to be reached by the parties themselves during a period of 'reflection and consideration', although the courts would retain jurisdiction to approve agreements made and to make orders where mediation had either failed or had been impossible to arrange. By facilitating mediation, parties were not being forced (as this would be counterproductive) but it was strongly recommended. The 'stick' or 'carrot', depending on your view, was that the Legal Aid Board would only approve funding for representation in divorce proceedings if mediation was unsuitable.

Pilot studies for this arrangement were undertaken by the Legal Aid Board. The results were very disappointing but in hindsight not surprising. It should have been apparent that in private matters people do not tend to seek legal redress unless forms

---

30   Zander, M., *Cases and Materials on the English Legal System* (Cambridge: Cambridge University Press, 2007) pp. 141–150.
31   [1994] 1 All ER 34.

of ADR such as mediation are unlikely to work. Mediation requires a willingness to engage in discussion. Often couples have passed the point at which a calm discussion is possible. A good mediator will know that if they list the key issues in the case they should be able to negotiate around the issues not the personalities of the parties involved. But the parties by the stage of mediation appear to have given up hope of reconciliation and are now more interested in ending their marriage and reaching agreement on all ancillary matters.[32]

Given the disappointing findings of these pilot studies it was decided in June 1999 by the then Lord Chancellor, Lord Irvine, that the implementation of Part II of the Family Law Act 1996 would be delayed. By 2000 it became clear that Part II and its attempt to insert a formal mediation process into divorce was not going to be implemented. Zander stated that the 'abandonment of the project was plainly a setback for the mediation bandwagon'.[33] It could be explained as a setback if the formal use of mediation in divorce proceedings was a necessary development. However if the non-formal use of mediation, where couples are prepared to engage in a calm discussion about the state of their marriage, can still be accessed then it may have been a blip rather than an end to this form of ADR.

Both the interim and final report from Lord Woolf did demonstrate a commitment to the increased use of ADR. This became an important part of the CPR where under rule 1.4(2)(e) it states that once proceedings have commenced then the court will be under a duty to further the overriding objective of dealing with cases justly by encouraging the parties to use ADR if the court believes this to be appropriate. If time is required for the ADR to take place then under rule 26.4 the parties will be given the opportunity to try to settle the case by ADR. The rules are not meant to be broken! If it appears that one of the parties has adopted an unnecessary approach to ADR then they can be deprived of costs.[34] There is no presumption in favour of ADR as each case has to turn on its facts but the very fact that sanctions can be imposed does show the court treads a fine line between promoting ADR where appropriate and realising that forcing people into mediation, for example, helps no one in the long run as it is unlikely to succeed.

Despite the failure of Part II of the Family Law Act 1996 we have proceeded on the basis that the maximisation of choice in terms of ADR versus court proceedings does in turn maximise liberty as per Rawls' first postulate. It is now important, in offering a balanced picture of the impact of ADR, to consider the realities of its use in the civil justice system. If you imagined that a formal commitment (via the CPR) to generally informal processes would maximise use then you will be disappointed. Professor Zander begins his forensic examination of how ADR is not nearly as popular as Woolf had hoped by suggesting:

CPR - Civil procedure rules

---

32   A particularly insightful account of the 1996 Act and the rise and fall of Part II is presented by Reece, H., *Divorcing Responsibly* (Oxford: Hart, 2003).

33   Zander, M., *Cases and Materials on the English Legal System* (Cambridge: Cambridge University Press, 2007) p. 143.

34   See *Leicester Circuits Ltd v. Coates Industries plc* [2003] EWCA Civ 333. For a list of what factors need to be considered for a refusal to be deemed unreasonable see *Halsey v. Milton Keynes General NHS Trust* [2004] 1 WLR 3002.

While the 'mood music' of the courts is certainly therefore in favour of ADR, it is making slow headway on the ground as a means of resolving civil disputes.[35]

This gloomy picture should be of no surprise as Zander has often taken issue with some of the claims made by Woolf and his supporters in terms of reforming the civil justice process. That said, the figures speak for themselves. He cites the failure of Part II of the Family Law Act 1996 as a clear example of low take-up but he also refers to research undertaken by Professor Dame Hazel Genn[36] in 1996, 2002 and 2007 to show that take-up of ADR has been modest but there was an increase post-*Dunnett* v. *Railtrack plc*[37] where the courts became more interested in imposing or refusing costs on those who had unreasonably refused to engage in ADR. Dame Hazel confirms that if you pressure people into mediation they are less likely to settle as they did not want to mediate in the first place but only agreed for fear of a costs sanction. By 2007 the settlement rate post-mediation was around 42 per cent. Professors Peysner and Seneviratne[38] also conducted research, post-Woolf, in 2003–2004 and confirmed that ADR has not become incorporated into the court process. They identify that lack of both facilities and resources have had an impact on the take-up of ADR.

There is also the question of how ADR fits into the post-Human Rights Act era? To what extent are contemporary rules on ADR consistent with the requirements of Article 6? Is there a possible tension between the 'compulsory or semi-compulsory' nature of ADR and the right of access to the court? This is not, of course, to criticize the emphasis on ADR in the CPR, as ADR provides an alternative to costly and resource intensive litigation. CPR 1.4 (1) and (2) instructs the court to 'encourage' the use of ADR as a means of actively managing cases. These rules interface with CPR Part 26 that allows the court, in circumstances where it considers it appropriate, to stay proceedings and facilitate recourse to mediation. Both parties must consent to ADR.

There does appear to be the inherent problem of 'facilitation' of mediation. Lord Woolf's judgment in *Anufreijeva* v. *Southwark LBC* indicates that '[un]less a party is prepared to use ADR, it could have no access to the courts at all'.[39] This problem has been dealt with by Practice Direction B, which gives a district judge the power to hear the 'objections' to mediation, but also to direct that mediation should proceed. There are similar provisions in the Admiralty and Commercial Court Guide, which allows a judge to 'invite' parties to consider mediation if s/he considers it suitable, and to order an adjournment to 'encourage' the parties to so do. A judge can also issue an ADR order which requires the parties to take 'serious steps' to resolve their dispute through the appointment of a neutral mediator. It seems therefore that the judiciary are keen to emphasise, in accordance with the commitment to Article 6, that a line has to be drawn between encouraging and compelling ADR.

---

35   Zander, M., *Cases and Materials on the English Legal System* (Cambridge: Cambridge University Press, 2007) p. 146.

36   *The Central London County Court Pilot Mediation Scheme*, LCD Research Series (1998), *Court-based ADR initiatives for non-family civil disputes: the Commercial Court and the Court of Appeal* (2005) and *Mediating Civil Disputes: Evaluating Court Referral and Voluntary Mediation* (2007).

37   [2002] 1 WLR 2434.

38   *The Management of Civil Cases: the Courts and the Post-Woolf Landscape*, DCA Research Report 9/2005.

39   [2003] EWCA Civ 1406.

In 2008 Professor Dame Hazel Genn in the Hamlyn Lectures delivered a powerful message of concern at the way in which ADR was being promoted. Entitled *Judging Civil Justice* Dame Hazel portrays a vivid picture of the current shortfalls of the civil justice process. The emphasis of her lectures begin with:

> I want to focus on the decline of civil justice, the degradation of civil court facilities and the diversion of civil cases to private dispute resolution, accompanied by an anti litigation/anti adjudication rhetoric that interprets these developments as socially positive.[40]

The lectures are damning. They present an alarming assessment of the current civil justice process. Dame Hazel is particularly concerned with ADR and its main product, mediation, where she argues that justice has little do with it. Suggesting that:

> The outcome of mediation is not about *just* settlement, it is *just about settlement*[41]

Mediation is not working as it should and this is, in part, because the system needs to be clear as to who needs mediation and what is it needed for? Dame Hazel is also concerned about the quality of mediation, which is at present unregulated and unaccountable. This commentary further serves to highlight how reform must be principled and suitably resourced if it is to function effectively.

The empirical evaluations of Professors Peysner and Seneviratne, when accompanied by Professor Zander's and Professor Genn's gloomy but accurate commentary, suggest that ADR may not be nearly as successful as it was once hoped it would be. This is a clear example of where promotion can all too often undermine impact as it is seen that using a 'stick' (cost implications) to cajole individuals into ADR will increase the take-up rate, but means that the settlement rate is lower. The Department of Justice and the Treasury may decide that the settlement rate is too low for them to bother to promote ADR any more. This would be a shame as the option to engage in ADR does, on final analysis, maximise liberty because there is a choice to engage or not. The cost sanctions may improve post-Jackson but even if they do not the limit to liberty is not as extensive as it might have been if ADR is not available. Even if settlement rates are low the choice should be there for those parties who want to use it. Glasser suggested that 'among these needs are surely those of developing alternatives to the traditional processes'.[42] These alternatives continue to evolve and in time they may either become more embedded in the civil justice process or they will, like the 1996 Family Law Act reforms, simply wither away. On the one hand ADR maximises liberty. Rawls' only restriction was where constraints were required to protect liberty itself. The end of ADR would do nothing to protect liberty.

---

40   Genn, H., *Judging Civil Justice* (Oxford: Oxford University Press, 2010), p. 4.
41   Ibid., p. 117.
42   Glasser, C. (1993) 'Civil procedure and the lawyers – the adversary system and the decline of the orality principle', *Modern Law Review* 56(3): 324.

DISTRIBUTION OF RESOURCES: MEDICINE AND LAND

Aristotle founded the Western tradition of 'distributive justice' in arguing for money or honour to be equally distributed.[43] This distribution was to be based on merit and the resources available were to be allocated proportionately. Rawls provides a contemporary view for a just distribution in his second postulate, which states:

> Equality for all, both in the basic liberties of social life and also in distribution of all other forms of social goods, subject only to the exception that inequalities may be permitted if they produce the greatest possible benefit for those least well off in a given scheme of inequality.

We will illustrate the importance of a civil justice system to individuals by concentrating on two areas which are currently controversial. So that 'the basic liberties of social life' can be enjoyed equally by the rich and poor we shall consider one example of where there is an attempt for 'social goods' to be distributed equally and another example where the civil justice system would appear to be left wanting. Both examples are witness to how far the court processes are prepared to involve themselves in the resolution of disputes.

ALLOCATION OF MEDICAL RESOURCES: EQUALITY OR LOTTERY?

It is clearly the case that the world's medical resources are distributed unevenly.[44] The developing countries often find themselves running Cinderella services which fail to preserve the lives of their citizens for want of sometimes basic equipment or drugs. This inadequate distribution of resources on the world stage comes at a time when there exist increasingly pandemic levels of infectious diseases.[45] This inequality does suggest that on a global level Rawls' notion of distributing goods equally is not apparent (Rawls himself realised that his theory of justice was limited to the nation state). But what happens nationally?

In the UK the National Health Service[46] was set up in 1948 under the National Health Service Act 1946. The aim of this legislation was to provide the whole population with free and comprehensive health care and to provide access to other social services, which in time would improve the nation's health and reduce the need for intervention. The funding for this service was to come from National Insurance contributions which would be taken at source from an individual's salary and this would

---

43   Aristotle, *The Nicomachean Ethics* (Oxford: Oxford University Press, 1925) pp. 741–748.
44   See Mason, J.K. and Laurie, G.T., *Mason and McCall Smith's Law and Medical Ethics* (Oxford: Oxford University Press, 2010) p. 377.
45   This is certainly the case for HIV and tuberculosis infection.
46   A lively account of the set-up of the NHS and its almost immediate problems can be found in Jackson, E., *Medical Law* (Oxford: Oxford University Press, 2010) p. 34.

ensure that, although not actually free, health care was free at the point of delivery. It was a masterful endeavor. The architect of this plan, Aneurin Bevan, was the first Secretary of State for Health and his vision had seen the development of a system which became the envy of the world. This really was a system, which attempted to distribute resources equally, regardless of birth or wealth.

As early as 1951 it became clear that the demand for health care resources was outstripping National Insurance contributions and so to assist in financing the system the introduction of nominal prescription charges took place so that those who could afford to would pay an additional sum for medicines. This continued to work in accordance with distribution on the basis of merit and individuals were not excluded on the grounds of inability to pay. Since 1948 successive governments have continued to prop up the NHS with increased subsidies from the gross national product of the nation and while funding has increased rapidly the perceived quality of service has decreased.

Emily Jackson[47] explains that blame cannot all be laid at the door of the architects of the NHS. She explains that a number of factors have contributed to the present problems with resource allocation in the NHS. Initially the NHS has been a success in that life expectancy is far higher than it was in the 1940s. This means that much of the NHS budget is spent on the elderly and as the elderly sector grows so the demands on limited resources grows. Second, advances in technology have meant that procedures available now are beyond the imagination of those who designed and implemented the NHS. This also means that patient expectations as to what is available and what can be done has increased. This is in line with a growing understanding by the population that the NHS is not a 'free' service for which they should be grateful. It is a (sometimes) free at the point of delivery service which extensive funding continues to prop up. This has meant that demand for the primary services of visiting a general practitioner is often viewed as an entitlement and people insist on visiting their doctor when their ailment may often heal by its own accord. Another problem with dwindling effective distribution of resources is that more than half the resources for the NHS are spent on salaries. Hard-working professional people work for the service and ought to be rewarded adequately but this has, in recent years, continued to place an enormous strain on already strained resources. Finally it is worth remembering that this scarcity of resources is not a national phenomenon. It is a global one. Everyone wants medical assistance to ensure they can live for as long as possible. This expectation is not without its casualties.

Given this expensive exercise in 'balancing the books' it has become clear that difficult decisions need to be made where the resources are inevitably finite. Although it is still the case that the provision of accident and emergency support continues without the cash registers ringing, it has become clear that non-emergency procedures are more difficult to obtain. Medicines that may improve a patient's quality of life may also be difficult to obtain and this is again due to difficult rationing decisions where limited budgets cannot be stretched any more. In this world the possibility of success in any given treatment becomes less and less attractive to those who decide on resource

47   Ibid., p. 34.

allocation and it is the probable, the safe, which becomes the norm. Since 1980 the housekeeping exercise of ensuring finances are spent wisely in the NHS fell to the district health authorities whose task it is to purchase health care services on behalf of the local population. While it was thought this would ensure that local needs would be prioritised, it has resulted in something of a lottery where a person's postcode can literally decide whether or not they are able to receive medical treatment.[48]

Historically the decision as to whether a particular procedure was undertaken or a particular drug was to be administered was a clinical one. While the local district health authorities will consult with clinicians over a particular procedure, they do now have a responsibility to consider the wider local demands on their budgets. In addition the National Institute for Health and Clinical Excellence (NICE)[49] was established in 1999 with a remit to promote clinical excellence in the health service so as to provide advice and guidance as to what treatments are best for patients on a national scale. It was hoped that NICE would deal with the problem of the emerging postcode lottery for treatment because it would adopt a national view to complement the local view taken by the health authorities. This attempt to redress any perceived inequalities in the distribution of resources was, in reality, difficult to see because as commentators have conceded the decisions of NICE have largely been 'unashamedly moulded to a large extent by their economic effect'.[50]

With the problem of limited resources identified and the local and national attempts to ensure that the distribution of 'social goods' is guaranteed it would appear that civil justice, in its widest sense, is ensured. It is therefore perhaps difficult to see how the civil justice system becomes involved in this process. The answer is that in recent years as difficult decisions have been made and litigants have been disappointed by those decisions reached so they have attempted to use the courts to seek redress. The most fertile avenue for litigation came from the statutory provision in the National Health Service Act 1977[51] which placed a duty on the Secretary of State for Health to produce a comprehensive health service. This duty could be exercised as he or she thinks necessary to meet all reasonable requirements but clearly if a litigant believes the duty has not been exercised to meet their reasonable requirements then litigation can follow.

The classic case concerned with resource allocation and an indication of whether the courts would be prepared to assist the disappointed litigant came in *Hincks*.[52] In this case, patients in an orthopaedic hospital claimed that they had waited too long for treatment because there was a shortage of facilities. They claimed that the health authority and the Secretary of State were in breach of their statutory duties. At first instance the court decided that as the duty to provide services was accompanied by the words 'to such an extent as he considers necessary' so this discretion could only be successfully challenged if the actions of the Secretary of State frustrated the Act or the

48   For a critical discussion of the different methods of resource allocation which are possible see Newdick, C., *Who Should We Treat?* (Oxford: Oxford University Press, 2005).

49   For a wider discussion see Mason, J.K. and Laurie, G., *Mason and McCall Smith's Law and Medical Ethics* (Oxford: Oxford University Press, 2010) p. 378.

50   Ibid., p. 384.

51   S.3 as amended in 2006.

52   *R. v. Secretary of State for Social Services, ex p Hincks* [1979] 123 Sol Jo 436.

policy. On appeal it was held that a failure on behalf of the Secretary of State could only exist if the Minister's[53] action was thoroughly unreasonable. This was a very difficult legal hurdle for the litigants to jump and they once again lost.

When budget holding became a more local issue in 1980[54] it appeared that the lines of accountability could be more clearly drawn and in the *Walker*[55] case the surgery of a baby had been postponed five times due to a lack of skilled nursing staff. This was a non-urgent operation and the court, supported on appeal, stated that the health authority could not be compelled to perform the operation as they had not acted unreasonably. This position was confirmed in a similar case, which this time was urgent,[56] and so the message appeared to be that the civil justice trial process could not be used for litigants to demand performance of a statutory duty unless the decision not to perform was unreasonable. There is of course also a political point to be made here. If the courts had opened the floodgates to permit those suffering delay because of a shortage of resources to either force action or receive redress for failure to act this would have deprived the NHS even further of valuable resources which it can ill-afford to spend.

In the case of *B*,[57] a highly publicised case, funding for what would be an ineffective treatment was refused by the health authority. At first instance the door was left ajar for effective redress when Laws LJ explained that the health authority would have to explain their decision for not providing the necessary resources in this case. He said:

> Where the question is whether the life of a ten year old child might be saved, by more than a slim chance, the responsible authority must in my judgement do more than toll the bell of tight resources. They must explain the priorities that have led them to decline to fund the treatment.[58]

This was overturned on appeal as it was felt unnecessary for health authorities to explain their decision. Bingham LJ in the Court of Appeal said that:

> Difficult and agonising judgements have to be made as to how a limited budget is best allocated to the maximum advantage of the maximum number of patients.[59]

There have been a number of well-publicised cases involving cancer treatments where a Primary Care Trust (PCT) has found their decision not to treat quashed via judicial review. In *R. (Rogers) v. Swindon NHS PCT* (2006)[60] a decision not to fund a yet to be licensed cancer drug called Herceptin was deemed unlawful. In *R. (Otley)* v.

---

53   For a discussion of the case see Mason, J.K. and Laurie, G., *Mason and McCall Smith's Law and Medical Ethics* (Oxford: Oxford University Press, 2010) p. 385.
54   By virtue of the Health Services Act 1980.
55   *R. v. Central Birmingham Health Authority, ex p Walker* [1987] 3 BMLR 32 CA.
56   *R. v. Central Birmingham Health Authority, ex p Collier* [1987] 6 January.
57   *R. v. Cambridge Area Health Authority, ex p B (A Minor)* [1995] 25 BMLR 5.
58   Ibid. p. 17.
59   *R. v. Cambridge Area Health Authority, ex p B (A Minor)* [1995] 1 WLR 898.
60   *R. (Rogers) v. Swindon NHS PCT* (2006) EWCA 392.

Barking and Dagenham NHS PCT (2007)[61] a decision not to fund an unapproved cancer drug was deemed irrational and unlawful. Finally in *R. (Ross) v. West Sussex Primary Care Trust* [2008][62] the PCT were again deemed to be acting unlawfully in denying Mr Ross access to a drug that was available in 'exceptional circumstances'. Herring (2011)[63] tells us that these cases all demonstrate the willingness of the court to look behind the decisions taken and to ensure that PCT's are accountable for the decisions taken and they closely follow their published guidelines.

These cases involved treatment for cancer, which would have literally been a matter of life or death. When there has been a seemingly less urgent need to fund treatment the position of the court is less clear. In *R. v. North West Lancashire Health Authority, ex parte A and Others*[64] the applicants suffered from gender identity dysphoria and it had long been thought that they should have had gender reassignment surgery. Although clinical need was apparent these cases were lowered in priority due to pressures on the authority's budget. The applicants wanted to seek treatment outside of the authority's area and they were refused. This refusal was quashed by the court and the Court of Appeal upheld this decision. In *AC v. Berkshire West PCT* (2010)[65] however it was decided that genital surgery was 'core' for these purposes but breast augmentation for the treatment of gender identity disorder was not.

These cases demonstrate the courts' increasing willingness to adjudicate effectively and sympathetically to the extent that the blanket raising of resources as a defence to a decision not to treat will likely be insufficient in future. This is certainly the view of Newdick.[66] King has argued[67] that the Human Rights Act 1998 has ensured that questions of resource allocation are no longer no-go areas for the courts. He says:

> A new fault line has emerged under the Human Rights Act 1998. The non-justiciability doctrine no longer applies. The notion of a judicial 'no-go area' of resource allocation has effectively been put to rest where human rights are at issue.[68]

At the same time as the courts have allowed litigants to use judicial review fruitfully so legislation has also made changes to the operation of the NHS. Firstly the NHS Act 2006 has changed the Secretary of State's duty for health care to be one of promotion rather than provision. This is a particularly watered down obligation. Secondly the NHS now has a Constitution. S.2 of The Health Act 2009 requires NHS bodies to have regard to the constitution and its key provisions. The Constitution is wide ranging but as well as accounting for patients' rights it also refers to their responsibilities. It is unclear what legal status the provisions of this Constitution may have. Key provisions concerning access to services, assessment of need and treatment abroad are all heavily watered down with phrases such as 'as considered necessary', 'in

---

61   *R. (Otley) v. Barking and Dagenham NHS PCT* (2007) EWHC 1927.
62   *R. (Ross) v. West Sussex Primary Care Trust* [2008] EWHC 2252.
63   Herring, J. *Medical Law* (Oxford: Oxford University Press, 2011) pp. 23–28.
64   [2000] 1 WLR 977.
65   *AC v. Berkshire West PCT* (2010) EWHC 1162.
66   Newdick, C., *Who Should We Treat?* (Oxford: Oxford University Press, 2005).
67   King, J. (2007) 'The justiciability of resource allocation', *Modern Law Review*, 70(2): 197.
68   Ibid., p. 224.

certain circumstances' and 'unreasonable grounds' and so the extent of their justiciability is currently unclear.

The distribution of the 'social good' of medicine in the UK is increasingly based on equality principles where everyone should be able to access the services required. This is in accordance with Rawls' postulate. The civil justice trial process is now being used to ensure that those disappointed by these rationing decisions can use the courts to hold those who have their hands on the purse strings and make these decisions accountable.

USE OF LAND BY MINORITIES: THE GYPSY'S LOT

While the availability of medicine is critical to a nation's health, so the availability of land is also crucial if only to ensure that people have somewhere to live. When examining resource allocation we were particularly concerned about equality of access for all. We now turn our attention to how the civil justice process has been used to attempt to secure occupational land rights for one of our minority groups: the Gypsy.

According to Barnett[69] Gypsies were first recorded in the sixteenth century.[70] She goes on to explain that the legal system's response to them has been one of 'expulsion, repression, discrimination and uneasy tolerance'.[71] Barnett importantly acknowledges the difficulty associated with accommodating minorities within any given domain. For the past 50 years the Gypsy has caused problems for the legislature and the courts not just in terms of deciding who is a Gypsy but also how and when their occupation of land will be legal.

The Highways Act 1959 offered no definition of 'Gypsy'. It merely decided they would be guilty of an offence if they encamped on a highway. The Caravan Sites Act 1968 decided that 'Gypsies' would be broad in definition as it is 'clear that "Gypsies" do not constitute a cohesive and separate group within our society'.[72] The courts decided that 'Gypsy' should be construed as meaning 'any person having a nomadic way of life'.[73] This wide definition saw the courts struggle when considering whether a sign saying 'no travellers' outside a public house was in contravention of the Race Relations Act 1976.[74] Although the court recognised that it was difficult to identify gypsies as a cohesive whole they did take the view that they were still a racial group who deserved protection under the 1976 Act.

The wide definition of 'Gypsy' proved to be a blessing and a curse because under s.16 Caravan Sites Act 1968 local authorities had to make site provision for all nomadic peoples. This would have included 'new age travellers' under the Race Relations Act 1976 but it did not apply to the Caravan Sites Act 1968 because the

---

69   Barnett, H. (1995) 'The end of the road for gypsies', *Anglo American Law Review* 24(2): 133.
70   In 1530 an Act was passed which prevented gypsies from entering the realm.
71   Barnett, H. (1995) 'The end of the road for gypsies', *Anglo American Law Review* 24(2): 133.
72   Ibid., p. 142.
73   *Mills v. Cooper* [1989] 2 WLR 17.
74   *The Commission for Racial Equality v. Dutton* [1989] 2 WLR 17.

latter legislation did not consider race but the currently adopted way of life as central to its decision making. A series of cases[75] saw the courts wrestle with local authority decisions to take possession of land which had been inhabited by Gypsies. Barnett argues that these decisions generally show that attempts to distinguish between 'real' Gypsies and others who appear to have been, on occasion, living a nomadic lifestyle ensured restrictive practices could be exercised and the statutory duty to provide accommodation was limited in its impact. The restrictions it appears did not end there. S.6 Caravan Sites Act 1968 imposed a duty for the local authority to provide adequate accommodation 'so far as may be necessary'. This 'get out' clause along with other statutory provisions[76] was supposed to effectively balance the needs of the gypsies and the concerns of the community. The legislation was meant to ensure that 'no Gypsy residing in or resorting to the area is without a suitable place to go',[77] but in reality there was a significant shortfall in lawful sites provided for gypsies.

The duty prescribed under the Caravan Sites Act 1968 was subsequently repealed by the Criminal Justice and Public Order Act 1994. Part V strengthens the provisions of the Public Order Act 1986 to enable a police officer to move on trespassers to land where they have been asked to leave. This is usually in response to violent or threatening behaviour on the part of the Gypsy or if there are six or more vehicles on the land. If the gypsies fail to abide by this provision then this can result in the vehicles being seized. The 1994 Act is committed to finding permanent housing for Gypsies. This is, according to Barnett, 'anathema'[78] to travelling Gypsies. In addition s.225 Housing Act 2004 requires Local Authorities to carry out an assessment of the 'needs' of Gypsies and Travellers in their district.

The language used by the government is punitive. Circular 1/94 confirms that Gypsies wanting a nomadic existence should be permitted one but this should only ever be within the confines of the law. This means that at the present time Gypsies are to be encouraged to purchase their own land for their sites so that the local authorities do not have to provide sites for them. The problem here is that just as occupation of the land can be controversial so obtaining the land with the correct planning provision can also be very difficult.

The difficulty of obtaining planning permission was raised in *South Bucks* v. *Porter*, *Wrexham CBC* v. *Berry* and *Chichester DC* v. *Keet and Searle*[79] where it was noted:

> In the case of Gypsies, the problem [i]s compounded by the features peculiar to them: their characteristic [nomadic] lifestyle debarred them from access to conventional sources of housing provision. Their attempts to obtain planning permission almost always met with failure: statistics quoted by the European Court . . . [found that] 90% of applications made by Gypsies had been refused whereas 80% of all applications had

---

75   *Greenwich London Borough Council* v. *Powell* [1959] 1 AC 995; *Horsham District Council* v. *Secretary of State for the Environment* (1989) *The Guardian*, October 31; *R.* v. *Shropshire County Council ex p Bungay* [1990] 23 HLR 195; *R.* v. *South Hams District Council ex p Gibb and others* [1993] EGCS 179.
76   S.6(2) and s.12 Caravan Sites Act 1968.
77   Department of the Environment Consultation Paper.
78   Barnett, H. (1995) 'The end of the road for gypsies', *Anglo American Law Review* 24(2): 161.
79   [2003] 2 WLR 1547.

been granted. But for many years the capacity of sites authorized for Gypsies had fallen far short of that needed.|

The tide did appear to be turning. [In *South Bucks* v. *Porter*, *Wrexham CBC* v. *Berry* and *Chichester DC* v. *Keet and Searle*[80] it became apparent that the court were prepared to consider an applicant's Article 8 rights under the European Convention on Human Rights when it comes to the granting of planning permission.[81] [Historically Lord Scarman had said that 'the courts should be reluctant to accommodate individual rights in a manner that compromised effective enforcement of planning policy'[82] At this time, post-*Porter*, it did not initially appear to be the path being taken by the courts.[83] By the time the Court of Appeal ruled on *Smith* v. *Buckland*[84] in 2007 it would appear that to respect Gypsy human rights, domestic law does now provide, when they reside on local authority sites, some procedural safeguards against conviction.]

[By 2011 however the issue of Gypsies and where they live was once again in the spotlight. The Dale Farm protests\ (of which the image at the front of this chapter is taken) [involved the residents of Dale Farm.] Home[85] explores the foundations of this dispute and the legal arguments around this forced eviction. [Dale Farm is a site of around 2.5 hectares in Essex, England. English Gypsies had lived in the area of Dale Farm for many years. In 1987 one of these families obtained planning permission on the site known as Oak Lane. When a scrap metal dealer lost his permission to continue his business he then sold his land to Gypsies. The sale took place and Irish Travellers arrived in 1998. They bought land on the legal site. Dale Farm itself was then purchased and subdivided into plots. A planning application was refused for there to be 20 plots on the site and in 2003 a public local inquiry was held. Residents were given two years to find alternative accommodation. No alternatives were found and the plots had now grown to 50. At one stage Dale Farm housed over 1,000 people. The local council attempted to secure compliance with the enforcement notices but were unsuccessful. By 2011 the council finally succeeded in clearing the site. Ninety families were cleared in September 2011 and by October the clearance was complete. These clearances were an unedifying spectacle. There were riot police sent in to clear Gypsies and Travellers from the site they had called home for at least 10 years. The Gypsies and Travellers had lost their battle at Dale Farm but polarised opinion at the same time. The Council of Europe's Commissioner for Human Rights produced a report identifying the struggles of Roma people to live in Europe.[86] The Prime Minister, David Cameron was rather less supportive:

80   [2003] 2 WLR 1547.
81   For a discussion of the case and its potential impact see Loveland, I. (2002) 'Injunctions, planning enforcement and human rights', *Modern Law Review* 65(6): 906.
82   Ibid., p. 922.
83   See *Leeds City Council (Respondents)* v. *Price and others (FC)* [2006] UKHL 10 where Article 8 rights were not upheld as the right of local authorities to evict was upheld.
84   EWCA Civ. 1318.
85   Home, R. (2012) 'Forced eviction and planning enforcement: the Dale Farm gypsies', *International Journal of Law in the Built Environment*, p. 178.
86   Hammarberg, O., *Human Rights of Roma and Travellers in Europe*, Council of Europe, Commissioner for Human Rights, Strasbourg, 2011.

What I would say is that it is a basic issue of fairness; everyone in this country has to obey the law including the law about planning permission and about building on green belt land. Where this has been done without permission it is an illegal development and those people should move away.]

Hansard HC vol 532 col 353

[Home[87] suggests that the events at Dale Farm saw a shift of opinion against Gypsy and Travellers with a view to enabling local authorities to be far more resolute in the upholding of their planning laws against this minority group. The result was a world wide spectacle of minorities being removed by riot police and the majority supporting this action.]

['The history of Gypsies is one characterized by intolerance'][88][It would appear that this intolerance has also involved reluctance by the community to allow this minority group to live the nomadic life they crave./When statute attempted to prescribe a duty on local authorities to find sites for the Gypsy caravans this legislation was littered with exceptions. Gypsies then became victims of the community's mistrust of 'new-age travellers' when the Criminal Justice and Public Order Act 1994 was passed] [The result was that the community decided that instead of providing sites for Gypsies the local authority would expect the Gypsy to purchase their own land for their own sites./ [This seemed equitable enough but it then emerged that when Gypsies applied for the requisite planning permission to turn the land they had purchased into a site they were on most occasions refused] Human rights jurisprudence may save the Gypsy in the long run but at the moment case law and the particularly violent events at Dale Farm suggest that success for the Gypsy, when either seeking legal redress or subject to legal sanction, is patchy. The distribution of this social good; that is, land, would appear to be sporadic for this minority and while Rawls always insisted 'that inequalities may be permitted if they produce the greatest possible benefit for those least well off in a given scheme of inequality' the Gypsy's lot appears to be a precarious one. They are clearly subject to inequalities when one considers the success rate of those planning applications and they are often the least well-off individuals in society.]

ACCESS TO JUSTICE: ACCESS TO LEGAL REPRESENTATION

[It can be argued that a central right of an individual who is trying to secure access to justice is that they should have access to legal representation. In criminal cases statute ensures[89] that an individual has the right to legal advice following arrest] [The civil justice system is rather less generous in its funding of litigation] [There are practical reasons for this. The effect of losing a civil case is not, generally, as catastrophic as

---

87   Home, R. (2012) 'Forced eviction and planning enforcement: the Dale Farm gypsies', *International Journal of Law in the Built Environment*, p. 187.

88   Barnett, H. (1994) 'A privileged position? Gypsies, land and planning law', *The Conveyancer* (Nov/Dec): 464.

89   S.58 Police and Criminal Evidence Act 1984.

losing a criminal case where the latter could involve the loss of liberty. There are a wide range of methods of funding litigation. For now it is important to return to the final postulate of Rawls where he states there should be:

> 'Fair equality of opportunity' and the elimination of all inequalities of opportunity based on birth or wealth.

Here for our purposes we shall be considering access to legal representation both for the commencement and defence of civil actions as an example of where the law should be providing 'fair equality of opportunity'. Clearly if you have sufficient resources then such actions will not be prohibited but it is also clear that there are hostages to the limitations that have been placed on the funding of litigation.

First, it is clear that solicitors are under a professional duty to ensure that their clients are clear as to the options available to them. Under the Solicitors' Costs Information and Client Care Code 1999 solicitors are to discuss with their clients how the funding of their case is to be managed. The traditional method of payment is termed a retainer and it involves the client paying an agreed hourly rate with the solicitor. There is also legal expenses insurance which some clients have access to. This is usually the case with home and motor insurance policies. There also exists after-the-event insurance where a premium is paid in an attempt to cover the possibility of paying the successful party's costs. Such premiums can be very expensive given the risk involved. If a solicitor wishes to take on a case where the client cannot afford the costs then the solicitor may choose only to recover costs if the claim is successful. Historically such agreements were thought to be illegal and unenforceable because they 'savour of champerty and maintenance'.[90] This is still the case and actions which come from those litigants who cannot afford these costs will normally be recommended for a conditional fee agreement (CFA). The CFA can be used where a solicitor agrees that a client will be liable for the costs if the action is successful. Here the usual costs and a success fee will be payable. This success fee cannot be more than 100 per cent of the solicitor's usual fees. Finally, limited funding may be available for civil cases from the Legal Services Commission (LSC). The criteria for allocation can be strict although if a case is particularly deserving it may receive full public funding. There are some actions which are excluded from assistance though. These include boundary disputes, the making of wills, conveyancing and, controversially, defamation and malicious falsehood.[91]

The result is that in the civil justice system an interesting dichotomy emerges. Given the restrictions in entitlement only those with modest means can secure financial assistance from the LSC. If a litigant is of significant means then they will be able to afford the litigation. That must mean there is a group in the middle who are neither entitled nor blessed with sufficient funds. The result for them is a distinct non-access

---

[90]   Ibid., pp. 50–51. 'Maintenance' refers to supporting litigation without just cause and 'champerty' is an advanced form of this on the basis the solicitor seeks to obtain a share in the proceeds of the suit.
[91]   Controversial because following *Steel v. UK* [2005] it was held that a denial of public funding for a libel case was in breach of the European Convention on Human Rights.

to justice. That said, Zander[92] points out that there is an interesting anomaly here. We spend much of our time being critical of the current limits to the funding of legal aid in the UK and yet an international comparison[93] suggests that we have the highest per capita expenditure on legal aid of any country in the world. This is for both criminal and civil litigation but perhaps, as with medical resources, there will never be enough!

Up until now we have been talking generally about those who wish to bring an action against someone. This is not to say the aforementioned methods of funding do not apply to individuals defending a case but the issue of financing a defence in a civil case is perhaps more critical in the civil justice process. If the civil justice system does not fund your defence to a claim against you then you could, if unsuccessful, find yourself financially ruined. The most celebrated case where this happened in the recent history of civil justice was in the now infamous 'McLibel' case.

Whilst the 'McLibel' case is considered later in this book its importance here is in the current restriction on funding for defending an action brought against someone. The facts of the 'McLibel' case are well known[94] but the key point was that in an aggressive leafleting exercise Helen Steel and Dave Morris, among others, broadly attacked the McDonald's Corporation for their working practices as well as holding them largely responsible for the growth in consumerism, corporatism and materialism. Their leaflet entitled 'McCancer, McDisease and McGreed' was distributed widely. While the protest by Steel and Morris may not have been wise it was certainly effective. It must have been as McDonald's reacted very strongly to the leaflet by infiltrating the group who were disseminating it and finally a libel action was brought against Steel and Morris. The trial took place in June 1994 and became the longest trial in British history, lasting for 313 days. The significance here was that because the case against Steel and Morris was for libel it was excluded from public funding. This was the case in 1994 due to the Legal Aid Act 1988 and it would also be true today under the Access to Justice Act 1998.[95]

This was a true battle between 'David and Goliath' as Steel and Morris had nothing to defend themselves with whereas McDonald's secured high levels of expensive legal representation. The result was never really in doubt given the inflammatory nature of the comments made by Steel and Morris. However, interestingly the claims made by them that McDonald's food was unhealthy by virtue of its fat and salt content were received with sympathy by the Court of Appeal. The result was that, according to Vick and Campbell:[96]

92   Zander, M., *Cases and Materials on the English Legal System* (Cambridge: Cambridge University Press, 2007) p. 629.

93   Flood, J. and White, A. (2006) 'What's wrong with legal aid? Lessons from outside the UK', *Civil Justice Quarterly* 25: 80–98.

94   Nicholson, M.A. (2000) 'McLibel: A case study in English Defamation Law', *Wisconsin International Law Journal* 18: 1–114.

95   Although they could obtain special authorisation from the Lord Chancellor.

96   Vick, D.W. and Campbell, K. (2001) 'Public protests, private lawsuits, and the market: the investor response to the McLibel case', *Journal of Law and Society* 28(2): 218.

Most observers concluded at the time of the High Court's verdict that McDonald's had won the battle but lost the war, suffering a tremendous public relations backlash in the United Kingdom, the United States and elsewhere.]

[Not only were Steel and Morris not able to fund a defence because public funding is not available for defamation proceedings, but the law of defamation was to all intents and purposes curtailing their right to trial under Article 6 and freedom of expression under Article 10 of the European Convention on Human Rights. Having been denied an appeal to the House of Lords, Steel and Morris decided to take their case to Strasbourg in an attempt to assert their Convention rights.]

[At Strasbourg the applicants were successful. The Court found that the denial of legal aid violated their rights under Article 6(1) as it contributed to an unacceptable inequality between Steel and Morris and McDonald's.[97] We have claimed elsewhere in this book that there is a general commitment to 'equality of arms' so this should not be of any great surprise. [The Court recognised that there was no absolute right to legal aid but each case should be assessed and it seems the Court were not in favour of the blanket ban on public funding for defamation cases given the 'David and Goliath' spectre that followed.] This seems a sensible criticism of the present rules, especially if individuals are having to defend themselves in cases where the stakes are so high. Scolnicov has argued that as a result of the decision of the European Court of Human Rights the law 'should be rectified . . . by change in the provision of legal aid'.[98] It seems that Rawls' final postulate with its emphasis on equality of opportunity is, in the context of legal aid for civil justice, left wanting. [Recent changes to the provision of legal aid under Legal Aid, Punishment of Offenders Act 2012 will do nothing to improve this situation.] For a fairer, more just distribution of resources, reform is required.

CONCLUSION

To imagine civil justice is to imagine a system which provides the opportunity for disputing parties to resolve their disagreements in an effective and expeditious way while remembering that a good decision is a just decision. An examination of the system in light of the Woolf reforms has at best shown that the present process is better than before[99] but not nearly as effective as it could be. At this stage we can ask whether Dickens would have been any happier assessing the process than he was some 170 years ago? Holdsworth[100] tells us: 'What Dickens is concerned with is the machinery by which the law was enforced, the men who enforced it, the conditions in

---

97   The Court also accepted Steel and Morris' Article 10 claim. They felt that free speech here was akin to that given to journalists and they had made a valuable contribution to the debate.

98   Scolnicov, A. (2005) 'Supersized speech – McLibel comes to Strasbourg', *Cambridge Law Journal* 311–314.

99   Although Zander, M., *Cases and Materials on the English Legal System* (Cambridge: Cambridge University Press, 2007) p. 140 argues that on balance the disadvantages outweigh the advantages. This view does not appear to be that of most.

100   Holdsworth, W., *Charles Dickens as a Legal Historian* (New Haven: Yale University Press, 1928), p. 7.

which these men lived, and the actual effects of the rules of law, substantive and adjective, upon the men and women of his day. Hence we get in his books that account of the human side of the rules of law and their working'. When we then consider some of the current issues in civil justice, when judged against Rawls' criteria and Dickens' vision we can see that uncertainty and injustice do remain for some who seek recourse to a system designated for just dispute resolution.

16

IMAGINING CRIMINAL JUSTICE

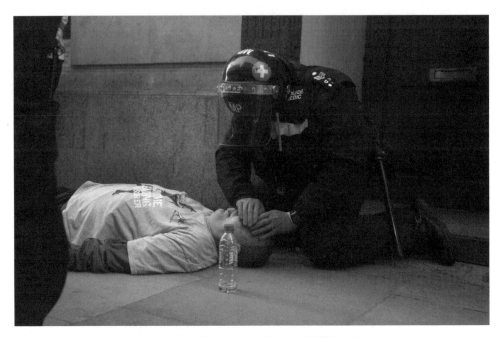

Figure 16.1 Ian Tomlinson. Photo by Oli Scarff/Getty Images, Copyright 2009 Getty Images

The criminal sanction is at once prime guarantor and prime threatener of human freedom. Used providently and humanely it is guarantor; used indiscriminately and coercively it is threatener. The tensions that inhere in the criminal sanction can never be wholly resolved in favour of guaranty and against threat. But we can begin to try.

Herbert Packer, 1968, *The Criminal Sanction*, 366

INTRODUCTION: A FORTUNE WITH HOSTAGES?

Traditional accounts of criminal justice tend to assume that there exists a system with a collection of seamless processes, which begins with intervention by the police and ends in the punishment of the offender. Such accounts are useful to demonstrate how the institutions of the criminal justice system work but their assumption that the process operates in an objective fashion with one common aim and a seamless 'system' is unfounded. Since Herbert Packer's famous account[1] of how the criminal justice process of any country can be evaluated by considering whether its processes are committed to crime control or due process far more attempts have been made to try and understand the underlying values within any criminal justice system. In England and Wales more recent academic commentary has concerned itself with the inherent conflicts and dilemmas that are faced by those who practise within the criminal justice process.[2] These practitioners face competing values every day in their work and an appreciation of this encourages any reader to recognise how each practitioner within each institution has its own 'working credos'[3]. With such variations within each institution it is difficult to see how there can be one seamless process with a single aim. The criminal justice system is best understood therefore as a series of processes with many of its practitioners working with different values. This could suggest chaos but in fact it is at worst organised chaos because the machinery of the institution tends to drive through a particular course and practitioners often work beneath the radar to preserve their own working credos.

Once we understand that the system is not objective, it is not uniform, we can begin to imagine what criminal justice is and how it impacts upon an individual. The majority of us lead law-abiding lives and so will not encounter the criminal justice system. However it is important that those who do encounter the system should be subject to practices, which are defensible and bear critical scrutiny. Some who encounter the process will be guilty but there will also be those who are innocent and yet have been a victim of a miscarriage of justice. These miscarriages may be due to discriminatory police practices, it may be due to incompetent scientific evidence or the over reliance of the court on expert testimony. In imagining criminal justice we need to remember that where mistakes are made by those who have power within the process so this power when abused, can have critical consequences. These people are often hostages to the fortune of the process.

But our story is not simply one of mistakes. It is also a story of the battle for power. It involves a consideration of the arguments that continue to rage within any evaluation of the criminal justice process. The battle between the judiciary and the executive/legislature over the sentencing of a convicted person and also over the effects of an expansionist policy towards the use of prison continue to haunt the processes we think about. In these battles we would expect to be supportive of the executive/legislature for their task is to represent us in our liberal democracy. However sometimes they too become blinkered in their search for fortune (in the form of re-election and the consolidation of political power) that they forget that there will be hostages to their decision making. Helena Kennedy warns us of how even the most benevolent of governments with significant influence over the legislature[4] can often forget how powerful they have become and the responsibility which accompanies that power. She says:

----

1   Packer, H. (1968) *The Limits of the Criminal Sanction* (Stanford: Stanford University Press)
2   See in particular Rutherford, A., *Criminal Justice and the Pursuit of Decency* (Oxford: Oxford University Press, 1993).
3   A term used by Rutherford, which is later considered in Liebling, A. with Arnold, H. *Prisons and their Moral Performance* (Oxford: Oxford University Press, 2004).
4   Given the fact that our government is almost exclusively selected from the legislature the term executive/legislature is used to demonstrate how powerful the executive in the UK is.

[Once people 'are the state' or have their hands on the levers of the state they have amnesia about the meaning of power and its potential to corrupt. They forget the basic lessons that safeguards and legal protections are there for the possible bad times which could confront us, when a government may be less hospitable, or when social pressures make law our only lifeline. They forget that good intentions are not enough, that scepticism about untrammelled power is essential. No state should be assumed benign, even the one you are governing.[5]]

[The state is therefore not benign. The criminal justice process with its institutions who advance their commitment to 'justice' are not benign either.] The process may be littered with good intentions but whilst those intentions manifest themselves into practices which marginalise or vilify the few then our imagining of criminal justice soon becomes the darkest of visions.

POLICING: LOCAL BATTLES AND NATIONAL WARS

We begin our tour through the criminal justice process by considering the current extent of police powers and some of the controversies, which have emerged during the exercising of those powers. Policing in England and Wales has long been considered to be by consent.[6] This means that those who are policed tacitly consent to allow the police to have powers, which enable the police to preserve public order, ensure citizen safety and to protect citizen property where appropriate. This has been the traditional view of policing since reforms to policing were carried out during the nineteenth century. Any evaluation of policing in the twenty-first century can see that although there continues to be widespread support for the police there has, over the last thirty years, been a decline in policing by consent. This is in part due to the fragmentation of local communities where those being policed have felt for some years that the powers possessed by the police have become too intrusive and are being used in a discriminatory way to target particular groups within that local community. Whilst these local battles continue to rage we have also seen developments on the world stage which has led to increased police powers which have been implemented in an attempt to respond to the perceived increased threat of terrorism.[7] These powers have also proved controversial in their use by police. The result being a general recognition that heightened policing may be a necessity but a far keener eye is now placed on how the police exercise these powers, both locally and nationally, to ensure they are used carefully.

5   Kennedy, H., *Legal Conundrums in our Brave New World* (London: Sweet and Maxwell, 2004) pp. 41–42.
6   For a fuller discussion of policing by consent and its efforts at attainment see Joyce, P., *Criminal Justice: An Introduction to Crime and the Criminal Justice System* (Abingdon: Routledge, 2012).
7   Although terrorist threats have been local to the UK since the 1970s due to the troubles in Northern Ireland the extent of these threats have been heightened since 9/11 and the death of 3,017 people.

Local battles

Policing has always been a local business. Historically policing was organised and controlled by the local community. This arrangement, with 43 police forces in England and Wales, has continued and so there is not currently a national police force. That said in recent years there have been legislative reforms, which have resulted in greater centralisation,[8] and indeed the home office suggests that they 'fund the police and have overall responsibility as overseer and coordinator'.[9] This localised arrangement means that each police force is permitted, within limits, to target its resources at particular priorities within that local community.[10] Local justice has always been preferred as a means of targeting local problems. There would be little point directing valuable resources towards preventing a particular type of crime, which is a concern for one police force but not for another. This division has been particularly noted when considering the priorities for policing in rural as opposed to urban areas. One 'local' problem[11] for the London Metropolitan Police Service since the publication of the MacPherson report[12] has been how to deal with the criticism by that report that the service is 'institutionally racist'. There have been a whole host of initiatives[13] to attempt to combat this charge. However on a local level there remains a crucial test of how racist,[14] or not, the police are. This is in their day to day exercising of their stop and search powers.

Historically, with the exception of Londoners,[15] there was no police power to stop and search. Any police officer stopping and attempting to search a citizen could be sued for assault. This changed in 1984 when s.1 of the Police and Criminal Evidence Act (PACE) permitted police, on reasonable suspicion, to stop and search any person or vehicle that the police believed were carrying stolen goods or other prohibited items. This search was limited to a search of bags or pockets. This new power was seen as a crucial development for the police as they had argued they could not prevent or detect crime if they were unable to detect people carrying stolen goods and prevent people who were in possession of items, which may be criminal[16] or facilitate a future crime.[17]

8   For an excellent discussion of the structure of the police and issues currently facing them see Uglow, S., *Criminal Justice* (London: Sweet and Maxwell, 2002) p. 35.

9   See http://www.homeoffice.gov.uk/police/about/?version=3 for an overview.

10   Although Uglow (2002) questions how far this is really possible given that the 'Home Office increasingly lays down a general strategy, which all forces are expected to follow' (p. 54). Suggesting the Home Office tacitly direct affairs!

11   Racial discrimination is a concern for all police but is more critical for those areas where there are large populations of people from ethnic minority groups.

12   *Report of the Inquiry into the Matters Arising from the Death of Stephen Lawrence* (Home Office, 1999).

13   The Home Office website cites an increase in defining racists incidents, more community and race relations training for police officers and the mobilisation of the Independent Police Complaints Commission to independently review police actions. There has also been an attempt to increase the recruitment of minority ethnic police officers. See http://www.homeoffice.gov.uk/police/about/?version=3 for more details.

14   This refers to a police officer being racist in their decision-making rather than an institution whose processes discriminate against those from an ethnic minority background.

15   S.66 Metropolitan Police Act 1839.

16   Possession of drugs which s.23 Misuse of Drugs Act 1971 did permit stop and search on the basis of reasonable suspicion.

17   Possession of a dangerous weapon.

All stop and searches have to be recorded and each police force publishes statistics on those searches in their annual reports. The controversy surrounding the exercising of these powers was considered in MacPherson and does remain an indicative measure of the working practices of police officers.

To stop and search an individual there must be 'reasonable suspicion' on the part of the police officer. It is the formation of this suspicion, based around societal stereotypes and discriminatory beliefs, which causes the most concern. As Sanders *et al.* have stated 'police working rules do not impact equally upon all sections of society'.[18] It has become apparent that black people in deprived socio-economic conditions are no more likely to commit crimes than their white counterparts[19] and yet they figure disproportionately in the stop and search figures. The same is true for those who are unemployed and low paid.[20] Back in 1970, prior to the supposed rigours of PACE, Lord Devlin stated that:

> suspicion arises at or near the starting point of an investigation of which obtaining of prima facie proof is the end . . . Prima facie proof consists of all admissible evidence. Suspicion can take into account matters that could not be put in evidence at all.
> *Shaaban Bin Hussien* v. *Chong Fook Kam* [1970] AC 942 at 948–949

This view tended to grant police officers *carte blanche* to stop who they wanted even though they had no statutory power to do so.[21] Things did not appear to improve after PACE. Sanders *et al.* explain that in 2007/8 a black person was over 7 times and an Asian person 2.2 times more likely to be subject to a stop and search by a police officer than a white person.[22] They explain that this could be due to both direct and indirect discrimination. The direct discrimination is where the stop and search is founded by police prejudice and reliance on negative stereotypes (all black people are drug users and all Asians, especially Muslims, are terrorists). Indirect discrimination occurs where the exercising of police powers is based on criteria, which inadvertently results in unjustified disparities. It could also be due to black people actually exhibiting behaviour, which is objectively more suspicious.[23] We should not assume that the reasons are easy to locate within the police officer on the street exercising reasonable suspicion. It could be a combination of all three. The problem is that even if black people are exhibiting behaviour which is objectively more suspicious which makes the stop and search 'legitimate' their over representation in the figures does suggest that direct and/or indirect discrimination is also apparent and this does need to be addressed.

To understand how the exercising of stop and search powers is racially discriminatory we need to understand what the motivation is of those who exercise these powers.

---

18   Sanders, A., Young, R. and Burton, M., *Criminal Justice* (Oxford: Oxford University Press, 2010) p. 177.
19   Ibid., p. 178.
20   We are concentrating on the issue of race here in light of the MacPherson report.
21   With the exception of Londoners. We have already stated there was no statutory power to stop and search and yet police officers often did in a particularly arbitrary way. An assault claim could follow against an officer but few individuals would know this and in accordance with 'policing by consent' would submit to a search if asked.
22   See Sanders, A., Young, R. and Burton M., *Criminal Justice* (Oxford: Oxford University Press, 2010) p. 98.
23   Sanders *et al.* describe this as 'legitimate factors' at p. 98.

Quinton *et al.*[24] conducted an extensive survey of those who stop and are searched and noted that one police officer said 'you see someone and you just know he's not right'. Decisions are often based on instinct and experience which by its nature can be negatively grounded in racial prejudice. This research confirmed that those who experienced stop and search often found the experience aggressive and intimidating. It also stated that: 'the legal requirement of reasonable suspicion is probably not fulfilled for some searches'.[25] This research confirms the 'suspicions' long held over the use of stop and search and it seems apposite that: 'the aggravation, distrust and resentment currently caused was seen to outweigh any perceived positive outcomes'.[26]

Quinton *et al.*'s research was conducted directly after the MacPherson report was published in an attempt to offer some guidelines on good practice for the use of stop and search powers. It now remains to ask if things have improved. Foster *et al.*[27] conducted research, which attempted to assess the impact of the MacPherson report on the London Metropolitan Police Service. They indicate that some improvements are apparent[28] but now police are very anxious about stopping and searching for fear of being accused of being racist. This does suggest that police have become more aware of how their behaviour can be construed as being racist. It is also understandable that police officers may find themselves working in a more defensive way. We should however have no problem with this. Police make decisions to stop and search and these decisions should be defensible. Police officers may well be anxious about exercising those powers but it is an anxiety, which should inform and assist in their decision to stop and search. It is not a decision which should be taken lightly. Foster *et al.* do offer a caveat to the many positives they identify by suggesting that: 'Forces – perhaps understandably – have tended to focus on those changes that were most obviously identifiable and achievable'.[29] Changes in attitude, especially in the canteen and on the streets, may prove rather more difficult to alter over such a short period of time.

On final analysis Bowling and Phillips[30] remain sceptical. They conclude that as of 2007 black people in England and Wales were now six times more likely to be stopped and searched based on their numbers in the general population. They argue that unlawful racial discrimination continues to operate and this can be supported in two ways. Firstly they argue that this does have an unfavourable impact on those people of African Caribbean origin because it continues to undermine any trust and confidence that these communities may have ever held for the police. Secondly they point to evidence which continues to show damning examples of police prejudice towards

---

24   Quinton, P., Bland, N. and Miller, J., *Police Stops, Decision-making and Practice* (London: Home Office: Police Research Series Paper 130, 2000).

25   Ibid., p. 5.

26   Quinton, P., Bland, N. and Miller, J., *Police Stops and Searches: Lessons from a programme of research* (Briefing Note) (London: Home Office, 2000), p. 5.

27   Foster, J., Newburn, T. and Souhami, A., *Assessing the Impact of the Stephen Lawrence Inquiry* (London: Home Office Research Study 294, 2005).

28   Racist language in the workplace appears to have been eliminated although those black and minority ethnic officers interviewed tended to suggest this was something of a cosmetic change.

29   Foster, J., Newburn, T. and Souhami, A., *Assessing the Impact of the Stephen Lawrence Inquiry* (London: Home Office Research Study 294, 2005) p. viii.

30   Bowling, B. and Phillips, C. (2007) 'Disproportionate and Discriminatory: Reviewing the Evidence on Police Stop and Search', *Modern Law Review* 70(6): 936–961.

ethnic minorities. One cited example is a film in 2003 which used covert recordings to show extreme racism was alive and well in a National Police Training Centre. Officers were shown demonstrating extreme racial hatred and even admiration for those who murdered Stephen Lawrence.[31] The film also showed a serving police officer boasting about his use of discretion in stopping and searching people from ethnic minority backgrounds. Their final rallying cry is for: 'the police power to detain a person on the street for the purpose of a search should be restricted to situations where a constable has a genuine and reasonable belief that wrongdoing is afoot, rather than the merest of suspicions'.[32] A sound sentiment but we are left imagining how 'genuine and reasonable belief' will be construed by a serving officer who appears to be confronted with, if not thoroughly adhering to, the stereotypical views of police officers about those from ethnic minority backgrounds.

In this discussion of the use and/or abuse of police power a recent case concerning the death of a 47-year-old civilian has highlighted once more the tragic fall out from excessive use of police power. Tomlinson was a newspaper vendor who was caught up in the protests that took place during London's G20 Summit in April 2009. He was not a protestor. He tragically died on that day. It was initially suggested by the Metropolitan Police Service that they had no contact with Tomlinson on that day and indeed protestors had attacked the police who were trying to offer him medical assistance. As the days went by it became clear that there was a substantial range of evidence to directly contradict the initial position taken by the Metropolitan Police Service. In spite of video footage which showed a Simon Harwood, a Territorial Support Group officer, striking and pushing Tomlinson just before he collapsed the Crown Prosecution Service in 2010 decided not to prosecute this officer at that time.[33] At the inquest in 2011 a verdict of unlawful killing was returned and the CPS reviewed the case and proceeded to prosecute Harwood for manslaughter. In July 2012 he was found not guilty. Harwood has since been dismissed from the Metropolitan Police Service for gross misconduct. The authors chose to mark this incident and so inserted an image of Tomlinson at the beginning of this chapter.

The fall out from the case has been understandably extensive and one particular method of containing public order known as 'kettling' has come under scrutiny once more. 'Kettling' is a widely used tactic to control large crowds or protestors. It involves the cordoning of an area where the police can determine the exit point. Police have regularly used this method and its use has now been deemed lawful by the ECtHR in *Austin and others v. the UK* (39692/09, 40713/09 and 41009/09). The applicants claimed that Article 5 of the Convention was violated when protestors and passers by were essentially held captive for up to 7 hours. The ECtHR did not believe that there

---

31   A teenager who was killed in 1993 in South East London for simply being black. His murder prompted the MacPherson review. It took 19 years for two of his killers to be brought to justice. Gary Dobson and David Norris were found guilty in January 2012 and a life sentence for both was passed.

32   Bowling, B. and Phillips, C. (2007) 'Disproportionate and Discriminatory: Reviewing the Evidence on Police Stop and Search', *Modern Law Review* 70(6): 961.

33   An effective analysis of the case and the media frenzy surrounding it can be found at Greer, C. and McLaughlin, E. (2012) 'THIS IS NOT JUSTICE', Ian Tomlinson, Institutional Failure and the Press Politics of Outrage', *British Journal of Criminology* 52: 274.

was a violation of the Article. The Court held that police had been required to contain a large crowd of people in difficult conditions and this was the 'least intrusive' means of protecting the public from violence.[34]

National wars

The 'war on terror' is now a common feature of crime prevention and detection in this country. Police appear to tour the streets in far greater numbers than they did prior to 9/11 and 7/7[35] and we as citizens are all encouraged to be far more vigilant as we go about our everyday lives. Such a response is understandable. But it is also responsible for instilling a growing sense of paranoia between citizens. Imagine the following: a young Asian man in his 20s gets on to a busy bus or a busy underground carriage in London with a large rucksack on his back. He is wearing traditional Muslim dress. Some people will not notice him, but others may flinch, even momentarily, and worry that the man is in fact a suicide bomber. That worry is borne out of experience for some people and media filled fear for others. Such paranoia is understandable if not legitimate. To combat this fear we expect our government and our police force to keep us safe. The methods for ensuring that safety may appear draconian but we often think they are necessary given the current climate. The 'war on terror' is the defence for policing which would otherwise appear indefensible. The reality is that for these policing methods to be truly defensible there is no greater time for them to be defended than in times of fear for national security. As John Wadham has commented: 'Draconian anti-terrorist laws . . . have a far greater impact on human rights than they ever will on crime'.[36]

Since the 'war on terror' began after 9/11 the law enforcement agencies have been granted ever more extensive powers to attempt to counter terrorism. The head of the Anti-Terrorist Branch of the Metropolitan Police said: 'public safety demands earlier intervention'.[37] Earlier intervention required greater stop and search powers than were already in existence. Moeckli[38] charts the increase in police powers. The Terrorism Act 2000 had already created a power for police officers to carry out blanket stop and searches. The Anti-Terrorism Crime and Security Act 2001 introduced new powers of the Treasury to freeze terrorist funds and control orders on terrorist suspects can be imposed under the Terrorism Act 2005. The Terrorism Act 2006 gave police the power to detain terrorist suspects for up to 28 days and the Counter-Terrorism Act 2008 extended this limit to 42 days. The Terrorism Prevention and Investigation Measures Act 2011 abolished control orders and introduced a new regime, which is designed to protect the public from terrorism. Our interest here is once again to consider how far

---

34   http://www.humanrightseurope.org/2012/03/judges-reject-police-kettling-human-rights-appeal/

35   7/7 refers to the terrorist attacks, which took place in 2005 in London. 56 people died and over 700 were injured. It was the largest and deadliest terrorist attack on London in history.

36   *The Guardian*, 14 November 1999.

37   House of Commons Home Affairs Committee, *Fourth Report of Session 2005–6: Terrorism Detention Powers*, HC 910-I, 54.

38   Moeckli, D. (2007) 'Stop and Search Under the Terrorism Act 2000: A Comment on *R (Gillan)* v. *Commissioner of Police for the Metropolis*', *Modern Law Review* 70(4): 654.

these powers have impacted upon individual liberty. Just as the stop and search powers under PACE could be seen to be disproportionately aimed at Black citizens so the terrorist powers have been disproportionately applied to Asian citizens. Moeckli suggests that after 9/11 the searches of Asian persons rose by 302 per cent. Black and Asian people were more likely to be stopped under the provisions of the Terrorism Act 2000 than white people.

There is apparently inevitability to this rise. Hazel Blears, Home Office Minister at the time, stated that it 'inevitably means that some of our counter-terrorist powers will be disproportionately experienced by people in the Muslim community'.[39] The Chief Constable of the British Transport Police at that time was even blunter when he said: 'We should not waste time searching old white ladies. It is going to be disproportionate. It is going to be young men, not exclusively, but it may be disproportionate when it comes to ethnic groups'.[40] Moeckli suggests that this strategy is tantamount to ethnic profiling and when exploring the judgments in the *Gillan*[41] case he explores how this form of profiling can be compatible within the European Convention on Human Rights, which under Article 14 prohibits discrimination. Lord Scott in *Gillan* comments that the stop and search powers under Terrorism Act 2000 may 'require some degree of stereotyping in the selection of the persons to be stopped and searched and arguably therefore, some degree of discrimination'. He felt this would be validated by existing legislation which permits discrimination on the grounds of race[42] if this is for the purpose of safeguarding national security. This in itself is, to Moeckli, difficult to defend. Targeting terrorists is the purpose of the Terrorism Act 2000 not persons of Asian appearance who may, just may, be involved in terrorist activity. This is difficult to defend in the context of Article 14, which can be mobilised when the Article 8 right to privacy has been infringed. Moeckli[43] is also more concerned on a practical level with the use of Asian appearance as a factor, which defends this discriminate form of stop and search. He points out that only half of those who are Asian are Muslim and so the criteria are too broad. Many who are stopped will not be Muslim and, secondly, the overwhelming majority of those who are Muslim have nothing to do with terrorism. These broad criteria serve once again to alienate the ethnic minority communities and give police the power to interfere with people's lives. The justification is that these people are of a particular ethnic origin and the current threat means that this interference is inevitable. Inevitable for some though not for all.

Terrorist attacks are tragic. They often involve an indiscriminate taking of civilian life and represent a breakdown in the democratic process, which is there to ensure that dissatisfied citizens can voice their concerns about national and international developments, which affect them either directly or indirectly. Increased powers of policing may be necessary to contain the threat of terror and to ensure national security is

---

39   Hazel Blears quoted in House of Commons Home Affairs Committee, *Sixth Report of Session 2004–5: Terrorism and Community Relations*, HC 165-I, 46.
40   Dodd, V., 'Asian Men Targeted in Stop and Search', *The Guardian*, 17 August 2005.
41   *R (Gillan)* v. *Commissioner of Police for the Metropolis* [2006] 2 AC 307.
42   See Race Relations (Amendment) Act 2000.
43   Moeckli, D. (2007) 'Stop and Search Under the Terrorism Act 2000: A Comment on *R (Gillan)* v. *Commissioner of Police for the Metropolis*', *Modern Law Review* 70(4): 667.

maintained. However these powers should not be used at any cost. One tragic reminder of the need to defend decisions taken in times of heightened security is the death of Jean Charles de Menezes. Jean Charles, 27, was a Brazilian National who had been living in London since 2002. On 22 July 2005 he was shot dead by Metropolitan Police armed officers. The armed officers shot him eight times. Following his death it transpired that the police had been following Jean Charles believing that he fitted the description of a terrorist suspect who had been foiled the previous day in their attempt to blow up a London Underground train. Mystery surrounds the identity of the armed officers who shot him. This was a tragic case of mistaken identity.[44] Alarming too was the response of the police to the incident. Initially it was claimed that Jean Charles had been wearing bulky clothes in the height of summer, he had jumped over the ticket barrier, which added to the officers suspicions and had not responded when challenged before he was shot. The Independent Police Complaints Commission later confirmed that none of this was true. It would appear that eyewitnesses and police fabricated these details in an attempt to provide some 'justification' for the incident. Public reaction appeared mixed.[45] Some appeared to recognise that the police had made a split-second decision and it was tragic. It appeared to some that it was collateral damage in the 'war on terror'. Three weeks earlier 52 people had died, excluding 4 suicide bombers, in the 7/7 attacks and it was understandable that the police should be vigilant and tragedies happen. Others were far more critical believing this to be a further example of police brutality. What does appear evident is that the exercising of police powers needs to be based on more accurate intelligence if such incidents are to be avoided. Jean Charles was Brazilian and mistook for a naturalised British Citizen who was originally from Ethiopia. One man was South American, the other of African descent. Ethnic profiling in this instance had tragic consequences. As Moeckli[46] speculates: 'One wonders whether the shooting of Jean Charles de Menezes . . . was not a tragic consequence of the over reliance on stereotypical characteristics such as ethnic appearance in anti terrorism operations'. The lesson is clear. When police powers are increased for the protection of citizens from terrorist attack they need to be employed even more carefully to ensure that citizens do not become as vulnerable to the police as they do to the terrorist attack. Lucia Zedner explains it best when she concludes:

> The London bombings were a stark reminder both of the threat posed by terrorist acts to fundamental rights and the importance of security measures in protecting them. Yet, when the pursuit of security is permitted to proceed at such a speed and with such sway as to trample basic liberties, it runs counter to the very purpose of securing liberty. One of the ironies of pursuing security is that whilst claiming to protect liberty from one source – terrorism, it diminishes the protection of liberty from another – the state.[47]

---

44   Although it is not suggested that it would have been fine for Hussain Osman, the suspected terrorist who the officers mistook de Menezes to be, to have been shot dead, unless he demonstrated an immediate threat to public safety.

45   BBC News, 'Is police anti-terror policy justified?', 26 July 2005.

46   Moeckli, D. (2007) 'Stop and Search Under the Terrorism Act 2000: A Comment on *R (Gillan)* v. *Commissioner of Police for the Metropolis*', *Modern Law Review* 70(4): 667.

47   Zedner, L. (2005) 'Securing Liberty in the Face of Terror: Reflections from Criminal Justice', *Journal of Law and Society* 32(4), December 2005.

POWERS OF ARREST AND HUMAN RIGHTS

Is there, then, a principled way that we could approach policing? To what extent are the common law principles and rules that ensure that police powers are limited and used in an accountable way? What is the relationship between the common law and human rights law when it comes to police powers? These are the questions that animate our discussion in the following section of the chapter. Our focus is on powers of arrest because this defines the point at which the citizens liberty is suspended and they enter the criminal justice process.

The common law has always understood that arrest serves a valid function in the apprehension of criminals or those suspected of being criminals. However, it is a power that can be easily abused. The common law has therefore attempted to safeguard individual liberty, or 'the sense of freedom from arbitrary detention'. Indeed, the protection of 'personal freedom' is fundamental to the libertarian conscience of the common law that Lord Bingham described as 'dating back to Chapter 39 of Magna Carta 1215'.[48] Liberty is given specific form in the writ of habeas corpus, the right to damages for false imprisonment and the narrow interpretation of any exceptions to the 'most basic guarantee of individual freedom'.[49] While it is true to say that the common law provides remedies for unlawful arrest, we need to look critically at the constitution of arrest in both common law, and the Police and Criminal Evidence Act (PACE) 1984. The critical issue is: does the common law achieve a balance between crime control and due process? We will examine this question by considering the 'threshold' for a valid arrest. This is a fundamental concern, as the test itself must ensure that powers of arrest are not easy to abuse, whilst acknowledging the practical issues that face a police officer making an arrest.

As argued earlier in *Shaaban bin Hussien* v. *Chong Fook Kam*,[50] Lord Devlin pointed out that the threshold condition or the 'test of reasonable suspicion . . . has existed in the common law for many years'. *In Dumbell* v. *Roberts*,[51] Scott J explained that reasonable grounds for 'suspicion of guilt' are a 'safeguard' designed for the 'protection of the public'. However, as he also argued, the 'requirement is very limited' and falls far short of the evidence required for conviction. Moreover, suspicion can be based on matters that are not 'admissible evidence'.[52] The problem is precisely this 'malleability'[53] of the standard required for arrest. One would have thought that if the common law were so committed to the protection of civil liberties, it would have required a far more exacting threshold. In order to investigate these issues, we need to look in more detail at the contemporary law defining arrest.

Powers of arrest without warrant are now primarily defined by statute. However, as has been pointed out, PACE preserves[54] the 'ancient' power of the citizen's arrest,

---

48   A. v. *Home Secretary* [2004] UKHL 56; [2005] HRLR 1.
49   *Austin* v. *Metropolitan Police Commissioner* [2005] HRLR 20, para 37.
50   *Shaaban bin Hussien* v. *Chong Fook Kam* [1970] AC 942, at 948.
51   *Dumbell* v. *Roberts* [1944] 1 All ER 326, at 329.
52   Supra, at 329.
53   Feldman, D., *Civil Liberties and Human Rights in England and Wales* [Oxford: OUP, 2002] p. 332.
54   PACE at 24(4) and (5).

and this informs the way in which arrest powers are described by the Act.[55] The most important section is 24(4). An individual can make an arrest if there are reasonable grounds for suspecting that an arrestable offence is in the process of being committed or when an arrestable offence has been committed. The powers of arrest given to police officers are more extensive. A police officer can arrest on reasonable grounds of suspicion that an arrestable offence has been committed. In other words, an officer is effectively protected from a civil action if he makes an arrest and an offence has not been committed.[56] A constable also has a preventative power of arrest[57] that is not available to a private citizen.[58]

PACE preserves the fundamental common law safeguard on arrest: the threshold of reasonable suspicion. But how do the courts understand this key term? The requirement of 'reasonable suspicion' is based on the information available to the arresting officer at the time that s/he makes the arrest.[59] The court has determined that this issue must be assessed at the time of arrest and not from the perspective of hindsight.[60] It is also necessary to acknowledge that an arrest may be based on a 'spur of the moment' decision.[61] So, critical questions relate to what the officer knew or had in mind when he or she made the arrest. But how are we to understand the concept of reasonable suspicion? One of the central authorities is *Castorina v. Chief Constable of Surrey*.[62] The trial judge defined 'reasonable cause'[63] as an 'honest belief founded upon reasonable suspicion leading an ordinary cautious man to the conclusion that the person arrested was guilty of the offence'. This argument was based on the authority of *Dumbell v. Roberts* that applied to arrests the principle that 'everyone is innocent until proven guilty'. The Court of Appeal disagreed, asserting that the proposed test was too severe and should be objective. The trial judge's reference to 'honest belief' was misleading, as it raised questions of subjective belief.

Thus, it would appear that reasonable cause does not mean that an ordinary cautious man would conclude that the person was guilty of the offence; it would be enough to suspect that he was guilty. *Castorina* was further elaborated in *Holgate-Mohammed v. Duke*.[64] The House of Lords determined that: 'where a police officer reasonably suspects an individual of having committed an arrestable offence, he may arrest that person with a view to questioning her at the police station'.[65] This decision can only be judicially reviewed if the constable acted improperly by taking something irrelevant into account.

---

55   Robertson, G., *Freedom, the Individual and the Law* [London: Penguin, 1993] p. 10.
56   PACE 24(6).
57   PACE 24(7).
58   The only exception is the power to make an arrest when an imminent breach of the peace is anticipated. A citizen (as well as a constable) may then make a preventative arrest.
59   See *Redmond-Bate* v. *DPP* [1999] Crim LR, 998. This principle is elaborated by a later case: *Clarke* v. *DPP* [14 November 1997, unreported]. It must be made clear to the court what the officer had in mind when he or she made the arrest. See Bailey, S. Harris D. and Ormerod, D. *Civil Liberties* (London: Butterworths, 2001) p. 281.
60   *Redmond Bate* v. *DPP*, 163 JP 789 DC.
61   *G.* v. *Chief Superintendent of Police*, Stroud, 86 Cr.App. R.92 DC.
62   *Castorina* v. *Chief Constable of Surrey* [1988] 138 NLJ 180, CA.
63   Under 2(4) of the Criminal Law Act 1967, now 24(6) PACE.
64   *Holgate-Mohammed* v. *Duke* [1984] 1 All ER 1054.
65   Ibid.

Commentators have pointed out that this case law errs too far on the side of crime control. The law also allows the space for the investigation of crime to be based on 'hunches'. An arrest is made to provide reasons for either confirming or denying a police officer's 'feeling' that an individual has committed an offence. The courts have shown themselves unwilling to question those decisions that arresting officers have made. Moreover, s.25 of PACE created arrest powers for non-arrestable offences. The fact that the courts have been careful to construe this power narrowly indicates that there may be due process constraints over these additional police powers. However, it would be wrong to suggest that the courts have always taken this approach to arrest powers.

While in some cases the courts are attempting to control power of arrest, in others they have been less interventionist. For instance, the police make extensive use of common law breach of the peace powers – both to make arrests and to take steps short of arrest. In *Chief Constable of Cleveland Police* v. *McGrogan*,[66] powers of arrest for breach of the peace were construed narrowly but in *Austin*,[67] the court was less willing to examine the use of breach of peace powers.[68] As these powers are useful in policing public order situations, it is likely that the court does not want to interfere unduly with operational decisions, although it will censure more extreme abuses.

We can observe a similar pattern in relation to the court's consideration of the safeguards on the power of arrest. At common law, it was necessary for the person making the arrest to make it clear to the person under arrest by either physical means or through clear oral communication that s/he had been arrested.[69] PACE supplements the common law with further requirements. An arrest under PACE has to meet with the formalities contained in s.28(1). Section 28 states that the arrest is not lawful until the person arrested is told of the reason for arrest, and this must be done as soon as is practicable after the arrest. Moreover, the person arrested must be informed of the ground of the arrest under s.28(3). In s.28(3) an arrest is not lawful unless the arrestee is informed of the ground for arrest: *Christie* v. *Leachinsky*[70] gives the reason:

> a person is *prima facie* entitled to personal freedom [and] should know why for the time being his personal freedom is being interfered with . . . No one, I think, would approve of a situation in which when the person arrested asked for the reason, the policeman replied: 'that has nothing to do with you: come along with me . . .'. And there are practical considerations . . . if the charge . . . is then and there made known to him, he has the opportunity of giving an explanation of any misunderstanding or of

---

66   *Chief Constable of Cleveland Police* v. *McGrogan* [2002] 1 FLR 707, CA (Civ. Div.).
67   *Austin* v. *Metropolitan Police Commissioner* [2005] HRLR 20, para 37.
68   A related issue is the extent to which the courts are willing to question the arrest power of private security guards. Given the privatisation of policing, this matter should be given more attention than it presently receives.
69   In terms of the common law definition of arrest, the element of compulsion is also essential. The arresting officer must, therefore, indicate that the suspect is under arrest either physically or orally. The problem in relation to indicating arrest by oral means alone is that it may not indicate the required compulsion. See *Alderson* v. *Booth* [1969] 2QB 216. Note: the requirements under s.28 are strictly separate from this necessity to indicate that the detainee is under compulsion.
70   *Christie* v. *Leachinsky* [1947] AC 573.

calling attention to the other persons for whom he may have been mistaken, with the result that further inquiries may save him from the consequences of false accusation . . .[71]

This statement suggests that the courts take the requirements of s.28 with great seriousness. The words spoken on arrest are important as they specify the reason for the arrest and thus give the detained person the factual basis for any legal challenge. If there were no requirement to give reasons or the courts allowed a valid arrest to be constituted by vague and imprecise reasons, the law would not effectively prevent the arbitrary use of power. Viscount Simonds' words in *Wilson v. Chief Constable of Lancashire Constabulary*[72] are an instructive guide to the court's attitude. An arresting officer is not entitled to 'keep to himself' the grounds of arrest or give an untrue ground. Indeed, failure to inform the detained person of the correct grounds for arrest constituted false imprisonment. However, at the same time, the requirement to give reasons for arrest cannot hinder the practical task of making an arrest. The words used by the arresting officer need not be technically correct[73] – it is a matter of 'substance . . . and turns on the elementary proposition that . . . a person is . . . entitled to his freedom and is only required to submit to restraints on his freedom if he knows in substance the reason why it is claimed that this restraint should be imposed'.[74]

ARTICLE 5

To what extent is the common law consistent with European human rights?

Article 5 is an essential element of human rights, as it is concerned with limiting the power of the state, and preserving the liberty of the individual. In *Kurt v. Turkey*,[75] the ECtHR stressed that:

'the fundamental importance of the guarantees contained in Article 5 for securing the right of individuals in a democracy to be free from arbitrary detention at the hands of

---

71   Ibid.

72   *Wilson v. Chief Constable of Lancashire Constabulary, Daily Telegraph*, 5 December 2000, CA (Civ Div), pp. 587–88.

73   In *Lewis v. The Chief Constable* [1991] 1 All ER 206, CA, the plaintiffs were told of the fact of the arrest but the police delayed telling them the grounds. The court stated that an arrest arose as a question of fact from the deprivation of a person's liberty: as it was a continuing act, what had started as an unlawful arrest could *become* a lawful arrest; in other words an arrest becomes lawful once a ground is given. *DPP v. Hawkins* [1988] 1 WLR 1166 is authority for the fact that if it is not practicable for reasons to be given at the time of the arrest, the arrest is lawful and remains so until such time as reasons should be given. The arrest does not need to be confirmed by words such as 'I arrest you'; a statement of the fact of the arrest is sufficient. Zander (The Police and Criminal Evidence Act 1984 (Sweet and Maxwell: London, 1995) pp. 74–75) suggests that the *Abbassey* [1990] 1 All ER 193 has the key statement of the law here. There was no need for the technical or precise language to be used, provided the person knew that they had been arrested. This was a question of fact to be answered by the jury. However, the reason given must be the correct reason. 'If an incorrect reason is given the arrest is unlawful' – see *DPP v. Edwards* [1993 DC]; see also *Mullady v. DPP* [1997 DC].

74   Ibid.

75   *Kurt v. Turkey* (1998) 27 EHRR 373, para 122.

the authorities' [and to the need to interpret narrowly any exception to] 'a most basic guarantee of individual freedom'.[76]

This statement of general principle appears broadly consistent with the values articulated by the common law courts. But, as always, the devil is in the detail. It is necessary to take a close look at Article 5. Article 5(1) states the fundamental guarantee: deprivation of liberty can only take place in the circumstances stated in the Article, and only 'in accordance with a procedure prescribed by law'. The remainder of 5(1) covers these circumstances. They range from the requirement that detention should be 'after conviction by a competent court' through to arrest for non-compliance with a court order, to detention of various classes of persons. This basic summary gives some sense of the range of the Article. As we need to focus on what it tells us about arrest, we are not concerned with the challenges to mandatory life sentences, the confinement of the mentally ill or the concept of the 'supervision of minors' that emerge in Article 5 jurisprudence. Although this approach does limit our understanding of the Article, it does allow us to focus on the paradigmatic instance of the suspension of a person's liberty.

So far as this first paragraph of the Article is concerned, our focus is on 5(1)(c), which states that detention is lawful to the extent that it is based on 'reasonable suspicion' and 'effected for the purpose of bringing [an individual] . . . before the competent legal authority'. How is reasonable suspicion defined?

The ECtHR has held that 'the "reasonableness" of the suspicion on which an arrest must be based forms an essential part of the safeguard against arbitrary arrest and detention'. Article 5(1)(c) requires that some facts exist which 'would satisfy an objective observer that the person concerned may have committed the offence', although the court pointed out that reasonableness depends on the facts of the case.[77] A fair proportion of the cases brought against the UK in relation to this point concern anti-terrorism legislation in Northern Ireland. Anti-terrorism legislation tends to allow arrest to take place on the basis of information that, for reasons of security, can be withheld from the person arrested or even from the court. The jurisprudence of the Convention attempts to balance a tension between competing values. It recognises that non-disclosure is justifiable but that the concept of reasonableness should not be exploited by the state and its agencies. Thus, the state is under a duty under Convention law to reveal at least some information that justifies detention.[78]

What is the nature of this information? The test is not too stringent. Information used to justify an arrest does not have to be of the quality to justify charges against the detainee. It can be linked to an arrest, the purpose of which is to question the detainee about the suspicion that might have arisen that made the arrest necessary in the first place.[79] In O'Hara,[80] for instance, the applicant was arrested on suspicion of murder.

---

76   Ibid.
77   *Fox, Campbell and Hartley* v. *United Kingdom*, judgment of 30 August 1990, Series A no. 182, p. 16, § 32.
78   Ibid., pp. 16–18.
79   *Brogan and Others* v. *United Kingdom*, judgment of 29 November 1988, Series A no. 145-B, p. 29, § 53, and *Murray* v. *United Kingdom*, judgment of 28 October 1994, Series A no. 300-A, p. 27, § 55.
80   *O'Hara* v. *United Kingdom*, judgment of 16 October 2001.

He was held and questioned for over six days – but remained silent. The ECtHR did not find a breach of Article 5(1)(c), partly because the applicant had not raised this issue in the domestic courts. On the facts, it was thus legitimate to rely on the evidence of informers to justify the detention. Brogan[81] is largely consistent with this position. It was possible to rely on evidence that could not be produced in court and, to the extent that it was not possible to show that the investigations were motivated by bad faith, the detention of those suspected of terrorist offences was justifiable.

We will look in detail at *Murray* v. *UK*[82] to determine what is at stake in these terrorism cases. Murray had been arrested under section 14 of the Northern Ireland (Emergency Provisions) Act 1978 on suspicion of being involved with the procurement of arms for a terrorist organisation, the Irish Republican Army [IRA]. Before the ECtHR, Murray argued that the arresting officer did not have the 'requisite suspicion' to justify the arrest. The ECtHR began its judgment by referring to the political context of the case, noting that: 'due account will be taken of the special nature of terrorist crime, the threat it poses to democratic society and the exigencies of dealing with it'.[83] The question for the ECtHR was whether this was sufficient, given that Article 5(1) laid down a standard of 'reasonable suspicion'.

In *Fox*, the ECtHR had held that reasonable suspicion 'presupposed' facts that would 'satisfy an objective observer that the person concerned may have committed the offence'.[84] Importantly, though, reasonableness required that all relevant circumstances be taken into account. This, of course, meant that the specific concern with the investigation of terrorist offences had to be taken seriously. The 'risk of loss of life and human suffering' requires that the authorities 'act with utmost urgency'. It may be necessary to act on information from sensitive or secret sources. This may be 'reliable' but cannot be made known to the suspect for fear of compromising the sources. Therefore the standard that justifies 'reasonable suspicion' cannot be the same as that used in 'conventional crime', but this does not mean that 'reasonableness' can be 'stretched' to the point that the 'safeguards' put in place by Article 5 are negated.[85] By the same token, the Article cannot be interpreted to 'put disproportionate difficulties in the way of the police authorities of the Contracting States in taking effective measures to counter organised terrorism'. This element of appreciation means that the ECtHR will not require the compromise of secret sources of information in anti-terrorism cases. However, a government must 'furnish at least some facts or information capable of satisfying the Court that the arrested person was reasonably suspected of having committed the alleged offence'. This requirement becomes all the more serious when the relevant law sets the threshold of 'honest suspicion', which is not as exacting a standard as 'reasonable suspicion'.[86]

Following *Brogan*,[87] the threshold of suspicion falls below that required to bring charges. The length of detention also had to be taken into account. On the facts of the

....

81   *Brogan* v. *UK*, supra n. 79.
82   *Murray* v. *UK*, supra n. 79.
83   Ibid., para 47.
84   Supra n. 77.
85   Supra n. 77, para 51.
86   Ibid.
87   Brogan, supra n. 79.

instant case, it had been limited to the maximum period allowed by the Act, which was four hours. The ECtHR's balancing act required them to acknowledge the need to combat terrorism but not to restrict the protection offered by Article 5. The following paragraph is worth citing in full:

> As to the present case, the terrorist campaign in Northern Ireland, the carnage it has caused over the years and the active engagement of the Provisional IRA in that campaign are established beyond doubt. The Court also accepts that the power of arrest granted to the Army by section 14 of the 1978 Act represented a bona fide attempt by a democratically elected parliament to deal with terrorist crime under the rule of law.[88]

From this position, the ECtHR can approach the government's argument much more positively than the Commission and attach a much greater level of credibility to the evidence against Murray. Applying *Fox*, though, the government still had to show that there were some facts to justify honest suspicion. The ECtHR considered that the fact that Murray had associated with her brothers in the United States, that they were prosecuted for attempting to procure arms, and that the evidence showed that they were liasing with someone 'trustworthy' in Northern Ireland, was sufficient to pass the minimum standard.

We now turn from our consideration of the legitimate grounds of detention to the second paragraph of the Article that specifies the safeguards that should operate. These have been described as 'elementary' and an 'integral' part of Article 5. They state that a person who has been arrested should know that this is the case.[89] The Article requires that: 'any person arrested must be told, in simple, non-technical language that he can understand, the essential legal and factual grounds for his arrest'. The ECtHR has also held that whilst it is necessary that the detained person must be promptly[90] told that s/he is under arrest, the arresting officer need not tell the detainee everything. Indeed, there appears to be something of a sliding scale. If a person is arrested on the basis that s/he has committed a crime, it is not necessary to specify the precise crime or charge nor even to use a particular form of language.[91] Extradition proceedings require a lower threshold still,[92] although the court has insisted on the requirements of promptness.[93]

The fundamental reason for this safeguard is to allow the detained person to 'challenge' the lawfulness of his/her arrest. This links together paragraphs (2) and (4) of Article 5. An equally important requirement is that the person is told 'promptly'. There is a great deal of case law on this element of the Article, and we can only review the fundamental reason for this particular requirement. The court's explanation of the

---

88   Ibid.
89   Fox, supra n. 77, para 40.
90   Promptness must be assessed on the facts of the case: See *Bordovskiy* v. *Russia*, no. 49491/99, 8 February 2005.
91   *X.* v. *Germany*, no. 8098/77, Commission decision of 13 December 1978, DR 16, p. 111.
92   *K.* v. *Belgium*, no. 10819/84, Commission decision of 5 July 1984, DR 38, p. 230.
93   See *Saadi* v. *UK Judgment*, 11 July 2006.

promptness requirement links it to protection against the 'arbitrary' powers of the state.[94] The court has further elaborated this point:

> Judicial control of interferences by the executive . . . is implied by the rule of law [this is] one of the fundamental principles of a democratic society . . . [and] is expressly referred to in the Preamble to the Convention[.][95]

Section 5(3) is seen to flow directly from the fundamental values of the Convention. The ECtHR's approach acknowledges the fine line that exists between legitimate policing and the use of power unchecked by law. This means that the ECtHR has been keen to interpret the word 'prompt' in a very narrow way, as it means a person has been kept from appearance before a judge or a court through an executive act that has not been justified before an independent body. Even in anti-terrorism cases, the ECtHR has insisted on the need to bring a detainee before a court.

If we link 5(3) with 5(4), we can understand more precisely the schema of the Article. Article 5(4) specifies that a detained person must have the opportunity to challenge the 'lawfulness of his detention'. This, in turn, requires further guarantees:

> Certain procedural and substantive guarantees ensure that judicial control: the judge (or other officer) before whom the accused is 'brought promptly' must be seen to be independent of the executive and of the parties to the proceedings; that judge, having heard the accused himself, must examine all the facts arguing for and against the existence of a genuine requirement of public interest justifying, with due regard to the presumption of innocence, a departure from the rule of respect for the accused's liberty, and that judge must have the power to order an accused's release.[96]

It would be far too limited to think in terms of the writ of habeus corpus to address these issues from the perspective of the common law.[97] Indeed, the ECtHR has suggested that in certain circumstances, the writ is itself too limited.[98]

....

94   The *Bozano* judgment of 18 December 1986, p. 23, para 54.
95   Ibid.
96   *S.B.C. v. United Kingdom* Judgment of 19 June 2001.
97   From the perspective of the common law, this gives us the terms in which to judge the operation of habeus corpus. Habeus corpus has been described as 'the fundamental instrument for safeguarding individual freedom against arbitrary and lawless state action' *Harris v. Nelson*, 394 US 286, 290–92 (1969). Although it is perhaps less important in English law today, it retains a hold on the legal imagination. It is the means by which the court can make a determination of the legality of a person's detention. As well as questioning the technical reasons for an arrest and detention, habeus corpus can also be used to enquire into the abuse of power. See *R v. Governor of Brixton Prison, ex parte Sarno* [1916] 2 King's Bench Reports 742 and *R v. Brixton Prison (Governor), ex parte Soblen* [1962] 3 All England Law Reports 641.
98   *X. v. United Kingdom*, Judgment of 5 November 1981, para 57: 'Although X. had access to a court which ruled that his detention was "lawful" in terms of English law, this cannot of itself be decisive as to whether there was a sufficient review of "lawfulness" for the purposes of Article 5 par. 4'. However, at para 58, the court commented: '58. Notwithstanding the limited nature of the review . . . the remedy of habeas corpus can on occasions constitute an effective check against arbitrariness in this sphere. It may be regarded as adequate, for the purposes of Article 5 para 4, for emergency measures for the detention of persons on the ground of unsoundness of mind. The authority empowered to order emergency detention of this kind must, in the nature of things, enjoy a wide discretion, and this inevitably means that the role of the courts will be reduced'.

What should we make of the terrorism context of these cases? Although the nature of terrorist offences means they must be policed in a different way to non-terrorist criminal activity, has the ECtHR taken into account the rights of the suspects in any meaningful way? Arguably, in some cases, and Murray would be a good example, there are factors that suggest the court has ceded too much to executive power.

Taking into account Murray's health, the fact that she had four young children and no previous criminal record, meant that there should be 'a higher level of suspicion', a 'stricter standard' put in place. Moreover, the interrogation was characterised by 'vague questions' and Murray could not therefore have come to the conclusion that she had been 'informed of the reasons for her arrest'.[99] According to the interpretation of the Article in Fox, the basic safeguard of Article 5(2) was that 'any person arrested must be told, in simple, non-technical language that he can understand, the essential legal and factual grounds for his arrest, so as to be able, if he sees fit, to apply to a court to challenge its lawfulness in accordance with paragraph 4'. The facts in the instant case suggest that this 'basic standard' had been breached.[100]

COURTROOM: SCIENCE AS TRUTH, EXPERTS AS TRUTH TELLERS

One area within the criminal justice system, which has increased dramatically, is the reliance on science in the courtroom. Whilst the English legal system has a long history of consulting expert advice on scientific matters the growing developments in forensic science have meant that reliance on science is greater than ever before. This should be welcomed. As Roberts confirms:

> The increasing use of science in the modern criminal process should be welcomed as an overwhelmingly positive development. Forensic science is good for justice in the same way that all modern science improves on the knowledge and technology of the past. Aeroplanes are more effective conveyances than hot-air balloons, key-hole surgery is preferable to treatment with leeches, and rape is easier to prove with DNA evidence than without it.[101]

It is the growth of reliance on DNA evidence which is to be particularly welcomed. Historically the criminal trial used witness testimony and statements by the accused along with documents and real evidence to attempt to establish truth. Alongside lawyer submissions and judicial directions this was thought to make for a court system which although adversarial did ensure that the truth was established. The celebrated miscarriages of justice cases[102] from the 1970s have all demonstrated the limitations of these methods. DNA is more foolproof. DNA evidence however is not to be relied on

---

99   Supra n. 32, Murray, para 6.
100   Ibid., para 7.
101   Roberts, P., 'Science, Experts and Criminal Justice', in McConville, M. and Wilson, G., *The Handbook of Criminal Justice* (Oxford: Oxford University Press, 2002), p. 259.
102   See the *Guildford Four*, *Birmingham Six* and *Maguire Seven*.

without caution. Uglow[103] considers an example where a sample taken from a scene of a burglary led to a suspect who lived 200 miles away, suffered from Parkinson's disease, who could not drive and could barely dress himself. His blood sample had been taken during a previous arrest and the police refused to accept his alibi when he protested his innocence. A retest established that there had been a mistake but it demonstrated that once DNA evidence is found its mythical qualities of absolute truth tends to dissuade even the most compelling counter evidence. These mistakes are likely to be increased where the growth of the DNA database continues. This database was set up in 1995 and by 2006 it had over four million different DNA stored on it. The database records the DNA of all those who are arrested. Given that this is when they are arrested rather than charged the use of DNA in this way is controversial, least because of its potential invasion of privacy and given the concerns about over reliance on it as a type of evidence. It is more foolproof than witness testimony but reliance on it should not be at the expense of all other evidence, which can, on balance, be compelling.

The increased use of scientific evidence is generally supported. Back in 1993 following the unmasking of the celebrated miscarriages of justice cases it became apparent that techniques of interrogation by the police were flawed and Mike McConville proclaimed that we should have 'more detection, less interrogation'.[104] Given our discussion of the potential and actual abuse of police powers earlier in this chapter this may be a desirable development. However it should not be utilised without caution. Scientific evidence has to be presented in the courtroom within the context of the adversarial system and Walker has commented that 'the evidential value of expert testimony has been overestimated in a number of instances only for it later to emerge that the tests being used were inherently unreliable, that the scientists conducting them were inefficient or both'.[105] In the case of the *Maguire Seven* the prosecution case was heavily based around the fact that the defendants had knowingly handled nitroglycerine for an unlawful purpose. The charge required a positive trace on the body or clothing of the defendants and innocent contamination had to be discounted. The scientific evidence presented at trial was used to construct a narrative of bomb preparation. In fact Stockdale asserts that later tests showed the 'brittle nature of legal extrapolation from scientific fact'[106] and there were a number of explanations as to how these traces of nitroglycerine could have found their way onto the defendant's bodies. By the time a successful appeal was granted all but one of the defendants had served their prison sentences. One of the defendants, Giuseppe Conlan, father of Gerard Conlon who was one of the *Guildford Four*, died in prison in 1980. He would never know that his name had been cleared. The *Maguire Seven* case reminds us that it is not just the accumulation of scientific evidence that is important but also its presentation in the courtroom. To demand more scientific evidence as though it is a panacea to all the problems associated with other forms of evidence is to look 'for a

103   Uglow, S., *Criminal Justice* (London: Sweet and Maxwell, 2002) p. 168.
104   M. McConville, 'Wanted: More Detection, Less Interrogation', *The Times*, 2 March 1993.
105   Walker, C. 'Miscarriages of Justice in Principle and Practice', in Walker, C, and Starmer, K. (eds) *Miscarriages of Justice*, (Oxford: Blackwell, 1999) pp. 53–54.
106   Stockdale, R., 'Forensic Evidence', in Walker, C. and Starmer, K. (eds) *Miscarriages of Justice* (Oxford: Blackwell, 1999) p. 133.

chimera – forms of evidence which can be presented in court unsullied by fallible human processes'.[107]

As well as the type of evidence presented and the over reliance on evidence which happens to be scientific, the reliance on and deification of the 'expert' has also led to calls for increasing caution surrounding the use of expert testimony. Concerns surrounding the jury attempting to understand scientific evidence are not new. Stephen[108] back in 1860 said that:

> Few spectacles, it might be said, can be more absurd and incongruous than that of a jury composed of twelve persons who, without any previous scientific knowledge or training are suddenly called upon to adjudicate in controversies in which the most eminent scientific men flatly contradict each other's assertions.

What has become clear in recent years is that there has been greater reliance on expert evidence usually because of increased sophistication in the collection of scientific data. This in turn has led to a more extensive use of the expert who often presents their findings as the truth, unable to recognise alternative explanations. The three cases here concern the phenomenon of Sudden Infant Death Syndrome (SIDS). This is where death occurs and following an autopsy the apparent cause is still unknown. This immediately presents us with a problem. We do not why the child has died so we speculate. And although we refute 'suspicious circumstances' we need to find out why. We turn to an expert to assist and through its informed, specialist, all knowing expert we believe what we are told. Why would we doubt the expert?

Our story begins with the case of Sally Clark. She was convicted of murdering two of her babies in November 1999. The murders took place within 14 months of each other. At her trial the expert paediatrician, Professor Sir Roy Meadow said that the chance of two babies dying as a result of SIDS[109] was 1 in 73 million. He had famously stated that: 'one sudden infant death in a family is a tragedy, two is suspicious and three is murder unless proven otherwise'. This became known as Meadow's law.[110] During her appeal against conviction in 2001 the Court of Appeal recognised that Meadow's had reached his calculation incorrectly but the appeal was still disallowed. Soon after Clark's failed appeal Angela Cannings[111] was convicted of a double murder when she had lost three babies to SIDS although she was only convicted of murdering two of her three children. This time the statistic of Meadow appeared to hover over the trial like the ghost at the feast. Given the media coverage it was unlikely the jury had not learned of Meadow's erroneous calculation.[112] At this trial, in response to a suggestion that the prevalence of death to Angela Cannings' children could be attributed to a medical condition was refuted when he said:

---

107   Ibid., p. 150.
108   Stephen, J.F. 'On Trial by Jury: and the Evidence of Experts' (1860) *Two Papers Read before the Juridical Society*, 236.
109   Colloquially known as a 'cot death'.
110   See M. Taylor, 'Cot death expert to face investigation', *The Guardian*, December 19 2003.
111   For a lively discussion of the case see Ward, T. (2004) 'Experts, Juries and Witch-hunts: From Fitzjames Stephen to Angela Cannings', *Journal of Law and Society* 31(3), 2004.
112   See Nobles, R. and Schiff, D. (2004) 'A story of miscarriage: Law in the Media', *Journal of Law and Society* 31(2), for a discussion of the Sally Clark case and the media's presentation of that case.

Well, is it possible it is a condition that is not yet understood by doctors or described by them? and that must always be a possibility, but nevertheless as a doctor of children I am saying these features are those of smothering.[113]

The Court of Appeal noted in Cannings' appeal that:

Experts in many fields will acknowledge the possibility that later research may undermine the accepted wisdom of today. 'Never say never' is a phrase which we have heard in many different contexts from expert witnesses.[114]

It would seem however that this was a concession that Meadow was reluctant to acknowledge.

Soon after this case the second appeal of Sally Clark was heard and this time it was decided that Meadow's statistics were manifestly wrong and grossly misleading. Clark was freed having spent over three years in prison. Just before the successful appeal of Angela Cannings in 2003 another woman, Trupti Patel was charged with killing three of her babies. This time there was no conviction as Patel's grandmother appeared as a witness and explained that five of her twelve children had died within six weeks of birth. There was a genetic defect here which could account for the deaths. As could be commonly concluded multiple deaths made a genetic link just as likely as a case of serial murder.

As an expert, Professor Sir Roy Meadow had been raised up by the trial system. Deified as an expert who had explained how the death of Sally Clark's children could not have been anything but murder. However following these cases he was investigated and in December 2005 the General Medical Council (GMC) found him guilty of serious professional misconduct. Meadow appealed to the High Court in 2006 and was successful. The GMC then appealed to the Court of Appeal who upheld Meadow's appeal. He had been cleared of serious professional misconduct but would never act as an expert again. It would appear that Meadow had been too focussed on confirming his own suspicions without considering the alternative explanations for the SIDS. This was understandable in that he had long launched a crusade against those who wilfully injured their children. He was an early campaigner in the medical recognition of Munchausen Syndrome by proxy and it seems he became so focussed on the prosecution and conviction of those he thought were guilty that he forgot that he was an expert opinion not the only expert opinion. He had also miscalculated his statistics and this meant there could be an alternative explanation. He was likened to a Witchfinder General by Jenkins[115] who suggested that during Meadow's court appearances:

The courts of justice are the same as tried the Salem witches. They summon juries to pass public judgement on these wretched women, calling in aid a witch-finder general, the hawkish Professor Sir Roy Meadow . . . Sir Roy is said to possess the courtroom presence of Judge Danforth in Arthur Miller's Salem witches play, *The Crucible*. He can whip any jury into finding these women guilty.

113   As quoted in *R. v. Cannings* [2004] 1 All ER 725.
114   See *R. v. Cannings* [2004] 1 All ER 725.
115   S. Jenkins, 'Trupti Patel and the Rotten Courts of Salem', *The Times*, 13 June 2003.

The criminal justice system had asked a medical expert to offer an explanation as to how the deaths of these children had occurred. Professor Sir Roy Meadow offered such an explanation but that explanation was from someone who had forgotten to recognise the limits of his own opinion. He had offered a view but it appeared he delivered a verdict. Delivering a verdict in the adversarial trial is the task of the jury not the expert and Meadow ultimately paid the price for his folly. There is a tragic end to our story though. In March 2007 Sally Clark was found dead at her home, four years following her release from prison. Her death reminds us of the very real costs often borne by victims of miscarriages of justice and her case serves as a reminder of why 'expert' testimony too has its flaws.[116]

SENTENCING: ART OR SCIENCE?

Once an offender has been convicted they will be sentenced. There has long been a power struggle between the judiciary and the executive over who controls sentencing. Believing it to be an art the judiciary have argued that sentencing, to be just, has to be very carefully navigated to consider not only the offence committed but the offender themselves. As one judge explained:

> At the end of the day, the exercise of discretion in sentencing must remain in human hands. You cannot programme a computer to register the 'feel' of a case, or the impact that a defendant makes upon the sentencer.[117]

The executive on the other hand have argued for there to be far more consistency in application and this has meant the pursuit of statutory penalties for offences which limit the extent of judicial discretion. This has really been a battle for control over punishment because increasingly successive governments adopt an agenda of taking crime seriously and part of this agenda is the attempt to exert pressure on the judiciary to mete out harsher punishments. This is not to suggest that the judiciary have never administered harsh punishments but they have generally demonstrated a reluctance to lose their own discretion in favour of satisfying the executive's political aspirations of the day. This battle has seen a number of key twists and turns which we shall now explore.

Thomas[118] explains that in early English criminal law sentencing was a straight-forward matter. If a person committed a felony[119] then they would receive the death penalty. If a person committed a misdemeanour[120] they would be subject to an

116   See Taylor, N. and Wood, J., 'Victims of Miscarriages of Justice', in Walker, C. and K. Starmer (eds) *Miscarriages of Justice* (Oxford: Blackwell, 1999) p. 247.
117   Judge Cooke, 'The Practical Problems of the Sentencer', in Pennington, D. and Lloyd-Bostock, S. (eds) *The Psychology of Sentencing* (Oxford: Centre for Socio Legal Studies, 1987) p. 58.
118   Thomas, D., 'The Sentencing Process', in McConville, M. and Wilson, G., *The Oxford Handbook of Criminal Justice* (Oxford: Oxford University Press, 2002) p. 473.
119   This would now be an indictable offence.
120   This would now be a summary offence.

unlimited fine or an unlimited prison sentence. The law was harsh and unforgiving. Over a period of time the judiciary developed procedures which mitigated the harshness of the law. One such procedure was known as the 'benefit of clergy'. If a defendant was convicted of a felony they were sentenced to death. One way of avoiding this was if the defendant was a priest. Being a priest meant the defendant could be dealt with by the ecclesiastical court. There existed no formal records as to who was or was not a priest and so the only measure was the defendant's literacy. A defendant would be asked in court to read extracts from the bible to demonstrate their membership of the clergy. Although most defendants could not read many would learn extracts from the bible verbatim and recite them when prompted in the courtroom. This would result in the felon's release. This early circumvention of the common law demonstrated a common dilemma for judges and one they still face today. What right do they have to circumvent the existing law? Their answer: it is in the interests of justice to do so.

The 'benefit of clergy' dwindled in importance during the eighteenth century and it was then that the power for judges in sentencing was at its apogee. They could transport the offender if friends of the offenders could secure a royal pardon. The pivotal point for the Judge was where they either decided to sentence the offender to death or they granted a temporary reprieve for the offender to seek the royal pardon. The operation of this discretion was totally arbitrary and did according to Thomas result in 'a lottery of justice'.[121] Whilst the exercising of power in an arbitrary way is always frowned upon the key principle of establishing judicial discretion in the sentencing process is a key feature in the argument by the judiciary that sentencing is an art not a science.

By the nineteenth century sentencing was still very much in the hands of the judiciary but statutes were passed, prompted by the executive, to further restrict judicial discretion. Fixed penalties were enforced so that it was clear that if you were guilty of murder then the death penalty followed. Given that the death penalty[122] had been reduced in scope so that it only remained for the most serious of offences this meant there could be no further justification for the judiciary to depart from the existing legislative provisions. By the end of the nineteenth century consistency in sentencing was again seen as elusive and so by 1907 the Court of Criminal Appeal was established. This court was charged with ensuring that there was parity in sentencing. If a defendant believed their sentence was excessive then they could appeal to this appellate court that would have a sense of how similar cases were being dealt with across the country. It was also hoped that the spectre of appeal would encourage the judiciary to be more consistent in their decisions on sentencing. Just as the executive had attempted to curb excessive disparity in the awarding of sentences by the creation of the Court of Criminal Appeal, so the executive had also widened sentencing powers to include probation, which after 1907 was an alternative to custody.

By the time the Court of Criminal Appeal was renamed the Court of Appeal (Criminal Division) in 1964 it had become clear that the plea for consistency had not

---

121   Thomas, D., 'The Sentencing Process', in McConville, M. and Wilson, G., *The Oxford Handbook of Criminal Justice* (Oxford: Oxford University Press, 2002) p. 473.
122   Ibid., p. 474.

been overly successful. Few defendant's appealed against sentencing and there was a lack of systematic reporting and analysis of sentencing decisions. This was altered after 1964 thanks to the work of Lord Chief Justice Parker and the arrival of the Judicial Studies Board[123] but by 1991 there was still a feeling that the executive wanted to use sentencing as a tool by which they could demonstrate their commitment to tougher sentencing. In fact their statutory enshrinement of 'just desserts' in the Criminal Justice Act 1991 demonstrated a commitment to proportionality which the judiciary had arguably always worked towards anyway. Ordinal and cardinal proportionality[124] had always been used to ensure that similar cases received similar sentences taking into account any mitigation or aggravating factors. The 1991 Act also introduced the custody threshold under s.2(2)(a) where it was made clear to the judiciary when they should be sentencing a defendant to custody. This was largely ignored by the judiciary. Believing the custody threshold was a matter for 'recognising elephants' they did not believe a statutory provision could explain when custody should be used. The judges, with their experience, felt they knew when custody was appropriate. By the late 1990s the Court of Appeal had come to all but ignore the 1991 Act.

By 1996 there was a real concern that the executive had prompted the legislature to legislate far beyond what was reasonable and the judges felt their 'art' of sentencing was being reduced to a science as the executive began to legislate for mandatory sentencing.[125] Mandatory sentencing clips the judicial wings in that it prescribes what sentences must be awarded for what offences. The Crime (Sentences) Act 1997 saw offenders who were convicted for a second time of a violent or sex offence were to receive an automatic life sentence. Similarly if an offender was convicted of domestic burglary and already had two previous convictions for similar offences then they would receive a mandatory sentence of three years. This was popularly known as the 'three strikes and you are out rule'. These reforms had taken place during a period of penal populism where the Conservative Administration, desperate to show they were responding to perceived increases in crime had decided that sentences needed to be harsher. Lord Chief Justice Taylor was publicly very critical of these reforms feeling they were ill considered and symptomatic of an executive interference, which should be ceased immediately. Lord Donaldson was equally concerned that interference with the judicial power to sentence posed a threat to the individual citizen who was excessively punished because politicians had decided that an example needed to be set. Finally Lord Hailsham, a former Lord Chancellor, had argued that the legislation imposed upon the independence of the judiciary.[126] There was however a critical loophole in the 1997 legislation. The provisions for the second life sentence stated that the

---

123   The old training forum for judges to keep abreast of new developments. This is now called the Judicial College.

124   Cardinal proportionality is where offences are considered among themselves so a rape is considered against another rape. Ordinal proportionality is where different offences are considered against each other so for example a burglary is compared with a rape.

125   A very public battle emerged between the then Lord Chief Justice, Lord Taylor and the Home Secretary, Michael Howard. See Ashworth, A., *Sentencing and Criminal Justice* (Cambridge: Cambridge University Press, 2010) for more details.

126   This controversy is discussed further by Joyce, P. (2006) *Criminal Justice: An Introduction to Crime and the Criminal Justice System* (Devon: Willan, 2006) p. 254.

automatic life sentence should be imposed 'unless there were genuinely exceptional circumstances' which the court would have to justify. In 2000 the Court of Appeal effectively quashed this rule by arguing that as long as the defendant posed no substantial risk to the public the life sentence did not need to be passed. Again consistency and 'honesty in sentencing'[127] had been used to defend the passing of the Crime (Sentences) Act 1997 but the judiciary had seen an out with the 'exceptional circumstances' section and seized upon it to limit the impact of the legislation.

Further attempts have been made to promote consistency in sentencing. The Labour Government had been as keen as the Conservative Government had been to add to the list of mandatory punishments for offences committed.[128] They had however adopted a more conciliatory approach by establishing the Sentencing Advisory Panel (SAP) in 1998 whose task it was to stimulate sentencing guidelines. Given that the membership included senior judges it would appear a sense of co-operation was being fostered between all those involved and influencing the sentencing function. The Criminal Justice Act 2003 also established the Sentencing Guidelines Council (SGC) whose job it was to provide sentencers with comprehensive and practical guidance. Again membership was mixed but this time it was chaired by the Lord Chief Justice. The Coroners and Justice Act 2009 then established the Sentencing Council, which assumed the role of both the SAP and the SGC. Its task is to:

> . . . promote greater consistency in sentencing, whilst maintaining the independence of the judiciary.[129]

It seems that in this long battle to keep sentencing as an art rather than reducing it to a science a fine balance has been reached. The executive will now continue to allow the judiciary, with all their experience, to carry out the sentencing function as though it were an art but will ensure on some consistency which in turn will ensure it is marginally scientific in its approach. This balance is however subject to change. Recent legislative changes have sought to continue to exercise some control over the sentencing function and the impact of these changes have yet to be felt.[130] It is a clever judiciary that continues to find ways of retaining their power base just as they had done when they introduced the benefit of clergy some centuries before.[131]

As a coda to this discussion of the judiciary and sentencing it is interesting to note a development, which recognises why judges and not the executive should control

---

127   The mantra used by Michael Howard during the passing of the Crime (Sentences) Act 1997 to defend mandatory sentences.
128   See Crime and Disorder Act 1998 and Youth Justice and Criminal Evidence Act 1999.
129   See http://sentencingcouncil.judiciary.gov.uk/index.htm
130   See Legal Aid Sentencing and Punishment of Offenders Act 2012 which finally removes the controversial imprisonment for public protection which was introduced under the Criminal Justice Act 2003 and modified under the Criminal Justice and Immigration Act 2008. The full effects of this sentence can be found at http://www.prisonreformtrust.org.uk/uploads/documents/unjustdesertsfinal.pdf
131   Of course it could be argued that the judiciary have no right to circumvent the will of the people via their elected representatives. Andrew Ashworth argues that more consistency in sentencing is required and the judiciary should be required to be consistent. The author agrees but clearly legislative sledgehammers should not be used to trounce judicial discretion. Better judicial discretion is maintained and navigated through a path towards some relative consistency. The judiciary need to believe they are controlling sentencing as they believe is their function within the constitution.

sentencing. The example here is the historic power of the Home Secretary to fix and review the tariff of a prisoner serving a life sentence. The Court of Appeal has long issued guideline judgments which sets out the proper approach which is to be adopted by a judge in dealing with offences within a particular category. They are not meant to be prescriptive but they usually indicate a tariff or range in which judges, according to the severity of the offence, will impose a sentence. Things have always been slightly different for those convicted of murder. This offence carries a mandatory sentence of life imprisonment. Since 1948 the Home Secretary has had the power to decide when a life prisoner can be released from prison. Under s.29 Crime (Sentences) Act 1997 the Home Secretary was able to decide on the date of release for the lifer on licence and they were also able to set the tariff, which saw them decide how long a lifer should remain in prison. As this power was a judicial one the separation of powers had once again long been compromised.

By 2004 this position had become untenable. A series of cases before the courts, since the Human Rights Act 1998 had come into force, had been critical of the Home Secretary's power and the decision in the *Anderson* case[132] finally withdrew the power. A panel of seven Law Lords decided that the court rather than the Home Secretary should decide on the tariff for a lifer convicted of murder. The Home Secretary's sentencing role was seen to be in direct conflict with the Article 6 right to a fair trial as per the European Convention on Human Rights. The right to a fair trial demands an independent and impartial tribunal. The Home Secretary was not independent or impartial. The reaction by the executive was one of anger and the then Home Secretary, David Blunkett, insisted he would circumvent the rule with legislation. The result was s.269 Criminal Justice Act 2003 which requires the court to have regard to certain principles when setting a tariff for a convicted murderer. Once again however there is a loophole in the legislation in the form of the term 'normally' which allows the court to consider all factors and continue to be creative in their exercising of their function.

The change in the law that took place cannot be underestimated. Firstly the reiteration by the judiciary of the role of the judge in sentencing is important at a time when questions continue to be asked as to the legitimacy of that role. Lord Steyn views the separation of power to be critical here and has argued that:

> . . . nowhere outside Britain, even in democracies with the weakest forms of separation of powers, is the independence of the judiciary potentially compromised in the eyes of citizens by relegating the status of the highest court to the position of subordinate part of the legislature. And nowhere outside Britain is the independence of the judiciary potentially compromised in the eyes of the citizen by permitting a serving politician to sit as a judge at any level . . .[133]

In addition an infamous case in English legal history demonstrates the potential injustice that can befall a defendant under that power which was once held by the Home Secretary. Myra Hindley was convicted of killing four children with her partner Ian Brady in 1966. At trial the judge imposed a life sentence, as was mandatory, along

132   R. v. *Secretary of State for the Home Department ex p Anderson* [2002] UKHL 46.
133   Lord Steyn, 'The Case for a Supreme Court' (2002) *Law Quarterly Review* 382: 383.

with a tariff of 25 years. This meant she was due for parole in 1990. By 1985 the then Home Secretary, Leon Brittan decided, under his political power to extend tariffs that she would in fact serve 30 years before being eligible for parole. By 1990, following revelations of further involvement in other murders, the then Home Secretary, David Waddington imposed a whole life tariff on Hindley insisting she would never leave prison. Hindley was not notified of this decision until 1994 when the prison service were told they were obliged to inform all prisoners of when they could expect to be considered for parole. Between 1997 and 2000 Hindley appealed against the whole life tariff a total of three times each time arguing that she was a reformed prisoner who no longer posed a risk to the public. All three appeals were rejected. Hindley died in prison in November 2002. Two weeks later the House of Lords confirmed in the *Anderson*[134] decision that the Home Secretary should no longer decide on the tariff for convicted murderers. Hindley's crimes were clearly abhorrent but the decisions by successive Home Secretaries to alter her tariff and prevent her consideration for release were political and not based on sound legal principle. It is not clear whether Hindley would have ever been released from prison even if the power to set tariffs had been with a judge rather than a politician. Although not a sympathetic figure Hindley did prove, ironically, to be a victim of the partiality of the criminal justice process in this regard.

OVERCROWDED PRISONS: A CRISIS OF NUMBERS AND CONDITIONS

Convicted offenders sometimes receive custodial sentences. They are then sent to prison to serve those sentences. According to Cavadino and Dignan[135] there exists a penal crisis. This crisis is concerned with a number of issues, which impact upon the legitimacy of the process and more importantly the lives of prisoners. There currently exists a managerial crisis, a crisis of security, a crisis of control and authority, a crisis of accountability and a crisis of legitimacy. The impact of these crises should not be underestimated but it is the crisis of numbers which impacts upon prison conditions which is most worrying at this time. At the time of writing there are 86,158 prisoners in custody.[136] The last decade has consistently seen records broken as to the number of prisoners in custody and if an expansionist policy were the present and previous government's aim then the numbers would point to success. This unprecedented increase does however have its casualties. Cavadino and Dignan explain that as many of the current prison cells were designed for single occupancy at least 22 per cent of the prison population are being held in overcrowded conditions.[137]

Overcrowded prisons feed the crisis of conditions. This crisis is three-fold[138] in that it involves the physical accommodation that prisoners have to live in, the repressive

134   *R. v. Secretary of State for the Home Department ex p Anderson* [2002] UKHL 46.
135   Cavadino, M. and Dignan, J., *The Penal System* (London: Sage, 2007).
136   Her Majesty's Prison Service Population Figures as of 23 November 2012. Can be accessed at: http://www. justice.gov.uk/statistics/prisons-and-probation/prison-population-figures
137   Cavadino, M. and Dignan, J., *The Penal System* (Sage: London, 2007) p. 214. This figure is likely to be much higher five years on.
138   Ibid., p. 215.

regimes they are often subject to[139] and the breakdown with family ties that often occurs as a result of local prisons being full and inmates being transported around the country to places difficult for visitors to travel to. This final consequence is said to feed offender bitterness and hostility whilst in prison which then contributes to their recidivism upon release.[140] We will contain our discussion to the physical accommodation and its related conditions as this has the most direct impact upon the prisoner's life and reminds us of a political battle that was once won by the executive but which proved the judiciary to see into the future and the developments that would occur. The Howard League of Penal Reform has commented on how two or more prisoners are often housed in cells designed for one and they are using unscreened toilets which 'fail to provide them with the most basic of human rights'.[141] These 'inhuman and degrading conditions'[142] are not new but the current prison crisis of numbers and overcrowding is likely to exacerbate rather than reduce these squalid conditions. The practice of prisoners 'slopping out' their overnight waste did come to an end in 2006 but this some fifteen years after the Woolf Report cried out for a cap on prison numbers and a review of prison conditions.

The Woolf Report was in response to the Strangeways and other prison riots in 1990. Lord Justice Woolf chaired the enquiry that followed these prison disturbances. His terms of reference were to: 'inquire into the events which began on April 1st 1990 and the action taken to bring it to a conclusion, having regard also to the serious disturbances which occurred shortly thereafter in other prison establishments'.[143] Interestingly sentencing practice was not included in these terms of reference for fear that Woolf would comment on the expansionist policy that the government of the day was beginning to adopt following a dip during the 1980s. The key point to Woolf's approach was he believed that there was no single cause to a riot. This meant that there was no simple solution or action, which will prevent this from happening again. There were a total of twelve recommendations. Most significant for the discussion here was that, in light of prison conditions and the executive thirst for recourse to the prison, a new prison rule should be implemented which would prevent an establishment holding more prisoners than is provided for in its normal certified level of accommodation. This recommendation was never adopted in the package of reforms that followed the publication of the report. Woolf also wanted the executive power of release to be used if prisons became overcrowded.[144]

By 2007 Cavadino and Dignan comment that Woolf's call for a new prison rule to limit overcrowding appears 'fanciful'.[145] And yet a member of the judiciary had asked for an executive power, to continue to fill up prisons beyond their natural capacity, to

139   For example, it was reported in 2006 that the Lord Chief Justice announced that overcrowding was proving 'fatal' for prisoner treatment. In fact he said that drug addicts were often committing offences in order to access treatment in prison. See http://www.guardian.co.uk/uk/2006/may/30/ukcrime.prisonsandprobation

140   Cavadino, M. and Dignan, J., *The Penal System* (Sage: London, 2007) p. 215.

141   Howard League for Penal Reform, Campaign to End Prison Overcrowding, 2012, accessed at http://www.howardleague.org/overcrowding/

142   As confirmed by the European Committee for the Prevention of Torture (1991).

143   Woolf, H. and Tumim, S., *Prison Disturbances April 1990*, Cm 1456 (London, HMSO, 1991).

144   Woolf, H. and Tumim, S., *Prison Disturbances April 1990*, Cm 1456 (London: HMSO, 1991) para 1.189.

145   This classification is confirmed by Cavadino and Dignan in Cavadino, M. and Dignan, J., *The Penal System* (Sage: London, 2007) p. 215.

be curtailed. Lord Woolf had been wrong about one thing though. He had declared that prison overcrowding was a thing of the past and yet prisons are now overcrowded beyond anything he could have imagined. Answers to the current problem could be 'increasing prison capacities or crisis driven changes in sentencing'.[146] The problem with these solutions is they tend to be short term and isolated. Losel offers a more profound course of change when he suggests that a reduction in the prison over-crowding crisis may come if we improve offender rehabilitation which will reduce recidivism. He also advocates a reduction in short term incarceration and a greater commitment by government to developmental prevention and early intervention.[147]

Back in 1987 Vivien Stern described our prisons as 'bricks of shame'.[148] Woolf commented in 1991 that justice itself is compromised if prisoners are held in over-crowded conditions that are 'inhumane and degrading, or are otherwise wholly inap-propriate'.[149] Twenty years on, in spite of recent calls to reductionism,[150] the prison numbers have escalated beyond what could have ever been imagined. Crowded cells see prisoners sitting on toilets as a means of sitting down whilst eating their meals.[151] This time has seen improvements in prison conditions but there are still improvements to be made and these tend to be compromised when overcrowding is at such a peak. The prison service, in collusion with the government, suggests they have a useable opera-tional capacity of 90,995. This would suggest at the time of writing that there are still 4,837 places going spare! Cavadino and Dignan are however suspicious of the method of calculating these figures suggesting they 'mask the true extent of the problem'.[152] The Prison Reform Trust has suggested[153] that one very serious effect of this prison over-crowding is the incidence of self-harm increases. This cannot be defensible. The experi-ence of prison for the prisoner is directly affected by this commitment to an expansionist policy, which at the present time cannot keep up with its own enlargement.

CONCLUSION: DREAMS AND NIGHTMARES

Sanders *et al.* believe that the time has come to 'set the primary goal of the criminal justice system as the promotion of freedom of all citizens and social groups alike'.[154] This dream is a noble one. To promote freedom within a process that often prizes crime control over due process and routinely discriminates against vulnerable groups within society may be desirable but is it realistically attainable? At the beginning

---

146   Losel, F. (2007) 'Counterblast: The Prison Overcrowding Crisis and Some Constructive Perspectives for Crime Policy', *Howard Journal* 513.

147   Ibid., pp. 513–515.

148   Book title.

149   Woolf, H. and S. Tumim, S., *Prison Disturbances April 1990*, Cm 1456 (London: HMSO, 1991) para 10.19.

150   See Kenneth Clarke at http://www.guardian.co.uk/society/2012/feb/02/kenneth-clarke-wipe-slate-clean-exoffenders, however the new Justice Secretary, Chris Grayling, is less reductionist in tone. See http://www.guardian.co.uk/politics/2012/sep/20/chris-grayling-take-hardline-prison

151   See http://www.prisonreformtrust.org.uk/subsection.asp?id=333

152   Cavadino, M. and Dignan, J., *The Penal System* (Sage: London, 2007) p. 213.

153   See http://www.prisonreformtrust.org.uk/subsection.asp?id=333

154   See Sanders, A., Young, R., and Burton, M., *Criminal Justice* (Oxford: Oxford University Press, 2010) p. 746.

Packer said we should try. We should try to attain the unattainable for if we stop trying we will fall even further short of finding guaranty and eliminating threat. This chapter has considered some of the winners and the losers in our current criminal justice processes. The winners appear to be the state and its vast machinery charged with delivering justice in a way that satisfies many. It should satisfy all but on final analysis it is a process, which is left wanting. The losers are those who have suffered nightmares at the hands of a process, which in both its structures and its practices has left critics believing that it is a process in need of repair. We only need the process to be fair when we encounter it. On this evidence the many will hope they don't encounter for fear of being treated like the few.

17

CONCLUSION

The apparent government, composed of poor devils, is in the pay of the financiers. For one hundred years, in this poisoned country, whoever has loved the poor has been considered a traitor to society. A man is called dangerous when he says that there are wretched people. There are laws against indignation and pity, and what I say here could not go into print.[1]

I

Rather than revisit and recap exhaustively on the themes that have run through *The Politics of the Common Law*, we want to offer some final points for reflection that return to our key arguments. Lon L. Fuller has been a frequent point of reference. It thus seems fitting to leave him with the (more or less) last word:

> The lawyer's highest loyalty is at the same time the most intangible. It is a loyalty that runs, not to persons, but to procedures and institutions. The lawyer's role imposes on him a trusteeship for the integrity of those fundamental processes of government and self-government upon which the successful functioning of our society depends. . .[2]

Fuller's approach to the law was motivated by what he called a 'morality of aspiration'. Lawyers should strive to make the law best it could be. But, Fuller did not want to give a substantive purpose to the legal order. He preferred to think in terms of precepts: in particular lawyers must endeavour to keep 'communication [about the human condition] open'. Fuller's morality of aspiration animates the paragraph cited above. Legal officials are trustees for 'fundamental processes' of law and government. Whilst we would agree with some of Fuller's sentiments, we feel that his argument is not quite right. It tends to reify legal processes. For instance, he argues above that the lawyer's 'loyalty' is 'not to persons, but to procedures and institutions. Why is it necessary to de-couple people from processes? Perhaps it is explicable by Fuller's desire (as a good liberal), not to mandate 'ends' for the law. Our point would be that it is impossible to think about processes without people; indeed, our thinking about the ends of the law (to the extent that it is a theme in this book) is built on this fundamental idea. So, we have been more prescriptive than Fuller in arguing that courts must have moral authority, and (to a large extent) this authority comes from recognising the moral personhood of citizens.

---

1   Monsieur Choulette Anatole France, *The Red Lily*, Chapter VII.
2   Fuller (1978: 371).

We are aware that our argument has its problems. Consider our reading of Lord Bingham's speech in what was loosely called 'the torture case'.[3] His argument acknowledged that the common law's rhetoric is not always matched by reality. Human rights are often compromised. However, this does not mean that ideas of dignity and respect are irrelevant. If nothing else, they remain critical principles that allow us to structure our own uses of public reason: to study the extent to which a particular case may or may not articulate fundamental values. Due process values are particularly vital in this sense. They can be used to confront claims to states of emergency and/or of the fight against terror. Due process values, even if compromised in legislation, ensure a critical use of public reason. Officials, who may be tempted or under great pressure, might be encouraged to follow procedures that would render abuse open to scrutiny.

So, we should not separate our consideration of processes from the critical public culture that should animate a democracy and ensure that institutions are open and transparent to the people that they serve. To put this point in a slightly different way. Human rights are the rights of (all) humans: processes do not function in the absence of people. To the extent that principles are distanced from people it leads to a dangerous reification of legal processes. Integrity may become limited to the internal coherence of a system, rather than facilitating and structuring the relationship between an institution and the broader values it is meant to embody and protect.

II

At the level of human rights adjudication, there is no real distinction between law making by the judges, and law making by Parliament. Judicial decisions that articulate human rights values and protect people from power are elaborations of principles of the rule of law. These decisions address the black hole at the centre of the constitution: the illegitimacy of a sovereign Parliament that appears irrelevant to many people, influenced by powerful commercial and financial interests and elected by a dwindling number of voters. Amidst a public life characterised by popular disengagement from politics, the justification of Parliament as the 'voice of the people' is increasingly weak.

----

3   *A. and others v. Secretary of State for the Home Department (No 2)* [2005] UKHL 71. To recap the main themes: *A.* concerned the uses of torture evidence gathered abroad without the connivance of British authorities. Lord Bingham was adamant that such evidence could neither be admitted in a court of law nor used in the tribunal set up to hear appeals against arrest and detention of foreign terror suspects, the Special Immigration Appeals Commission (SIAC). However – and we will not comment on this here – in obiter (para 47) he seems to allow that the authorities can act on such evidence if they came across it. They could thus arrest individuals on the basis of information gained by torture. 'I am prepared to accept . . . that the Secretary of State does not act unlawfully if he certifies, arrests, searches and detains on the strength of what I shall for convenience call foreign torture evidence. But by the same token it is, in my view, questionable whether he would act unlawfully if he based similar action on intelligence obtained by officially-authorised British torture. If under such torture a man revealed the whereabouts of a bomb in the Houses of Parliament, the authorities could remove the bomb and, if possible, arrest the terrorist who planted it. There would be a flagrant breach of Article 3 for which the United Kingdom would be answerable, but no breach of Article 5(4) or 6'. Article 3 relates to torture, Articles 5 and 6 to detention and trial. His judgment is constructed in widening webs of articulation: first he considers the classic common law, then ideas on abuse of process; he then moves onto the European Law on Human Rights and Public international law, before finally considering academic and other concerned persons' views on the international prohibition of torture.

However, empowering the judiciary is not ultimately the answer to this failure of democratic culture and accountability. Repairing British democracy is a much broader task. For the moment, though, a judiciary that looks critically at the failures of British democracy and brings to bear the principles of European and International normative orders, is perhaps the best option available for maintaining a principled constitutional order.

III

The first part of the book was focused on the post colonial and on law's part in the construction of plural communities. We were very much concerned with the forms of life that the law either destroys or makes possible. We see the common law as bound up with a vast repository of narratives that are accounts of the law's proper role in the social and political world. We have seen the rhetorical appeal of arguments that linked the common law with the development of a 'spirit' of a 'people'. The assumption that the law speaks for 'the people' can be deeply problematic. For example in Nazi Germany, the law was given the role of embodying the 'volk', the people of the soil. It followed that those who were not members of the volk fell outside the law. Indeed, as many scholars have shown, it is just this exclusion from law that prepares for the extermination of those who are no longer citizens. Ideas of the volk and the exclusive racial order of a people are corrupt and exhausted concepts. There is no such thing as a pure people/race. We are all mongrels; the products of hybrid cultures – vast patterns of migration and dislocation that have displaced and scattered different people speaking different languages throughout different cultures of the world (which were never coherent in the first place). If the common law speaks to us today, it must talk polyglot; differently accented as it addresses us as people in our various circumstances.

IV

We have also seen due process as an index to the democratic nature of the courts. This is a problematic argument, and like II and III above begs more questions than it answers. Consider the following argument:

> Law reflects but in no sense determines the moral worth of a society. The values of a reasonably just society will reflect themselves in a reasonably just law. The better the society, the less law there will be. In Heaven there will be no law, and the lion will lie down with the lamb. The values of an unjust society will reflect themselves in an unjust law. The worse the society, the worse law there will be. In Hell there will be nothing but law, and due process will be meticulously observed.[4]

4   Gilmore (1977: 109).

The 'moral worth' of society is only, in part, due to legal values. Law reflects, but does not determine, the 'values of a reasonably just society'. One must look 'outside' of the law to understand its values. This is why, in Chapter 2, we were so concerned with the historical processes that have produced the contemporary sense of moral personhood and human rights. But note the interesting twist in the passage above. Its inspiration is anarchist: a good society would not need law. Hell is due process. What does this mean?

We have perhaps been hinting at this argument throughout the book. Purely formal due process produces a very narrow notion of the law. Formal equality, or equality before the law, is an essential component of the rule of law. However, we have suggested that unless law takes at least some account of the resources that people have access to the courts is limited. We considered this theme in Chapter 13 when we looked at legal aid, but the point can be generalised. It is necessary to acknowledge a tension between two ideas of justice: justice according to the law (due process) and distributive justice.

We briefly examined a theory of distributive justice in Chapter 15. However, as we saw, it is difficult to see law in distributive terms. We can extend that argument a little. Inequality and poverty are realities that law (and even human rights) finds hard to either understand or remedy. Our example of post-colonial development and our analysis in Chapter 5 suggests that human rights and injustice exist side by side. Perhaps it is not the 'job' of law to respond to poverty, but, conversely law helps constitute the socio-economic global order. Capitalist societies developed rights through ideas of property ownership and human right. Claims such as the right to share the city or other resources, remain in tension with the primacy of property rights. Why is there no right not to be poor? Indeed, the historical, economic, cultural and ideological processes that have coordinated the market and democracy takes us to the blind spot of human rights: the right to a fair trial exists alongside law's inability to deal with material inequality. To return to the passage above, it may be that the observation of due process is indeed an index of injustice.

V

Scholars of due process have engaged with these issues. Consider the following argument about the relationship between dignity and due process. Founding due process on dignity 'displaces the possessive, privatistic view of law, that of the isolated individual interested in getting what is his'.[5] But, to what extent does the idea of dignity allow a 'communal, interpersonal' vision of 'interaction between the citizen and his government'? Resnik thinks dignity is too limited a concept to further this account of social relations: '[d]ignity means preserving self inviolate from others'. Court processes 'only . . . confirm[s]. . . . egotistic separateness'.[6] So, what is the alternative? Resnik

---

5   Resnik (1987: 261).
6   Ibid.

favours an enhanced form of public dialogue, where the courts are part of an ongoing dialogue about communal values: and the creation of norms:

> I believe that . . . norms are generated in the course of the interaction among disputants and adjudicator, and among disputants, adjudicator, and the public. This is an interaction over time, during which the polity develops, learns about, and changes the norms that govern disputes.[7]

There are some similarities between Resnik's argument, and the positions we have elaborated in this book. However, before we sum up on this theme, we want to connect Resnik's arguments with those of Farina:

> We would see in due process the quintessential instance of rights as 'a form of communal dialogue' and realise that, of all adjudication, due process adjudication in particular could never be value-free, detached, abstract, universal, or final. We would understand that, especially at this point in our history, we *need* due process adjudication to be a consciously value-creating occasion that emphasises the relationship between government and its people, and elaborates the qualities and responsibilities of that relationship.[8]

It is worth clarifying the terms of the argument a little. The idea of participation discussed above, goes some way further than our discussion of participation within the context of the civil and criminal trial. Resnik and Farina are presenting a more radical account of due process. We would agree that due process should be 'value creating' in the realisation of the moral authority of the courts. Due process should also inform responsible relationships between lawyers and their clients in increasingly professionalised trial processes. We would also agree with the more radical suggestions that Resnik and Farina are making, although we have not got sufficient space in this book to develop our agreements and disagreements with their position. However, we can deal with one point. We don't believe that dignity is as narrow a concept as Resnik suggests.

There are the resources within law and human rights discourse to see dignity as an expression of our social nature as human beings. We touched upon this theme in Chapter 2. Dignity can be linked to terms like solidarity and seen as expressions of communal 'being together'. Perhaps this returns to our concern with the difficulties of separating law and politics. Although the institutional requirements of liberal democracy require us to observe separations between the institutions of law and politics, this can obscure the shared concern that both discourses have with articulating community. The 'limit' to the discourse on community that we alluded to above (IV) can thus be elaborated as follows.

The articulation of values that comes out of Farina and Resnik's work suggests that – in a radical democracy – citizens would not be left destitute: society and economy

---

7   Ibid.
8   Farina (1991: 271).

would be organised around communal welfare, and the rule of law seen as a link between formal and substantive equality. Whilst this may seem a utopian vision, it is one possible way of seeing the history that we recounted in Chapter 2 as unfinished: justice is still to come.

VI

Human rights provide a way of thinking about the common law. Whether or not this language becomes adopted as a general way of understanding the common law is open to question. We hope that we have also been alive to the way in which principles have developed at common law in an immanent manner. The principles of natural justice are a good example of common law ideas that are not expressed in terms of human rights, but, can be seen in terms of due process and Article 6. To repeat a point made in Chapters 12, 13 and 14, analysing the common law through Article 6 allows us to place common law ideas in an international context, and to test the common law against international standards. This is an essential element of an argument that has sought to examine the legitimacy of law; although, as we suggested above, questions of legitimacy raise problematic issues which take us to the limits of law within market economy.

VII

The final part of the book was focused upon matters of procedure. We wanted to engage our institutional imaginations. Procedural law is so frequently presented as dull or simply the province of the practitioner. To remain authentic to our theme, we considered it necessary to present procedure as an articulation of principles that (in part) return us to ideas of due process. However, the civil and criminal procedural systems are immensely complicated. The language of due process is not, in itself, sufficient. Thus an important element of our engagement was to be aware that civil and criminal procedure is animated by tensions. These reflect competing agendas about their function and the ways in which the system attempts to negotiate their inner tensions.

VIII

We have saved the most difficult point until last: how does this book fit into the law syllabus?

To the extent that the common law has been studied as part of an LLb syllabus, it has been done so through a subject called either Legal Method or English Legal System. As Kavanagh has pointed out, this tends to be the Cinderella subject of legal education – or at least Cinderella before the kiss. Its concern is with the drudgery of legal reasoning, with what remains behind the scenes, or at least somehow prior to the proper study of law. The subject is seen as either an irrelevance, or a trial for both those who have to teach it, and those who are forced to study it. In part, this is a valid response to courses (and indeed books) that are lacking in structure, imagination and any sense of the contemporary dynamics of the common law.

The subject thus needs to be reinvented. We hope that this book might re-orientate 'legal system' or 'legal method' and give the subject the coherence, foundations and provocations to creative and critical thinking that it is otherwise lacking. We believe the subject has a relationship to both public law and jurisprudence. Indeed, it should be presented in just such terms. Thus, rather than being cast adrift from the syllabus, 'legal system' can be informed by ideas drawn from those subjects that most directly engage in broader questions about the nature of law, its animating concerns and its possible futures.

London, 2013

POSTSCRIPT: A NOTE ON THE COVER IMAGES OF THE 1st AND 2nd EDITIONS

The images are taken from a sequence of photographs, *Gwendraeth House* (2000) by the Welsh artist Peter Finnemore. Throughout this book we have used images to provoke our thinking about the law; and Finnemore's work is exemplary in this respect. The photograph on the cover of the 1st edition of the book inspired many comments. It was testament to a kind of art that encourages thinking; makes connections that might not be obvious – or – rather stirs a level of thought that we want to 'get at' in this postscript.

We noticed a peculiar effect that the cover image had on readers of the book. People asked us about the image, and then went on to explain what *they* thought the image represented. Unlike conventional images of judges, wigs and gowns, here was something unusual. We think Finnemore's image taps into a kind of communal dream time; a mytho-poetic level of thinking that takes us 'moderns' back to the strange stories of law givers and the 'myths of the tribe' (or tribes). What does this mean?

Mark this page by keeping your thumb in the book, so you don't lose your place; so you can come back. Take a look at the cover image. A figure of a man against a grey sky with plastic animals dangling from his hands. We think this image echoes that of the striking front piece of Thomas Hobbes' *Leviathan* (1651) by Abraham Bosse. Bosse's illustration is one of the totemic images of modern law; after all, positivist jurisprudence traces its inheritance back to Hobbes. Perhaps the image of *Leviathan* is the image of positivism; this most un-visual of jurisprudences; this protestant exemplification of the word rather than the image. However, Finnemore's image both echoes and interrupts the Leviathan; instead of the corporate body of the *Leviathan*, the sublime power of community composed of the myriad bodies of the subjects of law, is a kind of bathetic deflation. Finnemore's image is, after all, just that of a man. A man having a joke? A strange modern shaman of the fields with his plastic fetishes?

Our interpretation of the image seems to combine contradictory associations: the sublime and the foolish; the sacred and the comic. The tensions evoked and focused by this image take us away from *Leviathan*, towards something else. This is the idea that the individual cannot simply be incorporated into the *Leviathan*. The sovereign power has to acknowledge that it does not and cannot speak for everyone. Indeed, there is a way of thinking about politics where the individual is protected from the community. This interpretation of the image evokes the concern with human rights that has been a major theme of this book. Finnemore's image articulates in a striking way the informing arguments of the politics of the common law.

But what might the image on the front of the 1st edition mean?

Against the backdrop of a rural family cottage, two men hold between them the garment of a deceased relative. What does this image represent? How does it relate to law? Our starting point was the idea that the law provides a home to those whom it gathers together in its name (*Leviathan*, again). However, this metaphor would have to be worked out at much greater length given the imposition of the common law on Wales. Indeed, the image takes us back to our concerns with the colonial order, as Wales and Ireland were the first territories colonised by the English. Other interpretations are possible. It is interesting that justice is represented as a woman. In the photograph, the body of the woman has gone but does her spirit live on? Is this an image that plays with

Figure 17.1 Photo © Peter Finnemore. 'But tho' those particular Variations and Accessions have happened in the Laws, yet they being only partial and successive, we may with just Reason say, They are the same English Laws now, that they were 600 Years since in the general. As the Argonauts Ship was the same when it returned home, as it was when it went out, tho' in that long Voyage it had successive Amendments, and scarce came back with any of its former Materials; and as Titius is the same Man he was 40 Years since, tho' Physicians tells us, That in a Tract of seven Years, the Body has scarce any of the same Material Substance it had before'. (Sir Mathew Hale, History of the Common Law of England, 1713).

idea of letter and spirit: the form of the law and its animus/anima? Is justice the spirit of the law?

These questions can be linked to Sir Matthew Hale's classic metaphor for the common law: the ship that took Jason and the Argonauts on their voyages. In some ways this takes us back to the beginning of the book, and the nomadic spirit of the common law abroad in the world. However, Sir Matthew Hale's metaphor is more precise. When the Argonaut's boat returned home to Iolcus it had been at sea so long and repaired so often that it had been completely rebuilt. The Argus came back the same and different.

Does this mythological image – this echo between Finnemore's image, Sir Matthew Hale and the story of the Argonauts – focus the meanings of the photograph? The common law made different from itself; a house to be built and re-built? We have certainly presented the common law as something that has become different from itself in the postcolonial period. In place of the English speaking people whose spirit is manifested in their law, we have found the plural, the polygot; in place of the history of the common law bringing order to those who need to be administered, we found something different: those who need justice; a dress, a spirit; *hiraeth*.

BIBLIOGRAPHY

Allan, T.R.S. (2003) 'Constitutional dialogue and the justification of judicial review', *Oxford Journal of Legal Studies* 23: 563–84.

Allison, J.W.F. (2007) *The English Historical Constitution – Continuity, Change and European Effects* (Cambridge: Cambridge University Press).

Alston, P. (1999) *The European Union and Human Rights* (Oxford: Oxford University Press).

Anderson, B. (1991) *Imagined Communities: Reflections on the Origin and Spread of Nationalism* (London: Verso).

Anderson, D. (2005) 'Burying the bones of the past', *History Today* 55(2): 2–3.

Anderson, D. (2005) *Histories of the Hanged* (London: Weidenfeld & Nicolson).

Anderson, D., Bennett, H. and Branch, D. (2006) 'A very British massacre', *History Today* 56(8): 20–2.

Andrews, N. (2003) *English Civil Procedure: Fundamentals of the New Civil Justice System* (Oxford: Oxford University Press).

Aristotle (1925) *The Nicomachean Ethics* (Oxford: Oxford University Press).

Armitage, A. (1995) *Comparing the Policy of Aboriginal Assimilation: Australia, Canada and New Zealand* (Vancouver: UBC Press).

Arnull, A. *et al.* (2002) *Accountability and Legitimacy in the European Union* (Oxford: Oxford University Press).

Ashworth, A. (2010) *Sentencing and Criminal Justice* (Cambridge: Cambridge University Press).

Ashworth, A.J. and Barsby, C. (2002) 'Human rights – post conviction change in the law', *Criminal Law Review*, 498–501.

Auden, W.H. (1976) *Collected Poems* (London: Random House).

Bailey, S.H., Harris, D.J. and Ormerod, D.C. (2001) *Civil Liberties* (London: Butterworths).

Baker, J.H. (1993) 'Statutory interpretation and parliamentary intervention', *Cambridge Law Journal* 52: 353.

Baker, J.H. (2002) *An Introduction to English Legal History*, 4th edn (London: Butterworth Lexis Nexis).

Bales, K. (1999) *Disposable People: New Slavery in the Global Economy* (Berkeley: University of California Press).

Balibar, E. and Wallerstein, I. (1991) *Race, Nation, Class: Ambiguous Identities* (London: Verso).

Ball, H. (1999) *Prosecuting War Crimes and Genocide: The Twentieth-Century Experience* (Kansas: University Press of Kansas).

Banton, M. (1991) 'The race relations problematic', *British Journal of Sociology* 42: 115–30.

Barber, B.R. (2003) *Fear's Empire: War, Terrorism, and Democracy* (New York: W.W. Norton & Co.).

Barnett, H. (1994) 'A privileged position? Gypsies, land and planning law', *The Conveyancer* (Nov/Dec): 454–64.

Barnett, H. (1995) 'The end of the road for gypsies', *Anglo American Law Review* 24(2): 133–67.

Baucom, I. (2005) *Specters of the Atlantic – Finance Capital, Slavery, and the Philosophy of History* (Durham and London: Duke University Press).

Beccaria, C., Bellamy, R. and Davies, R. (1995) *'On Crimes and Punishments' and Other Writings* (Cambridge, Cambridge University Press).

Becker, C.L. (1942) *The Declaration of Independence: A Study in the History of Political Ideals* (New York: Random House).

Bell, Derrick, *Race, Racism and American Law* (New York: Little Brown and Co, 1992), 62.

Bentham, J. (1928) *A Comment on the Commentaries*, Everett, C.W. (ed.) (Oxford: Clarendon Press).

Bentham, J. (1838) 'Principles of Judicial Procedure, With the Outlines of a Procedure Code' (Edinburgh: William Tait), Vol 2 of 11 vols.

Birks, P. (1985) *An Introduction to the Law of Restitution* (Oxford: Oxford University Press).

Blackstone, W. (1765) *Commentaries on the Laws of England*, vol. I [original edition 1765, used 9th edition as prepared by Wayne Morrison] (London: Cavendish Publishing).

Blankenburg, E. (1995) 'Access to justice and alternatives to courts', *Civil Justice Quarterly* 14(Jul): 176–89.

Bourdieu, P. (1977) *Outline of a Theory of Practice* (Cambridge: Cambridge University Press).

Bowling, B. and Phillips, C. (2007) 'Disproportionate and discriminatory: reviewing the evidence on police stop and search', *Modern Law Review* 70(6): 936–61.

Bracton (c. 1235) *De Legibus et Consuetudinibus Angliae* [On the laws and customs of England], fols 1b and 2.

Bratza, N. (2011) 'The Relationship between the UK Courts and Strasbourg', EHRLR 505.

Bridges, L. (2000) *Quality in Criminal Defences Services*, LSC.

Burger, W. (1982) 'Isn't there a better way? Annual Report on the State of the Judiciary, Remarks at the Mid-Year Meeting of the American Bar Association', *American Bar Association Journal* 68: 274, 275.

Burke, E. (1970) *Reflections on the Revolution in France* (London: Pelican).

Burns, R. (2000) 'A view from the ranks', *New Law Journal* 150: 1829–30.

Camenisch, P.F. (1983) *Grounding Professional Ethics in a Pluralist Society* (New York: New Haven Publications).

Cappelletti, M. (1993) 'Alternative dispute resolution processes within the framework of the World Wide Access to Justice Movement', *Modern Law Review* 56(3): 282–96.

Cardozo, B. (1921) *The Nature of the Judicial Process* (New Haven: Yale University Press).

Cassell (1902) *Cassells's History of England. Vol. I* (London: Cassell and Company).

Cavadino, M. and Dignan, J. (2007) *The Penal System* (London: Sage).

Chamberlain, M. (2011) '*Al-Rawi v. Security Services, Home Office v. Tariq*', *Civil Justice Quarterly* 30(4): 360–66.

Chrimes, S.B. (1965) *English Constitutional History*, 3rd edn (Oxford: Oxford University Press).

Churchill, W. (1997) *A Little Matter of Genocide: Holocaust and Denial in the Americas, 1492 to the Present* (San Francisco: City Lights Books).

Clayton, R. (2007) 'The Human Rights Act six years on: Where are we now?', *European Human Rights Law Review* (3): 11–16.

Clayton, R. and Tomlinson, H. (2000) *The Law of Human Rights* (Oxford: Oxford University Press).

Clayton, R. and Tomlinson, H. (2001) *Fair Trial Rights* (Oxford: Oxford University Press).

Cohn, M. (2007) 'Judicial activism in the House of Lords', *Public Law* 1: 95–115.

Coke, Edward (1797) 'The Second Part of the Institutes of the Laws of England' (London: E and R Brooke).

Cooke, R.K. (1987) 'The practical problems of the sentencer', in D. Pennington and S. Lloyd-Bostock (eds) *The Psychology of Sentencing* (Oxford: Centre for Socio-Legal Studies).

Corwin, E.S. (1911) 'The Doctrine of Due Process Before the Civil War', 24 *Harvard Law Review* 366-79.

Cownie, F. and Bradney, A. (1996) *English Legal System in Context* (London: Butterworths).

Craig, D. (2007) *EU Administrative Law* (Oxford: Oxford University Press).

Cross, R. and Harris, J.W. (1991) *Precedent in English Law* (Oxford: Clarendon).

Cunneen, C. (2010) 'Framing the crimes of colonialism', in Hayward and Presdee, ed., *Framing Crime: Cultural Criminology and the Image* (Abingdon, Oxon: Routledge GlassHouse).

De Burca, G. (1996) 'The quest for legitimacy in the European Union', *Modern Law Review* 359: 368–71.

De Certeau, M. (2006) *The Practice of Everyday Life* (Berkeley: University of California Press).

Dickens C., *Bleak House* (London: Penguin Classics, 2003)

Dicey, A.V. (1897) *Introduction to the Study of the Law of the Constitution* (London: Macmillan).

Dodd, V. (2005) 'Asian men targeted in stop and search', *The Guardian*, 17 August.

Donald, A., Gordon, J. and Leach, P. (2012) *The UK and the European Court of Human Rights, Equality and Human Rights Commission Research Report* (London: Equality and Human Rights Commission).

Douzinas, C. and Gearey, A. (2005) *Critical Jurisprudence* (Oxford: Hart Press).

Douzinas, C. (2000) *The End of Human Rights* (Oxford: Hart).

Duff, A., Farmer, L., Marshall, S. and Tadros, V. (2007) *The Trial on Trial* (Oxford: Hart).

Dworkin, R. (1986) *Law's Empire* (Cambridge, MA: Harvard University Press).

Dyrberg, P. (2002) 'Accountability and legitimacy: what is the contribution of transparency', in A. Arnull and D. Wincott (eds) *Accountability and Legitimacy in the European Union* (Oxford: Oxford University Press).

Ekins, R. (2003) 'A critique of radical approaches to rights consistent statutory interpretation', *European Human Rights Law Review* 6: 641–50.

Ellis, E. (ed.) (1999) *The Principle of Proportionality in the Laws of Europe* (Oxford: Hart).

Elkins, C. (2005) *Imperial Reckoning: The Untold Story of Britain's Gulag in Kenya* (New York: Henry Holt).

Equality and Human Rights Commission, Research Report 83, The UK and the European Court of Human Rights (2012) http://www.equalityhumanrights.com/uploaded_files/research/83._european_court_of_human_rights.pdf

Everson, E. (with Eisner, J.) (2007) *The Making of a European Constitution* (London: Routledge-Cavendish).

Ewing, K. (2005) 'The Futility of the Human Rights Act', *British Law Journal* 37: 41.

Ewing, K.D. and Tham, J.-C. (2008) 'The Continuing Futility of the Human Rights Act' *Public Law* 668.

Fanon, F. (1963) *The Wretched of the Earth* (New York: Grove Press).

Fanon, F. (1986) *Black Skin, White Masks* (trans. C. Lam Markmann) (London: Pluto).

Farina, C.R. (1991) 'Conceiving Due Process', *Yale J.L. & Feminism* (3): 189–279.

Feldman, D. (1999) 'Proportionality and the Human Rights Act 1998', in E. Ellis (ed.) *The Principle of Proportionality in the Laws of Europe* (Oxford: Hart Publishing) pp. 117–44.

Feldman, D. (2002) *Civil Liberties and Human Rights in England and Wales* (Oxford: Oxford University Press).

Fenwick, H., Masterman, R. and Phillipson, G. *et al.* (2007) *Judicial Reasoning under the UK Human Rights Act* (Cambridge: Cambridge University Press).

Ferguson, P.W. (2002) 'Human rights and their retrospective effect', *Scots Law Times* 2: 11–17.

Finberg, A.J. (1961) *The Life of J.M.W. Turner, R.A.*, 2nd edn (Oxford: Clarendon Press) p. 474.

Fionda, J. (2005) *Devils and Angels* (Oxford: Hart).

Fiss, O. (1979) 'The Forms of Justice', *Faculty Scholarship Series*. Paper 1220.

Fitzpatrick, P. (1987) 'Racism and the innocence of law', in P. Fitzpatrick and A. Hunt (eds) *Critical Legal Studies* (London: Blackwell) pp. 119–32.

Fitzpatrick, P. (1992) *The Mythology of Modern Law* (London: Routledge).

Fitzpatrick, P. (2001) *Modernism and the Grounds of Law* (Cambridge: Cambridge University Press).

Flood, J. and White, A. (2006) 'What's wrong with legal aid? Lessons from outside the UK', *Civil Justice Quarterly* 25: 80–98.

Foster, J., Newburn, T. and Souhami, A. (2005) 'Assessing the impact of the Stephen Lawrence Inquiry', *Home Office Research Study 294* (London: Home Office).

France, A. (1894) *Le Lys Rouge* (Paris: Calmann Lévy).

Frank, J. (1930) *Law and the Modern Mind* (New York: Brentano's).

Frankena, W.K. (1973) *Ethics*, 2nd edn (Englewood Cliffs: Prentice-Hall).

Freeman, M.D.A. (2001) *Lloyd's Introduction to Jurisprudence* (London: Sweet & Maxwell).

Fryer, P. (1984) *Staying Power* (London: Pluto Press).

Fryer, P. (1993) *Aspects of British Black History* (London: Index Books).

Fuller, L.L. (1978) 'The Forms and Limits of Adjudication', *Harvard Law Review* (92): 35–409

Galligan, D. (1996) *Due Process and Fair Procedure* (Oxford: Clarendon Press).

Gearty, C. (2004) *Principles of Human Rights Adjudication* (Oxford: Oxford University Press).

Genn, H. (1999) *Paths to Justice* (Oxford: Hart).

Genn, H. (2010) *Judging Civil Justice* (Oxford: Oxford University Press).

Gilmore, G. (1977) *The Ages of American Law* (New Haven: Yale University Press).

Gilroy, P. (1987a) 'The myth of black criminality', in P. Scraton (ed.) *Law, Order and the Authoritarian State* (Milton Keynes: WUL).

Gilroy, P. (1987b) *There Ain't No Black in the Union Jack: The Cultural Politics of Race and Nation* (London: Routledge).

Glasser, C. (1993) 'Civil procedure and the lawyers – the adversary system and the decline of the orality principle', *Modern Law Review* 56(3): 307–24.

Goodrich, P. (1986) *Reading the Law* (London: Basil Blackwell).

Goodrich, P. (1990) *Languages of Law* (London: Weidenfeld and Nicolson).

Goriely, T. (1994) 'Rushcliffe fifty years on: the changing role of civil legal aid within the welfare state', *Journal of Law and Society* 21(4): 545–66.

Gouldkamp, J. (2008) 'Facing up to actual bias', *Civil Justice Quarterly* 27(1): 32–9.

Greer, C. and McLaughlin, E. (2012) ' "THIS IS NOT JUSTICE", Ian Tomlinson, Institutional Failure and the Press politics of Outrage', *British Journal of Criminology* 52: 274.

Griffith, J.A.G. (1977) *The Politics of the Judiciary* (London: Fontana).

Griffith, J.A.G. (1979) 'The Political Constitution', 42 *Modern Law Review*.

Guardiola-Rivera, O. (2009) *Being Against the World. Rebellion and Constitution* (London: Routledge & Birkbeck Law Press).

Guillaum, C. (1995) *Racism, Sexism, Power and Ideology* (London: Routledge).

Habermas, J. (1989) 'The Crisis of the Welfare State, "On Society and Politics"', S. Seidman (ed.) (Boston: Beacon Press).

Hale, H. (1971) *The History of the Common Law* (Chicago: University of Chicago Press).

Hale, B. (2001) 'Equality and the judiciary', *Public Law* (Autumn): 489–504.

Hammarberg, O. (2011) *Human Rights of Roma and Travellers in Europe* (Strasbourg: Council of Europe, Commissioner for Human Rights).

Harpers Magazine (2003) 'We were calling to death', *Harpers Magazine* (February): 14–15.

Harris, B. (2002) 'Ongoing search', *Law Quarterly Review* 118(July): 408–27.

Harris, B.V. (2002) 'Final appellate courts overruling their own "wrong" precedents: the ongoing search for principle', *Law Quarterly Review* 118(July): 408–27.

Harris D.J., O'Boyle, M. and Warbrick, C. (1995) *Law of the European Convention on Human Rights* (London: Butterworths).

Hart, H.L.A. (1961) *The Concept of Law* (Oxford: Oxford University Press).

Held, D. (2001) 'Violence and Justice in a Global Age', in *After Sep. 11: Perspectives from the Social Sciences*. At http://www.ssrc.org/sept11/essays/held.htm

Hepple, B. (1992) 'Have twenty five years of race relations Acts in Britain been a failure?' in B. Hepple and E.M. Szyszczak (eds) *Discrimination: The Limits of the Law* (London: Mansell).

Herring, J. (2010) *Medical Law* (Oxford, Oxford University Press).

Hesiod (1983) 'Works and days' in *Hesiod: Theogony, Works and Days, Shield II* (trans. A.N. Athanassakis) (Baltimore: Johns Hopkins University Press).

Hilbink, L. (2007) *Judges beyond Politics in Democracy and Dictatorship: Lessons from Chile* (Cambridge: Cambridge University Press).

Hobbes, T. (1991 [1651]) in Richard Tuck (ed.) *Leviathan* (Cambridge: Cambridge University Press).

Hobbes, T. (1839) *Dialogue Between a Philosopher and a Student of the Common Laws of England* (London: Bohn).

Hochschild, A. (2005) *Bury the Chains – The British Struggle to Abolish Slavery* (London: Pan Macmillan).

Hoffman, D. and Rowe, J. (2003) *Human Rights in the UK* (Harlow: Pearson Longman).

Holdsworth, W. (1928a) *Charles Dickens as a Legal Historian* (New Haven: Yale University Press).

Holdsworth, W.S. (1928b) *Some Lessons from Our Legal History* (New York: Macmillan).

Holmes, C. (1998) *John Bull's Other Island* (London: Macmillan).

Holmes, O.W. (1881) [1923 reprint] *The Common Law* (Boston: Little Brown).

Home, R. (2012) 'Forced eviction and planning enforcement: the Dale Farm gypsies', *International Journal of Law in the Built Environment*, 4(3): 178–88.

Horne, A. (2010) 'A Case for Confirmation Hearings for Appointment to the New Supreme Court' *Judicial Review* 15(1).

Hough, C.M. (1919) 'Due Process of Law Today', 32 *Harvard Law Review*.

House of Commons Home Affairs Committee (2006) *Fourth Report of Session 2005–6: Terrorism Detention Powers HC 910-I*, 54.

House of Commons Home Affairs Committee (2005) *Sixth Report of Session 2004–5: Terrorism and Community Relations HC 165-I*, 46.

Hughes, K. (2012) 'The Right to know the case against you in civil claims', *Cambridge Law Journal* 71(1), 21–24.

Huntington, S.P. (1996) *The Clash of Civilizations and the Remaking of World Order* (London: The Free Press).

Ip, J. (2012) 'Al Rawi, Tariq and the Future of Closed Material Procedures and Special Advocates', *Modern Law Review* 75: 606–23.

Lord Irvine of Lairg (2012) 'A British Interpretation of Convention Rights', speech presented at the British Institute of International and Comparative Law, London.

Isaacs, J. (1999) *Spirit Country: Contemporary Australian Art* (Victoria: Hardie Grant Books).

Jackson, E. (2010) *Medical Law* (Oxford: Oxford University Press).

Jacob, J. (1987) *The Fabric of English Civil Justice* (London: Stevens and Sons).

Jacob, J. (2007) *Civil Justice in the Age of Human Rights* (Aldershot: Ashgate).

Jacobson, A. J. and Schlink, B. (eds) (2000) *Weimar: A Jurisprudence of Crisis*, Belinda Cooper (trans.) (Berkeley: University of California Press).

Jamieson, K.H. (1992) *Dirty Politics: Deception, Distraction and Democracy* (Oxford: Oxford University Press).

Janis, M.W., Bradley, A.W. and Kay, R.S. (2007) *European Human Rights Law* (Oxford: Oxford University Press).

Jenkins, S. (2003) 'Trupti Patel and the rotten courts of Salem', *The Times*, 13 June 2003.

Jordan, J. (1995) 'In the land of white supremacy', *The Progressive*, 18 June: 21.

Joseph, P. (1st edn 1993; 2nd edn 2001, 3rd edn 2007, 4th edn 2013) *Constitutional and Administrative Law in New Zealand*, 1st edn (Sydney: Law Book Co.).

Joseph, P. (2007) *Constitutional and Administrative Law in New Zealand*, 3rd edn (Wellington: Thomson Brookers).

Joyce, P. (2006) *Criminal Justice: An Introduction to Crime and the Criminal Justice System* (Devon: Willan).

Judt, T. (2005) *Post War: A History of Europe since 1945* (New York: Penguin Press).

Jurow, K. (1975) 'Untimely Thoughts: A Reconsideration of the Origins of Due Process of Law', 19 *American Journal of Legal History* 266–71.

Juss, S.S. (1993) *Immigration, Nationality and Citizenship* (London: Mansell).

Kavanagh, A. (2004) 'Statutory interpretation and human rights after Anderson: A more contextual approach', *Public Law* (Autumn) 537–45.

Kavanagh, A. (2009) 'Judging the judges under the Human Rights Act: deference, disillusionment and the "war on terror" ', *Public Law*, 287–304.

Kavanagh, A. (2010) 'Judicial Restraint in the Pursuit of Justice', *University of Toronto Law Review*, 24.

Kavanagh, A. (2010) 'Special Advocates, Control Order and the Right to a Fair Trial', *Modern Law Review* 75(3): 836ff.

Kelsen, H. ([1922] 1973) 'God and the State', trans. P. Heath, in O. Weinberger, (ed.) *Hans Kelsen – Essays in Legal and Moral Philosophy* (Dordrecht, Holland: D Reidel).

Kennedy, D. (1979) 'The Structure of Blackstone's Commentaries', 28 *Buffalo Law Review*.

Kennedy, H. (2004) *Legal Conundrums in our Brave New World* (London: Sweet and Maxwell).

King, J. (2007) 'The justiciability of resource allocation', *Modern Law Review* 70(2): 197–224.

King, M. (2003) *The Penguin History of New Zealand* (Auckland: Penguin Books).

Klug, F. (2003) 'Judicial deference under the Human Rights Act', *European Human Rights Law Review* 2: 125–33.

Kriegel, B. (1995) *The State and the Rule of Law* (trans. M.A. LePain) (New Jersey: Princeton University Press).

The Lawrence Inquiry (1999) Cm 4662-I (London: HMSO).

Le Sueur, A. (2000) 'Access to justice and human rights in the UK', *European Human Rights Law Review* 5: 457–75.

Leach, P. (2006) 'The effectiveness of the Committee of Ministers in supervising the enforcement of judgments of the European Court of Human Rights', *Public Law* 443–56.

Lenaerts, K. (2004) 'In the union we trust: trust enhancing principles of community law', *Common Market Law Review* 41: 317–43.

Lester, A. (2000) 'Politics of the Race Relations Act 1976', in M. Anwar, P. Roach and R. Sondhi (eds) *From Legislation to Integration; Race Relations in Britain* (London: Macmillan).

Lewis, J. (2007) 'The European ceiling on human rights', *Public Law*, 720–47.

Liebling, A. with Arnold, H. (2004) *Prisons and their Moral Performance* (Oxford: Oxford University Press).

Lord Denning (1979) *The Discipline of the Law* (London: Butterworths).

Lord Hailsham (1978) *The Dilemma of Democracy* (London: Collins).

Lord Irvine (1999) 'Activism and restraint: human rights and the interpretative process', *European Human Rights Law Review* 4: 350–402.

Lord Lugard, Frederick D. (1965) *The Dual Mandate in British Tropical Africa* (London: Frank Cass & Co Ltd).

Lord Steyn (2002) 'The case for a Supreme Court', *Law Quarterly Review* 118: 382.

Lord Steyn (2004) 'Dynamic interpretation amidst an orgy of statute', *European Human Rights Law Review* 3: 245–57.

Lord Steyn (2005) 'Democracy, The rule of law and the role of judges', *European Human Rights Law Review* 3: 243–53.

Losel, F. (2007) 'Counterblast: the prison overcrowding crisis and some constructive perspectives for crime policy', *Howard Journal of Criminal Justice* 46(5): 512–19.

Loveland, I. (2002) 'Injunctions, planning enforcement and human rights', *Modern Law Review* 65(6): 906–18.

Luban, D. (1994) *Legal Modernism* (Michigan: University of Michigan Press).

Lustgarten, L. (1980) *Legal Control of Discrimination* (London: Macmillan).

MacInnes, C. (1934) *England and Slavery* (London: Arrowsmith).

Macpherson, W. (1999) *The Stephen Lawrence Inquiry* (London: Home Office).

Mamdani, M. (1996) *Citizen and Subject* (Princeton: Princeton University Press).

Marx, K. (1975) 'On the Jewish Question', *in Early Writings* (New York: Vintage).

Mathew, P., Hunter, R. and Charlesworth, H. (1995) *Thinking about Law – Perspectives on the History, Philosophy and Sociology of Law* (Sydney: Allen & Unwin).

Maughan, C. and Webb, J. (2005) *Lawyering Skills and the Legal Process* (Cambridge: Cambridge University Press).

McConville, M. (1993) 'Wanted: more detection, less interrogation', *The Times*, 2 March 1993.

McCrudden, C., Smith, D.J. and Brown, C. (1991) *Racial Justice at Work* (London: Policy Studies Institute).

McHugh, P.G. (2001) *Aboriginal Title: The modern Jurisprudence of tribal land Rights* (Oxford: Oxford University Press).

McHugh, P.G. (2001) 'A History of Crown Sovereignty in New Zealand', in *Histories Power and Loss: Uses of the Past – a New Zealand Commentary*, A. Sharp and P. McHugh (eds) (Wellington: Bridget Williams Books).

McHugh, P.G. (2004) *Aboriginal Societies and the Common Law: A History of Sovereignty, Status and Self-Determination* (Oxford: Oxford University Press).

Mead, P. (1991) 'The obligation to apply European law', *European Law Review* 16(6): 490–501.

McIlwain, C.H. (1914) 'Due Process of Law in *Magna Carta*', *Columbia Law Review* 14(1): 27–51.

Miles, R. (1989) *Racism* (London: Routledge).

Miles, R. and Phizacklea A. (1987) *White Man's Country* (London: Pluto Press).

Moeckli, D. (2007) 'Stop and search under the Terrorism Act 2000: A comment on *R. (Gillan) v. Commissioner of Police for the Metropolis*', *Modern Law Review* 70(4): 654.

Morgan, J. (2004) 'Privacy torts: out with the old, out with the new', *Law Quarterly Review* 120(July): 393–98.

Morrison, T. (1992) *Playing in the Dark: Whiteness and the Literary Imagination* (London: Routledge).

Morrison, W. (2005) 'Rethinking Penal Narratives in Global Context', in Pratt, J. Brown, D. Brown, M. Holdsworth, S. and Morrison, W. (eds) *The New Punitiveness* (Devon: Willan).

Morrison, W. (2006) *Criminology, Civilisation and the New World Order* (London: Routledge-Cavendish).

Mowbray, A. (2007) *Cases and Materials on the European Convention on Human Rights* (Oxford: Oxford University Press).

Murphy, T. (1997) *The Oldest Social Science: Configurations of Law and Modernity* (Oxford: Oxford University Press).

Newdick, C. (2005) *Who Should We Treat?* (Oxford: Oxford University Press).

Nicholson, M.A. (2000) 'McLibel: A case study in English Defamation Law', *Wisconsin International Law Journal* 18: 1–114.

Nicol, D. (2004) 'Statutory interpretation and human rights after Anderson', *Public Law*, 274.

Nicol, D. (2006) 'Law and politics after the Human Rights Act', *Public Law*, 722–51.

Nicol, D. (2010) *Constitutional Protection of Capitalism* (Oxford: Hart).

Nobles, R. and Schiff, D. (2004) 'A story of miscarriage: law in the media', *Journal of Law and Society* 31(2): 221–44.

Packer, H. (1968) *The Limits of the Criminal Sanction* (Stanford: Stanford University Press).

Paine, T. (1791) *The Rights of Man*.

Pannick, D. (1989) *Judges* (Oxford: Oxford University Press).

Partington, M. (2003) *Introduction to the English Legal System*, 2nd edn (Oxford: Oxford University Press).

Paul, K. (1997) *Whitewashing Britain; Race and Citizenship in the Postwar Era* (Ithaca: Cornell University Press).

Penner, J. (2003) 'Legal Reasoning and the Authority of Law' in Paulson, S., Pogge, T. and Meyer, L.(eds.), *Rights, Culture, and the Law: Themes from the Legal and Political Philosophy of Joseph Raz* (Oxford: Oxford University Press), 71–97.

Peysner, J. and Seneviratne, M. (2005) *The Management of Civil Cases: the Courts and the Post-Woolf Landscape.* DCA Research Report 9/2005 (London: Department for Constitutional Affairs).

Phillips, C. and Bowling, B. (2002) 'Racism, ethnicity, crime and criminal justice' in M. Maguire, R. Morgan and R. Reiner (eds) *The Oxford Handbook of Criminology* (Oxford: Oxford University Press) pp. 579–619.

Phillipson, G. (2007) in Fenwick *et al.* (ed.) *Horizontal Effect after Campbell in Judicial Reasoning under the UK Human Rights Act* (Cambridge: Cambridge University Press).

Pollock, F. and Maitland, F.W. (1898) *History of English Law*, 2nd edn, vol. I (Cambridge: Cambridge University Press).

Potter, H. (1943) *An Historical Introduction to English Law*, 2nd edn (London: Sweet & Maxwell Ltd).

Purdy, J. (1999) 'Postcolonialism: The Emperor's New Clothes?', in *Laws of the Postcolonial*, Eve Darian-Smith and Peter Fitzpatrick (eds) (Ann Arbor: University of Michigan Press).

Quinton, P., Bland, N. and Miller, J. (2000a) 'Police stops, decision-making and practice', Police Research Series Paper 130 (London: Home Office).

Quinton, P., Bland, N. and Miller, J. (2000b) 'Police Stops and Searches: Lessons from a programme of research', *Briefing Note* (London: Home Office).

R (Jackson) v. Attorney General [2005] UKHL 56.

Raz, J. (1979) 'The Rule of Law and its Virtue', in *The Authority of Law: Essays on Law and Morality* (Oxford: Clarendon Press).

Reece, H. (2003) *Divorcing Responsibly* (Oxford: Hart).

Reeder, R. P. (1910) 'The Due Process Clause and the Substance of Individual, Rights', 58 *Univ. of Penn. L. Rev.* 191–204.

Resnik, J. (1987) 'Due Process: A Public Dimension', *Faculty Scholarship Series*. Paper 915 (New Haven: Yale University Press).

Reynolds, H. (1971) *An Indelible Stain? The Question of Genocide in Australia's History* (Camberwell: Penguin Viking).

Reynolds, H. (1987) *The Law of the Land* (Camberwell: Penguin Books Australia).

Roberts, P. (2002) 'Science, experts and criminal justice', in M. McConville and G. Wilson (eds) *The Handbook of Criminal Justice* (Oxford: Oxford University Press).

Roberts, P. and Zuckerman, A. (1994) *Criminal Evidence* (Oxford: Oxford University Press).

Robertson, G. (1993) *Freedom, the Individual and the Law* (London: Penguin).

Rubinstein, W.D. (2004) *Genocide: A History* (London: Pearson, Longman).

Rutherford, A. (1993) *Criminal Justice and the Pursuit of Decency* (Oxford: Oxford University Press).

Sales, P. (2012) 'Strasbourg Jurisprudence and the Human Rights Act: A Response to Lord Irvine', *Public Law* (2).

Sanders, A., Young, R. and Burton, M. (2010) *Criminal Justice* (Oxford: Oxford University Press).

Sartre, J.P. (1963) 'Preface', to F. Fanon, *The Wretched of the Earth* (New York: Grove Press).

Scolnicov, A. (2005) 'Supersized speech – McLibel comes to Strasbourg', *Cambridge Law Journal* 64, 311–14.

Sedley, S. (1995) 'Human rights: a twenty first century agenda', *Public Law* (3): 386–440.

Sedley, S. (2001) 'The common law and the political constitution', *Law Quarterly Review* 117(Jan): 68–70.

Seuffert, N. (2006) *Jurisprudence of National Identity: Kaleidoscopes of Imperialism and Globalisation from Aotearoa New Zealand* (Aldershot: Ashgate Publishing).

Sharp, A. (1900) *Justice and the Maori: The Philosophy and Practice of Maori Claims in New Zealand Political Arguments Since the 1970s* (Auckland: Oxford University Press).

Sharp, G. (1773) 'Granville Sharp's diary', *Gloucestershire Archives*, 19 April 1773, Ref: D3549 13/4/2 book G.

Sharp, G. (1786) 'Granville Sharp's letter to the Archbishop of Canterbury', *Gloucestershire Archives*, 1 August 1786, Ref: D3549 13/1/C3.

Sharp, G. (1820) *Prince Hoare, Memoirs of Granville Sharp* (London: Henry Colburn).

Shyllon, F.O. (1974) *Black Slaves in Britain* (Oxford: Oxford University Press).

Sibley, D. (1995) *Geographies of Exclusion: Society and Difference in the West* (London: Routledge).

Sime, S. (2011) *A Practical Approach to Civil Procedure* (Oxford: Oxford University Press).

Simpson, A.W.B. (1973) 'The common law and legal theory', *Oxford Essays in Jurisprudence* (Oxford: Clarendon Press).

Simpson, A.W.B. (1984) *Cannibalism and the Common Law* (Chicago: University of Chicago Press).

Simpson, A.W.B. (2001) *Human Rights and the End of Empire* (Oxford: Oxford University Press).

Sivandan, A. (1982) *A Different Hunger* (London: Pluto Press).

Slapper, G. and Kelly, D. (2006) *English Legal System* (Oxford: Routledge-Cavendish).

Slapper, G. and Kelly, D. (2012) *English Legal System* (Oxford: Routledge).

Slaughter, Anne- Marie (1997) 'The Real New World Order' 76 *Foreign Affairs* 183.

Solomos, J. (1993) *Race and Racism in Britain* (London: Macmillan).

Solum, L.B. (1994) 'Procedural Justice', *Southern California Law Review* 78:181–321.

Stannard, D.E. (1992) *American Holocaust: The Conquest of the New World* (Oxford: Oxford University Press).

Starmer, K. (2003) 'Two years of the Human Rights Act', *European Human Rights Law Review* 1: 14–23.

Stephen, J.F. (1860) 'On trial by jury: and the evidence of experts', *Two Papers Read before the Juridical Society* 236.

Stevens, R. (2002) *The English Judges: Their Role in the Changing Constitution* (Oxford: Hart).

Steyn, J. (2004), 'Dynamic Interpretation Amidst an Orgy of Statutes' EHRLR 245.

Stockdale, R. (1999) 'Forensic evidence', in C. Walker and K. Starmer (eds) *Miscarriages of Justice* (Oxford: Blackwell).

Summers, S. (2007) *Fair Trials* (Oxford: Hart).

Sumption, J. (2011) 'Judicial and political decision making: The uncertain boundary', *F.A. Mann Lecture*, Lincoln's Inn, London, 9 November. Available at: http://www.legalweek. com/digital_assets/3704/MANNLECTURE_final.pdf

Taguieff, P.-A. (1988) *La Force du Prejuge, Essai Sur Le Racisme et Ses Doubles* (Paris: Editions la Decouverte).

Tate, W. (2003) 'Pre-Wi Parata: early native title cases in New Zealand', *Waikato Law Review* 6.

Taylor, M. (2003) 'Cot death expert to face investigation', *The Guardian*, December 19 2003.

Taylor, N. and Wood, J. (1999) 'Victims of miscarriages of justice', in C. Walker and K. Starmer (eds) *Miscarriages of Justice* (Oxford: Blackwell).

Thomas, D.A. (2002) 'The sentencing process', in M. McConville and G. Wilson (eds) *The Oxford Handbook of Criminal Justice* (Oxford: Oxford University Press).

Tomkins, A. (2002) 'In Defence of the Political Constitution', *Oxford Journal of Legal Studies* 22(1): 157–75.

Tomkins, A. (2005) *Our Republican Constitution* (Oxford: Hart).

Tomkins, A. (2010) 'The Role of Courts in the Political Constitution', *University of Toronto Law Review* 60(1): 1–22.

Trechsel, S. (2005) *Human Rights in Criminal Proceedings* (Oxford: Oxford University Press).

Tuitt, P. (2004) *Race, Law, Resistance* (London: Glasshouse Press).

Twining, W. (1992) *How to Do Things with Rules* (London: Weidenfeld and Nicolson).

Uglow, S. (2002) *Criminal Justice* (London: Sweet & Maxwell).

Usher, J.A. (1998) *General Principles of EC Law* (London: Longman).

Van Caenegem, R.C. (1986) *Judges, Legislators and Professors: Chapters in European Legal History* (Cambridge: Cambridge University Press).

Van Cleve, G. (2006) 'Sommersetts Case and its Antecedents', *Law and History Review* 24(3).

Van Dijk, Van Hoof, G. (eds) (2006) *Theory and Practice of the European Convention on Human Rights* (Antwerp: Intersentia).

Vick, D.W. and Campbell, K. (2001) 'Public protests, private lawsuits, and the market: the investor response to the McLibel case', *Journal of Law and Society* 28(2): 204–41.

Wadham, J. (2003) *The Human Rights Act 1998* (Oxford: Blackstone Press).

Waldron, J. (2010) 'The Rule of Law and the Importance of Procedure', *New York University School of Law, Public Law Research Paper No. 10–73*.

Walker, C. (1999) 'Miscarriages of justice in principle and practice', in C. Walker and K. Starmer (eds) *Miscarriages of Justice* (Oxford: Blackwell).

Wall, I.R. (2011) *Humam Rights and Constituent Power: Without Model or Warranty* (Abingdon: Routledge).

Wallerstein, I. and Balibar, E. (1991) *Race, Nation, Class* (London: Verso).

Walvin, J. (1992) *Black Ivory – A History of British Slavery* (London: Fontana Press).

Ward, A. (1999) *An Unsettled History: Treaty Claims in New Zealand Today* (Wellington: Bridget Williams Books).

Ward, T. (2004) 'Experts, juries and witch-hunts: from Fitzjames Stephen to Angela Cannings', *Journal of Law and Society* 31(3): 369–86.

Watson, A. (1985) *The Evolution of Law* (Baltimore: Johns Hopkins University Press).

Weber, M. (1978) *Economy and Society*, Guenther Roth & Claus Wittich (eds) (Berkeley: University of California Press).

Weinrib, E.J. (1995) *The Idea of Private Law* (Cambridge, MA: Harvard University Press).

Williams, G. (1973) *Learning the Law*, 9th edn (London: Stevens).

Williams, P. (1997) 'The Genealogy of Race: Towards a Theory of Grace', *Reith Lectures* (London: BBC).

Wilson, B. (1988) 'The making of a constitution: approaches to judicial interpretation', *Public Law* (3): 370–84.

Wollstonecraft, Mary. *A Vindication of the Rights of Woman*. Printed at Boston, by Peter Edes for Thomas and Andrews, Faust's statue, no. 45, Newbury-street, MDCCXCII. [1792]; Bartleby.com, 1999. www.bartleby.com/144/.

Woolf, H. and Tumim, S. (1991) 'Prison Disturbances April 1990', *Cm 1456* (London: HMSO).

Young, A.L. (2010) 'Deference, Dialogue and the Search for Legitimacy', *Oxford Journal of Legal Studies* 30 (4): 815–31

Young, K.E. and Connelly, N. (1981) *Policy and Practice in the Multi-Racial City* (Report) (London: Policy Studies Institute).

Zander, M. (1995) *The Police and Criminal Evidence Act 1984* (London: Sweet & Maxwell).

Zander, M. (2007) *Cases and Materials on the English Legal System* (Cambridge: Cambridge University Press).

Zedner, L. (2005) 'Securing liberty in the face of terror: reflections from criminal justice', *Journal of Law and Society* 32(4): 507–33.

Zimmerer, J. (2004) 'Colonialism and the Holocaust: Towards an archaeology of genocide', in A. Dirk Moses (ed.) *Genocide and Settler Society* (New York: Berghan Books).

Zuckerman, A. (2010) 'Closed material procedure – denial of natural justice: Al Rawi v. The Security Service [2011] UKSC', *Civil Justice Quarterly* 30(4): 349–359.

INDEX

Items appearing in footnotes are indicated by the abbreviation 'n' and illustrations are indicated by page references in italic